Critical Thinking, Thoughtful Writing

A Rhetoric with Readings

SIXTH EDITION

Critical Thinking, Thoughtful Writing

A Rhetoric with Readings

JOHN CHAFFEE, PhD

Director, Center for Philosophy and Critical Thinking,
City University of New York

Susan Carlson

Composition Department, Kaplan University

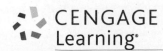
CENGAGE
Learning·

Australia · Brazil · Japan · Korea · Mexico · Singapore · Spain · United Kingdom · United States

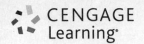

Critical Thinking, Thoughtful Writing, Sixth Edition
John Chaffee

Product Director: Monica Eckman

Product Manager: Margaret Leslie

Senior Content Developer: Leslie Taggart

Development Editor: Craig Leonard

Content Coordinator: Sarah Turner

Product Assistant: Cailin Barrett-Bressack

Media Developer: Janine Tangney

Marketing Brand Manager: Lydia LeStar

Senior Content Project Manager:
Aimee Chevrette Bear

Art Director: Hannah Wellman

Manufacturing Planner: Betsy Donaghey

Rights Acquisition Specialist: Ann Hoffman

Production Service: Tania Andrabi,
Cenveo® Publisher Services

Text Designer: Liz Harasymczuk

Cover Designer: Sarah Bishins

Cover Image: DEA/A. Dagli Orti/Getty Images

Compositor: Cenveo Publisher Services

Design Icons: © Involved Channel/
Shutterstock.com; © VLADGRIN/
Shutterstock.com

For product information and technology assistance, contact us at
Cengage Learning Customer & Sales Support, 1-800-354-9706

For permission to use material from this text or product, submit all requests online at **www.cengage.com/permissions.** Further permissions questions can be emailed to **permissionrequest@cengage.com.**

Library of Congress Control Number: 2013949591

ISBN-13: 978-1-285-44303-4

ISBN-10: 1-285-44303-9

Cengage Learning
200 First Stamford Place, 4th Floor
Stamford, CT 06902
USA

Cengage Learning is a leading provider of customized learning solutions with office locations around the globe, including Singapore, the United Kingdom, Australia, Mexico, Brazil and Japan. Locate your local office at **international.cengage.com/region.**

Cengage Learning products are represented in Canada by Nelson Education, Ltd.

For your course and learning solutions, visit **www.cengage.com.**

Purchase any of our products at your local college store or at our preferred online store **www.cengagebrain.com.**

Instructors: Please visit **login.cengage.com** and log in to access instructor-specific resources.

Printed in the United States of America
1 2 3 4 5 6 7 17 16 15 14 13

For Jessie and Joshua

Brief Contents

Part 1 Tools for Thinking, Reading, and Writing 1

1 The Thinking-Writing Model: Rhetoric, Situation, and Process 3

2 Reading: Making Meaning 29

3 Writing: Using Independent Thought and Informed Beliefs 59

4 Thinking: Becoming More Creative and Visually Aware 95

5 Drafting: Making and Analyzing Decisions 131

6 Revising: Using Language Thoughtfully 169

Part 2 Thinking and Writing to Shape Our World 205

7 Writing to Describe and Narrate: Exploring Perceptions 207

8 Writing to Classify and Define: Exploring Concepts 239

9 Writing to Compare and Evaluate: Exploring Perspectives and Relationships 285

10 Writing to Speculate: Exploring Cause and Effect 343

Part 3 Thinking and Writing to Explore Issues and Take Positions 377

11 Writing to Analyze: Believing and Knowing 379

12 Writing to Propose Solutions: Solving Problems 437

13 Writing to Persuade: Constructing Arguments 479

14 Writing About Investigations: Thinking About Research 537

Contents

Part 1   Tools for Thinking, Reading, and Writing   1

CHAPTER 1   The Thinking-Writing Model: Rhetoric, Situation, and Process   3

Thinking Critically About Visuals
Learn to think critically about what you see on page 10.

Thinking and Writing in College   3
Becoming a Critical Thinker and Thoughtful Writer   4
  Qualities of a Thoughtful Writer   4
The Thinking-Writing Model   5
Rhetoric and the Writing Situation   8
  Purpose   8

Thinking Critically About New Media
Learn to think critically about new media on page 12.

  Audience   9
  Subject   9
  Writer   9
  Writing Thoughtfully, Thinking Creatively, Thinking Critically   18
The Writing Process   19
  The Recursive Nature of the Writing Process   19
  Generating Ideas   20
  Keeping a Journal or Blog   20
  Defining a Focus   20
  Organizing Ideas   21
  Drafting   21
  Revising, Editing, and Proofreading   22
  Collaborating   25

CHAPTER 2   Reading: Making Meaning   29

Thinking Critically About Visuals
Learn to think critically about what you see on page 52.

Reading in College, Reading for Life   29
  Reading Actively   32
  Review the Table of Contents or Chapter Outlines   32
  Read the Introductory Paragraphs and the Concluding Paragraphs or Summary   33
  Scan the Reading Assignment, Taking Particular Note of Section Headings, Illustrations, and Diagrams   33

© iStockPhoto.com/ratluk

Gemstone Images/First Light/Corbis

    Annotating   33

    Summarizing   34

Reading Critically   34

    Asking Questions   34

    Using a Problem-Solving Approach   37

Practicing Active and Critical Reading: One Student's Approach   38

    Using Metacognitive Strategies   42

Making Meaning   54

    Semantic Meaning (Denotation)   54

    Perceptual Meaning (Connotation)   54

    Syntactic Meaning   55

    Pragmatic Meaning   56

Thinking Critically About New Media
Learn to think critically about new media on page 36.

CHAPTER 3   **Writing: Using Independent Thought and Informed Beliefs**   **59**

From Insight to Writing to Informed Beliefs (and Back Again)   59

Thinking Actively and Writing   61

    Influences on Your Thinking   61

Thinking Independently   62

    Viewing a Situation from Different Perspectives   65

    Supporting Diverse Perspectives with Reasons and Evidence   66

Developing Informed Beliefs   69

Experiences That Affect Beliefs   70

■Writing Project: An Experience That Influenced a Belief   82

    The Writing Situation   83

    The Writing Process   85

STUDENT WRITING: Eli Sharp's Writing Process   88

    Alternative Writing Projects   93

Colin Young-Wolff/PhotoEdit

Thinking Critically About Visuals
Learn to think critically about what you see on page 67.

Thinking Critically About New Media
Learn to think critically about new media on page 60.

CHAPTER 4   **Thinking: Becoming More Creative and Visually Aware**   **95**

Creative Thinking, Critical Viewing, and Writing   95

    Creativity in Selecting a Topic   95

    Moving from Topic to Thesis   96

    Creativity in Generating Ideas   97

Brenda Ann Kenneally/Corbis

Thinking Critically About Visuals
Learn to think critically about what you see on page 105.

Creative and Critical Thinking About Images   103
 Images and the Writing Situation   103
Reading Images Critically   104
 Semantic Meaning (Denotation)   104
 Perceptual Meaning (Connotation)   104
 Syntactic Meaning   105
 Pragmatic Meaning   106
Living Creatively   106
Becoming More Creative: Understand and Trust the Process   107
 Eliminate the Voice of Judgment   110
 Establish a Creative Environment   111
 Make Creativity a Priority   112
Where Do Ideas Come From?   112
■ Writing Project: Imagining Your Life Lived More Creatively   120
 The Writing Situation   121
 The Writing Process   122
STUDENT WRITING: Jessie Lange's Writing Process: Freewriting   126
 Alternative Writing Projects   128

Thinking Critically About New Media
Learn to think critically about new media on page 108.

Thinking Critically About Visuals
Learn to think critically about what you see on page 132.

Thinking Critically About New Media
Learn to think critically about new media on page 152.

| CHAPTER 5 | Drafting: Making and Analyzing Decisions | 131 |

Decisions While Drafting   132
Decisions in Your Life   136
 An Organized Approach to Making Decisions   136
 Step 1: Define the Decision and Its Goals Clearly (Audience)   137
 Step 2: Consider All Possible Choices (Subject)   137
 Step 3: Gather All Relevant Information and Evaluate the Pros and Cons of Each Possible Choice (Purpose)   138
 Step 4: Select the Choice That Seems Best Suited to the Situation   138
 Step 5: Implement a Plan of Action and Monitor the Results, Making Necessary Adjustments   139
 Analyzing Decisions   140
■ Writing Project: Analyzing a Decision to Be Made   154
 The Writing Situation   154
 The Writing Process   156
STUDENT WRITING: Wendy Agudo's Writing Process   159
STUDENT WRITING: Cynthia Brown's Writing Process   162
 Alternative Writing Projects   166

CHAPTER 6   Revising: Using Language Thoughtfully   169

Recognizing Effective Use of Language   170
   Language, Thinking, and Learning   170
Making Decisions When Revising Drafts   172
   Specific Decisions to Make at Several Levels   173
Using Language Ethically   181
   Improving Vague Language   181
   Using Figurative Language   183
Using Language to Influence   189
   Euphemistic Language   190
   Clichés   194
   Emotive Language   194
■ Writing Project: The Impact of Language on Our Lives   196
   The Writing Situation   198
   The Writing Process   199
STUDENT WRITING: Jessie Lange's Writing Process   201
   Alternative Writing Projects   203

Schalkwijk/Art Resource, NY

Thinking Critically About Visuals
Learn to think critically about what you see on page 190.

Thinking Critically About New Media
Learn to think critically about new media on page 184.

Part 2   Thinking and Writing to Shape Our World   205

CHAPTER 7   Writing to Describe and Narrate: Exploring Perceptions   207

Thinking Critically About Perceptions   208
   Becoming Aware of Your Own Perceptions   208
   Noting Differences in People's Perceptions   211
Writing Thoughtfully About Perceptions   214
   Writing Objectively and Subjectively   214
   Contrasting Objective and Subjective Writing   215
Chronological Relationships   220
   Narratives   220
   Writing About Processes   220
   Examples of Process Writing   221
■ Writing Project: A Narrative Showing the Effect of a Perception   229
   The Writing Situation   229
   The Writing Process   231

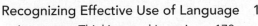

Radius Images/Jupiter Images

Thinking Critically About Visuals
Learn to think critically about what you see on page 211.

Thinking Critically About New Media
Learn to think critically about new media on page 212.

STUDENT WRITING: Joshua Chaffee's Writing Process   233
   Alternative Writing Projects   236

Thinking Critically About Visuals
Learn to think critically about what you see on page 249.

Thinking Critically About New Media
Learn to think critically about new media on page 246.

CHAPTER 8   Writing to Classify and Define: Exploring Concepts   239

What Are Concepts?   240
   The Importance of Concepts   241
   The Structure of Concepts   242
   The Process of Classifying   243
Forming Concepts   244
Applying Concepts   248
   Determining the Requirements of a Concept   248
   Analyzing Complex Concepts   250
A Casebook on the Evolving Concept of "Family"   251
Using Concepts to Classify   264
   Classifying People and Their Actions   265
   Writing and Classifying   266
Defining Concepts   267
Writing Thoughtfully to Define Concepts   268
■ Writing Project: Defining an Important Concept   269
   The Writing Situation   270
   The Writing Process   272
STUDENT WRITING: Nawang Doma Sherpa's Writing Process   275
STUDENT WRITING: Jorden Carlsen's Writing Process   278
   Alternative Writing Project   282

Thinking Critically About Visuals
Learn to think critically about what you see on page 304.

CHAPTER 9   Writing to Compare and Evaluate: Exploring Perspectives and Relationships   285

Perceptions and Perspectives   285
   Selecting Perceptions: Why Do We Notice the Things We Notice?   289
   Organizing Perceptions   290
   Interpreting Perceptions   291

Casebook: Perception and Reality in the Sandy Hook
Elementary School Shooting   291

How Perspective and Language Affect Perceptions:
A Focused Study of the Assassination of Malcolm X   305

    The New York Times (February 22, 1965)   306

    Life (March 5, 1965)   306

    The New York Post (February 22, 1965)   306

    Associated Press (February 22, 1965)   307

    The Amsterdam News (February 27, 1965)   307

    Changes in Perceptions and Perspectives   308

Obtaining More Accurate Perceptions:
Adjusting the Lenses   309

    Develop Awareness   309

    Get Input from Others   310

    Find Evidence   310

    Keep an Open Mind   310

Writing Thoughtfully About Perspectives   324

    Comparison and Contrast   324

    Thinking in Comparisons   324

    Analogy   329

Writing Project: Comparing Perspectives on an Issue or Event   330

    The Writing Situation   331

    The Writing Process   333

STUDENT WRITING: Jennifer Wade's Writing Process   337

    Alternative Writing Project: Comparing Two Reviews   341

Thinking Critically About New Media
Learn to think critically about new media on page 286.

CHAPTER 10   Writing to Speculate: Exploring Cause and Effect   343

Abid Katib/Getty Images

Thinking Critically About Visuals
Learn to think critically about what you see on page 350.

Kinds of Causal Relationships   343

    Causal Chains   345

    Contributory Causes   346

    Interactive Causes   347

Ways of Testing Causes   349

    Necessary Condition and Sufficient Condition   349

    Immediate Cause and Remote Cause   350

Identifying Causal Fallacies   351

    Questionable Cause   351

    Misidentification of the Cause   352

**Thinking Critically
About New Media**
Learn to think
critically about new
media on page 352.

Buyenlarge/Getty Images

**Thinking Critically
About Visuals**
Learn to think
critically about
what you see on
page 408.

**Thinking Critically
About New Media**
Learn to think
critically about new
media on page 392.

Post Hoc Ergo Propter Hoc   353

Slippery Slope   354

Detecting Causal Claims   355

Exploring Cause and Effect: Modern Agriculture and Social Impact   356

Writing Thoughtfully About Causal Relationships   365

■ Writing Project: Exploring Some Causes of a Recent Event   365

The Writing Situation   366

The Writing Process   368

STUDENT WRITING: Daniel Eggers' Writing Process   371

Alternative Writing Project: Utopias and Dystopias   376

Part 3   Thinking and Writing to Explore Issues and Take Positions   377

**CHAPTER 11   Writing to Analyze:
Believing and Knowing   379**

Ways of Forming Beliefs   379

Beliefs Based on Personal Experience   381

Beliefs Based on Indirect Experience   388

Evaluating Sources and Information   389

How Reliable Is the Source?   389

What Are the Source's Purposes and Interests?   390

How Knowledgeable or Experienced Is the Source?   390

Was the Source Able to Make Accurate Observations?   390

How Reputable Is the Source?   391

How Valuable Is Information from This Source?   391

Believing and Knowing   396

Knowledge and Truth   397

Understanding Relativism   397

Understanding Falsifiable Beliefs   397

Climate Change and Truth   398

Ways of Presenting Beliefs   409

Reporting Factual Information   411

Inferring from Evidence or Premises   412

Judging by Applying Criteria   422

Distinguishing Among Reports, Inferences, and Judgments   424

Presenting Beliefs in Your Writing   425

■ Writing Project: Analyzing Influences on Your Beliefs About a Social
or Academic Issue   426

The Writing Situation   426

The Writing Process   429

STUDENT WRITING: Jessie Lange's Writing Process   432

Alternative Writing Project: Evolving Beliefs in an Academic Field   434

CHAPTER 12 Writing to Propose Solutions: Solving Problems   437

Problems in Personal and Civic Life   438

Basics of the Problem-Solving Method   438

   1. What Is the Problem?   439

   2. What Are the Alternatives?   439

   3. What Are the Advantages and/or Disadvantages of Each Alternative?   439

   4. What Is the Solution?   439

   5. How Well Is the Solution Working?   440

The Problem-Solving Method in Detail   441

   Before You Begin: Accepting the Problem   443

   Step 1: What Is the Problem?   444

   Step 2: What Are the Alternatives?   447

   Step 3: What Are the Advantages and/or Disadvantages of Each Alternative?   449

   Step 4: What Is the Solution?   450

   Step 5: How Well Is the Solution Working?   452

Solving Social Problems   454

Taking a Problem-Solving Approach to Writing   465

■Writing Project: Proposing a Solution to a Problem   466

   The Writing Situation   466

   The Writing Process   469

STUDENT WRITING: Joshua Bartlett's Writing Process   472

   Alternative Writing Projects: Community Problems, Community Solutions   476

Thinking Critically About Visuals Learn to think critically about what you see on page 455.

Thinking Critically About New Media Learn to think critically about new media on page 456.

CHAPTER 13 Writing to Persuade: Constructing Arguments   479

Principles of Argument   479

   Classical Concepts of Argument   480

   Modern Concepts of Argument   481

Thinking Critically About Visuals Learn to think critically about what you see on page 482.

Lucas Oleniuk/The Toronto Star/ZUMApress

© Library of Congress

Recognizing Arguments   491
    Two Friends Argue: Should Marijuana Be Legalized?   491
Arguments as Inferences   499
    Constructing Arguments to Decide   500
    Constructing Arguments to Explain   500
    Constructing Arguments to Predict   500
    Constructing Arguments to Persuade   500
Evaluating Arguments   500
    Truth: How True Are the Supporting Reasons?   501
    Validity: Do the Reasons Support the Claim or Conclusion?   501
    Soundness: Is the Argument Both True and Valid?   502
Forms of Argument   503
    Deductive Reasoning   503
    Other Deductive Forms   505
    Inductive Reasoning   507
    Causal Reasoning   508
    Empirical Generalization   508
More Fallacies: Forms of False Reasoning   511
    Hasty Generalization   511
    Sweeping Generalization   511
    False Dilemma   512
    Begging the Question   513
    Red Herring   513
    Fallacies of Relevance   513
Deductive and Inductive Reasoning in Writing   523
■Writing Project: Arguing a Position on a Significant Issue   524
    The Writing Situation   525
    The Writing Process   527
Principles for Writing Responsible Arguments   528
STUDENT WRITING: Will Portman's Writing Process   530
    Alternative Writing Project: The Pursuit of Happiness   534

Thinking Critically About New Media
Learn to think critically about new media on page 486.

| CHAPTER 14 | **Writing About Investigations: Thinking About Research** | **537** |

Rewards of Research   537
Starting with Questions   538
    Questions That Identify Your Topic   538
    Questions That Focus Your Topic   538

Thinking Critically About Visuals
Learn to think critically about what you see on page 547.

Courtesy of Factcheck.org

Searching for Information 539
  Finding Electronic and Print Sources in the Library 539
  Primary and Secondary Sources 540
  Collecting Information from Experts and from the Field 540
Using Information 542
  Evaluating Sources for a Research Project 543
  Moving from Questions to Thesis 548
Understanding Plagiarism and Using Information Ethically 548
Taking Notes 550
  Deciding When to Take Notes 550
  Quoting and Paraphrasing 551
  Using Common Knowledge 552
  Characteristics of Effective Note-Taking Systems 552
  Summarizing 555
Preparing an Annotated Bibliography 556
Integrating Source Material 557
  Introducing Sources 557
  Establishing Your Voice 558
  Choosing Point of View 559
The Logic Behind Documentation 560
  Reasons for Documentation 560
  The Logic of MLA Style 561
Working Thoughtfully on Research Projects 562
  Time 562
  Planning and Outlining 563
  Formats and Models 564
  Collaboration 564
■ Writing Project: A Research Paper 564
  The Writing Situation 565
  The Writing Process 567
Annotated Student Research Paper: The Writing Situation
and Writing Process in Action 571
  Chris Buxton-Smith's Writing Situation 571
  Chris Buxton-Smith's Writing Process 572
  Chris Buxton-Smith's Working Outline 573
  Sample Annotated Research Paper (MLA) 574

Appendix 583
Index 605

Thinking Critically About New Media Learn to think critically about new media on page 544.

Readings

COLIN POWELL. *From* My American Journey (Chapter 1, page 15)

NATALIE GOLDBERG. "Writing Is Not a McDonald's Hamburger"
(Chapter 1, page 23)

SERGIO TRONCOSO. Why Read? (Chapter 2, page 30)

SONJA TANNER. On Plato's Cave (Chapter 2, page 39)

JULIA ALVAREZ. "Grounds for Fiction" (Chapter 2, page 44)

ANNIE DILLARD. *From* An American Childhood (Chapter 3, page 70)

STEPHEN JAY GOULD. Reversing Established Orders (Chapter 3, page 73)

JANE SMILEY. "The Case Against Chores" (Chapter 3, page 80)

DANIEL H. PINK. "Revenge of the Right Brain" (Chapter 4, page 112)

BILL BREEN. "The 6 Myths of Creativity" (Chapter 4, page 116)

FREDERICK DOUGLASS. *From* Narrative of the Life of Frederick Douglass,
an American Slave (Chapter 5, page 140)

MICHAEL SHERMER. The Doping Dilemma (Chapter 5, page 144)

MALCOLM X with ALEX HALEY. *From* The Autobiography of Malcolm X
(Chapter 6, page 170)

DONALD M. MURRAY. "The Maker's Eye: Revising Your Own Manuscripts"
(Chapter 6, page 176)

MARTIN LUTHER KING JR. "I Have a Dream" (Chapter 6, page 185)

DANIEL PIPES. "Beslan Atrocity: They're Terrorists—Not Activists"
(Chapter 6, page 191)

TEMPLE GRANDIN. "Animal Feelings" (Chapter 7, page 215)

ATUL GAWANDE. "The Learning Curve" (Chapter 7, page 222)

KATE RICE. "New 'Non-Traditional' American Families" (Chapter 8, page 251)

JOHN BERMAN. "What Makes a Family? Children, Say Many Americans"
(Chapter 8, page 259)

JOEL KOTKIN. "The Rise of Post-Familialism: Humanity's Future?"
(Chapter 8, page 260)

TED ANTHONY. "Connecticut School Shooting 'An Attack On America'"
(Chapter 9, page 293)

DAN BAUM. "The Price of Gun Control" (Chapter 9, page 294)

WAYNE LA PIERRE. Response to Newtown, Connecticut massacre by Wayne La Pierre, CEO of the National Rifle Association on December 21, 2012 (Chapter 9, page 296)

JEFF MCMAHAN. "Why Gun 'Control' Is Not Enough" (Chapter 9, page 298)

LISA WADE. "The (Terrifying) Transformative Potential of Technology" (Chapter 9, page 301)

JOE SCARBOROUGH. Comments made on *Morning Joe* (Chapter 9, page 303)

BENJAMIN FRANKLIN. "Remarks Concerning the Savages of North America" (Chapter 9, page 311)

ZITKALA-SA (GERTRUDE SIMMONS BONNIN). *From* The School Days of an Indian Girl (Chapter 9, page 316)

TED STEINBERG. "A Natural Disaster, and a Human Tragedy" (Chapter 9, page 325)

GRAIN.ORG. GMOs: Fooling—Er, "Feeding"—the World for 20 Years (Chapter 10, page 357)

THE EDITORS OF SCIENTIFIC AMERICAN. Do Seed Companies Control GM Crop Research? (Chapter 10, page 360)

RICHARD MANNING. Eating the Genes: What the Green Revolution Did for Grain, Biotechnology May Do for Protein (Chapter 10, page 362)

B. C. "Homeless in Prescott, Arizona" (Chapter 11, page 382)

ROB MANNING. Hard Times: A Family Escapes Homelessness (Chapter 11, page 384)

JOE LAWLOR. Newport News Mom Escapes Homelessness (Chapter 11, page 386)

KEN CALDEIRA. The Great Climate Experiment: How Far Can We Push the Planet? (Chapter 11, page 398)

PATRICK BUCHANAN. Global Warming: Hoax of the Century (Chapter 11, page 403)

TYLER HAMILTON. Why Media Tell Climate Story Poorly (Chapter 11, page 405)

STEPHEN JAY GOULD. "Evolution as Fact and Theory" (Chapter 11, page 416)

NICHOLAS CARR. Is Google Making Us Stupid? (Chapter 12, page 458)

ALEXIS C. MADRIGAL. The Perfect Technocracy: Facebook's Attempt to Create Good Government for 900 Million People (Chapter 13, page 495)

IN CONGRESS, JULY 4, 1776. The Declaration of Independence (Chapter 13, page 517)

ELIZABETH CADY STANTON. Declaration of Sentiments and Resolutions (Chapter 13, page 519)

Thinking-Writing Activities

Recalling a Learning Experience   4

Analyzing a Writing Experience   7

How Well Do You Communicate?   15

Expressing a Deeper Meaning   26

Why Do You Read?   31

Taking a Reading Inventory   32

Previewing a Reading Assignment   33

A Problem-Solving Approach to Reading   38

Your Reactions   42

Practicing Metacognition   43

Reading Worksheet   43

Reading Strategies   43

Syntactic Meaning   56

Pragmatic Meaning   57

Blogging   60

Active and Passive Influences   62

Evaluating Beliefs   64

Two Sides of a Belief   66

Viewing Different Perspectives   68

Creating a Belief Map   69

Create a Mind Map   98

Recalling a Creative Writing Experience   106

Reflecting on Past Inhibitions to Creativity   107

Creative "Crowdsourcing"   109

Analyzing a Previous Decision   136

Facebook Troubleshooting   153

Preparing for Decisions   153

Language That Offends   170

Using the Revision Method   176

Vague Language   182

Creating Similes and Metaphors   185

Thinking Critically About Euphemisms   191

Cliché and Proverb   194

Evaluating Emotive Language   196

What Do You Sense Right Now?   209

Comparing Your Perceptions with Those of Others   211

Detecting and Analyzing Faulty Perceptions on the Web   213

Creating Objective and Subjective Descriptions   219

Writing Process Descriptions   222

Changing Your Concepts   240

Diagramming Concepts   244

Forming a Concept   247

Media as a Concept   247

Exploring the Concepts of Masculine and Feminine   250

Classification and Your Self   265

Classification and Ethics   266

Identifying Classifications   267

Using Wikimedia to Collaborate and Communicate   287

Differing Perspectives   288

Five Accounts of the Assassination of Malcolm X, 1965   308

Creating a Causal Chain   346

Creating a Causal Chain   347

Identifying Causal Patterns   348

Diagnosing Causal Fallacies   355

Evaluating Causal Claims   356

Identifying Beliefs   381

The Origin of a Belief   389

Evaluating a Source of a Belief   391

Identifying Internet Hoaxes   395

Weighing Your Beliefs and Knowledge   397

Identifying Reports, Inferences, and Judgments   410

Evaluating Factual Information   412

Factual and Inferential Beliefs   415

Analyzing an Incorrect Inference   416

Analyzing Judgments   424

Analyzing a Problem Solved Previously   440

Analyzing a Problem in Your Life   454

Reading Print vs. Reading Online   457

Analyzing Argumentative Writing   480

Freedom of Speech on the Internet   487

Establishing Agreement   490

Analyzing a Dialogue   495

Evaluating Deductive Arguments   506

Analyzing Empirical Generalization   510

Analyzing Fallacies   516

Developing Research Questions   538

Identifying Research Questions   539

Learning About Your Library   540

Interviews, Questionnaires, and Observations   542

Evaluating Print and Web Sources   543

Evaluating the Quality of Two Websites with Contrasting
   Perspectives on an Issue   546

Going from Questions to Thesis   548

Plagiarism in the News   550

Creating Your Own Note-Taking Methods   554

Learning About the Methods of Experienced Note Takers   554

Learning to Summarize   555

Creating an Annotated Bibliography   557

Clarifying Who Is Talking   559

Citing and Paraphrasing   560

Explaining the MLA System   562

Leo Tolstoy eloquently observed that "the relations of word to thought, and the creation of new concepts, is a complex, delicate, and enigmatic process unfolding in our soul." Writers and teachers of writing have long recognized intricate relationships between the extraordinary human processes of thought and language. This insight, which helps beginning college students become thoughtful writers, informs the comprehensive approach of *Critical Thinking, Thoughtful Writing: A Rhetoric with Readings,* Sixth Edition. The synergy in what experts in the thinking process (philosophers and psychologists, for example) understand about learning can be powerfully integrated with the critical thinking process as understood by teachers of writing and composition, especially in an age of increasingly complex channels of information and media.

Critical Thinking, Thoughtful Writing: A Rhetoric with Readings, Sixth Edition, presents an integrated approach to teaching the thinking, writing, and reading skills—of both verbal and visual texts—that first-year composition students need in order to successfully meet the challenges of academic work, as well as of the professional workplace. As students develop higher-order thinking abilities, they learn to articulate their ideas through writing and the creation of multimodal texts. And as they develop their abilities to navigate the writing process, students learn to think coherently, precisely, and creatively. This approach integrates the development of thinking skills with composing skills so they not only reinforce each other but also become inseparable.

This book stimulates and guides students to think deeply and beyond superficialities, to refuse to be satisfied with the first idea they have, to look objectively at multiple perspectives on complex issues, and to formulate their own informed conclusions. It encourages students to develop an interest in conducting research and in delving into possibilities rather than settling for easy answers. It challenges students to be independent in their thinking and courageous in their convictions. And it shows them how to organize information, interpret different perspectives, solve challenging problems, analyze complex issues, and communicate their ideas clearly.

Advantages of a Critical Thinking Framework

The critical thinking framework of this text helps instructors and students in the following ways:

- **By providing an intellectual and thematic framework** that helps writing teachers place rhetorical concerns in a meaningful context. *Critical Thinking, Thoughtful Writing* challenges and guides students to think and write about important topics that build on their cognitive activities and critical explorations.

This process enables students to improve both the technical aspects of their writing (coherence, organization, detail, grammar, and mechanics) and the quality of their writing (depth, insight, and sophistication).

- **By leading students to understand the reciprocal relationship** between the process of thinking and the process of writing. The text stimulates students to explore their own composing processes, gradually mastering the forms of thought and critical thinking that are the hallmark of mature and thoughtful writing.

- **By helping students to appreciate that reading is a thinking activity** rather than a series of decoding skills. This understanding accelerates and enhances reading development. Students are better able to understand and develop the interrelated thinking abilities that the reading process comprises, including solving problems, forming and applying concepts, and relating ideas to larger conceptual frameworks.

Content and Organization

MOVEMENT FROM THE PERSONAL TO THE SOCIAL

The book moves logically from introducing creative and critical thinking to explaining how these tools can be used in different kinds of writing. Part One helps students understand themselves as thinkers and writers; the Writing Projects in this section ask them to write from their own experiences and observations. Part Two explores important thinking patterns and language issues; here, the Writing Projects ask them to incorporate ideas and perspectives from others into their expository writing. Part Three uses an increasing number of sources as students work with problem solving, argumentation, and research. This logical progression pulls students beyond their personal experiences and pushes them to think and write about challenging issues and concepts, while seeing how social issues are connected with their own lives. The practical strategies will help students address writing assignments in other academic classes and in the workplace.

FOUR INTEGRATED ELEMENTS TO EACH CHAPTER

1. **Critical Thinking Focus** examines the thinking skill central to each chapter. Examples of critical thinking skills are thinking about thinking, thinking creatively, making decisions, evaluating perspectives, using causal reasoning, conceptualizing, constructing knowledge, solving problems, and developing reasoned arguments.

2. **Writing Focus** provides strategies and Thinking-Writing Activities that draw upon the chapter's critical thinking skill.

3. **Reading Focus** comprises 43 professional readings (essays, articles, or book chapters) and 13 student essays, on themes including creativity, decision making,

politics and culture, gender, language, problem solving, and arguments on timely and provocative topics. Each chapter offers three or more pieces of professional writing (such as essays, investigative reporting, and editorials, as well as some imaginative genres) and at least one student essay. The readings reflect the critical thinking focus in each chapter and provide the basis for assignments that initiate students' writing.

4. **Writing Project** builds on the reading themes and skills developed through the chapter's activities. These carefully structured projects move systematically through stages toward a finished project, providing guidance for each stage of the writing process. Each chapter includes at least one student example of the completed Writing Project.

SPECIAL FEATURES

Practical Critical Thinking Strategies for Writing and for Evaluating Images This book introduces the process of thinking critically as a practical and powerful approach to writing, to the critical evaluation of electronic and visual media, and to life in general. For example, in learning a thoughtful approach for making decisions, students apply the decision-making process to revising drafts, as well as to making important decisions in other areas of their lives. By developing their problem-solving abilities, students become able both to compose a problem-solving essay and to be more effective in solving problems beyond the classroom.

Comprehensive Thinking-Writing Model The Thinking-Writing Model introduced in Chapter 1 (pages 5–8) and reinforced throughout the book provides a clear graphic representation of the writing process and of the connections between critical thinking and thoughtful writing, as well as creative thinking and inventive writing.

Creative Thinking to Enrich the Writing Process The book shows that creative thought can and should be an integral part of academic writing. All aspects of the writing process can be approached creatively, including selecting a topic, generating ideas and drafting, using specific details, and writing introductions and conclusions. In learning to think creatively, students discover strategies to make their writing more inventive, while also infusing creative energy into other areas of their lives.

Emphasis on Collaboration The value of collaboration in thinking and writing is emphasized throughout, with this special icon highlighting Thinking-Writing Activities and other material specifically designed for collaboration and peer review. Critical thinking is emphasized in actively exploring ideas, listening to others, and carefully evaluating opinions and arguments, and it provides a context for collaborative learning. Students learn to examine their own opinions more analytically and relate these opinions to the world at large. They learn to assess alternative points of view in dialogue with others, contributing to their development into a community of concerned thinkers and writers.

Cross-Disciplinary Approach Recognizing that first-year composition courses prepare students to write in all of their courses and after college, this book presents examples, selections, and assignments from sociology, psychology, linguistics, history, business, cultural studies, economics, and the natural and hard sciences.

Critical Thinking as a Tool for Living The book views learning to think, write, and read as integral dimensions of an individual's personal growth and transformation. It aims to help students grow. While learning how to think and write, students are encouraged to apply these critical and creative thinking skills to all facets of their lives, enabling them to make enlightened decisions, solve challenging problems, analyze complex issues, communicate effectively, nurture creative talents, and become more thoughtful and socially aware citizens.

New to the Sixth Edition

The sixth edition of *Critical Thinking, Thoughtful Writing* includes a number of revisions designed to help students become more fully engaged in the writing process.

- **REVISED: Expanded Writing Projects.** The Writing Projects have been expanded to help students more fully interact with the writing process. Each project includes an expanded overview, as well as specific questions and examples, to help transition students from conceptualizing the writing situation to engaging with the writing process. Each project also includes a redesigned section dedicated to peer review, revision, and editing and proofreading.

- **NEW: Reflection on Writing Questions.** Students have an opportunity to practice their critical thinking skills by responding to several questions in the new Reflection on Writing section following each essay.

- **NEW: Annotations to Accompany the Student Essays.** Student essays now include annotations that offer insight into the structure, style, and content of each essay and that reflect the theme or focus of each chapter.

- **NEW: Readings.** The sixth edition has a number of new readings by a variety of noteworthy authors (Michael Shermer, Will Portman, Kate Rice, Joel Kotkin, Dan Baum, Ken Caldeira, and Jeff McMahan) covering timely and provocative topics, including gun control in the aftermath of the shootings at Sandy Hook Elementary School, the changing concept of what it means to be a family, the pros and cons of genetically modified foods, and the debate surrounding the science of global warming.

- **NEW: Visuals.** Each chapter features a new chapter-opening photo, as well as new photos within each chapter.

- **NEW: Four-Color Design.** The sixth edition features a four-color interior design.

Supplements

Book Companion Website Visit the book companion website to access valuable course resources. Students will find an extensive library of interactive exercises and animations that cover grammar, diction, mechanics, punctuation, research, and writing concepts, as well as a complete library of student papers and a section on avoiding plagiarism. The site also offers a downloadable Instructor's Manual.

Online Instructor's Manual Available for download on the book companion site, the Instructor's Manual introduces instructors not only to the text, but also to critical thinking as a course. Features include sample syllabi; a writing inventory template; chapter-by-chapter teaching suggestions; a Test of Critical Thinking Abilities; a bibliography of additional readings, films, and videos for use with the text; and classroom handouts.

The Authors

Critical Thinking, Thoughtful Writing is the result of collaboration of two authors. John Chaffee is Director of the Center for Philosophy and Critical Thinking, and Professor of Philosophy at The City University of New York. His best-selling textbook *Thinking Critically,* going into its eleventh edition, presents a comprehensive, language-based approach to learning that helped define the field of critical thinking. His introduction to philosophy text, *The Philosopher's Way,* has been acclaimed as a genuinely innovative contribution to the field. As Director of Writing Across the Curriculum (WAC) at Kaplan University, Susan Carlson implemented the WAC program, directed the Composition Department as well as the Writing Center, and piloted several programs designed to improve student writing and retention. She has presented at numerous conferences, including the European Writing Centers Association at the American University of Paris, and also co-edited *The Kaplan Guide to Successful Writing.* Susan left her administrative role to return to teaching composition, work on a novel, and write and illustrate a children's book.

Acknowledgments

The following reviewers offered wise insights to and suggestions for the manuscript in this or earlier editions: Belinda Adams, Navarro College; Sonya Alvarado, Eastern Michigan University; Catherine Amdahl, Harrisburg Area Community College; Kathryn Bartle Angus, California State University, Fullerton; Jeanelle Barrett, Tarleton State University; Sally M. Baynton, San Antonio College; Larry Beason, University of South Alabama; Bruce Beckum, Colorado Mountain College; Patricia Bizzel, College of the Holy Cross; Bradley W. Bleck, Spokane Falls Community College; Paul Bodmer, Bismarck State College; Stephanie Byrd, Cleveland State University; Linda Caine, Prairie State College; Jamie Carey, Cerritos College; Peter Caster, University of

South Carolina, Upstate; Christine Caver, University of Texas, San Antonio; Frankie Chadwick, University of Arkansas at Little Rock; William Church, Missouri Western State College; Sherry Cisler, Arizona State University; Gina Claywell, Murray State University; Huey Crisp, University of Arkansas at Little Rock; Sarah Dangelantonio, Franklin Pierce College; Lisette Davies Ward, Santa Barbara City College; Charlie Davis, Boise State University; Damian Doyle, University of Colorado at Boulder; Thomas Fink, LaGuardia College; Adam Fischer, Bowie State University; Olive Fisher, Bluegrass Community College; Kim Grewe, Wor-Wic Community College; Christina Havlin, ECPI University; Judith A. Hinman, College of the Redwoods; Mark Hoffman, Borough of Manhattan Community College, CUNY; Martha M. Holder, Wytheville Community College; Elizabeth Hooper, University of Texas, San Antonio; Margaret Hosty, Tarrant County College; Marhsalla Hutson, The University of Texas of the Permian Basin; Frederick T. Janzow, Southeast Missouri State University; Margaret Johnson, Idaho State University; John H. Jones, Jacksonville State University; Dipo Kalejaiye, Prince George's Community College; John Kinkade, University of Southern Indiana; Robert Koppelman, Broward College; Chikako D. Kumamoto, College of DuPage; Laura La Flair, Gaston College; Anna M. Lang, University of Indianapolis; Shirley Wilson Logan, University of Maryland; Lewis Long, Irvine Valley College; Cheryl R. Lyda, Idaho State University; Linda McHenry, Fort Hays State University; Mary Kate McMaster, Anna Maria College; Catherine Moran, Bristol Community College; Paul J. Morris II, Pittsburgh State University; Andrea Muldoon, University of Wisconsin—Stout; Joan Mullin, University of Toledo; Robbi Nester, Irvine Valley College; Lisa Nicholas, University of Southern Indiana; Elizabeth A. Nist, Anoka-Ramsey Community College; John Regan, Boston University; Susan Rinaldi, Northeastern University; Shirley Roberts, Brookhaven College; Jeffrey Roessner, Mercyhurst College; Denise Rogers, University of Louisiana at Lafayette; Kenneth Rosenauer, Missouri Western State College; Nicholas Schevera, College of Lake County; Isaiah Smithson, Southern Illinois University; Byrin Stay, Mount St. Mary's College; Judith L. Steele, Mid-America Christian University; Kay Stokes, Hanover College; Leslie Stoupas, Colorado Mountain College; John T. Stovall, National-Louis University; Michael Thomas, College of the Redwoods; William Vaughn, Central Missouri State University; Elizabeth Wahlquist, Brigham Young University; Jane Armstrong Woodman, Northern Arizona University.

John Chaffee would also like to thank Christine McMahon and Barbara Stout for the dedication and expertise they brought to the unique project of extending his work in critical thinking to the field of composition. Their approaches to teaching writing and their active involvement in the composition field have contributed significantly to a text that is practical, effective, and adaptable to a variety of instructional contexts.

As has been the case for the last several decades, I have been privileged to work with a stellar team of individuals at Cengage Learning who are exemplary professionals and also valued friends. Lyn Uhl, Publisher, has been steadfast in her personal and professional support of *Critical Thinking, Thoughtful Writing*, and I am deeply grateful. My thanks also go to the Executive Editor Monica Eckman for her efforts on behalf of the book. Margaret Leslie, Acquisitions Editor, provided wise guidance and crucial decisions in overseeing this revision of *Critical Thinking, Thoughtful Writing:* her steady hand at the helm and insightful suggestions at key junctures were essential. My heartfelt thanks go to Leslie Taggart, who in her role as Senior Development Editor provided the comprehensive direction and creative vision for this splendid edition that will be crucial for its success. It was a special pleasure working with the Development Editor Craig Leonard. Craig was the invaluable core of the revision, instrumental in shaping every element of this new edition with a conscientious attention to detail and unwavering commitment to excellence. I am appreciative of the excellent support provided by the Assistant Editor Sarah Turner and also the Editorial Assistant Cailin Barrett-Bressack. Thanks also go to Janine Tangney in her role as Associate Media Editor. I am indebted to the Marketing staff for their talented and innovative efforts on behalf of *Critical Thinking, Thoughtful Writing:* Marketing Director Stacey Purviance; Marketing Development Manager Erin Parkins; and Marketing Coordinator Justin Lacap. I extend special appreciation to the production team, for their dedicated and talented efforts on behalf of the book: Corinna Dibble and Cenveo Publisher Services.

A special acknowledgment goes to Joyce Neff at Old Dominion University for her superb work in writing the earlier editions of the Instructor's Resource Manual. I am particularly indebted to the members of the English Department at LaGuardia College for their creative collaboration in linking the writing and critical thinking programs, a process that was initially supported with funding from the National Endowment for the Humanities.

My children, Jessie and Joshua, and my wife, Heide Lange, have provided ongoing love, support, and guidance that have enhanced this book and brought purpose and meaning to my life. I would also like to remember my parents, Charlotte Hess and Hubert Chaffee, who taught me lasting lessons about the most important things in life.

Tools for Thinking, Reading, and Writing

CHAPTER 1   The Thinking-Writing Model: Rhetoric, Situation, and Process

CHAPTER 2   Reading: Making Meaning

CHAPTER 3   Writing: Using Independent Thought and Informed Beliefs

CHAPTER 4   Thinking: Becoming More Creative and Visually Aware

CHAPTER 5   Drafting: Making and Analyzing Decisions

CHAPTER 6   Revising: Using Language Thoughtfully

Writing, reading, and creating text and images are how our minds explore and explain our world. The use of language and images is what makes us human; it is how we argue, how we tell stories, how we learn, how we creatively and politically express ourselves. To write is to use language thoughtfully, with a sense of audience and purpose. When you write, you pay close attention to the words that you choose, the structure of your paragraphs, the images you create. You contemplate your subject, search for exactly the right word to describe an observation, draw together different pieces of evidence to persuade a reader to think as you do. Writing helps you make sense of yourself and your world by illuminating your thought processes; writing is your mind in motion, working to clarify and understand. Learning to read critically helps you to become more aware of the strategies available to thoughtful writers. Reading texts and critically viewing images engage your mind with other conversations and open up additional perspectives.

Thinking clearly and critically about your reading strategies and your writing process will greatly enhance your ability to express yourself in all areas of your life. Part One of this book sharpens your awareness of the relationships among thinking, reading, writing, and creating texts and images and introduces you to ways of becoming a critical thinker and reader and a thoughtful writer.

Although the process of becoming a critical thinker involves solitary activities like reading, writing, and reflecting, it is a process that is also quite social in nature. Our minds develop in unique ways by exchanging ideas with others: discussing, debating, and questioning. When was the last time you experienced a mental "lightbulb" go off when working with others?

CHAPTER 1

The Thinking-Writing Model:
Rhetoric, Situation, and Process

I write to understand as much as to be understood.

—Elie Wiesel

CRITICAL THINKING FOCUS:
Thinking through writing

WRITING FOCUS:
The writing process

READING THEME:
Writing as self-expression

WRITING ACTIVITY:
Reflecting on past critical thinking

Thinking and Writing in College

The writer E. M. Forster once remarked, "How do I know what I think until I see what I say?" What did he mean by this? That you can't write better than you think! In many ways college is a whole new world. Not only are you expected to do more work in your courses, but you also are expected to work at a higher level: to *write more analytically,* to *think more conceptually,* and to *read more critically* than ever before. As a college writer, a citizen, or a member of a profession, you are expected to write with depth, insight, and analytical understanding. In order to achieve this level of sophistication in writing, you need to develop comparably advanced thinking abilities.

Becoming an effective writer enables you to represent your experience with clarity and precision. As you may have learned from your communication experiences thus far, the very process of using language serves to generate ideas. As a vehicle for creating and communicating your ideas, writing can be thought of as a catalyst that stimulates your personal and intellectual development. Since the writing process also enlarges your understanding of the world, becoming an effective writer is at the heart of your education.

To improve your writing abilities, you need to write on a regular basis, integrating writing into your life as a vital and natural element. Therefore, this book offers you Thinking-Writing Activities. These can be done in various ways: out of class or in, individually or in pairs or groups, and in whatever format your instructor specifies. Your instructor might ask you to record your responses in a journal to be reviewed periodically or in a class website or online forum. Your writing may also be shared with classmates or used as a basis for discussion. The work you do for the Thinking-Writing Activities will help to prepare you for the Writing Projects that conclude each chapter. These will give you an opportunity to think deeply about important subjects, to express your own distinctive point of view in a thoughtful and organized fashion, and to analyze the ideas of others from a variety of sources. Collaborative Activities provide the opportunity to enrich your writing by working with other students.

Thinking-Writing Activity

RECALLING A LEARNING EXPERIENCE

Recall a memorable learning experience that you have had, either in school or outside. Describe that experience and explain why it has had a lasting impact on you. Discuss how the experience has contributed to your development as a thinker and writer.

Becoming a Critical Thinker and Thoughtful Writer

Who is a critical thinker, and how do you become one? Traditionally, when people refer to a critical thinker, they mean someone who has developed an understanding of today's complex world, a thoughtful perspective on ideas and issues, the capacity for insight and good judgment, and sophisticated reasoning and language abilities. Critical thinkers are able to

- Articulate their ideas clearly and persuasively in writing
- Understand and evaluate what they read
- Discuss ideas in an informed, productive fashion

By questioning and analyzing, by evaluating and making sense of information, you examine your own thinking and that of others. And by clearly expressing your ideas in writing, you enter a larger community of thinkers and writers who enrich and sharpen your own thoughts through their responses. These thinking and writing activities help you reach the best possible conclusions and decisions.

QUALITIES OF A THOUGHTFUL WRITER

A thoughtful writer is a person who thinks critically while moving through the process of writing. This writer reflects deeply on the ideas to be expressed and thinks carefully about the language and organization needed to meet the goals of the writing situation. In short, a thoughtful writer is a critical thinker. No collection of writing tips and strategies will ever enable you to write thoughtfully if you're not thinking critically.

Throughout this text, we focus on four qualities that characterize critical thinkers and thoughtful writers, and we will tie these thinking-writing qualities into specific stages of the writing process.

- Curious
- Open-minded
- Knowledgeable
- Creative

Let's explore these qualities in greater depth.

Curious   Thoughtful writers explore situations with probing questions that penetrate beneath the surface of issues, instead of being satisfied with superficial explanations. (They *want* to learn, to discover . . . .)

Open-minded   Thoughtful writers explore their subjects from many different perspectives, willing to listen carefully to every viewpoint and evaluate each perspective carefully and fairly. Rather than being locked in to one point of view or a single, limited framework, they strive to understand and communicate the complex dimensions of their themes. For example, if they are writing about a social issue, they strive to present different perspectives on the issue as they reason their way to an informed conclusion.

Knowledgeable   Thoughtful writers always work to support their opinions with facts, evidence, and reasons. They recognize that opinions have value only to the extent that they are *informed* opinions. On the other hand, if they lack knowledge of the subject, they acknowledge this and set out to research what they need to know.

Creative   Thoughtful writers strive to develop inventive approaches to subjects; their writing is fresh and imaginative, avoiding clichés and tired conventions. They seek to break out of established patterns of thinking and approach themes and ideas from innovative directions.

Thinking critically by carefully exploring your thinking process is one of the most satisfying aspects of being a mature, educated human being. Analogously, *writing thoughtfully* involves thinking critically as you move through the process of writing so that you can express your ideas effectively.

The Thinking-Writing Model

The paradox of acquiring any complex ability is that in the best of all possible worlds, you would learn all the component parts of the activity at the same time. For example, learning to drive a car requires you master a variety of component skills that operate simultaneously: watching the road ahead, steering, applying the appropriate pressure on the gas pedal, braking, keeping a proper distance from other vehicles, watching for traffic signs and traffic lights, keeping an eye open for pedestrians, and so on. Yet a book on driving, or a video, focuses on one skill at a time because that is how information is presented most easily. Somehow you have to make the leap from learning all of the skills separately in a linear, step-by-step fashion to using them all at the same time, in complex relationships with one another.

Learning the complex skills of thinking critically and writing thoughtfully poses a similar dilemma. Although it is essential to learn each of the component parts of these processes, what distinguishes critical thinkers and thoughtful writers is that they can use all of these individual skills simultaneously.

The visual Thinking-Writing Model (Figure 1.1) presents each of these processes in relationship to the others. As you work on the various chapters and activities in this book, you will become more familiar with the different dimensions of the thinking-writing process.

As you examine the model, the writing process typically begins with a series of questions. What is the *Purpose* of this communication? What is the *Subject?* Who is the

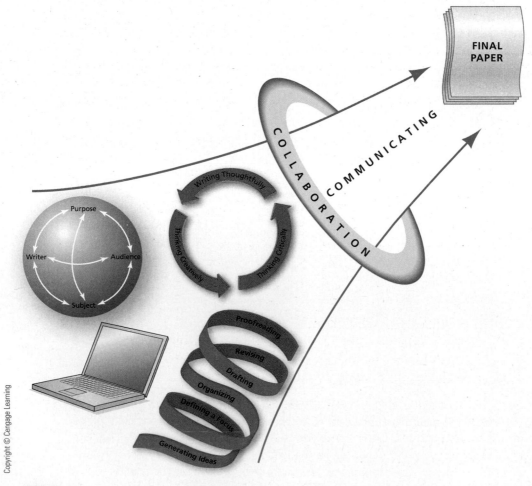

FIGURE 1.1
The Complete Thinking-Writing Model

Audience? Who is the *Writer,* and what is the writer's perspective? Engaging these questions utilizes our core abilities to *Think Creatively* about ideas we want to communicate, *Think Critically* in order to organize and clarify these ideas, and *Write Thoughtfully* by using the appropriate vocabulary and language forms to communicate our ideas.

The writing process itself is dynamic and holistic. The key elements of the process are *Generating* ideas, *Defining* a focus, *Organizing, Drafting, Revising,* and *Proofreading.* For most writers, these activities rarely occur in a neat, orderly sequence: the process is much more organic and recursive. Effective writers also *Collaborate* with other people in order to help them produce the highest quality of writing, and their assistance can occur at any stage in the writing process.

At the very center of the model is *Communicating,* the process by which we share our thoughts, feelings, and experiences. Communication creates miraculous moments when our minds touch and engage other minds. The word *communicating* comes from the Latin word *communicare,* which means "to share, to impart, to make common." As members of a social species, we need to share thoughts and feelings with other human beings. As technologies allow speedier and speedier communication throughout the world, critical thinking and thoughtful writing are evermore vital to the survival and progress of humanity.

This book is designed to offer you opportunities to build on the strengths you have and to grow as a critical thinker and thoughtful writer. The following Thinking-Writing Activity asks you to reflect on your own thinking-writing process as a starting point.

Thinking-Writing Activity

ANALYZING A WRITING EXPERIENCE

Describe in detail a writing experience that you found particularly satisfying or successful: for example, a paper you wrote for school, a market analysis you created for your company, or a letter in which you expressed important thoughts and feelings. After completing your description, answer the following questions in your journal or notebook.

- What was your goal or purpose in writing?
- What was the reaction of the people who read it—your audience?
- How did you think of the key ideas you included?
- How did you organize your ideas?
- Did you use other sources (such as readings) to provide support and context for your writing?
- In what ways did you revise your writing?
- How did you feel after completing your writing?

Your analysis will probably demonstrate that you already use many of the abilities that are integral to the Thinking-Writing Model. Carefully examine the Thinking-Writing

Model in Figure 1.1. Before long, the model will become familiar, and you will be able to use it as a powerful guide to strengthen and clarify your thinking and writing. Let's explore the various dimensions of the Thinking-Writing Model and see how they work together to produce clear thinking and effective writing.

Rhetoric and the Writing Situation

Writers have reasons to write, someone to whom they wish to write, a subject about which they have something important to say, and a sense of self as a writer that they want to project. Although these ideas are of great importance today, they are not new. They come from the study of *rhetoric,* the principles developed in ancient times for speaking and writing effectively. Rhetoric is the art of inventing or discovering your ideas, arranging them in the most persuasive way, and then expressing them in suitable language in order to have the desired effect on their audiences. Today the word *rhetoric* has both a negative and a positive meaning: language that is insincere and not to be taken seriously—"mere rhetoric"—and the positive meaning with which this book is concerned, the study of the principles and rules for effective writing.

We begin our study of rhetoric with the components of the writing situation: purpose, audience, subject, and writer. In Figure 1.2, these four components appear in the first part of the model because they need to be considered when the writer begins to write, but they also need to be thought about at every stage of writing and communicating. To help you develop your rhetorical skills, these components are discussed individually at the beginning of each of the Writing Projects in subsequent chapters.

PURPOSE

Every act of writing has a *purpose.* When you complete a paper for a college course, you hope to show your instructor that you have understood and can both apply and communicate concepts relevant to the class. In a business setting, your aim is to

FIGURE 1.2
The Writing Situation

Copyright © Cengage Learning

transmit information or requests in a memo or a report; in your civic life, you want to advocate for community interests through letters or petitions; in your private life, you may text, email, write in your journal, or post to Facebook or a blog so you can later recall events and feelings. A crucial part of becoming a thoughtful writer is maintaining a clear sense of the specific audience and purpose for whatever subject you are writing about.

AUDIENCE

Thoughtfully considering *audience* is critical during the entire writing process but especially during the early stages while forming ideas and considering the purpose of your writing. You may be writing only for yourself (in a diary, for instance), but most of your writing will be read by someone else. Your audience may be an individual receiving your letter, people visiting your blog, coworkers reading your memo, or your instructor grading your paper. If your writing is not clear, you risk communicating the wrong message. Consider the language you use to convey your ideas. You would, for example, communicate with the local school board differently than you would with a group of biologists. A skilled writer thoughtfully targets his or her audience. What the writer says is exactly what the audience hears, and there is no room for misunderstanding.

Thoughtful writers are able to put themselves in their readers' place and view their own writing through their readers' eyes. This perspective-taking helps them craft their writing so that it will best communicate the ideas, arguments, experiences, and emotions they seek to convey. In other words, they think about how much background information their audience will need (or won't need) to understand the intended message. Skilled writers anticipate potential audience questions, biases, and feelings so they can proactively address these in the writing itself. By acknowledging the audience, writers build a relationship based on trust and confidence.

SUBJECT

Writing has to be about someone or something—a *subject*. Sometimes the subject originates in your own experience, but often it comes from ideas and information provided by others. Much of college writing involves responding to ideas and concepts presented in textbooks, lectures, or research sources. Today much of the research you will do for college begins on the Internet, so the ability to find and evaluate online sources is crucial. Writing tasks are typically designed so that you can demonstrate your understanding of the ideas presented and so that you can apply, analyze, synthesize, or evaluate the ideas being expressed. The quality of your writing depends on the quality of your thinking as you process, organize, and present ideas in order to communicate your own informed perspective on the subject.

WRITER

A writer's personality and other characteristics can affect what is written, produced, and even interpreted by an audience. Gender, ethnicity, religion, culture, social standing, and education are just some of the factors influencing a writer's approach

Thinking Critically About Visuals

Perspective-Taking and Audience

The composition of a given audience can vary greatly, and it is important that the speaker is aware of who the audience is and what their needs will be. Consider how the tone, content, and length of a speech can impact a general audience—that is, one composed of people of varying backgrounds.

© iStockPhoto.com/ratluk

Many audiences consist of a specific group of people. In some ways, it is easier for the speaker to tailor his or her message to a specific group; however, it is still critical to consider the tone, content, and length of a speech. For example, if you were speaking to a group of baseball or soccer fans, it would not be necessary to define common lingo such as "being credited with an assist," "fighting off a pitch," or a "yellow card." Neglecting to provide definitions for terms unfamiliar to a more general audience, however, could be problematic in that they could feel lost or disconnected from the content.

Oberhaeuser/Caro/Alamy

Try asking yourself audience-centered questions while preparing your message: *Who is my audience? What do they expect from my speech? How do I grab (and keep) their attention? What is the most effective language to use? What do I want my audience to take away?* These same principles apply to a piece of writing since it, too, has an audience.

Paul Doyle/Alamy

Although speaking to a group of children (or even teenagers) may appear to be an easy task, an audience of young people can actually be quite challenging. What are some of the issues you (as a speaker/writer) would have to consider with this specific audience?

Van Hilversum/Alamy

It is also critical to consider any preexisting beliefs people might have when addressing an audience. An effective speaker (and writer) will make sure members of the audience feel comfortable and respected. It is the responsibility of the writer and the speaker to be professional and sensitive to the needs of the audience.

NEW MEDIA & THOUGHTFUL WRITING

How to Write for the New Media

When we express ourselves in writing, our audience is not able to hear our vocal inflections or see our gestures and body language. The impression we make depends completely on what we write. The same holds true for the use of texting and email, which have changed the way many people communicate at work, in social settings, in the classroom, and at home. Consider the following questions:

- What are some of the differences among communicating via text or email, the spoken word, or another form of writing?

- Do you think a text or email is easier to misunderstand than other styles of writing? Why or why not? For example, have you ever
  - Received a text or email you thought was sarcastic, cruel, or too blunt?
  - Sent one that was misinterpreted?
  - Received "hoax" virus warnings?
  - Received chain letters promising unbelievable rewards?
  - Received jokes you didn't want?

- In your opinion, has the popularity of texting or email changed the nature or frequency of these kinds of messages as compared to paper mail? If so, how has that happened? The central point is that in order to be an effective communicator in any medium, we have to be continually aware of our audience, asking ourselves the questions "How will my message be received or interpreted?" and "What 'voice' will be most successful in communicating my intended message?"

Writing is similar to speaking in this regard. Have you noticed that you speak differently to different groups of people in different situations? Depending on whether and where you work, you may notice that your choice of words and even grammatical constructions vary from those you use when speaking with, for example, family members. For that matter, how you speak to children is probably different from how you speak to siblings or to parents and other elders. You have different "speaking personalities" in different situations.

What different texting or email personalities do you have? What steps can you take to ensure that you come across as you intend when you text or use email? These are "language landmines" that you want to keep in mind as you compose and send your texts, emails, and tweets. Writing for new media effectively means developing a new set of writing strategies especially adapted to this new digital medium. In the following article, "How to Write for the New Media," author Neal Jansons identifies some of the writing strategies to work at developing.

How to Write for the New Media

by Neal Jansons

Here are some tricks and tips for developing a new media writing style.

1. Go Short

In school and literature, often we are taught that more is better. If you can slip in more detail, another source, or another idea, you should. Well, this is just plain wrong in the new media. Here we have to capture a reader who with the click of a mouse can be somewhere else. They are not a professor paid to read a paper or a book-reader sitting and relaxing in a nook. They are on a computer and working in a very "hot" (interactive) medium. **Keep your posts and articles between 400 and 700 words.** If you absolutely *must* go longer, consider splitting the post up into a series. DO NOT go for the "multi-pager." It does not work, nobody reads it and if you keep trying to write your *magnum opus* you will lose readers.

2. Avoid Big Blocks of Texts

Break your articles up into multiple paragraphs. What seems like over-formatting in a book or magazine can be perfect for a post because of the difference in how they are read. People's eyes react differently to text on a screen. **Use pictures, changes in font size, and lists to break your content up into meaningful chunks.** The goal is that at any point a person could finish up a section in just a few seconds and easily come back for the next chunk later.

3. Avoid the Passive Voice

In school we learn to speak in the passive voice to record facts. This makes things very "objective" and "neutral" sounding, but is not what people are looking for online. There are a billion other things they could be reading that can all be objective, but they will read *your* work because it is *yours*. **Make your writing drip with active verbs and your own personality.** Let your voice come through so strongly that the reader will hear you in their head.

4. Lead the Reader

The formatting of online content is always a problem, but the best thing you can do is let your content guide the reader's eyes and mind. **Use lists, headings, and text styling to lead the reader's eyes to the important points.** This is what is sometimes called the "Command to Look" from a book by the same name.

(Continues)

NEW MEDIA & THOUGHTFUL WRITING (CONTINUED)

5. Make Your Content "Hot"

This is the internet, web 2.0 thank you very much, and we want our content to be dynamic. We want links, video, and the ability to converse. **Pepper your articles with interactivity,** even to the point of asking questions for your readers to answer. If you refer to something, link it (but only the first time!), if you say there was a video, include it in the post.

6. K.I.S.S.

Keep it simple. No, really. Really simple. Avoid clarifying clauses, complicated thoughts, and involved sentences. This is not to say you can't write difficult ideas . . . just break them down. **Tell them what you are going to tell them, tell them, then tell them what you told them.** The reason for this is (again) about how people read on the internet. Since people are always multi-tasking, being able to come back to an article and read it in little chunks without losing the thread of the thought is absolutely necessary.

Final Word

Following these simple steps you can increase your reader loyalty and the usefulness of your posts. People will be able to get what they need from your content easily and efficiently, which will make your posts and articles appealing and useful, which means

and attitude. How the writer uses language can make a difference, too, as can the writer's state of mind (happy, sad, angry, etc.).

The relationship of the writer to the audience also plays a role in this complex relationship. For example, it is acceptable to use an informal writing style (slang, contractions, abbreviations, etc.) when texting friends or posting to Facebook. College students, however, are expected to write with authority and formality as they participate in larger conversations with educated authors. If an essay is about your own life and experiences, you automatically have that authority, since no one knows your life better than you do. But many college assignments related to course materials expect you to write with authority. That is why the library and the Internet are so important: by gathering, analyzing, synthesizing, and evaluating information, you can become knowledgeable on nearly any topic. One of the worst ways for a college writer to begin a speech or paper is "I don't know much about this subject, but here goes." Instead, do your research and equip yourself to communicate your ideas with confidence and professionalism.

people will come back to read more and pass on your work to other potential readers and clients. **Help your readers read and they will stay loyal, make them work too hard and they will just click something else.**

Source: From WriteNewMedia.com blog by Neal Jansons. Reprinted by permission of the author.

Thinking-Writing Activity

HOW WELL DO YOU COMMUNICATE?

How do you come across to your audience, and what can you do to improve the clarity of your message? One approach is to look through your sent email or text files and examine past messages. Ask yourself, "Was this message written in a way that best communicated my intended meaning, or could there have been misinterpretations?" and "How could I revise the message to make it less vague or ambiguous?" Once you have revised some of these older texts or emails, think of some strategies to help make your future texts or emails more successful in communicating the meaning you intend such as "I should make more use of examples to illustrate my point."

From *My American Journey*

by Colin Powell

In the following excerpt from his best-selling autobiography *My American Journey*, former Secretary of State Colin Powell writes with authority about his life. Powell was born in New York City to immigrant parents from Jamaica. He attended public schools in the city, graduating from the City College of New York with a degree in geology. As a student at CCNY, he participated in ROTC, receiving a commission as an Army second lieutenant upon graduation. Powell served for thirty-five years, rising to the rank of four-star general and holding, from 1989 through 1993, the position of Chairman of the Joint Chiefs of Staff, the highest military position in the Department of Defense.

Powell's name has often been mentioned as a candidate for public office. He has been awarded two Presidential Medals of Freedom and the Congressional Gold Medal, among other military honors and decorations.

I have made clear that I was no great shakes as a scholar. I have joked over the years that the CCNY [City College of New York] faculty handed me a diploma, uttering a sigh of relief, and were happy to pass me along to the military. Yet, even this C-average student emerged from CCNY prepared to write, think, and communicate effectively and equipped to compete against students from colleges that I could never have dreamed of attending. If the Statue of Liberty opened the gateway to this country, public education opened the door to attainment here. Schools like my sister's Buffalo State Teachers College and CCNY have served as the Harvards and Princetons of the poor. And they served us well. I am, consequently, a champion of public secondary and higher education. I will speak out for them and support them for as long as I have the good sense to remember where I came from.

Shortly before the commissioning ceremony in Aronowitz Auditorium, Colonel Brookhart called me into his office in the drill hall. "Sit down, Mr. Powell," he said. I did, sitting at attention. "You've done well here (in ROTC). You'll do well in the Army. You're going to Fort Benning soon."

He warned me that I needed to be careful. Georgia was not New York. The South was another world. I had to learn to compromise, to accept a world I had not made and that was beyond my changing. He mentioned the black general Benjamin O. Davis, who had been with him at West Point, where Davis was shunned the whole four years by his classmates, including, I assumed, Brookhart. Davis had gotten himself into trouble in the South, Brookhart said, because he had tried to buck the system. The colonel was telling me, in effect, not to rock the boat, to be a "good Negro." . . .

The Army was becoming more democratic, but I was plunged back into the Old South every time I left the post. I could go into Woolworth's in Columbus, Georgia, and buy anything I wanted, as long as I did not try to eat there. I could go into a department store and they would take my money, as long as I did not try to use the men's room. I could walk along the street, as long as I did not look at a white woman. . . .

5   One night, exhausted and hungry, I locked up the house and headed back toward the post. As I approached a drive-in hamburger joint on Victory Drive, I thought, okay, I know they won't serve me inside, so I'll just park outside. I pulled in, and after a small eternity, a waitress came to my car window. "A hamburger, please," I said.

She looked at me uneasily. "Are you Puerto Rican?" she asked.

"No," I said.

"Are you an African student?" She seemed genuinely trying to be helpful.

"No," I answered. "I'm a Negro. I'm an American. And I'm an Army officer."

10   "Look, I'm from New Jersey," the waitress said, and "I don't understand any of this. But they won't let me serve you. Why don't you go behind the restaurant, and I'll pass you a hamburger out the back window."

Something snapped. "I'm not that hungry," I said, burning rubber as I backed out. As I drove away, I could see the faces of the owner and his customers in the restaurant windows enjoying this little exercise in humiliation. . . .

Racism was still relatively new to me, and I had to find a way to cope psychologically. I began by identifying my priorities. I wanted, above all, to succeed at my Army career. I did not intend to give way to self-destructive rage, no matter how provoked. If people in the South insisted on living by crazy rules, then I would play the hand dealt me for now. If I was to be confined to one end of the playing field, then I was going to be a star on that part of the field. Nothing that happened off-post, none of the indignities, none of the injustices, was going to inhibit my performance. I was not going to let myself become emotionally crippled because I could not play on the whole field. I did not feel inferior, and I was not going to let anybody make me believe I was. I was not going to allow someone else's feelings about me to become my feelings about myself. Racism was not just a black problem. It was America's problem. And until the country solved it, I was not going to let bigotry make me a victim instead of a full human being. I occasionally felt hurt; I felt anger; but most of all I felt challenged. I'll show you!

QUESTIONS FOR READING ACTIVELY

1. What audience do you think Powell had in mind while writing? Identify a specific audience, either one person or a group of persons, to whom you would recommend this reading.

2. Describe the writer as specifically as you can. What is your attitude toward him, now that you have read this? Does this represent any change in your attitude toward Powell?

QUESTIONS FOR THINKING CRITICALLY

1. Describe an experience in which you were the victim of discrimination or prejudice. How did it make you feel? How did you deal with it?

2. Colin Powell was determined to achieve his goals, despite many obstacles. Describe in your own words the thinking approach he used to deal with the pervasive racism that he encountered.

3. Powell concludes his autobiography with an affirmation regarding the United States that seems particularly relevant in these perilous times: "We will come through because our founders bequeathed us a political system of genius, a system flexible enough for all ages and inspiring noble aspirations for all time. We will continue to flourish because our diverse American society has the strength, hardiness, and resilience of the hybrid plant we are."

   Explain whether you agree with Powell that America's ethnic diversity is a source of strength and resilience, and list the reasons why or why not.

QUESTION FOR WRITING THOUGHTFULLY

1. What purpose or purposes do you think Powell had in mind while writing? How does he try to achieve his purpose(s)? List two specific examples from the reading to support your answer.

WRITING THOUGHTFULLY, THINKING CREATIVELY, THINKING CRITICALLY

The next part of the Thinking-Writing Model, Figure 1.3, indicates the reciprocal relationships among writing thoughtfully, thinking creatively, and thinking critically. The ability to be creative is one of the four qualities that distinguish critical thinkers and thoughtful writers. When you first decide to write something, you need to come up with some initial ideas to write about. Your ability to *think creatively* makes producing such ideas possible. When you think creatively, you discover ideas—and connections among ideas—that are illuminating, useful, often exciting, sometimes original, and usually worth developing. We can define *thinking creatively* as discovering and developing ideas that are unusual and worthy of further elaboration.

Simultaneously (or *almost* simultaneously), these beginning ideas find form in language expressed in writing. Yet the process of writing thoughtfully elaborates and shapes the ideas that you are trying to express, especially if you are to bring your critical thinking abilities to bear on this evolving process. This extraordinarily complex process typically takes place in a very natural fashion as creative thinking and critical thinking work together to produce thoughtful writing, which, in turn, gives form to your ideas and communicates them to others.

Effective writers not only use each of these processes but also are able to integrate them. For example, it is impossible to write thoughtfully without creating ideas that reflect your vision of the world or without using your critical thinking abilities to evaluate the accuracy and intelligibility of your writing. Unfortunately, these essential abilities are not always taught explicitly. Too often, writing is emphasized as a way of putting words together in conventional forms, not as a dynamic means of personal expression that liberates us to articulate our creative perspectives—tempered by critical evaluation.

FIGURE 1.3
Core Abilities

The Writing Process

THE RECURSIVE NATURE OF THE WRITING PROCESS

A perfect piece of writing does not happen immediately, nor does it happen on its own. All writers must go through a process beginning with generating ideas and ending with meticulous editing and a final proofreading. This process is not linear, but instead is recursive—that is, the writer often loops back through previous steps to make sure the message, and the writing itself, is as clear as possible. Despite the many different writing forms and contexts, the basic elements of the writing process remain constant:

- Generating ideas
- Defining a focus (main idea or *thesis*)
- Organizing ideas into various thinking patterns
- Drafting
- Revising, editing, and proofreading
- Collaborating, which can weave through all these activities

These elements of the writing process occur within the writing situation as a result of creative and critical thinking, and they are depicted in the third part of the Thinking-Writing Model (Figure 1.4). For most writers, these activities rarely occur in a neat, orderly sequence. Instead, writers move in different ways, from generating ideas to drafting to more generating to organizing to revising to generating to editing—around and around—as they develop ideas and clarify them. And each

Copyright © Cengage Learning

FIGURE 1.4
The Writing Process

element of the writing process depends on the writer's awareness of subject, audience, and purpose.

You have probably discovered that the process of writing does not merely express your thinking; it also stimulates your thoughts. As you write your thoughts and, if needed, research your subject, new ideas can bubble to the surface and inspire different directions to explore. As you develop and organize your thoughts into a draft, you may find the need to cultivate new ideas or refine the ones you already have. This is a natural and necessary part of the writing process. Collaboration plays a key role in the process, too. Turning to others for feedback helps you gain the perspective of a potential audience, and this, in turn, can help you improve the way you express yourself and your ideas.

GENERATING IDEAS

We have seen that most writing efforts begin with identifying something to write about—a subject. Since ideas are not created in isolation but are almost always related to a particular subject, you expand ideas by exploring that subject. Some writing projects have very specific requirements; others may be more open-ended. In most cases, however, you will be expected to come up with your own ideas. Even when you are responding to an assigned subject or a reading selection, you are typically expected to offer an original insight or viewpoint. As a thoughtful writer, you are expected to be open-minded, creative, and curious. At this stage of generating ideas, a number of strategies are useful, such as brainstorming, creating mind maps, freewriting, and asking key questions to stimulate your creative thinking. These strategies will be explored in depth in Chapter 4 if you are interested in taking a look ahead.

KEEPING A JOURNAL OR BLOG

Keeping a journal or blog is rewarding in many ways. The process of writing stimulates your mind and helps shape your thinking, while the end product is a record of your thoughts and feelings. You can return to these ideas at any time and use them as a starting point for a finished piece of writing. Personal journal entries should be freely written, with no concern for punctuation or polished prose. Let your ideas flow, write them in a notebook or a computer file, and make journaling a part of your daily life. A blog, or online journal, is less private, but equally rewarding, and allows you to participate in larger communities and conversations. Just remember that you will have a virtual audience and should approach your online writing accordingly.

DEFINING A FOCUS

After generating ideas to write about, academic writers must define a focus (which is related to purpose). Academic writing is expected to have a focus; your audience will expect more than a list of facts. Your main idea—known as a thesis or, for argumentative writing, a claim—will organize and direct your thinking. Your thesis or claim should guide your exploration of the subject. Of course, a variety of main ideas can develop out of any particular situation, so you may need to redefine your initial working thesis as you draft your paper.

Sometimes you will need to research, draft, and organize before you are ready to define your focus, but other times you might need to refocus your thesis as you are drafting. Each writer must find the path that works best for his or her particular needs. This is an organic process—one that develops naturally, based on needs, in each writing situation.

ORGANIZING IDEAS

Once you have a tentative thesis or claim, you may be ready to plan the organization of your paper. But at this point or even earlier, you may realize that you don't have enough information on your subject to fulfill your purpose. Remembering that a thoughtful writer is knowledgeable, you may need to generate more ideas or consult other sources of information in order to write with authority. When you are ready to begin organizing, ask yourself, "What are my main points, and how should they be presented to my audience?" You can use a variety of thinking patterns as you organize your writing, such as reporting chronologically, comparing and contrasting, or dividing and classifying. Your choice of thinking pattern will depend on the subject you are exploring, your purpose, and your audience. We will examine these patterns in later chapters.

It usually helps to have a tentative organization plan or outline to guide your drafting, but often your organization changes as you draft and revise. This is a natural and productive part of most people's writing processes.

DRAFTING

Drafting begins when you start writing. *What* you write reflects the work you did during the initial stages of the writing process: generating ideas, defining a focus, and thinking about an organizational structure. The more effort you put into these initial stages, the easier it will be to compose a draft—but don't expect your initial draft to be perfect or feel finished. In fact, your initial draft should undergo substantial revision until it finally represents your mind's best work. That said, during the drafting stage, don't obsess over crafting perfect sentences, creating ideal metaphors, or using optimal words. You'll have time to do that later, and quite frankly, time spent perfecting now could be time wasted, since, during the revision stage, you might delete sentences or even paragraphs because they no longer support your thesis or claim. The most important goal in drafting is to get started. Get those vague and evolving ideas onto paper where they can be examined, reflected upon, and refined.

You might find it useful to draft sections of your essay by following your organization plan, but be prepared to let the writing process take you to new places that you didn't anticipate. The process of writing is a catalyst for your thinking process and can inspire new ideas and lead you in unexpected directions. Trusting your writing/thinking process can lead to creative breakthroughs that will enrich your original plan.

Keep in mind that *what* you are drafting—a summary, an argument, a report—will influence the way you express and organize your thinking. Much of your academic writing will be in the form of essays in which you are expected to take a position, analyze a concept, or interpret a subject. The structure normally used to organize ideas in an essay typically reflects the basic questions raised when you discuss ideas with others. As you draft, keep in mind the questions of a hypothetical audience (from Mina Shaughnessey's book *Errors and Expectations*):

What is your point? (stating the main idea)

I don't quite get your meaning. (explaining the main idea)

Prove it to me. (providing examples, evidence, and arguments to support the main idea)

So what? (drawing a conclusion)

REVISING, EDITING, AND PROOFREADING

Thinking and writing are recursive processes that compel us to continually revise our thinking and writing. Whatever your drafting style is, once you have committed your ideas to a draft, you must be able to go back and "re-see" (the origin of the word *revise*) your draft as clearly as possible.

Skilled writers understand that there are significant differences among the revising, editing, and proofreading stages of the writing process and approach these stages in a logical manner:

1. *Revising* focuses on the larger elements in a piece of writing such as purpose, focus, major concepts, and supporting materials and how they work together to effectively communicate your ideas. During the revision process, you may add or cut significant parts of your writing, and even change the overall structure so that your ideas flow more logically. Make sure that your introduction clearly defines your purpose and focus (your thesis) and that the conclusion adequately summarizes and then wraps up the essay and leaves the reader with something of value.

2. *Editing* takes place after revising and focuses on medium-sized elements such as logical transitions between paragraphs, sentence structure, language and word choice, style, rhythm, and voice. It is also a good time to check your references and citations to make sure they fit and are in the correct documentation style (see the Appendix). Try reading your paper aloud to see how it flows. If you stumble over a particular passage, it is likely you'll need to make some adjustments.

3. *Proofreading* focuses on the small (but critical) elements and is the final step. Look at the essay under a microscope, so to speak, and check for errors in spelling, punctuation, and other mechanical issues. Also look for consistency in verb tense and check for typos. Because this is the last step in the writing process, you want to be sure the essay is the very best it can be.

Most writers have a hard time looking at their own writing objectively. Because they wrote it, everything makes sense—even if parts of the writing are confusing to someone else. Sometimes a writer likes certain words, sentences, or clever ideas and does not want to change them. Thoughtful writers, however, have learned how to be critical readers of their own work and accept the fact that major changes might be needed. As they go through the revision process, they have a Reader/Editor voice in their heads that asks useful questions, similar to those posed during the drafting stage:

Have you made your main point clear?

Have you proved your point to your audience by giving enough information and examples?

Could you reorganize any of your ideas to help your audience understand more easily?

As mentioned earlier, it is smart to wait until you are satisfied with the overall content and organization of your essay before you spend time editing elements like sentence structure and transitions. From there, you can proofread and work on even finer details. But keep in mind the recursive nature of the thinking and writing process—sometimes while editing or proofreading, you might see content and organization problems that require more revision!

Finally, writers and researchers in most disciplines share their drafts with colleagues for feedback and additional perspective, a collaborative process called *peer review*. It is an integral part of the writing process that can (and should) be woven through all stages to ensure quality and clarity. We will explore collaboration at the end of this chapter and strategies for peer review in Chapter 3.

"Writing Is Not a McDonald's Hamburger"
by Natalie Goldberg

Natalie Goldberg has been acclaimed as much for her intuitive, compassionate teaching of writing as for her own well-received prose, Natalie Goldberg's 1986 book *Writing Down the Bones* (from which "Writing Is Not a McDonald's Hamburger" is excerpted) has become a touchstone not only for aspiring writers but also for anyone wishing to live more creatively. Goldberg has continued to mine her personal life, her deeply engaged study of Zen Buddhism, and her painterly observations of the natural world (particularly the landscape around her home in Taos, New Mexico) in such books as *Wild Mind: Living the Writer's Life* (1990), *Long Quiet Highway: Waking Up in America* (1993), and *Thunder and Lightning: Cracking Open the Writer's Craft* (2000). Goldberg lives with her partner in Taos, New Mexico, and St. Paul, Minnesota.

Sometimes I have a student who is really good right from the beginning. I'm thinking of one in particular. The air was electric when he read, and he was often shaking. The writing process split him open; he was able to tell about being fourteen

Source: From *Writing Down the Bones: Freeing the Writer Within,* by Natalie Goldberg, © 1986 by Natalie Goldberg. Reprinted by arrangement with The Permissions Company, Inc., on behalf of Shambhala Publications Inc., Boston, MA. www.shambhala.com.

years old in a mental hospital, about walking the streets of Minneapolis tripping on LSD, about sitting next to the dead body of his brother in San Francisco. He said he had wanted to write for years. People told him he should be a writer, but anytime he sat down to write he couldn't connect the words on paper with the event or his feelings.

That is because he had an idea of what he wanted to say before he came to paper. Of course, you can sit down and have something you want to say. But then you must let its expression be born in you and on the paper. Don't hold too tight; allow it to come out how it needs to rather than trying to control it. Yes, those experiences, memories, feelings, are in us, but you can't carry them out on paper whole the way a cook brings out a pizza from the oven.

Let go of everything when you write, and try at a simple beginning with simple words to express what you have inside. It won't begin smoothly. Allow yourself to be awkward. You are stripping yourself. You are exposing your life, not how your ego would like to see you represented, but how you are as a human being. And it is because of this that I think writing is religious. It splits you open and softens your heart toward the homely world.

When I'm cranky now, miserable, dissatisfied, pessimistic, negative, generally rotten, I recognize it as a feeling. I know the feeling can change. I know it is energy that wants to find a place in the world and wants friends.

5   But yes, you can have topics you want to write about—"I want to write about my brother who died in San Francisco"—but come to it not with your mind and ideas, but with your whole body—your heart and gut and arms. Begin to write in the dumb, awkward way an animal cries out in pain, and there you will find your intelligence, your words, your voice.

People often say, "I was walking along [or driving, shopping, jogging] and I had this whole poem go through my mind, but when I sat down to write it, I couldn't get it to come out right." I never can either. Sitting to write is another activity. Let go of walking or jogging and the poem that was born then in your mind. This is another moment. Write another poem. Perhaps secretly hope something of what you thought a while ago might come out, but let it come out however it does. Don't force it.

The same student mentioned above was so excited about writing that he immediately tried to form a book. I told him, "Take it slow. Just let yourself write for a while. Learn what that is about." Writing is a whole lifetime and a lot of practice. I understood his urgency. We want to think we are doing something useful, going someplace, achieving something—"I am writing a book."

Give yourself some space before you decide to write those big volumes. Learn to trust the force of your own voice. Naturally, it will evolve a direction and a need for one, but it will come from a different place than your need to be an achiever. Writing is not a McDonald's hamburger. The cooking is slow, and in the beginning you are not sure whether a roast or a banquet or a lamb chop will be the result.

QUESTIONS FOR READING ACTIVELY

1. What purpose or purposes do you think Goldberg had in mind while writing? Specify any one thing in the reading that helps you to identify her purpose.

2. What audience do you think she had in mind while writing? What other audiences might benefit from reading this? What audiences might not benefit?

3. What is her subject? Be as specific as you can in describing it. What is her attitude toward her subject?

QUESTIONS FOR THINKING CRITICALLY

1. Goldberg, a Zen Buddhist, claims in paragraph 3 that she believes "writing is religious." How does she define and understand "religious," and what specific qualities of writing make it a "religious" activity or experience? Do you agree with her definition of "religious"? Compare your own definition of a "religious" activity or mindset with Goldberg's.

2. Athletes often describe their feeling at peak performance as being "in the flow." Goldberg describes something similar about the process of inspiration. Describe a time when you felt like you were "in the flow" of an activity (physical, artistic, or intellectual). How did you get "in the flow"? Is there a specific strategy or ritual that you use to help you get "in the flow"?

QUESTION FOR WRITING THOUGHTFULLY

1. Goldberg uses an amusing metaphor to describe what writing is *not*. Do you agree with her metaphor? Create other metaphors that describe your feeling about writing (especially academic writing).

COLLABORATING

When you work with other people in the writing process, you participate in collaboration. You can collaborate with others at every stage of the thinking and writing process. People can help one another generate ideas, identify a main idea to pursue, or suggest possible approaches and ways of organizing. Some entire pieces of writing, especially in business, are produced collaboratively by a team of writers. Since collaborating can occur in all writing process activities, the line representing collaboration circles around them in the model in Figure 1.1.

Writers often discover new perspectives when others review drafts of their writing. This is the moment when writers get a sense of how effective their efforts at communication are. No matter how clearly you try to keep your audience in mind as you write, you may not succeed at first. There is no substitute for having your audience (or people like your intended audience) let you know what you have and have not communicated clearly. With their suggestions, you can improve and refine your writing so that it will better convey what you intended. As a critical thinker and informed writer, you will learn to work with others in developing your thinking and writing, welcoming their advice when you are the sole author and contributing well when you are part of a writing team. Opportunities for collaborating are marked throughout the book with the icon pictured at the beginning of this section.

Of course, in writing collaboratively, you also have a responsibility to respond critically to the writing of others. *Critical* is related to *criticize*, which means "to question and evaluate." Unfortunately, the ability to criticize is often used destructively to tear down someone else's thinking. Criticism, however, should be *constructive*—analyzing for the purpose of developing better understanding. To develop your abilities to think critically and write thoughtfully, it is important to offer and receive constructive criticism.

Becoming a critical thinker and a thoughtful writer does not simply involve mastering certain life skills; it affects the entire way that you view the world and live your life. You already use critical thinking in many aspects of your life: how you make decisions, how you relate to others, and how you deal with controversial issues. These abilities can be improved with information, strategies, and practice, and you will continue to develop them as you move forward through college and your career.

Thinking-Writing Activity

EXPRESSING A DEEPER MEANING

This Thinking-Writing Activity gives you an opportunity to apply some of the ideas we have been exploring in this chapter. Think of a place—or, if you can, go and visit a place—that has special meaning for you, a place that led you to a realization about life. Write a description that effectively communicates *where* you are as well as expressing a deeper kind of meaning. What kind of meaning, exactly, is up to you and depends on the feelings that the place evokes. Reach deep within yourself and discover an analogous feeling to articulate in your writing.

- Consider the audience for whom you are writing and the purpose you would like to accomplish.

- After writing your first draft, *revise* your paper to more fully express your feelings and ideas.

- Add details that communicate your meaning as specifically as possible.

- Craft your sentences so that they flow together and create a consistent "picture" of the place you are describing. *Edit* and *proofread* your writing.

- Share your paper with your classmates. Ask them what feelings and ideas your description communicated to them.

- As a group, discuss which steps of the writing process for this assignment came easily and which required more effort.

- Becoming a critical thinker and a thoughtful writer requires that you be curious, open-minded, knowledgeable, and creative.

- The components of any writing situation include the purpose, audience, subject, and writer.

- The writing process involves generating ideas, defining a focus, organizing ideas, drafting, revising, editing, and proofreading.

- Collaborating with others can be helpful at any stage of the writing process. The constructive criticism of others can help the writer gain different and valuable perspectives.

Students who study abroad are often faced with a language barrier—not only in terms of speech, but also when it comes to reading and writing. Have you ever come across an unfamiliar word, phrase, or allusion while reading? How do you cope with unfamiliar language?

Reading:
Making Meaning

"Read not to contradict nor to believe, but to weigh and consider."

—FRANCIS BACON

CRITICAL THINKING FOCUS:
Reflecting on reading and making meaning

WRITING FOCUS:
Thinking about rhetorical choices and writing in response to reading

READING THEME:
Using your response to reading as a subject for writing

WRITING ACTIVITY:
Evaluating and reflecting on writings

Reading in College, Reading for Life

Let's begin this chapter with a question: What does it mean to read? Not so long ago, to "read" meant to turn the pages of a book, a newspaper, or an owner's manual. Reading was a physical activity that required daylight or a lamp, and texts were physical objects that you carried around in a backpack or briefcase. When you went to the library, it was usually to check out a book that would be returned two weeks later. When you woke up in the morning, you read a newspaper as you drank your coffee. And when you got home from classes, you stayed up late into the night with your textbooks and a dictionary.

Times have changed, though, and so have our reading habits. The physical act of reading—opening a book, turning pages, flipping back and forth, underlining, inserting a bookmark—seems at times to be almost quaint or old-fashioned in the digital age of e-readers and the Internet. Yet reading—the deciphering of, and interacting with, ideas and language—is at the core of a liberal education.

Reading is certainly a critical component of education, but it is also a necessary part of life. It is difficult to imagine making it through the day without reading something: a sign, an email or text, a recipe, instructions, a prescription, the ticker at the bottom of the nightly news—the list goes on and on. But we also read for pleasure, and we read to help satisfy our curiosity about the world in which we live. Reading exercises our mind, encourages our imagination, broadens our horizons and perspectives, and can help us enrich our vocabulary. Avid readers are generally well-spoken—and, more often than not, have strong writing skills.

Although most of us might do most of our "reading" without ever getting near a book, the fundamental skills of deciphering, understanding, and interacting with *the text* are universal and, yes, important. Sergio Troncoso, author of five books including *The Last Tortilla and Other Stories,* is passionate about reading and feels that we are in "the crisis of our times." His blog post "Why Read?" was written in 2012.

Why Read?

by Sergio Troncoso

I believe this is the crisis of our times: we are losing readers, we are forgetting why reading is important as well as pleasurable, and we are becoming accustomed to a culture focused primarily on images. What happened to our long-term attention span? Why are logic and fact-based analysis overshadowed by rhetoric and politics? Why can't we slow down? Why do we believe responding in real time on Twitter and Facebook is 'meaningful involvement' with society or family? Why is reading more important than ever?

Over the past few weeks, I have been reading Edith Wharton's novels at night, and have marveled at the modernity of the protagonists, from Lily Bart to Undine Spragg, and at Wharton's ability to keep the story moving, the characters evolving, and the reader surprised. I like to learn from good novelists, and I am learning from Wharton.

I have timed my reading to finish whenever a Yankee game is on the Yes Network, and if no game is at hand, then at least *Storage Wars* or *American Pickers*. That's it. That's about the only TV I watch, or I feel is worth watching. My kids rarely watch TV, and my wife only watches the news, if that. They do see episodes of *The Office*, *The Daily Show*, and *The Colbert Report* on their computers, which prompts me to consider whether I should cut cable TV once and for all. But I don't. Not yet. I want to, but I don't.

Since Aaron and Isaac were toddlers, my wife and I read to them. Every night. Thirty minutes for Laura. Thirty minutes for me. This was our religion through their grade school years. Not surprisingly Aaron and Isaac as high-school students are enthusiastic readers for pleasure. After school, they are as likely to guffaw at Stephen Colbert on their MacBooks as they are to read their novels in bed. But this family culture of reading, if you can call it that, took years to foment, took attention and care to implement and nurture, and took active dismissal of what I would call the normal American culture of not reading.

I am often asked how I became a reader, in part because many know that I grew up poor along the Mexican-American border of El Paso, Texas. My parents did not read to me. They could read and did read in Spanish, but most of my reading was in English. My parents did hand me two or three dollars for paperback books I ordered at South Loop School from Scholastic Books every other Friday. But more importantly, they left me alone. They left me alone with my massive collection of paperbacks, and they never disparaged my love of reading. The opportunity to read and the space to read are as important as having your parents read to you. I still remember the lime-green bookshelves my handy father built in my room. These bookshelves housed my treasures. I have never forgotten how he took the time to do what mattered to me.

So I don't know if you are made a reader, or if you are born a reader. What I do know is that reading widely—reading beyond your time and culture, reading different genres, reading in different languages—changes your perspective profoundly. Television becomes a bore, and what is said and done on television is amusing. But it's rarely

Source: http://chicolingo.blogspot.com/2012/05/why-read.html. Used with permission from the author.

important. The crisis of the day or the outrage of the day becomes just more inane shouting to get your attention. On the Internet, online status updates are interesting little notes about your life, but never more than that. It's not really who you are, and well, a serious reader would know that. But you worry about the others. Those who don't read. Those who take television as the truth. Those who sell stocks at the clarion call of another 'crisis,' or buy gold as they anticipate a Mayan apocalypse, or attack an 'other' because 'they' are after us, aren't they?

Yes, I worry about our American culture and how it is shaping us. It's short-term-ism, if you can call it that, its obsession with fluff and images, its endless talk about who stunned in what dress. Are any of us ever going to look like Victoria Secret models? Will any of us ever get a chance to date them?

We are not 'censored' in the traditional way in the United States: writers are not beaten or killed because of their words, and no Ministry of Truth enforces an official version of what can be printed and thought. But in this culture of images, we are censoring ourselves. That may be more insidious and long-lasting. What I mean is that we disparage long-term complexity, and extol superficiality. We ignore reading, and lavish time on images. To read, in my mind, is to consider and to think. To see an image is to react. What happens when we start believing the world and what is important in it are only these reactions and prejudices? What have you become when the most expected of you is simply to press a 'Like' button? What kind of gulag is it when its inhabitants are too stupid to understand they are its prisoners?

Because I live in a different milieu of my own creation, and also because I'm rather humorless unless the joke is really quick and clever and insightful, I'd rather be reading and catch a Yankee game afterwards. For me, that's the perfect night. I can kiss my wife goodnight, and kiss my boys goodnight too (yes, remarkably, they still let me), and know that I am happy to do things the simple way, the slow way. I focus on how I find meaning in my life over the long-term. That is how I work to be free.

Thinking-Writing Activity

WHY DO YOU READ?

Consider what Sergio Troncoso said about the importance of reading and how losing readers is "the crisis of our times." In a paragraph or two, describe your past and current reading habits. For example, did you grow up in an environment that encouraged reading for pleasure? What do you read now, and how often do you read? Have your reading habits changed over time? If so, describe how, and then explain your feelings about whether or not this might be a crisis of our times.

Critical thinkers and thoughtful writers are avid readers. But there is more to it than simply reading. In order to fully absorb and engage with a text, a reader needs to read actively and critically. The following sections will help you hone this necessary skill, and whatever, however, or wherever you plan to communicate in your professional life, these fundamental reading skills will make you a better writer and communicator.

READING ACTIVELY

To read actively is to work at deciphering the many layers of a text. An active reader has a dictionary (online or print) at hand, along with annotating tools, plenty of time, and the will to jot down questions and comments on the printed page (or printout), in a reading journal, or in a word processing document. When you read actively, you give your full concentration and attention to the text. (Passive reading, on the other hand, is usually marked by boredom and daydreaming. If you look up from the page or screen and can't remember what you were just "reading," you weren't really reading at all—you were just looking at words.)

Active reading is also productive reading. You have a sense, as you begin to read, of what you might expect to discover. Active—and critical—reading also implies *re*reading; the following strategies will require you to work through a new text at least twice, becoming familiar with its structure as you delve into its content.

The following strategies for active reading will help to make any reading task—academic, professional, or even leisurely—more productive. They also apply equally to print texts and websites.

REVIEW THE TABLE OF CONTENTS OR CHAPTER OUTLINES

The table of contents and chapter outlines of a book or website provide you with the general structure and organization of a text. By beginning with these elements, you can develop an overall understanding of the reading, the organization of its major ideas, and the way specific details fit into this organization. It's as if you are taking an aerial view of the territory you are going to explore, looking for key landmarks, examining the patterns of connecting roads, and developing a sense of the terrain.

Review the table of contents in this book, taking particular note of the topics that are covered and the way these topics are organized. Now look at where this chapter fits in relation to the overall design of the book. How do the topics of this chapter relate to the other topics in the book?

Thinking-Writing Activity

TAKING A READING INVENTORY

In your journal, respond to any or all of these questions. Your instructor may ask you to share and discuss your responses with other students.

1. Is there anyone in your life to whom you read—a child, an older person, a friend? (Or perhaps you read aloud as part of a religious service or a professional presentation.) In what contexts do you read aloud? How does reading aloud define or contribute to your relationship to your audience?

2. Who taught you to read? Do you remember learning to read? Have you helped anyone else learn to read?

3. What was the last thing you read out of sheer curiosity or pleasure? Were you surprised by your response to that text? Would you recommend it to a friend, or was this purely a "guilty" pleasure?

READ THE INTRODUCTORY PARAGRAPHS AND THE CONCLUDING PARAGRAPHS OR SUMMARY

After reviewing the table of contents or chapter outlines, review next the opening paragraphs and the closing paragraphs or summary. In academic textbooks, authors generally explain the major goals of the chapter in the introduction and then conclude by reviewing the key topics that have been explored. Reviewing these sections should help you fill in the mental map you are creating of the reading assignment and help you develop a plan for exploring the material.

Other kinds of writing—essays, journalism, blogs—often include a thesis statement in the opening paragraph and summarize the overall argument or problem in the concluding paragraph. Note the topic sentence of each paragraph, which will give you an overall sense of the text's structure and organization.

Review the opening and concluding sections of this chapter. What additional information have you gathered about the chapter?

SCAN THE READING ASSIGNMENT, TAKING PARTICULAR NOTE OF SECTION HEADINGS, ILLUSTRATIONS, AND DIAGRAMS

The next step is to scout the territory by completing a rapid scan of what lies ahead. Move quickly through the material, focusing on the section headings, boxed or shaded areas, illustrations, diagrams, and other defining features. This should help you continue to fill in and elaborate your mental map, noting key points, concepts, definitions, and relationships.

Quickly scan this chapter, noting the features mentioned above. What new information have you gathered as a result of this scouting process?

Thinking-Writing Activity

PREVIEWING A READING ASSIGNMENT

Select a reading assignment from one of your courses, and before beginning to read, apply the previewing strategies that we have been considering:

- Examine the table of contents or chapter outline.
- Read the introductory paragraphs and the concluding paragraphs or summary.
- Scan the reading assignment, taking particular note of section headings, illustrations, and diagrams.

Then write a short paragraph, reporting specifically what each of the three strategies showed you about the assignment.

ANNOTATING

Annotation is one of the most productive techniques that you will use to read actively. It involves writing, or entering, your reactions to a text as you are reading, either with pen or pencil on paper or with your computer's graphic tools to annotate something that you have downloaded. When annotating, you are talking *with* the text, not allowing it to talk *at* you.

Your annotations will reflect your agreement and disagreement with what you read, your questions, what you see as important ideas, where you see relationships among parts of the texts, and where you see connections with additional ideas. Some methods are

- Underlining and numbering key points
- Circling key words and drawing lines to show relationships—for example, between a main idea and support for it
- Using question marks to indicate parts that you do not understand
- Commenting on the author's ideas or language or writing techniques
- Noting connections with your life or with other texts

Most word processing programs include annotation features such as highlighting, changing a font color, or inserting comments and questions. To annotate an online source, either save the online text in your word processing file or simply print out the page and highlight it on paper. (Many websites for periodicals, newspapers, and journals offer a "printer-friendly" option for articles, which allows you to print only the text, on continuous pages, without having to "click" through each separate page or print out banner advertisements.)

SUMMARIZING

When you summarize a text, you use your own language to briefly and succinctly restate the author's main point. A summary follows the structure and organization of the original text and might directly quote (using quotation marks) particularly interesting or apt words and phrases. When you summarize, you do not comment on or evaluate the text (that comes later); instead, writing the summary is a cognitive tool to ensure that you understand both the content and the structure of the text.

Summarizing is a strategy that is most effective at your second or third reading of a text, after you have annotated the text and looked up any unfamiliar terms or concepts.

Reading Critically

After reading actively in order to understand the content of a text, a thoughtful reader looks at it again, this time to read it critically. As a critical reader, you will analyze the text and evaluate its ideas and methods of presenting them. You will think of other subjects or issues to which the text might be connected.

ASKING QUESTIONS

Asking questions will help you read critically. One set of useful questions is based on the components of writing that you learned in Chapter 1: purpose, audience, subject, and writer. It also helps to look at the context of the writing.

1. What is the *purpose* of the selection, and how is the author trying to achieve it?
2. Who is the intended *audience*, and what assumptions is the writer making about it?
3. What is the *subject* of the selection, and how would you evaluate its cogency and reliability?
4. Who is the *writer*, and what perspective does she bring to the writing selection?
5. What is the larger *context* in which this selection appears? Is the writer responding to a particular event or participating in an ongoing debate?

Some questions often used to generate writing also help with critical reading.

Questions of Interpretation   Questions of interpretation probe for relationships among ideas.

Is a *time sequence* given in this text? If so, what is its importance?

Is a *process of growth or development* explained in this text? If so, what is its importance?

What is *compared or contrasted* in this text? What are the purposes of any comparisons?

What is the *context* of the selection, and what contextual components might be significant (for example, the time of its writing, characteristics of that time, the relationship to other works by the same author, whether or not it is a translation)?

Are *causes* discussed in this text? If so, what is suggested about those causes and their effects?

Questions of Analysis   Questions of analysis look at parts of a text and the relationship of those parts to the whole, and at the reasoning being presented.

Is this text divided into identifiable *sections?* What are they? Are sections arranged logically?

What *evidence* or *examples* support the ideas presented in the text?

Does the text give *alternatives* to the ideas presented?

Questions of Evaluation   Questions of evaluation establish the truth, reliability, and applicability—the value—of the text. They usually address the effectiveness of the writing as well.

What is the *significance* of the ideas in this text?

What is the apparent level of *truth* in this text? What criteria for truth does it meet?

What are the sources of information in this text? Are they *reliable?* Why?

Can the ideas in this text be *applied* to other situations?

NEW MEDIA & THOUGHTFUL WRITING (& READING)

Amplifying with Audio

People who are blind or have vision impairments, or have dyslexia or other types of learning disabilities, may not be able to read or may have difficulty reading a printed page. To get the information they want, they might read in a Braille format, listen to audio recordings of someone reading, have someone read to them, or have a computer "read" to them with the aid of optical character recognition (OCR) software.

Even if you do not have vision problems or a learning disability, you may still benefit from hearing an audio version of something you have read. Some people learn better through certain types of stimuli. For example, many people consider themselves visual learners (they learn best by observing), while others consider themselves kinesthetic learners (they learn best by doing) or auditory learners (they learn best through listening). Some theorists would even argue that learning is optimized when it is multimodal—in other words, when you engage in more than one or all three types of learning.

Studying a reading in written form allows you to do things that an audio version does not—like observing spellings, paragraph length variety across the reading at a glance, and more. But, likewise, listening to an audio version of a reading provides experiences that the written version does not, particularly if the audio is provided by the author of the piece. For instance, when you listen to authors read their own work, you can more readily hear the tone, inflection, and pace they intended. This can be particularly helpful in studying certain types of literature and poetry.

You can find audio versions of popular fiction books at bookstores, on book websites, and in libraries in cassette and CD format. Some vendors may even offer the audio as an MP3 download. You have access to thousands of podcasts that can be downloaded from the iTunes Store, *Scientific American*, NPR, the Library of Congress, *The New York Times*, and more. And, with the advent of text readers (e.g., the Kindle and Nook), you can store and access a large number of books in one little lightweight, handheld device that can read to you.

Using audio recordings properly can positively augment your learning experience and should not be approached as a passive activity. A critical thinking and active learning perspective should be engaged regardless of which mode of learning stimuli you choose.

What is *effective* about the writing in this text? Clarity? The right tone? Appropriate—or imaginative—word choices? Organization?

Of course, you are not likely to ask all these questions about everything you read, and you will find other questions to ask as well.

USING A PROBLEM-SOLVING APPROACH

Successful readers often approach difficult reading passages with a problem-solving approach.

Step 1: *What is the problem?* What don't I understand about this passage? Are there terms or concepts that are unfamiliar? Are the logical connections between the concepts confusing? Do some things just not make sense?

Step 2: *What are the alternatives?* What are some possible meanings of the terms or concepts? What are some potential interpretations of the central meaning of this passage?

Step 3: *What is the evaluation of the possible alternatives?* What are the "clues" in the passage, and what alternative meanings do they support? What reasons or evidence supports these interpretations?

Step 4: *What is the solution?* Judging from my evaluation and what I know of this subject, which interpretation is most likely? Why?

Step 5: *How well is the solution working?* Does my interpretation still make sense as I continue my reading, or do I need to revise my conclusion?

Of course, expert readers go through this process very quickly, much faster than it takes to explain it. Although this approach may seem a little cumbersome at first, the more you use it, the more natural and efficient it will become. Let's begin by applying it to a sample passage. Carefully read the following passage from French philosopher Jean-Paul Sartre's "Existentialism Is Humanism," and use the problem-solving approach below to determine the correct meanings of the italicized concepts and the overall meaning of the passage.

> *Existentialism*, of which I am a representative, declares with greater consistency that if God does not exist there is at least one being whose existence comes before its essence, a being which exists before it can be defined by any conception of it. That being is man or, as Heidegger has it, the human reality. What do we mean by saying that *existence precedes essence*? We mean that man first of all exists, encounters himself, surges up in the world—and defines himself afterwards. If man as the existentialist sees himself as not definable, it is because to begin with he is nothing. He will not be anything until later, and then he will be what he makes of himself. Thus, *there is no human nature*, because there is no God to have a conception of it. Man simply is. Not that he is simply what he conceives himself to be, but he is what he wills, and as he conceives existence. *Man is nothing else but that which he makes of himself.* This is the first principle of existentialism. . . . If, however, it is true that existence is prior to essence, *man is responsible for what he is.* Thus, the first effect of existentialism is that it puts every man in possession of himself as

he is, and places the entire responsibility for his existence squarely upon his own shoulders. . . . That is what I mean when I say that man is *condemned to be free.* Condemned, because he did not create himself, yet is nevertheless at liberty, and from the moment that he is thrown into this world he is responsible for everything he does. . . . In life, a man commits himself, draws his own portrait and there is nothing but that portrait.

—Jean-Paul Sartre's "Existentialism Is Humanism."

Thinking-Writing Activity

A PROBLEM-SOLVING APPROACH TO READING

Step 1: What parts (if any) of Jean-Paul Sartre's passage do you find confusing?

Step 2: What are some possible definitions of the italicized words, and what are some potential interpretations of this passage?

Existentialism: (a) _____

                      (b) _____

Free: (a) _____

                      (b) _____

Overall Meaning: (a) _____

                      _____

Overall Meaning: (b) _____

                      _____

Step 3: What contextual clues can you use to help you define these concepts and determine the overall meaning? What knowledge of this subject do you have, and how can this knowledge help you understand this passage?

Step 4: Judging from your evaluation in Step 3, which of the possible definitions and interpretations do you think are most likely? Why?

Step 5: How do your conclusions compare with those of the other students in the class? Should you revise your definitions or interpretation?

For additional practice, you may select a challenging passage from a course textbook and apply the preceding problem-solving approach.

Practicing Active and Critical Reading: One Student's Approach

Here is how one student, Joshua Bartlett, used previewing, problem solving, annotating, and summarizing with an essay that his philosophy professor assigned, Sonja Tanner's "On Plato's Cave," to show students how ideas from more than 2,500 years ago can apply to their lives today.

Previewing   Because this was an instructor's handout, Joshua's previewing started with a look at the title, the first two paragraphs, and the concluding paragraph. Because this is a short essay, Joshua moved quickly to scanning, reading through, and annotating. He was a bit confused when he read the first paragraph, since the class had not yet begun studying Plato.

Problem Solving   Joshua realized that his major *problem* with this text was his lack of knowledge about Plato and Socrates. He decided that his *alternatives* were (1) to look them up in his philosophy textbook or the encyclopedia, or (2) to go on reading. He quickly *evaluated* the alternatives. Consulting his book or the encyclopedia would take some time, and he wanted to finish this assignment before he had to go to work. He knew that he would learn about Plato and Socrates next week in his class. His previewing had shown him that these problem paragraphs would be explained later in the essay. He *solved the problem* by deciding to go on reading. He felt that his solution *worked well* when he was able to summarize the essay.

Annotating   Joshua gave Tanner's essay a second and then a third reading, each time using a colored pen to draw his attention to specific points in the text. He underlined important points, placed question marks next to parts he did not understand, and commented on the writer's rhetorical strategies to better help him understand the writer's argument.

Summarizing   Joshua's philosophy professor asked the students to prepare a summary of the essay and be ready to share it with the class. She did this so that class discussion would be focused. Joshua took his annotations to class, too, so he was able to participate effectively. Here is his summary:

> "On Plato's Cave" claims that much of what we see, hear, and read may give us inaccurate images and projections of points of view and that we need to try to discover what is really solid, rather than believe what might not be. This essay begins by quoting Plato's description of human beings chained in a cave, seeing only reflections of people, animals, and material items. The essay connects this fantasy situation with our experiences with the media, and even with what parents and teachers tell us. The essay says that Plato tells of a person escaping from the cave and seeing the real world. It says that we, too, can climb out of darkness by understanding how received information and our resulting beliefs need to be examined so that we can have "substantiated knowledge."

On Plato's Cave
by Sonja Tanner

In the seventh book of Plato's dialogue *The Republic,* he offers an image of education in which humans are likened to prisoners in a cave. To understand this fully, we can attempt to render this image.

Source: On Plato's Cave by Sonja Tanner.

I guess we'll learn about Socrates next week— then I'll get this funny use of word.

spooky

? the ones in the cave? no

who?

ok—clearer than bonds

—or with a flashlight

aha! where?

important point

now it's making sense

important point

This whole paragraph is important

may be the thesis

They sure do!

!!

"Next, then," (Socrates) said, "make an image of our nature in its education and (want) of education, likening it to a condition of the following kind. See human beings as though they were in an underground cave-like dwelling with its entrance, a long one, open to the light across the whole width of the cave.

"They are in it from childhood with their legs and necks in bonds so that they are fixed, seeing only in front of them, unable because of the bond to turn their heads all the way around. Their light is from a fire burning far above and behind them. Between the fire and the prisoners there is a road above, along which we see a wall, built like the partitions puppet-handlers set in front of the <u>human beings</u> and over which they show the puppets."

"I see," (Glaucon) said.

"Then also see along this wall human beings carrying all sorts of artifacts, which project above the wall, and statues of men and other animals wrought from stone, wood, and every kind of material...." (514a1–515a2, Allan Bloom, trans.)

We see persons at the bottom of a cave, <u>chained so as</u> to prevent them from leaving the cave and from turning around to see what is behind them. Positioned in this way, they can only watch the shadows projected onto the back wall of the cave, by the passing of the artifacts in front of the fire. Behind the prisoners is a low wall which obscures the persons carrying these artifacts. This projection is like those we create around campfires, or in front of slide projectors, where a set of hands may look like a barking dog or a flying bird. A similar distortion takes place in the cave. Further up the cave is a fire and beyond that lies the cave's opening to the sunlight.

Having sketched what is happening within the cave literally, we must now try to <u>interpret what this image means figuratively.</u> When Glaucon remarks upon how strange these prisoners are, Socrates tells him <u>that they are like us</u>. How are we like these passive and helpless prisoners? <u>Do we ever receive information or entertainment without thinking about where it actually comes from?</u> Although Plato was writing over two thousand years before the invention of cathode ray tubes, the modern example of television may show us what he meant. If the projected images are analogous to those televised to us, then what might the <u>persons behind the wall represent? Acting as filters of information, they might be seen as television networks, advertisers, or the media in general.</u> They and their motivations for presenting information about the world to us through their particular perceptual lenses are obscured from view like the persons who pass behind the wall in the cave. As the chains prevent the prisoners from turning to see what is causing the images they watch, we are sometimes prevented by ignorance or uncritical thinking from recognizing the interests and persons served by the way in which information is presented to us. When we are unaware as to how perceptual lenses shape what it is we then believe, the information we receive and the beliefs we build upon this information may be distorted, like the shadows projected onto the wall. Many other persons shape the information we receive and the beliefs we hold. Authorities of all sorts fulfill this function—politicians, journalists, parents, teachers, writers and sometimes even ourselves.

Plato does not think us <u>doomed to</u> this unreflective state, however. Escape from the cave, though mysterious, is possible. Someone is apparently released from their bonds, turns around, and despite the confusion and pain from the dazzling light and arduous ascent, both of which they are unaccustomed to, is able to leave the cave. Just as when we leave a <u>matinee movie and enter</u> bright sunlight, we are at first dazzled and our eyes need a few moments to adjust to the light, the ascendant may experience disorientation or confusion upon first turning around. Turning from the shadows, this person discovers the objects causing these projections and the persons carrying them and, once outside the cave, the beings which these artifacts are made to resemble. <u>The journey upwards is one of turning from images to their originals, ending ultimately in one's view of the sun itself,</u> which, as the earth's <u>source of heat and light</u>, is a cause of all of the beings described in this allegory.

good comparison

!

But how is <u>escape</u> from chains which bind at the neck and legs possible? Does someone release the prisoner and force them up into the light, and if so, who is this and why do they do it? Perhaps we are taking this image too literally in seeing this as a physical journey. Taking a cue from the aforementioned example in which the <u>projections represent beliefs and information we take on uncritically,</u> perhaps this journey is not <u>physical but mental.</u> The chains <u>may signify</u> ignorance and the uncritical taking over of second-hand opinions or beliefs and, as such, the chains themselves may even be self-imposed. Such an <u>intellectual journey</u> begins with a recognition that what we see and believe are only images, and by turning away from such appearances towards reality.

escape → journey

another explanation

If the ascent <u>is intellectual,</u> rather than <u>physical,</u> a problem presents itself. Although Plato describes the release of a prisoner as though she or he were dragged up and out of the cave by the scruff of their neck, this type of force seems unlikely to guide an intellectual journey. Could one truly be <u>forced or compelled to think independently?</u> What else would motivate the journey? This is a particularly difficult question given the description of both ascent and return back into the cave as arduous, painful, and as subjecting one to derision and danger from the prisoners. What benefit could make good of undergoing such difficulties to leave the cave? We have been assuming here that the compulsion Plato describes as motivating the **ascent is a force external to the ascendant, but internal forces motivate us as well.** Why take the treacherous journey out of the cave? Perhaps simply because we <u>want</u> to. Our motivation upwards may be a desire for knowledge, as opposed to mere beliefs. If desire is the impetus for the <u>ascent,</u> this places <u>responsibility</u> for one's <u>education squarely on the shoulders of the individual.</u> We may have <u>assistance, encouragement and sometimes</u> even external forces compelling us upwards, but ultimately, our success depends <u>upon our own desire</u> for <u>knowledge and truth,</u> and our willingness to give up what we are accustomed to—the passive life and familiar comforts of cave-dwelling—for the rewards of rational and grounded knowledge.

repeats

probably not

hard to understand (read slow!)

!
Aha—again! The cave makes sense here
This sounds like my dad!

We are now able to locate ourselves on the (trajectory of enlightenment.) Looking at and discussing images are a first stage in education according to Plato and indeed that is precisely what we have done here thus far. The next step then seems to be turning away from the images we accept unreflectively and towards questions as to why we believe what we do, who or what are the sources of these beliefs, and how reliable are these sources, which can distinguish unfounded beliefs from substantiated knowledge. Maybe this ascent is undertaken by us on a regular basis, rather than simply once, in our lives.

important phrase
Here's the main point
One of those essays that leads up to it—doesn't state it at the beginning the way my English teacher wants us to do

Thinking-Writing Activity

YOUR REACTIONS

1. Write your reactions to the strategies for active and critical reading in this chapter. Which have you used before? How do they work for you? Which do you want to try now as you do your college reading?

2. How would you annotate "On Plato's Cave"?

3. Do you think that Joshua wrote an accurate summary of it? Would you summarize it differently?

If you can, share your reactions with classmates, and notice agreements and disagreements.

USING METACOGNITIVE STRATEGIES

Metacognition is a process we will be working on throughout this book. While *cognition* refers to the process of thinking, *metacognition* refers to a form of thinking *about* the thinking process. For example, think about what you will be doing this evening, and as you are thinking about this, make a special effort to stand outside your thinking process and observe it while it is going on. This process of becoming an observer to your own thinking process—"reflecting" on your thinking—may feel strange, but it is well within your power if you concentrate. In the following space, describe some of the characteristics of the thinking process that you observed yourself engaging in. For instance, did you find you were talking to yourself? Did your thinking make use of still or moving visual images? Did you feel ideas were rushing through your mind like a river, or were your thoughts organized in an orderly fashion? Did you find one idea led to another idea, which led to another idea, through a series of associations?

Characteristics of My Thinking Process:

1. _____

2. _____

3. _____

By participating in this activity you were actually engaging in the process of *metacognition,* working to become aware of the process you use to think about something.

While the process of reading is a thinking (cognitive) activity, expert readers also engage in metacognition while they are reading. In other words, they are aware of their thinking process as they are reading, and they use this awareness to improve their thinking. This awareness can be expressed as a variety of questions:

Goals: What are my goals in reading this passage? How well am I meeting these goals?

Comprehension: How well do I understand what I am reading? What parts do I understand, and what parts am I confused about?

Anticipation: What events are going to take place following the ones I am reading about? How will the author develop and elaborate on these ideas?

Author's Purpose: What is the author's point of view, and why did she adopt this particular perspective? How has her point of view affected the information she selected and the manner in which she presented this information?

Evaluation: Is this information accurate? Do the ideas make sense? What evidence and reasons does the author provide to support her perspective?

As you work to answer these questions, you are likely to find that you are *rereading* key sections, and this rereading is an essential part of the process of reading effectively.

Thinking-Writing Activity

PRACTICING METACOGNITION

Although developing metacognitive reading abilities is a complex process that takes place over time, you can begin using these strategies immediately. Select a chapter from one of your textbooks. As you read, make a conscious effort to ask—and to answer—metacognitive questions noted above. Record your experience, identifying the questions that you found yourself asking, and how the process of asking—and trying to answer—these questions while you were reading affected your understanding of the material. The metacognitive questions are part of a reading worksheet located below that you can use for reference later.

READING WORKSHEET

Reading Assignment: _____

Reading Environment: _____

Reading Schedule: _____

Date Due: _____

Day   *Time Planned for Reading*

_____   _____

_____   _____

READING STRATEGIES

Problem Solving

Step 1: What is the problem in understanding the reading?

Step 2: What are the possible meanings and interpretations?

Step 3: What are the contextual clues, reasons, or evidence?

Step 4: What meaning or interpretation is most likely?

Step 5: How well is my conclusion working?

Metacognition

What are my *goals* in reading this passage, and how well am I meeting these goals?

What parts do I *understand*, and what parts are *confusing*?

How will the author *elaborate* and *develop* ideas I am reading about?

What is the author's *point of view*, and why did she adopt this particular perspective?

Do the ideas *make sense?* What *evidence* and *reasons* support the ideas presented?

Annotation

··

"Grounds for Fiction"

by Julia Alvarez

Poet, novelist, and teacher Julia Alvarez was born in New York City but raised in the Dominican Republic. Her novel *In the Time of the Butterflies* (1994) is based on the true story of the four Mirabal sisters, who fought against the brutal Trujillo dictatorship, and her enormously popular *How the Garcia Girls Lost Their Accents* (1991) deftly explores the relationships among sisters. Both novels were critically acclaimed, nominated for and winning several important prizes. Her most recent novel, *Saving the World,* was published in 2006.

In recent years, Alvarez and her husband have started an organic coffee farm in the Dominican Republic; she recently brought a group of her American college students to the farm to work alongside local farmers and teach literacy classes in the community.

Every once in a while after a reading, someone in the audience will come up to me. *Have I got a story for you!* They will go on to tell me the story of an aunt or sister or next-door neighbor, some moment of mystery, some serendipitous occurrence, some truly incredible story. "You should write it down," I always tell them. They look at me as if they've just offered me their family crown jewels and I've refused them. "I'm no writer," they tell me. "You're the writer."

"Oh, you never know," I reply, so as to encourage them. What I should tell them is that writing ideas can't really be traded in an open market. If they could be, writers would be multimillionaires. Who knows what mystery (or madness) it is that drives us to our computers for two, three, four years, in pursuit of some sparkling possibility that looks like dull fact to everyone else's eyes. One way to define a writer is she who is able to make what obsesses her into everyone's obsession. I am thinking of Goethe, whose *Sorrows of Young Werther,* published in 1774, caused a spate of suicides in imitation of its young hero. Young Werther's blue frock coat and yellow waistcoat became the fad.

We have all been the victims of someone's too-long slide show of their white-water rafting trip or their recounting of a convoluted, boring dream. But a Mark Twain can turn that slide show into the lively backdrop of a novel, or a Jorge Luis Borges can take the twist and turn of a dream and wring the meaning of the universe from it.

But aside from talent—and granted, that is a big aside, one that comes and goes and shifts and grows and diminishes, so it is also somewhat unpredictable—how can we tell when we've got it: that seed of experience, of memory, that voice of a character or fleeting image that might just be grounds for fiction? The answer is that we can never tell. And so another way to define a writer is someone who is willing to find out. As James Dickey once explained to an audience, "I work on the process of refining low-grade ore. I get maybe a couple of nuggets of gold out of fifty tons of dirt. It is tough for me. No, I am not inspired."

"Are you all here because you want to muck around in fifty tons of dirt?" I ask my workshop of young writers the first day. Not one hand goes up unless I've told them the Dickey story first.

In fact, my students want to know ahead of time if some idea they have will   5
make a good story. "I mean, before I spend hours and hours on it," one young man explained. I told my students what Mallarmé told his friend the painter Degas, when Degas complained that he couldn't seem to write well although he was "full of ideas." Mallarmé's famous answer was, "My dear Degas, poems are not made out of ideas. Poems are made out of words." I told my student that if a young writer had come up to me and told me that he was going to write a story about a man who wakes up one morning and finds out that he has been turned into a cockroach, I would have told him to forget it. That story would never work. "And I would have stopped Kafka from writing his 'Metamorphosis,'" I concluded, smiling at my student, as if he might be a future Kafka.

"Well, it's just two pages," he grumbled. "And I have this other idea that might be better. About a street person who is getting Alzheimer's."

"Write both stories, and I'll read them and tell you what I think of them," I said. He looked alarmed. So I leveled with him. I told him that if he didn't want to spend hours and hours finding out if the kernel of an idea, the glimmer of an inspiration, the flash of a possibility would make a good story, he should give up the *idea* of wanting to be a writer.

As much as I can break down the process of writing stories, I would say that this is how it begins. I find a detail or image or character or incident or cluster of events. A certain luminosity surrounds them. I find myself attracted. I come forward. I pick it up, turn it around, begin to ask questions, and spend hours and weeks and months and years trying to answer them.

I keep a folder, a yellow folder with pockets. For a long time it had no label because I didn't know what to label it: WHATCHAMACALLITS, filed under *W*, or also under *W*, STORY-POEM-WANNABES. Finally, I called the folder CURIOSIDADES, in Spanish so I wouldn't have to commit myself to what I was going to do in English with these random little things. I tell my students this, too, that writing begins before you ever put pen to paper or your fingers down on the keyboard. It is a way of being alive in the world. Henry James's advice to the young writer was to be someone on whom nothing is lost. And so this is my folder of the little things that have not been lost on me; news clippings, headlines, inventory lists, bits of gossip that I've already sensed have an aura about them, the beginnings of a poem or a short story, the seed of a plot that might turn into a novel or a query that might needle an essay out of me.

10   Periodically, when I'm between writing projects and sometimes when I'm in the middle of one and needing a break, I go through my yellow folder. Sometimes I discard a clipping or note that no longer holds my attention. But most of my *curiosidades* have been in my folder for years, though some have migrated to new folders, the folders of stories and poems they have inspired or found a home in.

Here's one of these *curiosidades* that is now in a folder that holds drafts of a story that turned into a chapter of my novel *¡YO!* This chapter is in the point of view of Marie Beaudry, a landlady who, along with other narrators, gets to tell a story on Yolanda García, the writer. The little curiosity that inspired Marie's voice was a note I found in the trash of an apartment I moved into. It has nothing at all to do with what happens in my story.

Re and Mal: Here's the two keys to your father's apt. Need I say more excepting that's such a rotten thing you pulled on him. My doing favors is over as of this morning. Good luck to you two hard-hearted hannahs. I got more feeling in my little finger than the two of you got in your whole body.

Jinny

I admit that when I read this note, I wanted to move out of that apartment. I felt the place was haunted by the ghost of the last tenant against whom some violation had been perpetrated by these two hard-hearted hannahs, Re and Mal. Over the years that handwritten note stayed in my yellow folder and eventually gave me the voice of my character Marie Beaudry.

Here's another scrap from deep inside one of the pockets. It's the title of an article in one of my husband's ophthalmological journals: "Treatment of Chronic Postfiltration Hypotony by Intrableb Injection of Autologous Blood." I think I saved that choice bit of medical babble because of the delight I took in the jabberwocky phenomenon of that title.

'Twas brillig and the slithy toves
Did gyre and postfiltrate the wabe;
All hypotonious was the blood,
And autologous the intrableb.

from *Jabberwocky* by Lewis Carroll

I have not yet used it in a story or poem, but who knows, maybe someday you will look over the shoulder of one of my characters and see that he is reading this article or writing it. I can tell you that this delight in words and how we use and misuse them is a preoccupation of mine.

Maybe because I began my writing life as a poet, the naming of things has always interested me:

Mother, unroll the bolts and name
the fabrics from which our clothing came,
dress the world in vocabulary:
broadcloth, corduroy, denim, terry.

Actually, that poem, "Naming the Fabrics," besides being inspired, of course, by the names of fabrics, was also triggered by something I picked up while reading *The 1961 Better Homes and Garden Sewing Book*, page 45: "During a question and answer period at a sewing clinic, a woman in the audience asked this question: 'I can sew beautifully; my fitting is excellent; the finished dress looks as good as that of any professional—but how do I get up enough courage to cut the fabric?'" I typed out this passage and put it away. A few months later, this fear found its way from my yellow folder to my poem, "Naming the Fabrics":

I pay a tailor to cut his suits
from seersucker, duck, tweed, cheviot,
those names make my cutting hand skittish—
either they sound like sex or British.

Since I myself have no sewing skills to speak of, I didn't know about this fear that
seamstresses experience before cutting fabric. Certainly, the year 1961, when this sewing
book was published, brings other fears to mind: the Berlin Wall going up; invaders going
down to the Bay of Pigs; Trujillo, our dictator of thirty-one years, being assassinated in
the Dominican Republic. But this housewife in Indiana had her own metaphysical fears to
work out on cloth. "How do I get up enough courage to cut the fabric?" Her preoccupation
astonished me and touched me for all kinds of reasons I had to work out on paper.

You might wonder what a "serious writer" was doing reading *The 1961 Better Homes*   15
and Garden Sewing Book. Wouldn't my time have been better spent perusing Milton or Emily
Dickinson or even the *New York Review of Books* or *The Nation*? All I can say in my defense
is that I believe in Henry James's advice: be someone on whom nothing is lost. Or what
Deborah Kerr said in *Night of the Iguana*, "Nothing human disgusts me." I once heard a
writer on *Fresh Air* tell Terry Gross that one of the most important things he had ever learned
in his life was that you could learn a lot from people who were dumber than you. You can
also learn a lot from publications that are below your literary standards: housekeeping
books, cookbooks, manuals, cereal boxes, and the local newspapers of your small town.

These last are the best. Even if some of this "news" is really glorified gossip—so
what? Most of our classics are glorified gossip. Think of the Wife of Bath's inventory of
husbands or the debutante's hair-rape in "The Rape of the Lock." How about Madame
Bovary's steamy affair? Is what happened to Abelard over his Héloïse or to Jason for
pissing off Medea any less infamous than the John and Lorena Bobbit story of several
years ago? The wonderful Canadian writer Alice Munro admits that she likes reading
People magazine, and "not just at the checkout stand. I sometimes buy it." She goes
on to say that gossip is "a central part of my life. I'm interested in small-town gossip.
Gossip has that feeling in it, that one wants to know about life."

I've gotten wonderful stories from the *Addison Independent*, the *Valley Voice*, even
the *Burlington Free Press* that would never be reported in the *Wall Street Journal* or the
New York Times:

11-Year-Old Girls Take Car on Two-State Joyride

Two 11-year-old girls determined to see a newborn niece secretly borrowed their
grandfather's car, piled clothes on the front seat so they could see over the steering
wheel and drove more than 10 hours.

Neither one of them had ever driven a car before, said Michael Ray, Mercer
County's juvenile case worker. The youngsters packed the Dodge Aries with soda,
snacks, and an atlas for their trek from West Virginia to the central Kentucky town
of Harrodsburg. "They were determined to see that baby," said caseworker Ray.

You could write a whole novel about that. In fact, in Mona Simpson's latest novel,
A Regular Guy, eleven-year-old Jane di Natali is taught by her mother to drive their pickup
with wood blocks strapped to the pedals so her short legs can reach them. Little Jane
takes off on her own to see her estranged father hundreds of miles away. I wonder if Mona
Simpson got her idea for Jane's odyssey from reading about these two eleven-year-olds.

Here's another article I've saved in my yellow folder:

Misdiagnosed Patient Freed After 2 Years

A Mexican migrant worker misdiagnosed and kept sedated in an Oregon mental hospital for two years because doctors couldn't understand his Indian dialect is going home.

Adolfo Gonzales, a frail 5-foot-4-inch grape picker who doesn't speak English or Spanish, had been trying to communicate in his native Indian dialect of Trique.

Gonzales, believed to be in his 20s, was born in a village in Oaxaca, Mexico. He was committed in June 1990 after being arrested for indecent exposure at a laundromat. Charges later were dropped.

I couldn't get this story out of my head. First, I was—and am—intensely interested in the whole Scheherazade issue of how important it is to be able to tell our stories to those who have power over us. Second, and more mundanely, I was intensely curious about those charges that were later dropped: indecent exposure at a laundromat. What was Adolfo Gonzales doing taking his clothes off in a laundromat? Why was he in town after a hard day of grape picking? I had to find answers to these questions, and so I started writing a poem. "It's a myth that writers write what they know," the writer Marcie Hershman has written. "We write what it is that we need to know."

> The next payday you went to town
> to buy your girl and to wash your one
> set of working clothes.
> In the laundromat, you took them off
> to wring out the earth you wanted
> to leave behind you.

from "Two Years Too Late"

20   Of course, you don't even have to go to your local paper. Just take a walk downtown, especially if you live in a small town, as I do. All I have to do is have a cup of coffee at Steve's Diner or at Jimmy's Weybridge Garage and listen to my neighbors talking. Flannery O'Connor claimed that most beginners' stories don't work because "they don't go very far inside a character, don't reveal very much of the character. And this problem is in large part due to the fact that these characters have no distinctive speech to reveal themselves with." Here are some examples of my fellow Vermonters talking their very distinctive and revealing speech.

> He's so lazy he married a pregnant woman.
> I'm so hungry I could eat the north end out of a southbound skunk.
> The snow's butt-high to a tall cow.
> More nervous than a long-tailed cat in a room full of rocking chairs.
> I'm so sick that I'd have to get well to die.

Of course if, like Whitman, you do nothing but listen, you will also hear all kinds of bogus voices these days, speaking the new doublespeak. In our litigious, politically overcorrected, dizzily spin-doctored age, politicians and public figures have to use language so that it doesn't say anything that might upset anyone. Here's a list of nonterms and what they really stand for:

Sufferer of fictitious disorder syndrome:	Liar
Suboptimal:	Failed
Temporarily displaced inventory:	Stolen

Negative gain in test scores: Lower test scores
Substantive negative outcome: Death

We're back to "Treatment of Chronic Postfiltration Hypotony by Intrableb Injection of Autologous Blood," what Ken Macrorie in his wonderful book about expository writing, *Telling Writing,* calls "Engfish"—homogenized, doctored-up, approximate language that can't be traced to a human being.

I tend to agree with what Dickinson once said about poetry, "There are no approximate words in a poem." Auden even went so far as to say that he could pick out a potential poet by a student's answer to the question, "Why do you want to write poetry?" If the student answered, "I have important things to say," then he was not a poet. If he answered, "I like hanging around words listening to what they say," then maybe he was going to be a poet.

I got enmeshed in one such string of words when I visited the United Nations to hear my mother give a speech on violation of human rights. At the door an aide handed me the list of voting member countries and the names caught my eye: Dem Kampuchea, Dem Yemen, Denmark, Djibouti, Dominica, Dominican Republic, Ecuador, Egypt....When I got home, I started writing a poem, ostensibly about hearing my mother give that speech, but really because I wanted to use the names of those countries:

> I scan the room for reactions,
> picking out those countries
> guilty of her sad facts.
> Kampuchea is absent,
> absent, too, the South African delegate.
> I cannot find the United States.
> Nervous countries predominate,
> Nicaragua and Haiti,
> Iraq, Israel, Egypt.

from *"Between Dominica and Ecuador"*

But of course, it's not just words that intrigue writers, but the stories, the possibilities of human character that cluster around a bit of history, trivia, gossip.

For instance, Anne Macdonald's book, *Feminine Ingenuity,* inspired a character trait of the mother in *How the García Girls Lost Their Accents.* According to Macdonald, at the beginning of the twentieth century, 5,535 American women were granted patents for inventions, including a straw-weaving device, an open-eye needle for sewing hot-air balloons, and special planking designed to discourage barnacles from attaching themselves to warships. These intriguing facts gave me a side of the mother's character I would never have thought up on my own. Inspired by the gadgetry of her new country, Laura García sets out to make her mark: soap sprayed from the nozzle head of a shower when you turn the knob a certain way; instant coffee with creamer already mixed in; time-released water capsules for your potted plants when you were away; a key chain with a timer that would go off when your parking meter was about to expire. (And the ticking would help you find your keys easily if you mislaid them.)

Sometimes the inspiration is history. History . . . that subject I hated in school because it was so dry and all about dead people. I wish now my teachers had made me read novels to make the past spring alive in my imagination. For years, I wanted to write about the Mirabal sisters, but I admit I was put off by these grand historical abstractions. It wasn't until I began to accumulate several yellow folders' worth of vivid little details about them that these godlike women became accessible to me. One of my first entries came from my father, who had just returned from a trip to the Dominican Republic: "I met the man who sold the girls pocketbooks at El Gallo before they set off over the mountain. He told me he warned them not to go. He said he took them out back to the stockroom supposedly to show them inventory and explained they were going to be killed. But they did not believe him." I still get goosebumps reading my father's letter dated June 5, 1985. It went in my yellow folder. That pocketbook-buying scene is at the end of the novel I published nine years later.

25   So what are you to conclude from this tour of my yellow folder? That this essay is just an excuse to take you through my folder and share my little treasures with you? Well, one thing I don't want you to conclude is that this preliminary woolgathering is a substitute for the real research that starts once you have a poem or story going. In "Naming the Fabrics," for instance, though I was inspired by the plaintive question asked at a sewing clinic, I still had to go down to the fabric store and spend an afternoon with a very kind and patient saleslady who taught me all about gingham and calico, crepe and gauze. I spent days reading fabric books, and weeks working on the poem, and years going back to it, revising it, tinkering with it. For my story "The Tent," I had to call up the National Guard base near Champaign, Illinois, and get permission from the base commander to go observe his men setting up a tent. ("What exactly do you need this for?" he asked at least half a dozen times.) Sometimes I think the best reason for a writer to have a reputable job like being a professor at a university or a vice president of Hartford Insurance Company is so you can call up those base commanders or bother those salesladies in fabric stores as if you do have a real job. Otherwise, they might think you are crazy and lock you up like poor Adolfo Gonzales.

On the whole, I have found people to be kind and generous with their time, especially when you ask them to talk about something they know and care about. Many people have actually gone beyond kindness in helping me out. I remember calling up the local Catholic priest, bless his heart, who really deserves, I don't know, a plenary indulgence for tolerance in the face of surprise. Imagine getting an early-morning call (my writing day starts at 6:30, but I really don't do this kind of phone calling till about 7:30 since I do want my sources to be lucid). Anyhow, imagine an early-morning call at your rectory from a woman you don't know who asks you what is the name of that long rod priests have with a hole on one end to sprinkle people with holy water? I'd be lying if I tried to make drama out of the phone call and say there was a long pause. Nope. Father John spoke right up, "Ah yes, my aspergill."

One thing I should add—the bad news part of all this fun, but something writers do have to think about in this litigious age—what is grounds for fiction can also be, alas, grounds for suing. All three of my novels have been read by my publisher's lawyer for what might be libelous. Thank goodness Algonquin's lawyer is also a reader who refuses to vacuum all the value out of a book in order to play it safe. Still, I have had to take drinks out of characters' hands and make abused ladies disabused and make so many changes in hair coloring and hairstyle that I could start a literary beauty parlor.

But even if your fictional ground is cleared of litigious material, there might still be grounds for heartache. Your family and friends might feel wounded when they can detect— even if no one else can—the shape of the real behind the form of your fiction. And who would want to hurt those very people you write for, those very people who share with you the world you are struggling to understand in your fiction for their sake as well as your own?

I don't know how to get around this and I certainly haven't figured out what the parameters of my responsibility are to the real people in my life. One of my theories, which might sound defensive and self-serving, is that there is no such thing as straight-up fiction. There are just levels of distance from our own life experience, the thing that drives us to write in the first place. In spite of our caution and precaution, bits of our lives will get into what we write. I have a friend whose mother finds herself in all his novels, even historical novels set in nineteenth-century Russia or islands in the Caribbean where his mother has never been. A novelist writing about Napoleon might convey his greedy character by describing him spooning gruel into his mouth, only to realize that her image of how a greedy man eats comes from watching her fat Tío Jorge stuff his face with sweet habichuelas.

I think that if you start censoring yourself as a novelist—*this is out of bounds, that is* 30 *sacrosanct*—you will never write anything. My advice is to write it out, and then decide, by whatever process seems fair to you—three-o'clock-in-the-morning insomniac angst sessions with your soul, or a phone call with your best friend, or a long talk with your sister—what you are going to do about it. More often than not, an upset reaction has more to do with people's wounded vanity or their own unresolved issues with *you* rather than what you've written. I'm not speaking now of meanness or revenge thinly masquerading as fiction, but of a writer's serious attempts to render justice to the world she lives in, which includes, whether she wants it to or not, the people she loves or has tried to love, the people who have been a part of the memories, details, life experiences that form the whole cloth of her reality—out of which, with fear and a trembling hand, she must perforce cut her fiction.

But truly, this is a worry to put out of your head while you are writing. You'll need your energy for the hard work ahead: tons and tons of good *ideas* to process in order to get those nuggets of pure prose. What Yeats once said in his poem "Dialogue of Self and Soul" could well be the writer's pledge of allegiance:

I am content to follow to its source,
every event in action or in thought.

And remember, no one is probably going to pay you a whole lot of money to do this. You also probably won't save anyone's life with anything you write. But so much does depend on seeing a world in a grain of sand and a heaven in a wildflower. Maybe we are here only to say: house, bridge, aspergill, gingham, calico, gauze. "But to say them," as Rilke said, "remember oh, to say them in a way that the things themselves never dreamed of existing so intensely."

But this is too much of an orchestral close for the lowly little ditty that starts with a newspaper clipping or the feel of a bolt of gingham or a cup of coffee at the Weybridge Garage. The best advice I can give writers is something so dull and simple you'd never save it in your yellow folder. But go ahead and engrave it in your writer's heart. If you want to be a writer, anything in this world is grounds for fiction.

QUESTIONS FOR READING ACTIVELY

1. In rereading the essay, highlight all the cultural allusions Alvarez makes—the writers she cites, the paintings she mentions, the literary characters who obsess her, even the tabloid news stories she finds entertaining. Using the Internet (and working with partners, if you like), look up any allusions that are unfamiliar, and annotate your text by writing explanations of those

Thinking Critically About Visuals

Denotation and Connotation in Images

This photo shows what appear to be the hands of both a male and a female, presumably the mother and father, holding a sleeping baby. This is the denotative meaning of this image. In other words, the literal, face-value meaning of the image. What is the connotative meaning? For example, do you see one person handing the baby off to the other, or do you see them both holding the baby equally?

Gemstone Images/First Light/Corbis

allusions in the margins. What is Alvarez's purpose for all these allusions? How do you, as a reader, respond to the breadth of her interests?

2. How does Alvarez demonstrate the four qualities of an active, thoughtful, and critical reader? In what ways is she curious, open-minded, knowledgeable, and creative in her reading and her use of what she reads?

3. After you have annotated the essay to clarify any unfamiliar allusions, respond to any or all of the previous metacognitive reading questions.
   Do any portions of the essay resist your questioning? Compare notes with your classmates—what is most difficult about Alvarez's essay, and why?

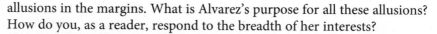

QUESTIONS FOR THINKING CRITICALLY

1. An *apologia* is a kind of argument, a defense that someone writes to explain and justify his or her actions, beliefs, or opinions. It's different from an *apology*, in which someone admits wrongdoing. In what ways does Alvarez present an apologia for herself as a writer? How, conversely, would she respond to a writer who might feel compelled to offer an apology for something he or she had written?

This photograph shows a bombed-out building with flowers growing in the foreground. How would you describe the denotative and connotative meaning of this photo? Why do you think the photographer decided to include the flowers in the foreground?

© prasit chansareekorn/ShutterStock.com

2. What does it mean to be *inspired*? (Look up the word; are you surprised by its etymology?) Where does Alvarez find inspiration? Look into the creative habits of another artist (in any medium) whose work you admire. From where does she draw her inspiration?

QUESTION FOR WRITING THOUGHTFULLY

1. Get an empty folder. For one week, make an effort to put anything in that folder that catches your interest—an email from a friend, a photograph from the newspaper, the menu from a coffee shop, the stub from a movie ticket. At the end of the week, dump the contents of the folder on your desk. What story do these scraps tell you about yourself? About your life? Can you arrange them into any sort of "narrative," either creative or very close to true? You could also exchange folders with a classmate. What stories could you tell about your classmate based on what's in his or her folder?

Making Meaning

Words are not simple entities with one clear meaning that everyone agrees on. Instead, most words are complex, multidimensional carriers of meaning; their exact meaning often varies from person to person. These differences in meaning can lead to disagreements and confusion. To understand how words function, you have to examine the way that words serve as vehicles to express meaning.

Words arouse a variety of ideas, feelings, and experiences. Taken together, these responses express the total meaning of the words for each individual. Linguists believe that this total meaning is actually composed of four different types of meaning:

- Semantic meaning
- Perceptual meaning
- Syntactic meaning
- Pragmatic meaning

Let us examine each of them in turn.

SEMANTIC MEANING (DENOTATION)

The *semantic meaning* of a word expresses the relationship between a *linguistic event* (speaking or writing) and a *nonlinguistic event* (an object, idea, or feeling). For example, saying "chair" relates to an object you sit in, while saying "college education" relates to the experience of earning an academic degree through postsecondary study.

The semantic meaning of a word, also referred to as its *denotative meaning*, expresses the general properties of the word, and these properties determine how the word is used within its language system. How do you discover the general properties that determine word usage? Besides examining your own knowledge of the meaning and use of words, you can check dictionary definitions. They tend to focus on the general properties that determine word usage. For example, a dictionary definition of *chair* might be "a piece of furniture consisting of a seat, legs, and back, and often arms, designed to accommodate one person."

However, to understand a word's semantic meaning fully, you often need to go beyond defining its general properties to identifying examples that embody those properties. If you are sitting in a chair or can see one from where you are, examine its design. Does it embody all the properties identified in the definition? (Sometimes unusual examples embody most, but not all, the properties of a word's dictionary definition—for example, a beanbag chair lacks legs and arms.) If you are trying to understand the semantic meaning of a word, it is generally useful to see both the word's general properties and examples that illustrate them.

PERCEPTUAL MEANING (CONNOTATION)

The total meaning of a word also includes its *perceptual meaning*, which expresses the relationship between a linguistic event and an individual's consciousness. For each of us, words elicit personal thoughts and feelings based on previous experiences and past associations. A person might relate saying "chair" to his favorite chair in his living room or the small chair that he built for his daughter. Perceptual meaning also includes an individual's positive and negative responses to the word. When you read or hear the word *book,* what positive or negative feelings does it arouse? What about *textbook? Mystery book? Comic book? Cookbook?* In each case, the word probably elicits distinct feelings, and these contribute to the meaning each word has for you. For this reason, perceptual meaning is also sometimes called *connotative meaning,* the literal or basic meaning of a word plus all it suggests or connotes to you.

SYNTACTIC MEANING

A third component of a word's total meaning is its *syntactic meaning,* which defines its relation to other words in a sentence. The syntactic meaning defines three relationships among words:

- *Content:* words that express the major message of the sentence
- *Description:* words that elaborate or modify the major message of the sentence
- *Connection:* words that join the major message of the sentence

For example, in the sentence "The two novice hikers crossed the ledge cautiously," *hikers, ledge,* and *crossed* represent the content, or major message, of the sentence. *Two* and *novice* describe *hikers,* and *cautiously* elaborates on *crossed.*

At first, you may think that this sort of relationship among words involves nothing more than semantic meaning. The following sentence, however, clearly demonstrates the importance of syntactic meaning in language: "Invisible fog rumbles in on lizard legs." Although *fog* does not *rumble,* and it is not *invisible,* and the notion of moving on *lizard legs* seems incompatible with *rumbling,* the sentence does "make sense" at some level of meaning—namely, at the syntactic level. One reason it does is that there are three basic content words—*fog, rumbles,* and *legs*—and two descriptive words—*invisible* and *lizard.*

The third major syntactic relationship is connection. Connective words join ideas, thoughts, or feelings being expressed. For example, you could connect content meaning to either of the two sentences in the following ways:

The two novice hikers crossed the ledge cautiously *after* one of them slipped.

Invisible fog rumbles in on lizard legs, *but* acid rain doesn't.

When you add the content words *one, slipped,* and *rain doesn't,* you join the ideas, thoughts, and feelings they represent to the ideas, thoughts, and feelings expressed earlier (*hikers crossed* and *fog rumbles*) by using the connective words *after* and *but.*

The second reason that "Invisible fog rumbles in on lizard legs" makes sense at the syntactic level of meaning is that the words of that sentence obey the syntax, or order, of English. Most English speakers would have trouble making sense of "Invisible rumbles legs lizard on fog in"—or of "Barks big endlessly dog brown the," for that matter. Because of syntactic meaning, each word in the sentence derives part of its total meaning from the ways in which it is combined with the other words in that sentence.

PRAGMATIC MEANING

The fourth element that contributes to the total meaning of a word is its *pragmatic meaning*. The pragmatic meaning of a word involves the person who is writing and the situation in which the word is written. For example, the statement "That

Thinking-Writing Activity

SYNTACTIC MEANING

Look at the following sentences and explain the difference in meaning between the two in each pair.

1. a. The process of obtaining an *education at college* changes a person's future possibilities.

    b. The process of obtaining a *college education* changes a person's future possibilities.

2. a. She felt *happiness* for her long-lost brother.

    b. She felt the *happiness* of her long-lost brother.

3. a. The most important thing to me is *freedom from* the things that restrict my choices.

    b. The most important thing to me is *freedom* to make my choices without restrictions.

4. a. Michelangelo's painting of the Sistine Chapel ceiling represents his *creative* genius.

    b. The Sistine Chapel ceiling represents the *creative* genius of Michelangelo's greatest painting.

5. a. I *love* the person I have been involved with for the past year.

    b. I am *in love* with the person I have been involved with for the past year.

student likes to borrow books from the library" allows a number of pragmatic interpretations:

1. Was the writer outside looking at *that student* carrying books out of the library?

2. Did the writer have this information because he or she is a classmate of *that student* but did not actually see the student carrying books?

3. Was the writer in the library watching *that student* check the books out?

The correct interpretation or meaning of the sentence depends on what was actually taking place in the situation—in other words, its pragmatic meaning, which is also called its *situational meaning*.

The four types of meanings you just examined—semantic, perceptual, syntactic, and pragmatic—create the total meaning of a word. That is, all the dimensions of a word—all the relationships that connect linguistic events with nonlinguistic events, with your consciousness, with other linguistic events, and with situations in the world—make up the meaning you assign to the word. Later, we will build on the ideas of this section.

Thinking-Writing Activity

PRAGMATIC MEANING

For each of the following sentences, try describing a pragmatic context that identifies the person writing and the situation for which it is being written.

1. A *college education* is currently necessary for many careers that formerly required only high school preparation.

2. The utilitarian ethical system is based on the principle that the right course of action is that which brings the greatest *happiness* to the greatest number of people.

3. The laws of this country attempt to balance the *freedom* of the individual with the rights of society as a whole.

4. "You are all part of things, you are all part of *creation*, all kings, all poets, all musicians, you have only to open up, to discover what is already there." —Henry Miller

5. "If music be the food of *love*, play on."—Shakespeare

After completing the activity, compare your answers with those of your classmates. In what ways are the answers similar or different? Analyze the ways in which different pragmatic contexts (persons speaking and situations) affect the meanings of the italicized words.

CHAPTER 2   Summary

- To get the most out of what you are reading, you need to read actively and critically. Reading actively involves reviewing the tables of contents or chapter outlines; reading the introductory paragraphs and the concluding paragraphs or summary; scanning the reading assignment, taking particular note of section headings, illustrations, and diagrams; annotating; and summarizing.

- Reading critically entails asking questions of interpretation, analysis, and evaluation, and using a problem-solving approach.

- Metacognition (or thinking about your thinking) can aid active critical reading.

- To get the full meaning of what you read, you should consider the semantic, perceptual, syntactic, and pragmatic meanings of the words and how they are being used together.

Becoming an independent, critical thinker requires examining situations from different perspectives. Your own writing and thinking will have greater significance and meaning to you (and to others) as you push the limits of your own understanding. Breakthroughs in thinking lead to vital, lively writing and insightful, informed beliefs. Do you know of any current research that is challenging people's beliefs?

Writing:
Using Independent Thought and Informed Beliefs

"The mere process of writing is one of the most powerful tools we have for clarifying our own thinking."

—JAMES VAN ALLEN

From Insight to Writing to Informed Beliefs (and Back Again)

Thinking, writing, reading—these are the tools you use to understand your world, develop relationships with others, and make intelligent decisions in your quest to live a meaningful life. The underlying theme of this book is the way these potentially powerful tools are intrinsically related to one another. Every day you make choices in many areas of your life, choices that are guided by the beliefs you have developed. Successful choices are generally the product of enlightened beliefs that we have developed as a result of thinking critically, reading actively, and writing thoughtfully, as well as through lived experience. Whether the choices involve how best to write a research paper, enliven your social life, or pursue a challenging career, these fundamental abilities provide you with the means to construct beliefs that will guide your choices.

This chapter extends and deepens the four core qualities listed below and explores other related qualities that characterize critical thinkers, active readers, and thoughtful writers.

- Thinking actively
- Thinking independently
- Viewing a situation from different perspectives
- Supporting diverse perspectives with evidence and reasons

The chapter then presents readings in which authors think critically by reflecting on experiences that have affected their beliefs. Concluding the chapter is a Writing Project that asks you to think critically and write thoughtfully about an experience that had an important impact on a belief that you held or hold. You should keep this Writing Project in mind as you read the chapter and work on the Thinking-Writing Activities.

CRITICAL THINKING FOCUS: **Thinking about thinking**

WRITING FOCUS: **Reflecting on experiences**

READING THEME: **Experiences that have affected beliefs**

WRITING ACTIVITY: **Writing about beliefs**

WRITING ACTIVITY: **How beliefs and perspectives influence writing**

WRITING PROJECT: **Recalling the impact of experience on a belief**

NEW MEDIA & THOUGHTFUL WRITING

Blogs

As we mentioned in Chapter 1, keeping a journal or blog is rewarding in a number of ways. An additional benefit of journaling in blog format is that you can get feedback on your writing through the comments section (provided you decide to make that section "open" under your privacy settings). People who visit your blog may offer useful constructive criticism, alternative viewpoints on your topic, or additional sources for exploring your ideas further. Being open to feedback from every possible source inevitably will enrich your writing experience. Charles Darwin wrote in his seminal work *The Origin of Species* (1859) "that something might perhaps be made out of this question [about the origin of species] by patiently accumulating and reflecting on all sorts of facts which could possibly have any bearing on it."

Another useful way you can use blogs to enhance your writing experience is to take advantage of a blog aggregator, such as Blogger.com, Bloglines.com, or Reddit.com. You can add the RSS (or "really simple syndication" feed) URLs for the blogs or newsfeeds you are interested in, and the aggregator will keep track of all of them for you, showing you at a glance when a blog or newsfeed has a new posting and allowing you to read that posting on the aggregator's page. If you have a particular interest or research topic you want to learn more about, you can add blogs and newsfeeds on that topic that present differing viewpoints, and, in this way, you can stay well informed on a subject you may want to write about.

Thinking-Writing Activity

BLOGGING

Go to a site like Blogger.com or Reddit.com, and use the site's aggregator options to start keeping track of blogs and newsfeeds on the topics you will be investigating for this class (and other classes, too, if you like). Then create your own blog, and share the address with your classmates. Blog about your ideas for writing topics, and provide links to your potential research sources. Throughout the course, visit your classmates' blogs, and leave constructive feedback via the comments section. Also remember to check back on your own posts to read the comments left there. You may find your classmates have provided very helpful suggestions.

Thinking Actively and Writing

When you think critically, you are *actively* using your intelligence, knowledge, and abilities to deal effectively with life's situations. Similarly, when you write thoughtfully, you act in the following ways:

- You *become involved* in the subject you are writing about, and because the writing process stimulates your thinking, you often discover ideas that you were unaware of until you started writing. Also, if you keep a journal or notebook and make writing part of your daily life, you find yourself more involved in and more reflective about your world.
- You *take initiative* as you develop confidence in your writer's voice, so you express your own perspectives instead of imitating the ideas of others.
- You *follow through* as you revise and edit in order to produce your best effort.
- You *take responsibility* for your work. That is, you begin assignments promptly and schedule enough time to complete them. Though your professors will guide you, and your classmates and writing center tutors will make suggestions about your drafts, you are in charge of your writing, and it is up to you to complete it honestly and well.

When you are thinking actively, you are not just waiting for something to happen. You are engaged in the process of achieving goals, making decisions, analyzing issues, and writing thoughtfully.

INFLUENCES ON YOUR THINKING

As our minds grow and develop, we are exposed to influences that encourage us to think actively. We also, however, have many experiences that encourage us to think passively. For example, some analysts believe that when people, especially children, spend much of their time watching television or playing video games instead of reading and writing, they are being encouraged to think passively, thus inhibiting their intellectual growth.

You are influenced to think passively if an employer gives you detailed instructions for performing every task that permit no exception or deviation. On the other hand, when an employer gives you general areas of responsibility within which you are expected to make thoughtful and creative decisions, you are being stimulated to think actively and independently. Of course, certain people or activities can act as either active or passive influences, depending on specific situations and your individual responses. For example, consider employers. If you are performing a routine, repetitive task—such as a summer job in a peanut-butter cracker plant, hand-scooping 2,000 pounds of peanut butter a day—the very nature of the work encourages passive, uncritical thinking (although it might also lead to creative daydreaming!).

In college, you will find that your course work and professors encourage you to think actively by expecting you to apply, analyze, synthesize, and evaluate the information you are acquiring. Professors may assign independent research projects, give essay exams, and require you to write papers in which you must bring your informed perspective to the course material.

Thinking Independently

Answer the following questions on the basis of what you believe to be true.

	Yes	*No*	*Not Sure*
1. Is the earth flat?			
2. Is the soul immortal?			
3. Should marijuana be legalized?			
4. Should music lyrics and videos be censored?			
5. Should we always follow the "Golden Rule" ("Do unto others as you would have them do unto you")?			

Thinking-Writing Activity

ACTIVE AND PASSIVE INFLUENCES

Here is a list of some of the influences we all experience in our lives, along with space for adding others you are aware of. As you read through the list, place an *A* next to items that you believe influence you to think actively and a *P* next to items that make you more passive.

Activities	*People*
Reading	Family members
Writing	Friends
Watching television	Employers
Surfing the Internet	Advertisers
Drawing and painting	Teachers
Playing video games	Police officers
Playing sports	Religious leaders
Listening to music	Politicians
_____	_____
_____	_____

Identify one important influence in your life that stimulates you to think actively; then identify one that encourages you to think passively. Write explanations of how each has affected your thinking. Provide at least two specific examples for each influence.

....

Your responses to these questions reveal aspects of the way your mind works and of the beliefs you have developed that you express in your speaking and writing. How did you arrive at these conclusions? Your views on these and many other issues probably had their beginnings with your family, especially your parents or other adults who raised you. When you were little, you were very dependent on those adults, and you were influenced by the way they saw the world. As you grew up, you learned how to think, feel, and behave in various situations. Very likely your teachers included your brothers and sisters, friends, religious leaders, instructors, books, and the media. You absorbed most of what you learned passively, without even being aware of doing so. Many of your ideas about the issues raised in the five questions you just answered probably were shaped by experiences you had while growing up.

As a result of your ongoing experiences, however, your mind—and your thinking—has continued to mature. Instead of simply accepting the views of others, you have gradually developed the ability to examine your earlier thinking and to decide how much of it still makes sense to you and whether you should accept it. Now, when you think through important ideas, use this standard when making a decision: Are there good reasons or evidence that supports this thinking? If so, you can actively decide to adopt the ideas. If not, you can modify or reject them.

How do you know when you have examined and adopted beliefs yourself instead of simply borrowing them from others? One indication of having thought

Frank Cotham/The New Yorker Collection/cartoonbank.com

"I keep my core beliefs written on my palm for easy reference."

your beliefs through is being able to explain why you believe in them, giving the reasons that led you to your conclusions.

Still, not all reasons and evidence are equally strong or accurate. For example, in Europe before the fifteenth century, the common belief that the earth was flat was supported by the following reasons and evidence:

> *People of Authority:* Many educational and religious authorities taught that the earth was flat.
>
> *Recorded References:* The written opinions of scientific experts supported belief in a flat earth.
>
> *Observed Evidence:* No person had ever circumnavigated the earth.
>
> *Personal Experience:* From a normal vantage point, the earth *looks* flat.

Thinking-Writing Activity

EVALUATING BELIEFS

For each of the five beliefs you expressed at the beginning of this section, explain how you arrived at it, and state the reasons and evidence that you believe support it.

1. *Example:* Is the earth flat?
   Belief: No, it is round.
   Reasons/Evidence:
   a. People of Authority: My parents and teachers taught me this.
   b. Recorded References: I read about the earth in science textbooks and saw films and videos.
   c. Observed Evidence: I have seen a sequence of photographs taken from outer space that show the earth as a globe.
   d. Personal Experience: When I flew across the country, I could see the horizon line changing.
2. Is the soul immortal?
3. Should marijuana be legalized?
4. Should music lyrics and videos be censored?
5. Should we follow the "Golden Rule" in our relationships with others?

To evaluate the strength and accuracy of the reasons and evidence you identified for holding your beliefs on the five issues, address questions such as the following:

> *People of Authority:* Are the authorities knowledgeable in this area? Are they reliable? Have they ever given inaccurate information? Do other authorities disagree with them?
>
> *Recorded References:* What references support your belief? What are the credentials of the authors? Do other authors disagree with their opinions? On what reasons and evidence do the authors base their opinions?
>
> *Observed Evidence:* What are the source and foundation of the evidence? Can the evidence be interpreted differently? Does the evidence support the conclusion?

Personal Experience: What were the circumstances under which the experiences took place? Were distortions or mistakes in perception possible? Have other people had either similar or conflicting experiences? Are there other explanations for your experiences?

As a college writer, you are going to apply these questions to material you encounter while gathering information for essays, projects, or reports. The opposite of thinking for yourself is simply accepting the thinking of others without examining or questioning it. Learning to become an independent thinker is a complex, ongoing process.

VIEWING A SITUATION FROM DIFFERENT PERSPECTIVES

Critical thinkers listen to other views and new ideas, and examine them carefully. No one person has *all* the answers! Your beliefs represent just one perspective on whatever problem you want to solve or situation you are trying to understand. In addition to your own particular viewpoint, there may be others, equally important, that you need to consider if you are to develop a more complete understanding of the problem or situation. Learning to think critically and write thoughtfully, in fact, requires this.

Audience and Perspective   Effective writing depends on always having a clear sense of your readers, the audience for whom you are writing. The ability to remain focused on that audience includes being able to see things from their point of view, to think empathetically within their frame of reference, and to understand their perspective. Perspective taking is essential to becoming a thoughtful writer. To begin with, exploring topics from a variety of vantage points is often the best way to present a comprehensive analysis of the subject you are writing about. When you are tied to only one perspective, your writing tends to be one-sided and superficial. In order to produce your most accomplished writing, you need to be open to the informed comments and suggestions of others and flexible enough to use that feedback to refine your writing.

For most of the issues and problems you will explore and write about in college, one viewpoint is simply not adequate to provide a full and satisfactory understanding. To increase and deepen your knowledge, you must seek other perspectives. In academic and professional writing, you will be expected to seek actively (and *listen to*) other people's viewpoints. It is often very difficult to see things from points of view other than your own; if you are not careful, you can make the serious mistake of assuming that the way you see things is the way they really are.

In order to identify with perspectives other than your own, then, you also have to work to grasp the reasons for these alternate viewpoints. This approach, which stimulates you to evaluate your beliefs critically, is enhanced by writing. Writing about beliefs encourages people to explain their reasons for holding them and provides a vehicle for sharing their thinking with those who have contrasting points of view.

Thinking-Writing Activity

TWO SIDES OF A BELIEF

Describe in detail a belief about which you feel very strongly. Then explain the reasons or experiences that led you to this belief. Next, describe a point of view that differs from your belief. Identify some of the reasons someone would have that point of view.

Purpose and Perspective   Being open to new ideas and different viewpoints means being *flexible* enough to change or modify one's own ideas in the light of new information or better insight. People do have a tendency to cling to the beliefs they were brought up with and the conclusions they have arrived at. If you are going to continue to grow and develop as a thinker, however, you have to be willing to change or modify your beliefs when evidence suggests that you should.

In contrast to open and flexible thinking, *un*critical thinking tends to be one-sided and close-minded. People who think uncritically are convinced that they alone see things as they really are and that everyone who disagrees with them is wrong. It is very difficult for them to step outside their own viewpoints and look at issues from other people's perspectives. Words often used to describe this type of person include *dogmatic, subjective,* and *egocentric.*

SUPPORTING DIVERSE PERSPECTIVES WITH REASONS AND EVIDENCE

When you are thinking critically, you can offer sound reasons for your views. As a thoughtful writer, you cannot simply take a position on an issue or make a claim; you have to back up your views, reinforcing them with information that you feel supports your position. There is an important distinction between *what* you believe and *why* you believe it.

If you want to know all sides of an issue, you have to be able to give supporting reasons and evidence not just for your own views but also for the views of others.

Consider whether or not cell phone use should be allowed while driving. As you try to make sense of this issue, you should attempt to identify not just the reasons for your view but also the reasons for other views. Following are reasons that support each view of this issue.

Issue

Cell phone use while driving should be prohibited.	Cell phone use while driving should be permitted.
Supporting reasons:	*Supporting reasons:*
1. Studies show that using cell phones while driving increases accidents.	1. Many people feel that cell phones are no more distracting than other common activities in cars.

Thinking Critically About Visuals

Understanding Different Sides of Complex Issues

As critical thinkers and thoughtful writers, we have an obligation to appreciate diverse perspectives on complex issues and develop informed opinions that are supported by compelling reasons. Have you ever taken part in or attended a protest or a demonstration regarding an issue that was important to you? Although it is essential to stand up for what we believe, how can we also try to appreciate why people on different sides of the issue have conflicting perspectives?

Colin Young-Wolff / PhotoEdit

Now see if you can identify additional supporting reasons for each of these views on cell phone use while driving.

For each of the following issues, identify reasons that support each side.

Issues

1. Multiple-choice and true/false exams should be given in college-level courses.

1. Multiple-choice and true/false exams should not be given in college-level courses.

2. It is better to live in a society in which the government plays a major role in citizens' lives.

3. The best way to reduce crime is to impose long prison sentences.

4. When a couple divorces, the children should choose the parent with whom they wish to live.

2. It is better to live in a society that minimizes the role of the government in citizens' lives.

3. Long prison sentences will not reduce crime.

4. When a couple divorces, the court should decide all custody issues regarding the children.

Thinking-Writing Activity

VIEWING DIFFERENT PERSPECTIVES

Seeing different perspectives is crucial to getting a more complete understanding of ideas expressed in passages you read. Read the two passages that follow. Then, for each passage, do these four things:

1. Identify the main idea of the passage.
2. List the reasons that support the main idea.
3. Develop another view of the main issue.
4. List the reasons that support the other view.

PASSAGE 1:

If we want auto safety but continue to believe in auto profits, sales, styling, and annual obsolescence, there will be no serious accomplishments. The moment we put safety ahead of these other values, something will happen. If we want better municipal hospitals but are unwilling to disturb the level of spending for defense, for highways, or for household appliances, hospital service will not improve. If we want peace but still believe that countries with differing ideologies are threats to one another, we will not get peace. What is confusing is that up to now, while we have wanted such things as conservation, auto safety, hospital care, and peace, we have tried wanting them without changing consciousness, that is, while continuing to accept those underlying values that stand in the way of what we want. The machine can be controlled at the "consumer" level only by people who change their whole value system, their whole worldview, their whole way of life. One cannot favor saving our wildlife and wear a fur coat.

* * * *

PASSAGE 2:

Most wicked deeds are done because the doer proposes some good to himself. The liar lies to gain some end; the swindler and thief want things which, if honestly got, might be good in themselves. Even the murderer may be removing an impediment to normal desires or gaining possession of something his victim keeps from him. None of these people usually does evil for evil's sake. They are selfish or unscrupulous, but their deeds are not gratuitously evil. The killer for sport has no such comprehensible motive. He prefers death to life, darkness to light. He gets nothing except the satisfaction of saying,

"Something which wanted to live is dead. There is that much less vitality, consciousness, and, perhaps, joy in the universe. I am the Spirit that Denies." When a human wantonly destroys one of humankind's own works, we call him Vandal. When he wantonly destroys one of the works of God, we call him Sportsman.

Developing Informed Beliefs

The process of developing informed beliefs is ongoing and lifelong. It is also a process that is essential for you to achieve success and happiness, since your beliefs constitute the "map" you use to guide your choices. If your belief map is accurate, your choices will reflect a clear understanding of the world. However, if your belief map is inaccurate or incomplete, you are in jeopardy of making ineffective or wrong-headed choices.

Developing informed beliefs involves the core qualities of a critical thinker and thoughtful writer to which we have been referring: *curious, open-minded, knowledgeable, creative.* The themes of this chapter complement these qualities:

- *Thinking actively* provides the impetus for asking questions, keeping an open mind, seeking knowledge, and being inventive.
- *Thinking independently* is achieved by being curious, going beyond familiar points of view, engaging in research to develop one's own informed opinions, and transcending conventional norms to achieve creative insights.
- *Viewing situations from different perspectives* is the essence of questioning narrow points of view in order to become truly open-minded. Perspective taking is also the vehicle one uses to develop genuine knowledge and achieve creative insights.
- *Supporting diverse perspectives with reasons and evidence* is the outgrowth of questioning, open-minded explorations, and utilization of one's knowledge.

Thinking-Writing Activity

CREATING A BELIEF MAP

Just as maps help you navigate your way through unfamiliar territory, belief mapping is a creative strategy for visualizing a path through new and challenging ideas. You can use belief mapping to help you better understand the origins of your own beliefs and positions, as well as to plan ways to become a more active and independent thinker. In Chapter 4, we will explore how to use mapping and other visual strategies to help plan writing assignments.

To create a belief map, return to the topics in the Thinking-Writing Activity on page 62 and follow these guidelines:

- Select a topic (either an activity or a person) that has had a *passive* influence on your thinking. This is the starting point of your journey.
- Next, select a topic (again, an activity or a person) that has had an *active* influence on your thinking. This is the route you will travel.

- Finally, select a personal, academic, or career goal. This is your destination.
- Using any visual or artistic medium that appeals to you (such as a simple pencil sketch, a collage, or graphic-arts software), create a map that shows how the active influences on your thinking will help you navigate from your starting point to your goal. What kinds of obstacles might you expect along the way? How would you visually represent those obstacles? How would you describe them to someone on a similar journey?

Experiences That Affect Beliefs

In the following narratives, three writers reflect on learning experiences that caused them to evaluate and in some cases revise beliefs about themselves, the world in which they live, other people, and ways to live their lives.

As you read the selections, keep in mind one set of critical reading questions that we identified in Chapter 2.

- Who is the *writer*, and what perspective does he or she bring to the writing selection?
- What is the *subject* of the selection, and how would you evaluate its cogency and reliability?
- Who is the intended *audience,* and what assumptions is the writer making about it?
- What is the *purpose* of the selection, and how is the author trying to achieve it?

Following each selection are questions designed to stimulate and guide your critical thinking, active reading, and thoughtful writing.

From *An American Childhood*

by Annie Dillard

Annie Dillard's engagement with nature and its reflection of the spiritual life informs her extensive creative and nonfiction writing. A poet, novelist, and essayist, Dillard won the Pulitzer Prize for her memoir *Pilgrim at Tinker Creek* (1974). Her close observations of the environment and her ongoing spiritual quests combine in her views on writing, as in this passage from "Write Till You Drop": "The sensation of writing a book is the sensation of spinning, blinded by love and daring. It is the sensation of a stunt pilot's turning barrel rolls, or an inchworm's blind rearing from a stem in search of a route. At its worst, it feels like alligator wrestling, at the level of the sentence." In the following memoir, she describes how her parents encouraged her early explorations of the natural world.

Source: From *An American Childhood* by Annie Dillard, pp. 147–149. Copyright © 1987 by Annie Dillard. Reprinted by permission of HarperCollins Publisher.

After I read *The Field Book of Ponds and Streams* several times, I longed for a microscope. Everybody needed a microscope. Detectives used microscopes, both for the FBI and at Scotland Yard. Although usually I had to save my tiny allowance for things I wanted, that year for Christmas my parents gave me a microscope kit.

In a dark basement corner, on a white enamel table, I set up the microscope kit. I supplied a chair, a lamp, a batch of jars, a candle, and a pile of library books. The microscope kit supplied a blunt black three-speed microscope, a booklet, a scalpel, a dropper, an ingenious device for cutting thin segments of fragile tissue, a pile of clean slides and cover slips, and a dandy array of corked test tubes.

One of the test tubes contained "hay infusion." Hay infusion was a wee brown chip of grass blade. You added water to it, and after a week it became a jungle in a drop, full of one-celled animals. This did not work for me. All I saw in the microscope after a week was a wet chip of dried grass, much enlarged.

Another test tube contained "diatomaceous earth." This was, I believed, an actual pinch of the white cliffs of Dover. On my palm it was an airy, friable chalk. The booklet said it was composed of the silicaceous bodies of diatoms—one-celled creatures that lived in, as it were, small glass jewelry boxes with fitted lids. Diatoms, I read, come in a variety of transparent geometrical shapes. Broken and dead and dug out of geological deposits, they made chalk, and a fine abrasive used in silver polish and toothpaste. What I saw in the microscope must have been the fine abrasive—grit enlarged. It was years before I saw a recognizable, whole diatom. The kit's diatomaceous earth was a bust.

All that winter I played with the microscope. I prepared slides from things at hand, as the books suggested. I looked at the transparent membrane inside an onion's skin and saw the cells. I looked at a section of cork and saw the cells, and at scrapings from the inside of my cheek, ditto. I looked at my blood and saw not much; I looked at my urine and saw long iridescent crystals, for the drop had dried.

All this was very well, but I wanted to see the wildlife I had read about. I wanted especially to see the famous amoeba, who had eluded me. He was supposed to live in the hay infusion, but I hadn't found him there. He lived outside in warm ponds and streams, too, but I lived in Pittsburgh, and it had been a cold winter.

Finally late that spring I saw an amoeba. The week before, I had gathered puddle water from Frick Park, it had been festering in a jar in the basement. This June night after dinner I figured I had waited long enough. In the basement at my microscope table I spread a scummy drop of Frick Park puddle water on a slide, peeked in, and lo, there was the famous amoeba. He was as blobby and grainy as his picture; I would have known him anywhere.

Before I had watched him at all, I ran upstairs. My parents were still at the table, drinking coffee. They, too, could see the famous amoeba. I told them, bursting, that he was all set up, that they should hurry before his water dried. It was the chance of a lifetime.

Father had stretched out his long legs and was tilting back in his chair. Mother sat with her knees crossed, in blue slacks, smoking a Chesterfield. The dessert dishes were still on the table. My sisters were nowhere in evidence. It was a warm evening; the big dining-room windows gave onto blooming rhododendrons.

Mother regarded me warmly. She gave me to understand that she was glad I had found what I had been looking for, but that she and Father were happy to sit with their coffee, and would not be coming down.

She did not say, but I understood at once, that they had their pursuits (coffee?) and I had mine. She did not say, but I began to understand then, that you do what you do out of your private passion for the thing itself.

I had essentially been handed my own life. In subsequent years my parents would praise my drawings and poems, and supply me with books, art supplies, and sports equipment, and listen to my troubles and enthusiasms, and supervise my hours, and discuss and inform, but they would not get involved with my detective work, nor hear about my reading, nor inquire about my homework or term papers or exams, nor visit the salamanders I caught, nor listen to me play the piano, nor attend my field hockey games, nor fuss over my insect collection with me, or my poetry collection or stamp collection or rock collection. My days and nights were my own to plan and fill.

When I left the dining room that evening and started down the dark basement stairs, I had a life, I sat with my wonderful amoeba, and there he was, rolling his grains more slowly now, extending an arc of his edge for a foot and drawing himself along by that foot, and absorbing it again and rolling on. I gave him some more pond water.

I had hit pay dirt. For all I knew, there were paramecia, too, in that pond water, or daphniae, or stentors, or any of the many other creatures I had read about and never seen: volvox, the spherical algal colony; euglena with its one red eye; the elusive glassy diatom; hydra, rotifers, water bears, worms. Anything was possible. The sky was the limit.

QUESTIONS FOR READING ACTIVELY

1. Examine the structure of Dillard's essay. How much time passes over the course of the essay, and how can you tell? When does she "pause" in her narrative, and why?

2. In paragraph 11, Dillard asks a rhetorical question (a question that a writer does not answer, but leaves to the reader). Although it's just one word, what is the full meaning of that question? How would you, as a reader, answer it, based on what you know of Dillard's parents? Based on your own parents or your own experience as a parent?

QUESTIONS FOR THINKING CRITICALLY

1. When Annie Dillard rushed to share her discovery of the amoeba with her parents, they politely declined. What reaction had she expected, and what did this reveal about her beliefs regarding her relationship with her parents?

2. Her parents' lack of interest in this and other passions in her life led her to a conclusion: "I had essentially been handed my own life." Explain why you think she reached this conclusion.

3. Based on your own experience, do you believe that the best way to achieve "your own life" is through your parents' lack of involvement in your life?

4. The author states that "you do what you do out of your private passion for the thing itself." This "private passion" is a kind of curiosity, a key characteristic of a critical thinker. Describe a "private passion" of your own that you pursue not to please others but because of your personal curiosity and enthusiasm.

> ### QUESTION FOR WRITING THOUGHTFULLY
>
> 1. Compare the vocabulary of the final paragraph with the rest of the essay. Why do you think Dillard concludes her essay with this kind of language?

"Reversing Established Orders"

by Stephen Jay Gould (1941–2002)

From *Leonardo's Mountain of Clams and the Diet of Worms: Essays on Natural History*

Stephen Jay Gould started his academic career as a professor of geology at Harvard University but expanded his interests into evolutionary biology. He was curator of invertebrate paleontology at Harvard's Museum of Comparative Zoology and a writer with a gift for translating complex scientific theories into informed, but witty, prose that nonscientists can understand and enjoy. His essays appeared in magazines such as *Natural History* and *Discover* and were collected in the books *Ever Since Darwin, The Panda's Thumb, The Flamingo's Simile,* and *Leonardo's Mountain of Clams and the Diet of Worms*, in which the following essay appears. This essay illustrates the ongoing process by which natural scientists use inferences to discover factual information and to construct theories explaining that information.

We all know how the world works. A fisherman asks his boss in Shakespeare's *Pericles:* "Master, I marvel how the fishes live in the sea," and receives the evident response, "Why, as men do a-land; the great ones eat up the little ones." Consequently, when humorists invent topsy-turvy worlds, they reverse such established orders and then emphasize the rightness of their absurdity. Alice's Wonderland works on the principle of "sentence first—verdict afterwards." In Gilbert and Sullivan's town of Titipu, the tailor Ko-ko, condemned to death by decapitation, is elevated instead to the rank of Lord High Executioner because—it is so obvious; after all—a man "cannot cut off another's head until he's cut his own off." Pish-tush explains all this in a spirited song with a rousing chorus: "And I am right, and you are right, and all is right too- loora-lay."

Social and literary critics of the so-called postmodernist movement have emphasized, in a cogent and important argument often buried in the impenetrable jargon of their discourse, that conventional support for established orders usually relies upon claims for the naturalness of "dualisms" and "hierarchies." In creating dualisms, we divide a subject into two contrasting categories; in imposing hierarchy upon these dualisms, we judge one category as superior, the other as inferior. We all know the dualistic hierarchies of our social and political lives—from righteous versus infidel of centuries past to the millionaire CEOs who deserve tax cuts versus single mothers who should lose their food stamps in our astoundingly mean-spirited present. The postmodernists correctly argue that such dualisms and hierarchies represent our own constructions for political utility (often nefarious), rather than nature's factual and inevitable dictate. We may choose to parse the world in many other ways with radically different implications.

Our categorizations of nature also tend to favor dualistic hierarchies based upon domination. We often divide the world ecologically into predators and prey, or anatomically into complicated and dominant "higher" animals versus simpler and subservient "lower" forms. I do not deny the utility of such parsings in making predictions that usually work—big fish do generally eat little fish, and not vice versa. But the postmodernist critique should lead us to healthy skepticism, as we scrutinize the complex and socially embedded reasons behind the original formulations of our favored categories. Dualism with dominance may primarily record a human imposition upon nature, rather than a lecture directed to us by the birds and bees.

Natural historians tend to avoid tendentious preaching in this philosophical mode (though I often fall victim to such temptations in these essays). Our favored style of doubting is empirical: if I wish to question your proposed generality, I will search for a counterexample in flesh and blood. Such counterexamples exist in abundance, for they form a staple in a standard genre of writing in natural history—the "wonderment of oddity" or "strange ways of the beaver" tradition. (Sorry to be so disparaging—my own ignoble dualism, I suppose. The stories are terrific. I just often yearn for more intellectual generality and less florid writing.)

5   Much of our fascination with "strange cases" lies in their abrogation of accepted dualisms based on dominance—the "reversing established orders" of my title. As an obvious example, and paragon of this literature, carnivorous plants have always elicited primal intrigue—and the bigger and more taxonomically "advanced" the prey, the more we feel the weirdness. We yawn when a Venus's flytrap ensnares a mosquito, but shiver with substantial discomfort when a large pitcher plant devours a bird or rodent.

I keep a file marked "Reversals" to house such cases. I have long been on the lookout for optimal examples, where all three of the most prominent dualisms based on dominance suffer reversal: predator and prey, high and low, large and small— in other words, where a creature from a category usually ranked as small in body, primitive in design, and subject to predation eats another animal from a category generally viewed as bigger, anatomically superior, and rapacious. I now have four intriguing examples, more than enough for an essay. Since we postmodernists abjure hierarchical ranking, I will simply present my stories in the nonjudgmental chronological order of their publication (though postmodernism in this sense—and truly I am not a devotee of this movement—may be a cop-out and an excuse, for not devising a better logical structure for this essay!).

* * * *

1. FROGS AND FLIES. Frogs eat flies. If flies eat frogs, then we might as well be headed for bedlam or the apocalypse. My colleague Tom Eisner of Cornell University is revered throughout our profession as the past master of natural oddities with important and practical general messages. One day in August 1982, at a small pond in Arizona, Eisner and several colleagues noted thousands of spadefoot toads congregating on the muddy shore as they emerged to adulthood in near synchrony from their tadpole stage. Eisner and colleagues described their discovery in a technical publication:

Spaced only centimeters apart in places, they were all of minimal adult size (body length, 1.5 to 2 cm [less than an inch]). Conspicuous among them were toads that were dead or dying, apparently having been seized by a predator in the mud and drawn partly into the substrate, until only their head, or head and trunk, projected above ground. We counted dozens of such semisubmerged toads.

They then dug deeper and to their great surprise, found the predator "a large grublike insect larva, subsequently identified as that of the horsefly *Tabanus punctifer*." In other words, flies can eat toads! (Although astonishment may be lessened in noting that the tiny toads are much smaller than enormous fly larvae.) Unusually large insects and maximally small vertebrates have also been featured in the few other recorded cases of such reversals—frogs, small birds, even a mouse, consumed by praying mantids, for example.

The fly larvae force themselves into the mud, rear end first, until their front end, bearing the mouthparts, lies flush with the surface. The larvae then catch toads by hooking their pointed mandibles into the hind legs or belly, and then dragging the toad partway into the mud. The larvae—please remember that many tales in natural history are not pleasant by human standards—then suck the toad dry (and dead) by ingesting blood and body fluids only.

I loved the wry last sentence of the paper by Eisner and his colleagues—unusual in   10
style for a technical article, but odd stories have always permitted some literary license:

> The case we report is a reversal of the usual toad-eats-fly paradigm, although . . . the paradigm may also prevail in its conventional form. Adult *Scaphiopus* [the spadefoot toad] might well on occasions have predatory access to the very *Tabanus* flies that as larvae preyed upon their conspecifics.

J. Greenberg, reporting for *Science News* (November 5, 1983), began his commentary with the emotional impact of such reversals:

> This is the Okeechobee Fla. Little League team thrashing the New York Yankees; this is Wally Cox beating out Burt Reynolds for the girl; this is Grenada invading the United States. "This is unlike anything I've ever seen," says Thomas Eisner.

* * * *

2. LOBSTERS AND SNAILS. Decapod crustaceans (lobsters, crabs, shrimp) eat snails, as all naturalists know. In fact, the classic case of an extended evolutionary "arms race," elegantly documented over many years by my colleague Geerat Vermeij, involves increased strength of crab claws correlated with ever more efficient protective devices (spines, ribs, thicker and wavier shells) in snails over geological time. Land crabs are the overwhelmingly predominant predator of my own favorite subject for research, the Caribbean land snail *Cerion*. If snails eat decapods, we might as well retire.

Amos Barkai and Christopher McQuaid studied rock lobsters and whelks (snails of middling size) in waters around two islands, Marcus and Malgas, located just four miles apart in the Saldanha Bay area of South Africa. On Malgas, as all God-fearing folk would only rightly suspect, rock lobsters eat mollusks, mostly mussels and several species of whelks. Barkai and McQuaid write in their 1988 account: "The rock lobsters usually attacked the whelks by chipping away the shell margin with their mouth parts."

The local lobstermen report that, twenty years ago, rock lobsters were equally common on both islands. But lobsters then disappeared from Marcus Island, for unclear reasons, perhaps linked to a period of low oxygen in surrounding waters during the 1970s. In the absence of lobsters as the usual top predator, extensive mussel beds have become established, and the population density of whelks has soared. Barkai and McQuaid asked themselves: "Why do rock lobsters not recolonize Marcus Island despite the high availability of food?"

15   In an attempt to answer their own question, they performed the obvious experiment— and made an astonishing discovery. The food has become the feeder—this time by overwhelming in number, not equaling in size (the whelks are much smaller than the lobsters). The conventional passive voice of scientific prose does not convey excitement well, but a good story easily transcends such a minor limitation. So, in Barkai and McQuaid's own words; and without any need for further commentary from me (I would only be tempted to make some arch and utterly inappropriate statement about slave revolts—Spartacus and all that):

> One thousand rock lobsters from Malgas Island were tagged and transferred to Marcus Island . . . The result was immediate. The apparently healthy rock lobsters were quickly overwhelmed by large numbers of whelks. Several hundreds were observed being attacked immediately after release and a week later no live rock lobsters could be found at Marcus Island . . . The rock lobsters escaped temporarily by swimming, but each contact with the substratum resulted in several more whelks attaching themselves until weight of numbers prevented escape. On average each rock lobster was killed within fifteen minutes by more than three hundred *Burnupena* [whelks] that removed all the flesh in less than an hour.*

Sic semper tyrannis.

* * * *

3. FISH AND DINOFLAGELLATES. Fish don't generally eat dinoflagellates; why should they even deign to notice such microscopic algae, floating in the plankton? But dinoflagellates certainly don't eat fish; the very notion, given the disparity in sizes, is ludicrous to the point of incomprehensibility.

Dinoflagellates do, however, *kill* fish, by indirect mechanisms long known and well studied for their immense practical significance. Under favorable conditions, dinoflagellate populations can soar to 60 million organisms per liter of water. These so-called blooms can discolor and poison the waters—"red tide" is the most familiar example—leading to massive deaths of fish and other marine organisms.

J. M. Burkholder and a group of her colleagues from North Carolina State University have studied toxic blooms associated with fish kills in estuaries of the southeastern United States. The largest event resulted in the death of nearly one million Atlantic menhaden in the estuary of the Pamlico River. The oddity of this case lies not in the killing of fish per se, a common consequence of dinoflagellate blooms. We have always regarded the deaths of fishes and other marine organisms during red tides as passive and "unintended" results of dinoflagellate toxins, or other consequences of massive algal populations during blooms. No one had supposed that dinoflagellates might

*Amos Barkai and Christopher McQuaid.

actively kill fish as an evolved response for their own explicit advantage, including a potential nutritional benefit for the algal cells. And yet the dinoflagellates do seem to be killing and eating fishes in a manner suggesting active evolution for this most peculiar reversal.

The dinoflagellate lives in a dormant state, lying on the sea floor within a protective cyst. When live fish approach, the cyst breaks and releases a mobile cell that swims, grows, and secretes a powerful, water-soluble neurotoxin, killing the fish. So far, so what?—though the presence of fish does seem to induce activity by the dinoflagellate (breaking of the cyst), thus suggesting a direct link. Anatomical and behavioral evidence both suggest that dinoflagellates have actively evolved their strategy for feeding on fishes. The swimming cell, breaking out from the cyst, grows a projection, called a peduncle, from its lower surface. The cells seem to move actively toward dead or dying fishes. Flecks of tissue, sloughed off from the fish, then become attached to the peduncle and get digested. The authors describe this reversal at maximum disparity in size among my four cases:

> The lethal agent is an excreted neurotoxin. [It] induces neurotoxic signs by fish including sudden sporadic movement, disorientation, lethargy and apparent suffocation followed by death. The alga has not been observed to attack fish directly. It rapidly increases its swimming velocity to reach flecks of sloughed tissue from dying fish, however, using its peduncle to attach to and digest the tissue debris.

* * * *

4. SPONGES AND ARTHROPODS. Among invertebrates, sponges rank as the lowest of the low (the bottom rung of any evolutionary ladder), while arthropods stand highest of the high (just a little lower than the angels, that is, just before vertebrates on a linear list of rising complexity). Sponges have no discrete organs; they feed by filtering out tiny items of food from water pumped through channels in their body. Arthropods grow eyes, limbs, brains, and digestive systems; many live as active carnivores. Most arthropods wouldn't take much notice of a lowly sponge, but we can scarcely imagine how or why a sponge might subdue and ingest an arthropod. [20]

However, in a 1995 article, crisply titled "Carnivorous Sponges," J. Vacelet and N. Boury-Esnault of the Centre d'Oceanologie of Marseille have found a killer sponge (about as bizarre as a fish-eating dinoflagellate—but both exist). Relatives of this sponge, members of the genus *Asbestopluma*, have only been known from very deep waters (including the all-time record for sponges at more than 25,000 feet), where behavior and food preferences could not be observed. But Vacelet and Boury-Esnault found a new species in a shallow-water Mediterranean cave (less than one hundred feet), where scuba divers can watch directly.

The deep sea is a nutritional desert, and many organisms from such habitats develop special adaptations for procuring large and rare items (while relatives from shallow waters may pursue a plethora of smaller prey). *Asbestopluma* has lost both filtering channels through the body and the specialized cells (called choanocytes) that pump the water through. So how does this deep-water sponge feed?

The new species grows long filaments that extend out from the upper end of the body. A blanket of tiny spicules, or small skeletal projections, covers the surface of the filaments. The authors comment: "The spicule cover . . . gives the filaments a 'Velcro'-like adhesiveness"—the key to this feeding reversal at maximal anatomical distance for invertebrates. The sponge captures small crustaceans on the filaments— and they can't escape any more than a fuzz ball can detach itself from the Velcro lining of your coat pocket. The authors continue: "New, thin filaments grew over the prey, which was completely enveloped after one day and digested within a few days." The sponge, in other words, has become a carnivore.

Four fascinating stories to give us pause about our preconceptions, particularly our dualistic taxonomies based on the domination of one category over another. The little guys sometimes turn tables and prevail—often enough, perhaps, to call the categories themselves into question.

25   I see another message in these reversals—a consequence of the reassessment that must always proceed when established orders crumble, or merely lose their claim to invariance. In our struggle to understand the history of life, we must learn where to place the boundary between contingent and unpredictable events that occur but once and the more repeatable, lawlike phenomena that may pervade life's history as generalities. (In my own view of life, the domain of contingency looms vastly larger than all Western tradition, and most psychological hope, would allow. Fortuity pervades the origin of any particular species or lineage. *Homo sapiens* is a contingent twig, not a predictable result of ineluctably rising complexity during evolution. . . .)

The domain of lawlike generality includes broad phenomena not specific to the history of particular lineages. The ecological structure of communities should provide a promising searching ground, for some principles of structural organization must transcend the particular organisms that happen to occupy a given role at any moment. I imagine, for example, that all balanced ecosystems must sustain more biomass as prey than as predators—and I would accept such statements as predictable generalities, despite my affection for contingency. I would also have been willing to embrace the invariance of other rules for sensible repetition—that single-celled creatures don't kill and eat large multicellular organisms, for example. But these four cases of reversed order give me pause.

In a famous passage from the *Origin of Species*, Charles Darwin extolled the invariance of certain ecological patterns by using observed repetition in independent colonizations to argue against a range of contingently unpredictable outcomes:

When we look at the plants and bushes clothing an entangled bank, we are tempted to attribute their proportional numbers and kinds to what we call chance. But how false a view is this! Every one has heard that when an American forest is cut down, a very different vegetation springs up; but it has been observed that the trees now growing on the ancient Indian mounds, in the Southern United States, display the same beautiful diversity and proportion of kinds as in the surrounding virgin forests. What a struggle between the several kinds of trees must here have gone on during long centuries, each annually scattering its seeds by the thousand; what war between insect and insect—between insects, snails, and other animals with birds and beasts of prey—all striving to increase, and all feeding on each other or on the trees or their seeds and seedlings, or on the other plants which first clothed the ground and thus checked the growth of the trees! Throw up a handful of feathers, and all must fall to the ground according to definite laws; but how simple is this problem compared to the action and reaction of the innumerable plants and animals which have determined, in the course of centuries, the proportional numbers and kinds of trees now growing on the old Indian ruins!*

But the same patterns do not always recur from adjacent starting points colonized by the same set of species. Even the most apparently predictable patterns of supposedly established orders may fail. Remove the lobsters from waters around one South African island, and a new equilibrium may quickly emerge—one that actively excludes lobsters by converting their former prey into a ganging posse of predators!

Thus, I sense a challenge in these four cases, a message perhaps deeper than the raw peculiarity of their phenomenology—and the resulting attack upon our dualistic and hierarchical categories. We do not yet know the rules of composition for ecosystems. We do not even know if rules exist in the usual sense. I am tempted, therefore, to close with the famous words that D'Arcy Thompson wrote to signify our ignorance of the microscopic world (*Growth and Form*, 1942 edition). We are not quite so uninformed about the rules of composition for ecosystems, but what a stark challenge and what an inspiration to go forth: "We have come to the edge of a world of which we have no experience, and where all our preconceptions must be recast."

QUESTIONS FOR READING ACTIVELY

1. In your own words, define the concept of *dualism with dominance* (paragraph 3). What is Gould's opinion of this concept and the ways in which it has been used to explain the natural world?

2. How is Gould's argument structured? What does Gould himself think about this method for structuring his argument?

QUESTIONS FOR THINKING CRITICALLY

1. How could you use what Gould calls "counterexamples" in biology (paragraph 4) to better develop your own perspectives and beliefs about a wide variety of issues?

2. In paragraph 15, Gould notes that "The conventional passive voice of scientific prose does not convey excitement well, but a good story easily transcends such a minor limitation." Compare Gould's sense of excitement and curiosity with Annie Dillard's recollection of her first sighting of an amoeba (page 71). What qualities of critical thinking and thoughtful writing do these two authors share?

QUESTIONS FOR WRITING THOUGHTFULLY

1. How would you describe the audience Gould had in mind as he wrote this essay? Point out examples of Gould's language choices, allusions to scientific or cultural concepts, and other places in the essay where you think Gould is

Source: Origin of Species, Charles Darwin (1859).

specifically appealing to this audience. Which parts of the essay do you find most accessible and appealing, and why? Which parts are most challenging for you?

2. What is the "message" that Gould sees in these reversals of seemingly established orders? In an essay, define that message in your own words and describe how it either challenges or upholds your own beliefs.

"The Case Against Chores"
by Jane Smiley (b. 1949)

Novelist and literature professor Jane Smiley has explored everything from the history of Greenland to thoroughbred horse racing in her fiction. A native of California, Smiley lived and taught for many years in Iowa. The influence of that state's proud rural culture is deeply felt in her novel *A Thousand Acres,* which won the Pulitzer Prize in 1991. Using the great Shakespearean tragedy *King Lear* as her inspiration, Smiley captured the vast sense of loss and despair felt by many Midwestern farm families during the rural economic crisis of the 1980s. Smiley's essays and book reviews have appeared in a range of periodicals. "The Case Against Chores" was originally published in *Harper's Magazine* in 1995.

I've lived in the upper Midwest for twenty-one years now, and I'm here to tell you that the pressure to put your children to work is unrelenting. So far I've squirmed out from under it, and my daughters have led a life of almost tropical idleness, much to their benefit. My son, however, may not be so lucky. His father was himself raised in Iowa and put to work at an early age, and you never know when, in spite of all my husband's best intentions, that early training might kick in.

Although "chores" are so sacred in my neck of the woods that almost no one ever discusses their purpose, I have over the years gleaned some of the reasons parents give for assigning them. I'm not impressed. Mostly the reasons have to do with developing good work habits or, in the absence of good work habits; at least habits of working. No such thing; as a free lunch any job worth doing is worth doing right, work before play, all of that. According to this reasoning, the world is full of jobs that no one wants to do. If we divide them up and get them over with, then we can go on to pastimes we like. If we do them "right," then we won't have to do them again. Lots of times, though, in a family, that *we* doesn't operate. The operative word is *you.* The practical result of almost every child-labor scheme that I've witnessed is the child doing the dirty work and the parent getting the fun: Mom cooks and Sis does the dishes; the parents plan and plant the garden, the kids weed it. To me, what this teaches the child is the lesson of alienated labor: not to love the work but to get it over with; not to feel pride in one's contribution but to feel resentment at the waste of one's time.

Another goal of chores: the child contributes to the work of maintaining the family. According to this rationale, the child comes to understand what it takes to have a family, and to feel that he or she is an important, even indispensable member of it. But come on. Would you really want to feel loved primarily because you're the one who gets the floors mopped? Wouldn't you rather feel that your family's love simply exists all around you, no matter what your contribution? And don't the parents love their children anyway, whether the children vacuum or not? Why lie about it just to get the housework done? Let's be frank about the other half of the equation too. In this day and age, it doesn't take much work at all to manage a household, at least in the middle class—maybe four hours a week to clean the house and another four to throw the laundry into the washing machine, move it to the dryer, and fold it. Is it really a good idea to set the sort of example my former neighbors used to set, of mopping the floor every two days, cleaning the toilets every week, vacuuming every day, dusting, dusting, dusting? Didn't they have anything better to do than serve their house?

Let me confess that I wasn't expected to lift a finger when I was growing up. Even when my mother had a full-time job, she cleaned up after me, as did my grandmother. Later there was a housekeeper. I would leave my room in a mess when I headed off for school and find it miraculously neat when I returned. Once in a while I vacuumed, just because I liked the pattern the Hoover made on the carpet. I did learn to run water in my cereal bowl before setting it in the sink.

Where I discovered work was at the stable, and, in fact, there is no housework like horsework. You've got to clean the horses' stalls, feed them, groom them, tack them up, wrap their legs, exercise them, turn them out, and catch them. You've got to clip them and shave them. You have to sweep the aisle, clean your tack and your boots, carry bales of hay and buckets of water. Minimal horsekeeping, rising just to the level of humaneness, requires many more hours than making a few beds, and horsework turned out to be a good preparation for the real work of adulthood, which is rearing children. It was a good preparation not only because it was similar in many ways but also because my desire to do it, and to do a good job of it, grew out of my love of and interest in my horse. I can't say that cleaning out her bucket when she manured in it was an actual joy, but I knew she wasn't going to do it herself. I saw the purpose of my labor, and I wasn't alienated from it.

Probably to the surprise of some of those who knew me as a child, I have turned out to be gainfully employed. I remember when I was in seventh grade, one of my teachers said to me, strongly disapproving, "The trouble with you is you do only what you want to do!" That continues to be the trouble with me, except that over the years I have wanted to do more and more.

My husband worked hard as a child, out-Iowa-ing the Iowans, if such a thing is possible. His dad had him mixing cement with a stick when he was five, pushing wheelbarrows not long after. It's a long sad tale on the order of two miles to school and both ways uphill. The result is, he's a great worker, much better than I am, but all the while he's doing it he wishes he weren't. He thinks of it as work; he's torn between doing a good job and longing not to be doing it at all. Later, when he's out on the golf course, where he really wants to be, he feels a little guilty, knowing there's work that should have been done before he gave in and took advantage of the beautiful day.

Good work is not the work we assign children but the work they want to do, whether it's reading in bed (where would I be today if my parents had rousted me

5

out and put me to scrubbing floors?) or cleaning their rooms or practicing the flute or making roasted potatoes with rosemary and Parmesan for the family dinner. It's good for a teenager to suddenly decide that the bathtub is so disgusting she'd better clean it herself. I admit that for the parent, this can involve years of waiting. But if she doesn't want to wait, she can always spend her time dusting.

QUESTIONS FOR READING ACTIVELY

1. What kinds of reasons and evidence does Smiley offer to support her argument? Do you consider these reasons and evidence to be authoritative? What does her choice of reasons and evidence reveal about Smiley's intended audience?

2. How does Smiley use rhetorical questions to appeal to her readers? What is your reaction to these questions?

QUESTIONS FOR THINKING CRITICALLY

1. How does the concept of dualism with dominance described by Stephen Jay Gould in "Reversing Established Orders" (page 73) apply to Smiley's description of "chores" as part of a family dynamic?

2. In paragraph 5, Smiley makes a startling analogy. What is it? Do you agree? How might student writer Eli Sharp (page 88) respond to that analogy?

3. In what ways do Jane Smiley's (page 80) and Annie Dillard's (page 70) childhoods resemble each other? What kinds of arguments do both writers make for the benefits of encouraging curiosity and independence in children? Do you agree or disagree?

QUESTION FOR WRITING THOUGHTFULLY

1. What experience did Smiley have that changed her beliefs about chores? At what point in her essay does she describe this experience? Does the placement of that information have an impact on the reader? Try rewriting her essay with the information about that experience introduced at a different point. What is the effect?

Writing Project

AN EXPERIENCE THAT INFLUENCED A BELIEF

The Thinking-Writing Activities and the readings and questions in this chapter have encouraged you to become an active thinker, to examine your beliefs, and to observe how some thoughtful people have reflected on their learning experiences. As you work on this project, reread what you wrote for the activities and think about the events discussed in the readings.

Project Overview and Requirements

Think back to an experience that had an important influence on a belief you once held. The belief might be about yourself, about another person involved in the experience, or about the issue that the experience illustrates. The experience may have helped form your current belief or perhaps even strengthened your existing belief.

In an essay, begin by explaining your original belief and include, if possible, the sources of your belief (see pages 64 and 65). Next, describe the experience itself, and, finally, reflect on how that experience influenced your current belief.

Follow your instructor's directions related to the length and format of your essay, and carefully review The Writing Situation and The Writing Process below before you get started.

THE WRITING SITUATION

Before committing your ideas to paper, it is important to consider the writing situation—purpose, audience, subject, and writer—since they are the corner-stones of an effective piece of writing.

Purpose   Your primary purpose for this essay is to clearly describe your belief to your readers, narrate your experience (tell your story) in an interesting way, and effectively connect the two. You do not need to convince your readers that they should adopt your belief. Instead, you should show them what your belief is and how the experience you had impacted that belief. A secondary purpose for this essay is to increase your understanding of your own belief, your ability to evaluate that belief, and your recognition and comprehension of other people's beliefs.

Audience   When you write about your own experiences, you are an important part of the audience. This form of writing, as you have seen in Annie Dillard's essay (page 70), acts as a catalyst for self-discovery by encouraging you to reflect on your past experiences. As you write, your guiding ideas should include these questions:

- How effectively am I communicating the reality of this experience?
- How effectively have I analyzed the significance of this experience and the impact that it had?

You will also be writing for the other readers with whom you'll share this piece of writing. Consider these questions when thinking about your audience:

- How much information about my belief should I include to help my readers understand it and know where it came from?

- How much background information is necessary in order for my audience to fully understand the situation?
- What details of the experience should I include to make it real for my readers? What details can I leave out?

In other words, you need to put yourself in your readers' position and view your writing through their eyes.

Subject   Writing about one's own experience (an autobiographical narrative) is a popular and effective mode of communication. While a belief or idea is typically abstract or hypothetical, a personal experience is concrete and generally more expressive. Have you ever witnessed someone using a story or personal experience to illustrate a point he or she was trying to make? A good narrative can make an idea come to life and facilitate a meaningful, memorable connection with your audience. One goal of this writing project is to demonstrate that connection and interaction.

As you think about your own beliefs and experiences, try to identify a belief that will interest an audience and an experience that you can write about using concrete, vivid details. Although the subject or belief you plan to write about might be somewhat abstract, your experience was real—and the narrative you create of that experience will help you convey meaning.

In a later chapter, you will consider narration again and be reminded that a story illuminates an idea but does not necessarily prove that the idea is true.

Writer   This Writing Project, like the others in Part 1 of this book, asks you to use your own experience as the basis of an essay. This makes you the authority on the subject, which should give you confidence. Your challenges are to shape your story and to connect it directly to your belief.

To help you more fully explore and develop your idea, review the Thinking-Writing Activities you completed earlier in this chapter, and then answer the following four questions before moving on to The Writing Process:

1. In a simple sentence, describe the belief you would like to write about; then briefly describe the experience that influenced this particular belief. For example:

   > I never gave that much thought about where my food came from, but now that I understand how what I eat affects my health, I am a huge proponent of eating only organic foods.

2. What are the key details of your experience an audience will need to know in order to understand why you hold this particular belief? For example, if your sister told you she only eats organic food, why did she tell you this? What was the context of your conversation? Was it because your sister was suffering from health issues? How did her actions cause you to modify your beliefs about your own health and eating organically?

3. How can you make key details interesting to your audience? Think about the time the initial experience took place, the setting, and the people (if any) involved. How can you paint a vivid picture of your experience for your audience? For example, if you were writing about your sister and your beliefs about eating organic foods, you could describe the place where your beliefs started to change like this:

> When I walked into my sister's backyard, my jaw dropped. She had built a chicken coop under the branches of a maple in the far corner of the lot, and there were several large vegetable gardens along the fence. The vines of cucumber, squash, and watermelon tumbled onto what little was left of the lawn. She had huge pots of heirloom tomatoes on the patio, and green beans scrambled up trellises attached to the garage. My world changed when I realized that lunch was a matter of picking what to pick and that my sister, free from the aliments that had plagued her for years, was now the picture of health.

4. As the writer, how can you convey that you are the expert—that, through your experience, you have gained something valuable? For example, you could show how an experience inspired you to learn more and how the process of learning helped further shape your beliefs:

> My sister's actions inspired my belief that organic food is the key to health, but it wasn't until I read books like *The Omnivore's Dilemma* by Michael Pollan that I truly understood why I had to be more knowledgeable and responsible.

THE WRITING PROCESS

One of this book's main goals is to help you discover the strengths and weaknesses of your current writing practices and expose you to a process of writing that is more productive and effective. The following writing process is a sensible path thoughtful writers use to compose nearly any piece of writing. It begins by generating ideas and defining a focus and includes organizing ideas into a meaningful order, composing a draft, revising the draft, and, finally, editing and proofreading the draft.

Generating Ideas   Think about a suitable experience to write about—one that had a profound effect on your belief and that may have implications for other people's lives. Next, ask yourself questions and jot down your responses and ideas. This exercise is often referred to as pre-writing and is an important part of the writing process. Here are a few questions that can help you generate ideas:

- What happened? Outline the major events of the experience.
- How did you respond? What were your thoughts, reactions, and feelings?

- What roles did other people play? Was the location important? Recall specific details about what people did and said, and about the setting, to make your retelling vivid for your audience.

- What was the result of the experience? How did it affect your belief?

- As you reflect on it, what was the experience's value for you? How has it influenced your life?

You may also look ahead to Chapter 4 for more pre-writing techniques and ways to generate ideas.

Defining a Focus   In a few sentences, summarize the main point you wish to make in your essay, given your subject, audience, and purpose. Then evaluate your focus: Is it specific enough for you to convey it clearly in an essay? Is it interesting so that your audience will find it worth reading about? Is it thoughtful so that it serves the purpose of reflection?

At this point, consider whether or not the experience you have chosen is an appropriate subject for your purpose and audience. If not, you can begin again by looking for another experience to write about.

Organizing Ideas   Think about how you can order the elements of your experience. Will you start at the beginning and describe them chronologically? Or will you start at a later point in time and use a flashback to the beginning of the experience? Where will you include your observations and reflections about the experience: at the end or at various places throughout?

Drafting   The draft you are writing for this project includes three parts: your belief, your experience, and the connection between the two. It can help to write out each part separately and then work on connecting these parts together. A draft is the first written version of your essay and will likely be rough. Focus on writing out your ideas without worrying too much about grammar and punctuation. There will be time to polish your writing during the revision stage.

Drafting Hints

1. Spread out all the work you did while generating ideas and defining a focus so that you can easily refer to it while writing the draft.

2. Keep writing! Get all of your ideas down, and focus on making corrections later.

3. If you are working on a computer, be sure to save your work often!

4. If you must take a break, be sure to reread what you have written to get back into the flow of your ideas.

Revising Your Essay: An Experience That Influenced a Belief

Peer Review Groups

There are many revision strategies that writers use to get an audience's reactions to their work. Some take place independently, where a single reviewer reads and comments on the writing, while other strategies rely on open discussion. Either way, your classmates, or peers, can help you see where your draft is successful and where it needs improvement. If your instructor allows class time for peer review, have a draft ready so you can benefit from this activity. This particular revision strategy takes place in the classroom and works best with groups of three or four.

Note: If you are working in an online classroom, you can post or email drafts of your paper and ask for written responses to questions 5–7 below.

1. The group selects a timekeeper, who allots 10 minutes to each writer (or more, depending on paper length requirements). After 10 minutes, the group must move on to the next writer's work.
2. One person begins by reading aloud his or her draft while group members simply listen.
3. The writer next reads his or her writing aloud a second time. Do not skip this step.
4. Group members listen and write notes or comments.
5. The writer then asks each group member this question and jots down their responses: "What questions do you have about my original belief and its sources?"
6. The writer next asks each member these questions and takes notes: "What questions do you have about the experience I described? What else do you need to know about it?"
7. The writer then asks each member these questions and records their responses: "Do you understand why my belief changed as a result of this experience and what my belief is now? What could I add to make my writing clearer?"

Revision

As soon as possible after peer review, revise your draft based on your peers' responses. Think about each of the following questions. As you consider ways to improve your draft based on your answers to each question, stop and make changes to your draft before you move on to the next question.

- How could you improve the first paragraph? How could you get your readers' attention and make them want to read on?

- How could you improve the order of your draft? Could you rearrange some paragraphs?
- How could you improve the flow of your draft? Where would transitions help your audience?
- How could you improve your sentences? Reading your draft aloud can be beneficial here. Pay particular attention to sentences that are difficult to read aloud. If you trip over certain passages, chances are your audience will have trouble following them, too! Could you shorten long, hard-to-read sentences or write them as two sentences? Where could you use parallel structure to make your sentences more graceful?

Editing and Proofreading

After you prepare a final draft, check for use of standard grammar and punctuation. Proofread carefully for omitted words and punctuation marks. Run your spell-checker program, but be aware of its limitations. Proofread again to detect the kinds of errors the computer can't catch. You should also refer to "A Step-by-Step Method for Revising Any Assignment" on the inside front cover of this book.

Your essay should now be completed to the very best of your ability, and, of course, you will need to submit a copy to your instructor by the due date. If you have time, try to share your essay with friends or family. They might be able to offer further feedback and might enjoy reading about your experience. Would other people who were involved in the experience want to know how it affected you? Would someone with whom you currently have a relationship understand you better by reading it?

The following essay shows how one student responded to this assignment.

STUDENT WRITING

Eli Sharp's Writing Process

In response to an assignment asking him to agree or disagree with a belief expressed in one of the assigned readings, Eli Sharp, a student at City College of San Francisco, chose to disagree with Jane Smiley's belief expressed in "The Case Against Chores" (page 80) that children should not be assigned chores. The assignment also required Sharp to consult other sources and cite them according to MLA style.

To begin generating ideas, Sharp started with his own immediate emotional reaction to Smiley's essay. "The hardest part was getting out of my reactive emotional response," he wrote in response to a query from his professor. "I was trying to be in an inquiring and open-minded state, rather than just defending my own belief."

The move from personal, subjective experience to a broader outlook was supported by Sharp's reading of other sources, an eclectic mix of authors and philosophers whose own insights into childhood helped Sharp to refine his own argument. "I knew that I wanted to convince my audience, my professor and classmates, of the soundness of my belief, so I had to work through my emotional reaction and more closely examine the bases for my own belief in the value of chores," he said. As he worked, Sharp kept track of the necessary source information and was careful to ensure that everything he quoted, paraphrased, or summarized was correctly cited both in the body of the essay and on the works-cited page that is required for MLA papers.

As you read Eli Sharp's essay, note how he often refers to specific points made in "The Case Against Chores." These references both support Eli's own argument and help his audience—even an audience that might not be familiar with Smiley's essay—understand the larger context.

An Argument for Chores
by Eli Sharp

In her essay "The Case Against Chores," Jane Smiley argues that children are both immediately and ultimately better off it they are not required by their parents, family, or other guardians to do household chores. She succinctly sums up the conventional rationales for assigning chores and dismisses them. In her own upbringing she "wasn't expected to lift a finger," and the closest she came to cleaning up after herself was "to run water in [her] cereal bowl before setting it in the sink." All the same, she developed work habits and skills tending a stable, as, she explains, she "wasn't alienated from [the work]" (73).

Sharp sets up his essay by first introducing Jane Smiley's argument against chores.

Smiley seems, first of all, to assume that the reader will share in her high opinion of herself as a well-known academic and a professional writer. True, she is esteemed by her peers and enjoys an elevated social status. But are these the only qualities that chore-doling Iowans want to engender in their children? I would argue that all too often those who make a living with their minds are viewed not with awe or respect by those who do so with their hands, but with some degree of suspicion, mistrust, and the sense that somehow such people are shirking "real work."

In the second paragraph, Sharp uses language that makes it clear he does not agree with Smiley, and he begins to deconstruct her argument.

Be this as it may, I find Smiley's argument unconvincing on many grounds. I think she's guilty of faulty inductive reasoning, or "hasty generalization," in claiming that because she turned out so well, most other children will too. And again, when, having "[. . .] over the years gleaned some of the *reasons* parents give for assigning [chores,]" (italics mine), she assumes her work in this regard is done (72). If she's gleaned some of the reasons and remains unimpressed, the other ones couldn't possibly be any better. Even in her title Smiley seems a bit grandiose in her assessment of her own views. It's not just "A" case against chores; it's "The" case against chores.

Sharp points out a logical fallacy in Smiley's argument to show his audience why he is not convinced of Smiley's lofty ideals.

Perhaps Smiley most compromises the validity of her argument in my eyes with her comment about learning to run some water in her cereal bowl before setting it

Source: An Argument for Chores by Eli Sharp.

in the sink. Is this a chore? I hardly consider a rudiment of self-accountability, such as cleaning up after herself, to be a chore. Maybe one of those reasons for assigning tasks that she didn't glean was that children should be weaned of the idea that they can expect to be served by others, including their parents. Or is this only true of certain segments of society, those who are to learn how to serve?

Whatever Smiley's views on wider issues may be, I see the case for assigning chores to children at some stage of their development and dependence on the family as being far more sound, reasonable, and convincing than that against. For one, not all children will opt for such benevolent pastimes as stable cleaning, in the absence of assigned chores. In his short but wonderfully lucid and honest essay on his own boyhood misbehavior, Andrew O'Hagan writes, "We all took and assigned roles in cruel little dramas of our own devising. Our talk would be full of new and interesting ways to worry or harass our parents . . . ." He goes on to describe a twelve-year-old neighbor girl who claimed to grind up lightbulbs and put them in her father's porridge (43). While I don't suggest that assigning chores would have any influence whatsoever on such behavior, O'Hagan's point in mentioning this questionable claim is that the idea was lauded by him and his boyhood friends. Having some chores to do can keep children from having too much time on their hands to hang around with their peers and get into trouble. "Something happened when we all got together . . . ," O'Hagan writes, "We were competitive, deluded, and full of our own small powers. . . . As only dependents can be, we were full of our own independence" (40–41). Chores can help remind children of their dependence.

Smiley makes much of the insufficiency of this argument and stresses the idea that children should be loved, valued, and accepted for who they are, not what they do for the family. On the latter point, of course, I agree. However, it is the transition from dependence on the family to dependence on society, and the relative independence required, which interests me here. I suggest that some transitional stage, involving the introduction to the rules and mores of the society in which the family lives, is highly desirable. In a capitalist state society like ours, where semi-socialist institutions are required to play a subordinate role to "free enterprise," or unregulated competitive organizations, it greatly behooves a child to learn that her society does *not* value her for who she "is," but precisely for what she does, or what she's "worth" in terms of wealth, as the case may be. I don't contend that this situation owes to any specific historical cause, much less a particular political or social agenda, but that it is a normal extension of human nature, in absence of understanding and acknowledgement of a higher law. In this sense I follow Jean-Jacques Rousseau as he writes:

> Such was . . . the origin of society and law, . . . which irretrievably destroyed natural liberty, eternally fixed the law of property and inequality, converted clever usurpation into unalterable right, and, for the advantage of a few

Sharp makes it clear that his biggest issue with Smiley's "case" goes beyond the idea of "chores" to the idea of being personally accountable or responsible.

Sharp now begins to define his own argument and finally provides his thesis statement.

Notice how Sharp admits he agrees with one of Smiley's points. Do you think this gives Sharp more credibility as a writer? Will an audience be more likely to trust him?

ambitious individuals, subjected all mankind to perpetual labour, slavery, and wretchedness.* (79)

I believe the facts of daily life bear out this view despite the best efforts and intentions of the leaders and shapers of our society. President John F. Kennedy, in his inaugural address of January 20, 1969 (as examined by Robert Bellah in his essay on civil religion), spoke: "The same revolutionary beliefs for which our forebears fought are still at issue around the globe—the belief that the rights of man come not from the generosity of the state but from the hand of God." Nonetheless, the address concludes, "Here on earth God's work must truly be our own." Of this speech Bellah astutely observes that "It might be argued that the passages quoted reveal the essentially irrelevant role of religion in the very secular society that is America. . . . [Religion] gets only a sentimental nod . . . , before a discussion of the really serious business with which religion has nothing whatever to do" (41). The laws that govern our daily lives, in the modern world, are economic, not moral, and it is to a child's benefit to be prepared for this realization. Without entering into the question of the advisability of bringing children into such a world in the first place, I submit that the least parents can do is to *gradually* wean their child from the loving, nurturing environment of the family into the so-called "working world."

"She also taught me 'to speak the truth and shame the Devil!'" writes the poet and author Robert Graves of his mother. "Her favourite biblical exhortation went: 'My son, whatever thy hand findeth to do, do it with all thy might'" (32). This exhortation, central to many of the world's religions, sheds light on another possible advantage of chores. They give the child the opportunity to discover the simple pleasure of exertion itself.

Chores tend to be simple, manual labor. Growing up in northern Michigan, in a home built by my parents and their friends and heated entirely with wood-burning ovens, I have extensive experience with chores of this type. It really was an unusual amount of physical labor for boys (my brother and I) in the twentieth century. Felling, cutting, and splitting cordwood; shoveling masses of snow; gardening; composting; mowing; and occasionally harvesting maple sap, in addition to the usual household chores, were all on the list.

While Smiley says she took straight to stable work without the least outside obligation, there's no way I would have worked like I did without having my tasks clearly outlined for me. And, more to the point, I learned to enjoy physical labor, even in harsh conditions. The work was not oppressive, monotonous, dangerous, arbitrary, or, by a far cry, to someone else's reward and my detriment.

I was not a driven child, and I am not a driven adult. Having chores to do helped me better appreciate my leisure time. "Oh the happy, happy, never-to-be-recalled days of childhood!" writes the great novelist Lev Tolstoy. "How could one fail to love and

Source: Jean-Jacques Rousseau.

Notice the details Sharp uses to describe his personal experience.

Why do you suppose Sharp uses this quotation from Tolstoy? As Sharp's audience, do you feel more connected to the essay knowing that this type of feeling is not isolated?

cherish memories of such a time? Those memories refresh and elevate the soul and are a source of my best enjoyment" (52). So it is with me. The sheer physical, sensory enjoyment of the world is my abiding memory of childhood. My early childhood was virtually pure leisure, and chores were imposed on me only later in life, gradually. I often didn't want to do them beforehand, and made this very clear, but I also often enjoyed doing them once I started, and better enjoyed my meals and beverages and slept better afterward. There were more chores in winter than summer, and less daylight to do other things anyway. Still, I was never excessively tasked and spent more time playing than working, even in winter.

In view of all these advantages of assigning chores to children, all borne out in my own experience, I think the most significant is the lesson of self-accountability to be gleaned from these tasks. Children learn first-hand how much work goes into maintaining their own comfort and well-being. They may decide that such experience is unpleasant and distasteful and spend much of their adult lives seeking "better service," or expecting to be cleaned up after. But it is my opinion that they are far less likely to do so with the added experience of having been required, at some stage of their development, to take part in the daily work and maintenance of their own household.

Sharp's conclusion leaves the audience with something of value. Even though he admits this is his own experience, it is still clear that there are inherent benefits to having chores.

Works Cited

Bellah, Robert N. "Civil Religion in America." *Daedalus* 134 (Fall 2005): 40–55. Print.

Graves, Robert. *Goodbye to All That*. New York: Doubleday, 1957. Print.

O'Hagan, Andrew. "Bad Bastardness." *Leopard 3, Frontiers*. Ed. Christopher MacLehose. London: Harvill, 1994. 38–44. Print.

Rousseau, Jean-Jacques. "On the Origin of Inequality." *Rousseau/Kant (13/14)*. Trans. G.D.H. Cole (1913). Chicago: Great Books Foundation, 1955. 22–109. Print.

Smiley, Jane. "The Case Against Chores." *Critical Thinking, Thoughtful Writing*. By John Chaffee. 4th ed. Boston: Houghton, 2008. 71–73. Print.

Tolstoy, L. N. *Childhood, Boyhood, Youth*. Baltimore: Penguin, 1972. Print.

REFLECTION ON WRITING

1. Is the writer, Eli Sharp, successful in regard to being open-minded and inquiring in this essay as opposed to being reactive and emotional? Do you find passages that teeter on sounding emotional?

2. Sharp used a number of outside sources to support his claim that children should have chores. Are there any authors or philosophers that could have been added to the essay to help support his claim? Are there any that should have been left out?

3. Does Sharp neglect to provide clear evidence in any passages such that you might not be convinced by his rebuttal to Smiley's essay? If so, where would you like to see more evidence?

ALTERNATIVE WRITING PROJECTS

- An Author's Change in Belief

  Explain how one of the authors of the readings in this chapter changed or strengthened one or more beliefs. Be sure to present in your own words the author's original belief, what circumstances changed or strengthened it, and what it was after these circumstances. Give the title and author's name, probably at the beginning of your essay, and put quotation marks around any of the author's words that you use.

- A Friend's or Relative's Belief

  Interview a friend or relative about one of that person's most important beliefs. Prepare your questions ahead of time, and write down the answers carefully. Look ahead to later chapters for some guidelines on conducting an interview. Use what your friend or relative tells you as the basis for an essay about this belief, how it developed, and what it means in the life of the person who holds it.

- A Belief That You Have Observed

  Look around your community. Can you see evidence of some belief in action? For example, is there evidence that people believe in keeping up (or showing off) their homes or gardens or cars? Is there evidence of a belief in helping one's neighbors or in keeping to oneself? Is there evidence of a belief in the importance of education, political action, sports, or nice clothes? Use your observation as the basis for an explanation of the belief that you have noticed and your thinking about its significance.

CHAPTER 3 | Summary

- Thinking actively as part of your writing process requires that you become involved, take initiative, follow through, and take responsibility.
- Part of thinking actively involves becoming aware of the influences on your thinking.
- By continually reexamining your long-held beliefs, holding them up to the scrutiny of reason and evidence, and comparing them to the different perspectives of others, you can ensure that your beliefs are your own and not just those passed down from other people.
- Developing informed beliefs involves being curious, open-minded, knowledgeable, and creative and is a lifelong process.

Creativity is not a talent possessed only by the likes of poets, painters, and musicians. Instead, creativity is a natural human ability that should be a central part of everyone's life. What role does creativity play in your thinking and writing process?

Thinking:
Becoming More Creative and Visually Aware

"You must expect the unexpected, because it cannot be found by search or trail."

—HERACLITUS

Creative Thinking, Critical Viewing, and Writing

C reative writing is often thought of as imaginative fiction, poetry, or drama, for which the author invents characters and situations. Creativity also plays an important role in expository writing, in which facts, ideas, and concepts are explored, developed, and argued.

You use creative thinking in the way you select and narrow your topic (if you are allowed to pick your own topic), in the way you generate and research ideas, in the way you organize ideas, and in the way you focus on your ideas with your thesis. You also use creative thinking to develop ideas with carefully chosen details and examples. Creative thinking helps you develop analogies and metaphors to help your readers grasp your ideas. Finally, creative thinking allows you to write imaginative, inviting introductions that will make your readers eager to read further, and to write carefully crafted conclusions that tie in elegantly with your introductions. Of course, your critical thinking abilities are also involved in all these steps, helping you to decide which of your creative ideas to include and which to discard.

The challenge to be creative in your writing is a difficult one, but the possibilities for creativity are vast. Focusing on the following four areas for creativity in expository writing will help you further develop the creative thinking abilities you may already have. This chapter deals with the first two.

- Creativity in selecting a topic
- Creativity in generating ideas, researching, and drafting
- Creativity in using specific details and examples
- Creativity in writing introductions and conclusions

CREATIVITY IN SELECTING A TOPIC

The topic of an essay is the subject you write about, one of the four components of the writing situation. Some topics are personal and ask you to draw on your own life experiences, others are impersonal and clearly require research, and still

CRITICAL THINKING FOCUS:
The qualities of a creative thinker

WRITING FOCUS:
Generating original ideas

READING THEME:
The creative thinking process

WRITING ACTIVITIES:
Tapping into creativity

WRITING PROJECT:
Imagining your life lived more creatively

others are a blend of the personal and impersonal. Furthermore, some topics are fairly specific, such as "Write about your favorite sports figure" or "Write about the effects of the war in Iraq." Others are more general: "Write about some aspect of political science." A first step is to think creatively about how to shape an assigned topic into one that interests you and that you can handle in the assigned length. A visual way to do this is to "narrow with arrows."

> My favorite sports figure → my favorite football player → my favorite
> quarterback → Eli Manning
>
> Effects of the war in Iraq → different types of effects → social effects → effects
> on national security → effects on airports and passengers
>
> Political science → elections → the 2008 presidential election → Obama's
> victory → why he won

Notice that, at any point, the arrows could take you in a different direction.

> My favorite sports figure → my favorite baseball player → my favorite
> shortstop → Derek Jeter
>
> Effects of the war in Iraq → different types of effects → financial effects →
> effects on the price of oil → long-term effects on energy consumption
>
> Political science → elections → the 2008 presidential election → new
> campaign strategies → candidates' use of social media to advertise
> and communicate

MOVING FROM TOPIC TO THESIS

A topic is what you are going to write about, and a thesis is what you are going to say about it. Once you have narrowed your topic, try turning it into a question. For example:

> Why is Eli Manning my favorite sports figure?
>
> What are the effects of the war in Iraq on energy consumption in the United
> States?
>
> How did Obama manage to win the 2008 presidential election?

The answer to your question will eventually turn into your thesis. First, if the answer to your question requires research, read as much as you can about your topic. You might end up modifying your question or changing it completely. This is fine and part of the creative thinking, critical viewing, and writing process. If you are working with a personal topic, take notes related to whether or not you have enough information to answer your question. You can broaden or narrow your topic question as you proceed. When you think that you have enough information, try answering your question in a complete sentence. This will become your tentative thesis.

> Eli Manning's amazing athletic ability, great leadership skills, and
> generous contributions to our community make him my favorite sports figure.

The war in Iraq has a rippling effect on America's economy: the rising price of oil contributes to inflation.

Barack Obama won the 2008 presidential election because he ran a strategic and modern campaign, he got the endorsement of well-respected leaders, and his intelligent and empassioned speeches inspired and motivated large segments of the population.

Once you have a tentative thesis, you will likely modify it during the writing process as new ideas surface or additional research changes your outlook on the topic. This is a natural part of the writing process, so embrace it. If you are willing to put in the time and effort, the results will show in your writing.

CREATIVITY IN GENERATING IDEAS

Books about writing sometimes make it sound as though generating ideas, researching, and drafting are three entirely separate stages in the writing process. While this is partly true, in reality, writers will often find themselves getting new ideas while researching, or writing the draft only to realize more research or brainstorming is needed. It is natural to loop back through these stages until all the pieces finally work together.

Here are some strategies your open and curious mind can use to develop creative ideas in your writing. Your journal, blog, or notebook is a good place to practice these strategies.

Brainstorming   Brainstorming is an activity in which, working individually or with a group of people, you list all the ideas you can think of related to a given topic. The goal is to produce as many ideas as possible in a specific time period. While you are engaged in this idea-generating process, it is important to relax and let your mind run free. These guidelines should help you:

- Set a timer and keep thinking until it goes off.
- Go for quantity. You want to generate as many ideas as you can.
- Write down *all* the ideas you generate.
- Build on ideas.
- Don't criticize or discard any ideas.
- Don't worry about spelling or mechanics—just get your ideas down on paper.

Imagine, for example, that you are assigned the following topic for a research paper:

There are many problems that students face on college campuses. Identify one such problem, and then write a research paper that analyzes the causes of and possible solutions, to the problem. Why does the problem occur, and what can be done to deal with it? Your paper should include relevant research findings, as well as your own perspective on this problem.

Using the brainstorming strategy with a friend, you might come up with a list that includes the following student problems on your campus:

parking	classes too large
library closed too early	not enough access to computers
political tensions	plagiarism
binge drinking	use of drugs
registration too complicated	tests and papers coming in clumps
not enough social activities	some teachers just lecturing
increasing thefts	curriculum not well organized
financial aid cutbacks	

Mind Maps   *Mind maps* are visual presentations of the various ways ideas can be related to one another. For example, the Thinking-Writing Model is represented as a mind map in Figure 4.1. Mind maps are also a powerful approach for writing, helping you generate ideas and begin organizing them into various relationships. They are well suited to the writing process for a number of reasons. First, the organization grows naturally, reflecting the way your mind naturally makes associations and arranges information. Second, the organization can easily be revised to reflect new information and your developing understanding of how it should be organized. Third, you can express a range of relationships among the various ideas. Fourth, instead of being identified once and then forgotten, each idea remains an active part of the overall pattern, suggesting new possible relationships. Fifth, you do not have to decide initially on a beginning, subpoints, and so on; you can do this after your pattern is complete, so you save time and avoid frustration. For example, imagine that from your list of problems on campus you select "abuse of alcohol" as a paper topic. Your mind map might resemble Figure 4.1.

Thinking-Writing Activity

CREATE A MIND MAP

For this activity, you will experiment with a mind map. Your instructor will direct your choice of topic.

These guidelines should help you:

- Draw a circle in the middle of the page, and write your topic in the circle.
- Draw a few lines coming out from the circle, and label them with ideas about your topic.
- See which of your lines you could develop further. Then draw more lines from those, and label them with ideas and details about those aspects of your topic.
- Keep going until you have no more ideas about the topic or until you see a section of your map developing into a cluster of ideas that you could write about.

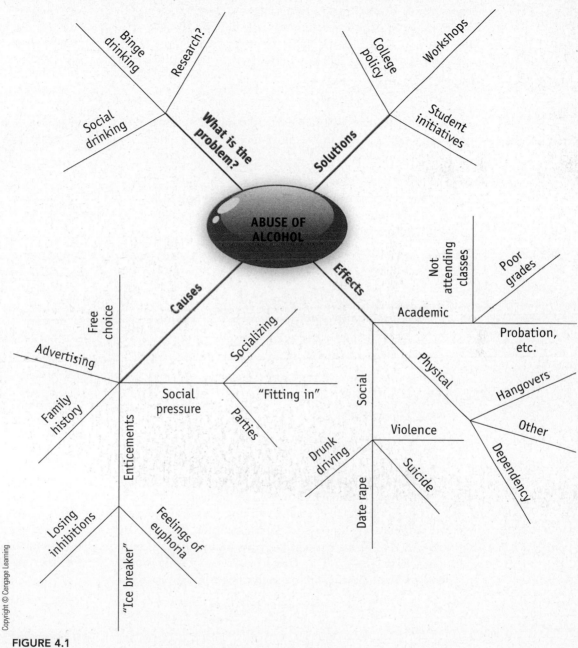

FIGURE 4.1
Mind Map

Freewriting   *Freewriting* is sometimes referred to as *stream of consciousness* writing. Instead of simply listing ideas, you write free-flowing sentences without worrying about spelling, grammar, or punctuation. The goal is to quickly develop and record your ideas without inhibitions or obstacles and allow your creative mind to take over. These guidelines should help you get started:

- Set a timer and keep writing until it goes off.
- Write at a steady, comfortable pace for the entire time. If you get stuck, it is OK to write "I am stuck. I can't think of any more ideas. I hope I get another idea" until a new idea comes to you. Don't stop writing!
- Don't criticize or make corrections.
- After the time limit is up, read carefully what you have written. Think about it for a few minutes. Then try the process again, starting with the most interesting ideas from your first try.

An example of freewriting about the problem of alcohol abuse might begin something like this:

Alcohol is a real problem on campus. Every party, that's all people do, is drink too much and then get silly. I think it's ok for people to drink some if they want to. They say it relaxes them and makes it easier to talk to strangers. But it's out of control, and that's a problem. There are a lot of students that drink all the time. They must be failing their classes, they sleep until noon, and they look lousy. There's got to be a better way to socialize and have fun with people besides getting bombed out of your mind....

Questioning   *Asking questions* that explore a topic provides another strategy for generating ideas, just as asking questions about a topic supports critical reading. In fact, the ability to ask appropriate and penetrating questions about visual and written texts is one of the most powerful thinking and communicating tools writers possess. Asking questions enables them to go beyond the obvious, to think, read, see, and write in ways that are in-depth, complex, and articulate. Questions come in many different forms and are used for many different purposes. For instance, questions can be classified in terms of the ways people organize and interpret information. The following are six such categories of questions:

1. Fact   4. Synthesis
2. Interpretation   5. Evaluation
3. Analysis   6. Application

Thoughtful writers ask appropriate questions from all of these categories. Listed next is a description of the six categories of questions, along with sample questions from each category.

1. **Questions of Fact.** Questions of fact seek to determine the basic information of a situation: who, what, when, where, how, why. The following seek information that is relatively straightforward and objective:

Who, what, when, where, how, why?

Describe _____.

2. **Questions of Interpretation.** Questions of interpretation seek to select and organize facts and ideas, discovering the relationships among them. Examples of such relationships include the following:

   Chronological relationships—relating things in time sequence

   Process relationships—relating aspects of growth, development, or change

   Comparison/contrast relationships—relating things in terms of their similar or different features

   Causal relationships—relating events in terms of the way some are responsible for causing others

   These questions can help you discover relationships:

   Can you retell _____ in your own words?

   What is the *main idea* of _____?

   What is the *time sequence* relating the following events: _____?

   What are the steps in the *process of growth* or *development* in _____?

   How would you *compare* and *contrast* the features of _____ and _____?

   What was/were the *cause(s)* of _____? What was/were the *effect(s)* of _____?

3. **Questions of Analysis.** Questions of analysis seek to separate an entire process or situation into its component parts and understand the relation of these parts to the whole. These questions or statements attempt to classify various elements, outline component structures, articulate various possibilities, and clarify the reasoning being presented:

   What are the *parts* or *features* of _____?

   Classify according to _____.

   Outline/diagram/web _____.

   What *evidence* can you present to support _____?

   What are the *possible alternatives* for _____?

   Explain the *reasons* you think _____.

4. **Questions of Synthesis.** The goal of questions of synthesis is to combine ideas to form a new whole or to arrive at a conclusion, making inferences about future events, creating solutions, and designing plans of action:

   What would you *predict/infer* from _____?

   What ideas can you *add to* _____?

   How would you *create/design* a new _____?

   What might happen if you *combined* _____ with _____?

   What *solutions/decisions* would you suggest for _____?

5. **Questions of Evaluation.** The aim of evaluation questions is to help you make informed judgments and decisions by determining the relative value, truth, or reliability of things. The process of evaluation involves identifying your criteria or standards and then determining to what extent the things being evaluated meet those standards.

How would you evaluate _____ and what *standards* would you use?

Do you *agree* with _____? *Why or why not?*

How would you *decide* about _____?

What *criteria* would you use to *assess* _____?

6. **Questions of Application.** The purpose of application questions is to help you take the knowledge or concepts you have gained in one situation and apply them to other situations.

How is _____ *an example* of _____?

How would you *apply* this rule/principle to _____?

Additional Tips for Generating Ideas

- When brainstorming, write down every idea, no matter how unusable it may seem at the time.
- Use the recorder on your smartphone or call yourself and leave a voice mail if an idea strikes you while you are out.
- Talk to other people about your topic. Knowledgeable people will add information; those unfamiliar with the topic will ask useful questions.
- Ask a librarian for research suggestions.
- Note conflicting information or opinions. They are the heart of academic discussion.
- Search at Yahoo! or Google for businesses or organizations that can provide information.
- Identify and interview experts on your topic. (Be sure to acknowledge them as sources.)
- Scan television schedules for related programs.
- Search online for sources of information.
- When drafting, don't necessarily begin with the introduction. Instead, begin with whatever section is easiest to write.
- Be willing to modify your thesis as you go along so that you don't lock yourself into a position too early.
- Avoid premature organization; draft sections on separate pages or as separate computer files. Then try arranging them in various orders.
- If you are interrupted while drafting, read what you have already written to get back into the flow.

Creative and Critical Thinking About Images

Many professional writers in a variety of contexts integrate images with their texts. From college and military recruitment brochures to advertisements to a company's annual reports, images work in both a subtle and an overt way to persuade us to do, believe, or buy something. As a creative thinker and thoughtful writer, you should begin to pay attention to the relationships between images and text in what you read. You should also think about the ways in which images can inspire, support, and reflect your own written work.

IMAGES AND THE WRITING SITUATION

Just as writers consider audience, subject, and purpose as they think through their writing and conduct their research, so, too, do creators of images (painters, cartoonists, graphic artists, photographers, and others). Whether they are recording events as they happen or reflecting imaginatively on their personal experiences, visual artists in all media are fundamentally aware that they are *communicating*—that, even without words, their images will tell a story, make an argument, show a process, or provide information.

Images and Your Audience   In your college career, you will often be asked to present information in a visual manner. Classes in the sciences and social sciences require you to present numerical data in the form of charts, graphs, and maps. In the visual arts and humanities, you may be asked to analyze a painting's message and style or to describe a film director's approach to setting a scene. Be sure to ask your instructors for each of your classes how to locate, correctly cite, and usefully include images in your own essays and research papers.

Images and Your Subject   Creative thinking teaches us that there are many different ways of experiencing and communicating information. When you use any of the idea-generation strategies discussed earlier in this chapter, try to incorporate visual as well as verbal descriptions and information. You could collect images from magazines, books, and online sources, printing them out or scanning them electronically to create a kind of visual "mind map." Or you could look online at sites such as the National Archives, *Flickr.com,* and Google Images, all of which allow you to search for images using key words related to your subject.

Images and Your Purpose   When you have gathered images that relate to your topic, you can use questions of fact, interpretation, analysis, synthesis, evaluation, and application (pages 100–102) to help you sort through the visuals and select those that best support your purpose in writing. For example, a witty or satirical editorial cartoon about the federal response to Hurricane Katrina might be appropriate for an argument essay in which you analyze the political impact of that disaster, but for a paper about the storm's long-term environmental effects, you would be better served by a map showing the loss of land or a satellite photograph showing the extent of flood damage.

Reading Images Critically

As you search for images to use in your essays, reports, and arguments, remember that the content of an image—just like the content of a text—is composed of elements that work together to convey a message. Some of these elements are similar to those you consider when evaluating a piece of writing: setting, point of view, relationships between characters, an objective or subjective perspective. Other elements are specifically visual: the use of color, the manipulations of Photoshop or other image-moderating techniques, cropping (cutting), and the arrangement of images on a page or screen. And, of course, images are frequently accompanied by text that describes and contextualizes what you are seeing; this text, called a *caption,* should also be a part of your critical interpretation of visual evidence.

In Chapter 2, we explored four different types of meaning: semantic, perceptual, syntactic, and pragmatic. Each of these four kinds of meaning can also apply to your critical "reading"—or viewing—of visual content. Let's see how each type of meaning can be used to understand how just one compelling image can convey many different layers of meaning.

SEMANTIC MEANING (DENOTATION)

As we learned in Chapter 2, the denotative or *semantic meaning* of a word expresses the relationship between the word itself and an idea or feeling. When you think about the relationship between images and ideas, beginning with the denotative (or literal) meaning can help you to understand its larger purpose and argument. Photographers and artists refer to the *composition* of an image—the arrangement of elements within the frame—and that is one way to think of a picture's denotative meaning. The photograph in the *Thinking Critically About Visuals* box, for example, shows an urban scene with a boy holding a bird. The caption supplied with the photograph, however, gives us a richer level of context. You already know that a denotative or semantic reading of a word is enriched by understanding both its general properties and specific examples. Were you asked to imagine, or draw, a picture of a boy holding a bird, your image might be very different—and probably much more bucolic. The caption, however, adds a level of specificity to the picture's semantic message. The picture might *literally* be about a boy with a bird, but its *connotative* message is far more powerful—and far less lovely.

PERCEPTUAL MEANING (CONNOTATION)

Just as words can elicit personal and subjective feelings, so do images. You would respond quite differently to the picture if the boy, Feliciano, were smiling. Here, too, the relationship between an image and its caption is important to analyze. Remember that the images you see in the media are captured by one kind of journalist (a photographer, a cameraperson) but later interpreted by reporters and editors in the newsroom. The interpretation that a journalist gives to a visual image can profoundly affect the way an audience interprets that image. Visually, the composition of the *Thinking Critically About Visuals* photograph conveys a definite connotative or *perceptual meaning:* the boy is sad; the background is littered and abandoned; the overall sense is of urban blight. The words in the caption accompanying the photograph reinforce this meaning: *vacant lots, slumlords, dump, addicts.*

Learning to critically examine the relationships between the words and the images in a news report can help you dig deeper into an issue's impacts—and can also help you detect bias. This relationship between images and their larger contexts can be described as syntactic meaning.

SYNTACTIC MEANING

A word's *syntactic meaning* (see page 55 in Chapter 2) depends on its relationships with other words—relationships of content, description, and connection. The content of a photograph or image is similar to its semantic meaning—What's this all about? But once you begin to connect that content to the way it is verbally described (by a caption, in this case), as well as visually composed (what is most

Thinking Critically About Visuals

Analyzing and Interpreting Visuals

August 6, 2001. Feliciano holds up a bird that mistakenly got into some oil paint that was dumped in one of the vacant lots in the neighborhood along Broadway in Brooklyn. Local slumlords pay addicts a few dollars to dump construction debris, and much of it ends up in the nearest lot. The bird died despite Feliciano's efforts to save it.

The caption above notes that the bird died "despite Feliciano's attempts to save it." What does that statement suggest about the relationship between the photographer and his subject? Why are the boy and the bird so close to the front of the image (and, therefore, close to you as a reader) instead of the slick of dumped paint?

Brenda Ann Kenneally/Corbis

important or dominant in the frame; what is the emotional impact of the image; what is the relationship between the photographer and the subject?), you begin to unravel the image's syntactic meaning. A third level of syntactic meaning has to do with the connection of these ideas and their ability to make sense—to convey a larger, more meaningful idea. The *Thinking Critically About Visuals* photograph and its caption work together to make a profound argument about urban pollution and its littlest victims. That that image and caption work so well together to make such a clear, direct argument contributes to our understanding of the fourth type of meaning: pragmatic, or situational.

PRAGMATIC MEANING

This final type of meaning has to do with the context or situation of the image—who created it, who or what is in it, and the ultimate purpose of and audience for the image. You'll find that many journalists and media outlets will attempt to give context and meaning to a large-scale catastrophe by focusing on the specific lives it impacts. The photographer who took the picture on page 105, Brenda Ann Kenneally, is renowned for her work documenting troubled urban families; you can find many portfolios of her work online.

Thinking-Writing Activity

RECALLING A CREATIVE WRITING EXPERIENCE

1. Write about a time when you expressed yourself creatively in writing. It may have been in an important email, a memorable poem, or a paper for a school course. Respond to the following questions as you recall the writing experience:

   • What was the writing situation that required your creativity?

   • How did you go about finding a creative idea or approach?

   • Was it successful?

   • How do you feel as you recall this experience?

2. Share your experience with the class, and listen carefully to the experiences of other students. On the basis of your own writing experience and those of your peers, make some inferences or general statements about creativity.

Living Creatively

We human beings have a nearly limitless capacity to be creative; our imaginations give us the power to conceive of new possibilities and to put these innovative ideas into action. Using creative resources in this way enriches our lives and brings a special meaning to our activities. Although we might not go to the extreme of saying that the uncreative life is not worth living, it is surely preferable to live a life enriched by the joys of creativity.

Many people think that being creative is beyond them, that creativity is a mysterious gift bestowed on only a chosen few. One reason for this misconception is that people often confuse being "creative" with being "artistic"—skilled at art, music, poetry, imaginative writing, drama, or dance. Although artistic people are certainly creative, there are an infinite number of ways to be creative that are *not* artistic. Being creative is a state of mind and a way of life. As the writer Eric Gill expresses it: "The artist is not a different kind of person, but each one of us is a different kind of artist."

Are you creative? Yes! Think of all the activities that you enjoy: cooking, styling a wardrobe, raising children, playing sports, rapping, dancing, repairing an engine, blogging, designing a web page. Whenever you are investing your own personal ideas, applying your own personal stamp, you are being creative. To the extent that you are expressing your unique ideas developed through inspiration and experimentation, you are being creative. Similarly, if your moves on the dance floor or the basketball court express your distinctive personality, you are being creative, as you are when you stimulate the original thinking of your children or make your friends laugh with your own brand of humor. Living life creatively means bringing your perspective and creative talents to all the areas of your life.

Becoming More Creative: Understand and Trust the Process

Although the forces that discourage you from being creative are powerful, they can nevertheless be overcome with four productive strategies:

- Understand and trust the creative process.
- Eliminate the "Voice of Judgment."
- Make creativity a priority.
- Establish a creative environment.

Thinking-Writing Activity

REFLECTING ON PAST INHIBITIONS TO CREATIVITY

Reflect on your own creative development, and describe some of the fears and pressures that inhibit your own creativity. For example, have you ever been penalized for trying a new idea that didn't work out? Have you ever suffered the wrath of the group for daring to be different and violating the group's unspoken rules? Do you feel that your life is so filled with responsibilities and demands that you don't have time to be creative?

Discovering your creative talents requires that you understand how the creative process operates and then have confidence in the results it produces. There are no fixed procedures or formulas for generating creative ideas because creative ideas by definition go beyond established ways of thinking to the unknown and the innovative. As the ancient Greek philosopher Heraclitus once said, "You must expect the unexpected, because it cannot be found by search or trail."

THINKING CRITICALLY ABOUT NEW MEDIA

Creative Applications

The world is changing at warp speed, and many of these changes have to do with what is popularly termed the "new media," forms of information and communication technologies that were made possible by the creation of the Internet, wireless phones, and text communication devices. Virtually every aspect of our lives has been affected by the development and use of these technologies, including the way we think and write, communicate with one another, research and gather information, develop and sustain relationships, create our sense of self-identity, and construct "virtual" realities that have complex connections to the space-and-time world in which we go about the business of living. For example, it used to be that communicating with someone else involved speaking in person, writing a letter, or talking on a landline telephone. We can now speak by cell phone directly to most anyone on the planet from wherever we are whenever we want. What's more, we can use the technologies of email, instant messaging, text messaging, or twittering to stay socially connected to a large number of people on a continual basis. And through the development of social networking sites like Facebook, YouTube, and LinkedIn, people have been able to create "virtual communities." These virtual communities transcend geographical boundaries, and as the new media critic and writer Howard Rheingold explains, these globalized societies are self-defined networks that resemble what we do in real life. "People in virtual communities use words on screens to exchange pleasantries and argue, engage in intellectual discourse, conduct commerce, make plans, brainstorm, gossip, feud, fall in love, create a little high art and a lot of idle talk."

However, accompanying this new universe of possibilities provided by new media are many risks and challenges that, more than ever, make it necessary to develop and apply our critical thinking abilities as we navigate our way through this digital universe. To this end, I have included a number of readings in this edition that address various aspects of new media, and, in addition, each chapter contains a section on "Thinking Critically About New Media." It's essential that we have the strategies and insight to make sure that these powerful new vehicles of communication are used to enhance our lives, not complicate and damage them.

One of the themes of this chapter has been creative thinking, and new media have offered an unprecedented opportunity to roam far and wide in our search for information that will enrich our creative endeavors. But new media also afford us the chance to gather many different perspectives on our projects, with others' ideas serving as catalysts to our creative imaginations. For example, the columnist David Pogue suggests that companies should use what he calls "crowdsourcing" to generate new ideas. To try this out, he asked his Twitter followers for their best tech-product enhancement ideas. He reports that "They responded wittily, passionately—and immediately (this is Twitter, after all)." Ideas that were tweeted back included

- Cell phone batteries that recharge through kinetic motion as you walk around
- Technology that lets you use your hand as a TV remote control (the TV recognizes your gestures)
- A camera warning that responds to voice commands and also tells you if your thumb is in the way of the lens
- Laptop computers with built-in solar panels for charging batteries
- Music players that can be shifted to "Karaoke mode"

Thinking-Writing Activity

CREATIVE "CROWDSOURCING"

Following up on David Pogue's ingenious use of "crowdsourcing" to generate creative ideas, try some crowdsourcing of your own to generate innovative ideas to improve the quality of your life. Send several queries out to your network of friends asking them for their creative ideas, and then compile these into a master list that you share with everyone (be sure to give credit!). Here are some possible topics:

- Ideas for organizing the many activities in your life more efficiently
- Ideas for making studying more entertaining *and* effective
- Ideas for having a party with a totally unique theme

Although there is no fixed path to creative ideas, there are activities you can pursue that make the birth of creative ideas possible. In this respect, generating creative ideas is similar to gardening. You need to prepare the soil; plant the seeds; ensure proper watering, light, and food; and then be patient until the ideas begin to sprout. Following are some steps for cultivating your creative garden.

Absorb yourself in the task: Creative ideas don't occur in a vacuum. They emerge after a great deal of work, study, and practice. For example, if you want to come up with creative ideas in the kitchen, you need to learn more about the art of cooking. The more knowledgeable you are, the better prepared you will be to create innovative dishes. Similarly, if you are developing a creative perspective for a college research paper, you need to immerse yourself in the subject, becoming knowledgeable about the central concepts and issues. Absorbing yourself in the task "prepares the soil" for your creative ideas.

Allow time for ideas to incubate: After absorbing yourself in the task or problem, the next stage is to stop working on it. When your conscious mind stops actively working on the task, the unconscious dimension of your mind continues working—processing, organizing, and ultimately generating innovative ideas and solutions. This process is known as *incubation* because it mirrors the process in which baby chicks gradually evolve inside the egg until the moment when they break out through the shell. In the same way, your creative mind is at work while you are going about your business until the moment of *illumination,* when the incubating idea finally erupts to the surface of your conscious mind. People report that these illuminating moments—when their mental lightbulbs go on—often occur when they are engaged in activities completely unrelated to the task. For example, you may suddenly realize how to organize your research paper while you are working out at the gym.

Seize on the ideas when they emerge and follow them through: Generating creative ideas is of little use unless you recognize them when they appear and then act on them. Too often people don't pay much attention to these ideas when they occur, or they dismiss them as too impractical. Have confidence in your ideas, even if they seem a little strange. Many of the most valuable inventions in history began as improbable ideas ridiculed by the popular wisdom. For example, the idea of Velcro started with burrs covering the pants of the inventor as he walked through a field, and Post-It notes resulted from the accidental invention of an adhesive that was weaker than normal. In other words, thinking effectively means thinking creatively and thinking critically. After you use your *creative thinking* abilities to generate innovative ideas, you must employ your *critical thinking* abilities to evaluate and refine those ideas and design a practical plan for implementing them. For example, you should write down your creative idea about organizing your research paper and then begin drafting to see if it will work.

ELIMINATE THE VOICE OF JUDGMENT

The biggest threat to your creativity lies within yourself, the negative *Voice of Judgment (VOJ).* This term was coined by Michael Ray and Rochelle Myers, the authors of *Creativity in Business,* a book based on a Stanford University course. The VOJ can undermine your confidence in every area of your life, including your creative activities. For example, when you are drafting a paper, the VOJ may whisper:

"This is a stupid idea, and no one will like it."

"Even if I could pull this idea off, it probably won't amount to much."

These statements, and countless others like them, have the ongoing effect of making you doubt yourself and the quality of your creative thinking. As you lose confidence, you become more timid, reluctant to follow through on ideas and present them to others. After a while your cumulative insecurity will discourage you from even generating ideas in the first place, and you will end up simply conforming to established ways of thinking and the expectations of others. In so doing, you surrender an important part of yourself, the vital and dynamic creative core of your personality.

How do you eliminate this unwelcome and destructive inner voice? There are a number of effective strategies. Remember, though, that the fight, although worth the effort, will not be easy.

Become aware of the VOJ: You have probably been listening to the negative messages of the VOJ for so long that you may not even consciously be aware of it. To conquer the VOJ, you first need to recognize it when it speaks.

Restate the judgment in a more accurate or constructive way: Sometimes there is an element of truth in our self-judgments, but we may have blown the reality out of proportion. For example, if you receive a low grade on a writing assignment, your VOJ may say, "You're a failure." But you need to assess the situation accurately: "I got a low grade on this paper—I wonder what went wrong and how I can improve my performance in the future."

Get tough with the VOJ: You can't be a wimp if you hope to overcome the VOJ. Instead, you have to be strong and determined, responding as soon as the VOJ appears: "I'm throwing you out and not letting you back in!" You may feel peculiar at first, but this will soon become an automatic response when those negative judgments appear.

Create positive voices and visualizations: The best way to destroy the VOJ for good is to replace it with positive encouragement. As soon as you have stomped on, say, the judgment "You're a jerk," replace it with "No, I'm an intelligent, valuable person with many positive qualities and talents." Similarly, make extensive use of positive visualization—"see" yourself performing well on assignments, being entertaining and insightful with other people, and succeeding gloriously in your courses and activities.

Use other people for independent confirmation: The negative judgments coming from the VOJ are usually irrational, but until they are dragged out into the light of day for examination, they can be very powerful. Sharing your VOJ with people you trust is an effective strategy because they can provide an objective perspective that will reveal the irrationality and destructiveness of negative judgments.

ESTABLISH A CREATIVE ENVIRONMENT

An important part of eliminating the negative voice in your mind is to establish environments in which your creative resources can flourish. This means finding or developing physical environments conducive to creative expression, as well as supportive social environments. Sometimes working with other people can be stimulating and energizing to your creative juices; at other times, you may need a private place to work without distraction. You have to find the environment(s) best suited to your own creative process; then make a special effort to do your work there.

The people in your life who form your social environment play an even more influential role in encouraging or inhibiting your creative process. When you are surrounded by people who are positive and supportive, their presence will increase your confidence and encourage you to risk expressing your creative vision. They can stimulate your creativity by providing you with fresh ideas and new perspectives. By engaging in brainstorming, they can help you generate ideas and then later can help you figure out how to refine and implement the most valuable ones.

MAKE CREATIVITY A PRIORITY

Having diminished the negative VOJ in your mind, established a creative environment, and committed yourself to trusting your creative gifts, you are now in a position to live and write more creatively. But how do you actually do this? Start small. Identify some habitual patterns in your life, and break out of them. Choose new experiences whenever possible—for example, order unfamiliar items from a menu, get to know people outside your circle of friends, or deliberately choose a new type of introduction for a paper—and strive to develop fresh perspectives on aspects of your life. Resist falling back into the ruts you were in previously; remember that living things are supposed to be continually growing, changing, and evolving, *not* acting in repetitive patterns like machines.

Where Do Ideas Come From?

Creativity is the process we use to discover and develop ideas that are unusual and worthy of further elaboration. But how do we get creative ideas? Where do they come from? The following readings from the worlds of science and business may give us some clues.

"Revenge of the Right Brain"
by Daniel H. Pink

When I was a kid growing up in a middle-class family, in the middle of America, in the middle of the 1970s, parents dished out a familiar plate of advice to their children: Get good grades, go to college, and pursue a profession that offers a decent standard of living and perhaps a dollop of prestige. If you were good at math and science, become a doctor. If you were better at English and history, become a lawyer. If blood grossed you out and your verbal skills needed work, become an accountant. Later, as computers appeared on desktops and CEOs on magazine covers, the youngsters who were really good at math and science chose high tech, while others flocked to business school, thinking that success was spelled MBA.

Tax attorneys. Radiologists. Financial analysts. Software engineers. Management guru Peter Drucker gave this cadre of professionals an enduring, if somewhat wonky, name: knowledge workers. These are, he wrote, "people who get paid for putting to work what one learns in school rather than for their physical strength or manual skill." What distinguished members of this group and enabled them to reap society's greatest rewards, was their "ability to acquire and to apply theoretical and analytic knowledge." And any of us could join their ranks. All we had to do was study hard and play by the rules of the meritocratic regime. That was the path to professional success and personal fulfillment.

Source: From "Revenge of the Right Brain" by Daniel H. Pink, in *WIRED* magazine, Issue 13.02, February 2005. Adapted from *A Whole New Mind: Moving from the Information Age to the Conceptual Age*, copyright © Daniel H. Pink, published in March, 2005, by Riverhead Books. Printed by permission of the publisher.

But a funny thing happened while we were pressing our noses to the grindstone: The world changed. The future no longer belongs to people who can reason with computer-like logic, speed, and precision. It belongs to a different kind of person with a different kind of mind. Today—amid the uncertainties of an economy that has gone from boom to bust to blah—there's a metaphor that explains what's going on. And it's right inside our heads.

Scientists have long known that a neurological Mason-Dixon line cleaves our brains into two regions—the left and right hemispheres. But in the last 10 years, thanks in part to advances in functional magnetic resonance imaging, researchers have begun to identify more precisely how the two sides divide responsibilities. The left hemisphere handles sequence, literalness, and analysis. The right hemisphere, meanwhile, takes care of context, emotional expression, and synthesis. Of course, the human brain, with its 100 billion cells forging 1 quadrillion connections, is breathtakingly complex. The two hemispheres work in concert, and we enlist both sides for nearly everything we do. But the structure of our brains can help explain the contours of our times.

Until recently, the abilities that led to success in school, work, and business were   5 characteristic of the left hemisphere. They were the sorts of linear, logical, analytical talents measured by SATs and deployed by CPAs. Today, those capabilities are still necessary. But they're no longer sufficient. In a world upended by outsourcing, deluged with data, and choked with choices, the abilities that matter most are now closer in spirit to the specialties of the right hemisphere—artistry, empathy, seeing the big picture, and pursuing the transcendent.

Beneath the nervous clatter of our half-completed decade stirs a slow but seismic shift. The Information Age we all prepared for is ending. Rising in its place is what I call the Conceptual Age, an era in which mastery of abilities that we've often overlooked and undervalued marks the fault line between who gets ahead and who falls behind.

To some of you, this shift—from an economy built on the logical, sequential abilities of the Information Age to an economy built on the inventive, empathic abilities of the Conceptual Age—sounds delightful. "You had me at hello!" I can hear the painters and nurses exulting. But to others, this sounds like a crock. "Prove it!" I hear the programmers and lawyers demanding.

OK. To convince you, I'll explain the reasons for this shift, using the mechanistic language of cause and effect.

The effect: the scales tilting in favor of right brain-style thinking. The causes: Asia, automation, and abundance.

Asia

Few issues today spark more controversy than outsourcing. Those squadrons of   10 white-collar workers in India, the Philippines, and China are scaring the bejesus out of software jockeys across North America and Europe. According to Forrester Research, 1 in 9 jobs in the US information technology industry will move overseas by 2010. And it's not just tech work. Visit India's office parks and you'll see chartered accountants preparing American tax returns, lawyers researching American lawsuits, and radiologists reading CAT scans for US hospitals.

The reality behind the alarm is this: Outsourcing to Asia is overhyped in the short term, but underhyped in the long term. We're not all going to lose our jobs tomorrow.

(The total number of jobs lost to offshoring so far represents less than 1 percent of the US labor force.) But as the cost of communicating with the other side of the globe falls essentially to zero, as India becomes (by 2010) the country with the most English speakers in the world, and as developing nations continue to mint millions of extremely capable knowledge workers, the professional lives of people in the West will change dramatically. If number crunching, chart reading, and code writing can be done for a lot less overseas and delivered to clients instantly via fiber-optic cable, that's where the work will go.

But these gusts of comparative advantage are blowing away only certain kinds of white-collar jobs—those that can be reduced to a set of rules, routines, and instructions. That's why narrow left-brain work such as basic computer coding, accounting, legal research, and financial analysis is migrating across the oceans. But that's also why plenty of opportunities remain for people and companies doing less routine work—programmers who can design entire systems, accountants who serve as life planners, and bankers expert less in the intricacies of Excel than in the art of the deal. Now that foreigners can do left-brain work cheaper, we in the US must do right-brain work better.

Automation

Last century, machines proved they could replace human muscle. This century, technologies are proving they can outperform human left brains—they can execute sequential, reductive, computational work better, faster, and more accurately than even those with the highest IQs. (Just ask chess grandmaster Garry Kasparov.) Consider jobs in financial services. Stockbrokers who merely execute transactions are history. Online trading services and market makers do such work far more efficiently. The brokers who survived have morphed from routine order-takers to less easily replicated advisers, who can understand a client's broader financial objectives and even the client's emotions and dreams.

Or take lawyers. Dozens of inexpensive information and advice services are reshaping law practice. At CompleteCase.com, you can get an uncontested divorce for $249, less than a 10th of the cost of a divorce lawyer. Meanwhile, the Web is cracking the information monopoly that has long been the source of many lawyers' high incomes and professional mystique. Go to USlegalforms.com and you can download—for the price of two movie tickets—fill-in-the-blank wills, contracts, and articles of incorporation that used to reside exclusively on lawyers' hard drives. Instead of hiring a lawyer for 10 hours to craft a contract, consumers can fill out the form themselves and hire a lawyer for one hour to look it over. Consequently, legal abilities that can't be digitized—convincing a jury or understanding the subtleties of a negotiation—become more valuable.

15   Even computer programmers may feel the pinch. "In the old days," legendary computer scientist Vernor Vinge has said, "anybody with even routine skills could get a job as a programmer. That isn't true anymore. The routine functions are increasingly being turned over to machines." The result: As the scut work gets offloaded, engineers will have to master different aptitudes, relying more on creativity than competence. Any job that can be reduced to a set of rules is at risk. If a $500-a-month accountant in India doesn't swipe your accounting job, TurboTax will. Now that computers can emulate left-hemisphere skills, we'll have to rely ever more on our right hemispheres.

Abundance

Our left brains have made us rich. Powered by armies of Drucker's knowledge workers, the information economy has produced a standard of living that would have been unfathomable in our grandparents' youth. Their lives were defined by scarcity. Ours are shaped by abundance. Want evidence? Spend five minutes at Best Buy. Or look in your garage. Owning a car used to be a grand American aspiration. Today, there are more automobiles in the US than there are licensed drivers—which means that, on average, everybody who can drive has a car of their own. And if your garage is also piled with excess consumer goods, you're not alone. Self-storage—a business devoted to housing our extra crap—is now a $17 billion annual industry in the US, nearly double Hollywood's yearly box office take.

But abundance has produced an ironic result. The Information Age has unleashed a prosperity that in turn places a premium on less rational sensibilities—beauty, spirituality, emotion. For companies and entrepreneurs, it's no longer enough to create a product, a service, or an experience that's reasonably priced and adequately functional. In an age of abundance, consumers demand something more. Check out your bathroom. If you're like a few million Americans, you've got a Michael Graves toilet brush or a Karim Rashid trash can that you bought at Target. Try explaining a designer garbage pail to the left side of your brain! Or consider illumination. Electric lighting was rare a century ago, but now it's commonplace. Yet in the US, candles are a $2 billion a year business—for reasons that stretch beyond the logical need for luminosity to a prosperous country's more inchoate desire for pleasure and transcendence.

Liberated by this prosperity but not fulfilled by it, more people are searching for meaning. From the mainstream embrace of such once-exotic practices as yoga and meditation to the rise of spirituality in the workplace to the influence of evangelism in pop culture and politics, the quest for meaning and purpose has become an integral part of everyday life. And that will only intensify as the first children of abundance, the baby boomers, realize that they have more of their lives behind them than ahead. In both business and personal life, now that our left-brain needs have largely been sated, our right-brain yearnings will demand to be fed.

As the forces of Asia, automation, and abundance strengthen and accelerate, the curtain is rising on a new era, the Conceptual Age. If the Industrial Age was built on people's backs, and the Information Age on people's left hemispheres, the Conceptual Age is being built on people's right hemispheres. We've progressed from a society of farmers to a society of factory workers to a society of knowledge workers. And now we're progressing yet again—to a society of creators and empathizers, pattern recognizers, and meaning makers.

But let me be clear: The future is not some Manichaean landscape in which 20
individuals are either left-brained and extinct or right-brained and ecstatic—a land in which millionaire yoga instructors drive BMWs and programmers scrub counters at Chick-fil-A. Logical, linear, analytic thinking remains indispensable. But it's no longer enough.

To flourish in this age, we'll need to supplement our well-developed high tech abilities with aptitudes that are "high concept" and "high touch." High concept involves the ability to create artistic and emotional beauty, to detect patterns and opportunities, to craft a satisfying narrative, and to come up with inventions the world didn't know it was missing. High touch involves the capacity to empathize, to understand the subtleties of human interaction, to find joy in one's self and to elicit it in others, and to stretch beyond the quotidian in pursuit of purpose and meaning.

Developing these high concept, high touch abilities won't be easy for everyone. For some, the prospect seems unattainable. Fear not (or at least fear less). The sorts of abilities that now matter most are fundamentally human attributes. After all, back on the savannah, our caveperson ancestors weren't plugging numbers into spreadsheets or debugging code. But they were telling stories, demonstrating empathy, and designing innovations. These abilities have always been part of what it means to be human. It's just that after a few generations in the Information Age, many of our high concept, high touch muscles have atrophied. The challenge is to work them back into shape.

Want to get ahead today? Forget what your parents told you. Instead, do something foreigners can't do cheaper. Something computers can't do faster. And something that fills one of the nonmaterial, transcendent desires of an abundant age. In other words, go right, young man and woman, go right.

QUESTION FOR READING ACTIVELY

1. Identify and describe the social forces that the author believes are responsible for moving us from the Information Age to the Conceptual Age.

QUESTION FOR THINKING CRITICALLY

1. Explain the differences among what the author characterizes as the Industrial Age, the Information Age, and the Conceptual Age. Why does he feel that being a "knowledge worker" will be no longer sufficient for achieving success in the new Conceptual Age?

QUESTION FOR WRITING THOUGHTFULLY

1. According to the author, the thinking abilities associated with left-brain thinking are linear, logical, and analytic, while the thinking abilities associated with right-brain thinking involve artistry, empathy, inventiveness, and seeing the big picture. Using examples, explain how being able to think in both of these ways is advantageous for most careers.

"The 6 Myths of Creativity"
by Bill Breen

Bill Breen is the senior editor of *Fast Company*, a print and online magazine that has covered the business of new media and technology since the dot-com boom of the mid-1990s. A graduate of Colorado College (BA) and Trinity College, Dublin (MA),

Breen studied literature in preparation for his career as a "word wrangler." Breen has written extensively on environmental issues, as well as on business and technology.

Creativity

These days, there's hardly a mission statement that doesn't herald it, or a CEO who doesn't laud it. And yet despite all of the attention that business creativity has won over the past few years, maddeningly little is known about day-to-day innovation in the workplace. Where do breakthrough ideas come from? What kind of work environment allows them to flourish? What can leaders do to sustain the stimulants to creativity—and break through the barriers?

Teresa Amabile has been grappling with those questions for nearly thirty years. Amabile, who heads the Entrepreneurial Management Unit at Harvard Business School and is the only tenured professor at a top B-school to devote her entire research program to the study of creativity, is one of the country's foremost explorers of business innovation.

Eight years ago, Amabile took her research to a daring new level. Working with a team of PhDs, graduate students, and managers from various companies, she collected nearly 12,000 daily journal entries from 238 people working on creative projects in seven companies in the consumer products, high-tech, and chemical industries. She didn't tell the study participants that she was focusing on creativity. She simply asked them, in a daily email, about their work and their work environment as they experienced it that day. She then coded the emails for creativity by looking for moments when people struggled with a problem or came up with a new idea.

"The diary study was designed to look at creativity in the wild," she says. "We wanted to crawl inside people's heads and understand the features of their work environment as well as the experiences and thought processes that lead to creative breakthroughs."

Amabile and her team are still combing through the results. But this groundbreaking 5 study is already overturning some long-held beliefs about innovation in the workplace. In an interview with Fast Company, she busted six cherished myths about creativity. (If you want to quash creativity in your organization, just continue to embrace them.) Here they are, in her own words.

1. Creativity Comes from Creative Types

When I give talks to managers, I often start by asking, Where in your organization do you most want creativity? Typically, they'll say R&D, marketing, and advertising. When I ask, Where do you not want creativity? Someone will inevitably answer, "Accounting." That always gets a laugh because of the negative connotations of creative accounting. But there's this common perception among managers that some people are creative, and most aren't. That's just not true. As a leader, you don't want to ghettoize creativity; you want everyone in your organization producing novel and useful ideas, including your financial people. Over the past couple of decades, there have been innovations in financial accounting that are extremely profound and entirely ethical, such as activity-based costing.

The fact is, almost all of the research in this field shows that anyone with normal intelligence is capable of doing some degree of creative work. Creativity depends on a number of things: experience, including knowledge and technical skills; talent; an ability to think in new ways; and the capacity to push through uncreative dry spells. Intrinsic motivation—people who are turned on by their work often work creatively—is especially critical. Over the past five years, organizations have paid more attention to creativity and innovation than at any other time in my career. But I believe most people aren't anywhere near to realizing their creative potential, in part because they're laboring in environments that impede intrinsic motivation. The anecdotal evidence suggests many companies still have a long way to go to remove the barriers to creativity.

2. Money Is a Creativity Motivator

The experimental research that has been done on creativity suggests that money isn't everything. In the diary study, we asked people, "To what extent were you motivated by rewards today?" Quite often they'd say that the question isn't relevant—that they don't think about pay on a day-to-day basis. And the handful of people who were spending a lot of time wondering about their bonuses were doing very little creative thinking.

Bonuses and pay-for-performance plans can even be problematic when people believe that every move they make is going to affect their compensation. In those situations, people tend to get risk averse. Of course, people need to feel that they're being compensated fairly. But our research shows that people put far more value on a work environment where creativity is supported, valued, and recognized. People want the opportunity to deeply engage in their work and make real progress. So it's critical for leaders to match people to projects not only on the basis of their experience but also in terms of where their interests lie. People are most creative when they care about their work and they're stretching their skills. If the challenge is far beyond their skill level, they tend to get frustrated; if it's far below their skill level, they tend to get bored. Leaders need to strike the right balance.

10 3. Time Pressure Fuels Creativity

In our diary study, people often thought they were most creative when they were working under severe deadline pressure. But the 12,000 aggregate days that we studied showed just the opposite: People were the least creative when they were fighting the clock. In fact, we found a kind of time-pressure hangover—when people were working under great pressure, their creativity went down not only on that day but the next two days as well. Time pressure stifles creativity because people can't deeply engage with the problem. Creativity requires an incubation period; people need time to soak in a problem and let the ideas bubble up.

In fact, it's not so much the deadline that's the problem; it's the distractions that rob people of the time to make that creative breakthrough. People can certainly be creative when they're under the gun, but only when they're able to focus on the work. They must be protected from distractions, and they must know that the work is important and that everyone is committed to it. In too many organizations, people don't understand the reason for the urgency, other than the fact that somebody somewhere needs it done today.

4. Fear Forces Breakthroughs

There's this widespread notion that fear and sadness somehow spur creativity. There's even some psychological literature suggesting that the incidence of depression is higher in creative writers and artists—the depressed geniuses who are incredibly original in their thinking. But we don't see it in the population that we studied.

We coded all 12,000 journal entries for the degree of fear, anxiety, sadness, anger, joy, and love that people were experiencing on a given day. And we found that creativity is positively associated with joy and love and negatively associated with anger, fear, and anxiety. The entries show that people are happiest when they come up with a creative idea, but they're more likely to have a breakthrough if they were happy the day before. There's a kind of virtuous cycle. When people are excited about their work, there's a better chance that they'll make a cognitive association that incubates overnight and shows up as a creative idea the next day. One day's happiness often predicts the next day's creativity.

5. Competition Beats Collaboration

There's a widespread belief, particularly in the finance and high-tech industries, that internal competition fosters innovation. In our surveys, we found that creativity takes a hit when people in a work group compete instead of collaborate. The most creative teams are those that have the confidence to share and debate ideas. But when people compete for recognition, they stop sharing information. And that's destructive because nobody in an organization has all of the information required to put all the pieces of the puzzle together.

6. A Streamlined Organization Is a Creative Organization

Maybe it's only the public-relations departments that believe downsizing and restructuring actually foster creativity. Unfortunately, I've seen too many examples of this kind of spin. One of my favorites is a 1994 letter to shareholders from a major U.S. software company: "A downsizing such as this one is always difficult for employees, but out of tough times can come strength, creativity, and teamwork."

Of course, the opposite is true: Creativity suffers greatly during a downsizing. But it's even worse than many of us realized. We studied a 6,000-person division in a global electronics company during the entire course of a 25 percent downsizing, which took an incredibly agonizing 18 months. Every single one of the stimulants to creativity in the work environment went down significantly. Anticipation of the downsizing was even worse than the downsizing itself—people's fear of the unknown led them to basically disengage from the work. More troubling was the fact that even five months after the downsizing, creativity was still down significantly.

Unfortunately, downsizing will remain a fact of life, which means that leaders need to focus on the things that get hit. Communication and collaboration decline significantly. So too does people's sense of freedom and autonomy. Leaders will have to work hard and fast to stabilize the work environment so ideas can flourish.

Taken together, these operating principles for fostering creativity in the workplace might lead you to think that I'm advocating a soft management style. Not true. I'm pushing for a smart management style. My thirty years of research and these 12,000 journal entries suggest that when people are doing work that they love and they're allowed to deeply engage in it—and when the work itself is valued and recognized— then creativity will flourish. Even in tough times.

15

QUESTIONS FOR READING ACTIVELY

1. In your own words, describe the "6 Myths of Creativity."

2. How did Teresa Amabile, the Harvard Business School professor who studies creativity in the workplace, design her research? What kinds of information was she looking for? What seems especially surprising or interesting about her approach to research?

3. Who is the audience for Bill Breen's article? How can you tell?

QUESTION FOR THINKING CRITICALLY

1. Compare Daniel Pink's description of the kind of thinking that is necessary to be successful in today's business world ("Revenge of the Right Brain," page 112) with the qualities that Amabile identifies as motivating creativity in business. How is the advice similar or different?

QUESTIONS FOR WRITING THOUGHTFULLY

1. Select one of the "6 Myths of Creativity" that has special application to your own studies, work, or life. How has this myth challenged or blocked your ability to be creative? In an essay, describe the myth in your own words, and devise a plan for overcoming this challenge or block and becoming more creative.

2. In your experience, which of the four strategies for becoming more creative (page 107) is most important for innovation and success? In your response, refer to Daniel Pink's essay (page 112) or Teresa Amabile's research.

Writing Project

IMAGINING YOUR LIFE LIVED MORE CREATIVELY

According to a French proverb, "Only he who does nothing makes a mistake." For this chapter's writing project, you will need to think creatively and imagine the changes you would like to see in your life. This may be difficult, but it can help you avoid future regrets related to the things you could have done in life, but didn't.

Project Overview and Requirements

Imagine how some part of your life could be more satisfying or exciting. You will need to focus on one or more specific areas of your life such as an important relationship, your college work, or your dream job. Visualize how your future will be when you creatively transform this part of your life.

Next, think about what you must do in the present to achieve this imagined goal. You may start by creating a list of ideas, and you will need to locate images that inspire or evoke your goal, as well as how you plan to achieve it.

In an essay, write about your "life lived more creatively," and be sure to include your thesis in the introduction, main points detailing how you will achieve your goal, and, finally, your conclusion. Follow your instructor's directions related to essay length, format, and so on, and review The Writing Situation and The Writing Process sections below to help get you started.

THE WRITING SITUATION

Begin by considering the key elements of the Thinking-Writing Model: purpose, audience, subject, and writer.

Purpose   Your purpose is to use the strategies for thinking, living, and writing this chapter presents to create a new vision of your own life. Doing this will require you to step back from your life; to become an observer of how you have lived, or are living, or might be living; and then to create a potentially different vision.

Your essay will begin with, and include, at least one actual image.

Audience   You have an interesting and varied audience, and it begins with you. Who else could be more interested in this particular subject? Beyond yourself, you may choose to show your writing to key people in your life, especially if any of them would be affected by the changes you propose. Their reactions to your early draft could be very helpful as you revise.

Your classmates may be part of your audience if your writing is going to be shared with them. All the readers mentioned so far will be interested in what you say, and especially in the changes you propose, so include enough background information about how your life was, or is, for them to understand the impact of those changes.

Subject   Thinking and writing about our own lives can be exciting yet challenging. Often we are so busy just living our lives that we don't take time to think about how they might be different. We begin to think that whatever *is* has to be.

A potential problem is that you may believe that there is little in your life that can be changed. You are not necessarily being asked to propose major changes. What you end up writing about could be a different life or simply a richer, more fully realized version of your life now.

Writer   As the expert on your own life, you write with authority on this project. If you are the creative type, you should welcome the chance to let your imagination go! If you consider yourself unimaginative, take this opportunity to develop your creative side, using any of the strategies discussed in this chapter.

The following four questions will help you explore and develop your ideas related to imagining your life lived more creatively. You may also want to look back at your responses to the Thinking-Writing Activities earlier in this chapter for inspiration. After you have your thoughts in writing, it will be easier to move on to The Writing Process, which includes more ways to generate ideas.

1. Of the ideas you came up with related to making creative improvements to your life, which one seems the most exciting or important? Here is an example of one person's idea:

   Although I enjoy my career and am considered successful, there is a part of me that yearns to express my feelings through painting. I used to paint when

I was younger, but haven't had the time now that my career has taken off. My goal is to publicly exhibit and sell my paintings.

2. Describe (for yourself and your audience) why you feel this is a realistic or attainable goal. For example:

> I feel like I don't have much time to paint, but I notice that I spend at least three hours each evening watching television. If I cut out television, and if I turn the junk room above the garage into a studio, I will have more time (and a good place) to paint. Cleaning out the room above the garage will take a lot of work (and a possible yard sale), and I will need to discipline myself to spend time in the studio.

3. Since this is an improvement you would really like to make, what are the underlying reasons you feel your life would be better?

> I love to paint because it gives me a way to express my thoughts and feelings without having to speak or write—something I do all day at work. Aside from coming up with a pleasing or thought-provoking composition and color scheme, I like the physical process of applying paint to the canvas. I lose myself in that process, and all my worries seem to disappear. I love my career, but it is filled with meetings, deadlines, and lots of pressure. When I paint, it is just me, my thoughts, and the canvas—and the world slows down.

4. How can you describe your sense of creativity to someone who does not know you?

> Creativity comes from many different places and manifests itself in many ways. Some people are creative in the way they manage employees, while others are creative when it comes to raising money, designing clothes, or marketing products. I am creative when it comes to expressing my thoughts on canvas. I am a painter.

THE WRITING PROCESS

The following sections guide you through the stages of the writing process. Try to be particularly conscious of how creative thinking can help you discover and connect ideas.

Generating Ideas   Review your responses to the Thinking-Writing Activities in this chapter. You will probably see a number of ideas that pertain to this project. Then, to discover more ideas and a possible focus, follow these suggestions and jot down your responses.

- Think about two or three things you do that are particularly important to you. How might they become more satisfying if you became more creative in your approach?

- Envision your life five years from now. What activities do you hope to be involved in? How could they be shaped by creative thinking? What would your ideal job situation be?

- Recall an event from the past in which you experienced a creative breakthrough. What was your flash of insight? Can you apply that creative insight to your current situation or future life?

- Choose a situation and brainstorm or ask questions about it.

- For a week, keep a journal about how you experience your work and work environment each day. (See "The 6 Myths of Creativity," page 116.) What situations seem to inspire your creativity? What situations stifle your creativity?

- Collect images that suggest "creativity" to you, even if you can't quite articulate *why* they seem creative.

- Ask yourself if you have enough ideas to begin drafting your paper. If not, you may want to try again by examining another aspect of your life.

Defining a Focus   After reviewing the material you created, consider which area of your life would be most exciting to focus on. Then write a few sentences about that change. For example:

> I think that I would like to be a more creative cook. Why? How? So that my housemates and I can have more enjoyable meals when it's my turn in the kitchen; so that I can really enjoy cooking. . . . Some ways that I can do this are to take a cooking course, check some really different cookbooks out of the library—like from other countries or other regions, or vegan, or barbecue. I should spend some time with my uncle who makes such good one-dish meals, find some tasty websites and watch some of those cooking shows instead of surfing away.

This writer has a focus: to become a better cook. Next, she must decide how to draft her thesis. It should be a clear, simple statement, but one that also provides a "blueprint" for her overall essay.

> *Simple statement:* I want to change my life by becoming a more creative cook.
>
> *Blueprint sentence:* I plan to become a more creative cook by taking a cooking course, checking some good cookbooks out of the library, spending more time with my uncle, finding some tasty websites, and watching some cooking shows.

If you do write a blueprint sentence, consider whether you have listed the changes in an order that your audience can easily comprehend. Once you have established an order, use it to structure your essay.

Organizing Ideas   After you have decided on a focus, you can

- Describe your current or past situation
- Describe some changes you would like to make or wish you had made
- Describe the improved situation
- Select images that more specifically reflect your situation and/or your goal

Does this thinking suggest a logical method of organization? Is that organization effective, or is it too stodgy for a paper about creative thinking? How about narrating the events from a future perspective, after you have made some changes?

Map out an organizational plan that you think might work. Consult with your instructor if you are taking a creative approach to organization.

Drafting   As you translate your ideas into coherent writing, consider the three distinct components that will make up your essay: your present situation, the changes you would make, and how your life would be different. You may want to write about each component separately and then think about connecting them together in the draft. This can also help the revision process go more smoothly.

Drafting Hints

1. If you are drafting on a word processor, double or even triple space. Be sure to save your work every few minutes if your program does not do so automatically.

2. Consider drafting the three components of this essay as three separate files. You could name them "Present Situation," "Changes," and "New and Different Life." Then you can easily copy and paste them to see what organization would work best.

3. If you are drafting by hand, skip lines and write on only one side of the paper. That way you can easily rearrange them if you decide to reorganize.

Revising Your Essay: Imagining Your Life Lived More Creatively

Peer Review—Silent Writer

One of the best revision strategies is to get an audience's reactions to your draft. Your classmates can help you see where your draft is already successful and where it needs improvement. If your instructor allows class time for peer review, have a draft ready.

This peer review introduces a different approach than the one used in Chapter 3. In this approach, the writer is silent after reading the draft aloud twice and listens as peers respond. Groups of three or four work best, and be sure to carefully follow all six steps below.

1. The group selects a timekeeper, who allots 10 minutes to each writer (or more, depending on paper length requirements). After 10 minutes, the group must move on to the next writer's work.

2. One person begins by reading his or her draft aloud while group members listen, giving the writer their full attention.

3. The writer then reads the draft aloud a second time. Group members listen again, this time taking notes.

4. Group members read their comments to the writer. Responses must be specific in order to help the writer revise his or her work. Here are some examples:

Weak response: "I like it. It sounds okay to me." (The writer receives no specific help.)

Marginally useful: "I thought the description of your new neighborhood was entertaining." (The writer receives encouragement.)

Useful: "Can you give me an example of the kind of task you would perform in your new job?" (The writer learns what information the reader needs.)

Very useful: "I was confused when you said your aunt came into the room. I thought you said earlier that you were alone in the house." (The writer receives specific feedback related to an essential clarification.)

5. The writer listens to questions and comments and may take notes but does not answer or respond aloud. The writer may ask questions after all group members have commented.

6. Continue the process until each group member has used 10 minutes of response time.

Revision

As soon as possible after peer review, revise your draft based on your peers' questions and comments. Work through the checklist below, and reread your revised draft out loud, slowly. Think about each of the following questions.

- Is your thesis a clear, simple statement, but also one that provides a "blueprint" for your overall essay?

- Does your draft flow smoothly from one idea to the next? Remember that you need to balance creativity with the needs of your audience. Is there a more creative way to arrange your essay without sacrificing details needed to engage your audience?

- Do the transitions between sections of your essay help your audience follow your ideas?

- Is your use of language creative? Could you provide more specific adjectives and adverbs?

- Have you given your essay an inventive title that will make your audience want to read it?

Editing and Proofreading

To prepare your final draft, edit for standard grammar and punctuation. Proofread carefully to detect omitted words and punctuation errors. Run your spell-checker program, but be aware of its limitations. Finally, ask someone you trust to proofread after you are finished. Also, you may want to look ahead to Chapter 6 and review "A Step-by-Step Method for Revising Any Assignment" on the inside front cover of this book. This checklist will help you revise your essay and polish your final draft.

The following essay shows how one student responded to the idea of living a more creative life. Before writing, the student used one of the methods on pages 107–110 for generating ideas.

STUDENT WRITING

Jessie Lange's Writing Process: Freewriting

I have to write a paper about a legend I didn't even understand. There are stairs going up a tower to a place that is a kind of nirvana, a place of happiness, but you can only reach the top if you don't believe in the legend itself. Hello? If you don't believe it, why would you spend your time climbing up? OK, OK, I needed to think. Usually getting outside helps me think better so I tried that up at our place in the country. I did have a great experience. I saw some deer in the mist at night. They were really hard to see and when I put up my lamp to get more light, instead of seeing them better, they almost disappeared in the light. So I turned out the light and I could see them better in the dark. I'm thinking that maybe this is like the legend. The opposite of what you would expect happens. Maybe the legend is about trying too hard. I'll try this angle and see what happens.

Notice how Lange's "Voice" in the opening paragraph almost sounds confessional. Does this help her connect with the audience? Can we relate to her?

Discovering Creativity by Not Looking for It
by Jessie Lange

There have been numerous times when I have sat in front of a blank computer screen, a writing assignment in hand, feeling completely uninspired and uncreative. Without having even begun I think, "Now what?" There have been numerous times when I've just started filling up that screen with meaningless, dry words that really have no effect on me or anyone else. Yes, I'm getting the job done, but not the job I'd like—not my best work, not anywhere near it. One thing that I've found in my life is that in your most uncreative ruts sometimes you can't pull yourself out all on your own. You can't always, sitting in an idea-less vacuum, turn on the creativity. Sometimes you will save yourself time and produce a much more fulfilling piece

Source: Discovering Creativity by Not Looking for It by Jessie Lange.

of work if you take the time out to go *out* of the world of your blank screen. For me this has always meant literally getting outdoors, because somehow it always seems that I find *outside* what I've been looking for *inside*.

© Stephane Bidouze/Shutterstock.com

It was the first English assignment of my senior year of high school—an interpretation of a Buddhist legend—and I was struggling with its meaning. The legend is about a set of stairs leading to the top of the tower from where you can see the "whole horizon" and the "loveliest landscape"—a symbol of attaining nirvana. The paradox in the legend is that you can only reach the top if you do not believe in the legend itself. How would those who believe, then, ever reach the top? How can you even start the climb without making the conscious decision to do so?

Lange places her story during her "senior year of high school." This is an important detail because it shows the reader that she is fairly young. She also introduces a Buddhist legend that is central to her essay.

Being in the country on weekends has many benefits, one of them being that I could go outside to clear my head. I lit my Williams Sonoma oil lamp and walked out into the night that offered the occasional drizzle and a strong breeze that ruffled the leaves of the tree I lay down under. I was there for an hour, feeling the drops on my face and the dampness settling into my body, before it happened. I rolled over and looked out into the field, because I sensed something the way that you can and will when you're listening with your entire body. Farther out, right before the lawn becomes high grass and eventually woods, were four white shapes moving across my line of vision. The same deer I casually glanced at during the day were like ghosts grazing out there at night. Just faint, light vaporous figures against the pitch black. That moment was like seeing the "whole horizon." Those animals, moving with such grace, were unaware of my presence. For all they knew, I was another tree silently overseeing their nightly ritual. Watching these beasts—because that's

In this paragraph, Lange intentionally uses concrete details to place her story (and audience) in nature.

In the final half of the third paragraph, Lange presents a metaphor that helps her (and her audience) understand the Buddhist legend.

Lange revels her epiphany and connects her carefully crafted metaphor to her new understanding of the Buddhist legend and creativity.

what they are, wonderfully wild animals—I was witnessing a scene that could have taken place in this same spot on this same night hundreds or thousands of years before. I reached for my lantern and turned up the flame, holding it in front of me for a better view. This light, however, obstructed my vision rather than illuminating it. It was only when I put the flame aside and cupped my hands around my eyes, creating a deeper darkness, that I could really see the deer.

And then I realized that perhaps that was why only those who do not believe the legend ever climb the stairs of the tower—because when you actively search for things, like holding the light, perhaps you prevent yourself from seeing them. Had I not put my writing aside and taken that walk, I would never have found this answer, the answer I was looking for. I wrote my English essay and I also learned something about creativity in my own life. Some of your most creative moments happen when you're not looking. In the journey up the steps of the tower toward creativity, sometimes it is not those who are keenly searching for a victory of sorts, but those who are instead turning down the light, that begin the climb.

REFLECTION ON WRITING

1. Jessie Lange begins her essay by describing herself sitting in front of a blank computer screen. As her audience, what does this do for you? Is this a successful introduction to her essay?

2. Can you find evidence of how Jessie's freewriting exercise helped her generate ideas for her essay?

3. Jessie spends time focusing on concrete details in her essay ("occasional drizzle," "strong breeze that ruffled the leaves," "light vaporous figures against the pitch black," etc.). Recall how, in Chapter 3, you wrote an essay about an experience that influenced a belief. In describing your experience, you likely included specific details to paint a vivid picture for your audience. In Jessie's essay, does her level of detail draw you in? What other ways might the details she used add to (or detract from) the essay?

ALTERNATIVE WRITING PROJECTS

- Write an essay explaining your original, creative solution to a physical problem, one involving a piece of equipment, the use of space, overcoming some barrier, or a similar situation. Be sure to incorporate images that illustrate the problem, the solution, or both. Here are some examples:
  - Crowd control or better seating at concerts and sporting events
  - A device that makes some activity easier or more accessible for the disabled
  - A new design or redesign of highways and roads in your area
  - An imaginative new tool or transportation device

- Write an essay explaining your original, creative solution to a social problem, such as homelessness, tensions between racial groups, or drug use among young teenagers.
- Write an essay explaining your original, creative plan for the perfect house, the perfect party, or the perfect vacation.

CHAPTER 4   Summary

- Creative ways to generate ideas include brainstorming, using mind maps, freewriting, and questioning.
- Six types of questions can help you generate ideas and narrow your topic: questions of fact, interpretation, analysis, synthesis, evaluation, and application.
- Images are a form of communication, too, and should be considered from a critical thinking perspective.
- In evaluating images, you should identify their audience, subject, and purpose to help determine their semantic, perceptual, syntactic, and pragmatic meanings.
- You can live a more creative life by eliminating the "Voice of Judgment," establishing a creative environment, and making creativity a priority.

The decisions we make on a daily basis run the gamut from simple to complex, trivial to momentous. The stronger your critical thinking abilities are, the better equipped you will be to make important decisions. Your analytical skills, knowledge, experience, training, confidence, and even intuition, all play a key role in the decision-making process. When is the last time you had to make an important decision? How did you analyze the situation in order to make the best decision possible?

Drafting:
Making and Analyzing Decisions

"The strongest principle of growth lies in human choice."

—GEORGE ELIOT

CRITICAL THINKING FOCUS: **Decision making in writing and in life**

WRITING FOCUS: **Making decisions about drafts**

READING THEMES: **Extraordinary decisions**

WRITING ACTIVITIES: **Analyzing and preparing**

WRITING PROJECT: **Analyzing a decision to be made**

A decision is a kind of commitment. You make decisions, of varying degrees of importance and impact, every day of your life. How carefully you approach that decision, how thoughtfully you evaluate your choices, and how meaningfully you follow through on your commitment to what you have decided vary with the degree of that decision's importance. For example, a knowledgeable and open-minded evaluation of your current lifestyle might lead you to decide to make a few fundamental changes—you might resolve to get more exercise, drink less on the weekends, opt for salad instead of fries. Your decision to live more healthfully might be based on the advice of your doctor and the example set by an athletic friend, but until you *commit* yourself to that decision, you're never going to succeed at lowering your cholesterol or waking up refreshed on Monday morning.

When you decide on a topic for an essay, you are also making a commitment. In the previous chapter, we looked at the process of deciding on a topic—engaging your creativity, your curiosity, your open-mindedness, and your knowledge in order to *decide* on the most engaging and appropriate topic for you to write about. In this chapter, we'll examine strategies for following through on that decision, applying those same four qualities to the decision making inherent in each stage of the drafting process.

In addition, this chapter includes essays by and about people forced to make extraordinary decisions under the most perilous circumstances. Their insight, creativity, strength, and thoughtfulness are truly inspiring.

Thinking Critically About Visuals

What's My Next Move?

Our success in life depends on developing the ability to solve challenging problems in organized and creative ways. Through research, we can gather relevant information to help evaluate the pros and cons of a situation or problem, and then make an educated decision. Learning to interpret charts and statistics can be a valuable critical thinking skill. How would you interpret the "Balancing loans vs. earnings" chart?

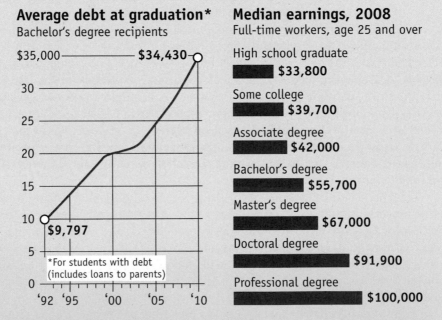

Balancing loans vs. earnings

U.S. college students are graduating with increasing levels of debt, but higher education still means higher earnings.

Average debt at graduation*
Bachelor's degree recipients

$35,000 — $34,430
30
25
20
15
10 — $9,797
5
*For students with debt (includes loans to parents)
0
'92 '95 '00 '05 '10

Median earnings, 2008
Full-time workers, age 25 and over

High school graduate
$33,800

Some college
$39,700

Associate degree
$42,000

Bachelor's degree
$55,700

Master's degree
$67,000

Doctoral degree
$91,900

Professional degree
$100,000

Source: From: http://www.thedailyaztec.com/2012/11/bachelors-degrees-are-losing-their-value/balancing-college-loans-vs-potential-future-earnings/. © 2012 All rights reserved. Distributed by McClatchy-Tribune News Services-MCT.

Decisions While Drafting

Most decisions made while drafting a piece of writing are not made in a "first this, then that" sequential order. As Chapter 1 points out, writing processes are usually recursive. Ideas are generated, drafts are made, more ideas come, revisions are necessary, more planning, peer review, maybe more drafting—back and forth until the writer says this is it. However, throughout this recursive process, writers must make decisions on subjects, audiences, purposes, and specific ideas and words.

Actually, there is a *first decision*. That is, of course, to take the step from generating ideas to drafting. Some people do this easily; others postpone it. You need to understand your own tendency here and be sure to have some strategies that get you going. Some of the strategies in Chapter 4 used to generate ideas are also useful for beginning to draft. For example,

- *Freewriting* on the selected topic. This can get a draft started, especially if you resolve to write and not stare at the screen or the blank page. Try not to worry about making your sentences perfect—just get your ideas down on paper.

- *Listing ideas about the topic and then expressing the ideas in sentences.*

- *Deciding to write on the topic for a set amount of time,* maybe half an hour.

- *Deciding to draft a specific section first,* usually the one you know most about.

Before and during the drafting process, consider the following decisions you will need to make—they are all a part of the writing situation.

Decide What Your Purpose for Writing Is   Usually in college and at work, the purpose is clear. You want to complete the lab report or the English paper to fulfill the assignment as well as you can, or you want your proposal or your application to be accepted. However, if you are composing an email to go to your family list about reunion plans or a letter to the editor about a community problem, you might need to define your purpose. Do you want family members to help? Do you want the city council to act?

In your notebook or a separate file, complete the following sentences to help you decide:

My purpose(s) for this (essay, email, memo) is(are) to:

_____

In order to fulfill my purpose, I should:

_____

These sentences will probably not be part of your draft, but they can help you decide what to include in your essay.

Decide Who Your Audience Is and What Its Needs Are   As with purpose, the primary audience is often obvious in college and workplace writing—the instructor or the supervisor—but your classmates and fellow workers might be an audience, too. You often know what those audiences expect, since assignments and office formats are usually explicit. If you are writing for family members or community groups, as you draft, you should think about what background information is necessary or superfluous, what tone is suitable, what level of vocabulary is appropriate, and what special needs that audience may have.

In your notebook or a separate file, complete the following statements:

My audience is:

_____

My audience will expect:

_____

My audience will need to know:

_____

My audience already knows:

_____

Decide What Your Subject Is and Why It Is Interesting   As we have seen, your subject for writing can be drawn from your personal experience, or it can be a topic assigned by an instructor. If you are allowed to choose a subject, now is the time to exercise your creativity. Try the Creativity and Topic Selection suggestions (as well as Creativity in Generating Ideas) presented in Chapter 4 (pages 95–97).

Decide Who You Are as a Writer   Finding your voice and taking a stand are key steps not only of the writing process but also of your intellectual development. To make a decision about what voice and tone to use in your paper, consider again your audience and purpose. Are you speaking as someone who is an expert on an issue, writing on a subject about which you have considerable personal experience? Alternatively, are you writing for an audience of experts whose conversation about a subject or issue you would like to join? As you read more widely in a variety of disciplines and attend lectures and seminars by experts in a range of fields, you will become more familiar with the different voices and vocabularies used to express ideas for specific audiences. As your knowledge increases, it will be time for you to experiment with different voices and approaches to convey that knowledge.

Decide on a Working Thesis   This is a time to be open-minded. After some drafting, you need to think again about the thesis you may have started with or think about formulating one if you have not yet done so. Reread the material in Chapter 4 (beginning on page 96), Moving from Topic to Thesis Statement. As you draft your essay, you will decide exactly how to state (and where to place) your thesis statement.

In your notebook or a separate file, complete the following statements to help you decide:

As I see it now, the basis for this piece is:

_____

Or perhaps it is better stated as:

_____

Decide What Information to Use and What More You Need   Review your idea-generating activities. Look again at your tentative thesis. What information do you need to support it and to fulfill your purpose? Think about what you know; think about what you should know more about. Think about what your audience needs to know. The Critical Reading Questions of Interpretation, Analysis, and Evaluation in Chapter 2 (page 35) can be helpful in this decision.

In your notebook or a separate file, complete the following statements:

The ideas about _____ *are important to my thesis.*

I need to know more about _____

My audience needs to know _____

Decide When to Outline to Bring Order to Your Draft   Some writers make an outline or a plan before drafting; some writers outline after drafting; some writers do not outline but instead revise and redraft until they are satisfied with the organization of the piece.

A rough (or informal) outline, which indicates the order of sections but is not carefully formatted, can help you structure your essay. Sometimes a draft benefits from being outlined more than once. Formal outlines, with logical patterns of letters, numbers, sentences, and phrases, can be done when a piece is close to being finished. Ask your instructor for formal outline specifications if you are asked to do one, or if you want to be sure about your paper's organization.

In your notebook or a separate file, outline the material in your draft, using an informal or a formal system as you find helpful.

Decide on an Introduction and a Conclusion   Although you will look carefully at these parts of your draft as you revise and refine, don't forget to work out possible beginnings and endings as you draft.

Explore as many different types of introductions and conclusions as you can. Some kinds of writing, such as lab reports, have standard formats that specify how to construct your introduction and conclusion, but in other cases, you will have options. Here are a few strategies to consider when constructing your introduction:

- Background information or context
- A relevant anecdote
- A quotation or proverb that relates to the topic
- A striking statement (to be contradicted or supported)
- The problem to be addressed in the paper
- Questions connected to the content of the paper
- The who, what, where, when, how, and why of the paper's focus
- The claim, thesis, or main point
- Combinations of these types

Here are several strategies you can use when crafting your conclusion:

- A summary of the paper's information
- A recommendation or call for action
- An apt quotation or proverb
- A telling anecdote

- The thesis or main point restated or stated at the end instead of the beginning
- A suggestion of the need for more discussion of the issue

A conclusion must provide a sense of closure to the piece; readers should recognize it as an ending (you should not have to write "The End"!).

Neither introductions nor conclusions should be apologetic ("I don't know much about this, but . . ."); nor should their tone differ from that of the body of the paper.

Decisions in Your Life

Throughout your life, you will continue to make decisions and to deal with decisions others make that affect your life. Recalling a previous decision about your education, your relationships, your athletic activities, or any other part of your life will remind you of how important those choices are.

Thinking-Writing Activity

ANALYZING A PREVIOUS DECISION

Think back to an important decision you made that turned out well, and describe the experience as specifically as possible by reconstructing the reasoning process you used to make your decision.

- How did you *define* the decision to be made?
- What *choices* did you consider?
- What were the various *pros and cons* of each possible choice?
- What specific plan of action did you use to implement your ideas?
- How did you review your decision to make any necessary adjustments?

Using a method to help you decide about important issues will help you make intelligent decisions and avoid poor choices.

AN ORGANIZED APPROACH TO MAKING DECISIONS

As you were reflecting on the successful decision you wrote about in the previous Thinking-Writing Activity, you probably noticed your mind working in a systematic way as you thought your way through the decision-making process. Of course, we often make important decisions with less thoughtful analysis by acting impulsively and are later forced to cope with the consequences. Our intuitions can be a useful guide to success when they are *informed intuitions*—based on lessons learned from past experience and thoughtful reflection. Naturally, there are no guarantees that careful analysis will lead to a successful result—there are often too many unknown elements and factors beyond our control. But we can certainly improve our success rate by becoming more knowledgeable about the decision-making process.

This approach consists of five steps. As you master these steps, you will be able to apply them in a natural and flexible way.

STEP 1: DEFINE THE DECISION AND ITS GOALS CLEARLY (AUDIENCE)

This seems like an obvious step, but decision making frequently goes wrong at the starting point. For example, imagine that you are trying to decide on an academic major. In order to make an informed decision, you have to project yourself into the future, imagining the career that will be right for you. Your goals will likely include

- Financial security
- Personal fulfillment
- An opportunity to make use of your special talents
- Employment opportunities and job security

Keeping these goals in mind as you consider various majors will give you the greatest success in discovering the field that best suits you. Your audience for this thinking exercise includes not just yourself but also anyone who can help you achieve those goals. The more specific your definition of the decision—and its goals—is, the clearer your analysis and the greater the likelihood of your success will be. Here's a strategy you can use to best define your decision:

STRATEGY: Write a one-page analysis describing your decision-making situation that defines your goals as clearly and specifically as possible. Write for an audience beyond yourself. Your audience might be your parents, your partner, or your career counselor.

STEP 2: CONSIDER ALL POSSIBLE CHOICES (SUBJECT)

Successful decision makers explore all possible choices, not simply the obvious ones. In fact, the less obvious choices often turn out to be the most effective ones. For instance, one student couldn't decide whether to major in accounting or business management. While discussing his situation with his friends, he revealed that his real interest was in website design. Although he was very talented, he considered this area only a hobby, not a possible career choice. His friends pointed out that designing websites could prove to be his best career opportunity, but he first needed to see it as a possibility.

STRATEGY: List as many possible choices for your situation as you can—obvious and not obvious, practical and impractical. Ask other people for additional suggestions, and keep an open mind—don't censor or prejudge any ideas. Evaluating many different possibilities will help you select a truly interesting and engaging subject.

STEP 3: GATHER ALL RELEVANT INFORMATION AND EVALUATE THE PROS AND CONS OF EACH POSSIBLE CHOICE (PURPOSE)

Each of the possible choices you identified will have certain advantages and disadvantages, so it is essential that you analyze these pros and cons in an organized fashion. This analysis will help you to define and focus your purpose. In the case of the student discussed in Step 2, the career choice of accounting might, on the one hand, offer advantages like ready employment opportunities, the flexibility of working in many different situations and geographical locations, a moderate to high income, and job security. On the other hand, disadvantages might be that accounting does not reflect the student's deep and abiding interest, that he might become bored with it over time, and that the career might not result in the personal challenge and fulfillment that he needs.

> STRATEGY: Analyze the pros and cons of each of your possible choices. The "pro" list will likely help you to visualize the true purpose motivating your choice.

In many cases, you may lack sufficient information to make an informed choice. Unfortunately, this has never prevented people from plunging ahead anyway, making a decision that is more a gamble than an informed choice. But it makes much more sense to seek out the information you need in order to determine which of your choices has the best chance of success. In the case of the student, he would need certain crucial information to determine which career would be best for him: What sort of academic preparation and experience are required for the various careers? What are the prospects for employment in these areas, and how well do the positions pay? What are the day-to-day activities in each career? How happy are the people in the various careers?

> STRATEGY: For each possible choice that you have identified, create questions regarding information you need; then obtain that information. Your purpose here is to clarify the resources you need to achieve your goal.

STEP 4: SELECT THE CHOICE THAT SEEMS BEST SUITED TO THE SITUATION

The first three steps are designed to help you analyze your decision situation: to define clearly the decision in terms of your goals, to generate possible choices, and to evaluate the pros and cons of the choices you have identified. In the fourth step, you must synthesize what you have learned, weaving together all the various threads into a conclusion that you consider your best choice. In academic writing, synthesis often evolves from the drafting process as you discern new connections among different perspectives and resources. How do you do this? There is no one simple way to identify your best choice, but the following strategy will help guide your deliberations:

> STRATEGY: Identify and prioritize the goal(s) of your decision situation, and determine which of your choices best meets these goals.

This process will probably involve reviewing and perhaps refining your definition of the decision situation. For example, for the student we have been discussing, goals included choosing a career that would (a) provide financial security, (b) provide personal fulfillment, (c) make use of special talents, and (d) offer plentiful work opportunities along with job security.

Once identified, these goals can be ranked in order of priority, which will then suggest what the best choice would be. If the student ranks goals *a* and *d* at the top of the list, a choice of accounting or business administration may make sense. However, if the student ranks goals *b* and *c* at the top, pursuing a career in website design and illustration may be the best selection.

Project yourself into the future, imagining as realistically as you can the consequences of each possible choice. Write your thoughts down, and discuss them with your friends or colleagues.

STEP 5: IMPLEMENT A PLAN OF ACTION AND MONITOR THE RESULTS, MAKING NECESSARY ADJUSTMENTS

Once you have made your best choice, you need to develop and implement a plan of action. The more specific your plan, the greater the likelihood of its success. If, for instance, the student in the example in Step 2 decides to pursue a career in website design, his plan should include reviewing the major that best meets his needs, discussing his situation with students and faculty in that department, planning what courses to take, and perhaps speaking with people working in the field. This step of the decision-making process is similar to the work of creating a research plan for writing (Chapter 14).

> STRATEGY: Create a plan that details the steps you would take to implement your decision, along with a time line for taking these steps.

Naturally, your plan is merely a starting point. As you actually begin taking the steps in your plan, you may discover that you need to make changes and adjustments. You might find new information that suggests that your choice may be wrong. For example, as the student takes courses in HTML and design, he may realize that his interest in the field is not as serious as he once thought and that although he likes this area as a hobby, he does not want it to be his life's work. In this case, he should reconsider his other choices, perhaps adding some choices that he did not contemplate before.

> STRATEGY: After implementing your choice, evaluate its success by identifying what is working and what is not; then make the necessary adjustments to improve the situation.

Summary for Making Decisions in Writing and in Life

1. Define the decision and its goals clearly.
2. Consider all possible choices.
3. Gather all relevant information and evaluate the pros and cons of each possible choice.
4. Select the choice that seems best suited to the situation.
5. Implement a plan of action and monitor the results, making necessary adjustments.

ANALYZING DECISIONS

The following readings illustrate decisions of tremendous, life-altering import. Frederick Douglass describes how he and fellow slaves made the momentous decision to escape to the North in 1835. Michael Shermer uses "game theory" to explore the ethics surrounding "doping" in sports.

From *Narrative of the Life of Frederick Douglass, an American Slave*

by Frederick Douglass

Frederick Bailey was born into slavery in 1818, his mother a field worker and his father rumored to be her white master. He spent his early childhood with his grandmother. When he was six years old, his grandmother brought him to the Lloyd Plantation, one of the oldest and largest plantations in Maryland. Frederick only saw his mother once more; she died when he was seven years old.

In 1825, Frederick was sent to live at the Baltimore home of Hugh and Sophia Auld. Sophia, a religious woman, began to teach Bailey (not yet known as Douglass) to read—until she was abruptly forbidden to continue the lessons by her husband, who believed that teaching a slave to read and write was too dangerous. Douglass quickly realized that literacy was a powerful tool for gaining his freedom.

In 1838, after laboring at various plantations and in a Baltimore shipyard, Douglass decided to flee north to New York City. Through the Underground Railroad, Douglass and his wife then moved further north to New Bedford, Massachusetts. To further protect himself from bounty hunters looking for runaway slaves, Frederick Bailey changed his name to Frederick Douglass. In 1845, he published the autobiographical *Narrative of the Life of Frederick Douglass, an American Slave,* which quickly became a bestseller.

During the Civil War, Douglass met several times with President Abraham Lincoln. After the Civil War, Douglass was perhaps the most important black advocate for equal rights and suffrage (the right to vote) in America. Douglass died in Washington, D.C., on February 20, 1895.

Source: From *Narrative of the Life of Frederick Douglass, an American Slave* by Frederick Douglass (1818–1895).

At the close of the year 1834, Mr. Freeland again hired me of my master, for the year 1835. But, by this time, I began to want to live ~ *upon free land* ~ as well as ~ *with freeland;* ~ and I was no longer content, therefore, to live with him or any other slave-holder. I began, with the commencement of the year, to prepare myself for a final struggle, which should decide my fate one way or the other. My tendency was upward. I was fast approaching manhood, and year after year had passed, and I was still a slave. These thoughts roused me—I must do something. I therefore resolved that 1835 should not pass without witnessing an attempt, on my part, to secure my liberty. But I was not willing to cherish this determination alone. My fellow-slaves were dear to me. I was anxious to have them participate with me in this, my life-giving determination. I therefore, though with great prudence, commenced early to ascertain their views and feelings in regard to their condition, and to imbue their minds with thoughts of freedom. I bent myself to devising ways and means for our escape, and meanwhile strove, on all fitting occasions, to impress them with the gross fraud and inhumanity of slavery. I went first to Henry, next to John, then to the others. I found, in them all, warm hearts and noble spirits. They were ready to hear, and ready to act when a feasible plan should be proposed. This was what I wanted. I talked to them of our want of manhood, if we submitted to our enslavement without at least one noble effort to be free. We met often, and consulted frequently, and told our hopes and fears, recounted the difficulties, real and imagined, which we should be called on to meet. At times we were almost disposed to give up, and try to content ourselves with our wretched lot; at others, we were firm and unbending in our determination to go. Whenever we suggested any plan, there was shrinking—the odds were fearful. Our path was beset with the greatest obstacles; and if we succeeded in gaining the end of it, our right to be free was yet questionable—we were yet liable to be returned to bondage. We could see no spot, this side of the ocean, where we could be free. We knew nothing about Canada. Our knowledge of the north did not extend farther than New York; and to go there, and be forever harassed with the frightful liability of being returned to slavery—with the certainty of being treated tenfold worse than before—the thought was truly a horrible one, and one which it was not easy to overcome. The case sometimes stood thus: At every gate through which we were to pass, we saw a watchman—at every ferry a guard—on every bridge a sentinel—and in every wood a patrol. We were hemmed in upon every side. Here were the difficulties, real or imagined—the good to be sought, and the evil to be shunned. On the one hand, there stood slavery, a stern reality, glaring frightfully upon us,—its robes already crimsoned with the blood of millions, and even now feasting itself greedily upon our own flesh. On the other hand, away back in the dim distance, under the flickering light of the north star, behind some craggy hill or snow-covered mountain, stood a doubtful freedom—half frozen—beckoning us to come and share its hospitality. This in itself was sometimes enough to stagger us; but when we permitted ourselves to survey the road, we were frequently appalled. Upon either side we saw grim death, assuming the most horrid shapes. Now it was starvation, causing us to eat our own flesh;—now we were contending with the waves, and were drowned;—now we were overtaken, and torn to pieces by the fangs of the terrible bloodhound. We were stung by scorpions, chased by wild beasts, bitten by snakes, and finally, after having nearly reached the desired spot,—after swimming rivers, encountering wild beasts, sleeping in the woods, suffering hunger and nakedness,—we were overtaken by our pursuers, and, in our resistance, we were shot dead upon the spot! I say, this picture sometimes appalled us, and made us

> rather bear those ills we had,
> Than fly to others, that we knew not of.

In coming to a fixed determination to run away, we did more than Patrick Henry, when he resolved upon liberty or death. With us it was a doubtful liberty at most, and almost certain death if we failed. For my part, I should prefer death to hopeless bondage.

Sandy, one of our number, gave up the notion, but still encouraged us. Our company then consisted of Henry Harris, John Harris, Henry Bailey, Charles Roberts, and myself. Henry Bailey was my uncle, and belonged to my master. Charles married my aunt: he belonged to my master's father-in-law, Mr. William Hamilton.

The plan we finally concluded upon was, to get a large canoe belonging to Mr. Hamilton, and upon the Saturday night previous to Easter holidays, paddle directly up the Chesapeake Bay. On our arrival at the head of the bay, a distance of seventy or eighty miles from where we lived, it was our purpose to turn our canoe adrift, and follow the guidance of the north star till we got beyond the limits of Maryland. Our reason for taking the water route was, that we were less liable to be suspected as runaways; we hoped to be regarded as fishermen; whereas, if we should take the land route, we should be subjected to interruptions of almost every kind. Any one having a white face, and being so disposed, could stop us, and subject us to examination.

5   The week before our intended start, I wrote several protections, one for each of us. As well as I can remember, they were in the following words, to wit:—

"This is to certify that I, the undersigned, have given the bearer, my servant, full liberty to go to Baltimore, and spend the Easter holidays. Written with mine own hand, & c., 1835."

WILLIAM HAMILTON,

"Near St. Michael's, in Talbot county, Maryland."

We were not going to Baltimore; but, in going up the bay, we went toward Baltimore, and these protections were only intended to protect us while on the bay.

As the time drew near for our departure, our anxiety became more and more intense. It was truly a matter of life and death with us. The strength of our determination was about to be fully tested. At this time, I was very active in explaining every difficulty, removing every doubt, dispelling every fear, and inspiring all with the firmness indispensable to success in our undertaking; assuring them that half was gained the instant we made the move; we had talked long enough; we were now ready to move; if not now, we never should be; and if we did not intend to move now, we had as well fold our arms, sit down, and acknowledge ourselves fit only to be slaves. This, none of us were prepared to acknowledge. Every man stood firm; and at our last meeting, we pledged ourselves afresh, in the most solemn manner, that, at the time appointed, we would certainly start in pursuit of freedom. This was in the middle of the week, at the end of which we were to be off. We went, as usual, to our several fields of labor, but with bosoms highly agitated with thoughts of our truly hazardous undertaking. We tried to conceal our feelings as much as possible; and I think we succeeded very well.

After a painful waiting, the Saturday morning, whose night was to witness our departure, came. I hailed it with joy, bring what of sadness it might. Friday night was a sleepless one for me. I probably felt more anxious than the rest, because I was, by common consent, at the head of the whole affair. The responsibility of success or failure lay heavily upon me. The glory of the one, and the confusion of the other, were alike mine. The first two hours of that morning were such as I never experienced before, and hope never to again. Early in the morning, we went, as usual, to the field. We were spreading manure; and all at once, while thus engaged, I was overwhelmed with an indescribable feeling, in the fulness of which I turned to Sandy, who was near by, and said, "We are betrayed!" "Well," said he, "that thought has this moment struck me." We said no more. I was never more certain of any thing.

The horn was blown as usual, and we went up from the field to the house for breakfast. I went for the form, more than for want of any thing to eat that morning. Just as I got to the house, in looking out at the lane gate, I saw four white men, with two colored men. The white men were on horseback, and the colored ones were walking behind, as if tied. I watched them a few moments till they got up to our lane gate. Here they halted, and tied the colored men to the gate-post. I was not yet certain as to what the matter was. In a few moments, in rode Mr. Hamilton, with a speed betokening great excitement. He came to the door, and inquired if Master William was in. He was told he was at the barn. Mr. Hamilton, without dismounting, rode up to the barn with extraordinary speed. In a few moments, he and Mr. Freeland returned to the house. By this time, the three constables rode up, and in great haste dismounted, tied their horses, and met Master William and Mr. Hamilton returning from the barn; and after talking awhile, they all walked up to the kitchen door. There was no one in the kitchen but myself and John. Henry and Sandy were up at the barn. Mr. Freeland put his head in at the door, and called me by name, saying, there were some gentlemen at the door who wished to see me. I stepped to the door, and inquired what they wanted. They at once seized me, and, without giving me any satisfaction, tied me—lashing my hands closely together. I insisted upon knowing what the matter was. They at length said, that they had learned I had been in a "scrape," and that I was to be examined before my master; and if their information proved false, I should not be hurt.

[Douglass and his companions were caught, jailed, and released to their owners.]

QUESTIONS FOR READING ACTIVELY

1. Frederick Douglass and many other nineteenth-century abolitionist writers used biblical metaphors to describe the experience of slavery and the quest for freedom. (In the next chapter, on page 185, you'll see how Martin Luther King, Jr., also uses biblical imagery to describe the moral imperative for civil rights.) How effective are the religious images and allusions that Douglass makes? (Some of these allusions are quite subtle; for example, his use of the word *betrayed* in paragraph 8.) What does this language suggest about Douglass's audience?

2. In this excerpt, Douglass describes at least one major decision that he makes. Describe, in your own words, one such decision. What steps did he take before making a commitment to that decision? Which factors were most important to him in making that decision?

QUESTIONS FOR THINKING CRITICALLY

1. Throughout his *Narrative*, Douglass emphasizes the power of literacy. Would Douglass and Malcolm X (page 170 in Chapter 6) share a common definition of *literacy*?

2. To inspire his close friends and fellow slaves at the Freeland home, Douglass "talked to them of our want of manhood, if we submitted to our enslavement without at least one noble effort to be free." What does he mean? What is a "noble effort to be free," and have you ever made such an effort? Are *you* truly "free" to make decisions about how you live your life?

QUESTION FOR WRITING THOUGHTFULLY

1. In academic writing, students are often discouraged from using the first person in making an argument. How would the impact of Douglass's argument be affected if he had written in the third person? When is one person's experience enough for an argument to be completely authoritative and effective?

The Doping Dilemma
by Michael Shermer

For a competitive cyclist, there is nothing more physically crushing and psychologically demoralizing than getting dropped by your competitors on a climb. With searing lungs and burning legs, your body hunches over the handlebars as you struggle to stay with the leader. You know all too well that once you come off the back of the pack the drive to push harder is gone—and with it any hope for victory.

I know the feeling because it happened to me in 1985 on the long climb out of Albuquerque during the 3,000-mile, nonstop transcontinental Race Across America. On the outskirts of town I had caught up with the second-place rider (and eventual winner), Jonathan Boyer, a svelte road racer who was the first American to compete in the Tour de France. About halfway up the leg-breaking climb, that familiar wave of crushing fatigue swept through my legs as I gulped for oxygen in my struggle to hang on.

To no avail. By the top of the climb Boyer was a tiny dot on the shimmering blacktop, and I didn't see him again until the finish line in Atlantic City. Later that night Jim Lampley, the commentator for ABC's Wide World of Sports, asked what else I might have done to go faster.

"I should have picked better parents," I deadpanned. We all have certain genetic limitations, I went on, that normal training cannot overcome. What else could I have done?

Plenty, and I knew it. Cyclists on the 1984 U.S. Olympic cycling team had told me how they had injected themselves with extra blood before races, either their own—drawn earlier in the season—or that of someone else with the same blood type. "Blood doping," as the practice is called, was not banned at the time, and on a sliding moral scale it seemed only marginally distinguishable from training at high altitude. Either

Source: http://www.scientificamerican.com/article.cfm?id=the-doping-dilemma.

way, you increase the number of oxygen-carrying red blood cells in your body. Still, I was already 30 years old and had an academic career to fall back on. I was racing bikes mostly to see how far I could push my body before it gave out. Enhancing my performance artificially didn't mesh well with my reasons for racing.

But suppose I had been 20 and earning my living through cycling, my one true passion, with no prospects for some other career. Imagine that my team had made performance-enhancing drugs part of its "medical program" and that I knew I could be cut if I was not competitive. Finally, assume I believed that most of my competitors were doping and that the ones who were tested almost never got caught.

That scenario, in substance, is what many competitive cyclists say they have been facing since the early 1990s. And although the details differ for other sports such as baseball, the overall doping circumstances are not dissimilar. Many players are convinced that "everyone else" takes drugs and so have come to believe that they cannot remain competitive if they do not participate. On the governance side, the failure of Major League Baseball to make the rules clear, much less to enforce them with extensive drug testing throughout the season, coupled with its historical tendency to look the other way, has created an environment conducive to doping.

Naturally, most of us do not want to believe that any of these stellar athletes are guilty of doping. But the convergence of evidence leads me to conclude that in cycling, as well as in baseball, football, and track and field, most of the top competitors of the past two decades have been using performance-enhancing drugs. The time has come to ask not if but why. The reasons are threefold: first, better drugs, drug cocktails and drug-training regimens; second, an arms race consistently won by drug takers over drug testers; and third, a shift in many professional sports that has tipped the balance of incentives in favor of cheating and away from playing by the rules.

Gaming Sports

Game theory is the study of how players in a game choose strategies that will maximize their return in anticipation of the strategies chosen by the other players. The "games" for which the theory was invented are not just gambling games such as poker or sporting contests in which tactical decisions play a major role; they also include deadly serious affairs in which people make economic choices, military decisions and even national diplomatic strategies. What all those "games" have in common is that each player's "moves" are analyzed according to the range of options open to the other players.

The game of prisoner's dilemma is the classic example: You and your partner are arrested for a crime, and you are held incommunicado in separate prison cells. Of course, neither of you wants to confess or rat on the other, but the D.A. gives each of you the following options:

1. If you confess but the other prisoner does not, you go free and he gets three years in jail.
2. If the other prisoner confesses and you do not, you get three years and he goes free.
3. If you both confess, you each get two years.
4. If you both remain silent, you each get a year.

The table below, called the game matrix, summarizes the four outcomes:

PRISONER'S DILEMMA	MY OPPONENT'S STRATEGY	
	COOPERATE [remain silent]	DEFECT [confess]
MY STRATEGY COOPERATE [remain silent]	One year in jail [High Payoff]	Three years in jail [Sucker Payoff]
DEFECT [confess]	No jail time [Temptation Payoff]	Two years in jail [Low Payoff]

With those outcomes, the logical choice is to defect from the advance agreement and betray your partner. Why? Consider the choices from the first prisoner's point of view. The only thing the first prisoner cannot control about the outcome is the second prisoner's choice. Suppose the second prisoner remains silent. Then the first prisoner earns the "temptation" payoff (zero years in jail) by confessing but gets a year in jail (the "high" payoff) by remaining silent. The better outcome in this case for the first prisoner is to confess. But suppose, instead, that the second prisoner confesses. Then, once again, the first prisoner is better off confessing (the "low" payoff, or two years in jail) than remaining silent (the "sucker" payoff, or three years in jail). Because the circumstances from the second prisoner's point of view are entirely symmetrical to the ones described for the first, each prisoner is better off confessing no matter what the other prisoner decides to do.

Those preferences are not only theoretical. When test subjects play the game just once or for a fixed number of rounds without being allowed to communicate, defection by confessing is the common strategy. But when testers play the game for an unknown number of rounds, the most common strategy is tit-for-tat: each begins cooperating by remaining silent, then mimics whatever the other player does. Even more mutual cooperation can emerge in many-person prisoner's dilemma, provided the players are allowed to play long enough to establish mutual trust. But the research shows that once defection by confessing builds momentum, it cascades throughout the game.

In cycling, as in baseball and other sports, the contestants compete according to a set of rules. The rules of cycling clearly prohibit the use of performance-enhancing drugs. But because the drugs are so effective and many of them are so difficult (if not impossible) to detect, and because the payoffs for success are so great, the incentive to use banned substances is powerful. Once a few elite riders "defect" from the rules (cheat) by doping to gain an advantage, their rule-abiding competitors must defect as well, leading to a cascade of defection through the ranks. Because of the penalties for breaking the rules, however, a code of silence prevents any open communication about how to reverse the trend and return to abiding by the rules.

It was not ever thus. Many riders took stimulants and painkillers from the 1940s through the 1980s. But doping regulations were virtually nonexistent until Tom Simpson, a British rider, died while using amphetamines on the climb up Mont Ventoux in the 1967 Tour de France. Even after Simpson's death, doping controls in the 1970s and 1980s were spotty at best. With no clear sense of what counted as following the rules, few perceived doping as cheating. In the 1990s, though, something happened to alter the game matrix.

The EPO Elixir

That "something" was genetically engineered recombinant erythropoietin: r-EPO. Ordinary EPO is a hormone that occurs naturally in the body. The kidneys release it into the bloodstream, which carries it to receptors in the bone marrow. When EPO molecules bind to those receptors, the marrow pumps out more red blood cells. Chronic kidney disease and chemotherapy can cause anemia, and so the development of the EPO substitute r-EPO in the late 1980s proved to be a boon to chronically anemic patients—and to chronically competitive athletes.

Taking r-EPO is just as effective as getting a blood transfusion, but instead of hassling with bags of blood and long needles that must be poked into a vein, the athlete can store tiny ampoules of r-EPO on ice in a thermos bottle or hotel minifridge, then simply inject the hormone under the skin. The effect of r-EPO that matters most to the competitor is directly measurable: the hematocrit (HCT) level, or the percentage by volume of red blood cells in the blood. More red blood cells translate to more oxygen carried to the muscles. For men, the normal HCT percentage range is in the mid-40s. Trained endurance athletes can naturally sustain their HCT in the high 40s or low 50s. EPO can push those levels into the high 50s and even the 60s. The winner of the 1996 Tour de France, Bjarne Riis, was nicknamed Mr. 60 Percent; last year he confessed that he owed his extraordinary HCT level to r-EPO.

The drug appears to have made its way into professional cycling in the early 1990s. Greg LeMond thinks it was 1991. Having won the Tour de France in 1986, 1989 and 1990, LeMond set his sights on breaking what would then have been a record of five Tour de France victories, and in the spring of 1991 he was poised to take his fourth. "I was the fittest I had ever been, my split times in spring training rides were the fastest of my career, and I had assembled a great team around me," LeMond told me. "But something was different in the 1991 Tour. There were riders from previous years who couldn't stay on my wheel who were now dropping me on even modest climbs."

LeMond finished seventh in that Tour, vowing to himself that he could win clean the next year. It was not to be. In 1992, he continued, "our [team's] performance was abysmal, and I couldn't even finish the race." Nondoping cyclists were burning out trying to keep up with their doping competitors. LeMond recounted a story told to him by one of his teammates at the time, Philippe Casado. Casado learned from a rider named Laurent Jalabert, who was racing for the Spanish cycling team ONCE, that Jalabert's personal doping program was entirely organized by the ONCE team. That program, LeMond said, included r-EPO, which LeMond refused to take, thereby consigning himself to another DNF ("did not finish") in 1994, his final race.

Some who did go along with the pressure to dope paid an even higher price. Casado, for instance, left LeMond's team to join one that had a doping program—and died suddenly in 1995 at age 30. Whether his death resulted directly from doping is not known, but when HCT reaches around 60 percent and higher, the blood becomes so thick that clots readily form. The danger is particularly high when the heart rate slows during sleep—and the resting heart rates of endurance athletes are renowned for measuring in the low 30s (in beats per minute). Two champion Dutch riders died of heart attacks after experimenting with r-EPO. Some riders reportedly began sleeping with a heart-rate monitor hooked to an alarm that would sound when their pulse dropped too low.

Trapped in an Arms Race

Just as in evolution there is an arms race between predators and prey, in sports there is an arms race between drug takers and drug testers. In my opinion, the testers are five years away from catching the takers—and always will be. Those who stand to benefit most from cheating will always be more creative than those enforcing the rules, unless the latter have equivalent incentives. In 1997, because there was no test for r-EPO (that would not come until 2001), the Union Cycliste International (UCI), the sport's governing body, set an HCT limit for men of 50 percent. Shortly afterward, riders figured out that they could go higher than 50, then thin their blood at test time with a technique already allowed and routinely practiced: injections of saline water for rehydration. Presto change-o.

Willy Voet, the *soigneur,* or all-around caretaker, for the Festina cycling team in the 1990s, explained how he beat the testers in his tell-all book, *Breaking the Chain:*

> Just in case the UCI doctors arrived in the morning to check the riders' hematocrit levels, I got everything ready to get them through the tests....I went up to the cyclists' rooms with sodium drips....The whole transfusion would take twenty minutes, the saline diluting the blood and so reducing the hematocrit level by three units—just enough.
>
> This contraption took no more than two minutes to set up, which meant we could put it into action while the UCI doctors waited for the riders to come down from their rooms.

How did the new rules of the doping game change the players' strategies? I put the question directly to Joe Papp, a 32-year-old professional cyclist currently banned after testing positive for synthetic testosterone. Recalling the day he was handed the "secret black bag," Papp explained how a moral choice becomes an economic decision: "When you join a team with an organized doping program in place, you are simply given the drugs and a choice: take them to keep up or don't take them and there is a good chance you will not have a career in cycling."

When Papp came clean, professional cycling slapped him with a two-year ban. But the social consequences were far worse than that. "The sport spit me out," he lamented to me. "A team becomes a band of brothers,...but with a team of dopers there's an additional bond—a shared secret—and with that there is a code of silence. If you get busted, you keep your mouth shut. The moment I confessed I was renounced by my friends because in their mind I put them at risk. One guy called and threatened to kill me if I revealed that he doped."

Papp was never a Tour-caliber cyclist, however, so perhaps the game matrix—with its implications for the rider's own cycling career—is different at the elite level. Not so, as I learned from another insider. "For years I had no trouble doing my job to help the team leader," said Frankie Andreu, who was the *superdomestique,* or lead pacer, supporting Lance Armstrong throughout much of the 1990s. "Then, around 1996, the speeds of the races shifted dramatically upward. Something happened, and it wasn't just training." Andreu resisted the temptation as long as he could, but by 1999 he could no longer do his job: "It became apparent to me that enough of the *peloton* [the main group of riders in a cycling race] was on the juice that I had to do something." He began injecting himself with r-EPO two to three times a week. "It's not like Red Bull, which gives you instant energy," he explained. "But it does allow you to dig a little deeper, to hang on to the group a little longer, to go maybe 31.5 miles per hour instead of 30 mph."

The Doping Difference

One of the subtle benefits of r-EPO in a brutal three-week race like the Tour de France is not just boosting HCT levels but keeping them high. Jonathan Vaughters, a former teammate of Armstrong's, crunched the numbers for me this way: "The big advantage of blood doping is the ability to keep a 44 percent HCT over three weeks." A "clean" racer who started with a 44 percent HCT, Vaughters noted, would expect to end up at 40 percent after three weeks of racing because of natural blood dilution and the breakdown of red blood cells. "Just stabilizing [your HCT level] at 44 percent is a 10 percent advantage."

Scientific studies on the effects of performance-enhancing drugs are few in number and are usually conducted on nonathletes or recreational ones, but they are consistent with Vaughters's assessment. (For obvious reasons, elite athletes who dope are disinclined to disclose their data.) The consensus among the sports physiologists I interviewed is that r-EPO improves performance by at least 5 to 10 percent. When it is mixed in with a brew of other drugs, another 5 to 10 percent boost can be squeezed out of the human engine. In events decided by differences of less than 1 percent, this advantage is colossal.

Italian sports physiologist Michele Ferrari, as knowledgeable on doping as he is controversial (because of his close affiliation with elite athletes who have tested positive for doping or been accused of same), explains it this way: "If the volume of [red blood cells] increases by 10 percent, performance [the rider's net gain in output of useful kinetic energy] improves by approximately 5 percent. This means a gain of about 1.5 seconds per kilometer for a cyclist pedaling at 50 kilometers per hour in a time trial, or about eight seconds per kilometer for a cyclist climbing at 10 kph on a 10 percent ascent."

In the Tour de France, those numbers imply that a cyclist who boosts his HCT by 10 percent will cut his own time by 75 seconds in a 50-kilometer (31-mile) time trial, a race typically decided by a few seconds. On any of the numerous 10-kilometer (six-mile) climbs in the Alps and the Pyrenees, on grades as steep as 10 percent, that same blood difference would gain the rider a whopping 80 seconds per climb. If any of the top cyclists are on the juice, their erstwhile competitors cannot afford to give away such margins. That is where the game matrix kicks into defection mode.

Nash Equilibrium

In game theory, if no player has anything to gain by unilaterally changing strategies, the game is said to be in a Nash equilibrium. The concept was identified by mathematician John Forbes Nash, Jr., who was portrayed in the film *A Beautiful Mind*. To end doping in sports, the doping game must be restructured so that competing clean is in a Nash equilibrium.

That is, the governing bodies of each sport must change the payoff values of the expected outcomes identified in the game matrix. First, when other players are playing by the rules, the payoff for doing likewise must be greater than the payoff for cheating. Second, and perhaps more important, even when other players are cheating, the payoff for playing fair must be greater than the payoff for cheating. Players must not feel like suckers for following the rules.

In the game of prisoner's dilemma, lowering the temptation to confess and raising the payoff for keeping silent if the other prisoner confesses increases cooperation. Giving players the chance to communicate before they play the game is the most effective way to increase their cooperation. In sports, that means breaking the code of silence. Everyone must acknowledge there is a problem to be solved. Then drug testing must be done and the results communicated regularly and transparently to all until the test results are clean. That will show each player that the payoff for playing fair is greater than the payoff for cheating, no matter what the other players do.

Here are my recommendations for how cycling (and other sports) can reach a Nash equilibrium in which no one has any incentive to cheat by doping:

1. Grant immunity to all athletes for past (pre-2008) cheating. Because the entire system is corrupt and most competitors have been doping, it accomplishes nothing to strip the winner of a title after the fact when it is almost certain that the runners-up were also doping. With immunity, retired athletes may help to improve the antidoping system.

2. Increase the number of competitors tested—in competition, out of competition, and especially immediately before or after a race—to thwart countermeasures. Testing should be done by independent drug agencies not affiliated with any sanctioning bodies, riders, sponsors or teams. Teams should also employ independent drug-testing companies to test their own riders, starting with a preseason performance test on each athlete to create a baseline profile. Corporate sponsors should provide additional financial support to make sure the testing is rigorous.

3. Establish a reward, modeled on the X prizes (cash awards offered for a variety of technical achievements), for scientists to develop tests that can detect currently undetectable doping agents. The incentive for drug testers must be equal to or greater than that for drug takers.

4. Increase substantially the penalty for getting caught: one strike and you're out—forever. To protect the athlete from false positive results or inept drug testers (both exist), the system of arbitration and appeals must be fair and trusted. Once a decision is made, however, it must be substantive and final.

5. Disqualify all team members from an event if any member of the team tests positive for doping. Compel the convicted athlete to return all salary paid and prize monies earned to the team sponsors. The threat of this penalty will bring the substantial social pressures of "band of brothers" psychology to bear on all the team members, giving them a strong incentive to enforce their own antidoping rules.

That may sound utopian. But it can work. Vaughters, who is now director of the U.S. cycling team Slipstream/Chipotle, has already started a program of extensive and regular in-house drug testing. "Remember, most of these guys are athletes, not criminals," he says. "If they believe the rest are stopping [the doping] and feel it in the speed of the peloton, they will stop, too, with a great sigh of relief."

Hope springs eternal. But with these changes I believe the psychology of the game can be shifted from defection to cooperation. If so, sports can return to the tradition of rewarding and celebrating excellence in performance, enhanced only by an athlete's will to win.

QUESTIONS FOR READING ACTIVELY

1. In his essay, Shermer details a compelling argument for ending the practice of doping. How does he construct and support his argument? Which parts of his argument are the most convincing and why? How has Shermer incorporated research into his essay?

2. In paragraph 8, Shermer writes, "The time has come to ask not if but why" in regard to the top competitors in several popular sports using performance-enhancing drugs. Is this point central to his argument? Why is it no longer useful to ask *if*? As a reader, does knowing *why* help support this argument?

QUESTIONS FOR THINKING CRITICALLY

1. Part of Shermer's argument centers around understanding game theory, and he used the prisoner's dilemma to show how people choose strategies that will "maximize their return in anticipation of the strategies chosen by the other players." Aside from the examples in this essay (doping and the prisoner's dilemma), what might be another real-world example where game theory plays a role?

2. In Shermer's recommendations for how cycling "can reach a Nash equilibrium," he encourages the disqualification of *everyone* on a team if just one team member is caught doping. Even if, hypothetically, a mandate like this might help end the practice of doping, is this fair to everyone else on the team if they are not doping? What are some of the complications that might arise from this rule?

QUESTIONS FOR THOUGHTFUL WRITING

1. Analyze the structure of Shermer's essay, and describe how he introduces his topic, presents evidence, discusses counterpoints, and arrives at a conclusion. Are there sections of the essay where too much (or not enough) information is presented to convince you that the practice of doping must end? Point out those sections, and describe what information you felt was excessive (or missing).

2. Think of another current social problem, and describe it in one paragraph. Next, what is the average person's role in aiding or ending this problem? In your second paragraph, explore the average person's role in regard to the decisions he or she may or may not make—decisions that can affect the outcome of or solution to the problem.

NEW MEDIA & THOUGHTFUL WRITING

Issues with Communication

New media have created a rapidly expanding universe of possibilities, and with this expansion comes the need to expand one's critical thinking abilities to successfully navigate our way through unfamiliar terrain.

In this section, we are going to briefly consider the way new media have affected our relationships with others. As is obvious, online communication has greatly expanded the frequency of our contact with others, as well as the number of people with whom we are in touch. But with this ease of communication have come new challenges as well. For example, how many times have you regretted impulsively pressing the "send" button on a message written in the heat of the moment? For most of us, this is an all too frequent occurrence. As a rule of thumb, it's often a good idea to delay sending our composed message until we've had an opportunity to let things settle and review it with fresh vision. This also goes for important messages we send, professional or otherwise. We can almost always improve the content and clarity of our message by giving ourselves time to think about it for a while. It's helpful to recognize also that emailing and text messaging can sometimes encourage a weakening of our inhibitions or internal censors, emboldening us to write things that we would probably not say in person. Again, making a practice of revisiting our message before sending it will doubtless save us from those next-day "How could I?" moments. And, finally, we should always remind ourselves that email and text messages are usually stripped down to the essentials, lacking the rich context that is provided when we are speaking to someone. Without our tone of voice, body language, or detailed articulation, the words and tone are often ambiguous, a situation that can easily lead to misunderstandings. Just because *we* know what we intend to say doesn't mean that the other person will interpret it in the same way. So when sending significant communications via new media, the watchword is "Handle with care." Make the time and effort to say precisely what you intend in a way that leaves minimal chance that the recipient will take it any other way.

Analogously, social networking sites like Facebook and MySpace have opened up a Pandora's box of trouble. These sites provide the unprecedented opportunity for individuals to create a "virtual self," building records of their social identities via descriptions, comments, photographs, and music. In addition to serving as powerful models of social communication, such public displays of private information play to the twin human impulses of showmanship and voyeurism. But problems arise when the "wrong" people visit our site and learn things about us we would never want them to know. For example, 30 percent of today's employers are using Facebook to check out potential employees prior to hiring! There are a number of ways to protect yourself from embarrassment, whether it's an employer, your parent, or your romantic partner. To begin with, you can think carefully about what you post on the site and also exercise care in who you invite to have access. Too often items are posted or people are invited without any consideration of future consequences and complications. Additionally, you can create lists of people in different categories—for example, professional, family, close friends, casual friends—and then regulate who gets to see what through the site's settings. It may seem like a bother, but in the long run you will likely be thankful you took the time to take these basic precautions.

Thinking-Writing Activity

FACEBOOK TROUBLESHOOTING

Sometimes it's easier to detect problems that others face than to view our own potential problems. With this in mind, work with a group of friends to identify potential trouble spots (inappropriate disclosures, incriminating photographs). Once you have compiled the areas of concern, devise strategies for erasing the problems and avoiding similar difficulties in the future. In this regard, you might develop a list of criteria or "ground rules" to guide you in your posting and also strategies for organizing your page to head off problems before they occur.

Thinking-Writing Activity

PREPARING FOR DECISIONS

1. Make a list of whatever important decisions in your academic or personal life you have to make now or will have to make in the near future.

2. Select one decision, and apply the five-step decision-making method that begins on page 132. As you think through your decision, be sure to identify all your possible choices and to follow your thoughts wherever they lead.

There are no guarantees in life. Our decisions may or may not turn out well. Still, following an organized method for making decisions can at least assure us of having explored and evaluated many possible choices and then having selected the one that seemed to best meet our needs. In other words, we will know that we made the best decision that we could have at the time.

Writing Project

ANALYZING A DECISION TO BE MADE

This chapter includes both readings and Thinking-Writing Activities that encourage you to reflect on drafting and decision making. Be sure to reread what you wrote for those activities; you may be able to use your responses to complete this project.

Project Overview and Requirements

For this essay, you will analyze a decision you must make now or in the near future. Be sure to select a decision for which you already have considerable information or want to obtain more. Include all five steps of the decision-making method beginning on page 132. Once your draft is complete, you will revise it to the best of your abilities.

THE WRITING SITUATION

For this project, consider the key elements of the Thinking-Writing Model detailed below (and also found on pages 5–8 in Chapter 1).

Purpose   Use this opportunity to work through an important real-life decision to obtain the best possible outcome. If others will be involved in or affected by this decision, your paper can show them your best thinking about it, making them more likely to agree with your decision. Practice the creative and critical thinking involved in the five-step decision-making method, and be sure to carefully work through the revision process.

Audience   An essay about a decision implies at least two potential audiences. In describing a decision you made and the process of making that decision, you could be writing for people who are faced with similar circumstances or a closely related predicament. For example, perhaps you are considering moving to a new city or country with many unknowns and risks, as Frederick Douglass did. Through describing your commitment to a decision, even at its most difficult, you can inspire people who have to make a similar decision.

Subject   Decisions can be challenging to think about and difficult to make. Sometimes we haven't enough information to make an intelligent choice; sometimes we *think* we know what the right decision is yet are reluctant to actually make it. Therefore, we often tend to put off decision making for as long as possible. Keep in mind that not making a decision is, in a way, making a decision to do nothing. For this assignment, try to identify a decision that will have significant consequences. It may be what area to major in, whether to get a part-time job, whether to participate in a sport or other extracurricular activity, or whether to get a dog. The more significant the decision, the more helpful this assignment will be to you.

Writer   You approach this Writing Project as the expert on the subject, since you are analyzing one of your own decisions. One challenge here is to distinguish between your own expertise about the decision-making situation and your audience's need for enough background and information. Another challenge is to focus on the material provided earlier in this chapter because this assignment moves away from *recollecting experience* and asks you to apply the decision-making process to a decision you need to make soon.

For example, Michael Shermer demonstrates his knowledge of game theory, and uses striking examples and compelling reasoning to analyze the complex, ethical facets of doping in sports.

Now that you have given some thought to purpose, audience, subject, and writer, work through the following four questions to analyze a decision you must make. You may also want to look back at your responses to the Thinking-Writing Activities earlier in this chapter for inspiration. After you have your thoughts in writing, it will be easier to move on to The Writing Process, which includes more ways to generate ideas.

1. Describe the real-life decision you would like to make in one or two clear sentences. Here is one writer's description:

   I have the opportunity to start my own business. I am torn, however, between the excitement and potential of this new venture and my current salaried position that offers security and important benefits like health insurance.

2. List and describe people who may be interested in the analysis of the decision you must make (your audience). For example:

   My wife, of course, and my father—who moved in with us a few years ago due to failing health—are the people who would be most interested in my decision to either start my own business or stick with my current career. Both are supportive of whichever path I choose, but I want to be sure they both see that I have given this decision a lot of thought. I also want to be sure my decision does not have a negative effect on our finances and quality of life—especially now that I am taking care of my father. My sister, whom I would employ if I opened the new business, would be interested in my analysis as well. I also think that anyone in a similar situation might be interested in the way I plan to weigh the pros and cons of each option in order to make the smartest choice possible.

3. Is there any additional information you will likely need to make your decision? For example:

   I would like to start my own landscaping business, and although there appears to be a growing demand for these services, I would like to investigate this assumption. I also want to check into the types of permits or licenses I would have to obtain, equipment (cost and depreciation), and so on. I also want to find out how other landscaping businesses operate and the profits they make.

4. Once you make your decision, there is still work to be done. Now you will need to implement a plan of action. In a sentence or two, explain your plan of action and how you might need to make adjustments.

> If I choose to stay in my current position, I won't need a plan of action. If I choose to start my own business, I will need to put together a business plan, approach the bank for financing, decide how to best market my new business, build a customer database, and more. I am an organized person and feel comfortable creating schedules, time lines, and databases. These tools will help me see where adjustments might need to be made as I work to grow the business.

THE WRITING PROCESS

The following sections will guide you through the stages of generating, planning, drafting, and revising as you work on an essay about making a decision.

Generating Ideas   Try to be particularly conscious of both the creative and the critical thinking you do while making your decision and the critical thinking and decision making you do as you refine your writing. The following steps will help you come up with ideas and focus:

1. Is there a decision you must make in the near future? If so, you can accomplish two important things at once: writing your paper and making your decision.

2. Think about how much additional information you would need to evaluate possible choices for this decision. Do you have enough time to locate and absorb this information and still meet your deadline for this project?

3. Describe the decision-making situation and your goals as clearly as you can.

4. Now that you have defined the decision you need to make, brainstorm as many possible options as possible. Ask others involved in the decision to help.

5. Eliminate choices that you know are impractical or undesirable.

6. Determine what information you must find for each remaining choice. Locate that information.

7. Write each choice on a separate sheet of paper. Then divide the paper into two columns: pros and cons. Write as much as you can in each column.

8. For each column, freewrite for five minutes on what would happen and how you would feel if you selected that choice.

9. Freewrite for five minutes on how you would know if any given choice was the right one.

Defining a Focus   Write a tentative thesis statement that clarifies your decision-making situation. You might write something like "After thinking about the situation carefully, I realize that I have only two possible choices." Or you might "blueprint" your paper by naming the possible choices: "My choices for housing next year come down to these three: living with my aunt, sharing an apartment with my friend, or looking for a live-in job situation." You may even decide to announce your decision in your thesis statement: "After carefully weighing my options, I have decided to major in business administration." Or you may find a more creative way to state your thesis.

Organizing Ideas   The five-step method for making decisions fits well with essay structure. Your description of the decision-making situation might be the beginning of an introduction, to be completed by your thesis statement. You could include your goals in the introduction or state them in a separate paragraph. Each of the potential choices, explained in as much detail as possible along with the pros and cons of that choice, could serve as a body paragraph. Your decision as to the best choice and your plan for monitoring it could be the essay's conclusion.

Drafting   Begin with the easiest part to draft. Your description of the decision-making situation could begin the introduction, but consider what, if any, additional information your audience might need in order to understand the situation. The introduction can end with your tentative thesis statement.

In either your conclusion or your thesis statement, name the choice you have selected. You may want to explain why if you think your reason may not be obvious to your audience. Remember to explain how you will monitor the results of your decision.

Revising Your Essay: Analyzing a Decision to Be Made

Peer Response

One of the best revision strategies is to get an audience's reactions to your draft. Here are some questions to ask your peers about this assignment:

- What questions do you have about my decision-making situation and my goals?
- What questions do you have about the alternative choices I described? What else do you need to know about them? Can you suggest any others?
- Do you understand why I am making this decision?
- What could I add to clarify why this choice is best for me?

Armed with the information from peer review, you are now ready to begin revising by using the method presented in Chapter 6, starting on page 174. If possible, use the following directions for revising with a word processor.

Revision

For this strategy, you will be using a computer to revise your work by creating a series of files. This strategy will give you a complete record of your work so you can track how each draft changes.

1. Call your first draft Decision 1, and print and save it.

2. Create a new file called Decision 2 by copying and pasting the text you created in Decision 1. In this file, make changes to the draft as a whole using the answers you received during peer review and your own answers to the "Think Big" revision questions on page 174. Print and save this draft.

3. Consider the "Think Medium" revision questions to evaluate your individual paragraphs. Create a new file called Decision 3 by copying and pasting Decision 2. Then make whatever changes are suggested by your answers to the "Think Medium" questions on pages 174–175. Print and save this draft.

4. Consider the "Think Small" questions to evaluate your individual sentences. Create a new file called Decision 4 by copying and pasting Decision 3. Then make whatever changes are suggested by your answers to the "Think Small" questions on page 175. Print and save this draft.

5. Finally, consider the "Think 'Picky'" questions. Create a new file called Decision 5 by copying and pasting Decision 4. Then make whatever changes are suggested by your answers to the "Think 'Picky'" questions on pages 175–176. Run the spelling and grammar checking features of your word processing program, and use your judgment about which suggested changes to make. Print and save this draft. Decision 5 should present your very best work. It is now ready to be submitted to your instructor and any other audience you select.

Editing and Proofreading

Editing and proofreading are the final critical components of any solid piece of writing. In steps 4 and 5 above, you practiced just this by considering the "Think Small" questions, as well as the "Think Picky" questions. Your essay should now be completed to the best of your ability, and, of course, you will need to submit it to your instructor by the due date.

Since this essay is based on a decision you had to make, consider other possible audiences that may be interested in your work. Do you want to share your ideas with any of the people involved in your decision-making situation? For example, would members of your family or your close friends benefit by reading it? If your paper is about a decision that others must also make, such as selecting a major, perhaps your student newspaper would be interested in publishing it as a model of good decision making that others could emulate.

The following essays show how two students responded to this assignment.

STUDENT WRITING

Wendy Agudo's Writing Process

Wendy Agudo began to compose the following essay after a chance remark her philosophy professor made in class. Wendy had already completed the Thinking-Writing assignment on page 136, reflecting on her decision in junior high to overcome her learning disability and earn the high grades she would need to go to college and pursue a career in television journalism. The day after she completed that assignment, her philosophy professor told her class that the French philosopher Jean-Paul Sartre had said that we were "condemned to be free." Wendy began with a freewriting to sort out her feelings about how that quotation related to her own experience and then used the five steps to organized decision making (pages 137–139) to begin to plan her paper.

> *Jean-Paul Sartre "we are condemned to be free"—it wasn't anyone's fault, the accident. I don't blame my parents. I don't blame anyone, and they don't blame each other. It just happened. Moving to America when I was really little was probably the best thing they could have done for me. Back in Ecuador it would have been really hard for me to get the help I needed. But still I wouldn't have had to learn a new language, and mami and papa wouldn't have had to work so hard and leave me alone for so much time when I really needed them. I'm angry with Lidia because she doesn't even know how easy she has it. Lidia has always had the family support and the money and the time to do whatever she wants, but all she wants to do is sit around talking on her celly to her boy. We're at work together and we're on deadline and I'm trying to get her to shut up and pay attention and she just rolls her eyes and says something in Albanian over the phone. She has no respect but I can't be jealous, that's not right either. Does she think about where she'll be in two years? in ten years?*

> 1. *Define the decision. I decided not to let my brain injury get in the way of my goals.*
>
> 2. *Consider all possible choices. I didn't have a choice. Either I succeed or I fail. It's up to me.*
>
> 3. *Gather all relevant information and evaluate the pros and cons of each choice.*
>   - *I could have stayed in the remedial class in junior high. PRO—less work. CON—where would I be today?*
>   - *I could ignore Lidia and let her screw up. PRO—not having to confront Lidia. CON—it's my job to confront her and make sure she's learning skills. If I don't help her, then I fail at some level.*
>   - *I could let Lidia learn for herself. It worked for me. You need to take responsibility for your own life.*

4. *Select the choice that seems best suited to the situation.* I can't boss Lidia around. She needs to find out for herself what the consequences of her lack of responsibility will be. Besides she won't listen to me. I can be a better example for everyone in the peer training program if I just get my own work done and set a high standard for myself.

5. *Implement a plan of action.* I owe it to my parents and to myself to succeed. I can't get jealous of Lidia or let her own decisions make my own work look bad.

Freedom

by Wendy Agudo

It's funny how some people always seem to have an excuse for everything, refusing to take responsibility for their actions. All of us have, at some point, shrugged our shoulders and made an excuse for behavior we should have regretted, or at least apologized for—being late to meet a friend, not having an assignment completed on time, not visiting an elderly relative. But making these excuses implies that we are not really in control of our own lives. When we make an excuse for our behavior, we are really saying that some other force—a train conductor, the weather, a computer, whatever—has more control over our lives than we do. To make excuses is to place limits on the extent of your personal freedom.

I see this kind of refusal to take responsibility all the time at my job. I work as a peer trainer for a small non-profit television station, teaching other young people (high school through age 25) how to use field and studio digital cameras, digital and analog video editing, and media literacy. I was fortunate enough to begin this work at the age of 18, and now at the age of 20 I consider myself very skilled and motivated. Because of my experience in a professional environment, I tend to have high expectations for my peers in this training program, who are my own age and often a little older. When they are late for a meeting, or careless with their work, or would rather go out and have fun than stay late and edit a story, I am very disappointed. I hear excuses like "I have no time because of school," or "my family this" and "my intelligence that." I could come up with many more compelling excuses myself, but yet I don't.

I believe that we all make choices in life, and that there is no reason for failure or self-pity. Many factors have contributed to my sense of responsibility, my stubbornness, and my loyalty to my family. But the most significant challenge I have faced—and that I could use as an excuse, but don't—has to do with my health.

I was born in Ecuador. When I was two years old, I accidentally fell from the second-story window of my parents' house. I landed on a pile of broken concrete

Source: *Freedom* by Wendy Agudo.

Agudo sets up her essay by revealing her thoughts about excuses and how they limit one's freedom in her introductory paragraphs.

Next, Agudo introduces the decision she had to make.

and suffered brain damage, which the doctor said would be permanent. My parents could have allowed this to be a limit on my freedom, but they refused. I know I was too young to think this, but I do know that somewhere around this time I didn't allow myself to let this keep me down. As I grew I got better. It was my choice to continue and get past it.

Or maybe it was just luck.

My story doesn't have an accidentally happy ending. After I recovered from the fall there were still limitations. I was slow to walk and speak, and was dyslexic. Then, when I was four years old, my family immigrated to the United States. I was enrolled in an English-speaking public school. Between my difficulties in reading, walking, and speaking, I had to work three times as hard as anyone else just to keep up. I stuttered and had a lisp, so even when I did manage to speak English, other children teased me. Due to my dyslexia I had trouble focusing and concentrating, so I had trouble reading. Eventually I was afraid to read anything. I saw all of the other kids round me finishing with two books before I was able to get through even one. I was so discouraged that I wanted to give up.

This is another example of freedom of choice. I could have chosen to work harder, to study more, but I allowed outside circumstances—my disability—to make the choice for me. I gave up, but giving up was my own choice. It wasn't determined for me and it wasn't something I couldn't avoid. I chose to give up out of my own free will. And that choice had consequences. For many years I had very low grades and was passed from one "special" classroom to another.

At some point during junior high I realized that I wasn't going to get anywhere with such low grades. I worked harder and harder and eventually got better. I defeated the dyslexia, but it hasn't gone away. I still have dyslexia, but it doesn't control me. At least now it's something that doesn't hold me back. Eventually, I graduated from high school with honors, and I am now enrolled in college and earning "A" grades. Not bad for someone with a damaged brain!

This brings me back to the high expectations I have for other people in my peer training program. Due to the fact that I had to work so hard to develop myself, I also developed what I call high standards. I look at another peer trainer, whom I will call Lidia, as a comparison. Lidia is five months older than I am, and is also an immigrant. Her family came to the United States from Albania when she was four years old, just like me. Her parents are both doctors, and she was raised with many privileges. Although we both grew up in the same New York City neighborhood, our lives were very different. For my parents to get here from Ecuador, they had to make a dangerous and lonely journey across South America by car and on foot. We had no family in America to welcome us, and my parents had to work illegally in

Notice the challenges Agudo faced and how she presents them in a matter-of-fact way.

Agudo defines the choice (or decision) she faced.

Agudo evaluates the pros and cons of her decisions and provides a comparison to illustrate her point.

sweatshops for many years. But Lidia's parents joined a large family of uncles, aunts, and cousins, and her parents were able to begin practicing medicine again within a year or two of their arrival.

I have read that the environment you grow up in determines the kind of life you lead. I guess that, based on that evidence, I should have been a mother when I was still a teenager, and shouldn't have gone to college at all. But environment doesn't determine everything, and freedom to choose your own destiny isn't limited because of one or two aspects. Even in poverty, even in prison—even with a damaged brain!—you still have the freedom to choose to work hard and to make the best of your circumstances.

Lidia is always complaining at work. She takes fewer college classes than I do, and only works ten hours at the television station each week (I work 30 hours, sometimes more). Yet she is always late for meetings, loses track of equipment, and doesn't take her work assignments seriously. She assumes that everything will be easy for her, and doesn't realize that that complacency limits the choices she can make about her life. When things go wrong, she makes excuses—her car broke down, or she was out late the night before. She doesn't know how fortunate she is, and she'll never achieve as much as she could.

I believe that freedom is unlimited, and your life is determined by matters of choice. If you choose to give up, to accept less of yourself, then you will forever limit your choices and your freedom. But if you choose to continue, no matter what the obstacles, you will eventually achieve your goals. I may be disappointed in other people, but I have never been disappointed in myself. My family has sacrificed too much for me to come this far, and I will not let them down.

Agudo concludes her essay by reiterating her point that excuses limit personal freedom.

STUDENT WRITING

Cynthia Brown's Writing Process

Cynthia Brown's approach to this writing project exhibits those qualities of creativity, open-mindedness, knowledge, and curiosity that are the hallmarks of a critical thinker. Rather than writing about a specific decision, Cynthia reflected on a key factor—time—and how her relationship to time shaped all the major decisions she had made in her life. Cynthia drew on readings from her writing class and notes from her philosophy class to inform her essay.

When I moved to New York, I thought I was going to go insane. As much as I loved the city, I could not bear to live here. However, I came to New York to attend college and decided it would be best to allow myself time to make this decision based on rationale as opposed to emotion. I spent the next two years carefully analyzing and weighing my options. With the passage of time, I have come to the conclusion that I cannot live the kind of life I want to live as a student if I stay in New York. I decided to transfer, upon graduation from my current college, to a small liberal arts college in the middle of nowhere. I used time to help me explore my options instead of feeling trapped within its confines. This allowed me to move through the two years with ease and come to a truly authentic decision regarding my life.

Freedom and the Constraint of Time
by Cynthia Brown

Do I believe that I am free?

The 18th-century French philosopher Baron d'Holbach says that we are drowning in a river, desperately trying to keep our heads above water, sinking, rising, sinking again, until we die. The American writer William James argued that we are free to act, to drag ourselves out of that river of circumstance any time we choose and set our own course. I believe that whatever your personal belief about the nature of your freedom, we are all captured and held by the whims of Time. Time is universal, preceding both existence and essence.

> Brown compares two philosophers with differing ideas related to free will and then moves into exploring her concept of time in relation to freedom.

Take, for example, measurement. Everything we know about the material world, everything we experience, is measured by time. Distance, stability, stamina, progress, relationships . . . the list is endless. We run, not a mile, but ten minutes. We travel, not by miles, but by hours. We wait, not with patience but in days. To an imaginary objective observer, an angel or an alien, humans would all seem to be motivated not by internal desires or the pursuit of knowledge, but by the hands of the clock. An alien wouldn't know that you decided to stop speaking with your boyfriend because you had fallen in love with someone else; the alien would notice that the clock on your bedroom wall said 3:37 pm, and could just as easily assume that the time determined your heart's action.

> Brown begins her analysis and extended definition of time by discussing our perceptions of time.

People wear wristwatches, follow the sun across the sky, track the phases of the moon. New technology helps us to process time faster so we don't waste a moment of it. We have cell phones and computers so we can work faster, multitask, move several concepts and relationships through time simultaneously. We are racing time, desperate to control it, bend it to our will. Yet time is a universal law, a rule we must abide by. We might think that we are free to make decisions about our own lives, but whatever we "choose" is ultimately changed, decayed, or unraveled by the passage of time.

> At the end of paragraph 3, Brown circles back to the question of free will and then skillfully reiterates her idea that time "trumps" free will.

When we look into the heavens, we see stars and wonder just how small we are. How long would it take me to travel to the next galaxy, the next universe?

Source: Freedom and the Constraint of Time by Cynthia Brown.

Ask a physicist and she will answer you in increments of time: light years. Our imaginations can travel as far into the universe as they may please in the shortest segment time has to give us. We feel we can take a shortcut and go where we please, sometimes inventing new universes where time does not exist. We feel, briefly, ecstatically, that we have beaten time—and then we wake up, or come down, and find ourselves in a place where we are alone and helpless, desperate to come back to the places and people we know.

Suppose we were to look back at our lives and what has shaped us. Wouldn't it be nice to go back and change everything, to disappear without knowledge of our present life and be given a chance to start all over again? Alan Lightman, a renowned physicist, explores this idea in his novel *Einstein's Dreams*. Many of his stories claim that time is an endless cycle, never giving in or relenting to our wishes. Our clocks repeat themselves in a circle. We fall in and out of love, looking back at time spent in our relationships as so much wasted time, hardly daring to allow ourselves to experience the emotion itself. We are simultaneously anticipating the future and regretting the past. We move forward, waiting for time to heal our wounds.

Although we created a calendar to help us move through and keep track of time, it is an endless cycle. Day into night. Hour into hour. The refugee boy from Sudan, lost on the dark North Dakota prairie, asks a friend: "Can you tell me, please, is it now night or day?" We ask Time to be responsible, ignoring our own role in our destiny. While we are thinking of everything that has gone wrong with our lives, Time is passing through us, creating us, owning us. We are creating ourselves in Time. Are we really making our decisions based on our experience and careful analysis, or are we allowing Time to take control and be our guide?

We slip in and out of awareness of time. We wake in the morning fresh from our dreams and instinctively look at the clock. Some mornings we rise and say, "Shit, I'm late for class. My professor is going to be so mad. He wears a watch." And here, we have a choice. Do we go late, or not go at all? Both of these decisions come with consequences. We weigh them as we brush our teeth and pull a sweater over our heads. Is the decision we make truly free, or are we simply responding to the urgency of the ticking clock?

It's possible to leave the technology of clocks and cell phones behind, but just like the Lost Boys of Sudan, we are still instinctively aware of the cycles of the sun. We cannot live without sunlight; we cannot imagine the universe without darkness. Our secrets are kept in the dark, and we reveal ourselves to each other by shining a light on our deepest truths. We are determined to live in light and

By implying that we do not allow ourselves "to experience the emotion itself," Brown illustrates how we rarely live in the moment, strengthening her idea that we are "captured and held by the whims of Time."

This is the second reference Brown makes to the Lost Boys of Sudan. Do you feel this strengthens her argument about freedom and time?

shadow, and from an early age we are trained to respond to the shifts from day to night and back again.

One of the earliest lessons I remember from preschool was how to tell time (tell it what? I wonder now…). We learned how to read the hands on a clock, and what the numbers on a digital dial meant; we were taught to "be on time," and were punished if we were late. As schoolchildren, responding to bells, we were taught to be driven by forces beyond what we can truly see—only measure (and isn't it ironic that we are not allowed to pray in schools? But that's another argument entirely). Were we learning because we were curious, eating because we were hungry, jumping up from our desks because we couldn't wait to get home? Or were we just responding, like a bunch of trained rats, to the sound of the bell?

And so we wait. We wait for time to tell us what will be and where we will end up next. Whether or not the alarm clock will let us live another day. All of our teachings and still we wait, for something as old as the universe itself, a force that will long outlast any choices or commitments or decisions we make. Time moves forward, carrying us with it whether we ask it to or not. For surely if we exist outside of this concept of time, lock ourselves in a windowless room for what we suspect are minutes, days, or years, we are certain to be driven to madness.

So when I am asked, "Are you free?"

I answer, "Well, I don't wear a wristwatch. Do you?"

Brown circles back to the notion of freedom in her conclusion and states she does not wear a wristwatch. Does this imply that she is free? Do you feel this is a strong conclusion to her essay?

REFLECTION ON WRITING

1. Wendy Agudo generated ideas for her essay through freewriting and then used the five steps to organized decision making to structure her paper. Using the five steps she followed, underline the passages that pertain to each step in the essay itself. Where, for example, did she define her decision? Where did she address the possible choices she had? Can you highlight the pros and cons she wrote about? Which choice was best for her situation? Finally, underline the one sentence that best describes her plan of action. Did you have a difficult time pinpointing any of these passages, or were they obvious?

2. Cynthia Brown's approach to writing was a little different than Wendy Agudo's. Although she spent a little time brainstorming, we are not able to tell if she used an outline to structure her paper. Considering that she wove the concept of time throughout her paper, can you point out where she may have used the five steps of the decision-making method to structure her paper? If Cynthia had used a different approach to the structure of her paper, would it have been as successful? Why or why not?

ALTERNATIVE WRITING PROJECTS

1. Write an essay in which you analyze a decision that must be made soon by a community or group to which you belong. Describe the circumstances leading up to this decision, and follow through the five steps of the decision-making method discussed in this chapter. When you consider alternate choices and their pros and cons, be sure to include the perspectives of several members of your community who will be affected by this decision.

2. The theme of the wandering pilgrim, or the prodigal son, is found in literature across cultures and time periods. What does it mean to "come home" after a life-changing experience? Is it more difficult to decide to run away or to decide to come home? Have you had a comparable experience? What led you away? Why did you decide to come home? How did the experience change you?

3. Have you ever talked someone out of what you knew was a bad decision? What were the circumstances of that decision? What was your relationship to the person making the decision? What was the most effective, or surprising, argument that you made to change that person's mind?

CHAPTER 5 | Summary

- When you begin to prepare your draft, you should first establish what your purpose for writing is. To determine this, you should ask yourself the following questions:

  - Who is my audience, and what are its needs?

  - What is my subject, and why is it interesting?

  - Who am I as a writer?

  - What should my working thesis be?

  - What information should I use and what more do I need?

  - When should I start outlining?

  - What should my introduction and conclusion be?

- In making decisions about your life, you should take an informed and strategic approach. Using the following organized steps should prove helpful:

  - Step 1: Define the decision and its goals clearly.

  - Step 2: Consider all possible choices.

  - Step 3: Gather all relevant information and evaluate the pros and cons of each possible choice.

- Step 4: Select the choice that seems best suited to the situation.
- Step 5: Implement a plan of action and monitor the results, making necessary adjustments.

- After following your decision-making plan through to completion, it is good practice to look back and analyze your decisions. By identifying decisions that aided in your success or failure, you learn important lessons about which strategies may be worth repeating and which should be avoided in the future.

Language and thinking are intertwined and have an intrinsic relationship. Language allows us to communicate what we are thinking, and we express our thoughts through language. As critical thinkers and thoughtful writers, we have a responsibility to express ourselves as clearly and truthfully as possible. What effect does language have on the way you express yourself? Does the language you use to communicate change depending on the situation?

Revising:
Using Language Thoughtfully

"Only where there is language is there world."

—ADRIENNE RICH

CRITICAL
THINKING FOCUS:
**Language and
power**

WRITING FOCUS:
**Revising
language to
clarify thinking**

READING THEME:
**Using language
ethically**

WRITING
ACTIVITIES:
**How language
affects writing**

WRITING PROJECT:
**The impact of
language on our
lives**

Every time we use language and images, we send messages about our thinking and ourselves. When we speak or write, we are not simply making sounds or writing symbols; we are conveying ideas, sharing feelings, and describing experiences. At the same time, language itself shapes and influences thinking. When language use is careless—vague, general, indistinct, imprecise, foolish, inaccurate—it leads to the same sort of thinking. The reverse is also true: clear, precise language leads to clear, precise thinking, speaking, and writing.

The careless or imprecise use of language can be more consequential than a mediocre grade or a boring essay. When you write, you assume an audience; even if your audience is "only" your instructor, you still take on the responsibility of enlightening, entertaining, and truth telling. That assumption of an audience, so fundamental to rhetoric, implies that you are writing from an *ethical* perspective. The word *ethics* comes from the Greek term *ethos,* or "character." What you say, and how you say it, reveals to your audience what kind of person you are.

To write ethically also implies that you have a *responsibility* toward your reader, your subject, and yourself. To be responsible to your reader means that you write clearly, choosing the most appropriate language and constructing a logical argument that your reader can easily follow. To be responsible to your subject requires you to be as truthful as you can, given what you know. If you are writing an argument, it is your responsibility as an ethical writer to present opposing viewpoints fairly and accurately. Finally, you are responsible to your *ethos,* or how you appear in your writing. A carefully written, logically organized, interestingly illustrated essay reveals the presence of a thoughtful, interesting, curious mind.

This chapter explores the ethical implications of language—how it is used on both a personal and a social level to provoke, to haunt, to challenge, and to heal. Activities in this chapter discuss the *revision* part of the writing process, that careful reconsideration of your sources, organization, and word choice before you present your "final" paper to your audience.

Thinking-Writing Activity

LANGUAGE THAT OFFENDS

Has your attention been drawn to the ethical or responsible use of language on your campus or in your workplace? For example, does your campus have a speech code that defines hate speech or otherwise proscribed language? Are there words you are uncomfortable using or hearing in the classroom or the office? Are you uncomfortable with that language because it offends you or because you worry about offending someone?

Recognizing Effective Use of Language

One effective way to develop your ability to use language ethically and responsibly in communicating your thoughts, feelings, and experiences is to read widely. Highly regarded writers use word meanings accurately. They also often use many action verbs, concrete nouns, and vivid adjectives to communicate effectively. Another way to become a more sensitive and responsive writer is by seeking feedback from readers. In this section, you will be using all these strategies.

When thinking about how to use language effectively, we must consider not only our course assignments but also all the other forms of communication in which we participate and the different media in which we do so. The same rules do not apply for all types of writing. For instance, writing successfully for new media requires a unique set of criteria. Think about how different a Facebook post is from a blog post, and how different a blog post is from an academic journal.

LANGUAGE, THINKING, AND LEARNING

The following excerpt from *The Autobiography of Malcolm X* chronicles his discovery of the power of language while he was serving time in prison. Frustrated by not being able to communicate his ideas in writing, he committed himself to mastering the use of words by copying the dictionary. As you read, pay special attention to the way Malcolm X uses language to share his experiences with us. Do you find his personal quest inspiring? Why?

From *The Autobiography of Malcolm X*

by Malcolm X with Alex Haley

Born as Malcolm Little in Omaha, Nebraska, the son of an activist Baptist preacher and a mother busy with her eight children, Malcolm X saw racial injustice and violence from a very young age.

Source: From *The Autobiography of Malcolm X* by Malcolm X and Alex Haley.

Malcolm dropped out of high school after a teacher's contemptuous discouragement of his ambitions to be a lawyer and became involved in criminal activities. After a conviction for burglary in Boston, he was sentenced to prison for ten years. (In the following excerpt from his autobiography, Malcolm X describes how he used this time for reflection and intellectual growth.) Paroled in 1952, Malcolm dropped the name Little (which he now referred to as his "slave name") and took up the name X to symbolize his lost African heritage.

In 1964, following a period of disappointment and disillusionment with Elijah Muhammad, Malcolm X broke with the Nation of Islam, within which he had held a prominent position. Returning to the spiritual roots of his conversion to Islam, he made a hajj, or pilgrimage, to Mecca in Saudi Arabia. The sight of so many Muslims of so many different races and colors was deeply moving to Malcolm X, and upon his return to America he began working toward healing and reconciliation for all Americans of all races.

Unfortunately, the enemies he had made and the fears he had provoked did not leave Malcolm X much time to share this message; three assassins shot him as he spoke at the Audubon Ballroom in Harlem on February 15, 1965.

Many who today hear me somewhere in person, or on television, or those who read something I've said, will think I went to school far beyond the eighth grade. This impression is due entirely to my prison studies.

It had really begun back in the Charlestown Prison, when Bimbi first made me feel envy of his stock of knowledge. Bimbi had always taken charge of any conversation he was in, and I had tried to emulate him. But every book I picked up had few sentences which didn't contain anywhere from one to nearly all of the words that might as well have been in Chinese. When I just skipped those words, of course, I really ended up with little idea of what the book said. So I had come to the Norfolk Prison Colony still going through only book-reading motions. Pretty soon, I would have quit even these motions, unless I had received the motivation that I did.

I saw that the best thing I could do was get hold of a dictionary—to study, to learn some words. I was lucky enough to reason also that I should try to improve my penmanship. It was sad. I couldn't even write in a straight line. It was both ideas together that moved me to request a dictionary along with some tablets and pencils from the Norfolk Prison Colony school.

I spent two days just riffling uncertainly through the dictionary's pages. I'd never realized so many words existed! I didn't know which words I needed to learn. Finally, just to start some kind of action, I began copying. In my slow, painstaking, ragged handwriting, I copied into my tablet everything printed on that first page, down to the punctuation marks. I believe it took me a day. Then, aloud, I read back, to myself, everything I'd written on the tablet. Over and over, aloud, to myself, I read my own handwriting.

I woke up the next morning, thinking about those words—immensely proud to realize that not only had I written so much at one time, but I'd written words that I never knew were in the world. Moreover, with a little effort, I also could remember what many of these words meant. I reviewed the words whose meanings I didn't remember. . . .

I was so fascinated that I went on—I copied the dictionary's next page. And the same experience came when I studied that. With every succeeding page, I also learned of people and places and events from history. . . . That was the way I started copying what eventually became the entire dictionary. . . . Between what I wrote in my tablet, and writing letters, during the rest of my time in prison I would guess I wrote a million words. I suppose it was inevitable that as my word-base broadened, I could for the first time pick up a book and read and now begin to understand what the book was saying. . . .

QUESTIONS FOR READING ACTIVELY

1. For whom is Malcolm X writing, and what is his purpose? (In fact, if you read closely, you might detect more than one assumed audience and many layers of purpose.) What language does he use and what images does he create to appeal to a specific audience?

2. Malcolm X describes the process of how learning words from a dictionary sparked a hunger for learning that lead to his being able to "pick up a book and read and now begin to understand what the book was saying." Explain the importance of his hunger for knowledge in terms of how it impacted his life.

QUESTIONS FOR THINKING CRITICALLY

1. Malcolm X envied one of the other inmates, Bimbi, because his stock of knowledge enabled him to take charge of any conversation he was in. Explain why knowledge—and our ability to use it—leads to power in our dealings with others. Describe a situation from your own experience in which having expert knowledge about a subject enabled you, through writing, to influence the thinking of other people.

2. At one point in this essay, Malcolm X explains how his experience of discovering and mastering language helped him feel free for the first time in his life. Explain what you think he means by this. Then describe a time in your life when you felt "truly free."

QUESTION FOR WRITING THOUGHTFULLY

1. Write an essay that describes your intellectual awakening. In what ways was it similar to or different from the experience of Malcolm X? What book, television show, movie, or event sparked your awakening? Describe how your awakening made you feel. What things have you done since your awakening to feed your curiosity and grow your knowledge?

Making Decisions When Revising Drafts

Revision is the key to producing your best possible work. It is very rare for a first draft to represent the most effective writing of which a person is capable. Most accomplished writers expect their work to undergo a number of revisions based on their own reevaluation and on feedback from others. The difference between outstanding and mediocre writing often depends on revision.

Many of the concepts in the five-step decision-making approach discussed in Chapter 5 can be applied to revising your drafts.

- You *define the decision and your goals* by identifying what in a draft needs to be revised and what should be left as it is.

- You *consider possible choices* for improving a draft, first with the larger components related to revising: composing and placing the thesis statement; presenting evidence; and logically arranging material in sequences, sections, or paragraphs. During the editing and proofreading stage, you then have various choices related to the words and sentence patterns you use in your essay.

- You *gather relevant information* and *evaluate the pros and cons* of the different choices in order to select the one that best meets the needs of the writing situation. Sometimes you may want to write down the different possibilities; in other instances, you may just try them out in your mind.

- After *implementing* your choices by revising a draft, you *evaluate* your writing by *reading it again,* slowly and completely, to be sure that the whole piece is as good as you can make it.

 Collaborating with classmates or other trusted readers in all these decisions will usually be very helpful. Other readers can see your drafts more objectively and can help you "re-see" and revise them.

SPECIFIC DECISIONS TO MAKE AT SEVERAL LEVELS

The following suggestions should help you revise your drafts.

Read your entire draft slowly and carefully. You may find, as many writers do, that reading out loud helps you to identify parts that don't "sound" right. Also, ask someone whose judgment you trust to read the draft and help you to decide what improvement is needed. If your class allows peer review either in person or online, be prepared for this opportunity by having a draft ready.

The next step is to determine at what level you should begin to make changes. As you have already learned in Chapter 1, revision means much more than correcting grammar, punctuation, and spelling. In fact, those corrections are often made during the final stage of writing—the editing and proofreading stage—to help separate them from the larger aspects of revision.

A helpful way to decide where to begin revising is to move through the following hierarchy of questions about your draft. If you find yourself answering any of the questions in a manner that suggests ways to improve your writing, stop and try to make the changes or additions to your draft before you move on to the next level. There is no point in worrying about punctuation if your draft lacks focus or good examples. Time you spend carefully editing now can be time wasted if you jump ahead too far.

At the same time, remember that revision, like all steps of the writing process, is recursive. You may detect content, organization, or wording problems while you are checking punctuation; you may fix a typo while you are rewording the thesis statement. The following hierarchy emphasizes the importance of focusing on major revisions first and then moving in closer to examine and correct the smaller (yet still important) details of your writing during the editing and proofreading stage. Keep in mind that you may move back and forth between these levels until you are comfortable with your final paper or essay but that it is best to start with the big issues and then focus in on the smaller issues.

For your convenience, "A Step-by-Step Method for Revising Any Assignment" appears on the inside front cover. Refer to this method as you reach the Revision section of each Writing Project in the following chapters. You can also use this method to help you review the work of others. It can be applied to any writing assignment!

A Step-by-Step Method for Revising Any Assignment

Revision

1. **Think big**. Look at the draft as a whole.
   - ☐ Does it fulfill the assignment's purpose in terms of topic and length?
   - ☐ Does it have a clear focus?
   - ☐ What parts of the draft, if any, do not relate to its focus?
   - ☐ How could the draft be reorganized to make it more logical for your audience?
   - ☐ What evidence could be added to help to accomplish your purpose?
   - ☐ How could the flow between paragraphs be made smoother?
   - ☐ Is your point of view about your subject consistent throughout?
   - ☐ After answering the questions above, decide how to make the needed improvements.
   - ☐ Once you have made improvements to your draft, run through this list again to be sure you have addressed everything. If you are comfortable with your draft as a whole, you can proceed to the next level of revision.

2. **Think medium**. Look at the draft paragraph by paragraph, starting with the introduction.
   - ☐ How well does the introduction lead into the paper? Does it grab the readers' attention and inspire them to keep reading? (For tips on creative introductions, see Chapter 5.)
   - ☐ Are the thesis and purpose of the paper apparent, clear, and effective?
   - ☐ Does the tone of the introduction match the tone of the rest of the draft?
   - ☐ Does each body paragraph support the thesis or purpose?
   - ☐ Does each paragraph present relevant, specific evidence about the subject not presented elsewhere?

☐ Which, if any, paragraphs should be combined or eliminated?

☐ Have you chosen or created useful and interesting visuals if needed?

☐ Which paragraphs use topic sentences effectively? Which do not?

☐ Where could you use transitions to improve the flow within or between body paragraphs?

☐ Examine the conclusion, and remember that it is your last opportunity to connect with the intended audience. How could the conclusion be more effective or memorable? (Chapter 5 has tips on writing creative and effective conclusions.)

☐ Does the tone of the conclusion match the overall tone of the paper?

☐ Once you have made improvements to your draft, run through this list again to be sure you have addressed everything before proceeding to the next level.

Editing and Proofreading

3. **Think small.** Look at the draft sentence by sentence.

☐ Which sentences are difficult to understand? How could they be reworded for clarity?

☐ Which, if any, sentences are so long (run-on sentences) that an audience could become confused or lose interest?

☐ Are there short, choppy sentences (or sentence fragments) that could be combined?

☐ Which sentences seem vague? How could they be clarified?

☐ Which, if any, sentences have errors in standard English grammar or usage? How could you correct them?

☐ Is the paper consistent and accurate in regard to verb tense (past, present, future)?

☐ Check for errors in punctuation (commas, semicolons, hyphens, periods, etc.).

☐ Check for other mechanical issues (such as quotation marks in the right places, use of italics, correct format for titles, and capitalization) and simple typos.

☐ Make necessary changes to your draft before proceeding to the next level.

4. **Think "picky."** Look at the draft as the fussiest critic might.

☐ Which words are not clear or not quite right in regard to the intended meaning? What words could be used instead?

☐ Are any words spelled incorrectly? (Run the spell-checker program on your computer if possible, but don't rely on it alone.)

☐ Are the pages numbered consecutively?

☐ Does the physical appearance of your draft meet the assignment's requirements for format (instructor or other requirements, APA or MLA, etc.)?

☐ Is there anything else you can do to improve your draft?

Thinking-Writing Activity

USING THE REVISION METHOD

Apply each step of the revision method above to an essay you have written for this course (your instructor will advise you about which one to select). Although this process may initially seem time-consuming and rather mechanical, you will soon begin to integrate these ideas in a more natural and flexible way. As you become more experienced as a writer, the revision method will eventually become an integral part of your writing process.

Beyond considering your own earlier experiences, you can deepen your understanding of revision by reading the following selection by an expert writer.

"The Maker's Eye: Revising Your Own Manuscripts"
by Donald M. Murray

Known as both a professional journalist and a brilliant teacher, Donald M. Murray won the Pulitzer Prize for his editorials in the *Boston Herald* in 1954. Since then, he taught writing at the University of New Hampshire and Boston University and was a columnist for *The Boston Globe*. He acted as a writing coach for several national newspapers and wrote poetry for many journals. While in retirement, he published his memoir, *My Twice-Lived Life,* in 2001. Murray died in 2006.

Murray has also authored several books on the craft of writing and teaching writing, including *Learning by Teaching, Expecting the Unexpected,* and *Crafting a Life in Essay, Story, Poem.* His work has been highly influential in the way writing is taught. In this selection, he describes his own revision process, one that has served him well.

When students complete a first draft, they consider the job of writing done—and their teachers too often agree. When professional writers complete a first draft, they usually feel that they are at the start of the writing process. When a draft is completed, the job of writing can begin.

That difference in attitude is the difference between amateur and professional, inexperience and experience, journeyman and craftsman. Peter F. Drucker, the prolific business writer, calls his first draft "the zero draft"—after that he can start counting. Most writers share the feeling that the first draft, and all of those which follow, are opportunities to discover what they have to say and how best they can say it.

To produce a progression of drafts, each of which says more and says it more clearly, the writer has to develop a special kind of reading skill. In school we are taught to decode what appears on the page as finished writing. Writers, however, face a different category of possibility and responsibility when they read their own drafts. To them the words on the page are never finished. Each can be changed and rearranged, can set off a chain reaction of confusion or clarified meaning. This is a different kind of reading, which is possibly more difficult and certainly more exciting.

Writers must learn to be their own best enemy. They must accept the criticism of others and be suspicious of it; they must accept the praise of others and be even more suspicious of it. Writers cannot depend on others. They must detach themselves from their own pages so that they can apply both their caring and their craft to their own work.

Such detachment is not easy. Science fiction writer Ray Bradbury supposedly puts   5
each manuscript away for a year to the day and then rereads it as a stranger. Not many writers have the discipline or the time to do this. We must read when our judgment may be at its worst, when we are close to the euphoric moment of creation.

Then the writer, counsels novelist Nancy Hale, "should be critical of everything that seems to him most delightful in his style. He should excise what he most admires, because he wouldn't thus admire it if he weren't . . . in a sense protecting it from criticism." John Ciardi, the poet, adds, "The last act of writing must be to become one's own reader. It is, I suppose, a schizophrenic process, to begin passionately and to end critically, to begin hot and to end cold; and, more important, to be passion-hot and critic-cold at the same time."

Most people think that the principal problem is that writers are too proud of what they have written. Actually, a greater problem for most professional writers is one shared by the majority of students. They are overly critical, think everything is dreadful, tear up page after page, never complete a draft, see the task as hopeless.

The writer must learn to read critically but constructively, to cut what is bad, to reveal what is good. Eleanor Estes, the children's book author, explains: "The writer must survey his work critically, coolly, as though he were a stranger to it. He must be willing to prune, expertly and hard-heartedly. At the end of each revision, a manuscript may look . . . worked over, torn apart, pinned together, added to, deleted from, words changed and words changed back. Yet the book must maintain its original freshness and spontaneity."

Most readers underestimate the amount of rewriting it usually takes to produce spontaneous reading. This is a great disadvantage to the student writer, who sees only a finished product and never watches the craftsman who takes the necessary steps back, studies the work carefully, returns to the task, steps back, returns, steps back, again and again. Anthony Burgess, one of the most prolific writers in the English-speaking world, admits, "I might revise a page twenty times." Roald Dahl, the popular children's writer, states, "By the time I'm nearing the end of a story, the first part will have been reread and altered and corrected at least 150 times. . . . Good writing is essentially rewriting. I am positive of this."

10   Rewriting isn't virtuous. It isn't something that ought to be done. It is simply something that most writers find they *have* to do to discover what they have to say and how to say it. It is a condition of the writer's life.

There are, however, a few writers who do little formal rewriting, primarily because they have the capacity and experience to create and review a large number of invisible drafts in their minds before they approach the page. And some writers slowly produce finished pages, performing all the tasks of revision simultaneously, page by page, rather than draft by draft. But it is still possible to see the sequence followed by most writers most of the time in rereading their own work.

Most writers scan their drafts first, reading as quickly as possible to catch the larger problems of subject and form, then move in closer and closer as they read and write, reread and rewrite.

The first thing writers look for in their drafts is *information*. They know that a good piece of writing is built from specific, accurate, and interesting information. The writer must have an abundance of information from which to construct a readable piece of writing.

Next, writers look for meaning in the information. The specifics must build a pattern of significance. Each piece of specific information must carry the reader toward meaning.

15   Writers reading their own drafts are aware of *audience*. They put themselves in the reader's situation and make sure that they deliver information which a reader wants to know or needs to know in a manner which is easily digested. Writers try to be sure that they anticipate and answer the questions a critical reader will ask when reading the piece of writing.

Writers make sure that the *form* is appropriate to the subject and the audience. Form, or genre, is the vehicle which carries meaning to the reader, but form cannot be selected until the writer has adequate information to discover its significance and an audience which needs or wants that meaning.

Once writers are sure the form is appropriate, they must then look at the *structure*, the order of what they have written. Good writing is built on a solid framework of logic, argument, narrative, or motivation which runs through the entire piece of writing and holds it together. This is the time when many writers find it most effective to outline as a way of visualizing the hidden spine by which the piece of writing is supported.

The element on which writers may spend a majority of their time is *development*. Each section of a piece of writing must be adequately developed. It must give readers enough information so that they are satisfied. How much information is enough? That's as difficult as asking how much garlic belongs in a salad. It must be done to taste, but most beginning writers underdevelop, underestimating the reader's hunger for information.

As writers solve development problems, they often have to consider questions of *dimension*. There must be a pleasing and effective proportion among all the parts of the piece of writing. There is a continual process of subtracting and adding to keep the piece of writing in balance.

20   Finally, writers have to listen to their own voices. *Voice* is the force which drives a piece of writing forward. It is an expression of the writer's authority and concern.

It is what is between the words on the page, what glues the piece of writing together. A good piece of writing is always marked by a consistent, individual voice.

As writers read and reread, write and rewrite, they move closer and closer to the page until they are doing line-by-line editing. Writers read their own pages with infinite care. Each sentence, each line, each clause, each phrase, each word, each mark of punctuation, each section of white space between the type has to contribute to the clarification of meaning.

Slowly the writer moves from word to word, looking through language to see the subject. As a word is changed, cut, or added, as a construction is rearranged, all the words used before that moment and all those that follow that moment must be considered and reconsidered.

Writers often read aloud at this stage of the editing process, muttering or whispering to themselves, calling on the ear's experience with language. Does this sound right—or that? Writers edit, shifting back and forth from eye to page to ear to page. I find I must do this careful editing in short runs, no more than fifteen or twenty minutes at a stretch, or I become too kind with myself. I begin to see what I hope is on the page, not what actually is on the page.

This sounds tedious if you haven't done it, but actually it is fun. Making something right is immensely satisfying, for writers begin to learn what they are writing about by writing. Language leads them to meaning, and there is the joy of discovery, of understanding, of making meaning clear as the writer employs the technical skills of language.

Words have double meanings, even triple and quadruple meanings. Each word has   25
its own potential for connotation and denotation. And when writers rub one word against the other, they are often rewarded with a sudden insight, an unexpected clarification.

The maker's eye moves back and forth from word to phrase to sentence to paragraph to sentence to phrase to word. The maker's eye sees the need for variety and balance, for a firmer structure, for a more appropriate form. It peers into the interior of the paragraph, looking for coherence, unity, and emphasis, which make meaning clear.

I learned something about this process when my first bifocals were prescribed. I had ordered a large section of the reading portion of the glass because of my work, but even so, I could not contain my eyes within this new limit of vision. And I still find myself taking off my glasses and bending my nose towards the page, for my eyes unconsciously flick back and forth across the page, back to another page, forward to still another, as I try to see each evolving line in relation to every other line.

When does this process end? Most writers agree with the great Russian writer Tolstoy, who said, "I scarcely ever reread my published writings, if by chance I come across a page, it always strikes me: all this must be rewritten; this is how I should have written it."

The maker's eye is never satisfied, for each word has the potential to ignite new meaning. This article has been twice written all the way through the writing process, and it was published four years ago. Now it is to be republished in a book. The editors make a few small suggestions, and then I read it with my maker's eye. Now it has been re-edited, re-vised, re-read, re-re-edited, for each piece of writing to the writer is full of potential and alternatives.

30   A piece of writing is never finished. It is delivered to a deadline, torn out of the typewriter on demand, sent off with a sense of accomplishment and shame and pride and frustration. If only there were a couple more days, time for just another run at it, perhaps then . . .

QUESTIONS FOR READING ACTIVELY

1. Murray quotes several authors in his essay, identifying each with a short phrase. Does that additional information influence how you read that quote and "listen" to its speaker? In what way?

2. Reread that same essay aloud to yourself, and see if your "ear's experience with language" suggests any additional changes.

QUESTIONS FOR THINKING CRITICALLY

1. Murray begins by contrasting the "student" and the "professional" writer. How do you, as a member of his audience, feel about your place in this comparison?

2. Compare the kind of writing that Murray is discussing to the writing that Malcolm X describes. How might Malcolm X interpret Murray's idea that "the words on the page are never finished"?

3. How does Murray establish his authority as a writer? Are you satisfied that he is someone whose advice you should follow? Why or why not?

QUESTIONS FOR WRITING THOUGHTFULLY

1. Murray identifies elements for writers to examine when critically reading their drafts: information, audience, form, structure, development, dimension, and voice. Reread any essay you have written for this course, paying attention to each of these elements. How would you revise the essay further to better express your meaning?

2. Find a published article on a topic about which you are passionate and knowledgeable. Then revise it, focusing on one or two of the elements that Murray identifies (information, audience, form, structure, development, dimension, and voice). Locate areas where you can cut text to make the meaning more precise.

3. Think about the times when you have received criticism of your writing, from peers, professors, siblings, or parents. Were you suspicious of the criticism you received? Why or why not? Have you ever given criticism to another writer who you felt was suspicious of you and your criticisms? What are some of the possible reasons for why we tend to be suspicious of criticism?

Using Language Ethically

Language reflects thinking, and thinking is shaped by language. Language not only provides multiple ways of expressing the same ideas, thoughts, and feelings but also helps to structure those thoughts. In turn, patterns of thinking breathe life into language.

The relationship between thinking and language is *interactive;* both processes are continually influencing each other in many ways. The interactive qualities of language also extend to its communicative purpose. We use language to persuade, to entertain, to inform, and to delight; yet we also know that language can be used to conceal the truth, to foment hatred, and to create terror. As a critical thinker, it is your ethical responsibility to continually evaluate the quality and reliability of what you communicate to others through text, visuals, and speech. Malcolm X recognized, at a personal level, how powerful language can be; later in this chapter, Daniel Pipes explains how language, used for unethical purposes, can cause tremendous damage.

When language use is sloppy—vague, general, indistinct, imprecise, foolish, inaccurate, and so on—it leads to the same sort of thinking. And the reverse is also true. Clear and precise language leads to clear and precise thinking, as shown in Figure 6.1. The opposite of clear, effective language is language that fails to help the reader picture or understand what the writer means because it is vague or ambiguous.

IMPROVING VAGUE LANGUAGE

Although our ability to name and identify gives us the power to describe the world in a precise way, we often tend to describe it in words that are imprecise and general. Such nonspecific words are termed *vague* words. Consider the following sentences:

- I had a *nice* time yesterday.
- That is an *interesting* book.
- She is an *old* person.

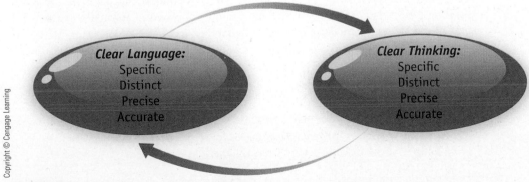

FIGURE 6.1
Clear Language and Clear Thinking

In each of these cases, the italicized word does not provide a precise description of the thought, feeling, or experience that the writer or speaker is trying to communicate. Vagueness occurs whenever a word is used to represent an area of experience without clearly defining it. A *vague word* is one that lacks a clear and distinct meaning.

Although the vagueness of general terms used to describe and measure can lead to confusion, other forms of vagueness are more widespread and often more problematic. Terms such as *good* and *enjoyable,* for example, are imprecise and unclear. Vagueness of this sort permeates every level of human discourse, undermines clear thinking, and is extremely difficult to combat. To use language clearly and precisely, you must develop an understanding of the way language functions and commit yourself to breaking the entrenched habit of using vague expression.

Thinking-Writing Activity

VAGUE LANGUAGE

Most words of general measurement—short, tall, big, small, heavy, light, and so on—are vague. The exact meanings of these words depend on the specific situation in which they are used and on the particular perspective of the person using them. For example, give specific definitions for the following italicized words by filling in the blanks. Then compare your responses with those of your classmates. Can you account for the differences in meaning?

1. A *middle-aged* person is one who is _____ years old.
2. A *tall* person is one who is over _____ feet _____ inches tall.
3. It's *cold* when the temperature is _____ degrees.
4. A person is *wealthy* when he or she is worth _____ dollars.

Vagueness is always a matter of degree. In fact, you can think of your descriptive/informative use of language as falling somewhere on a scale between extreme generality and extreme specificity. The following statements move from the general to the specific.

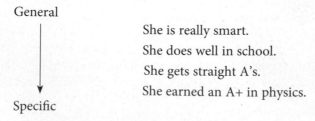

General

She is really smart.

She does well in school.

She gets straight A's.

She earned an A+ in physics.

Specific

Although different situations require various degrees of specificity, you should work to become increasingly more precise in your use of language.

When you are revising your own work, try to recognize and improve vague language, remembering your obligation to your audience to be as clear as possible. Be on the lookout for vague words such as *nice, good, fine, interesting, well, special, bad, really, very, old, young, situation,* and so on. Resist the temptation to improve vague words by putting *very* or *really* in front of them. Instead, if you have written, "The dessert was good," ask yourself, "How or why was it good?" Then substitute your answer for the vague word: "The dessert was full of fresh, plump strawberries flavored with orange juice and bits of mint." Now your audience can enjoy it with you!

USING FIGURATIVE LANGUAGE

Thus far in this section, we have been concerned with saying and writing exactly what we mean as precisely as possible. However, there is another way to use language to express thinking: to say something we do not literally mean. Of course, there are some writing situations for which figurative language is inappropriate, so when in doubt, check with your instructor. But when we do use figurative language effectively, our readers or listeners understand that we are not speaking literally but rather that we are speaking figuratively, using a figure of speech. Here we will focus on two figures of speech that may already be familiar: *simile* and *metaphor*.

Both simile and metaphor are based on a special kind of comparative thinking called an analogy, which is a limited comparison of two essentially unlike things for the purpose of illuminating or enriching our understanding. Analogies differ from the more common comparisons that examine the similarities and differences of two items in the same general category, such as two items on a menu or two methods of learning a language. Similes and metaphors focus on unexpected likenesses between items from different categories. Thus, when we compare a baby's skin to velvet, we may be calling attention to the skin's color or softness, but we are not suggesting that it makes a nice jacket or can be dyed different colors.

Consider the following example:

> Life's but a walking shadow, a poor player
> That struts and frets his hour upon the stage,
> And then is heard no more . . .
> —Shakespeare, *Macbeth*

In this famous metaphor, Shakespeare is comparing two things that at first seem to have nothing in common: life and an actor. Yet a closer look reveals that even though they are dissimilar in many ways, they share some undeniable similarities.

It is simple to distinguish similes from metaphors. Similes are explicitly stated comparisons that include the word *as, like,* or *than*. For example, "To the goalie, Mia Hamm's shot appeared as a photon of light." On the other hand, metaphors are implicitly stated comparisons, usually using some part of the verb *to be,* and do not include the word *as, like,* or *than*. Thus, it would be a metaphor to say, "To the goalie, Mia Hamm's shot was a photon of light."

NEW MEDIA & THOUGHTFUL WRITING

New Media Metaphors for Our World

The advent of new media has given us a large number of new concepts that we can use as metaphors to better understand our world. For example, "genetically modified organism" is no longer an obscure scientific phrase. In fact, its acronym, GMO, is commonly used today in everyday conversations about crops and food. In the article in Chapter 10, "GMOs: Fooling—Er, 'feeding'—the World for 20 Years," GRAIN (a nonprofit organization supporting small farmers) points out that plants are "complex living beings, not Lego blocks," and that we cannot "just flip a genetic switch and turn on high productivity" to feed the world. Using metaphors such as these helps a wider audience understand that crop plants are part of a much more complex system.

Thinking-Writing Activity

Identify five concepts from new media: hardware, wired, twittering, tagging, and so on—and then explain how they are or might be used as metaphors to shape and understand our world.

When should you use figurative language in your writing? Extensive reading will help you develop a feel for opportunities, but here are four suggestions:

- **When you have trouble finding the right words.** Powerful or complex emotions can make you speechless or make you say things like "Words cannot express what I feel." For example, if you are trying to describe your feelings of love for someone, you might write, "As breathtaking as the first rose in spring, this is the first great love of my life," or, "Like the fragile yet supple petals of the rose, my feelings are tender and sensitive."

- **When you want to express a profound thought in a strikingly original way.** For example, you want to express an idea about the meaning of life, which the simple word *life* does not convey. Shakespeare wrote, "(Life) is a tale/Told by an idiot, full of sound and fury,/Signifying nothing." Forrest Gump said, "Life is like a box of chocolates." You might write, "Life is a football game," or, "Life is an earthquake."

- **When you want to add an extra dimension to a description.** The scientist Alan Lightman recalls that he "would save [his] math problems for last, right before bedtime, like bites of chocolate cake awaiting [him] after a long and dutiful meal of history and Latin." You might write, "The spilled flour settled all over the apartment like a soft snow."

- **When you want to amuse your audience.** The great pool hustler Minnesota Fats wrote, "A pool player in a tuxedo is like a hotdog with whipped cream on it." By putting together two things that don't go together, like hotdogs and whipped cream, Minnesota Fats made his audience smile. You might write, "My twin brothers get along like ice cream and sauerkraut."

Thinking-Writing Activity

CREATING SIMILES AND METAPHORS

1. Use your creative thinking skills to create a simile for a subject of your own choosing, noting at least two points of comparison.

2. Now use your creative thinking skills to create a metaphor (implied analogy) for a subject of your own choosing, noting at least two points of comparison.

3. Create a metaphor for life that represents your feelings, and explain the points of similarity.

Figurative language that has become cliché is not effective. "He runs like a deer" and "I slept like a baby" were wonderful similes the first time they were used, but they have become old and tired: clichés. Use your creative thinking skills to write original, striking figures of speech.

Skillful speakers and writers are able to weave similes and metaphors together into a striking tapestry. As you read the following selection by Martin Luther King Jr., notice how he uses figurative language effectively, while being clear and precise about both the problem and the solution.

"I Have a Dream"

by Martin Luther King Jr.

The son of an influential Baptist minister, Martin Luther King Jr. began his involvement with the civil rights movement in 1955, when as a Baptist minister in Montgomery, Alabama, he led the Montgomery bus boycott after Rosa Parks, an African-American woman, heroically refused to give up her seat at the front of a public bus.

Greatly influenced by the nonviolent resistance of Mohandas K. Ghandi, King advocated an approach to protesting injustice that continues to resonate in progressive movements worldwide. Through education and outreach, marches, silent sit-ins at segregated lunch counters, and other acts of nonviolent resistance, King and his followers consistently met acts of barbarism with gestures of peace. He was awarded the Nobel Peace Prize in 1964.

And yet the violence he so peacefully—but forcefully—resisted eventually claimed him (as it did Ghandi). Dr. King was assassinated while standing on the balcony of the Lorraine Motel in Memphis, Tennessee, on April 4, 1968.

The speech that follows was delivered during the great March on Washington in 1963. That peaceful march and demonstration for human rights remains one of the most indelible images of twentieth-century American culture.

Five score years ago, a great American, in whose symbolic shadow we stand, signed the Emancipation Proclamation. This momentous decree came as a great beacon light of hope to millions of Negro slaves who had been seared in the flames of withering injustice. It came as a joyous daybreak to end the long night of captivity.

But one hundred years later, we must face the tragic fact that the Negro is still not free. One hundred years later, the life of the Negro is still sadly crippled by the manacles of segregation and the chains of discrimination. One hundred years later, the Negro lives on a lonely island of poverty in the midst of a vast ocean of material prosperity. One hundred years later, the Negro is still languishing in the corners of American society and finds himself an exile in his own land. So we have come here today to dramatize an appalling condition.

In a sense we have come to our nation's capital to cash a check. When the architects in our republic wrote the magnificent words of the Constitution and the Declaration of Independence, they were signing a promissory note to which every American was to fall heir. This note was a promise that all men would be guaranteed the unalienable rights of life, liberty, and the pursuit of happiness.

It is obvious today that America has defaulted on this promissory note insofar as her citizens of color are concerned. Instead of honoring this sacred obligation, America has given the Negro people a bad check; a check which has come back marked "insufficient funds." But we refuse to believe that the bank of justice is bankrupt. We refuse to believe that there are insufficient funds in the great vaults of opportunity of this nation. So we have come to cash this check—a check that will give us upon demand the riches of freedom and the security of justice. We have also come to this hallowed spot to remind America of the fierce urgency of *now*. This is no time to engage in the luxury of cooling off or to take the tranquilizing drugs of gradualism. *Now* is the time to make real the promises of Democracy. *Now* is the time to rise from the dark and desolate valley of segregation to the sunlit path of racial justice. *Now* is the time to open the doors of opportunity to all of God's children. *Now* is the time to lift our nation from the quicksands of racial injustice to the solid rock of brotherhood.

5   It would be fatal for the nation to overlook the urgency of the moment and to underestimate the determination of the Negro. This sweltering summer of the Negro's legitimate discontent will not pass until there is an invigorating autumn of freedom and equality. 1963 is not an end, but a beginning. Those who hope that the Negro needed to blow off steam and will now be content will have a rude awakening if the nation returns to business as usual. There will be neither rest nor tranquility in America until the Negro is granted his citizenship rights. The whirlwinds of revolt will continue to shake the foundations of our nation until the bright day of justice emerges.

But there is something that I must say to my people who stand on the warm threshold which leads into the palace of justice. In the process of gaining our rightful place we must not be guilty of wrongful deeds. Let us not seek to satisfy our thirst for freedom by drinking from the cup of bitterness and hatred. We must forever conduct our struggle on the high plane of dignity and discipline. We must not allow our creative protest to degenerate into physical violence. Again and again we must rise to the majestic heights of meeting physical force with soul force. The marvelous new militancy which has engulfed the Negro community must not lead us to a distrust of all white people, for many of our white brothers, as evidenced by their presence here today, have come to realize that their destiny is tied up with our destiny and their freedom is inextricably bound to our freedom. We cannot walk alone.

And as we walk, we must make the pledge that we shall march ahead. We cannot turn back. There are those who are asking the devotees of civil rights, "When will you be satisfied?" We can never be satisfied as long as the Negro is the victim of the unspeakable horrors of police brutality. We can never be satisfied as long as our bodies, heavy with the fatigue of travel, cannot gain lodging in the motels of the highways and the hotels of the cities. We cannot be satisfied as long as the Negro's basic mobility is from a smaller ghetto to a larger one. We can never be satisfied as long as a Negro in Mississippi cannot vote and a Negro in New York believes he has nothing for which to vote. No, no, we are not satisfied, and we will not be satisfied until justice rolls down like waters and righteousness like a mighty stream.

I am not unmindful that some of you have come here out of great trials and tribulations. Some of you have come fresh from narrow jail cells. Some of you have come from areas where your quest for freedom left you battered by the storms of persecution and staggered by the winds of police brutality. You have been the veterans of creative suffering. Continue to work with the faith that unearned suffering is redemptive.

Go back to Mississippi, go back to Alabama, go back to South Carolina, go back to Georgia, go back to Louisiana, go back to the slums and ghettos of our northern cities, knowing that somehow this situation can and will be changed. Let us not wallow in the valley of despair.

I say to you today, my friends, that in spite of the difficulties and frustrations of   10
the moment I still have a dream. It is a dream deeply rooted in the American dream.

I have a dream that one day this nation will rise up and live out the true meaning of its creed: "We hold these truths to be self-evident; that all men are created equal."

I have a dream that one day on the red hills of Georgia the sons of former slaves and the sons of former slaveowners will be able to sit down together at the table of brotherhood.

I have a dream that one day even the state of Mississippi, a desert state sweltering with the heat of injustice and oppression, will be transformed into an oasis of freedom and justice.

I have a dream that my four little children will one day live in a nation where they will not be judged by the color of their skin but by the content of their character.

I have a dream today.   15

I have a dream that one day the state of Alabama, whose governor's lips are presently dripping with the words of interposition and nullification, will be transformed into a situation where little black boys and black girls will be able to join hands with little white boys and white girls and walk together as sisters and brothers.

I have a dream today.

I have a dream that one day every valley shall be exalted, every hill and mountain shall be made low, the rough places will be made plain, and the crooked places will be made straight, and the glory of the Lord shall be revealed, and all flesh shall see it together.

This is our hope. This is the faith with which I return to the South. With this faith we will be able to hew out of the mountain of despair a stone of hope. With this faith we will be able to transform the jangling discords of our nation into a beautiful symphony of brotherhood. With this faith we will be able to work together, to pray together, to struggle together, to go to jail together, to stand up for freedom together, knowing that we will be free one day.

20   This will be the day when all of God's children will be able to sing with new meaning:

My country, 'tis of thee, Sweet land of liberty, Of thee I sing: Land where my fathers died, Land of the pilgrims' pride, From every mountain-side Let freedom ring.

And if America is to be a great nation, this must become true. So let freedom ring from the prodigious hilltops of New Hampshire. Let freedom ring from the mighty mountains of New York. Let freedom ring from the heightening Alleghenies of Pennsylvania!

Let freedom ring from the snowcapped Rockies of Colorado!
Let freedom ring from the curvaceous peaks of California!
But not only that; let freedom ring from Stone Mountain of Georgia!
Let freedom ring from Lookout Mountain of Tennessee!
Let freedom ring from every hill and molehill of Mississippi. From every mountainside, let freedom ring.

When we let freedom ring, when we let it ring from every village and every hamlet, from every state and every city, we will be able to speed up that day when all of God's children, black men and white men, Jews and Gentiles, Protestants and Catholics, will be able to join hands and sing in the words of the old Negro spiritual, "Free at last! free at last! thank God almighty, we are free at last!"

QUESTIONS FOR READING ACTIVELY

1. Of the rich metaphors King uses, which two or three do you find most effective or striking? Why?

2. This text is at once a speech and a sermon. Locate a recording of King's delivery of this great sermon, and listen to his delivery. How does King's voice, his emphasis on particular phrases, and his call-and-response engagement with his audience change the way you silently "read" the printed text?

3. The cadences and the figurative language of "I Have a Dream" are profoundly influenced by King's lifelong immersion in the African-American Baptist Church. Are those rhythms and biblical allusions familiar to you? Do you need to understand those allusions in order to fully appreciate the ethical and moral implications of his call to action?

QUESTIONS FOR THINKING CRITICALLY

1. Do you have faith in individual people, or in society as a whole, to address and correct a specific injustice? Describe an injustice that you have witnessed,

and evaluate how either individuals or a community has responded to that injustice.

2. King dreams of a nation where people are judged by the "content of their character"—their *ethic*. What is the content of your own character? How do you measure up to your own ethical ideals?

QUESTION FOR WRITING THOUGHTFULLY

1. King exhorts the marchers to "continue to work with the faith that unearned suffering is redemptive." In the same year as the March on Washington, Malcolm X delivered a speech in Detroit in which he noted that "there is nothing in our book, the Koran, that teaches us to suffer peacefully. Our religion teaches us to be intelligent. Be peaceful, be courteous, obey the law, respect everyone; but if someone puts his hands on you, send him to the cemetery." Can these two views be reconciled? How do you think injustice should best be fought? Describe your point of view in a short essay.

Using Language to Influence

Because of the intimate relationship between language and thinking, people naturally use language to influence the thinking of others. One of the reasons Dr. King's speech was so influential was that he invoked the cadences and the vocabulary of the Bible. President Bill Clinton used the same strategy when he promised Americans "a new covenant" between the government and the people. Later, George W. Bush became president after promoting an agenda of "compassionate conservatism." Conversely, the term *weapons of mass destruction* was so terrifying that many people believe it was one of the reasons that Congress voted to support the war in Iraq.

Manufacturers and advertising professionals choose language just as carefully to influence buying decisions. Americans are told that the Energizer bunny "keeps going and going." We are invited to "Join the Pepsi generation" and challenged to stop eating chips: "I bet you can't eat just one." And we are told over and over, "It's Miller time."

Whatever your political positions or buying habits, there are people who make a profession of using language to influence others' thinking. They are interested in influencing—and sometimes in controlling—your thoughts, feelings, and behavior. To avoid being unconsciously manipulated by these efforts, you need to be aware of how language functions. This knowledge will help you to distinguish actual arguments, information, and reasons from techniques of persuasion that others use to get you to accept their views without thinking critically. Three types of language often used to promote the uncritical acceptance of views are euphemistic language, clichés, and emotive language.

Thinking Critically About Visuals

Reading the Unwritten

Are citizens entitled to universal health care? In this mural, *The History of Medicine in Mexico, and the People Demanding Health,* which was created for a wall in the Hospital de la Raza in Mexico City, Mexico, the artist Diego Rivera dramatizes the struggle of the poor for access to a health care system that favors the rich. Murals like this have a rich history as a visual language to express important ideas. Who might be the audience for this mural, and what message did the artist want to communicate? Can you describe other murals that you have seen and what you thought their audiences and messages were intended to be?

Schalkwijk/Art Resource, NY

EUPHEMISTIC LANGUAGE

The term *euphemism* is derived from a Greek word meaning "to speak with good words." Using a euphemism involves substituting a pleasanter, less objectionable expression for a blunt or more direct one. For example, an entire collection of euphemisms exists to disguise the unpleasantness of death: *passed away, went to her reward, departed this life,* and *blew out the candle.*

Why do people use euphemisms? Probably to help smooth out the "rough edges" of life, to make the unbearable bearable and the offensive inoffensive. Sometimes people use them to make their occupations sound more dignified (a garbage collector, for instance, might be called a "sanitation engineer"). Sometimes euphemisms can be humorous, as are the following "New Euphemisms for Bad Stuff at School."

Course failure	Unrequested course reregistration
Incomplete course grade	An unrequited educational encounter
Suspension	Mandatory discontinued attendance
Absence	A non-school learning experience

Euphemisms can become dangerous, though, when they are used to evade or to create misperceptions of serious issues. An alcoholic may describe herself as a "social drinker," thus denying her problem and need for help. A politician may indicate that one of his statements was "somewhat at variance with the truth"— meaning that he lied. Another example would be to describe rotting slums as "substandard housing," making deplorable conditions appear reasonable and the need for action less urgent. In the following brief essay, foreign policy analyst Daniel Pipes argues against the use of euphemistic language to describe acts of terrorism.

Thinking-Writing Activity

THINKING CRITICALLY ABOUT EUPHEMISMS

Select an important social problem such as drug use, crime, poverty, juvenile delinquency, support for wars in other countries, racism, or unethical or illegal behavior in government. List several euphemisms commonly used to describe the problem; then explain how these euphemisms can lead to dangerous misperceptions and serious consequences.

"Beslan Atrocity: They're Terrorists—Not Activists"

by Daniel Pipes

Policy analyst Daniel Pipes is frequently consulted by media, industry, universities, and governments worldwide for his expert opinions and analysis of ongoing developments in the Middle East. He is the director of the Middle East Forum, a think tank that provides analysis about radical Islam to business, academic, and government entities. He was director of the Foreign Policy Research Institute from 1986 to 1993 and has been a board member of the United States Institute of Peace. The following article was written after Islamic terrorists took over a school in Beslan, Russia, in 2004, a siege that led to the deaths of 400 people. Most of the dead were children, their teachers, and their parents, who had been celebrating the first day of the school year.

"I know it when I see it" was the famous response by a U.S. Supreme Court justice to the vexed problem of defining pornography. Terrorism may be no less difficult to define,

Source: From "Beslan Atrocity: They're Terrorists—Not Activists," by Daniel Pipes, *New York Sun,* September 7, 2004. Reprinted with permission of Daniel Pipes.

but the wanton killing of schoolchildren, of mourners at a funeral, or workers at their desks in skyscrapers surely fits the know-it-when-I-see-it definition.

The press, however, generally shies away from the word *terrorist,* preferring euphemisms. Take the assault that led to the deaths of some four hundred people, many of them children, in Beslan, Russia, on September 3. Journalists have delved deep into their thesauruses, finding at least twenty euphemisms for terrorists:

Assailants—National Public Radio
Attackers—the Economist
Bombers—the *Guardian*
Captors—the Associated Press
Commandos—Agence France-Presse
refers to the terrorists both as
"members du commando" and
"commando"
Criminals—the *Times* (London)
25 Extremists—United Press International
Fighters—the *Washington Post*
Group—*The Australian*
Guerrillas—in a *New York Post* editorial
Gunmen—Reuters

Hostage-takers—the *Los Angeles Times*
Insurgents—in a *New York Times*
headline
Kidnappers—the *Observer* (London)
Militants—the *Chicago Tribune*
Perpetrators—the *New York Times*
Radicals—the BBC
Rebels—in a *Sydney Morning Herald*
headline
Separatists—the *Christian Science Monitor*
And my favorite:
Activists—the *Pakistan Times*

The origins of this unwillingness to name terrorists seems to lie in the Arab-Israeli conflict, prompted by an odd combination of sympathy in the press for the Palestinian Arabs and intimidation by them. The sympathy is well known; the intimidation less so. Reuters' Nidal al-Mughrabi made the latter explicit in advice for fellow reporters in Gaza to avoid trouble on the web site www.newssafety.com, where one tip reads: "Never use the word *terrorist* or *terrorism* in describing Palestinian gunmen and militants; people consider them heroes of the conflict."

The reluctance to call terrorists by their rightful name can reach absurd lengths of inaccuracy and apologetics. For example, National Public Radio's *Morning Edition* announced on April 1, 2004, that "Israeli troops have arrested twelve men they say were wanted militants." But CAMERA, the Committee for Accuracy in Middle East Reporting in America, pointed out the inaccuracy and NPR issued an on-air correction on April 26: "Israeli military officials were quoted as saying they had arrested twelve men who were 'wanted militants.' But the actual phrase used by the Israeli military was 'wanted terrorists.'"

5   (At least NPR corrected itself. When the *Los Angeles Times* made the same error, writing that "Israel staged a series of raids in the West Bank that the army described as hunts for wanted Palestinian militants," its editors refused CAMERA's request for a correction on the grounds that its change in terminology did not occur in a direct quotation.)

Metro, a Dutch paper, ran a picture on May 3, 2004, of two gloved hands belonging to a person taking fingerprints off a dead terrorist. The caption read: "An Israeli police officer takes fingerprints of a dead Palestinian. He is one of the victims (*slachtoffers*) who fell in the Gaza strip yesterday." One of the victims!

Euphemistic usage then spread from the Arab-Israeli conflict to other theaters. As terrorism picked up in Saudi Arabia such press outlets as *The Times (London)* and the Associated Press began routinely using *militants* in reference to Saudi terrorists. Reuters uses it with reference to Kashmir and Algeria.

Thus has *militants* become the press's default term for terrorists.

These self-imposed language limitations sometimes cause journalists to tie themselves into knots. In reporting the murder of one of its own cameramen, the BBC, which normally avoids the word *terrorist,* found itself using that term. In another instance, the search engine on the BBC web site includes the word *terrorist* but the page linked to [it] has had that word expurgated.

Politically correct news organizations undermine their credibility with such   10
subterfuges. How can one trust what one reads, hears, or sees when the self-evident fact of terrorism is being semi-denied?

Worse, the multiple euphemisms for *terrorist* obstruct a clear understanding of the violent threats confronting the civilized world. It is bad enough that only one of five articles discussing the Beslan atrocity mentions its Islamist origins; worse is the miasma of words that insulates the public from the evil of terrorism.

QUESTIONS FOR READING ACTIVELY

1. How are the terms listed by Daniel Pipes euphemistic? That is, why are these terms (in Pipes's opinion) less accurate, or less objectionable, than the term *terrorist?*

2. What does the word *wanton* (paragraph 1) mean, and what are the connotations of its use by Pipes to describe the actions of terrorists?

3. To what does Pipes attribute the use of euphemisms to describe terrorist actions?

4. What other euphemisms can you identify that are used to describe current events?

QUESTIONS FOR THINKING CRITICALLY

1. Go online to find more information about the attacks on the Beslan school. Which of the terms listed by Pipes did you find in the articles and analysis you consulted? Which term, based on your interpretations of the events, seems most accurate?

2. Working with a small group, look up each of the terms listed by Pipes in a good dictionary and in a thesaurus. In what ways are the derivations and usages of these terms similar, and in what ways are they different? Which words are considered to be synonyms for each other? Create a spectrum (see page 195) ranging from "most objectionable" to "least objectionable," and place each term at a point on that spectrum that reflects your research.

QUESTION FOR WRITING THOUGHTFULLY

1. The conservative Fox News network uses the term *homicide bombers,* as opposed to the more commonly used *suicide bombers,* to describe people who blow themselves up when they set off bombs meant to kill others as well. What is the difference between these two terms? Which term, in your opinion, is more accurate? In an extended definition essay (see page 268 in Chapter 8), explain your thinking.

CLICHÉS

Clichés function in a similar way to *euphemisms* in that they tend to dilute meaning and avoid the complexities of an issue. A cliché is an overused phrase, usually employing figurative language; it has been so often repeated that the phrase becomes an automatic pattern. For example, if someone says "Sly as a . . .," what word comes next? Or "Sharp as a . . ."? On page 184, in the discussion of figurative language, the point was made that clichés usually start off as fresh wordings. People like the way the phrase sounds and repeat it over and over, year after year. After a while, the phrase loses its freshness and also its clear reference to what is being discussed.

What does it really mean to be "drunk as a skunk"? First of all, skunks do not imbibe alcohol. But, more important, this cliché is not helpful to a discussion of intoxication. The issue may be a drinker's health or safety—or the safety of those around that person. What does it really mean to say that someone is "sly as a fox"? The issue may be manipulative behavior that can cause serious problems, not just wily strategies.

In addition, the use of clichés indicates lazy thinking. Imagine how clever it must have seemed the first time someone said in a meeting that the group should "think outside the box." Yet a person who uses that phrase now is not being clever, just repeating a tired phrase, and will probably be considered inarticulate. Clichés may not create serious problems in casual conversation, but they do cloud meaning and should not be used in your academic writing.

Thinking-Writing Activity

CLICHÉ AND PROVERB

Different societies and different time periods give rise to different clichés.

1. Write down two or three phrases that you consider to be clichés. Try to recall where you have read or heard them. Share this writing with classmates to see if they know these phrases and if they think that they are clichés.

2. Select a cliché from the list you discussed with your classmates, and then write a few sentences describing how that cliché could potentially cloud your thinking and obscure meaning.

3. Proverbs and famous quotations are also often repeated, but they function differently from clichés because they tend to *encourage* thinking. Write down a proverb or a famous quotation that you know, and write a few sentences about how it stimulates your thinking.

EMOTIVE LANGUAGE

What is your immediate reaction to each of the following words?

tyrant	*peaceful*	*disgusting*	*God*	*filthy*
mouthwatering	*bloodthirsty*	*freedom*	*jihad*	

Most of these words probably arouse strong feelings in you. In fact, this ability to evoke feelings accounts for the extraordinary power of language.

Certain words (like those just listed) are used to stand for the emotive areas of your experience. These emotive words symbolize the whole range of human feelings, from powerful emotions ("I detest you!") to the subtlest of feelings.

Emotive language often plays a double role: it not only symbolizes and expresses our feelings but also arouses or *evokes* feelings in others. When you tell someone, "You're my best friend," you usually are not simply expressing your feelings for the person; you also hope to inspire that person to have similar feelings for you. Even when communicating factual information, we make use of the emotive influence of language to interest other people in what we are saying.

Although an emotive word may be an accurate description of feelings, it is not the same as a factual statement because it is true only for the speaker—not for others. For instance, even though you may feel that a movie is "tasteless" and "repulsive," someone else may find it "exciting" and "hilarious." By describing your feelings about the movie, you are giving your personal evaluation, which often may differ from the personal evaluations of others (it is not unusual to see conflicting reviews of the same movie). A factual statement, on the other hand, is a statement with which rational people will agree, providing that suitable evidence to verify it is available (for example, the fact that mass transit uses less energy than automobiles). When emotive words are used in larger groups (such as sentences, paragraphs, compositions, poems, plays, or novels), they become even more powerful. Martin Luther King Jr.'s speech "I Have a Dream" (page 185) is a dramatic example of the force of effective emotive language.

One way to think about the meaning and power of emotive words is to see them on a scale or continuum, from mild to strong. For example:

overweight   fat   obese

The thinker Bertrand Russell used this continuum to illustrate how we perceive the same trait in various people:

- I am *firm.*
- You are *stubborn.*
- He/she is *pigheaded.*

We usually tend to perceive ourselves favorably ("I am firm"). I am speaking to you face to face, so I view you only somewhat less favorably ("You are stubborn"). But since a third person is not present, I can use stronger emotive language ("He/she is pigheaded"). Try this technique with two other emotive words:

1. I am . . .   You are . . .   He/she is . . .
2. I am . . .   You are . . .   He/she is . . .

Emotive words usually signal that a personal opinion or evaluation, rather than a fact, is being stated. Speakers occasionally do identify their opinions as opinions, using a phrase like "In my opinion" or "I feel that." Often, however, speakers do not identify their opinions as such because they want you to treat their judgments as facts. In these cases, the combination of the informative use and the emotive use of language can be misleading and even dangerous.

A final point to consider about emotive language is that it can be used in a reverse way, as we have seen in the section on euphemism. George Orwell gives examples of this in his classic essay "Politics and the English Language." He points out that such usages deliberately drain the emotion from terms in order to lessen the shock of the information being conveyed. "Defenseless villages are bombarded from the air, the inhabitants driven out into the country-side, the cattle machine-gunned, the huts set on fire with incendiary bullets: this is called *pacification.*"

Thinking-Writing Activity

EVALUATING EMOTIVE LANGUAGE

Identify examples of emotive language in the following passages, and explain how the writer is using that language to influence people's thoughts and feelings.

> We need another and a wiser and perhaps a more mystical concept of animals. Remote from universal nature, and living by complicated artifice, man in civilization surveys the creature through the glass of his knowledge and sees thereby a feather magnified and the whole image in distortion. We patronize them for their incompleteness, for their tragic fate of having taken form so far below ourselves. And therein we err, and greatly err. For the animal shall not be measured by man. In a world older and more complete than ours they move finished and complete, gifted with senses that you have lost or never attained, living by voices you shall never hear.
>
> —Henry Beston, *The Outermost House*

> Every criminal, every gambler, every thug, every libertine, every girl ruiner, every home wrecker, every wife beater, every dope peddler, every moonshiner, every crooked politician, every pagan Papist priest, every shyster lawyer, every white slaver, every brothel madam, every Rome-controlled newspaper, every black spider—is fighting the Klan. Think it over. Which side are you on?
>
> —From a Ku Klux Klan circular

Writing Project

THE IMPACT OF LANGUAGE ON OUR LIVES

This chapter explores the essential role of language in developing sophisticated thinking abilities. The goal of clear, effective thinking and communication is accomplished through the joint efforts of thought and language. Learning to use the appropriate language style, which depends on the social context in which you are operating, requires both critical judgment and flexible expertise with various language forms. Critically evaluating the pervasive attempts of advertisers and others to bypass your critical faculties and influence your thinking involves insight into the way language and thought create and express meaning. We will be examining these relationships between language and thought further in upcoming chapters.

The following Writing Project provides an opportunity for you to apply what you have learned in this chapter to your own writing.

Project Overview and Requirements

For this paper, you will discuss a specific aspect of your experience with language and analyze some way or ways in which words have affected you. Here are a few ideas to help you generate ideas:

- Write about a favorite poem or song lyric.
- Describe how the language of a religious ceremony or political statement influenced you.
- Discuss an advertisement that made you desire or reject a product.
- Explain how a statement made by someone close to you had a profound effect on you.
- Recount an event or situation, and describe its positive (or negative) effects.

The guidelines you need to consider are those involved in writing any paper that connects your personal experience with a complex issue.

1. Present your experience vividly, and use specific details.
2. Clearly state your point or thesis about the effect(s) the experience had on you. Think about the best place in your paper to do this.
3. Be explicit about the connections you see between your experience and the concepts about language that they illustrate. You may want to quote from the chapter. If you do, cite material as directed by your instructor.
4. Consider using some of the language techniques explored in this chapter (such as figurative language).
5. Whenever possible, connect your experience to concepts explained in this chapter (for example, the concept that what you say, and how you say it, reveals what kind of person you are, or that, as a critical thinker, it is your responsibility to evaluate the quality and reliability of what you communicate).

Follow your instructor's directions for topic limitations, length, format, and so on. Before you begin, be sure you understand The Writing Situation and The Writing Process below.

THE WRITING SITUATION

As with all of the Writing Projects you have completed so far, it helps to review the Thinking-Writing Model you learned about in Chapter 1: purpose, audience, subject, and writer.

Purpose   One purpose you have here is to connect abstract ideas about language with real-life experiences so that you and your readers can understand the concepts better. As with any writing project, another major purpose is to make your points clear and convincing to your audience.

Audience   As always, consider who could benefit from reading your paper. Perhaps your ideas would appeal to a larger audience, in which case you could submit your writing for publication in a popular magazine column, the opinion pages of your campus newspaper, or some other publication, website, or blog.

Subject   Because language is such a large subject, one involving fairly simple as well as very complex ideas, writing about a real-life experience can clarify—and test—the ideas you choose to write about.

Writer   Because this project draws on your own experience, you are in a position of authority. However, the project asks you to focus on an aspect of your experience that you might not have thought about before, and it requires an analytical approach rather than a narrative one, even though you may decide to tell of an event. Therefore, you will need a sort of double consciousness as a writer: you first want to recall your experience as directly as you can, but then you will have to distance yourself as you analyze the effect of language on the experience.

In this chapter, you have explored how language plays a role in your life. In addition to working through the following four questions, you may want to reflect on your responses to the Thinking-Writing Activities. The goal is to analyze and discuss how language has affected you.

1. Describe an experience where words or language had an effect on you. For example, one student wrote:

   > I drew pictures on anything and everything as a child, even on the barn walls at our farm, so it was only natural that I majored in art in college. Ms. Roberts, my professor in Art History, had a profound effect on me. Her lectures, packed with terms like Baroque, Rococo, Spatialism, and Transavantgarde, pulled me far away from the farm of my childhood and left me wandering the streets of Florence, Italy, and Paris, France.

2. Given that this experience had an effect on you, and possibly shaped who you are or how you think, who might be interested in reading your essay? For example:

   > My father and I have a good relationship, but sometimes I get the impression that he feels art is nothing more than a hobby for people with idle hands. I want

him to understand how Ms. Roberts inspired me to explore the role of art in society—how art is not simply a hobby. I also plan to use ideas from this writing project to help me create an artist's statement for an upcoming exhibit of my paintings, so explaining my transformation to a general audience will be critical.

3. Since your essay may contain complex ideas, how do you plan to relate them to your audience to help clarify meaning? For example:

> My initial "awakening" took place in a cavernous lecture hall as Ms. Roberts clicked through slides discussing artists and the periods to which they belonged. But it wasn't until I arrived in Florence and wandered the ornate halls of the Uffizi, and later that summer spent days in the Louvre in Paris, that the value and weight of Ms. Roberts's lectures nearly crushed me. I plan to explain the connections I made by comparing what I learned in the lecture hall to what I learned by visiting the cities where some of the major art periods took place. I am interested in how language can tell most of the story but not always the whole story. How can one, in words, fully describe how it feels to stand in front of Michelangelo's David?

4. How can you successfully relate the event or experience yet still analyze the effect of language on that experience? For example:

> I plan to present my experiences in chronological order (my childhood experience, my first course in Art History, and then my travels to Europe), but I also plan to analyze each experience and connect them—showing, basically, how they all shaped me—the language and the experience. Ultimately, the essay will come full circle as I end up back at the farm. After my travels, I turned one of the smaller barns into a studio.

THE WRITING PROCESS

The following sections will guide you through the stages of generating, planning, drafting, and revising as you work on this writing assignment.

Generating Ideas

1. Think of times when something you heard, read, or even said had an impact on you. Did someone use harsh language that upset you or comforting language that soothed you? Did you say something funny, helpful, embarrassing, or astute? Has a particular phrase ever made you want to do or try something? Why?

2. Do you find any common denominator among several experiences, or does one experience stand out and ask to be told as a single story?

3. Have your significant language experiences involved spoken words more often than written ones?

4. Have any of your experiences involved more than one language or more than one dialect or level of usage?

Defining a Focus   What do you want your audience to understand about the way the experience has affected you? If you are going to recount several experiences, is it important to make that clear in your thesis? Draft a thesis statement that makes a point about your experience(s).

Share your tentative thesis with classmates. Do they consider your idea worthwhile? Next, list things you might say to develop your thesis. How do your peers respond?

Organizing Ideas   The organization of this paper will depend on whether you are discussing one or more experiences. However you approach it, you will need to consider what arrangement will best help your audience understand the effects of your experience. If you are using specific concepts from the chapter, you will have to think about how and where to present them so that their relevance is clear. Using a mind map or a web may help you organize your ideas. Here is one possible format:

First experience	Second experience	Why the two experiences are related
Circumstances	Circumstances	_____
What was said	What was said	_____
How it affected you	How it affected you	_____

Drafting   Start with the part that will be easiest to write. Look at your freewriting, your possible thesis statement, and your list or map of ideas. Now, work those early-stage writings into a coherent draft. Remember that shaping ideas is your biggest concern at this stage. Trust yourself to speak about your own experiences and to explain what they mean to you.

After you have drafted enough material, give attention to paragraphs. Where does your material cluster into divisions? Which paragraphs need topic sentences? Where in the paragraphs should topic sentences be placed?

Draft an opening paragraph and a conclusion. What connections exist between them? Will they create an effective beginning and a good ending for your essay?

Revising Your Essay: The Impact of Language on Our Lives

Each author included in this chapter offers guidelines and inspiration for revising and clarifying your writing. What would Donald Murray, for example, draw your attention to? Are your word choices as specific, insightful, and sharp-eyed as Malcolm X's engagement with a dictionary would provide? Take your time revising, editing, and proofreading your writing to make your paper as effective as possible.

Peer Responses

Once your draft is ready for revision, you may decide to pass it along to your classmates or to a friend or family member in order to get some feedback. If you ask someone outside of class to review your writing, it will help to give that person a description of the assignment. You could also provide him or her a copy of "A Step-by-Step Method for Revising Any Assignment," located on the inside front cover of this book for additional guidance.

Revision

Begin your revision by referring to "A Step-by-Step Method for Revising Any Assignment," and focus on the "Think Big" and "Think Medium" sections under "Revision." These are the larger components of your paper.

Editing and Proofreading

After you are comfortable with the overall message your paper communicates, focus on your draft, sentence by sentence, as suggested in the "Editing" section of "A Step-by-Step Method for Revising Any Assignment." Finally, get "picky," and look at the smallest details—and remember that they, too, have an impact on the way the audience perceives you and the ideas you want to communicate.

The following essay shows how one student responded to this assignment. While revising, she applied concepts about language she had learned in this chapter.

STUDENT WRITING

Jessie Lange's Writing Process

Student Jessie Lange decided to write about an experience she had with her younger brother. She took the advice given, to start with the part that would be easiest to write. She began to describe her experience, which would become the third paragraph of her essay below, this way:

After my first four months of college, I returned home for the winter break. After all this, I returned home to be more affected by one word uttered by my younger brother than I had been by my classes.

Then Jessie thought about the precise language used in the readings in this chapter, and she realized that her readers would not know what "all this" meant and her readers also would not know how much younger her brother was. So she revised in this way:

After my first four months of college, I returned home for the winter break. After four months of reading inspirational writers, attending the lectures of powerful speakers, learning about language itself in my linguistics course, speaking French, and having discussions with intelligent professors who are at the top of their field, I returned home to be more affected by one word uttered by my twelve-year-old brother than I had been by any of the speaking and listening I'd engaged in first semester.

Jessie continued this process as she drafted and revised, and finally produced this essay.

Lange's brief analysis of language leads to her thesis statement: "In fact, just a few words often have more of an impact than long speeches and rambling sentences." She then uses a question to engage her audience. Her question also functions as a smooth transition into the body of her essay.

Lange uses *Kiss of the Spider Woman* as an example to illustrate her point. Even if her audience is not familiar with the play, she provides enough detail to make her point clear.

The Power of Language
by Jessie Lange

Language is indeed one of the most powerful things we possess. It is how we communicate our ideas, how we put our abstract feelings for others into words, and it is what we use to describe and evaluate our human experience. Being a "good speaker" in public is something we value highly as we do effective communication in our personal lives. One of the most incredible things about language is the power that just a phrase or even a single word can have. In fact, just a few words often have more of an impact than long speeches and rambling sentences. How does it happen that a small combination of letters can have such a tremendous effect on us?

In the play *Kiss of the Spider Woman* by Manuel Puig, one of the characters, Molina, comments on the power of language. Molina, a gentle soul and an expert storyteller, is desperately in love with the man with whom he is sharing a prison cell. "How does it happen that sometimes someone says something and wins someone else over forever?" he wonders. If only he knew, he could win the love of his cell-mate, Valentin. What Molina is acknowledging is that it doesn't take an infinite number of words to say something powerful. It can be a phrase or even a single word that has the most profound impact on others. In this case, it is the "one thing" uttered that causes another to fall in love with you. In the everyday, there are particular words and phrases that stay with us, that we roll over in our minds, repeating them to ourselves again and again. There are certain words that have such an impact that they stay with us eternally longer than the time it took to utter them. I recently had a personal experience with the effects of this.

After my first four months of college, I returned home for the winter break. After four months of reading inspirational writers, attending the lectures of powerful speakers, learning about language itself in my linguistics course, speaking French, and having discussions with intelligent professors who are at the top of their field,

Source: The Power of Language by Jessie Lange.

I returned home to be more affected by one word uttered by my twelve-year-old brother than I had been by any of the speaking or listening I'd engaged in first semester. My brother and I have always been extremely close. We do not have the "sibling rivalry" I so often hear about from others. And so being apart had been a struggle. The fact that we had been apart so long and the impending separation just a few weeks away were probably much of the reason his words had such an effect on me. We were saying goodnight one night and my brother who, in many ways, is a miniature me, was holding my hand. I'd just finished assuring him that he was the "bomb" and he was smiling at me. Somewhere out of his slim twelve-year-old frame a thought emerged in the form of speech: "I wish I could take you with me," he said. "Where?" I asked, thoroughly confused. His smile broadened. "Everywhere," he said matter-of-factly. Such a simple word but, to me, so profoundly meaningful, causing a complete overflow of emotion. I had visions of never letting go of his hand. Of bringing him to college with me, of going to school with him, of bringing him all through my life and never missing a day or a second of his getting older. Just one word: *Everywhere.*

If I've learned anything about language, it's that the cliché "quality, not quantity" definitely applies. It took one utterance from my brother to almost bring me to tears. With one word, I could imagine myself holding his fingers in mine wherever I went, wherever we went.

The third paragraph reveals Lange's personal experience. It effectively illustrates her point: "just a few words often have more of an impact than long speeches and rambling sentences." Notice the details she uses to purposefully describe her brother and the situation.

Lange's brief conclusion effectively summarizes what she learned from the experience. Her main point reverberates, and the audience is left with a memorable image.

REFLECTION ON WRITING

1. Consider the structure of Jessie Lange's essay, and ponder how, if the organization changed, it would affect the audience. If Jessie began the essay with the story about her brother uttering that magical word, "Everywhere," and then ended the essay with her thoughts and research on the power of language, would it be as powerful? Why or why not?

2. Several times in the essay, Jessie indicates that brevity, or conservative use of words, can have more impact than rambling sentences: "quality, not quantity" was the cliché she used. Can you think of a time when the brevity of language gave a particular message more power? What was the situation, the word (or words), and the effect?

ALTERNATIVE WRITING PROJECTS

1. Write an essay about the most current uses of emotive language. Be sure to have a focus, a main point that your examples support.

2. Write an essay about how names define or don't define who we are.

CHAPTER 6

Summary

- One effective way to develop your ability to recognize and use language effectively and ethically is to read widely.
- When making decisions when revising drafts, it is good practice to follow these steps:
  - Define your decision and your goals.
  - Consider possible choices.
  - Gather relevant information, and evaluate the pros and cons.
  - Implement your choice by drafting, and evaluate it by rereading what you wrote.
- Remember the following tips for revising your own writing or reviewing the writing of a peer:
  - Think big—look at the draft as a whole.
  - Think medium—look at the draft paragraph by paragraph.
  - Think small—look at the draft sentence by sentence.
  - Think "picky"—look at the draft as the fussiest critic might.
- You have a responsibility as a writer to use language ethically. One way to ensure your writing is ethical is to clear up any ambiguities or vagueness.
- Consider using figurative language, like similes and metaphors, when you
  - Have trouble finding the right words
  - Want to express a profound thought in a strikingly original way
  - Want to add an extra dimension to a description
  - Want to amuse your audience
- Euphemisms and clichés should be used carefully and sparingly to avoid diluting serious issues and making your ideas sound boring and unoriginal.
- Emotive words usually signal that a personal opinion or evaluation is being presented. These words possess the power to capture your audience's attention, but they should not be used as a substitute for presenting facts.

PART 2

Thinking and Writing to Shape Our World

CHAPTER 7   Writing to Describe and Narrate: Exploring Perceptions

CHAPTER 8   Writing to Classify and Define: Exploring Concepts

CHAPTER 9   Writing to Compare and Evaluate: Exploring Perspectives and
             Relationships

CHAPTER 10   Writing to Speculate: Exploring Cause and Effect

All of us actively shape, as well as discover, the world of our experience in which we live. Our world does not exist as a finished product waiting for us to perceive it, think about it, and describe it with words and pictures. Instead, we are active participants in composing our world, organizing and interpreting sensations to create a coherent whole. Many times, our shaping of this world will reflect basic thinking patterns that we rely on constantly whenever we think, act, speak, or write.

Part Two explores four basic ways of relating and organizing: relationships in space and time, relationships of classification and definition, relationships of comparison, and relationships of cause. The Writing Projects at the end of each chapter ask you to integrate ideas from other sources into your essays as you explore these relationships and the thinking/organizing patterns that develop from them.

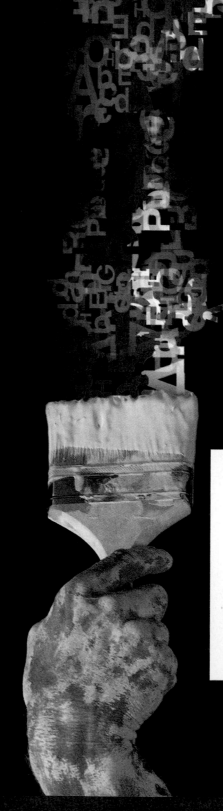

Images can convey a powerful message, and there is an intricate relationship between an image's *objective* attributes (what actually exists) and the *subjective* attributes dependent upon how we perceive that image (what we think exists). We view images through our own, unique lenses. As we strive to become critical thinkers and thoughtful writers, it is important to be cognizant of our perceptions as well as the perceptions of those around us.

Writing to Describe and Narrate:
Exploring Perceptions

". . . a thing is not seen because it is visible, but conversely, visible because it is seen . . ."

—PLATO

CRITICAL THINKING FOCUS: **Understanding perceptions**

WRITING FOCUS: **Detail and order in chronologies**

READING THEME: **Narratives and process descriptions**

WRITING ACTIVITIES: **Perceptions and descriptive writing**

WRITING PROJECT: **Narrative showing the effect of a perception**

The way we make sense of the world is through thinking, but our first experiences of the world come to us through our senses: sight, hearing, smell, touch, and taste. These senses are our bridges to the world, making us aware of what occurs outside us. The process of becoming aware of the world through our senses is known as *perceiving*.

This chapter, as well as Chapters 9 and 11, will explore the way the perceiving process operates and how it relates to the ability to think, read, and write effectively. In particular, these chapters examine the way each of us shapes personal experience by actively selecting from, organizing, and interpreting the information provided by our senses. In a way, we each view the world through a pair of individual "contact lenses" that reflect our past experiences and our unique personalities. As critical thinkers, we want to become aware of the nature of our own lenses in order to offset any bias or distortion they may be causing. We also want to become aware of the lenses of others so that we can better understand why they view things the way that they do.

Developing insight into the nature of people's lenses—our own and others'—is essential to becoming an effective writer. When we write, it's helpful to understand our own point of view, to be aware of our own biases. That doesn't mean that we should strive to be completely "objective." In fact, such absolute objectivity is not possible because we can never completely remove our personal lenses. However, understanding our lenses helps us achieve our goals as writers. For example, if we want to present our ideas objectively, then we can work to compensate for our inherent bias. On the other hand, if our intention is to persuade others, we may choose to enhance and strengthen our point of view.

Analogously, we need to understand the lenses of those in our audience if we are to communicate our thoughts and feelings effectively through our writing. This involves appreciating their point of view and understanding their biases. We can then use this knowledge to craft our writing, shape our language, and utilize the appropriate terminology and logic.

Once again, we can see the essential union of writing and thinking, communicating and knowing. This chapter will provide you with a foundation for understanding how you develop your beliefs and knowledge about the world and how you can communicate your ideas through clear, expressive, and compelling writing. Let's begin by exploring our main source of information—the perceiving process. Some of the most basic patterns of thinking and of presenting ideas draw directly on perceptions. This chapter will focus on three such patterns: description, process, and narrative.

Thinking Critically About Perceptions

BECOMING AWARE OF YOUR OWN PERCEPTIONS

At almost every waking moment of life, our senses are being bombarded by a tremendous number of stimuli: images to see, noises to hear, odors to smell, textures to feel, and flavors to taste. Experiencing all such sensations at once could create what the nineteenth-century American philosopher William James called "a bloomin' buzzin' confusion." Yet to us, the world usually seems much more orderly and understandable. Why is this so?

In the first place, our sense equipment can receive sensations only within certain limited ranges. For example, there are many sounds and smells that animals can detect but we cannot; animals' sense organs have broader ranges in these areas than ours do. A second reason we can handle sensory bombardment is that from the stimulation available, we select only a small amount on which to focus our attention. To demonstrate this, complete the following Thinking-Writing Activity.

This simple exercise demonstrates that for every sensation on which you focus, there are countless others that you are simply ignoring. If you were aware of everything that was happening at every moment, you would be completely overwhelmed. By selecting particular sensations, you are able to make sense of your world in a relatively orderly way. That is, you are *perceiving*, a process by which you actively select, organize, and interpret what is experienced by the senses.

It is tempting to think that our senses simply record what is happening out in the world, as if we were human camcorders. We are not, however, passive receivers of information, containers into which sense experience is poured. Instead, we are active participants who are always trying to understand the sensations we are encountering. As we perceive the world, our experiences are the result of combining the sensations we receive with our understanding of these sensations. For instance, examine the collection of markings in Figure 7.1. What do you see? If all you see is a collection of black spots, try turning the illustration sideways; you will probably perceive a familiar animal.

From this example, you can grasp how, when you perceive the world, you are doing more than simply recording what your senses experience; instead, you are actively making sense of these sensations. The collection of black spots suddenly became the figure of an animal because your mind was able to actively organize the spots into a pattern you recognized. Or think about times when you looked up at white, billowy clouds and saw different figures and designs. The figures you were perceiving were not actually in the clouds but were the result of your giving meaningful form to shapes you were experiencing.

Copyright © Cengage Learning

FIGURE 7.1
Recognizing a Pattern

The same is true for virtually everything we experience. Our perceptions of the world result from combining information provided by our senses with the way we actively make sense of this information. And since making sense of information is what we are doing when we are thinking, perceiving the world involves using our minds in an active way. Of course, we are usually not aware that we are using our minds to interpret sensations we are experiencing. We simply see the animal or the figures in the clouds as if they were really there.

Thinking-Writing Activity

WHAT DO YOU SENSE RIGHT NOW?

Respond to the following questions in writing, using a spontaneous, free-flowing style. Record your sensations as you experience them rather than first taking time to reflect and deliberate.

1. What can you *see?* (for example, the shape of the letters on the page, the design of the clothing on your arm)
2. What can you *hear?* (for example, the hum of the air circulator, the rustling of a page)
3. What can you *feel?* (for example, the pressure of the clothes against your skin, the texture of the page on your fingers)
4. What can you *smell?* (for example, the perfume someone is wearing, the odor of stale cigarette smoke)
5. What can you *taste?* (for example, the aftertastes of your last meal)

Compare your responses with those of your classmates. Did they perceive sensations different from the ones you perceived? If so, how do you explain these differences?

Actively Selecting, Organizing, and Interpreting Sensations   When we actively perceive the sensations we are experiencing, we are usually engaged in three distinct activities:

- *Selecting* certain sensations to pay attention to
- *Organizing* these sensations into a design or pattern
- *Interpreting* what this design or pattern means

In the case of Figure 7.1, you were able to perceive an animal because you selected certain markings to concentrate on, organized these markings into a pattern, and interpreted this pattern as representing a dog.

Of course, when we perceive, the three operations of selecting, organizing, and interpreting are usually performed quickly, automatically, and often simultaneously. Also, because they are so rapid and automatic, we are not normally aware of performing these operations.

Take a few moments to explore more examples that illustrate how you actively select, organize, and interpret your perceptions of the world. Carefully examine Figure 7.2. Do you see both the young woman and the old woman? If you do, try switching back and forth between the two images. As you do so, notice how, for each image, you are doing the following things:

- *Selecting* certain lines, shapes, and shadings on which to focus your attention
- *Organizing* these lines, shapes, and shadings into different patterns
- *Interpreting* these patterns as representing things you can recognize—a hat, a nose, a chin

So far, we have been exploring how the mind actively participates in the ways we perceive the world. By combining the sensations we are receiving with the way our minds select, organize, and interpret these sensations, we perceive a world that is stable and familiar. Thus, each of us develops a perspective on the world, one that usually makes sense to us.

The process of perceiving takes place on various levels. At the most basic level, *perceiving* refers to the selection, organization, and interpretation of sensations: for example, being able to perceive various objects such as a basketball. However, we also perceive larger patterns of meaning at more complex levels, as in watching the action of a group of people engaged in a basketball game. Although these are different situations, both engage us in the process of perceiving.

Mary Evans Picture Library

FIGURE 7.2
Young Woman/Old Woman

NOTING DIFFERENCES IN PEOPLE'S PERCEPTIONS

As we have noted, we are not usually aware of our active participation in perceiving the world. We normally assume that what we are perceiving is what is actually taking place. Only when we find that our perception of an event differs from others' perceptions of it are we forced to examine the manner in which we are selecting, organizing, and interpreting the event. Many artists and photographers believe that what an individual viewer sees in a picture mirrors something within the viewer himself.

In most cases, people in a group will have a variety of perceptions about what is taking place in the photograph below. Some will see the couple as engaged in a serious disagreement. Others may see them thoughtfully discussing a serious issue related to the baby on the bed. In each case, the perception depends on how the viewer is actively using his or her mind to organize and interpret what is taking place.

Thinking Critically About Visuals

Thinking-Writing Activity

COMPARING YOUR PERCEPTIONS WITH THOSE OF OTHERS

Carefully examine this photograph of a man and a woman sitting on a bed with a baby in the background, and then explore your reactions. What do you think is happening in this picture? Explain by answering the following questions.

1. Describe as specifically as possible what you perceive as taking place in the picture.
2. Describe what you think will take place next.
3. Identify which details of the picture inform your perceptions.
4. Compare your perceptions with those of your classmates. List several perceptions that differ from yours.

Radius Images/Jupiter Images

THINKING CRITICALLY ABOUT NEW MEDIA

Distinguishing Perception from Reality

Sure, the Internet is full of information, but much of this information is based on perceptions that are incomplete, biased, and outright false. How do we tell the difference between beliefs that are relatively accurate, objective, and factual and those that aren't? The short answer is that we need to come armed with our full array of critical thinking abilities, combined with a healthy dose of skepticism. Consider these examples.

Phony Journalism   "One could say my life itself has been one long soundtrack. Music was my life, music brought me to life, and music is how I will be remembered long after I leave this life. When I die there will be a final waltz playing in my head that only I can hear." When Dublin University student Shane Fitzgerald posted this poetic but phony quote on the Wikipedia obituary for the French composer Maurice Jarre, he said he was testing how our globalized, increasingly Internet-dependent media were upholding accuracy and accountability in an age of instant news. His report card: Wikipedia passed; journalism flunked. Although Wikipedia administrators quickly detected and removed the bogus quote, they weren't quick enough to prevent journalists around the world from cutting and pasting it to dozens of blogs and newspaper websites. And the offending quote continued its viral spread until, after a full month went by, Fitzgerald blew the whistle on his editorial fraud. His analysis? "I am 100 percent convinced that if I hadn't come forward, that quote would have gone down in history as something Maurice Jarre said, instead of something I made up. It would have become another example where, once anything is printed enough times in the media without challenge, it becomes fact."

Phony Degrees   Want a college degree—or even a Ph.D.—in engineering, medicine, philosophy, or virtually any subject you choose, without having to attend all of those classes and pay all of that tuition? No problem! Your options range from having to take a limited number of online courses to simply coming up with the right cash payment, and an official-looking diploma will be on its way before you can say *summa cum laude!* Phony degrees are nothing new: black markets in fake diplomas are known to have existed as far back as fourteenth-century Europe. But today's new media have raised the scam to a high art, with modern diploma mills providing detailed transcripts, verification services, and even fake accrediting agencies to legitimize fake schools. The only problem with using a phony degree to pad your resume? In addition to being uneducated and unqualified, of course, there's the likelihood of getting caught and watching your career disappear like invisible ink on a fraudulent diploma.

Counterfeit Websites   Counterfeit websites are sites disguising themselves as legitimate sites for the purpose of disseminating misinformation. For example, *www .martinlutherking.org* disseminates hateful information about one of the greatest African-American leaders of our era while pretending to be, on the surface, an "official" Martin Luther King Jr. site. While the home page depicts a photograph of King and his family and links titled "Historical Writings," "The Death of a Dream," and "Recommended Books," subsequent pages include defamatory allegations and links to white power organizations and literature.

Thinking-Writing Activity

DETECTING AND ANALYZING FAULTY PERCEPTIONS ON THE WEB

1. Here's an opportunity to put your critical thinking skills to use as a detective. Surf the Web, and identify at least one example of each of the misleading or bogus sites or advertisements listed below; then critically evaluate them in terms of their accuracy, authenticity, reliability, and objectivity.

   - Phony journalism
   - Phony degrees
   - Counterfeit websites

2. Spend a little time exploring one or more "hoax-busting" websites. You can use "hoax busting" or "hoax buster" as a search term in Google (or other search engine) to find results. Next, write your own personal guide to identifying and debunking false and misleading perceptions presented on the Web.

Writing Thoughtfully About Perceptions

Although the verb *describe* can be used to mean the giving of any detailed account, it more precisely indicates the reporting of sensory impressions: what you see, hear, feel, smell, or taste—your perceptions. Look back at the questions on page 209 to note how your five senses responded; also, reflect on what you have been reading about selecting, organizing, and interpreting sensations. This material should help you understand the two types of descriptions that you will be writing about in the Thinking-Writing Activity on page 219. You might also use objective and subjective descriptions in the writing you do for other college courses or in work situations.

WRITING OBJECTIVELY AND SUBJECTIVELY

Descriptions can be broadly divided into two categories: *objective,* involving as little judgment as possible, and *subjective,* involving whatever personal judgment is appropriate to a writer's purpose.

Objective descriptions are often expected in scientific, medical, engineering, and law enforcement writing. The purpose of an objective description is to help the audience sense an object or situation as it is. Later, judgments and implications can be drawn from objective descriptions, but the cleanest possible rendering is needed as a starting point. Of course, the selection and presentation of *any* ideas or information involve conscious and unconscious judgments. However, when objectivity is the purpose, you should try to perceive with as little bias as you can and to describe in language that is as neutral as possible. Personal beliefs or opinions do not figure into objective writing.

In other writing situations, descriptions are intended to be more subjective. Then the explicit purpose is to shape the audience's opinion of the object under scrutiny. Subjective descriptions occur in literary texts of all kinds: stories, poems, personal essays, and biographies; in argumentative pieces; and in personal writing such as letters to friends and journal entries. Think of how a novelist describes characters or settings; think of how an attorney might reword the police report's objective description of a victim in order to influence a jury; think of how you would describe your new special person to a close friend! You may want to use the first person (*I*) when writing a subjective description to help your audience realize that this description is how you see it. When writing a subjective description, you will be selecting details purposefully and using language that creates the effect that you want your audience to experience.

Objective Language	*Subjective Language*
A German shepherd	A vicious, snarling dog
A lake at night	A shimmering mirror of moonlight
Drove at 85 mph	Recklessly tore down the road
A six-foot five-inch man	A towering man
Quit my job	Told them to take their job and shove it
Filed for divorce	Got revenge on the lowlife
Won the election	Stole victory from the real winner

CONTRASTING OBJECTIVE AND SUBJECTIVE WRITING

The reading that follows has, as its subject, the abilities of animals to perceive and "feel." However, the reading is both "objective" and "subjective," as the author—who is autistic—writes about her own processes of thinking and feeling.

"Animal Feelings"
by Temple Grandin

Dr. Temple Grandin, a professor of animal science at Colorado State University, is renowned for her work on developing humane facilities for both the care and the slaughter of livestock. As a person with autism, she has written extensively on the ways in which people with autism perceive the world and the similarities between her own perceptions and those of animals. Her work was first brought to wide attention by neurologist and author Oliver Sacks in his book *An Anthropologist on Mars,* the title of which is Grandin's phrase for describing how she feels around "neurotypical" people. Grandin's books include *Thinking in Pictures: And Other Reports from My Life with Autism* (1996) and *Animals in Translation: Using the Mysteries of Autism to Decode Animal Behavior* (2005), from which the following selection is excerpted.

Animals Aren't Ambivalent

Mammals and birds have the same feelings people do. Researchers are just now discovering that lizards and snakes probably share most of these emotions with us, too. Just to give a couple of examples: the skink lizard in Australia is monogamous, and rattlesnake mamas here in the United States protect their young from predators the same way a mammal would. The fact that some snake mothers take care of their babies came as a big surprise, since researchers have always believed snakes weren't social at all and that mothers abandoned their babies after birth. We still don't know much about the social lives of snakes, but at least now we know that they *have* a social life.

We know animals and humans share the same core feelings partly because we know quite a bit how our core emotions are created by the brain, and there's no question animals share that biology with us. Their emotional biology is so close to ours that most of the research on the neurology of emotions—or *affective neuroscience*—is done with animals. When it comes to the basics of life, like getting eaten by a tiger or protecting the young, animals feel the same way we do.

The main difference between animal emotions and human emotions is that animals don't have *mixed emotions* the way normal people do. Animals aren't ambivalent; they don't have *love-hate* relationships with each other or with people. That's one of the reasons humans love animals so much; animals are loyal. If an animal loves you he loves you no matter what. He doesn't care what you look like or how much money you make.

Source: From "Animal Feelings," in *Animals in Translation: Using the Mysteries of Autism to Decode Animal Behavior,* Temple Grandin and Catherine Johnson, 2005, pp. 88–93. Reprinted with permission of the Authors.

This is another connection between autism and animals: autistic people have mostly simple emotions, too. That's why normal people describe us as *innocent*. An autistic person's feelings are direct and open, just like animal feelings. We don't hide our feelings, and we aren't ambivalent. I can't even imagine what it would be like to have feelings of love and hate for the same person.

5   Some people will probably think this is an insulting thing to say about autistic people, but one thing I appreciate about being autistic is that I don't have to deal with all the emotional craziness my students do. I had one fantastic student who flunked out of school because she broke up with her boyfriend. There's so much psychodrama in normal people's lives. Animals never have psychodrama.

Children don't, either. Emotionally, children are more like animals and autistic people, because children's frontal lobes are still growing and don't mature until sometime in early adulthood. I mentioned earlier that the frontal lobes are one big association cortex, tying everything together, including emotions like love and hate that would probably be better off staying separate. That's another reason why a dog can be like a person's child: children's emotions are straightforward and loyal like a dog. A seven-year-old boy or girl will race through the house to greet Dad when he comes from work the same way a dog will. I think animals, children, and autistic people have simpler emotions because their brains have less ability to make connections, so their emotions stay more separate and compartmentalized.

Of course, no one knows why an autistic *grown-up* has trouble making connections, since our frontal lobes are normal-sized. All we know right now is that researchers find "decreased connectivity among cortical regions and between the cortex and subcortex." The way I visualize it is that a normal brain is like a big corporate office building with telephones, faxes, e-mail, messengers, people walking around and talking—a big corporation has zillions of ways for messages to get from one place to another. The autistic brain is like the same big corporate office building where the only way for anyone to talk to anyone else is by fax. There's no telephone, no e-mail, no messengers, and no people walking around talking to each other. Just faxes. So a lot less stuff is getting through as a consequence, and everything starts to break down. Some messages get through okay; other messages get distorted when the fax misprints or the paper jams; other messages don't get through at all.

The point is that even though autistic people have a normal-sized neocortex including normal-sized frontal lobes, our brains *function* as if our frontal lobes were either much smaller or not fully developed. Our brains function more like a child's brain or an animal's brain, but for different reasons.

When the different parts of the brain are relatively separate from each other and don't communicate well, you end up with simple, clear emotions due to compartmentalization. A child can be furious at his mom or dad one second, then completely forget about it the next, because being mad and being happy are separate states. A child hops from one to the other depending on the situation.

10   You see the exact same thing with animals. Strong emotions in animals are usually like a sudden thunderstorm. They blow in and then blow back out. Two dogs who live together in the same house can be snarling one second, then go back to being best friends the next. Normal people need a lot more time to get over an angry emotion, and even when a normal adult does get over a bad emotion, he's made a lasting connection between the angry emotion and the person or situation that made him angry. When a

normal person gets furiously angry with a person he loves, his brain hooks up *anger* and *love* and remembers it. Thanks to his highly developed frontal lobes, which connect everything up with everything else, his brain learns to have mixed emotions about that person or situation.

Another big difference between animals and people is that animals probably don't have the complex emotions people do, like shame, guilt, embarrassment, greed, or wanting bad things to happen to people who are more successful than you. There are different schools of thought about simple and complex emotions, but the definition I use is brain-based. Simple emotions are the primary emotions such as fear and rage that come from the reptilian and the mammalian brains. Complex emotions, or secondary emotions, also come from the reptilian and the mammalian brains, but they light up the neocortex as well. The secondary emotions build on the primary emotions and involve more thought and interpretation. For instance, shame, guilt, and embarrassment probably all come out of the same primary emotion of *separation distress,* which I'll talk about shortly. Your culture and upbringing teach you when to feel shame versus when to feel embarrassment or guilt, but all three start out in the brain as the pain of being isolated.

I don't want to give the impression that animals *never* have more than one feeling at the same time. Later on I'll talk about the fact that cows often feel curious and afraid at the same time. (Jaak Panksepp, author of *Affective Neuroscience,* classifies curiosity as a core emotion.) Biologically it's possible for more than one basic emotional system to be activated in an animal's brain at the same time, so technically an animal is capable of experiencing a mixed emotion.

But in real life one emotion usually ends up completely replacing the other, and some of the core emotions probably do "turn off" others. For instance, brain research shows that play and rage are incompatible emotions, which anyone who has ever watched two dogs play fighting can tell you. Once in a while a play fight will turn into a real fight, and when that happens the two dogs don't show the slightest sign (friendly tail wags, toothy smiles) that they're experiencing happy play feelings along with angry fight feelings. Once a play fight has turned real, *all* of the dog's body language and vocal communication is angry.

No Freud for Dogs

Another huge difference between animals and people: I don't think animals have the defense mechanisms Sigmund Freud described in humans. Projection, displacement, repression, denial—I don't think we see these things in animals. Defense mechanisms defend against anxiety, and all defense mechanisms depend on repression in some way. Using repression, you push whatever it is you're afraid of down into your unconscious mind and focus your conscious mind on a stand-in. Or, in the case of the higher, more mature defense mechanisms, like humor, altruism, or intellectualization, you use humor, empathy, and thought to push away the "real" emotion, which is fear.

The reason I believe animals don't have Freudian defense mechanisms is that animals and autistic people don't seem to have repression. Or, if they do, they have it only to a weak degree. I don't think I have any of Freud's defense mechanisms, and I'm always amazed when normal people do. One of the things that blows my mind about normal human beings is denial. When I see a packing plant getting into a bad situation, I'll say, "That's not going to work," and everyone will immediately think I'm being really negative. But I'm not. It would be obvious to anyone outside the situation that what they're doing isn't going to work, but people inside the bad situation can't see it because their defense mechanisms protect them from seeing it until they're ready. That's denial, and I can't understand it at all. I can't even imagine what it's like.

15   That's because I don't have an unconscious. Normal people can push bad things out of their conscious minds into their unconscious minds, but I can't. Normal people can't always *keep* the bad stuff locked up, of course, but at least they have more freedom from it than I do. That's why I can't watch any violent movies with rape or torture scenes. The pictures stay in my conscious mind. Once they're there, I can't get rid of them. The only way I can block a bad image is by thinking about something else, but the bad image still pops back up in my mind, like a pop-up ad on the Internet. The way I think about it is that a normal brain has a built-in pop-up zapper, but my brain doesn't. To get rid of the pop-up image I have to consciously click on another screen.

I don't know *why* my brain doesn't have an unconscious, but I think it's connected to the fact that pictures are my "native language," not words. Lots of studies show that the language parts of your brain block your memory for images. Language doesn't *erase* your image memories; the images are still there, inside your head. But language keeps the images from becoming conscious. Psychologists call this *verbal overshadowing,* and I'll talk about it more in my chapter on animal thinking. For the time being, let's just say that while I don't know why I don't seem to have an unconscious, I think my problems with language have a lot to do with it. Language isn't a natural ability for me, so maybe the language parts of my brain don't have the same power to overshadow the pictures.

I know it's a leap to go from saying that I don't have an unconscious to saying I don't have defense mechanisms, but based on my personal experience I think it's true. No one has ever tried to test animals for defense mechanisms, but animals act as if they don't have them, either. You never see an animal act as if a dangerous situation is safe. You might see a dog act like he's not afraid when he is, but that's not the same thing. The dog knows there's danger and is using a standard dog strategy to avoid provoking the threatening dog any further.

A friend of mine has two dogs, one a gentle female collie and the other a macho golden retriever. (You might not have thought a golden retriever could be macho, but this one is.) When my friend walks the collie *alone* past the two ferocious-acting German shepherds down the street, the collie looks straight ahead and acts as if she's deaf and blind. She does this because staring is a provocation. She's averting her eyes to avoid challenging them.

The reason we can say the collie is only pretending not to be afraid of the other dogs when she's alone, instead of not feeling fear because she'd repressed it, is that she stops orienting to motion. All animals orient to movement. It's automatic. Since no dog can be oblivious to two German shepherds who are charging straight toward her, the collie has to consciously override her most basic orienting response. She has to *actively* ignore the other dogs.

QUESTIONS FOR READING ACTIVELY

1. Note which paragraphs of the excerpt from "Animal Feelings" are subjective and which paragraphs are objective. How does the subject of each paragraph influence whether or not the author, Temple Grandin, chooses the subjective or objective voice?

2. Grandin uses comparison and contrast effectively in this reading. What are the subjects and concepts that she compares and contrasts? What kind of evidence does she use to illustrate these comparisons?

3. What is the difference between "simple" and "complex" emotions?

QUESTION FOR THINKING CRITICALLY

1. Go online for more information about Temple Grandin and about autism. How do Grandin's history and writing challenge your perceptions of people with autism?

QUESTIONS FOR WRITING THOUGHTFULLY

1. Temple Grandin objectively considers and analyzes her own processes of perception in order to better understand the lives of animals. In a descriptive essay, analyze the ways in which you perceive a certain emotion or "feeling." What circumstances cause you to feel that emotion? Has your response to those circumstances changed as you have matured? Describe one or two key influences on how you perceive a specific circumstance, and tell how you have learned an emotional response.

2. In an objective essay, describe the behavior of an animal or a group of animals (wild or domestic) with which you are familiar. Before you begin, look up the term *personification*. In your essay, be particularly aware of moments when you personify the behavior that you are objectively observing and describing. How do audience and circumstance influence whether or not a writer might use personification to describe behavior? What does personification suggest about the limits of human perceptions?

Thinking-Writing Activity

CREATING OBJECTIVE AND SUBJECTIVE DESCRIPTIONS

Write two separate paragraphs in which you describe the same person or object in two different ways. Make one paragraph as objective as possible; make the other primarily subjective in order to create a particular impression for your readers. Each paragraph should have about six to eight sentences.

Which of these paragraphs will have a strong topic sentence? Why? Which may not have a topic sentence or may have one that makes no claim? Why?

Chronological Relationships

Chronological forms of writing organize events or ideas in a time sequence. The focus in chronological writing is on using description to illustrate growth, development, or change—from a person's life story to the steps in creating a favorite dish. The *chronological pattern* organizes a topic into a series of events in the time sequence in which they occurred. Many chronologies are narratives or stories. The process mode of thinking organizes an activity into a series of steps necessary for reaching a certain end. Here, the focus is on describing aspects of growth, development, or change, as you might do when explaining how to prepare a favorite dish or perform a new dance.

NARRATIVES

Perhaps the oldest and most universal form of chronological expression is the *narrative*, a story about real or fictional experiences. Many people who study communication believe that narrative is the starting point for other patterns of presentation because we often process our perceptions in storylike ways.

Every human culture has used narratives to pass on values and traditions from one generation to the next, as exemplified by such enduring works as the *Odyssey*, the Bible, and the Koran. One of America's great storytellers, Mark Twain, once said that a good story has to accomplish something and arrive somewhere. In other words, if a story is to be effective in engaging the interest of the audience, it has to have a purpose. The purpose may be to provide more information on a subject, to illustrate an idea, to lead the audience to a particular way of thinking, or to entertain. An effective narrative does not merely record the complex, random, and often unrelated events of life. Instead, it has focus, an ordered structure, and a meaningful point of view.

WRITING ABOUT PROCESSES

A second type of time-ordered thinking pattern is the *process relationship*, which describes events or experiences in terms of their development. From birth, we are involved with processes in every facet of life. They can be classified in various ways: *natural* (such as growing physically), *mechanical* (such as assembling a bicycle), *physical* (such as learning a sport), *mental* (such as developing a way of thinking), and *creative* (such as writing a poem).

Writing about a process involves two basic tasks. The first is to divide the process being analyzed into parts or stages. The second is to explain the movement of the process through these parts or stages from beginning to end. The stages identified should be separate and distinct and should involve no repetition or significant omissions.

Processes are explained for two purposes. One is to give instructions on how to do something, such as build a wall or set up a computer. Instructions will often use the pronoun *you* and imperative or command verb forms. This is an excellent example of grammar, meaning, and purpose working together. The other purpose of process writing is to describe a process but not necessarily teach someone to do it.

In your academic reading, you'll notice both kinds of process writing. For example, a biology textbook will explain the process of photosynthesis—something that your professor might expect you to understand but certainly not to do yourself! (If you could, you'd be green.) On the other hand, when your biology professor gives you instructions for dissecting a frog, those instructions describe a process that you are expected to do.

EXAMPLES OF PROCESS WRITING

Read the following two examples of process writing. What is the purpose of each? How can you tell? What are some words in each that indicate sequence?

> Jacketing was a sleight-of-hand I watched with wonder each time, and I have discovered that my father was admired among sheepmen up and down the valley for his skill at it: He was just pretty catty at that, the way he could get that ewe to take on a new lamb every time. Put simply, jacketing was a ruse played on a ewe whose lamb had died. A substitute lamb quickly would be singled out, most likely from a set of twins. Sizing up the tottering newcomer, Dad would skin the dead lamb, and into the tiny pelt carefully snip four leg holes and a head hole. Then the stand-in lamb would have the skin fitted onto it like a snug jacket on a poodle. The next step of disguise was to cut out the dead lamb's liver and smear it several times across the jacket of pelt. In its borrowed and bedaubed skin, the new baby lamb then was presented to the ewe. She would sniff the baby impostor endlessly, distrustful but pulled by the blood-smell of her own. When in a few days she made up her dim sheep's mind to accept the lamb, Dad snipped away the jacket and recited his victory: Mother him like hell now, don't ye? See what a hellava dandy lamb I got for ye, old sister? Who says I couldn't jacket day onto night if I wanted to, now-I-ask-ye?
>
> —Ivan Doig, *This House of Sky*

> If you are inexperienced in relaxation techniques, begin by sitting in a comfortable chair with your feet on the floor and your hands resting easily in your lap. Close your eyes and breathe evenly, deeply, and gently. As you exhale each breath let your body become more relaxed. Starting with one hand direct your attention to one part of your body at a time. Close your fist and tighten the muscles of your forearm. Feel the sensation of tension in your muscles. Relax your hand and let your forearm and hand become completely limp. Direct all your attention to the sensation of relaxation as you continue to let all tension leave your hand and arm. Continue this practice once or several times each day, relaxing your other hand and arm, your legs, back, abdomen, chest, neck, face, and scalp. When you have this mastered and can relax completely, turn your thoughts to scenes of natural tranquility from your past. Stay with your inner self as long as you wish, whether thinking of nothing or visualizing only the loveliest

of images. Often you will become completely unaware of your surroundings. When you open your eyes you will find yourself refreshed in mind and body.

—Laurence J. Peter, *The Peter Prescription*

Thinking-Writing Activity

WRITING PROCESS DESCRIPTIONS

Think about a process you know well. In one paragraph, instruct your audience on how to complete this process. For example, you could instruct a group of campers on how to build a lean-to.

For the second paragraph, explain the same process, but this time, avoid giving step-by-step instructions.

In the following essay, surgeon and writer Atul Gawande uses the description of a technical medical procedure to describe the ways in which young surgical residents become experienced, confident practitioners of their art.

"The Learning Curve"

by Atul Gawande

Atul Gawande received his M.D. from Harvard Medical School and an MPH from the Harvard School of Public Health. He is a doctor at a Boston hospital and a staff writer for *The New Yorker*, contributing essays on public health issues as well as specific cases and experiences from his own practice. A collection of these essays, *Complications: A Surgeon's Notes on an Imperfect Science*, was published in 2002.

The patient needed a central line. "Here's your chance," S., the chief resident, said. I had never done one before. "Get set up and then page me when you're ready to start."

It was my fourth week in surgical training. The pockets of my short white coat bulged with patient printouts, laminated cards with instructions for doing CPR and reading EKGs and using the dictation system, two surgical handbooks, a stethoscope, wound-dressing supplies, meal tickets, a penlight, scissors, and about a dollar in loose change. As I headed up the stairs to the patient's floor, I rattled.

This will be good, I tried to tell myself: my first real procedure. The patient— fiftyish, stout, taciturn—was recovering from abdominal surgery he'd had about a week earlier. His bowel function hadn't yet returned, and he was unable to eat. I explained to him that he needed intravenous nutrition and that this required a "special line" that would go into his chest. I said that I would put the line in him while he was in his bed, and that it would involve my numbing a spot on his chest with a local anesthetic, and then threading the line in. I did not say that the line was eight inches long and would go into his vena cava, the main blood vessel to his heart. Nor did I say how tricky the procedure could be. There were "slight risks" involved, I said, such as bleeding and lung collapse; in experienced hands, complications of this sort occur in fewer than one case in a hundred.

But, of course, mine were not experienced hands. And the disasters I knew about weighed on my mind: the woman who had died within minutes from massive bleeding when a resident lacerated her vena cava; the man whose chest had to be opened because a resident lost hold of a wire inside the line, which then floated down to the patient's heart; the man who had a cardiac arrest when the procedure put him into ventricular fibrillation. I said nothing of such things, naturally, when I asked the patient's permission to do his line. He said, "OK."

I had seen S. do two central lines; one was the day before, and I'd attended to   5
every step. I watched how she set out her instruments and laid her patient down and put a rolled towel between his shoulder blades to make his chest arch out. I watched how she swabbed his chest with antiseptic, injected lidocaine, which is a local anesthetic, and then, in full sterile garb, punctured his chest near his clavicle with a fat three-inch needle on a syringe. The patient hadn't even flinched. She told me how to avoid hitting the lung ("Go in at a steep angle," she'd said. "Stay *right* under the clavicle"), and how to find the subclavian vein, a branch to the vena cava lying atop the lung near its apex ("Go in at a steep angle. Stay *right* under the clavicle"). She pushed the needle in almost all the way. She drew back on the syringe. And she was in. You knew because the syringe filled with maroon blood. ("If it's bright red, you've hit an artery," she said. "That's not good.") Once you have the tip of this needle poking in the vein, you somehow have to widen the hole in the vein wall, fit the catheter in, and snake it in the right direction—down to the heart, rather than up to the brain—all without tearing through vessels, lung, or anything else.

To do this, S. explained, you start by getting a guide wire in place. She pulled the syringe off, leaving the needle in. Blood flowed out. She picked up a two-foot-long twenty-gauge wire that looked like the steel D string of an electric guitar, and passed nearly its full length through the needle's bore, into the vein, and onward toward the vena cava. "Never force it in," she warned, "and never, ever let go of it." A string of rapid heartbeats fired off on the cardiac monitor, and she quickly pulled the wire back an inch. It had poked into the heart, causing momentary fibrillation. "Guess we're in the right place," she said to me quietly. Then to the patient: "You're doing great. Only a few minutes now." She pulled the needle out over the wire and replaced it with a bullet of thick, stiff plastic, which she pushed in tight to widen the vein opening. She then removed this dilator and threaded the central line—a spaghetti-thick, flexible yellow plastic tube—over the wire until it was all the way in. Now she could remove the wire. She flushed the line with a heparin solution and sutured it to the patient's chest. And that was it.

Today, it was my turn to try. First, I had to gather supplies—a central-line kit, gloves, gown, cap, mask, lidocaine—which took me forever. When I finally had the stuff together, I stopped for a minute outside the patient's door, trying to recall the steps. They remained frustratingly hazy. But I couldn't put it off any longer. I had a page-long list of other things to get done: Mrs. A needed to be discharged; Mr. B needed an abdominal ultrasound arranged; Mrs. C needed her skin staples removed. And every fifteen minutes or so I was getting paged with more tasks: Mr. X was nauseated and needed to be seen; Miss Y's family was here and needed "someone" to talk to them; Mr. Z needed a laxative. I took a deep breath, put on my best don't-worry-I-know-what-I'm-doing look, and went in.

I placed the supplies on a bedside table, untied the patient's gown, and laid him down flat on the mattress, with his chest bare and his arms at his sides. I flipped on a fluorescent overhead light and raised his bed to my height. I paged S. I put on my gown and gloves and, on a sterile tray, laid out the central line, the guide wire, and other materials from the kit. I drew up five cc's of lidocaine in a syringe, soaked two sponge sticks in the yellow-brown Betadine, and opened up the suture packaging.

S. arrived. "What's his platelet count?"

10   My stomach knotted. I hadn't checked. That was bad: too low and he could have a serious bleed from the procedure. She went to check a computer. The count was acceptable.

Chastened, I started swabbing his chest with the sponge sticks. "Got the shoulder roll underneath him?" S. asked. Well, no, I had forgotten that, too. The patient gave me a look. S., saying nothing, got a towel, rolled it up, and slipped it under his back for me. I finished applying the antiseptic and then draped him so that only his right upper chest was exposed. He squirmed a bit beneath the drapes. S. now inspected my tray. I girded myself.

"Where's the extra syringe for flushing the line when it's in?" Damn. She went out and got it.

I felt for my landmarks. *Here?* I asked with my eyes, not wanting to undermine the patient's confidence any further. She nodded. I numbed the spot with lidocaine. ("You'll feel a stick and a burn now, sir.") Next, I took the three-inch needle in hand and poked it through the skin. I advanced it slowly and uncertainly, a few millimeters at a time. This is a big goddamn needle, I kept thinking. I couldn't believe I was sticking it into someone's chest. I concentrated on maintaining a steep angle of entry, but kept spearing his clavicle instead of slipping beneath it.

"Ow!" he shouted.

15   "Sorry," I said. S. signaled with a kind of surfing hand gesture to go underneath the clavicle. This time, it went in. I drew back on the syringe. Nothing. She pointed deeper. I went in deeper. Nothing. I withdrew the needle, flushed out some bits of tissue clogging it, and tried again.

"Ow!"

Too steep again. I found my way underneath the clavicle once more. I drew the syringe back. Still nothing. He's too obese, I thought. S. slipped on gloves and a gown. "How about I have a look?" she said. I handed her the needle and stepped aside. She plunged the needle in, drew back on the syringe, and, just like that, she was in. "We'll be done shortly," she told the patient.

She let me continue with the next steps, which I bumbled through. I didn't realize how long and floppy the guide wire was until I pulled the coil out of its plastic sleeve, and, putting one end of it into the patient, I very nearly contaminated the other. I forgot about the dilating step until she reminded me. Then, when I put in the dilator,

I didn't push quite hard enough, and it was really S. who pushed it all the way in. Finally, we got the line in, flushed it, and sutured it in place.

Outside the room, S. said that I could be less tentative the next time, but that I shouldn't worry too much about how things had gone. "You'll get it," she said. "It just takes practice." I wasn't so sure. The procedure remained wholly mysterious to me. And I could not get over the idea of jabbing a needle into someone's chest so deeply and so blindly. I awaited the X-ray afterward with trepidation. But it came back fine: I had not injured the lung and the line was in the right place.

My second try at placing a central IV line went no better than the first. The patient 20 was in intensive care, mortally ill, on a ventilator, and needed the line so that powerful cardiac drugs could be delivered directly to her heart. She was also heavily sedated, and for this I was grateful. She'd be oblivious of my fumbling.

My preparation was better this time. I got the towel roll in place and the syringes of heparin on the tray. I checked her lab results, which were fine. I also made a point of draping more widely, so that if I flopped the guide wire around by mistake again, it wouldn't hit anything unsterile.

For all that, the procedure was a bust. I stabbed the needle in too shallow and then too deep. Frustration overcame tentativeness and I tried one angle after another. Nothing worked. Then, for one brief moment, I got a flash of blood in the syringe, indicating that I was in the vein. I anchored the needle with one hand and went to pull the syringe off with the other. But the syringe was jammed on too tightly so that when I pulled it free I dislodged the needle from the vein. The patient began bleeding into her chest wall. I held pressure the best I could for a solid five minutes, but still her chest turned black and blue around the site. The hematoma made it impossible to put a line through there anymore. I wanted to give up. But she needed a line and the resident supervising me—a second-year this time—was determined that I succeed. After an X-ray showed that I had not injured her lung, he had me try on the other side, with a whole new kit. I missed again, and he took over. It took him several minutes and two or three sticks to find the vein himself, and that made me feel better. Maybe she was an unusually tough case.

When I failed with a third patient a few days later, though, the doubts really set in. Again, it was stick, stick, stick, and nothing. I stepped aside. The resident watching me got it on the next try.

* * * *

Surgeons, as a group, adhere to a curious egalitarianism. They believe in practice, not talent. People often assume that you have to have great hands to become a surgeon, but it's not true. When I interviewed to get into surgery programs, no one made me sew or take a dexterity test or checked to see if my hands were steady. You do not even need all ten fingers to be accepted. To be sure, talent helps. Professors say that every two or three years they'll see someone truly gifted come through a program—someone who picks up complex manual skills unusually quickly, sees tissue planes before others do, anticipates trouble before it happens. Nonetheless, attending surgeons say that what's most important to them is finding people who are conscientious, industrious, and boneheaded enough to keep at practicing this one difficult thing day and night for years on end. As a former residency director put it to me, given a choice between a PhD who had cloned a gene and a sculptor, he'd pick the PhD every time. Sure, he said, he'd bet on the sculptor's being more physically talented; but he'd bet on the PhD's being less "flaky." And in the end that matters more. Skill, surgeons believe, can be taught; tenacity cannot. It's an odd approach to recruitment, but it continues all the way up the ranks, even in top surgery departments. They start with minions with no experience in surgery, spend years training them, and then take most of their faculty from these homegrown ranks.

25   And it works. There have now been many studies of elite performers—concert violinists, chess grand masters, professional ice skaters, mathematicians, and so forth— and the biggest difference researchers find between them and lesser performers is the amount of deliberate practice they've accumulated. Indeed, the most important talent may be the talent for practice itself. K. Anders Ericsson, a cognitive psychologist and an expert on performance, notes that the most important role that innate factors play may be in a person's *willingness* to engage in sustained training. He has found, for example, that top performers dislike practicing just as much as others do. (That's why, for example, athletes and musicians usually quit practicing when they retire.) But, more than others, they have the will to keep at it anyway.

* * * *

I wasn't sure I did. What good was it, I wondered, to keep doing central lines when I wasn't coming close to hitting them? If I had a clear idea of what I was doing wrong, then maybe I'd have something to focus on. But I didn't. Everyone, of course, had suggestions. Go in with the bevel of the needle up. No, go in with the bevel down. Put a bend in the middle of the needle. No, curve the needle. For a while, I tried to avoid doing another line. Soon enough, however, a new case arose.

The circumstances were miserable. It was late in the day, and I'd had to work through the previous night. The patient weighed more than three hundred pounds. He couldn't tolerate lying flat because the weight of his chest and abdomen made it hard for him to breathe. Yet he had a badly infected wound, needed intravenous antibiotics, and no one could find veins in his arms for a peripheral IV. I had little hope of succeeding. But a resident does what he is told, and I was told to try the line.

I went to his room. He looked scared and said he didn't think he'd last more than a minute on his back. But he said he understood the situation and was willing to make his best effort. He and I decided that he'd be left sitting propped up in bed until the last possible minute. We'd see how far we got after that.

I went through my preparations: checking his blood counts from the lab, putting out the kit, placing the towel roll, and so on. I swabbed and draped his chest while he was still sitting up. S., the chief resident, was watching me this time, and when everything was ready I had her tip him back, an oxygen mask on his face. His flesh rolled up his chest like a wave. I couldn't find his clavicle with my fingertips to line up the right point of entry. And already he was looking short of breath, his face red. I gave S. a "Do you want to take over?" look. Keep going, she signaled. I made a rough guess about where the right spot was, numbed it with lidocaine, and pushed the big needle in. For a second, I thought it wouldn't be long enough to reach through, but then I felt the tip slip underneath his clavicle. I pushed a little deeper and drew back on the syringe.

30   Unbelievably, it filled with blood. I was in. I concentrated on anchoring the needle firmly in place, not moving it a millimeter as I pulled the syringe off and threaded the guide wire in. The wire fed in smoothly. The patient was struggling hard for air now.

We sat him up and let him catch his breath. And then, laying him down one more time, I got the entry dilated and slid the central line in. "Nice job" was all S. said, and then she left.

I still have no idea what I did differently that day. But from then on my lines went in. That's the funny thing about practice. For days and days, you make out only the fragments of what to do. And then one day you've got the thing whole. Conscious learning becomes unconscious knowledge, and you cannot say precisely how.

* * * *

I have now put in more than a hundred central lines. I am by no means infallible. Certainly, I have had my fair share of complications. I punctured a patient's lung, for example—the right lung of a chief of surgery from another hospital, no less—and, given the odds, I'm sure such things will happen again. I still have the occasional case that should go easily but doesn't, no matter what I do. (We have a term for this. "How'd it go?" a colleague asks. "It was a total flog," I reply. I don't have to say anything more.)

But other times everything unfolds effortlessly. You take the needle. You stick the chest. You feel the needle travel—a distinct glide through the fat, a slight catch in the dense muscle, then the subtle pop through the vein wall—and you're in. At such moments, it is more than easy; it is beautiful.

* * * *

It is 2 P.M. I am in the intensive-care unit. A nurse tells me Mr. G.'s central line has clotted off. Mr. G. has been in the hospital for more than a month now. He is in his late sixties, from South Boston, emaciated, exhausted, holding on by a thread—or a line, to be precise. He has several holes in his small bowel, and the bilious contents leak out onto his skin through two small reddened openings in the concavity of his abdomen. His only chance is to be fed by vein and wait for these fistulae to heal. He needs a new central line.

I could do it, I suppose. I am the experienced one now. But experience brings a new 35 role: I am expected to teach the procedure instead. "See one, do one, teach one," the saying goes, and it is only half in jest.

There is a junior resident on the service. She has done only one or two lines before. I tell her about Mr. G. I ask her if she is free to do a new line. She misinterprets this as a question. She says she still has patients to see and a case coming up later. Could I do the line? I tell her no. She is unable to hide a grimace. She is burdened, as I was burdened, and perhaps frightened, as I was frightened.

She begins to focus when I make her talk through the steps—a kind of dry run, I figure. She hits nearly all the steps, but forgets about checking the labs and about Mr. G.'s nasty allergy to heparin, which is in the flush for the line. I make sure she registers this, then tell her to get set up and page me.

I am still adjusting to this role. It is painful enough taking responsibility for one's own failures. Being handmaiden to another's is something else entirely. It occurs to me that I could have broken open a kit and had her do an actual dry run. Then again, maybe I can't. The kits must cost a couple of hundred dollars each. I'll have to find out for next time.

Half an hour later, I get the page. The patient is draped. The resident is in her gown and gloves. She tells me that she has saline to flush the line with and that his labs are fine.

40   "Have you got the towel roll?" I ask.

She forgot the towel roll. I roll up a towel and slip it beneath Mr. G.'s back. I ask him if he's all right. He nods. After all he's been through, there is only resignation in his eyes.

The junior resident picks out a spot for the stick. The patient is hauntingly thin. I see every rib and fear that the resident will puncture his lung. She injects the numbing medication. Then she puts the big needle in, and the angle looks all wrong. I motion for her to reposition. This only makes her more uncertain. She pushes in deeper and I know she does not have it. She draws back on the syringe: no blood. She takes out the needle and tries again. And again the angle looks wrong. This time, Mr. G. feels the jab and jerks up in pain. I hold his arm. She gives him more numbing medication. It is all I can do not to take over. But she cannot learn without doing, I tell myself. I decide to let her have one more try.

QUESTIONS FOR READING ACTIVELY

1. Why does Gawande conclude this essay as he does? How do you, as a reader, respond?

2. Obviously, Gawande is not writing for an audience of people who are about to perform the insertion of a large intravenous tube into the main blood vessel of the heart. Yet he gives a significant amount of detail as he describes the process of doing so. Each time he describes the insertion of such a tube, or "central line," his perceptions of the procedure change. What are the differences in Gawande's perceptions of each incident? What is Gawande's purpose for each description?

QUESTIONS FOR THINKING CRITICALLY

1. Gawande describes a kind of apprenticeship, a way in which knowledge and skills are passed along from one surgeon to another through example and practice. Is apprenticeship always the best way to learn, or teach, a particular skill or body of knowledge?

2. "Skill, surgeons believe, can be taught; tenacity cannot." Do you agree or disagree? Describe a time in your life when being *tenacious* helped you to overcome an obstacle, to master a skill, or to solve a problem.

3. Why does Gawande describe the experience in paragraph 33 as "beautiful"? What, exactly, is "beautiful" about it? Have you experienced that same kind of "beauty" in accomplishing something difficult?

QUESTION FOR WRITING THOUGHTFULLY

1. How does Gawande use chronology to organize his essay? Why is this a particularly effective organizational choice, given his subject and purpose?

Writing Project

A NARRATIVE SHOWING THE EFFECT OF A PERCEPTION

The readings and Thinking-Writing Activities in this chapter encourage you to become more aware of your perceptions, to use description to convey those perceptions, and to choose the appropriate organizing structure (chronology, narrative, and/or process) for writing about those perceptions.

Project Overview and Requirements

Think back to an experience when the perceptions of others had an influence on you. Their perceptions may have had an effect on how you understand yourself, on a skill or body of knowledge you were learning, or on a decision you had to make. Consider the following questions to get you started:

- When were you first made aware of this issue, conflict, idea, or skill?

- How did this other person (or persons) make his or her perceptions known to you?

- Were you initially in conflict with that other person, or have you always been in agreement?

- If there have been points of conflict in your relationship, did you learn and grow from them?

- How have your own perceptions grown and changed since knowing this other person (or persons)?

This project also includes a research component. Find a magazine or newspaper article that addresses the same (or similar) event or type of experience, and use a quotation or two from it to support your ideas. Document the quoted material according to your instructor's directions. If an academic documentation format such as that of the Modern Language Association (MLA) or American Psychological Association (APA) is required, be sure your entry conforms to that format. To see an example of a narrative showing the effect of a perception, jump ahead to the outline and essay by Joshua Chaffee, "We're All at Ground Zero," on page 234.

THE WRITING SITUATION

Begin by considering the key elements in the Thinking-Writing Model on pages 5–8 in Chapter 1 that are related to purpose, audience, subject, and writer, as well as The Writing Process below.

The following principles for writing narratives are not fixed rules; you may have good reasons for not following some of them. In general, though, they should help you write an effective essay.

1. Fully identify and describe the relevant issue so that the narrative has a meaningful context.

2. State your thesis well; place it effectively in your paper.

3. Use description to introduce your readers to the people involved and to help them clearly visualize the place. Consider whether subjective or objective description, or a combination of the two, will best serve your purpose.

4. Consider necessary details and tell your story as completely as possible, but avoid rambling excessively or leaving out important details or events.

5. Begin with a strong introduction—one that grabs your audience's attention. Your conclusion will be important, too, so consider reiterating your main point and leaving your audience with something memorable.

Purpose   You have a variety of purposes here, including the opportunity to recall and relate a significant experience. You can think about an issue that concerns you and learn more about it by finding and analyzing an article. In addition, you will be improving your ability to connect what you read with your own ideas, something you must do regularly as a college student. Most important, you can inform your classmates, your instructor, and your other readers about an issue that concerns you, or skill that interests you, and about the impact of other people's perceptions of that same issue.

Audience   As always, you are a member of your own audience and perhaps the person who will enjoy the narrative most, since it is connected with your life. Your classmates will be a good audience as well. They can learn from your narrative and share your experience, and they can be valuable as peer reviewers of your draft, reacting as intelligent readers who are also immersed in the assignment. Of course, anyone else who has had a similar experience would also benefit from reading your essay. Perhaps your campus newspaper would be interested. Finally, your instructor remains the audience who will judge how well you have planned, drafted, and revised. As a writing teacher, he or she cares about a clear focus, logical organization, specific details, and correctness. Keep these aspects in mind as you revise, edit, and proofread.

Subject   Although you and your readers are probably concerned about many perceptual issues, it is valuable to consider how an issue, and a person's perceptions of it, can have an effect on someone else.

Writer   You are in a dual position here. You are, of course, the expert on your own story. This is both an advantage and a disadvantage: no one can argue with you about your story, but you still need to remember that your audience was not there. You must provide them with sufficient background and description to make them feel as if they did share your experience, but you don't want to overwhelm them with details. Therefore, you will need to be selective as you decide what to include and what to omit. Also, remember that you are not the expert on the article from which you plan to quote, so analyze it carefully and decide what you would like to quote and where to best incorporate it into your essay.

Now that you have read about the purpose, audience, subject, and writer, review your responses to the Thinking-Writing Activities earlier in this chapter, and then answer the following four questions. Once you have a few ideas written down, it will be easier to move on to The Writing Process.

1. First, were you able to think of a time when someone's perceptions affected you? Write a sentence or two describing this situation. Here is one student's description:

   I was asked to help market a new small business by designing a social media campaign. This meant creating a website, Facebook, and Twitter account. Unfortunately, over time, I realized that the business owners' perceptions of customer satisfaction were vastly different from my perceptions, and this resulted in my resignation.

2. Describe people who may be interested in learning more about the perceptions that influenced you. For example:

   My coworkers, friends, and family may all be interested in what I have to say about this particular situation, but ultimately, I would like to submit my article to a magazine to help others who may find themselves in similar ethical dilemmas.

3. If differing perceptions were conflicting, how did you learn and grow from them? For example:

   At first, the business owners and I were in agreement that the customers' needs should come first and should help, in part, influence the direction of the business. Over time, though, it became clear that they had no interest in their customers whatsoever. I was afraid to quit, but my sense of right and wrong gave me the courage to stand up for what I believed in.

4. Since this project includes a research component, name and briefly describe a newspaper or magazine article that addresses a similar situation.

   I came across a helpful article in *Forbes* called "Ethics and the Five Deadly Sins of Social Media," posted on November 3, 2011, by David Vinjamuri. His descriptions of unreported endorsements, improper anonymity, compromising consumer privacy, overly enthusiastic employees, and using the online community to get free work will help support some of the points I plan to make in my essay.

THE WRITING PROCESS

The following sections will guide you through the stages of generating, planning, drafting, and revising as you work on a descriptive and illustrative narrative.

Generating Ideas

1. If you cannot immediately recall a meaningful experience you want to narrate, think about past events that were worrisome, frightening, amusing, or exciting. What was the event? What was the context of the event (and why was it worrisome, frightening, amusing, or exciting)?

2. You may be deeply involved in dealing with others' perceptions of issues because of who you are, where you live, or which organizations you support. If so, you should have no problem identifying a concern you want to address. If not, look around, talk with friends and family members, read newspapers and magazines, and watch the news. What issues strike you? How do you relate to them?

3. Think locally. Look at issues in your community or connected with your college or job. Then try to recall any experiences in which another person's perceptions had an impact on you.

Defining a Focus   Draft a thesis statement that connects your experience with the perception you plan to write about. You may want to emphasize the directness of the connection, or you may need to show that what is not obvious is indeed related. Perhaps you may wish to emphasize a time element: "I didn't understand at the time, but now I see that . . ." or "I knew at that moment that . . . ." You may want to focus on the impact this perception has had on your life.

Organizing Ideas   You could tell the story first and then connect it with the perceptual stereotype. Or you might make statements about the perception regularly throughout the narration as different events illustrate various aspects of the situation. In either case, your use of chronological order will help your audience follow the events of your story. Therefore, unless you see some serious reason not to do so, give background information first and then guide your audience through the time sequence of the events. You need to consider what arrangements will best help those in your audience see their connection to the issue. Be sure to select and place carefully the material quoted from your source and to incorporate it smoothly into your writing by introducing and commenting on it.

If you are using process writing in your essay, determine if the process itself can provide the organizational structure for the entire essay. Otherwise, be sure that each step of the process is clearly explained within each relevant paragraph.

Drafting   Begin with the easiest part to write, possibly the experience itself. Tell it fully; then plan to increase its effectiveness by including sharp details and a tight sequence of events at the revision stage. The paragraphs within the narrative may or may not have topic sentences. This is one of the differences between narration and exposition—while narration tells a story, exposition is more objective and direct. Here, you are telling a story, and since your purpose is to connect the experience with others' perceptions, you may want to have topic sentences for the paragraphs that do that.

After you have drafted the narrative, draft the paragraphs that state the thesis and make the connection between the experience and the issue. Then establish and write any necessary transitions.

Revising Your Essay: A Narrative Showing the Effect of a Perception

Remember that this essay is a narrative. Check to be sure that the purpose of your essay is clear, that you addressed the needs of your audience, that you considered the subject and how perceptions affect it, and also that you, as the writer, provided adequate background and description, including a quotation from an article.

Peer Responses

Once your draft is complete, pass it along to your classmates or to friends or a family member for feedback if possible. You could provide your reviewer a copy of "A Step-by-Step Method for Revising Any Assignment," located on the inside front cover of this book for additional guidance.

Revision

If you have received feedback, review it before beginning your revision. Refer to "A Step-by-Step Method for Revising Any Assignment," and focus on the "Think Big" and "Think Medium" sections under "Revision" first. These are the larger components of your paper.

Editing and Proofreading

Next, focus on your draft sentence by sentence, as suggested in the "Editing" section of "A Step-by-Step Method for Revising Any Assignment." Finally, look at the smallest details, and make any necessary corrections and modifications. These small details can have a big impact on the way the audience perceives you and the story you are communicating.

The following essay demonstrates how a student writer used a combination of description, process writing, and chronological ordering to illustrate how the perceptions of other people influenced his own decision. Your essay may benefit from using a combination of these rhetorical modes of writing as well.

STUDENT WRITING

Joshua Chaffee's Writing Process

Living so close to "Ground Zero," the site where the World Trade Center used to stand in New York City, Joshua Chaffee had an overwhelming number of perceptions, emotions, and experiences to sort through as he contemplated this essay. This experience was to define both how he perceived his community and how he understood himself. Joshua knew he wanted to draw upon his experience as he approached this essay, but he also knew that he had to be careful with his organization and his descriptions. Often, when writing about something so overwhelming—and something experienced, even at a distance, by so many people—it becomes difficult to stay focused on your audience and your purpose. Joshua brought in the perceptions of other people to balance his own feelings. Here is an excerpt from Joshua's rough outline for this essay.

1. *How did New Yorkers respond to 9/11?—keep it personal and specific; what did I personally witness? (Probably keep my emotions out of it—stick to what I perceived, not how I "felt"—that's too subjective and probably overwhelming. . . .)*

2. *Connect those perceptions to why I want to be a journalist. Can I talk to or find an article by another New York journalist who covered 9/11?—need to make a logical connection between 9/11 and why I want to be a journalist . . .*

3. *Incorporate as assignment for the "Feature Writing" course—how writing about New York (the La Frieda interview? the profile I did of Alan Kaufman and his pickle shop?) can give a voice to all New Yorkers, and connect that to my response to 9/11.*

4. *Conclusion?—maybe connect whatever I choose from "Feature Writing" to the behavior I witnessed on 9/11? A larger observation about why I love New York and want to stay here and do something for New Yorkers. . . .*

We're All at Ground Zero
by Joshua Chaffee

From my bedroom window, I can see the six-story remainder of the World Trade Center's steel siding, forked in the ground, shooting up towards its former resting place in the New York City skyline. The site is lit through the entire night with an otherworldly glow, and men are working there, at "Ground Zero," when I go to sleep and when I wake up.

Outside my house, hundreds of people gather to cheer and offer their gratitude towards the workers. Each night I have joined them. At one point, a truck stops beside the crowd and a fireman inside exclaims, "We've just contacted two Port Authority Police Officers on the second floor and we're digging them out right now!" What follows is an eruption of yelling and cheering far greater than I have ever heard.

In an interview I did with former *New York Times* columnist turned novelist Anna Quindlen, she told me, "September 11th was a time that made me proud of the journalism profession. Journalists provided a huge public service to people because they created an instant sense of community. It was a time when I seriously

Source: We're All at Ground Zero by Joshua Chaffee.

Joshua opens his essay with a descriptive image that helps the audience feel a sense of place.

considered writing columns again." After 9/11, Anna Quindlen re-affirmed her passion for journalism, while I discovered mine for the first time. It hit me on a Monday in late October of 2001.

About a month into the journalism course I was taking junior year, I found myself wedged in between Pat and Lisa La Frieda, scribbling madly onto a notepad because the air coolers in the meat locker were too loud for me to use my tape recorder. Outside the sun had yet to come up and, only weeks after September 11th, the air still smelled of ash. Inside, Pat La Frieda wore the same long, bloodstained white jacket and black knit cap characteristic of Italian-American butchers generations ago, when his grandparents owned La Frieda Meats. As he spoke to me, men hoisted sides of beef onto their shoulders while others sprayed the floor tiles with hoses to flush the blood into drains. The smell of cold, fresh meat permeated every corner of the long white room, a smell Pat relished as he slowly strolled past the lockers.

La Frieda Meats is located in Greenwich Village, one block east of the Hudson River and across the street from a controversial empty lot where an 18-story, luxury high-rise is planned to go up. The high-rise would be eight stories taller than any building near it, thus casting a long six-block shadow over the neighborhood. Pat had a lot to say on the topic. One question and he took off like a racehorse: "People have got to welcome advancement. You can't live in the past, saying how the Village used to be. Look, when my grandparents owned this meat packing business, they delivered the meat by horse drawn wagons every morning. Where would I be if I still used horses today!"

However, on the other side of me, his sister Lisa had a different point of view. Lisa is a large woman with heavy dark makeup. She jumped in, cutting off Pat, "Yeah, but you know what'll happen when they put in a luxury building? All the tenants will start screaming about my trucks coming in at four in the morning. And paying that much for an apartment, they probably got the right to complain." Sandwiched between Pat and Lisa, I tried to keep up with their words, which were barely audible above the meat coolers. I couldn't hold back a smile, though. Walking around a meat packing warehouse at six in the morning before school and talking to Pat and Lisa—I would rather be here than anywhere else, including my bed.

That Monday night I wrote about Pat and Lisa La Frieda, piecing their ideas into my article on the effects of the anticipated luxury high-rise. Hours later, I found myself still at my computer with a bowl of Chex Mix, writing and thinking about the interviews that morning. I understood what I had felt when I was standing in that frigid warehouse. I had realized my passion, and knew exactly what I wanted to be doing in the future. As a journalist, I have the opportunity to go out and have a

After quoting novelist Anna Quindlen (which sets the stage for the essay's focus), Joshua reveals when his perception about his life and career changed.

More vivid details ("scribbling madly," "smelled of ash," "long, bloodstained coat") convey a sense of place and time in the narration.

Joshua compares the different perceptions Pat and Lisa have.

Joshua reflects on the epiphany he had (mentioned in paragraph 3) and further describes his passion and desire to give people a voice.

half-hour conversation with some of the most interesting people—people I might otherwise never speak to. Then I come home and write about them; I give Pat and Lisa La Frieda a voice that they might never have used before—a voice that can be heard by hundreds of people.

The city is too big to know everyone's story. Most people don't know Alan Kaufman, the owner of the only remaining fresh pickle shop in the Lower East Side; or Joe Oliva, the 16-year security guard at Night Court, where every criminal arrested in Manhattan comes to be arraigned; or Chef José, the chef at a private Manhattan school, who was the head chef at United Airlines for most of his life. But, by opening up the worlds of everyone around us, journalists can unite a community.

This, I believe, is what Anna Quindlen meant by journalists creating "an instant sense of community," and this is what attracts me to the profession. Immediately after September 11, we all felt alone and frightened. But journalists showed us that everyone else was experiencing the same feelings, and that together we could help each other to understand and move on from what happened. When we are alone, our surroundings can seem overwhelming and unfriendly. But, through the telling of people's stories and the revealing of the true fabric of the city, New York can begin to feel as intimate as your family, and as small as a Village. All around the city people have come together. The city has united in a community of shared pain, devoted to its country and to each other. Everyone felt his or her hearts come down with those towers, but as we start to rebuild, we have each other for support.

Joshua returns to the quote by Anna Quindlen (from paragraph 3), and, after more fully describing how journalists create a sense of community, he brings the essay full circle and leaves the reader on a hopeful note.

REFLECTION ON WRITING

1. Why does Joshua Chaffee choose to begin his essay by depicting an image of the World Trade Center at Ground Zero?

2. Joshua's essay focuses on a turning point in his life. Try to pinpoint where, exactly, this takes place in the essay, and underline it. Do you feel this is the best place to address his turning point? Why or why not?

ALTERNATIVE WRITING PROJECTS

1. Ask someone with an interesting profession for permission to observe her or him at work. Keep careful notes, and if allowed, take audio and video recordings of that person at work. Write up an objective report of your findings. What were your perceptions of that kind of work before you began making your observations? How did your perceptions change? Next, draw up a list of questions for your subject based on your observations. As you ask your subject these questions, record his or her answers. Finally, write an

objective profile of a day in the life of that particular kind of worker, using his or her own subjective comments as illustrations and evidence.

2. Create a podcast walking tour of a part of your campus or your community. Your audience will be able to rely only on your ability to verbally evoke particular sights, smells, and circumstances, so your descriptions must be especially rich and accurate. Then exchange podcasts with another student, and offer each other constructive criticism on the quality of each other's language and the accuracy of each other's descriptions.

CHAPTER 7 Summary

- By actively selecting, organizing, and interpreting sensations, you can become better aware of your own perceptions. Then you will be better equipped to note the differences in the perceptions of others.

- To write thoughtfully, you need to know the difference between subjective perceptions, which include judgment, and objective perceptions, which include as little judgment as possible, and to strive to be as objective in your writing as you can.

- Chronological writing focuses on illustrating growth, development, or change and can take the form of a narrative or process essay.

Concepts allow us to make sense of our complex world and bring order to our lives. We form concepts by classifying things based on their similarities, and then by generalizing and interpreting that information. Some concepts can be rather abstract, and it is likely that people will interpret them differently. When discussing or writing about complex concepts, we rely on clear definitions to communicate as effectively as possible.

Writing to Classify and Define:
Exploring Concepts

"Our life is what our thoughts make it."

—MARCUS AURELIUS

Internet, *beauty, hip-hop culture, channel surfing, truth, bungee jumping, attitude,* and *thinking* are only a few examples of concepts in a world filled with them. As you speak and write, you refer to concepts you have formed. Your academic study involves learning new concepts as well, and success in college and in your career requires understanding the conceptualizing process.

When you read textbooks or listen to lectures and take notes, you have to grasp key concepts and follow them as they are developed and supported. Many courses require you to apply the key concepts you have learned to new sets of circumstances. When you write essays, conduct research, or participate in group projects, you are expected to focus on certain concepts, develop and present a thesis (itself a concept), and support it with relevant evidence.

Your academic writing will often require the definition of terms or concepts. Chapter 6 discussed the fact that words are complex carriers of meaning—with meanings varying from person to person. This chapter will explore further implications of this complexity as it pertains to your writing.

The Writing Project in the chapter asks you to write a full definition of a concept that is important to your life. As you write this essay, you will see that definition usually involves using all the patterns of thinking that Chapter 7 discussed.

Definition is a very important thinking and writing pattern. When you write an essay that defines a concept, that concept is the subject of your essay. A clear idea of your audience will help you determine the kind of illustrations you will need to provide, as well as the complexity of the language with which you describe those illustrations. Finally, the purpose of your essay (to demonstrate to your instructor that you have understood a concept, to introduce a complex concept to an audience unfamiliar with the subject, to explore how a concept has changed over time, and so on) will determine the rhetorical strategies you will use. The analytical activity of classification, which underlies defining, is essential to good thinking. Definition and classification rely on comparative relationships in order to establish categories by means of similarities and in order to distinguish among concepts within categories by identifying differences. Definitions usually include descriptions and sometimes employ causal, chronological, or process analyses to make distinctions or to show the development of a concept. Understanding the thinking patterns that you have already worked with and being able to use them effectively can ease the difficult task of defining concepts.

CRITICAL THINKING FOCUS:
The conceptualizing process

WRITING FOCUS:
Defining and applying concepts

READING THEME:
Gender issues

WRITING ACTIVITIES:
Concepts and classification

WRITING PROJECT:
Defining an important concept

To help you define significant concepts, this chapter will explain the conceptualizing process, present readings that involve definitions, and give you opportunities to define some terms that are significant in various aspects of your life.

What Are Concepts?

Concepts are general ideas that you use to organize your experience and, in so doing, bring order to your life. In the same way that words are the vocabulary of language, concepts are the vocabulary of thought. As organizers of your experience, concepts work in conjunction with language to identify, describe, distinguish, and relate all the various aspects of your world.

Developing expertise in the conceptualizing process improves your ability to form, apply, and relate concepts. This complex conceptualizing process is going on all the time in your mind, enabling you to think in a distinctly human way. When you form opinions or make judgments, you are applying and relating concepts.

How do you use concepts to organize and make sense of experience? Think back to the first day of the semester. For most students, this is a time to evaluate their courses by trying to determine which concepts apply.

- Will this course be interesting? Useful? Challenging?
- Is the instructor stimulating? Demanding? Understanding?
- Are the other students friendly? Intelligent? Conscientious?

Thinking-Writing Activity

CHANGING YOUR CONCEPTS

Identify an initial concept you had about an event in your life (starting a new job, attending college, getting married, and so on). After identifying your initial concept, describe the experiences that led you to change or modify your attitude toward or approach to that concept. Next, explain the new concept you formed to explain the situation. Your essay should include the following elements and use these rhetorical strategies:

- The initial concept (definition)
- New information gained through additional (possibly conflicting) experiences (narration and description)
- The new concept formed to explain the situation (definition)

Each of these descriptive words or phrases represents a concept you are attempting to apply so that you can understand what is occurring at the moment and also anticipate what will occur. As the course progresses, you gather more information from experiences in class. This information may support your initial concepts, or it may conflict with them. If it supports them, you tend to maintain them ("Yes, I can see that this is going to be a difficult course"). When the information you receive conflicts with your initial concepts, you tend to find new concepts to explain the situation ("No, I can see that I was wrong—this course isn't going to be as difficult as I first thought"). A diagram of this process might look something like the one in Figure 8.1.

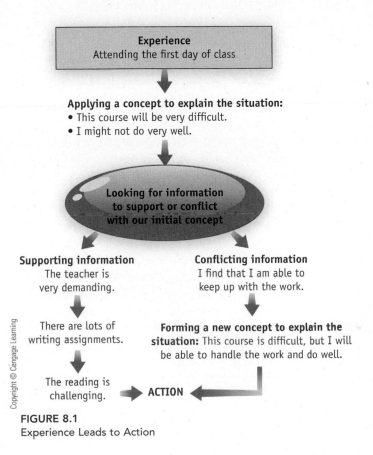

FIGURE 8.1
Experience Leads to Action

Throughout this thinking process, you are making evaluations that establish classifications of kinds or types: What *kind* of course—difficult? Easy? What *kind* of instructor? What *kind* of reading? What *kind* of student am I in relation to this course? And you are consciously or unconsciously using definitions that you have formulated: when I say "difficult course," I mean one that . . . . When I say "demanding instructor," I mean one who . . . . And so on.

THE IMPORTANCE OF CONCEPTS

Learning to understand and write about concepts will help you in every area of your life: academic, career, and personal. In college study, each academic discipline or subject uses many different concepts to organize experience, give explanations, and solve problems. Here is a sampling of college-level concepts: *entropy, subtext, Gemeinschaft, cell, metaphysics, relativity, parallel processing, prehistory, unconscious, aesthetic, minor key, interface, health, quantum mechanics, schizophrenia.* To make sense of how disciplines function, you need to understand what the concepts of that discipline mean, how to define them, how to apply them, and how they relate to other concepts.

Although each academic discipline has its own unique and specific concepts, some concepts change their definition according to the disciplinary "lens" used to interpret them. In the following passage from *Colour: Art & Science,* physiologist Trevor Lamb describes how the concept of *color* is understood by different academic disciplines.

> Although the idea of "colour" may seem a simple concept, it conjures up very different ideas for each of us. To the physicist, colour is determined by the wavelength of light. To the physiologist and psychologist, our perception of colour involves neural responses in the eye and the brain, and is subject to the limitations of our nervous system. To the naturalist, colour is not only a thing of beauty but also a determinant of survival in nature. To the social historian and linguist, our understanding and interpretation of colour are inextricably linked to our own culture. To the art historian, the development of colour in painting can be traced both in artistic and technological terms. And for the painter, colour provides a means of expressing feelings and the intangible, making possible the creation of a work of art. . . . In the field of colour, the arts and the sciences now travel in unison, and together they provide a rich and comprehensive understanding of the subject.

You will regularly present your understanding of definitions, of applications, and of relationships among concepts in your written work. You will also learn the methods of investigation, patterns of thought, and forms of reasoning that various disciplines use to form larger conceptual theories and methods. Successful completion of writing, research, and presentation assignments in your college courses will depend on your understanding of the key concepts that form the core of each discipline.

Regardless of their specific knowledge content, all careers require conceptual abilities, whether you are trying to apply a legal principle, develop a promotional theme, or devise a new computer program. Similarly, expertise in forming and applying concepts helps you make sense of your personal life, understand others, and make informed decisions. The Greek philosopher Aristotle said that the intelligent person is a "master of concepts."

THE STRUCTURE OF CONCEPTS

Concepts, in addition to being general ideas that you use to identify and organize your experience, are useful for distinguishing and connecting one thing to another. Concepts allow you to organize your world into patterns that make sense to you.

In their role of organizers of experience, concepts act to group aspects of your experience on the basis of their similarity. Consider the object that you usually write with: a notebook computer. The concept *notebook computer* represents an instrument that you use for writing. Now look around the classroom at other instruments people are using to write. You use the concept *notebook computer* to identify these as well, even though they may look quite different from yours. Thus, the concept *notebook computer* helps you not only to make distinctions in your experience by indicating how notebook computers differ from tablets, smartphones, or desktops but also to determine which items are similar enough to all be called notebook computers. When you put items into a group with a single description—such as *notebook computers*—you are focusing on their similarities:

- They use internal hard drives or external flash drives.
- They are used for writing, research, communication, and entertainment.
- They are portable.

Being able to see and name the similarities among certain things in your experience is the way you form concepts and is crucial for making sense of your world. If you were not able to do this, everything in the world would appear to be different, with its own individual name.

THE PROCESS OF CLASSIFYING

The process by which you group things on the basis of their similarities is known as *classifying*. Classifying is a natural human activity that goes on all the time. In most cases, however, you are not conscious of classifying something in a particular sort of way; you do so automatically. The process of classifying is one of the main ways that you order, organize, and make sense of your world. Because no two things or experiences are exactly alike, your ability to classify things into various groups is what enables you to recognize things in your experience. When you perceive a notebook computer, you recognize it as a *kind* of object you have seen before. Even though you may not have seen this particular notebook computer, you recognize that it belongs to a category of things that is familiar.

The best way to understand the structure of concepts is to visualize them by means of a model. Examine Figure 8.2. The *sign* is the word or symbol used to name or designate the concept; for example, the word *triangle* is a sign. The *referents* represent all the various examples of the concept; the three-sided figure we are using as our model is an example of the concept *triangle*. The *properties* of the concept are the features that all things named by the word or sign share in common; all examples of the concept *triangle* share the characteristics of being a polygon and having three sides. These are the properties that we refer to when we define concepts; thus, "a triangle is a three-sided polygon."

Let's take another example. Suppose you wanted to explore the structure of the concept *automobile*. The sign that names the concept is the word *automobile* or the symbol ⬲. Referents of the concept include the 1954 MG-TF currently residing in the garage, as well as the Ford Explorer parked in front of the house. The properties

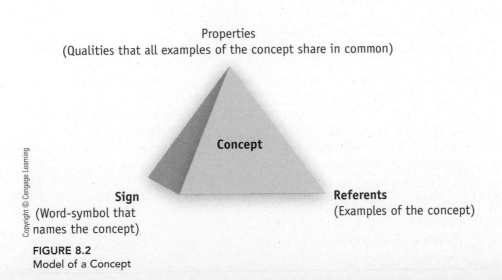

Properties
(Qualities that all examples of the concept share in common)

Concept

Sign
(Word-symbol that names the concept)

Referents
(Examples of the concept)

Copyright © Cengage Learning

FIGURE 8.2
Model of a Concept

Properties
Wheels, chassis, engine, seats for passengers

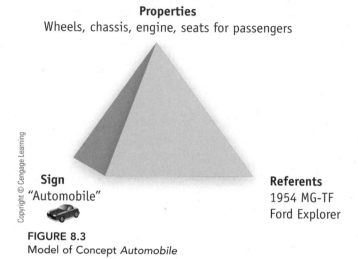

Copyright © Cengage Learning

Sign
"Automobile"

Referents
1954 MG-TF
Ford Explorer

FIGURE 8.3
Model of Concept *Automobile*

that all things named by the sign *automobile* include are wheels, a chassis, an engine, and seats. Figure 8.3 shows a conceptual model of the concept *automobile*.

Thinking-Writing Activity

DIAGRAMMING CONCEPTS

Using the model we have developed, diagram the structure of three of the following concepts: *dance, success, student, religion, music, friend*. Next, diagram the structure of two concepts of your own choice. Be sure to address the sign, properties, and referents for each concept.

Forming Concepts

You form—and apply—concepts to organize your experience, make sense of what is happening, and anticipate what may happen in the future. You form concepts by the interactive processes of *generalizing* (focusing on the common properties shared by a group of things) and *interpreting* (finding examples of the concept). The common properties form the necessary requirements that must be met in order for you to be able to apply the concept to your experience. If you examine the diagrams of concepts in the last section, you can see that the process of forming concepts involves moving back and forth between the referents (examples) of the concept and the properties (common features) shared by all examples of the concept. Let's further explore the way this interactive process of forming concepts operates.

Consider the following conversation between two people trying to form and clarify the concept *philosophy*.

A: What is your idea of what philosophy *means*?

B: Well, I think philosophy involves expressing important beliefs that you have— like discussing the meaning of life, assuming that there is a meaning.

A: Is explaining my belief about who's going to win the Super Bowl engaging in philosophy? After all, this is a belief that is very important to me—I've got a lot of money riding on the outcome!

B: I don't think so. A philosophical belief is usually a belief about something that is important to everyone—like what standards we should use to guide our moral choices.

A: What about the message that was in my fortune cookie last night: "Eat, drink, and be merry, for tomorrow we diet!"? This is certainly a belief that most people can relate to, especially during a holiday season! Is this philosophy?

B: I think that's what my grandmother used to call "foolosophy"! Philosophical beliefs are usually deeply felt views to which we have given a great deal of thought—not something plucked out of a cookie.

A: What about my belief in the Golden Rule—"Do unto others as you would have them do unto you"—because "What goes around comes around"? Doesn't that have the qualities that you mentioned?

B: Now you've got it!

As we review this dialogue, we can see that forming the concept *philosophy* works hand in hand with applying the concept to different examples. When two or more things work together in this way, we say that they *interact*. In this case, there are two parts of this interactive process.

We form concepts by generalizing, by focusing on the similar features among different things. In the previous dialogue, the things about which generalizations are being made are types of beliefs—beliefs about the meaning of life or about standards we use to guide our moral choices. By focusing on the similar features of these beliefs, the dialogue's two participants develop a list of properties philosophical beliefs share, including (1) beliefs dealing with important issues in life about which everyone is concerned and (2) beliefs reflecting deeply felt views—views to which people have given much thought. These common properties act as the requirements a viewpoint must meet to be considered a philosophical belief.

We apply concepts by interpreting, by looking for different examples of a concept and seeing if they meet the requirements of the concept we are developing. In the preceding dialogue, one participant attempts to apply the concept of *philosophy* to the following examples:

A belief about the outcome of the Super Bowl

A fortune cookie message: "Eat, drink, and be merry, for tomorrow we diet!"

Each of these proposed examples suggests the development of new requirements for the concept to help clarify how the concept can be applied. Applying a concept to different possible examples thus becomes the way we develop and gradually sharpen our idea of it.

Even when a proposed example turns out not to be a valid one, the process of questioning often clarifies our understanding of that concept. For instance, although the proposed example of a belief about the outcome of the Super Bowl turned out not to be an example of the concept *philosophy,* examining it helped clarify the concept and suggest other examples.

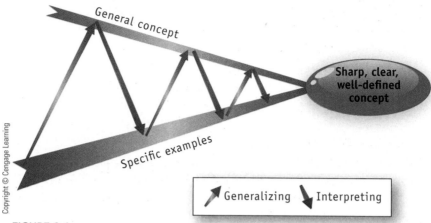

FIGURE 8.4
Movement from General Concept to Well-Defined Concept

The process of developing concepts involves a constant back-and-forth movement between generalizing and interpreting. As the back-and-forth movement progresses, we gradually develop a list of specific requirements for an example of the concept; at the same time, we gain a clearer sense of how the concept is defined. We are also developing a collection of examples that embody the qualities of the concept and demonstrate situations in which the concept applies. This interactive process is illustrated in Figure 8.4.

THINKING CRITICALLY ABOUT NEW MEDIA

Using New Media to Research a Concept

It's difficult to imagine, but it wasn't that long ago that if you wanted to research a subject, you had to physically go to the library and use the card catalog or periodical room to conduct your research. The creation of computers and the Internet has changed all of that, of course. Not only don't you have to go to a library, but also you don't even have to be sitting in front of a computer—through your smartphone or tablet, you literally have the world at your fingertips.

In this new information universe, it's not simply our mobility that has been revolutionized; it's also the *way* in which we're able to conduct research, roaming far and wide, with one link leading to another, and to another, and so on. It's very much the way in which our brain makes connections: spontaneously, dynamically, and at lightning speed.

Of course, as we've seen, with that boundless sea of information out there, it's essential that we keep our critical thinking abilities dialed up to the maximum so that we can distinguish the true from the false, objective from subjective, and fact from fiction.

Thinking-Writing Activity

FORMING A CONCEPT

Select a genre or style of music you are familiar with and perhaps enjoy. Next, consider the structure of the dialogue on philosophy you just read; then compose a dialogue about the type of music you chose. In the course of the dialogue, be sure to include the following:

1. Examples from which you are generalizing (such as specific bands)

2. General properties shared by various types of this music (e.g., "Jazz is a uniquely American form of music that uses complex rhythms and improvisation.")

3. Examples to which you are trying to apply the developing concept (such as the music of Marian McPartland, Miles Davis, or Thelonius Monk)

Forming concepts involves performing the operations of generalizing and interpreting together for two reasons:

1. You cannot form a concept unless you know how it might apply. If you have absolutely no idea what *jazz* or *philosophy* might exemplify, you cannot begin to form the concept, even in vague or general terms.

It's been said that in this new media age "We're drowning in information but we're starved for knowledge." The reason for this is that "information" is *not* "knowledge." As we have seen in earlier chapters, information doesn't become knowledge until the human mind has *acted* upon it: analyzing, synthesizing, applying, evaluating, *thinking critically* about it.

Thinking-Writing Activity

MEDIA AS A CONCEPT

What is your concept of what media are? Go through the process of generalizing, interpreting, and then narrowing your ideas until you have specific examples and a sharp, clear, well-defined concept. Now compare your results with those of your classmates.

2. You cannot gather examples of the concept unless you know what they might be examples of. Until you begin to develop some idea of what the concept *jazz* or *philosophy* might be (based on certain similarities among various things), you won't know where to look for examples of the concept (or how to evaluate them).

This interactive process of developing concepts by moving back and forth between generalizing and interpreting is the way that you usually form all concepts, particularly the complicated ones. In college, much of your education is focused on carefully forming and exploring key concepts such as *democracy, dynamic equilibrium*, and *personality*.

Applying Concepts

Making sense of our experience means finding the right concept to explain what is going on. To determine whether the concept we have selected fits a situation, we have to determine whether the requirements that form the concept are being met.

To figure out which concept applies to the situation, we must do the following:

1. Be aware of the properties that form the boundaries of the concept.
2. Determine whether the experience meets those requirements, for only if it does can we apply the concept to it.

If we have the requirements of the concept clearly in mind, we can proceed to figure out which of these requirements are met by the experience. This is how we apply concepts, which is one of the most important ways we have for figuring out what is taking place in our experience.

DETERMINING THE REQUIREMENTS OF A CONCEPT

In determining the requirements of a concept, we ask ourselves: *Would something still be an example of this concept if that thing did not meet this requirement?* If the answer to this question is *no*—that something would not be an example of this concept if it did not meet this requirement—we can say the requirement is a necessary part of the concept.

Consider the concept *dog*. Which of the following descriptions are requirements that must be met by an example of this concept?

1. Is an animal
2. Normally has four legs and a tail
3. Bites the mail carrier

It is clear that descriptions 1 and 2 are requirements that must be met to apply the concept *dog* because if we apply our test question—"Would something still be an example of this concept if that thing did not meet this requirement?"—we can say that the thing would not be an example of the concept *dog* if it did not fit the first two descriptions: if it was not an animal and did not normally have four legs and a tail.

Thinking Critically About Visuals

Fashion Statements as Concepts

There has always been a relationship between popular music and fashion, but this connection became even more prominent with the advent of music videos and MTV. For many performers today, fashion and dance choreography are an integral part of the overall music performance. For example, "Lady Gaga" (born Stefani Joanne Angelina Germanotta) uses elaborate costumes to frame her songs and has stated that "fashion is an inspiration for the song writing and her performances." We can contrast her "glam rock" (also exemplified by musicians like David Bowie, Freddy Mercury, Michael Jackson, and Madonna) with the fashion statements of other forms of music.

For example, in the mid-1970s, a grimmer countercultural youth movement was forming in New York City's underground music clubs and the streets of London. Punk, with its anarchic politics and shock-value fashion and music, had a bleak view of the potential for social change. However, just like the "glam rock" of Lady Gaga, and others, punk's fashion statements soon became part of the mainstream. What are some of the fashion statements of the forms of music with which you are familiar?

AP Photo/Peter Kramer

Playwright David Mamet has written: "The pursuit of Fashion is the attempt of the middle class to co-opt tragedy. In adopting the clothing, speech, and personal habits of those in straitened, dangerous, or pitiful circumstances, the middle class seeks to have what it feels to be the exigent and nonequivocal experiences had by those it emulates." In your own words, what is Mamet's argument about fashion? Can fashion choices that are meant to be political or social statements ever be frivolous, irresponsible, or counterproductive?

This does not seem to be the case, however, with description 3. If we ask ourselves the same test question, we can see that the thing might still be an example of the concept *dog* even if it did not bite the mail carrier. Even though some dogs do, in fact, bite mail carriers, this is not a requirement for being a dog.

Of course, there may be other things that meet these requirements but are not dogs. For example, a cat is an animal (description 1) that normally has four legs and a tail (description 2). What this means is that the requirements of a concept tell us only what attributes something must have to be an example of the concept. As a result, we often have to identify additional requirements that will define the concept more sharply. These requirements determine when the concept can be applied and indicate those things that qualify as examples of it. When we are able to identify all the requirements of the concept, we say these requirements are both necessary and sufficient for applying the concept.

ANALYZING COMPLEX CONCEPTS

Although dealing with concepts like *dog* and *cat* may seem simple, matters become somewhat confusing when you start analyzing the more complex concepts you will encounter in your academic study. For example, consider the concepts of *masculinity* and *femininity,* two of the more emotionally charged and politically contentious concepts in our culture. There are many different perspectives on what these concepts mean, what they should mean, and whether we should be using them at all. See if you can identify properties and examples of these two concepts by completing the following Thinking-Writing Activity.

Thinking-Writing Activity

EXPLORING THE CONCEPTS OF MASCULINE AND FEMININE

First, identify what you consider the essential properties (specific requirements that must be met to apply the concept) for the concepts of *masculinity* and *femininity.* Next, provide examples of people or behavior that illustrates these properties.

For example, you might identify "physical risk taking" as a property of the concept *masculinity*, and identify Russell Crowe as a person who illustrates this quality. Or you might identify "intuition" as a property of the concept *femininity*, illustrating this with the behavior "knowing without the conscious use of rational processes."

General Properties   *Specific Examples*

FEMININITY

1. _____   1. _____

2. _____   2. _____

3. _____   3. _____

MASCULINITY

1. _____   1. _____

2. _____   2. _____

3. _____   3. _____

Compare your list with those of your classmates. What similarities and differences do you notice? What factors might account for these similarities and differences? Save your responses—they may be useful to you later in this chapter when you draft your writing project.

A Casebook on the Evolving Concept of "Family"

The traditional concept of family in many parts of the world refers to a man and a woman (often married) with children. In Western culture, this traditional concept of family has been referred to as the "nuclear family," in the sense that the family functions as a self-contained "atom," unlike the "extended families" in days gone by. Our culture—and many other cultures around the world—has changed dramatically, and the concept of the family has changed with it. The idealized nuclear family, with the working father and the housewife mother, now represents less than 25 percent of the population. The following readings explore the phenomenon of the evolving concept of *family* and also pose the provocative question of whether we are entering a post-family era in which families may become an endangered species.

"New 'Non-Traditional' American Families"

By Kate Rice

Gina Smith and Heidi Norton of Northampton, Mass., have two sons. Norton is their biological mother, and Smith adopted them.

They live in a community in which there are several gay- or lesbian-headed households, but when they travel, they meet families with no experience with gay families and sometimes encounter clumsy questions.

While they may not fit the mold of what many Americans consider a typical family, they are a contemporary American family. There is no single typical American family anymore.

"We're in the midst of a major change in the way families and marriage are organized," says Stephanie Coontz, a college professor and author of *The Way We Never Were, American Families and the Nostalgia Trap* and *The Way We Really Are, Coming to Terms With America's Changing Families*. "It's distressing, because all of the rules we grew up with no longer work and so we're having to learn new ways of thinking about families."

Smith and Norton, both 39, head a family that helps others rethink their ideas of what a family is. When they're asked about themselves and their sons, Avery, 7, and Quinn, 3, they assume that questions are well-intended and that the clumsiness simply means that the questioner doesn't have the vocabulary to deal with the situation.

Source: January 19, 2013, http://abcnews.go.com/Health/story?id=118267&page=1.

"What's worked for us is stepping into the void and giving people some language to use," says Smith. "We would say things like, 'Avery is a very lucky boy who has two moms who love him,' so we just give them that language."

The 1950s Myth

Most children these days have buddies whose families are very different from their parents'. In fact, they quite possibly are growing up in such a family.

Most people still believe in the two-biological-married-parents-with-kids model, says Alexis Walker, editor of the National Council on Family Relations' Journal of Marriage and the Family (www.ncfr.org).

"Family is both a belief and a practice," she says.

When she asks her students at Oregon State University, where she is a professor of human development and family sciences, if they think their family will be a mom, a dad, and children, most raise their hands.

But practice is far different. When she asks if they come from a family like that, only a few put their hands up.

Americans have to deal with the great myth of the 1950s, an era in which 60 percent of families consisted of a breadwinning father and a stay-at-home mother. But this model was actually a 15-year-aberration, fueled by post-World War II prosperity and a GI bill of unprecedented generosity that funded the education of returning war veterans, according to Coontz, a professor of family and history at Evergreen State College, Olympia, Wash., and co-chairman of the Council on Contemporary Families (www.contemporaryfamilies.org)[.] The council's mission is to publicize the way the family is changing and to cover the consequences and implications of those changes.

Coontz says that for most of history, families have been co-provider families, with husband, wife and often children, all working to provide for the family.

"The fact is that families have always been diverse, and they've always been in flux and we've always been worried about it. As far back as colonial days people were complaining that the new generation of families was not like the old one," she says.

No Single Model

The 21st century child-rearing family can take any number of forms.

There's the 1950s model, one that is shrinking in number. An exact count is hard to come up with, but experts believe it's probably under 25 percent. Statistics show that today the majority of couples both earn income. Demographers estimate that only 50 percent of children will spend their entire childhood in a two-parent, married couple biological family, according to Coontz.

Increasingly common are blended families, couples with children from previous marriages as well as the current marriage. Then there are single parents, families with adopted children, gay families with adopted children or biological children, foster families, grandparents raising grandchildren, and so on.

Absent a single, cookie-cutter family model, the best definition of a healthy family is one that provides or performs certain core functions. These include basics such as food, shelter and economic support, according to Liz Gray, associate professor and family therapist in human development and family sciences at Oregon State University in Corvallis.

But a family does much more, providing love and affection, a sense of identity and a feeling of belonging. Families also provide a worldview or a spiritual belief that can help make sense of the world, as well as rules and boundaries for appropriate behavior and skills for dealing with the world.

More than a decade ago, Gray co-authored Nontraditional Families: A Guide For Parents (http://www.cyfernet.org/parent/nontradfam.html), which remains a highly useful piece for parents today. Looking back, Grey says she would never use the term "nontraditional," because today, those "nontraditional" families have become the norm.

Like any parents, Smith and Norton love to talk about how their family came to be, says Smith, and often handle curiosity by simply telling the story. Children had been part of each woman's life plan even before they met and fell in love 13 years ago, so it was only natural that they have children together. Smith says most people are accepting of their contemporary family.

"If you present yourself as comfortable with who you are as family, they'll take their cues from you," she says. She finds that the fact that she and Norton have such respect for themselves that others approach them and their sons with that same respect.

Tips: How to Deal

If you encounter a family that might once have been called nontraditional but aren't sure how to handle it, experts recommend first that you show respect no matter the others' family structure. Your children will closely follow your actions and their responses will mirror yours, as well. Some more of the experts' recommendations are below.

Look at your own family, your brothers, sisters, aunts, uncles, cousins, friends, neighbors. Odds are, you'll see a variety of family structures. That will give you an idea of what your children are encountering in school, and give you a way to discuss the issues with them.

Draw maps of families and extended families to help children understand family structure. Talk about it. Let children draw their own maps or pictures of families, then listen to what they have to say about it.

Your child has a friend whose family structure is one you're uncomfortable with. What do you do? Deal with it as though you were moving to a new neighborhood, suggests David Tseng, executive director of Parents, Families and Friends of Gays (www.pflag.org) in Washington, D.C. Be polite, respectful and curious to learn about others in a healthy and constructive way. It's important to recognize that your unspoken response influences your children as much as your spoken one.

Sometimes, you may disapprove of the family structure of one of your children's classmates. Mark Merrill, president of Family First, a non-profit research and communications organization (www.familyfirst.net) headquartered in Tampa, Fla., defines a family as any relationship of marriage, blood or adoption—but he limits that to heterosexuals. At the same time, he recognizes the reality of gay families. His response: "We are supposed to love everybody." And love, in Merrill's book, is not an emotion that leaps unsummoned from the heart. It is a decision to treat others, even those whose lifestyles you don't accept, with kindness and thoughtfulness and serve them in ways that are best for them.

Make a concerted effort within your own extended network of work colleagues and of friends to focus less on those who are like you and more on the diversity. "You want to be clear and deliberate about letting your kids know that this is America, this is the diversity of it and not to make a big deal of it," says James Morris, former president of the American Association for Marriage and Family Therapy (www.aamft.org) and assistant professor of marriage and family at Texas Tech University in Fredricksburg.

QUESTIONS FOR READING ACTIVELY

1. What is your definition of *family?* Describe your experiences as a family member growing up. What people comprised your family? Did the configuration of your family change over time?

2. The author, Kate Rice, quotes Alexis Walker when she says: "Family is both a belief and a practice." Professor Walker explains that her students tend to view a family in traditional terms, comprised of a mom, a dad, and children. Yet when she asks students if they come from a family like that, only a few put their hands up. How would you explain this discrepancy? Did you find the same "split perspective" in your response to the first question? Why or why not?

QUESTIONS FOR THINKING CRITICALLY

1. Liz Gray is quoted in the essay as saying a healthy family is one that provides certain core functions such as food, shelter, and economic support. Does that definition align with your concept of *family?* Why or why not?

2. Kate Rice contends that a family does much more than that by "providing love and affection, a sense of identity and a feeling of belonging. Families also provide a worldview or a spiritual belief that can help make sense of the world, as well as rules and boundaries for appropriate behavior and skill in dealing with the world." Do you believe that this more complex definition of *family* does a better job of articulating the boundaries of the concept of *family* does a better job of articulating the boundaries of the concept of *family?* Why or why not?

QUESTION FOR WRITING THOUGHTFULLY

1. Think about some of the experiences you have had related to family diversity and describe an event where you (or someone close to you) had to deal with questions or reactions to that diversity from others. What was the situation and reaction to the diverse or "non-traditional" family? How did the individuals involved contend with the situation? Was it handled well, or could it have been handled differently for a better outcome?

Pew Research

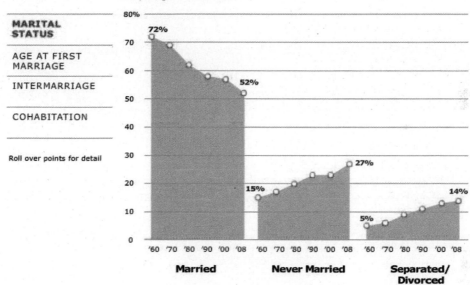

Current Marital Status
People Ages 18 and Older

MARITAL STATUS

AGE AT FIRST MARRIAGE

INTERMARRIAGE

COHABITATION

Roll over points for detail

NOTE: Widowed persons not shown.

SOURCE: Pew Research Center calculations of Decennial Census and American Community Survey data.

MARRIAGE | CHILDREN | HOUSEHOLD COMPOSITION

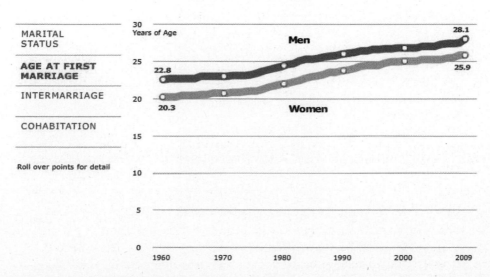

Median Age at First Marriage

MARITAL STATUS

AGE AT FIRST MARRIAGE

INTERMARRIAGE

COHABITATION

Roll over points for detail

SOURCE: U.S. Decennial Census and Current Population Survey data.

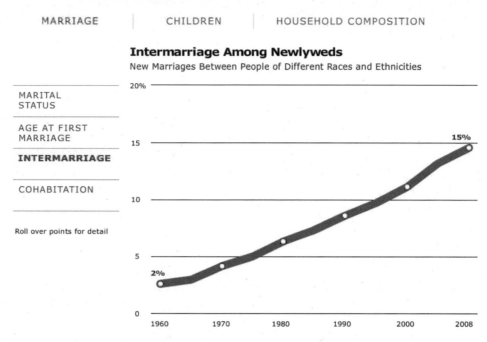

SOURCE: Pew Research Center calculations of Decennial Census and American Community Survey data.

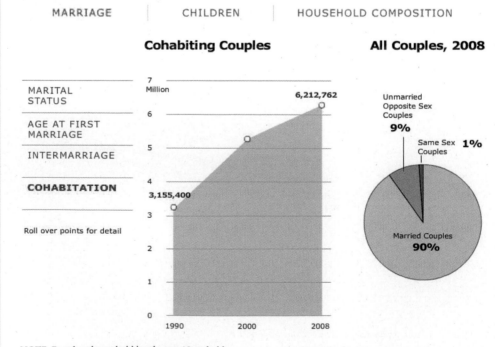

NOTE: Based on household heads ages 18 and older.

SOURCE: Pew Research Center calculations of Decennial Census and American Community Survey data.

MARRIAGE | CHILDREN | HOUSEHOLD COMPOSITION

Marital Status of Parents

Children Ages 17 and Younger Living With a Parent

MARITAL STATUS
OF PARENTS

COHABITING
PARENTS

BIRTHS TO
UNMARRIED
MOTHERS

Roll over points for detail

NOTE: Widowed parents not shown. Parents include biological, adoptive and stepparents.

SOURCE: Pew Research Center calculations of Decennial Census and American Community Survey data.

PEW RESEARCH CENTER

MARRIAGE | CHILDREN | HOUSEHOLD COMPOSITION

Children Living With A Cohabiting Parent

Children Ages 17 and Younger

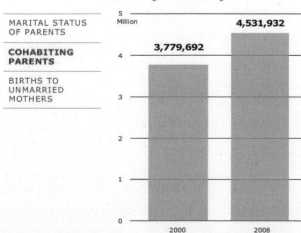

MARITAL STATUS
OF PARENTS

**COHABITING
PARENTS**

BIRTHS TO
UNMARRIED
MOTHERS

NOTE: Parents may be biological, adoptive or stepparents.

SOURCE: Pew Research Center calculations of Decennial Census and American Community Survey data.

PEW RESEARCH CENTER

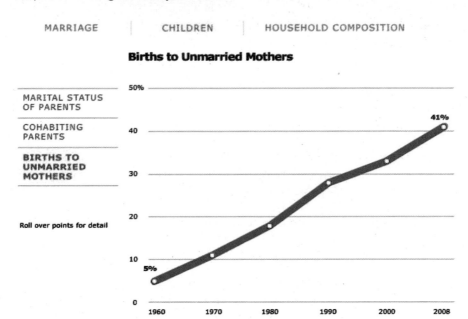

| MARRIAGE | CHILDREN | HOUSEHOLD COMPOSITION |

Births to Unmarried Mothers

MARITAL STATUS
OF PARENTS

COHABITING
PARENTS

**BIRTHS TO
UNMARRIED
MOTHERS**

Roll over points for detail

NOTE: 2008 data are preliminary.

SOURCE: Pew Research Center calculations of National Center for Health statistics.

PEW RESEARCH CENTER

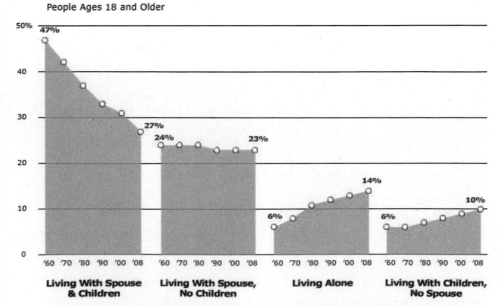

| MARRIAGE | CHILDREN | HOUSEHOLD COMPOSITION |

Household Composition
People Ages 18 and Older

Living With Spouse
& Children

Living With Spouse,
No Children

Living Alone

Living With Children,
No Spouse

NOTE: People in group quarters, other family households and non-family households not shown.

SOURCE: Pew Research Center calculations of Decennial Census and American Community Survey data.

"What Makes a Family? Children, Say Many Americans"

by John Berman

There's the Addams family, the first family and the Partridge family. But what really counts as family? It seems that children have a lot to do with it.

Brian Powell, a sociology professor at Indiana University, and his team tackled Americans' evolving definition of family—and their recognition of unmarried couples, gay and straight, as a family—in a book-length study, "Counted Out: Same-Sex Relations and Americans' Definitions of Family," and separate 2010 survey. Between 2003 and 2010, his team conducted three surveys involving more than 2,300 people.

The new research was released today.

"What we find is that people are moving away from a traditional definition of family and they're moving towards a modern definition of family," said Powell. "That includes a much greater array of living arrangements. They're including a much broader group of people, broader combination of people as families."

Besides the debate over same-sex marriage, the definition of family affects income tax filings, adoption and foster care practices, employee benefits and other matters.

The Census Bureau's definition of "family" remains traditional: "A family is a group of two people or more (one of whom is the householder) related by birth, marriage, or adoption and residing together."

Indeed, the "modern family" comes in many combinations—and so do Americans, according to the team's research.

The book's authors identified three clusters of Americans: "exclusionists" who hold onto a more narrow definition of family; "moderates" who are willing to count same-sex couples as family if children are involved; and "inclusionists" who have a very broad definition of family.

In 2010, almost everyone—99.8 percent—agreed that a husband, wife and kids count as a family. Ninety-two percent said that a husband and wife without the kids made a family.

"Children provide this, quote, 'guarantee' that move you to family status," Powell said. "Having children signals something. It signals that there really is a commitment and a sense of responsibility in a family."

83 Percent Say Unmarried Couples With Children Are a Family

For instance, 39.6 percent in 2010 said that an unmarried man and woman living together were a family—but give that couple some kids and 83 percent say that's a family.

Thirty-three percent said a gay male couple was a family. Sixty-four percent said they became a family when they added children. That number was 54 percent in 2003.

"People right now are really reevaluating their views about same-sex couples," Powell said.

In 2006, just over half of Americans surveyed—51 percent—said pets were part of the family.

Nearly 72 percent said in 2006 that it was better for a married woman to change her name and nearly 50 percent said the name change should be required. Fifty-four percent said it was OK for a man to take his wife's last name.

Sixty percent of Americans in 2010 said that if you considered yourself to be a family, then you were one.

Source: September 15, 2010, http://abcnews.go.com/WN/defines-family-children-americans-survey/ story?id=11644693

The shifts described in Powell's research pleased Jennifer Chrisler, executive director of the Family Equality Council, an advocacy group for same-sex families.

"People are taking a more expansive view of what a family is," said Chrisler. "But for any family that doesn't fit the 1960s Ozzie-and-Harriet mold, slow and steady doesn't feel fast enough."

So in the end, when it comes to defining "Family Ties" and determining "Family Matters," it's "All in the Family."

QUESTIONS FOR READING ACTIVELY

1. The article "What Makes a Family? Children, Say Many Americans" reports on the results of several polls regarding what counts as a *family*. What did the pollsters find out? How would you have responded to their questions?

2. Berman mentions that, in addition to same-sex marriage debates, "the definition of family affects income tax filings, adoption and foster care practices, employee benefits and other matters." What are some of the "other matters" that Berman did not touch on but that would affect families?

QUESTION FOR THINKING CRITICALLY

1. Berman points out that the book *Counted Out: Same-Sex Relations and Americans' Definitions of Family* identifies three "clusters" of Americans: exclusionists, moderates, and inclusionists. If you had to place your parents in one of these groups, which would it be and why? Which group would you place yourself in and why? What are some of the differences between your parents' perceptions and ideals and yours?

QUESTION FOR WRITING THOUGHTFULLY

1. In the beginning of the essay, Berman mentions the Addams family, the Partridge family, and the first family. Reflect on the highly visible or prominent families you were exposed to as a young person. Perhaps the families were fictional, like the Cleaver family in *Leave It to Beaver* or Armand Goldman and his partner, Albert, in the 1996 film *The Birdcage*. There also may be families you knew personally who made an impression on you. Choose one, and define the dynamics of that family, as well as your reaction to the family and how it may have formed some of your beliefs about what constitutes *family*.

"The Rise of Post-Familialism: Humanity's Future?"

by Joel Kotkin

This piece is the introduction to a new report on post-familialism from Civil Service College in Singapore, Chapman University, and Fieldstead and Company and authored by Joel Kotkin.

Source: Created October 12, 2012 - 05:42, http://www.joelkotkin.com/print/631.

For most of human history, the family—defined by parents, children and extended kin—has stood as the central unit of society. In Europe, Asia, Africa and, later, the Americas and Oceania, people lived, and frequently worked, as family units.

Today, in the high-income world and even in some developing countries, we are witnessing a shift to a new social model. Increasingly, family no longer serves as the central organizing feature of society. An unprecedented number of individuals—approaching upwards of 30% in some Asian countries—are choosing to eschew child bearing altogether and, often, marriage as well.

The post-familial phenomena has been most evident in the high income world, notably in Europe, North America and, most particularly, wealthier parts of East Asia. Yet it has bloomed as well in many key emerging countries, including Brazil, Iran and a host of other Islamic countries.

The reasons for this shift are complex, and vary significantly in different countries and cultures. In some countries, particularly in East Asia, the nature of modern competitive capitalism often forces individuals to choose between career advancement and family formation. As a result, these economies are unwittingly setting into motion forces destructive to their future workforce, consumer base and long-term prosperity.

The widespread movement away from traditional values—Hindu, Muslim, Judeo-Christian, Buddhist or Confucian—has also undermined familialism. Traditional values have almost without exception been rooted in kinship relations. The new emerging social ethos endorses more secular values that prioritize individual personal socioeconomic success as well as the personal quest for greater fulfilment.

To be sure, many of the changes driving post-familialism also reflect positive aspects of human progress. The change in the role of women beyond sharply defined maternal roles represents one of the great accomplishments of modern times. Yet this trend also generates new pressures that have led some women to reject both child-bearing and marriage. Men are also adopting new attitudes that increasingly preclude marriage or fatherhood.

The great trek of people to cities represents one of the great triumphs of human progress, as fewer people are necessary to produce the basic necessities of food, fibre and energy. Yet the growth of urban density also tends to depress both fertility and marriage rates. The world's emerging post-familial culture has been largely spawned in the crowded pool of the large urban centres of North America, Europe and, most particularly, East Asia. It is also increasingly evident in the fast growing cities of developing countries in south Asia, North Africa, Iran and parts of the Middle East.

The current weak global economy, now in its fifth year, also threatens to further slow family formation. Child-rearing requires a strong hope that life will be better for the next generation. The rising cost of urban living, the declining number of well-paying jobs, and the onset of the global financial crisis has engendered growing pessimism in most countries, particularly in Europe and Japan, but also in the United States and some developing countries.

This report will look into both the roots and the future implications of the post-familial trend. As Austrian demographer Wolfgang Lutz has pointed out, the shift to an increasingly childless society creates "self-reinforcing mechanisms" that make childlessness, singleness, or one-child families increasingly predominant.

Societal norms, which once almost mandated family formation, have begun to morph. The new norms are reinforced by cultural influences that tend to be concentrated in the very areas—dense urban centres—with the lowest percentages of married people and children. A majority of residences in Manhattan are for singles, while Washington D.C. has one of the highest percentages of women who do not live with children, some 70%. Similar trends can be seen in London, Paris, Tokyo and other cultural capitals.

A society that is increasingly single and childless is likely to be more concerned with serving current needs than addressing the future oriented requirements of children. Since older people vote more than younger ones, and children have no say at all, political power could shift towards nonchildbearing people, at least in the short and medium term. We could tilt more into a "now" society, geared towards consuming or recreating today, as opposed to nurturing and sacrificing for tomorrow.

The most obvious impact from post-familialism lies with demographic decline. It is already having a profound impact on fiscal stability in, for example, Japan and across southern Europe. With fewer workers contributing to cover pension costs, even successful places like Singapore will face this same crisis in the coming decade.

A diminished labour force—and consumer base—also suggest slow economic growth and limit opportunities for business expansion. For one thing, younger people tend to drive technological change, and their absence from the workforce will slow innovation. And for many people, the basic motivation for hard work is underpinned by the need to support and nurture a family. Without a family to support, the very basis for the work ethos will have changed, perhaps irrevocably.

The team that composed this report—made up of people of various faiths, cultures, and outlooks—has concerns about the sustainability of a post-familial future. But we do not believe we can "turn back the clock" to the 1950s, as some social conservatives wish, or to some other imagined, idealised, time. Globalisation, urbanisation, the ascendancy of women, and changes in traditional sexual relations are with us, probably for the long run.

Seeking to secure a place for families requires us to move beyond nostalgia for a bygone era and focus on what is possible. Yet, in the end, we do not consider familialism to be doomed. Even in the midst of decreased fertility, we also see surprising, contradictory and hopeful trends. In Europe, Asia and America, most younger people still express the desire to have families, and often with more than one child. Amidst all the social change discussed above, there remains a basic desire for family that needs to be nurtured and supported by the wider society.

Our purpose here is not to judge people about their personal decision to forego marriage and children. Instead we seek to launch a discussion about how to carve out or maintain a place for families in the modern metropolis. In the process we must ask—with full comprehension of today's prevailing trends—tough questions about our basic values and the nature of the cities we are now creating.

Notes

1. The United Nations Population Prospects defines the more developed world as Europe (including Russia and Eastern Europe, Canada, the United States, Australia, New Zealand and Japan). All other parts of the world are classified as the less developed world. This inexplicable definition leaves out Singapore, which had the fourth highest GDP per capita in the world in 2010, according to the International Monetary Fund. It also excludes Hong Kong, South Korea and a number of other regions. This report has reclassified the UN data into "higher income" and "medium and lower income" regions, with those above a 2010 GDP per capita $20,000 being "higher income."

2. Wolfgang Lutz, Vegard Skirbekk and Maria Rita Testa, "The Low Fertility Trap Hypothesis: Forces that may lead to further postponement and fewer births in Europe," Vienna Institute of Demography, *European Demographic Research Papers*, 2005.

3. Steven Klinenberg, *Going Solo: The Extraordinary Rise and Surprising Appeal of Living Alone* (New York: Penguin Press, 2012), p. 5; analysis on census data by Ali Modarres.

4. Radha Basu, "Retire on CPF Savings? Think Again," *The Straits Times*, March 21, 2012.

5. IBID.

QUESTIONS FOR READING ACTIVELY

1. Joel Kotkin's introduction to the report "The Rise of Post-Familialism: Humanity's Future" begins with a somewhat dire look at post-familialism but ends on a note of hope for the future. How does Kotkin use language (specific words and phrases) to define how the family is changing?

2. What are some of the passages in this report that you connected with personally? For example, do you know someone who has put off marriage or children for the sake of a career? What were the consequences? Describe two passages and your reactions to them.

QUESTIONS FOR THINKING CRITICALLY

1. Kotkin observes:

   > For most of human history, the family—defined by parents, children and extended kin—has stood as the central unit of society…. Today, in the high-income world and even in some developing countries, we are witnessing a shift to a new social model. Increasingly, family no longer serves as the central organizing feature of society. An unprecedented number of individuals are choosing to eschew child bearing altogether and, often, marriage as well.

   What are the factors that Kotkin cites to explain this changing nature of the family? Do you think that the family is in danger of becoming obsolete and at some point extinct? Why or why not?

2. Kotkin's report claims that "competitive capitalism" can make people choose between career and family. Consequently, "these economies are unwittingly setting into motion forces destructive to their future workforce, consumer base and long-term prosperity." Consider some of the larger issues facing our world today such as overpopulation, unemployment, world hunger, the depletion of natural resources, and global warming. If we are to, as Kotkin says, "carve out or maintain a place for families in the modern metropolis," what are some of the "tough questions" we might have to ask ourselves?

QUESTION FOR WRITING THOUGHTFULLY

1. Kotkin says that "for many people, the basic motivation for hard work in underpinned by the need to support and nurture a family" and that "without

a family to support, the very basis for the work ethos will have changed, perhaps irrevocably." Do you think this is true? Do you have other personal motivations to work? Define your career ambitions in relation to your overarching future goals. Use at least one quotation from Kotkin's report to help define and classify your future goals.

Using Concepts to Classify

When you apply a concept to an object, idea, or experience, you are in effect classifying it by placing it in a group of things that are defined by the properties or requirements of the concept. The same things can often be classified in many different ways. For example, if someone handed you a tomato and asked, "Which category does this tomato belong in, fruit or vegetable?" how would you respond? The fact is that a tomato can be classified as both a fruit and a vegetable because its botanical definition does not seem consistent with its uses as a food.

Let's consider another example. Imagine that you are walking on undeveloped land with some other people when you come across an area of soggy ground with long grass and rotting trees. One person in your group surveys the parcel and announces, "That's a smelly marsh. All it does is breed mosquitoes. It ought to be covered with landfill and

THE TREE, as seen by...

the planner...   the parks department...   the publisher...

400 LUXURY HOMES TO BE ERECTED ON THIS SITE

the highways department...   the developer...   the landscape architect.

built on so that we can use it productively." Another member of your group disagrees with the classification "smelly marsh," stating, "This is a wetland of great ecological value. There are many plants and animals that need this area and other areas like it to survive. Wetland areas also help to prevent the rivers from flooding, by absorbing excess water during heavy rains." Which person is right? Should the wet area be classified as a "smelly marsh" or as a "valuable wetland"? Actually, the wet area can be classified both ways. The classification that you select depends on your needs and your interests.

These examples illustrate how the way you classify reflects and influences the way you see the world, the way you think about the world, and the way you behave in the world. You classify many of the things in your experience differently than others do because of your individual needs, interests, and values. For instance, smoking marijuana might be classified by some as "use of a dangerous drug" and by others as a "harmless good time." Some view SUVs as "gas guzzlers"; others see the same cars as "safer, more comfortable vehicles." Some people categorize body piercing as "perverse abuse," while others think of it as "creative self-expression." The way you classify aspects of your experience reflects the kind of individual you are and the way you think and feel about the world.

CLASSIFYING PEOPLE AND THEIR ACTIONS

You also place people in various categories. The specific categories you select depend on who you are and how you see the world. Similarly, each of us is placed in a variety of classifications by other people. Here, for instance, are some of the categories in which certain people have placed this book's author:

Classification	People Who Classify Him
First-born son	His parents
Taxpayer	Internal Revenue Service
Tickler	His children
Bagel with cream cheese	Restaurant where he picks up his breakfast

Not only do you continually classify things and people and place them in various groups on the basis of common properties you choose to focus on, but also you classify ideas, feelings, actions, and experiences.

Thinking-Writing Activity

CLASSIFICATION AND YOUR SELF

List some of the different ways that you can be classified and identify the people who would classify you that way.

_____   _____

_____   _____

_____   _____

WRITING AND CLASSIFYING

The intellectual act of classifying is an essential part of writing in three ways.

First, writings themselves are classified into many different forms. You know this already, of course. Novels, poems, essays, news stories, blogs, emails, lab reports—the list is almost endless. And each of these forms of writing has subclassifications: science fiction, political blogs, romance novels, and so forth. Different classifications of writing, or *genres*, have different purposes and styles. You are aware of this as a reader. As a college writer, you must become more aware of using styles and formats appropriate to the kind of writing that you are doing for your classes.

Thinking-Writing Activity

CLASSIFICATION AND ETHICS

Each of these following classifications represents a separate legal concept, one with its own properties and referents (examples). Of course, even when you clearly understand what a particular concept means, the complexity of the circumstances surrounding it can make it difficult to determine which concept applies.

Classification	*Circumstance*	*Example*
1. Manslaughter	Killing someone accidentally	Driving while intoxicated
2. Self-defense	_____	_____
3. Premeditated murder	_____	_____
4. Mercy killing	_____	_____
5. Diminished capacity	_____	_____

Court cases raise complex and disturbing issues. During a trial, trying to identify the appropriate concept of the crime can be challenging. On top of that, trying to determine which of the related concepts—*guilty* or *not guilty*—applies can be even more challenging. This is also true of many of life's other complex situations: you must work hard at identifying appropriate concepts to apply to the circumstances you are trying to make sense of and then be prepared to change or modify these concepts on the basis of new information or better insights. Explain, for instance, why the killing of another person might be classified in different ways, depending on the circumstances.

Second, almost any piece of writing is organized by classifying material into sections, chapters, or paragraphs in which the content is sorted and arranged in logical ways. Usually, writers put similar material together so that readers can think about related items that have been assembled for their easy comprehension. You—and other writers—do this when you revise drafts to create good paragraphs that each focus on one idea. You do this when you are sorting your research notes into topics (or categories) in order to organize a paper, report, or presentation.

Third, much writing concentrates on presenting *kinds, categories, types,* or *classifications* of concepts. Readings in this chapter, for example, discuss different classifications of the concept of *family*. This book itself is divided into different categories of approaches to thinking and writing.

Thinking-Writing Activity

IDENTIFYING CLASSIFICATIONS

1. Think of any reading selection in this book that you recall as being well organized. Turn to it and see how the writer classified or sorted the material into logical arrangements. Note the classifications of information. Perhaps topic sentences of paragraphs will show you what the writer has done.

2. Share your observations with classmates. See if they agree.

3. How did analyzing this piece of writing provide ideas about organizing your own work?

Defining Concepts

When you define a concept, you usually identify the necessary properties or requirements that determine when the concept can be applied. In fact, the word *definition* is derived from a Latin word meaning "boundary." A definition provides the boundaries of whatever territory in your experience can be described by the concept.

Definitions also use examples of the concept being defined. Consider the following:

Oxymoron	A rhetorical figure in which incongruous or contradictory terms are combined as in *a deafening silence* and *a mournful optimist.*
	—*The American Heritage Dictionary of the English Language*
An edible	Good to eat and wholesome to digest, as a worm to a toad, a toad to a snake, a snake to a pig, a pig to a man, and a man to a worm.
	—Ambrose Bierce
Facts, theories	Facts and theories are different things, not rungs in a hierarchy of increasing certainty. Facts are the world's data. Theories are structures of ideas that explain and interpret facts. Facts do not go away when scientists debate rival theories to explain them. Einstein's theory of gravitation replaced Newton's, but apples did not suspend themselves in mid-air pending the outcome.
	—Stephen Jay Gould

Contrast these definitions with the one illustrated in the following passage from Charles Dickens' *Hard Times:*

> "Bitzer," said Thomas Gradgrind. "Your definition of a horse." "Quadruped. Graminivorous. Forty teeth, namely twenty-four grinders, four eye teeth, and twelve incisive. Sheds coat in the spring; in marshy countries sheds hoofs, too. Hoofs hard, but requiring to be shod with iron. Age known by marks in mouth." That (and much more) Bitzer. "Now girl number twenty," said Mr. Gradgrind, "you know what a horse is."

Although Bitzer has certainly done an admirable job of listing some of the necessary properties or requirements of the concept *horse,* it is unlikely that "girl number twenty" has any better idea of what a horse is than she had before, since Bitzer's definition relies exclusively on a technical listing of the properties characterizing the concept *horse* without giving any examples that might illustrate the concept more completely. Definitions like this, which rely exclusively on a technical description of the concept's properties, are not very helpful unless you already know what the concept means. A more concrete way of communicating the concept *horse* would be to point out various animals that qualify as horses and other animals that do not. You could also explain why they do not. (For example, "That can't be a horse because it has two humps and its legs are far too long.")

Even though examples do not take the place of a clearly understood definition, they are often very useful in clarifying, supplementing, and expanding such a definition. If someone asked you, "What is a horse?" and you replied by giving examples of different kinds of horses (thoroughbred racing horses, plow horses for farming, quarter horses for cowhands, circus horses), you certainly would be communicating a good portion of the meaning of *horse.* Giving examples of a concept complements and clarifies the necessary requirements for the correct use of that concept.

Giving an effective definition of a concept requires

- Identifying the general qualities of the concept, which determine when it can be correctly applied
- Classifying it, which means identifying its category, type, or "family"
- Using appropriate examples that embody its general qualities
- Differentiating it from other items in its classification

The process of providing definitions of concepts is basically the same process that you use to develop concepts.

Writing Thoughtfully to Define Concepts

Writing a full definition, often called an *extended definition,* is among the most important and most difficult of writing activities. Defining terms is a necessary part of college-level writing and speaking. For productive discussions about complex issues, all involved must agree on the meanings of significant terms, so clear definitions are often required. Difficulties arise because significant terms related to complex issues are usually abstract concepts, with possibilities of different definitions for different people. For example, the common political terms *conservative* and *liberal* often have varied meanings, even to people who identify themselves as one or the other.

No one has much trouble agreeing on definitions of physical objects. A table, a tree, a television set—not many arguments arise about what these objects are. But like *liberal* and *conservative,* concepts such as *religion, love, democracy, femininity,* and *masculinity* can be defined in different ways. If people discussing ideas like these do not establish definitions, their discussions will not be productive. Worse, these discussions sometimes lead to disagreements, arguments, and even wars. The readings and Thinking-Writing Activities in this chapter have been selected and planned to demonstrate the importance of definitions.

Notice how with both simple objects and complex concepts, defining is somewhat easier as long as a single word is being examined. As soon as modifying and classifying ideas are added, defining becomes more challenging and more significant to critical thinking. A *beautiful* table, a *good* tree to plant in a *small* yard, the *best* computer to buy for *your family room*—now these objects call for fuller definitions. The *kind* of democracy that can work in a country with a *history of despotism*, the *kind* of love that a *parent* might have for an *adult child*—these are the types of concepts that people must define in order to present arguments, to make decisions, to solve problems. These are the kinds of terms that you might want to define in the Writing Project in this chapter because they are the kinds that involve judgments; they are important to our lives because they influence our actions.

Clear, satisfying definitions can be as extended as book chapters, articles, or entire books; however, a definition often will be developed in a paragraph or two as a vital part of a paper or report. In the Writing Project for this chapter, you will write an essay that defines; you will see the need for using a variety of thinking/organizing patterns as you develop it. The guidelines for writing definitions are not fixed rules; there may be times when you would have good reasons for varying or adapting some of them. Try to use them, though, unless you have good reason not to.

Writing Project

DEFINING AN IMPORTANT CONCEPT

This chapter has included readings, questions, and Thinking-Writing Activities that encourage you to define concepts that affect your life. Be sure to reread what you wrote for the activities; you may be able to use some of that material in completing this project.

Project Overview and Requirements

For this project, you will write an essay that defines a concept that is currently important to you or to your future life. Clearly explain why this concept is significant to you and why it needs to be defined or even redefined.

Your essay must include material from two sources in addition to any dictionaries you consult for definitions. Integrate your sources into your essay in a meaningful way, and document them as your instructor advises (for example, using the APA or MLA format). After you have drafted your essay, revise it to the best of your ability, and as always, follow your instructor's directions for topic limits, length, format, and so forth.

For two examples of this type of essay, look ahead to the Student Writing section of this chapter beginning on page 275.

Begin by considering the key elements in the Thinking-Writing Model in Chapter 1 on pages 5–8. As you have seen in each project so far, the extended below will inspire deeper reflection and greater understanding of your writing task.

THE WRITING SITUATION

Purpose   One purpose for this project is to help you think about and formulate a definition that will be significant as you continue your college studies, decide on your profession, or enter a new phase in your personal life. Indeed, all of us need to be able to define the complex terms that are foundations for our thinking, our decisions, and our actions in life. Another purpose for this project is to help you improve your ability to present a full definition in order to clarify your own thinking and to increase your audience's understanding.

Audience   You have a multilevel audience. *You* are an important audience, for in facing the challenge of defining a complex concept, you can think more clearly about some aspect of your life. Your classmates can learn from your definition and can be a valuable, intelligent audience during the peer review process of your draft. You will also want to identify people outside your class who might enjoy or profit from reading your definition. If you are writing about a concept that impacts people in your community or on your campus, your paper can both share information and urge action

Subject   All of us need to be able to define abstract, complex terms that are foundations for our thinking, our decisions, and our actions in life. College courses, family life, spiritual concerns, and romantic relationships all involve concepts that need to be well defined. Clear definitions allow us to communicate our thoughts and feelings more accurately. They also help us more clearly understand the thoughts and feelings of others. Ultimately, clear definitions can help us avoid confusion and conflict. For this assignment, try to identify an important concept that is central to how you see yourself and your future. Concepts like *creative expression, enlightened free choice, authentic person, fulfillment, achieving potential, meaningful empathy, social responsibility, critical thinker,* and (of course) *thoughtful writer* are all examples with broad implications in a person's life.

Writer This project provides you with the opportunity to participate in the "conversation of ideas" that is the lifeblood of thoughtful, reflective people in a society. By defining a complex concept, you are explaining how the concept you have selected has personal meaning for you. You are also suggesting to others— your audience—how they might think about your analysis of the concept. The definition you propose may help them understand something in their experience more clearly, or it may provide an added meaning they have not previously considered. The outside sources integrated into your analysis ensure that your definition is grounded in a common understanding that goes beyond your own experience.

The following four questions will help you focus on the concept that you would like to define and explore in your paper. If you are not sure what you would like to write about, go back through your responses to the Thinking-Writing Activities earlier in this chapter in which you identified several concepts and explored definitions and properties. You can then move on to The Writing Process.

1. First, describe a concept that you find interesting and that has some sort of relationship to your life. Here is one writer's description:

   > When I was much younger, a friend of my mother's claimed I had "moxie." Over time, the thought of having moxie gave me the confidence to navigate tough decisions and take chances. I would like to explore the meaning of moxie—everything from the first mass-produced soft drink to Moxie Girlz dolls—and how the word still holds significance for me today.

2. Who may be interested in your extended definition of this concept? For example:

   > My friends and family will be interested, of course, but I also feel that this topic will have appeal to a much wider audience, especially young women who may need a little moxie themselves.

3. To effectively define a concept, it is critical that a writer is aware of signs, referents, properties, generalizations, interpretations, requirements, and classifications. With these key terms in mind, what is your plan for clearly describing the concept you have chosen? For example:

   > To me, having moxie means having courage or gumption, the backbone to do anything, but I plan to investigate the etymology of the word *moxie*, and tie in references to moxie in pop culture including the soda and a collection of "Moxie Girlz" dolls that uses "be true, be you" as a motivational message to girls. I also plan to show examples of my "inner moxie."

4. Once you have clearly defined your concept, what, ultimately, do you want your audience to learn?

Through my extended definition of moxie, I plan to show how having courage can result in positive changes to one's life.

THE WRITING PROCESS

The following sections will guide you through the recursive stages of generating, planning, drafting, and revising as you work on an essay in which you define a significant concept. Try to be particularly conscious of both the critical thinking you do as you articulate your definition and the critical thinking and decision making you do as you revise.

Generating Ideas

- Refer back to the responses you wrote for the questions for the readings on the concept of *family*. This concept is important in many people's lives, so perhaps you will write about it—or perhaps it will lead you to another concept to define.

- Think about the activities or concerns that are central to your life. Some of these are probably rather serious, as are the subjects discussed in this chapter, but some parts are surely more lighthearted, like sports you play or watch, television comedies, thriller movies, or parties.

- Next, think of concepts inherent in some of your activities, such as a satisfying relationship or what it means to be a good athlete, college student, or practitioner of your religion.

- Now, list the properties of two or three concepts that you have identified. Include specific examples. How should each example be classified?

- Think about why any of these concepts need to be defined or redefined. Do people agree on the meaning? Have you formulated a meaning that is more precise and accurate?

- Before you begin drafting, share your lists and thinking with classmates and, if you can, with people involved in the area in which the concept is important.

- Use as many thinking patterns as you can to discover ideas about your concept. What is it different from? Similar to? Analogous to? Describe it; think about what causes it; think about what effects it has.

- Look up the concept's key words in a good college-level dictionary and also in the *Oxford English Dictionary*. Ask your instructor or one of your college librarians to explain the *OED* to you. See if you can use any of your concept's word history in your definition.

- Freewrite for at least five minutes about why the concept is important to your life, why it needs to be defined, and what information needs to be in your definition.

Defining a Focus

- Look at your freewriting and the lists you created to see what main idea you are moving toward in your definition. Summarize your idea in one or two sentences.

- Next, build upon the sentences you just wrote to create a thesis statement. It should illustrate the key ideas in your definition. Recently, a student defining *freedom of religion* had this as her thesis sentence: "To me, freedom of religion means more than simply being able to practice our religions as we believe that we should; it also means that we must understand and respect other people's religions." Another student, working on a definition of today's *superwoman*, wrote, "The main properties of a superwoman are being capable, tenacious, and independent."

- Be sure that your thesis statement emphasizes the meaning of the concept that you are defining.

Organizing Ideas Essays emphasizing definition are not easy to organize because there are so many approaches to a clear definition of a complex concept. Because the thesis—the essence of the definition—needs to be placed in a context and explained in a number of ways, the question of where to state the thesis is especially crucial. This is the kind of essay in which it might come at the end. When you state the thesis at the end, you need to lead up to it or preview it throughout the essay. However, you will want to think of stating the thesis provisionally near the beginning and referring to it elsewhere in the paper as you establish your definition.

Identify the approaches that you have used in your generative writing and early drafts. Where have you used contrast, comparison, analogy, narration, and so on? The material developed by each of these approaches is likely to form a paragraph. The definitions that you have found in your dictionary and in the *Oxford English Dictionary* will need a paragraph or two to connect them with the definition that you are developing. As always, give careful thought to paragraphing. Rearrange your paragraphs to discover which order will best help your readers understand your definition. Because it is important that your readers understand the need for a definition, explaining that need is an effective way to begin. Explaining the significance of this concept in your life might be part of your introduction or conclusion.

Guidelines for Writing Definitions of Concepts

1. Establish the need for a definition. Why is it needed? Do people disagree on the meaning of the concept? Are there multiple meanings? Are earlier definitions no longer satisfactory? Is this a new concept or new terminology?

2. Carefully choose the word or words in which you state the concept. Definitions provide precision, so you need to be sure that you have presented the concept in the words that are most indicative.

3. Incorporate two kinds of dictionary definitions: the short one that gives meaning, as in a regular college dictionary, and a longer one that gives the history of the word's usage, which can be found in the *Oxford English Dictionary*. Word origins and past meanings can often illuminate the meaning that you want to present.

4. Be sure that you identify the category into which the concept fits.

5. Show comparative thinking. Point out similar concepts, but then make clear how your concept is distinct. Use analogies to illuminate the meaning of the concept.

6. Provide specific examples to show what the concept means. Illustrative anecdotes are often effective.

7. Include the meaning of the concept in the thesis statement. Give careful thought to where you state the thesis.

8. Throughout your definition, emphasize that you are establishing the meaning you believe the concept has within the context that you have identified.

9. Address the foregoing principles in separate paragraphs or sections of the definition. Provide each paragraph with a clear topic sentence whenever appropriate.

10. Document any sources that you use. Introduce source material into your definition, explain and comment on it, and cite it correctly.

Drafting   Be sure to accurately identify all sources in your draft. See the appendix for further guidelines on citing source material.

Begin with the easiest paragraph to draft. Explaining the concept's significance in your life is likely to be easy, since you are writing about your thoughts and feelings; showing the need for a definition should not be difficult because you are writing about one of your convictions. As you draft, be sure that each paragraph contains real-life examples that pertain to the meaning of the concept—unless for some good reason a specific paragraph does not need examples.

After you draft your paragraphs, make every effort to write topic sentences that focus on how the material in each paragraph helps to establish the meaning of your concept.

As you draft the conclusion, be sure that it provides a satisfying ending with some reference to the thesis and emphasis on the meaning of the concept.

Revising, Editing, and Proofreading   Use the step-by-step method on pages 174–176 in Chapter 6 to revise and polish your essay.

The following two essays use definition and classification to define concepts. The first essay explores the meaning of the term *freedom*; the second investigates the concept of *masculinity*.

Revising Your Essay: Defining an Important Concept

Once your draft is complete, take a break from your writing. When you come back to it, ask yourself if the writing fulfills the requirements of the project. Have you clearly defined a concept that affects your life? Do you feel your audience will understand your ideas based on what you have written?

Peer Responses

To help you decide if an audience will be able to clearly understand the concept you have defined, consider exchanging your draft with a peer for feedback. If you ask someone outside of class to review your writing, be sure to describe the goal of the assignment. Pay close attention to the feedback you receive.

Revision

As you revise your paper, use "A Step-by-Step Method for Revising Any Assignment," located on the inside front cover of this book for additional guidance. Remember to look at the larger components of your paper first.

Editing and Proofreading

Once you are comfortable with the concept you have defined and the overall flow of your paper, focus on the small details. Look at your draft sentence by sentence, and make clarifications if needed. Look for typos, spelling errors, and punctuation problems. Attention to detail shows your audience you truly care about the ideas you are communicating.

STUDENT WRITING

Nawang Doma Sherpa's Writing Process

An immigrant from the Himalayan nation of Nepal, student Nawang Doma Sherpa's perspective on *freedom* is informed both by the extraordinary challenges she faced, and choices she made in her life, and by her strong Buddhist faith. In her essay, she examines the concept of *freedom* through the lenses of both her immigrant experience and her faith, describing how achieving a sense of *freedom* has allowed her to define herself and her life. To generate ideas for her essay, she returned to her journal notes on the Thinking-Writing Activities she completed in this chapter.

General qualities of religion: I know what I believe, but everyone has their own very private reasons for what they believe in—it seems like everyone in my class has a different religion, but their faith—why they believe, or how they believe is the same. I think we're all looking for reasons for our lives. Why are we here?

<u>Classification? What kind of human activity is it?</u>: It's a mysterious activity. There has always been religion just as there have always been dreams. In Nepal our religion, Buddhism, determined so much—from how our days were structured to how we treated our parents and our neighbors. Here it seems like everyone has a different religion, or no religion at all. American society sometimes seems very religious—there's lots of talk about God and religion in politics for example—but it's not like the kind of everyday practice and discipline that I grew up with.

<u>What is my definition of religion?</u>: For me Buddhism is what I practice as well as what I believe. I live my life as a Buddhist, and it helps me to make rational choices about my life. Being free and contributing to make this world a better and more peaceful place is the only aim of Buddhism.

Sherpa's essay begins with two qualities or properties of freedom and implies the complexity of the relationship between freedom and responsibility.

Sherpa uses a quote to support her idea that we have freedom, but that with freedom comes responsibility. This concept is carefully woven throughout her essay.

Freedom for Enlightenment
by Nawang Doma Sherpa

Human freedom is dependent upon two qualities: our relationships with others, and our need to believe in a higher purpose for our lives. All the different roles that each of us plays in this world—child, student, peer, parent, and countless other relations—are intricate and interwoven with each other. In addition to the roles we each play, the mysterious phenomenon of religion both brings people together (as families and as entire societies) and drives them apart. In my own life, I have struggled with determining my freedom both in relationship to my family's traditions and expectations, and to my Buddhist faith.

I define myself on the basis of my achievements and flaws. In other words, I am who I am because of what I have done in my past—not because of the high goals and beautiful dreams I have set for my future. Both my own experience and the teachings of Buddhism have shown me that the future is both unpredictable and unknowable, but the past and present are reality and fact. The philosopher Jean-Paul Sartre noted that "man is nothing else but what he makes of himself," and I have come to share this view. We are free to determine our own fates, but we are not always fully aware of the responsibilities that come with this freedom. For me, religion and family duties helped me to

Source: Freedom for Enlightenment by Nawang Doma Sherpa.

acknowledge both my freedom and my responsibilities. However, it has not always been easy to accept these things.

I was born in Nepal into a middle class Sherpa family. They allowed me to pursue an education by attending a private girl's school for nine years and then a co-education school for another two years. After I graduated, I decided on my own to come to the United States. I moved to New York City, applied to college, and I now work to support myself and pay my tuition. This was a very unusual decision for a young girl from a traditional Nepalese family to make. Even though I am grown up, I still miss the love and care of my parents, especially the comfort of my mother's embrace and our home. My parents wanted me to stay in Nepal after I graduated, because it is traditional for girls of my social class to get married after they complete high school. But I made the decision to leave, to travel halfway around the world and live on very little money, entirely of my own free will. But if you ask me if I plan to spend the rest of my life away from Nepal, my family, and my home, I would not be able to answer you. I can only say that I will continue to make decisions based on my experience and my faith.

Sherpa helps her audience understand the lens through which she sees the world—the lens that shaped her ideas.

I practiced Buddhism, like most people in Nepal, and I feel free as a Buddhist. I could change my religion if I wanted to, because Buddhism encourages people to determine their own best choices for themselves rather than adhere strictly to one "perfect" or "correct" God. For me, Buddhism is rational. Ancestors have passed along the teaching of Buddha from generation to generation, and the core of that teaching is that we can free ourselves by understanding our inner self. The "eight-fold path" that all Buddhists follow determines how we relate to our selves and to each other: right speech, understanding, good deeds, determination, effort, awareness, thinking, and living. By understanding and accepting responsibility for our actions and beliefs, we achieve freedom. This makes us more responsible for who we are because by following this eight-fold path we will never hurt others and we will never fail in creating our image. Being free and contributing to make this world a better and more peaceful place is the only aim of Buddhism.

In this extended definition, Sherpa lays out the requirements of Buddhism. Note how she indicates that responsibility is central to Buddhism.

Freedom is possible, but with it comes responsibility. Freedom allows us to be conscious and aware, to explore and create new options and make choices that define us in the future. To deny your freedom is to deny responsibility for the choices that you make. I exercised free choice, and at the same time achieved freedom from my society's conservative expectations, by choosing to pursue a college education in America rather than getting married and staying in Nepal. But I have to accept the responsibility for this decision: my family misses me terribly, and I sometimes find it very difficult to balance work and school and to support myself financially. I am fortunate to have both the support of my family and the strength of my religion as I move forward into my future.

In her concluding paragraph, Sherpa skillfully reminds the audience that her concept of freedom is intricately tied to responsibility.

STUDENT WRITING

Jorden Carlsen's Writing Process

In response to an assignment asking him to develop an extended definition of an abstract concept related to the course readings, Jorden Carlsen, a student at City College of San Francisco, chose to explore the concept of *masculinity*.

Actually, I was stuck at first on choosing a topic. But masculinity is an interesting concept to me because its meaning is kind of vague; people aren't sure exactly what it means. So I thought it was open enough that I could come up with my own conclusions about it. What I wanted to do was to get the audience, my classmates and teacher, to agree that masculinity can be a positive ideal, and I didn't want to lose them along the way. I didn't want to make my essay too complex or outlandish.

To get started, I sat down and began writing ideas about masculinity on a piece of paper, just a list. From that, I could decide which direction to take. Then I began to do research. I used Google to find newspaper and magazine articles. I read about ten articles, and then I went back to my list to see which ideas I could support. Then I highlighted the parts of the articles I wanted to use to support these ideas.

I got rid of some of the ideas on my list and added some new ones. While I was doing this, I was able to write some sentences that I thought sounded good. These later became either topic sentences or supports in the body paragraphs of my essay.

Doing the research helped me get going. I could see that I could combine some of the ideas on my list to go together to form paragraphs. From there, I did an outline.

Deciding what ideas to use at the beginning was the hardest part. I began with what had attracted me to the topic, that the concept isn't exactly clear.

In the body, I decided to deal with some negative ideas about masculinity first and then move on to more positive ones and my own personal ideas. As I wrote, I actually convinced myself even more that my thesis was correct, that the concept of <u>masculinity</u> can be a positive tool for men. So my conclusion came right out of that. I was sold on the idea.

Carlsen sets up his essay by generalizing how others conceptualize masculinity and then moves into his thesis and definition of masculinity.

> ### Masculinity Makes a Good Man
> #### by Jorden Carlsen
>
> Nowadays it is difficult to pin down exactly what characteristics make someone a "real" man, and when most of us say a "real man," we mean a masculine man We know that such a man should be physically strong and not run away at the sight of a spider, but what else has come to mean a man is masculine? To some being
>
> *Source: Masculinity Makes a Good Man by Jorden Carlsen.*

masculine means that a man is never able to show any sign of weakness, and to others it means that all a man need do is be a good provider. I think there is more to it than that. I think that masculinity should be an ideal for men to live up to. It shouldn't limit a man's emotion or make him afraid to be seen as weak. Instead, the ideal of masculinity should be something that encourages men to live up to their full potential in life. It should be something that makes men want to be good providers, stay in good physical shape, and be generally reliable. Masculinity can and should be used as a tool to help men make the most of themselves.

For some people the idea of *masculinity* has become self-defeating. For them it has become synonymous with experiencing uncomfortable social pressures, denying their emotions, having unsavory world-views, or having a fear of showing any kind of weakness. Sara B. Kimmel explains one view of this present situation in her article "Measuring Masculine Body Ideal Distress: Development of a Measure." This article is mainly concerned with many men's dissatisfaction with their bodies and the stress this dissatisfaction causes them. Kimmel notes that "boys and men are comparing themselves to increasingly unattainable masculine body images and are thus increasingly likely to evaluate their body image negatively." For these men, wanting to have a body that they see as masculine has made them unhappy with the body they have. As bad as it may sound, I think slight dissatisfaction can be a good thing for people who are out of shape in that it can encourage them to exercise or eat right, but like many things, can go too far and do more harm than good by, for example, leading to steroid use or eating disorders.

Kimmel also mentions an instrument called "The Conformity to Masculinity Norms Inventory," which has been used to assess conformity to masculine norms in the dominant culture in U.S. society. I found something among the topics included in their survey disturbing. Two of the factors that were included in the "Masculinity Norms" were "Power over Women" and "Disdain for Homosexuals." Why is it [that] people see these things as masculine? I certainly cannot tell you. I believe that a man should respect people, not control or show disdain for them. Doing so can only display a man's insecurities and other shortcomings that take away from the depth of character that makes a real man.

Another drawback to masculinity is that some believe that a real man should not show his emotion, or even worse, not have any. Is this another example of something taken too far? I think it is possible that this belief could have its origins in men's need to do what needs to be done. It has served men best in the past to be able to put their emotions aside and deal with the task at hand, but when there is no task that needs to be done, men don't need to hide their emotions. Yet in his essay titled "Complexion," Richard Rodriguez wrote, "More important than any of this was

The topic sentence leads the reader into one aspect of the concept—the negative connotations of masculinity.

The third paragraph shows the reader Carlsen is still focusing on the negative aspects (or properties) of masculinity.

Carlsen's topic sentence keeps the audience focused on the negative aspects of masculinity.

the fact that a man never verbally revealed his emotions" (516). Through his writing Rodriguez is able to show his range of emotion, which displays his personal strength to face adversity and shows that being emotional can be a part of being a "real" man.

Carlsen begins to set the stage for his counterargument and turns the table, so to speak, on the definition of masculinity.

Having a weakness doesn't make a man less masculine; it makes him human. But for some reason it has become construed that for a man to be masculine, he cannot have any weakness. This had led to many kinds of negative consequences for men the world over. I believe this is a direct link to male violence. Many men now think that if anyone in any way, no matter how small, threatens to expose a weakness on their part, this person must be violently attacked in order to demonstrate that they are not weak. This has led to all kinds of despicable behavior from verbal attacks to gang warfare. These men don't see the irony that this behavior is covering up the bigger weakness of their own insecurity. Being vulnerable doesn't make men less masculine; it is how they handle the situation and themselves that makes them who they are.

Carlsen is now classifying the positive aspects of his concept of masculinity and provides a referent to illustrate how, even though the concept of working to provide for one's family has changed, it is still a property of masculinity.

What I believe to be basic to the view of what a man is supposed to be is his ability to provide. The pinnacle of manhood is his role of the hunter-gatherer. When a man can feed and clothe himself and his family, he is on the forefront of manliness. One of the main ideas in an article titled "Man-of-Action Heroes: The Pursuit of Heroic Masculinity in Everyday Consumption," written by Douglas B. Holt, professor of Marketing at the University of Oxford, and Craig J. Thompson, professor of Marketing at the University of Wisconsin, is that one of the main ideals of masculinity in America is that of a man who is a provider, what they call in the article "Breadwinner Masculinity" (427). These are the men who throughout history have been there for their families, clans, or villages, and have been able to keep everyone alive by bringing home the bacon. It may not always be glorious, but putting dinner on the table is often much more important to a culture's well-being than fighting on the battlefield. This is why men who work hard are seen as masculine. Advances in technology are taking working men farther and farther from hunting game and gathering crops, but that doesn't make them any less masculine. A man who spends eight hours a day doing quality control at the computer factory is putting dinner on the table just as much as an iron worker, and they both deserve the title of *masculine breadwinner*.

In this extended definition, Carlsen uses concrete details to redefine what the concept of masculinity looks like.

Take a moment to picture in your mind a masculine man. Chances have it that the man you saw wasn't extremely overweight or had arms that wouldn't stretch a rubber band put around his biceps. When most of us think of a masculine man, we tend to think of one who has an amount of physical prowess. This is mostly likely because strong men are more likely to be better protectors and better suited for the kind of physical labor that in the past kept our predecessors fed. This ideal can be good to encourage a man to stay healthy and in good shape. I know this from personal experience. When my running shoes have a fine layer of dust and I no longer recognize any of the people who work behind the counter at the gym, I know that I'm not living up to part of my potential. A man doesn't have to be an Olympic bodybuilder to have a masculine body. I see it more as a matter of physical ability. I don't do aerobic exercise because I think I'm fat. What gets my running shoes on is my personal drive to have physical stamina in case of the event I may need it, or want it. The physical side of masculinity is something that all men can tap into as encouragement to keep their body physically able, no matter their body type.

Much of what people perceive about masculinity is strength, but I think most people miss the most important strength of all: strength of character. This comes in many forms, from that of reliability to that of integrity. It's what I think about when I think about how a good man should behave. Real men do not take candy from children. They are the defenders of what is right and the ones who are willing to face risk for others. This is where the depth of masculinity lies. A man who is not a provider or [possessor] of any physical prowess will suddenly take on an air of masculinity when he stands up for what is right. Rodriguez wrote in his essay, "To be formal is to be steady. A man of responsibility, a good provider. Someone formal is also constant. A person to be relied upon in adversity" (515). This is from the part of the essay where he is describing one of the three F's, the concept of what it is to be a man. Living up to the masculine ideal of character isn't always the easiest form of masculinity, but it is the most fulfilling.

Masculinity can be a good ideal for a man to live up to. It also can be taken too far or interpreted in a bad way that takes away from a man's character or leads him to unhealthy behavior, but if viewed correctly, and in the right context, it can be a guide for all men to help them live up to their potential. It can give them drive in life to do things that they may not have otherwise seen or had the motivation to do. *Masculinity* is just a concept, but it is one that has the power to lead a man to be more than he is, and that makes it powerful.

Here, the extended definition continues as Carlsen connects "strength of character" to the concept of masculinity.

By urging his audience to view the concept of masculinity correctly, through the right lens and "in the right context," Carlsen concludes that his concept of masculinity is positive and powerful.

Works Cited

Holt, Douglas B., and Craig J. Thompson. "Man-of-Action Heroes: The Pursuit of Heroic Masculinity in Everyday Consumption." *Journal of Consumer Research* 31.2 (2004): 425–439. Print.

Kimmel, Sara B. "Measuring Masculine Body Ideal Distress: Development of a Measure." *International Journal of Men's Health* (Spring 2004): n. pag. Web. 18 Apr. 2005.

Rodriguez, Richard. "Complexion." *Great Writing*. Ed. Harvey S. Weiner and Nora Eisenberg. 3rd ed. San Francisco: McGraw, 2002: 513–516. Print.

REFLECTION ON WRITING

1. Nawang Doma Sherpa's essay, "Freedom for Enlightenment," not only shares the writer's personal ideas about freedom but also educates the audience about Buddhism and her concept of freedom. Underline the paragraph that most clearly defines Buddhism. How does Nawang Doma Sherpa lead up to this definition? By the time you get to the definition, do you feel you already know something important about the writer and her concept of freedom? If the definition of Buddhism were located in the first paragraph, do you feel the essay would have as much impact?

2. Jordan Carlsen takes a different approach to the overall structure of his essay, "Masculinity Makes a Good Man." How would you describe the structure he used to define the concept of masculinity? What was Carlsen's process of classifying in regard to using referents and properties?

ALTERNATIVE WRITING PROJECT

Compare and contrast how a distinctive concept (such as *family*, *masculinity* or *femininity*) is understood by two different cultures or social groups. You may draw upon your personal experience as part of your evidence to support your definition of a concept, and you might consider interviewing someone from a different culture or social group to compare the person's firsthand experiences with your own.

CHAPTER 8 | **Summary**

- Concepts are general ideas that you use to organize your experience and, in so doing, bring order to your life. They also distinguish and connect one thing to another.

- The process by which you group things on the basis of their similarities is known as classifying.

- You form concepts by the interactive processes of generalizing and interpreting.

- To determine whether the concept you have selected fits a situation, you have to determine whether the requirements that form the concept are being met. There are many different perspectives on what some complex concepts mean, what they should mean, and whether they should be used at all.

- When you apply a concept to objects, ideas, experiences, actions, or people, you are in effect classifying them by placing them in a group of things that are defined by the properties or requirements of the concept. The same things or individuals can often be classified in many different ways.

- When you define a concept, you usually identify the necessary properties or requirements that determine when the concept can be applied.

- For productive writing or discussions about complex issues, clear definitions are needed. Difficulties arise because significant terms related to complex issues are usually abstract concepts, which different people may define in various ways.

THINKING CRITICALLY ABOUT NEW MEDIA

Wikimedia

In your research, you may find various Wikimedia resources to be a useful starting point for your work. Wikipedia, a collaborative encyclopedia that was the first Wikimedia project, is written and edited entirely by volunteer contributors. There are now Wikipedia sites in more than 60 languages, and entries have been written in more than 100 languages. In an interview, Internet entrepreneur Jimmy Wales (founder of Wikimedia), pointed out that this diversity of perspective—bringing in marginalized cultures, voices, and languages to share their expertise with the world—is one of the greatest strengths of Wikimedia projects. "The Wikipedia for a lot of people harkens back to what we all thought the Internet was for in the first place," he observes. "When most people first started the Internet, they thought, oh, this is fantastic, people can communicate from all over the world and build knowledge and share information." Entirely nonprofit and volunteer-driven, Wikipedia is the ultimate expression of open-mindedness. Through a series of open-source, open-access chat rooms and other paths of communication, each Wikipedia entry is communally checked for accuracy, fairness, and the quality of its citations and illustrations. Until Wikipedia, print encyclopedias—for all their pretenses of objectivity—could only present one unified voice, one point of view, that was nearly impossible to amend or update once in print. With Wikipedia, both access to and control of information pass to a global community that uses the technology to collaborate, learn, and grow.

Wiki resources grow organically through collaboration and community. The various projects of Wikimedia itself are built by tens of millions of mostly anonymous users in collaboration with one another, sharing and checking their created knowledge together. Users compare specific entries with their own knowledge, perspectives, and perceptions, and amend or add to each entry based on their own experience and information. As a fully volunteer project, Wikipedia depends on the ability and integrity of each contributor. For example, Wikipedia contributors have created "active improvement teams" that have implemented policies to check all entries for bias, to screen for spam, and to set and adhere to encyclopedia standards.

To understand how people perceive the world, we have to understand their individual lenses, which influence how they actively select, organize, and interpret the events in their experience. A diagram of the process might look like Figure 9.1. A more comic demonstration of the different "lenses" we all wear provides the punchline of the *Dilbert* cartoon on page 289.

The software that structures all Wikimedia projects can be easily and freely adapted by anyone who wishes to create a communally edited website. You may, at some point in your academic career, be asked to create or participate in a wiki as a classroom project. The Wikimedia organization itself has branched out from Wikipedia to create wiki learning centers, online textbooks, dictionaries, a collection of quotations (in more than 30 languages), an archive of public-domain books and other texts, and even Wikispecies, a taxonomy database created by and for scientists but (as with all wikis) available to all.

Thinking-Writing Activity

USING WIKIMEDIA TO COLLABORATE AND COMMUNICATE

Later in this chapter, we will explore different perspectives on the 2012 shooting at Sandy Hook Elementary School. Gather into a group with two or three of your classmates and think of another mass shooting incident (e.g., at Columbine High School in 1999; at the movie theater in Aurora, Colorado, in 2012; at the Sikh temple in Oak Creek, Wisconsin, in 2012). Decide amongst yourselves who will research which aspects of the shooting and then do your research separately. Use a free wiki host site (e.g., *https://www.google.com/ sites*) as a place to compile your data, collaborate with your group members, and create your own web page about the shooting. The site should allow you to include whatever kind of media you would like (e.g., photos, video, audio, diagrams, and links), so use it to your advantage to highlight the different perspectives available regarding your subject. When the site is done, share it with the rest of your class and ask for their feedback.

Effective critical thinkers are aware of the lenses that they—and others—are wearing. People unaware of the nature of their own lenses can often mistake their own perceptions for objective truth, not having examined either the facts or others' perceptions of a given issue.

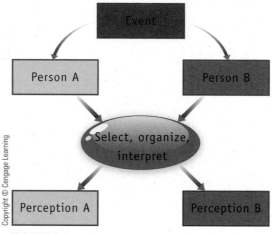

FIGURE 9.1
Differing Perceptions of an Event

Thinking-Writing Activity

DIFFERING PERSPECTIVES

Examine the following pairs of statements. In each pair, two people are being exposed to the same basic stimulus or event, yet the perception of one differs greatly from that of the other. Explain how the various perceptions might have developed.

1. a. That chili was much too spicy to eat.
      Explanation: _____

   b. That chili needed more hot peppers and chili powder to spice it up a little.
      Explanation: _____

2. a. People who wear lots of makeup and jewelry are very sophisticated.
      Explanation: _____

   b. People who wear lots of makeup and jewelry are ostentatious and overdressed.
      Explanation: _____

3. a. The music young people enjoy listening to is a highly creative cultural expression.
      Explanation: _____

   b. The music young people enjoy listening to is obnoxious noise.
      Explanation: _____

4. a. I really enjoy how stimulating and intellectually challenging this English class is.
      Explanation: _____

   b. This English class is too much work. All the teacher wants to do is make us think, think, think. It makes my head hurt.
      Explanation: _____

In the cartoon "The Investigation," each witness is giving what he or she (or it!) believes is an accurate description of the man in the center, and all are unaware that their descriptions are being influenced by who they are and the way that they perceive things.

SELECTING PERCEPTIONS: WHY DO WE NOTICE THE THINGS WE NOTICE?

We tend to select perceptions about subjects that have been called to our attention. For instance, at the age of three, one author's child suddenly became aware of beards. On entering a subway car, she would ask in a penetrating voice, "Any beards here?" and proceed to count them out loud. In so doing, she naturally focused her parents' attention—as well as that of other passengers—on beards.

Another aspect of our perceiving lenses is our tendency to notice what we need, desire, or otherwise find interesting. When we go shopping, we focus on whatever items we are looking for. Walking down the street, we tend to notice certain kinds of people or events while completely ignoring others. Even while watching a movie or reading a book, we tend to concentrate on and remember the elements most meaningful to us. Another person can perform *exactly* the same actions—shop at the same store, walk down the same street, read the same book, or go to the same movie—and yet notice and remember entirely different things.

Although we tend to focus on what is familiar, normally we are not aware of doing so. In fact, we often take for granted what is familiar to us—the taste of chili or eggs, the street that we live on, our family or friends—and normally don't think about how we perceive it. When something happens that makes the familiar seem strange and unfamiliar, though, we do become aware of our perceptions and start to evaluate them.

To sum up, we actively select our perceptions on the basis of

- What has been called to our attention
- What our needs or interests are
- What our moods or feelings are

THE INVESTIGATION

John Jonik/CartoonBank.Com

- What seems familiar or unfamiliar
- What our backgrounds are

The way in which we select perceptions is a paramount factor in shaping the lenses through which we view the world, and it influences our writing to a great extent. Our writing is based on the points we choose to make, the details we select to include. Even when different people are writing about the same subject, the results are often very different because their lenses and their perspectives lead them to make different selections.

ORGANIZING PERCEPTIONS

Not only do you actively select certain perceptions, but also you actively organize them into meaningful relationships and patterns. Carefully examine Figure 7.2 in Chapter 7 on page 210. Do you see both the young woman and the old woman?

If you do, try switching your perspective back and forth between the two images. As you do so, notice how for each image, you are doing the following things:

- *Selecting* certain lines, shapes, and shadings on which to focus your attention
- *Organizing* these lines, shapes, and shadings into different patterns
- *Interpreting* these patterns as representing things you can recognize—a hat, a nose, a chin

We naturally try to order and organize what we are experiencing into patterns and relationships that make sense to us. When we succeed in doing so, the completed whole means more than the sum of the individual parts. We are continually organizing the world in this way during virtually every waking moment. We do not live in a world of isolated sounds, patches of color, random odors, and individual textures. Instead, we live in a world of objects and people, language and music—a world in which all these individual stimuli are woven together. We are able to perceive this world of complex experiences because we can organize the individual stimuli we are receiving into relationships that have meaning for us.

This organizing process is integral to the writing process. When you write an essay, compose a letter, or create a story, you are actively organizing the ideas you selected to include various relationships. Instead of simply stringing together words, you are developing a coherent structure through which to communicate thoughts and feelings.

INTERPRETING PERCEPTIONS

Besides selecting and organizing perceptions, we actively interpret what we perceive: we are figuring out what something means. One of the elements that influences interpretations is the *context,* or overall situation, within which the perception is occurring. For example, imagine that you see a man running down the street. Your interpretation of his action will depend on the specific context. For example, is there a bus waiting at the corner? Is a police officer running behind him? Is the man wearing a jogging suit?

We are continually trying to interpret what we perceive, whether it is a design, someone else's behavior, or a social situation. As in the example of someone running down the street, many perceptions can be interpreted in more than one way. When a situation has more than one possible interpretation, it is ambiguous. The more ambiguous a situation is, the greater its number of possible meanings or interpretations.

Casebook: Perception and Reality in the Sandy Hook Elementary School Shooting

On the morning of December 14, 2012, Adam Lanza, age 20, shot and killed his mother as she lay sleeping. Then, armed with a Bushmaster XM-15 semi-automatic assault rifle and two handguns, he drove to Sandy Hook Elementary School. Wearing black clothes, earplugs, and a utility vest for carrying extra ammunition, he shot his way through a locked glass door and then proceeded to shoot and kill the principal, the school counselor, 4 teachers, and 20 first-grade students ranging in age from six to seven. With the police approaching, he fatally shot himself.

These are the basic facts of this horrific catastrophe about which there is fundamental agreement. However, in trying to understand *why* this event occurred and *how to prevent* events like this from occurring in the future, there are many competing points of view that reflect different perceptions of reality. Some view this primarily as the act of a deeply emotionally disturbed individual who had been taught to shoot by his gun-loving mother. Others view this as the symptom of a culture that is obsessed with guns and that has such lenient laws it is possible for virtually anyone to secure virtually any kind of weapon. For example, on the day before the Sandy Hook massacre, lawmakers in Michigan passed a bill that would allow people to carry concealed weapons in schools, and Ohio lawmakers passed a bill that would allow concealed guns in the statehouse. Still others view this as the product of a society in which gun violence is made to seem sexy and exciting in graphically violent movies, television shows, music, and hyper-realistic video games. Since the 1980s, firearms manufacturers have reacted to declines in demand for hunting rifles by increasingly focusing their production and marketing on pistols and "assault weapons." Those who view the Sandy Hook shooting as more than an isolated event point to similar events that have occurred on a regular basis in the United States, making schools the killing fields of our time:

- On July 20, 2012, suspect James Egan Holmes killed 12 people and wounded 58 in a movie theater in Aurora, Colorado, at a midnight screening of *The Dark Knight Rises.*

- On January 11, 2011, Jared Lee Loughner used a 9-mm Glock semiautomatic pistol with a high-capacity magazine to shoot 19 people, including U.S. Congressional Representative Gabrielle Giffords; 6 died.

- On April 16, 2007, Seung-Hui Cho, a student at Virginia Tech University, shot and killed 32 fellow students and faculty members and wounded 17 others with a 9-mm Glock semiautomatic pistol before committing suicide.

- On April 20, 1999, two students at Columbine High School in Colorado, using a Hi-Point 995 carbine and a shotgun, killed 12 students and 1 teacher and injured 21 before committing suicide.

The world's perception of these events was framed, shaped, and communicated through the media's reporting. And this reporting influences the beliefs we form regarding our understanding of what occurred and what, if anything, can be done to diminish the likelihood of similar events occurring in the future. As you read the following accounts, reflect on the interpretations that they are presenting, the reasons and evidence that support their interpretations, and the perceptions that you are forming (and have formed) as a result of these and other responses. Then consider and respond to the questions that follow each article.

"Connecticut School Shooting 'An Attack on America'"

by Ted Anthony

Pick a public elementary school somewhere in the continental United States and draw a half-mile circle around it. The odds are reasonable that you'll encounter some combination of the following:

A baseball field. A statue erected for war veterans. A municipal building. A community center. A polling place—probably the school itself. A library. A park. A basketball court crawling with kids playing pickup games.

In so many places, the school is the hub of civic life. Inside its walls, and around its grounds, are scattered the ideas and people and places that every day state the unspoken: When we talk of being American, this is what we mean.

It is for this reason that the excruciating saga of Newtown, Conn., has shaken the nation in a second way that is distinct from, yet of course related to, the actual death of so many young children.

Twenty-six lives ending so violently, so horrifyingly, is of course disruptive enough. But this event also disrupted the fundamental notion of what American community is. "Hurt a school and you hurt us all," The Chicago Tribune editorialized this week.

Americans have long had an unspoken social compact that says, hey—we build our lives around our schools because they're the bedrock of a society that makes sense. Without the sense of a strong school system—and, by extension, a safe school system—the whole grid buckles. Schools, where you pledge allegiance to the flag and gaze upon portraits of George Washington, have formed on a local level the civic contours of who we are as a nation.

"It's the place where you prepare to achieve the American dream—being president one day, going to outer space as an astronaut," says El Brown, a former teacher and the mother of a kindergartner in Fairfax, Va. "Classrooms are supposed to be where we build our tomorrows."

Schools are the field in which we farm our future. And when someone turfs that field so violently, leaving such chaos behind, it represents even more than the ugly notion of children dying violently. It feels, in some very visceral ways, like an act of war.

In remarks from the president on down during these jumbled days, the message comes through even when it's not said directly: In killing the children of Sandy Hook, Adam Lanza effectively attacked the American nest. He went after not only our young but two other precious commodities—our sense of what we might become, and the stories we tell about who we are. . . .

QUESTION FOR READING ACTIVELY

1. Ted Anthony makes the argument that the shooting at Sandy Hook Elementary School was an "attack on America." Does the evidence he presents support his argument? What do you consider to be the essay's strengths and weaknesses?

Source: © 2013 TheHuffingtonPost.com, Inc. (http://www.huffingtonpost.com/2012/12/19/connecticut-school-shooti_n_2329925.html).

QUESTIONS FOR THINKING CRITICALLY

1. Anthony also claims that "we build our lives around our schools because they're the bedrock of a society that makes sense." Do you feel this applies to all schools in the United States? Consider the current state of the public school system and the controversies surrounding it, such as financial issues, dilapidated buildings, ineffective teachers, dropout rates, and so forth. How does your experience compare to what Anthony believes?

2. As with many events of this significance, controversy surrounds the shooting at Sandy Hook Elementary School. When the news broke on December 14, 2012, the tragedy was quickly labeled one of the worst massacres in the history of the United States by the press. Shortly afterward, many were calling it a hoax—especially on the Internet. Considering what the American public witnessed as this tragedy unfolded, why has there been so much controversy surrounding Sandy Hook?

QUESTION FOR WRITING THOUGHTFULLY

1. Almost every town in America has experienced a tragedy, large or seemingly small, that affected the lives of its community. Describe an event that happened in your town or city, and focus on how it impacted your community. There were likely negative effects, but there may have been some positive effects as well.

"The Price of Gun Control"

by Dan Baum

When you write about guns, as I do, and a shooting like the one in the Aurora movie theater happens an hour from your house, people call. I've already done an interview today with a Spanish newspaper and with Canadian radio. Americans and their guns: what a bunch of lunatics.

Among the many ways America differs from other countries when it comes to guns is that when a mass shooting happens in the United States, it's a gun story. How an obviously sick man could buy a gun; how terrible it is that guns are abundant; how we must ban particular types of guns that are especially dangerous. The Brady Campaign to Prevent Gun Violence responded to the news with a gun-control petition. Andrew Rosenthal of the *New York Times* has weighed in with an online column saying that "Politicians are far too cowardly to address gun violence . . . which keeps us from taking practical measures to avoid senseless shootings."

Compare that to the coverage and conversation after Anders Behring Breivik murdered sixty-nine people on the island of Utøya in Norway, a year ago next Sunday. Nobody focused on the gun. I had a hard time learning from the news reports what type of gun he used. Nobody asked, "How did he get a gun?" That seemed strange, because it's much harder to get a gun in Europe than it is here.

But everybody, even the American media, seemed to understand that the heart of the Utøya massacre story was a tragically deranged man, not the rifle he fired. Instead of wringing their hands over the gun Breivik used, Norwegians saw the tragedy as the opening to a conversation about the rise of right-wing extremism in their country.

Rosenthal is wrong, by the way, that politicians haven't addressed gun violence. They have done so brilliantly, in a million different ways, which helps explain why the rate of violent crime is about half what it was twenty years ago. They simply haven't used gun control to do it. Gun laws are far looser than they were twenty years ago, even while crime is plunging—a galling juxtaposition for those who place their faith in tougher gun laws. The drop in violence is one of our few unalloyed public-policy success stories, though perhaps not for those who bemoan an "epidemic of gun violence" that doesn't exist anymore in order to make a political point.

It's true that America's rate of violent crime remains higher than that in most European countries. But to focus on guns is to dodge a painful truth. America is more violent than other countries because Americans are more violent than other people. Our abundant guns surely make assaults more deadly. But by obsessing over inanimate pieces of metal, we avoid looking at what brings us more often than others to commit violent acts. Many liberal critics understand this when it comes to drug policy. The modern, sophisticated position is that demonizing chemicals is a reductive and ineffective way to address complicated social pathologies. When it comes to gun violence, though, the conversation often stops at the tool, because it is more comfortable to blame it than to examine ourselves. . . .

40 percent of Americans own guns, and like it or not, they identify with them, personally. Guns stand in for a whole range of values—individualism, strength, American exceptionalism—that many gun owners hold dear. Tell a gun owner that he cannot be trusted to own a firearm—particularly if you are an urban pundit with no experience around guns—and what he hears is an insult. Add to this that the bulk of the gun-buying public is made up of middle-aged white men with less than a college degree, and now you're insulting a population already rubbed raw by decades of stagnant wages.

The harm we've done by messing with law-abiding Americans' guns is significant. In 2010, I drove 11,000 miles around the United States talking to gun guys (for a book, to be published in the spring, that grew out of an article I wrote for this magazine), and I met many working guys, including plumbers, parks workers, nurses—natural Democrats in any other age—who wouldn't listen to anything the Democratic party has to say because of its institutional hostility to guns. I'd argue that we've sacrificed generations of progress on health care, women's and workers' rights, and climate change by reflexively returning, at times like these, to an ill-informed call to ban firearms, and we haven't gotten anything tangible in return. Aside from what it does to the progressive agenda, needlessly vilifying guns—and by extension, their owners—adds to the rancor that has us so politically frozen and culturally inflamed. Enough.

President Obama, to his credit, didn't mention gun control in his comments today. Maybe that was just a political calculation; maybe, during an election year, he didn't want to reopen a fight that has hurt his party so dearly in the past. But maybe it's a hint of progress, a sign that we're moving toward a more honest examination of who we are.

1. According to Dan Baum, what is the price of gun control in America? Describe and expand on at least two significant points Baum makes in his essay.

1. Baum claims that even though "gun laws are far looser than they were twenty years ago," America has seen a drop in violent crime—"about half what it was twenty years ago." The media often paint a different picture, however. Explore several reliable websites related to "gun violence in America," and describe some of the discrepancies you find in regard to statistics. Why do these discrepancies exist?

2. Baum also contends that in our efforts to curb violence in America, we are making a mistake by focusing on guns. He states: "It's true that America's rate of violent crime remains higher than in most European countries. But to focus on guns is to dodge a painful truth. America is more violent than other countries because Americans are more violent than other people. . . .[B]y obsessing over inanimate pieces of metal, we avoid looking at what brings us more often than others to commit violent acts." Do you agree that "Americans are more violent than other people"? Should we not be focusing on gun control in our efforts to curb violence? Why or why not?

1. Compare and evaluate several statistics gathered from reliable print or online sources related to gun violence and gun ownership. Use these statistics and your evaluation of them to describe and support your thoughts related to gun control in America.

Response to Newtown, Connecticut massacre
by Wayne La Pierre, CEO of the National Rifle Association
on December 21, 2012

As reflected in the other articles in this section on the massacre of students and teachers of Newtown, Connecticut on December 14, 2012, many people believe that at least some of the responsibility for gun violence in this country is due to the absence of meaningful gun control laws. From this perspective, gun violence can be reduced by banning guns like military assault weapons, outlawing high capacity magazine clips, and instituting meaningful background checks for all people seeking to purchase guns. One of the most vocal opponents of any gun control restrictions is the leadership of the National Rifle Association (NRA) which cites Article 1 of the Constitution which grants citizens "the right to bear arms." (Contrary to the leadership of the NRA, the rank-and-file members of the NRA overwhelmingly support more restrictive background checks.)

Following the shootings at Sandyhook Elementary School, the leadership of the NRA did not issue a public statement until December 21, 2012. During those prepared remarks, the CEO of the NRA, Wayne La Pierre, did not make any reference to gun control initiatives or legislation. Instead, he advocated for having armed guards in every school, arguing that "The only thing that stops a bad guy with a gun is a good guy with a gun." From his perspective, the gun violence in this country is due to a number of factors unrelated to gun control restrictions, including the following:

- ". . .an unknown number of genuine monsters—people so deranged, so evil, so possessed by voices and driven by demons that no sane person can possibly comprehend them."

- ". . .a national media machine that rewards them (copycat killers) that rewards them with the wall-to-wall attention and sense of identity that they crave. . ."

- ". . .violent video games with names like Bulletstorm, Grand Theft Auto, Mortal Kombat, Splatterhouse, and. . .Kindergarten Killers."

- ". . .blood-soaked slasher films like 'American Psycho' and 'Natural Born Killers' that are aired like propaganda loops on 'Splatterdays'. . .

- ". . .a thousand music videos that portray life as a joke and murder as a way of life."

The answer of this gun violence, according to La Pierre, is to hire some of the "millions of qualified active and retired police; active reserve and retired military, security professionals" to be deployed, fully armed, in every school in the country in a "National School Shield Program." After all, La Pierre reasons, we protect other valued institutions in our country with armed protection, shouldn't we protect our most valuable institution, our schools?

QUESTION FOR READING ACTIVELY

1. La Pierre's remarks are emotive and call for action by Congress and the American people to create a National School Shield Program. What are some of the most effective arguments he makes? How does he use language to reach his audience?

QUESTIONS FOR THINKING CRITICALLY

1. As you learned earlier in this chapter, the way we select perceptions is an important part of shaping the lenses through which we view the world. Describe Wayne La Pierre's lens (consider his position as CEO of and affiliation with the NRA, as well as recent events) and how you feel it influences his perceptions.

2. La Pierre believes that the way to prevent massacres in schools is not by "demonizing lawful gun owners" but by placing armed officers in every school, contending that "The only thing that stops a bad guy with a gun is a good guy with a gun." He also argues that much of the blame rests on the manufacturers of vicious, violent video games and slasher films. How would you critically evaluate his claims and the reasoning upon which they are based?

QUESTION FOR WRITING THOUGHTFULLY

1. La Pierre states that "due to a declining willingness to prosecute dangerous criminals, violent crime is increasing again for the first time in 19 years," yet in the previous essay, Dan Baum says that America has seen a drop in violent crime—"about half what it was twenty years ago." Based on some of the research you have completed related to gun violence, support or refute La Pierre's statistic.

"Why Gun 'Control' Is Not Enough"
by Jeff McMahan

Americans are finally beginning to have a serious discussion about guns. One argument we're hearing is the central pillar of the case for private gun ownership: that we are all safer when more individuals have guns because armed citizens deter crime and can defend themselves and others against it when deterrence fails. Those who don't have guns, it's said, are free riders on those who do, as the criminally disposed are less likely to engage in crime the more likely it is that their victim will be armed.

There's some sense to this argument, for even criminals don't like being shot. But the logic is faulty, and a close look at it leads to the conclusion that the United States should ban private gun ownership entirely, or almost entirely.

One would think that if widespread gun ownership had the robust deterrent effects that gun advocates claim it has, our country would be freer of crime than other developed societies. But it's not. When most citizens are armed, as they were in the Wild West, crime doesn't cease. Instead, criminals work to be better armed, more efficient in their use of guns ("quicker on the draw"), and readier to use them. When this happens, those who get guns may be safer than they would be without them, but those without them become progressively more vulnerable.

Gun advocates have a solution to this: the unarmed must arm themselves. But when more citizens get guns, further problems arise: people who would once have got in a fistfight instead shoot the person who provoked them; people are shot by mistake or by accident.

And with guns so plentiful, any lunatic or criminally disposed person who has a sudden and perhaps only temporary urge to kill people can simply help himself to the contents of Mom's gun cabinet. Perhaps most important, the more people there are who have guns, the less effective the police become. The power of the citizens and that of the police approach parity. The police cease to have even a near-monopoly on the use of force.

To many devotees of the Second Amendment, this is precisely the point. As former Congressman Jay Dickey, Republican of Arkansas, said in January 2011, "We have a right to bear arms because of the threat of government taking over the freedoms we have." The more people there are with guns, the less able the government is to control them. But if arming the citizenry limits the power of the government, it does so by limiting

Source: © 2013 The New York Times (http://opinionator.blogs.nytimes.com/2012/12/19/why-gun-control-is-not-enough/).

the power of its agents, such as the police. Domestic defense becomes more a matter of private self-help and vigilantism and less a matter of democratically-controlled, public law enforcement. Domestic security becomes increasingly "privatized."

There is, of course, a large element of fantasy in Dickey's claim. Individuals with handguns are no match for a modern army. It's also a delusion to suppose that the government in a liberal democracy such as the United States could become so tyrannical that armed insurrection, rather than democratic procedures, would be the best means of constraining it. This is not Syria; nor will it ever be. Shortly after Dickey made his comment, people in Egypt rose against a government that had suppressed their freedom in ways far more serious than requiring them to pay for health care. Although a tiny minority of Egyptians do own guns, the protesters would not have succeeded if those guns had been brought to Tahrir Square. If the assembled citizens had been brandishing Glocks in accordance with the script favored by Second Amendment fantasists, the old regime would almost certainly still be in power and many Egyptians who're now alive would be dead. . . .

The logic is inexorable: as more private individuals acquire guns, the power of the police declines, personal security becomes more a matter of self-help, and the unarmed have an increasing incentive to get guns, until everyone is armed. When most citizens then have the ability to kill anyone in their vicinity in an instant, everyone is less secure than they would be if no one had guns other than the members of a democratically accountable police force.

The logic of private gun possession is thus similar to that of the nuclear arms race. When only one state gets nuclear weapons, it enhances its own security but reduces that of others, which have become more vulnerable. The other states then have an incentive to get nuclear weapons to try to restore their security. As more states get them, the incentives for others increase. If eventually all get them, the potential for catastrophe—whether through irrationality, misperception, or accident—is great. Each state's security is then much lower than it would be if none had nuclear weapons.

Gun advocates and criminals are allies in demanding that guns remain in private hands. They differ in how they want them distributed. Criminals want guns for themselves but not for their potential victims. Others want them for themselves but not for criminals. But while gun control can do a little to restrict access to guns by potential criminals, it can't do much when guns are to be found in every other household. Either criminals and non-criminals will have them or neither will. Gun advocates prefer for both rather than neither to have them.

But, as with nuclear weapons, we would all be safer if no one had guns—or, rather, no one other than trained and legally constrained police officers. Domestic defense would then be conducted the way we conduct national defense. We no longer accept, as the authors of the now obsolete Second Amendment did, that "a well-regulated militia" is "necessary to the security of a free state." Rather than leaving national defense to citizens' militias, we now, for a variety of compelling reasons, cede the right of national defense to certain state-authorized professional institutions: the Army, Navy, and so on. We rightly trust these forces to protect us from external threats and not to become instruments of domestic repression. We could have the same trust in a police force designed to protect us from domestic threats. . . .

Gun advocates will object that a prohibition of private gun ownership is an impossibility in the United States. But this is not an objection they can press in good faith, for the only reason that a legal prohibition could be impossible in a democratic state is that a majority oppose it. If gun advocates ceased to oppose it, a prohibition would be possible.

They will next argue that even if there were a legal prohibition, it could not be enforced with anything approaching complete effectiveness. This is true. As long as some people somewhere have guns, some people here can get them. Similarly, the legal prohibition of murder cannot eliminate murder. But the prohibition of murder is more effective than a policy of "murder control" would be.

Guns are not like alcohol and drugs, both of which we have tried unsuccessfully to prohibit. Many people have an intense desire for alcohol or drugs that is independent of what other people may do. But the need for a gun for self-defense depends on whether other people have them and how effective the protection and deterrence provided by the state are. Thus, in other Western countries in which there are fewer guns, there are correspondingly fewer instances in which people need guns for effective self-defense.

Gun advocates sometimes argue that a prohibition would violate individuals' rights of self-defense. Imposing a ban on guns, they argue, would be tantamount to taking a person's gun from her just as someone is about to kill her. But this is a defective analogy. Although a prohibition would deprive people of one effective means of self-defense, it would also ensure that there would be far fewer occasions on which a gun would be necessary or even useful for self-defense. For guns would be forbidden not just to those who would use them for defense but also to those who would use them for aggression. Guns are only one means of self-defense and self-defense is only one means of achieving security against attack. It is the right to security against attack that is fundamental. A policy that unavoidably deprives a person of one means of self-defense but on balance substantially reduces her vulnerability to attack is therefore respectful of the more fundamental right from which the right of self-defense is derived.

In other Western countries, per capita homicide rates, as well as rates of violent crime involving guns, are a fraction of what they are in the United States. The possible explanations of this are limited. Gun advocates claim it has nothing to do with our permissive gun laws or our customs and practices involving guns. If they are right, should we conclude that Americans are simply inherently more violent, more disposed to mental derangement, and less moral than people in other Western countries? If you resist that conclusion, you have little choice but to accept that our easy access to all manner of firearms is a large part of the explanation of why we kill each at a much higher rate than our counterparts elsewhere. Gun advocates must search their consciences to determine whether they really want to share responsibility for the perpetuation of policies that make our country the homicide capitol of the developed world.

QUESTION FOR READING ACTIVELY

1. Jeff McMahan presents an evaluation of gun control and asserts that "control" is not enough. Instead, he would like to see gun ownership banned in the United States. What are the primary comparisons he makes, and do you feel his argument is successful?

QUESTION FOR THINKING CRITICALLY

1. In contrast to what Wayne La Pierre proposed in the previous reading, McMahan argues that introducing more guns into the culture will only increase violence, not diminish it. Describe the reason that leads him to this conclusion, and then critically evaluate its soundness.

QUESTION FOR WRITING THOUGHTFULLY

1. McMahan argues that while prohibiting guns would "deprive people of one effective means of self-defense, it would also ensure that there would be far fewer occasions on which a gun would be necessary or even useful for self-defense" because "guns would be forbidden not just to those who would use them for defense but also to those who would use them for aggression." Consider a scenario in which this line of reasoning might apply. Describe the scenario, and evaluate how the outcome might be different depending on whether or not the parties involved had guns.

"The (Terrifying) Transformative Potential of Technology"

by Lisa Wade

When Adam Lanza walked into Sandy Hook Elementary School, he was carrying a Bushmaster .223 caliber Remington semiautomatic. This is the frightening weapon he used to take the lives of 27 people:

Richard Green/Commercial/Alamy

Source: http://thesocietypages.org/socimages/2012/12/20/the-transformative-potential-of-technology-the-bushmaster-223/. Published: 12/20/2012 12:30 pm.

The refrain—"guns don't kill people, people kill people"—does an injustice to the complicated homotechnocultural phenomenon that we call a massacre. Evan Selinger, at *The Atlantic*, does a wonderful job taking apart this phrase. It assumes an *instrumentalist* view of technology, where we bend it to our will. In contrast, he argues in favor of a *transformative* view: when humans interact with objects, they are transformed by that interaction. A gun changes how a person sees the world. Selinger writes:

> To someone with a gun, the world readily takes on a distinct shape. It not only offers people, animals, and things to interact with, but also potential targets.

In other words, if you have a hammer, suddenly all the world's problems look like nails to you (see Law of the Instrument). The wonderful French philosopher Bruno Latour put it this way:

> You are different with a gun in your hand; the gun is different with you holding it. You are another subject because you hold the gun; the gun is another object because it has entered into a relationship with you.

So, that's the homotechnological part of the story. What of the cultural?

At Sociological Images, Michael Kimmel observes that the vast majority of mass killings in the U.S. are carried out by middle-class, white males. "From an early age," he writes, "boys learn that violence is not only an acceptable form of conflict resolution, but one that is admired." While the vast majority of men will never be violent, they are all exposed to lessons about what it means to be a real man:

> They learn that if they are crossed, they have the manly obligation to fight back. They learn that they are entitled to feel like a real man, and that they have the right to annihilate anyone who challenges that sense of entitlement. . . They learn that "aggrieved entitlement" is a legitimate justification for violent explosion.

Violence is *culturally* masculine. So, when the human picks up the object, it matters whether that person is a man or a woman.

Bushmaster, the manufacturer of the weapon used by Lanza, was explicit in tying their product to masculinity. Though it has now been taken down, before the shooting visitors to their website could engage in public shaming of men who were insufficiently masculine, revoking their man card and branding them with the image of a female stick figure.

Their man card is "revoked" and Bushmaster has just the solution, which is to "reissue" a man card once a weapon is purchased.

Manliness is tied to gun ownership (and, perhaps, gun use). Whatever it is that threatens his right to consider himself a man, a gun is an immediate cure.

Many people are calling on politicians to respond to this tragedy by instituting stricter gun control laws and trying to reduce the number or change the type of guns in American hands. That'll help with the homotechnological part. But, as Kimmel argues, we also need to address the cultural part of the equation. We need to change what it means to be a man in America.

This post was co-written with Gwen Sharp and originally posted at Sociological Images.

Morning Joe

Joe Scarborough began his show *Morning Joe* Monday, December 17, 2012 addressing the school shooting at Sandy Hook Elementary School in Newtown, Connecticut.
Here's part of his remarks:

Today, we as a nation grieve. Today, we as a people feel helpless. Helpless to stop these random acts of violence that seem to be getting less random by the day.

It may the geographic proximity of Newtown to my hometown, or the fact my children's ages average those of the 20 young children tragically killed on Friday, or the fact my second son has Aspergers, or the fact that too many other facts associated with Friday's nightmare strike so close to home . . . that for me, there is no escaping the horrors visited upon the children and teachers of Sandy Hook.

The events that occurred in a short, violent outburst on Friday, December 14, 2012, were so evil that no words that I know of have yet been invented to sufficiently describe the horror experienced by 20 precious first grade students, their heroic principal, their anguished parents or the shocked New England town that will never be the same.

There is no way to capture the final moments of these children's short lives or the loss and helplessness their parents must feel today. There is nothing they can do, there is nothing any of us can do, to ease their pain this morning, or to cause these little children to run back into the loving arms of their family members this Christmas season.

Soon, we will watch the burials of these babies. We will hold up their parents in prayer. And we will hold our own children tighter as we thank God every afternoon watching them walk off their school bus and into our arms.

But every American must know—from this day forward—that nothing can ever be the same again.

We have said this before: after Columbine, after Arizona, after Aurora, after so many other numbing hours of murder and of massacre.

But let this be out true landmark; let Newtown be the hour after which, in the words of the New Testament, we did all we could to make all things new.

Politicians can no longer be allowed to defend the status quo. They must instead be forced to protect our children. Parents can no longer take "No" for an answer from Washington when the topic turns to protecting children.

The violence we see spreading from shopping malls in Oregon, to movie theaters in Colorado, to college campuses in Virginia, to elementary schools in Connecticut, is being spawned by the toxic brew of a violent pop culture, a growing mental health crisis and the proliferation of combat-styled guns.

Though entrenched special interests will try to muddy the issues, the cause of these sickening mass shootings is no longer a mystery to common-sense Americans. And blessedly, there are more common-sense Americans than there are special interests, even if it doesn't always seem that way. Good luck to the gun lobbyist or Hollywood lawyer who tries to blunt the righteous anger of ten million parents by hiding behind a twisted reading of our Bill of Rights.

Our government rightly obsesses day and night over how to prevent the next 9/11 from being launched from a cave in Afghanistan or a training base in Yemen. But perhaps

Source: © 2013 NBCUNIVERSAL (http://tv.msnbc.com/2012/12/17/scarborough-today-as-a-nation-we-grieve-and-today-as-a-people-we-feel-helpless/).

Thinking Critically About Visuals

The Aftermath of the Shooting at Sandy Hook Elementary School

What are some of the elements of this simple memorial for the children massacred at Newtown that make the photograph so profoundly heartbreaking?

now is the time to begin obsessing over how to stop the next attack on a movie theater, a shopping mall, a college campus or a first grade class.

The battle we now must fight, and the battle we must now win is for the safety and sanity of our children, and that is the war at home.

It's not all about guns, or all about violent movies and videogames. But we must no longer allow the perfect to be the enemy of the good. And we must not excuse total inaction by arguing that no single action can solve the problem and save our children.

I am a conservative Republican who received the NRA's highest ratings over 4 terms in Congress. I saw the debate over guns as a powerful, symbolic struggle between individual rights and government control. In the years after Waco and Ruby Ridge, the symbolism of that debate seemed even more powerful to my colleagues and me.

But the symbols of that ideological struggle have since been shattered by the harvest sown from violent, mind-numbing video games and gruesome Hollywood movies that dangerously desensitizes those who struggle with mental health challenges. Add military-styled weapons and high capacity magazines to that equation and tragedy can never be too far behind.

There is no easy ideological way forward. If it were only so simple as to blame Hollywood or the NRA, then our task could be completed in no time. But I come to you this morning with a heavy heart and no easy answers. Still, I have spent the past few days grasping for solutions and struggling for answers, while daring to question my long held beliefs on these subjects.

. . .

Abraham Lincoln once said of this great and powerful nation. . .

"From whence shall we expect the approach of danger? Shall some trans-Atlantic military giant step the earth and crush us at a blow? Never. All the armies of Europe and Asia. . .could not by force take a drink from the Ohio River or make a track on the Blue Ridge in the trial of a thousand years. No, if destruction be our lot we must ourselves be its author and finisher. As a nation of free men we will live forever or die by suicide."

For the sake of my four children, I choose life. And I choose change. It is time to turn over the tables inside the temple, for the sake of our children and for the sake of this great nation that we love.

QUESTION FOR READING ACTIVELY

1. In their article on guns, Gwen Sharp and Lisa Wade conclude that we need to address the "cultural part of the equation" and redefine "what it means to be a man in America." How can we, as a culture, begin to redefine what it means to be a man? Where do we start?

QUESTION FOR THINKING CRITICALLY

1. Sharp and Wade contend that weapons transform the people using them, taking issue with the NRA slogan, "Guns don't kill people, people do." Why do the authors believe what they do?

QUESTION FOR WRITING THOUGHTFULLY

1. Describe your experience with either guns or video games. It could be a personal experience or an experience of a friend or family member. How have your perceptions shaped your views over time? Describe your past perceptions and the key events and conversations that helped to shape your current perceptions.

How Perspective and Language Affect Perceptions: A Focused Study of the Assassination of Malcolm X

Chapter 6 of this book contains a passage written by Malcolm X (pages 170–172) when he was just beginning his life's work. A few years later, this work came to a tragic end with his assassination at a meeting in Harlem. As you read the following five accounts of his assassination, pay particular attention to how each author perceived the event, as well as the way in which they then present their accounts to the reader.

THE NEW YORK TIMES (FEBRUARY 22, 1965)

Malcolm X, the 39-year-old leader of a militant Black Nationalist movement, was shot to death yesterday afternoon at a rally of his followers in a ballroom in Washington Heights. The bearded Negro extremist had said only a few words of greeting when a fusillade rang out. The bullets knocked him over backwards.

A 22-year-old Negro, Thomas Hagan, was charged with the killing. The police rescued him from the ballroom crowd after he had been shot and beaten.

Pandemonium broke out among the 400 Negroes in the Audubon Ballroom at 160th Street and Broadway. As men, women and children ducked under tables and flattened themselves on the floor, more shots were fired. The police said seven bullets struck Malcolm. Three other Negroes were shot. Witnesses reported that as many as 30 shots had been fired. About two hours later the police said the shooting had apparently been a result of a feud between followers of Malcolm and members of the extremist group he broke with last year, the Black Muslims. . . .

Source: From *The New York Times*, February 22, 1965. Copyright © 1965 by *The New York Times* Co. Reprinted with permission.

LIFE (MARCH 5, 1965)

His life oozing out through a half dozen or more gunshot wounds in his chest, Malcolm X, once the shrillest voice of black supremacy, lay dying on the stage of a Manhattan auditorium. Moments before, he had stepped up to the lectern and 400 of the faithful had settled down expectantly to hear the sort of speech for which he was famous—flaying the hated white man. Then a scuffle broke out in the hall and Malcolm's bodyguards bolted from his side to break it up—only to discover that they had been faked out. At least two men with pistols rose from the audience and pumped bullets into the speaker, while a third cut loose at close range with both barrels of a sawed-off shotgun. In the confusion the pistol man got away. The shotgunner lunged through the crowd and out the door, but not before the guards came to their wits and shot him in the leg. Outside he was swiftly overtaken by other supporters of Malcolm and very likely would have been stomped to death if the police hadn't saved him. Most shocking of all to the residents of Harlem was the fact that Malcolm had been killed not by "whitey" but by members of his own race.

Source: "The Violent End of the Man Called Malcolm." From the March 5, 1965 *LIFE Magazine*. Copyright © 1965 The Picture Collection Inc. Reprinted with permission. All rights reserved.

THE NEW YORK POST (FEBRUARY 22, 1965)

They came early to the Audubon Ballroom, perhaps drawn by the expectation that Malcolm X would name the men who firebombed his home last Sunday. . . . I sat at the left in the 12th row and, as we waited, the man next to me spoke of Malcolm and his followers: "Malcolm is our only hope. You can depend on him to tell it like it is and to give Whitey hell."

There was a prolonged ovation as Malcolm walked to the rostrum. Malcolm looked up and said "A salaam aleikum (Peace be unto you)" and the audience replied "We aleikum salaam (And unto you, peace)."

Bespectacled and dapper in a dark suit, sandy hair glinting in the light, Malcolm said: "Brothers and sisters . . ." He was interrupted by two men in the center of the ballroom, who rose and, arguing with each other, moved forward. Then there was a scuffle at the back of the room. I heard Malcolm X say his last words: "Now, brothers, break it up," he said softly. "Be cool, be calm."

Then all hell broke loose. There was a muffled sound of shots and Malcolm, blood on his face and chest, fell limply back over the chairs behind him. The two men who had approached him ran to the exit on my side of the room, shooting wildly behind them as they ran. I heard people screaming, "Don't let them kill him." "Kill those bastards." At an exit I saw some of Malcolm's men beating with all their strength on two men. I saw a half dozen of Malcolm's followers bending over his inert body on the stage. Their clothes stained with their leader's blood.

Four policemen took the stretcher and carried Malcolm through the crowd and some of the women came out of their shock and one said: "I hope he doesn't die, but I don't think he's going to make it."

Source: Thomas Skinner, "I Saw Malcolm Die," *The New York Post*, February 22, 1965, p. 1. Copyright © 1965. Reprinted by permission of the *New York Post*.

ASSOCIATED PRESS (FEBRUARY 22, 1965)

A week after being bombed out of his Queens home, Black Nationalist leader Malcolm X was shot to death shortly after 3 (P.M.) yesterday at a Washington Heights rally of 400 of his devoted followers. Early today, police brass ordered a homicide charge placed against a 22-year-old man they rescued from a savage beating by Malcolm X supporters after the shooting. The suspect, Thomas Hagan, had been shot in the left leg by one of Malcolm's bodyguards as, police said, Hagan and another assassin fled when pandemonium erupted. Two other men were wounded in the wild burst of firing from at least three weapons. The firearms were a .38, a .45 automatic and a sawed-off shotgun. Hagan allegedly shot Malcolm X with the shotgun, a double-barrelled sawed-off weapon on which the stock also had been shortened, possibly to facilitate concealment. Cops charged Reuben Frances, of 871 E. 179th St., Bronx, with felonious assault in the shooting of Hagan, and with Sullivan Law violation—possession of the .45. Police recovered the shotgun and the .45.

Source: Paragraph on the assassination of Malcolm X, Associated Press, February 22, 1965. Reprinted by permission of the Associated Press.

THE AMSTERDAM NEWS (FEBRUARY 27, 1965)

"We interrupt this program to bring you a special newscast . . . ," the announcer said as the Sunday afternoon movie on the TV set was halted temporarily. "Malcolm X was shot four times while addressing a crowd at the Audubon Ballroom on 166th Street."

"Oh no!" That was my first reaction to the shocking event that followed one week after the slender, articulate leader of the Afro-American Unity was routed from his East Elmhurst home by a bomb explosion. Minutes later we alighted from a cab at the corner of Broadway and 166th St. just a short 15 blocks from where I live on Broadway. About 200 men and women, neatly dressed, were milling around, some with expressions of awe and disbelief. Others were in small clusters talking loudly and with deep emotion in their voices. Mostly they were screaming for vengeance. One woman, small, dressed in a light gray coat and her eyes flaming with indignation, argued with a cop at the St. Nicholas corner of the block. "This is not the end of it. What they were going to do to the Statue of Liberty will be small in comparison. We black people are tired of being shoved around." Standing across the street near the memorial park one of Malcolm's close associates commented: "It's a shame." Later he added that "if it's war they want, they'll get it." He would not say whether Elijah Muhammed's followers had anything to do with the assassination. About 3:30 P.M. Malcolm X's wife, Betty, was escorted by three men and a woman from the Columbia Presbyterian Hospital. Tears streamed down her face. She was screaming, "They killed him!" Malcolm X had no last words. . . . The bombing and burning of the No. 7 Mosque early Tuesday morning was the first blow by those who are seeking revenge for the cold-blooded murder of a man who at 39 might have grown to the stature of respectable leadership.

Source: Excerpt from the *Amsterdam News,* February 27, 1965/Reprinted by permission of the *New York Amsterdam News.*

Thinking-Writing Activity

FIVE ACCOUNTS OF THE ASSASSINATION OF MALCOLM X, 1965

Let's examine a situation in which a number of different people had differing perceptions about an event they were describing. After reading the accounts of the assassination of Malcolm X, analyze some of the differences in these perceptions by writing answers to the following questions.

1. What details of the events has each writer selected to focus on?

2. How has each writer organized the selected details? Remember that most newspapers give what they consider the most important information first.

3. How does each writer depict Malcolm X, his followers, the gunmen, and the significance of the assassination? Can you point out language that carries particular connotations or slants? How, in turn, does the language an author chooses to use affect your perception and interpretation of the text?

CHANGES IN PERCEPTIONS AND PERSPECTIVES

Just as journalists, scientists, and law enforcement officials change their perspectives after gaining increased knowledge, your ways of viewing the world will develop and change through the experiences you have, the knowledge you acquire, and your reflections on your experiences and knowledge. As you think critically about perceptions, you will learn more about how you make sense of the world. This understanding may strengthen your perceptions, or it may change them.

Obtaining More Accurate Perceptions: Adjusting the Lenses

So far, we have emphasized the great extent to which, by selecting, organizing, and interpreting, we directly affect our perceptions. We have suggested that each of us views the world through his or her own unique lenses, that no two of us perceive the world in exactly the same way. In addition, the sources on which we rely for the most up-to-date and ostensibly most accurate, objective information are themselves compromised by different and conflicting perceptions and perspectives as they try to negotiate enormous amounts of changing information.

Because we actively participate in selecting, organizing, and interpreting the sensations we experience, our perceptions are often incomplete, inaccurate, or subjective. To complicate the situation further, our own limitations in perceiving are not the only factors that can cause us problems. Other people often purposefully create perceptions and misperceptions. An advertiser who wants to sell a product may try to create the impression that our lives will be changed if we use it. Or a person who wants to discredit someone else may spread untrue rumors about her.

DEVELOP AWARENESS

The only way to correct the mistakes, distortions, and incompleteness of our perceptions is to become aware of the ordinarily unconscious process by which we perceive and make sense of the world. By doing so, we will be able to think critically about what is going on and to correct our mistakes and distortions. In other words, we can use our critical thinking abilities to create a clearer and more informed idea of what is taking place. We cannot rely on the validity of our perceptions alone. If we remain unaware of how our process of perceiving operates and of our active role in it, we will be unable to control it. We will be convinced that the way we see the world is the way the world is, even when our perceptions are mistaken, distorted, or incomplete.

Besides asking questions, we have to become aware of the personal perspectives that we bring to our perceptions. Each of us brings to every situation a whole collection of expectations, interests, fears, and hopes that can influence what we are perceiving.

Consider the following situations:

- You and your family have been advised to evacuate in the path of a forthcoming hurricane, but you remember from the experiences of people in New Orleans and Houston that to flee could leave your property vulnerable to looting or could result in a very long, hot, uncomfortable road trip that might not in the end have been necessary. How do you balance the recommendations of current authority with recent past experience?

- Your teacher asks you to evaluate the performance of a colleague who is giving a report to the group. You don't like this other student because he acts as if he's superior to everyone else in the group. How do you evaluate his report?
- You are asked to estimate the size of an audience attending an event that your organization has sponsored. How many people are there?

In each of these cases, your perceptions might be influenced by whatever hopes, fears, or prejudices you brought to the situation, causing your observations to be distorted or inaccurate. Although you usually cannot eliminate the personal feelings that influence your perceptions, you can become aware of these feelings and try to control them.

GET INPUT FROM OTHERS

The first step in critically examining your perceptions is to be willing to ask questions about them. As long as you believe that the way you see things is the only way to see them, you will not be able to recognize when your perceptions are distorted or inaccurate.

For instance, if you believe that your interpretation of the photo in the Thinking-Writing Activity on page 211 is the only correct one, you will probably not consider other interpretations. But if you are willing to entertain other possible interpretations, you will open the way to more fully developing your perception of what is taking place.

As noted in Chapter 7, critical thinkers strive to see things from different perspectives. One of the best ways to do so is by communicating with others. This means exchanging and critically examining ideas in an open and organized way. Engaging in dialogue is one of the main ways to check your perceptions—by asking others what their perceptions are and comparing and contrasting them with yours.

This is exactly what you did when you discussed the various possible interpretations of the "Thinking Critically About Visuals" photo in Chapter 7. By comparing your perceptions with those of your classmates, you developed a more complete sense of how differently events can be viewed, as well as an appreciation of the reasons supporting the different perspectives.

FIND EVIDENCE

Also, you should try to discover independent proof or evidence regarding your perceptions. You can evaluate the accuracy of your perceptions when evidence is available in the form of records, photographs, videotapes, or the results of experiments. What independent forms of evidence could verify your perceptions about the couple in the "Thinking Critically About Visuals" box in Chapter 7?

KEEP AN OPEN MIND

Thinking critically about perceptions means trying to avoid developing impulsive or superficial ones that you are unwilling to change. As explained in Chapter 3, a critical thinker is *thoughtful* in approaching the world and open to modifying his or her views in light of new information or better insights. Consider the following perceptions:

- Women are very emotional.
- Politicians are corrupt.
- All Muslims are potential terrorists.
- People who are good athletes are usually poor students.
- The government doesn't care about poor people.

These types of general perceptions are known as *stereotypes* because they express a belief about an entire group of people without recognizing the individual differences among members of the group.

For instance, it is probably accurate to say that there are some politicians who are corrupt, but this is not the same as saying that all, or even most, politicians are corrupt. Stereotypes affect our perceptions of the world because they encourage us to form inaccurate and superficial ideas about a whole group of people ("Teenagers are reckless drivers"). When we meet someone who falls into this group, we automatically perceive that person as possessing a stereotyped quality ("This person is a teenager, so he is a reckless driver"). Even if we find that the person does not fit our stereotyped perception ("This teenager is not a reckless driver"), this sort of superficial and thoughtless labeling does not encourage us to change our perceptions of the group as a whole. Instead, it encourages us to overlook the conflicting information in favor of our stereotyped perceptions ("All teenagers are reckless drivers—except this one"). In contrast, when we are perceiving in a thoughtful fashion, we try to see what a person is like as an individual instead of trying to fit him or her into a preexisting category.

Sometimes stereotypes are so built into a culture that it is difficult for a person to be aware of them until they are brought to his or her attention. The perspective, or view of the world, that the culture presents may not even acknowledge the possibility of other perspectives, so it can be very difficult for an individual to become aware of them and then to "switch lenses" to try to see a situation from those viewpoints.

True critical thinkers can and do switch lenses, and in their writing they help others to do so as well. The following two readings present varying perspectives on Native Americans. One was written by a famous eighteenth-century American; the other was written in the early twentieth century by a member of the Sioux Nation. As you read these accounts, think about what factors probably contributed to the writers' perspectives.

"Remarks Concerning the Savages of North America"
by Benjamin Franklin

Perhaps no other figure so captures the American imagination—or the America as once imagined—as Benjamin Franklin. Born into a family of Boston soapmakers, Franklin became a printer's apprentice to his brother, James, at the age of twelve. As brothers

Source: "Remarks Concerning the Savages of North America" by Benjamin Franklin (1706–1790).

tend to do, Benjamin and James quarreled repeatedly; in 1723, Benjamin ran away to Philadelphia. After several difficult years of hard work, Franklin was established enough in his own printing business to marry Deborah Read in 1730. He began publishing and contributing to a newspaper, the *Pennsylvania Gazette,* and in 1733 he started publishing *Poor Richard's Almanack.*

Franklin used his prominent position as a businessman and journalist to undertake civic initiatives that are still cornerstones of American communities. Franklin helped to establish the first free lending library, the first public hospital, and the first organized firefighting company in America. Politically, Franklin was elected to the Second Continental Congress in 1775 and helped to draft the Declaration of Independence. In 1776, Franklin was appointed the ambassador to the Court of Louis XVI for the American colonies. Franklin died at the age of eighty-four, back home in Philadelphia. His funeral was attended by 20,000 people.

In the following essay, excerpted from a longer work published in 1784, Franklin uses the term *savages* ironically. His admiration and respect for Native Americans is rooted in the diplomatic relationships he established with the Iroquois Nation in the 1760s. When, in 1763, a vigilante army of white settlers massacred a settlement of Conestoga Iroquois—including women and children—Franklin responded by mustering an army of Quakers and other citizens, including Governor Penn himself. The action probably saved more than one hundred Conestoga lives.

Savages we call them, because their Manners differ from ours, which we think the Perfection of Civility; they think the same of theirs.

Perhaps, if we could examine the Manners of different Nations with Impartiality, we should find no People so rude, as to be without any Rules of Politeness; nor any so polite, as not to have some Remains of Rudeness.

The Indian Men, when young, are Hunters and Warriors; when old, Counsellors; for all their Government is by Counsel of the Sages; there is no Force, there are no Prisons, no Officers to compel Obedience, or inflict Punishment. Hence they generally study Oratory, the best Speaker having the most Influence. The Indian Women till the Ground, dress the Food, nurse and bring up the Children, and preserve and hand down to Posterity the Memory of public Transactions. These Employments of Men and Women are accounted natural and honourable. Having few artificial Wants, they have abundance of Leisure for Improvement by Conversation. Our laborious Manner of Life, compared with theirs, they esteem slavish and base; and the Learning, on which we value ourselves, they regard as frivolous and useless. An Instance of this occurred at the Treaty of Lancaster, in Pennsylvania, *anno* 1744, between the Government of Virginia and the Six Nations. After the principal Business was settled, the Commissioners from Virginia acquainted the Indians by a Speech, that there was at Williamsburg a College, with a Fund for Educating Indian youth; and that, if the Six Nations would send down half a dozen of their young Lads to that College, the Government would take care that they should be well provided for, and instructed in all the Learning of the White People. It is one of the Indian Rules of Politeness not to answer a public Proposition the same day that it is made; they think it would be treating it as a light matter, and that they show it Respect by taking time to consider it, as of a Matter important. They therefore deferr'd their Answer till the Day following; when their Speaker began, by expressing their deep Sense of the kindness of the Virginia Government, in making them that Offer;

"for we know," says he, "that you highly esteem the kind of Learning taught in those Colleges, and that the Maintenance of our young Men, while with you, would be very expensive to you. We are convinc'd, therefore, that you mean to do us Good by your Proposal; and we thank you heartily. But you, who are wise, must know that different Nations have different Conceptions of things; and you will therefore not take it amiss, if our Ideas of this kind of Education happen not to be the same with yours. We have had some Experience of it; Several of our young People were formerly brought up at the Colleges of the Northern Provinces; they were instructed in all your Sciences; but, when they came back to us, they were bad Runners, ignorant of every means of living in the Woods, unable to bear either Cold or Hunger, knew neither how to build a Cabin, take a Deer, or kill an Enemy, spoke our Language imperfectly, were therefore neither fit for Hunters, Warriors, nor Counsellors; they were totally good for nothing. We are however not the less oblig'd by your kind Offer, tho' we decline accepting it; and, to show our grateful Sense of it, if the Gentlemen of Virginia will send us a Dozen of their Sons, we will take great Care of their Education, instruct them in all we know, and make *Men* of them."

Having frequent Occasions to hold public Councils, they have acquired great Order and Decency in conducting them. The old Men sit in the foremost Ranks, the Warriors in the next, and the Women and Children in the hindmost. The Business of the Women is to take exact Notice of what passes, imprint it in their Memories (for they have no Writing), and communicate it to their Children. They are the Records of the Council, and they preserve Traditions of the Stipulations in Treaties 100 Years back; which, when we compare with our Writings, we always find exact. He that would speak, rises. The rest observe a profound Silence. When he has finish'd and sits down, they leave him 5 to 6 Minutes to recollect, that, if he has omitted anything he intended to say, or has anything to add, he may rise again and deliver it. To interrupt another, even in common Conversation, is reckon'd highly indecent. How different this is from the conduct of a polite British House of Commons, where scarce a day passes without some Confusion, that makes the Speaker hoarse in calling *to Order;* and how different from the Mode of Conversation in many polite Companies of Europe, where, if you do not deliver your Sentence with great Rapidity, you are cut off in the middle of it by the Impatient Loquacity of those you converse with, and never suffer'd to finish it!

The Politeness of these Savages in Conversation is indeed carried to Excess, since it does not permit them to contradict or deny the Truth of what is asserted in their Presence. By this means they indeed avoid Disputes; but then it becomes difficult to know their Minds, or what Impression you make upon them. The Missionaries who have attempted to convert them to Christianity, all complain of this as one of the great Difficulties of their Mission. The Indians hear with Patience the Truths of the Gospel explain'd to them, and give their usual Tokens of Assent and Approbation; you would think they were convinc'd. No such matter. It is mere Civility.

A Swedish Minister, having assembled the chiefs of the Susquehanah Indians, made a Sermon to them, acquainting them with the principal historical Facts on which our Religion is founded; such as the Fall of our first Parents by eating an Apple, the coming of Christ to repair the Mischief, his Miracles and Suffering, &c. When he had finished, an Indian Orator stood up to thank him. "What you have told us," says he, "is all very good. It is indeed bad to eat Apples. It is better to make them all into Cyder. We are much oblig'd by your kindness in coming so far, to tell us these Things which you have heard from your Mothers. In return, I will tell you some of those we had heard from ours. In the Beginning, our Fathers had only the Flesh of Animals to subsist on; and if their Hunting was unsuccessful, they were starving. Two of our young Hunters, having kill'd a Deer, made a Fire in the Woods to broil some Part of it. When they were about to satisfy their Hunger, they beheld a beautiful young Woman descend from the Clouds, and seat herself on that Hill, which you see yonder among the blue Mountains. They said to each other, it is a Spirit that has smelt our broiling Venison, and wishes to eat of it; let us offer some to her. They presented her with the Tongue; she was pleas'd with the Taste of it, and said, 'Your kindness shall be rewarded; come to this Place after thirteen Moons, and you shall find something that will be of great Benefit in nourishing you and your Children to the latest Generations.' They did so, and, to their Surprise, found Plants they had never seen before; but which, from that ancient time, have been constantly cultivated among us, to our great Advantage. Where her right Hand had touched the Ground, they found Maize; where her left hand had touch'd it, they found Kidney-Beans; and where her Backside had sat on it, they found Tobacco." The good Missionary, disgusted with this idle Tale, said, "What I delivered to you were sacred Truths; but what you tell me is mere Fable, Fiction, and Falshood." The Indian, offended, reply'd, "My brother, it seems your Friends have not done you Justice in your Education; they have not well instructed you in the Rules of common Civility. You saw that we, who understand and practise those Rules, believ'd all your stories; why do you refuse to believe ours?"

When any of them come into our Towns, our People are apt to crowd round them, gaze upon them, and incommode them, where they desire to be private; this they esteem great Rudeness, and the Effect of the Want of Instruction in the Rules of Civility and good Manners. "We have," say they, "as much Curiosity as you, and when you come into our Towns, we wish for Opportunities of looking at you; but for this purpose we hide ourselves behind Bushes, where you are to pass, and never intrude ourselves into your Company."

Their Manner of entering one another's village has likewise its Rules. It is reckon'd uncivil in travelling Strangers to enter a Village abruptly, without giving Notice of their Approach. Therefore, as soon as they arrive within hearing, they stop and hollow, remaining there till invited to enter. Two old Men usually come out to them, and lead them in. There is in every Village a vacant Dwelling, called *the Strangers' House*. Here they are plac'd, while the old Men go round from Hut to Hut, acquainting the Inhabitants, that Strangers are arriv'd, who are probably hungry and weary; and every one sends them what he can spare of Victuals, and Skins to repose on. When the Strangers are refresh'd, Pipes and Tobacco are brought; and then, but not before, Conversation begins, with Enquiries who they are, whither bound, what News, &c.; and it usually ends with offers of Service, if the Strangers have occasion of Guides, or any Necessaries for continuing their Journey; and nothing is exacted for the Entertainment.

The same Hospitality, esteem'd among them as a principal Virtue, is practis'd by private Persons; of which Conrad Weiser, our Interpreter, gave me the following Instance. He had been naturaliz'd among the Six Nations, and spoke well the Mohock Language. In going thro' the Indian Country, to carry a Message from our Governor to the Council at Onondaga, he call'd at the Habitation of Canassatego, an old Acquaintance, who embrac'd him, spread Furs for him to sit on, plac'd before him some boil'd Beans and Venison, and mix'd some Rum and Water for his Drink. When he was well refresh'd, and had lit his Pipe, Canassatego began to converse with him; ask'd how he had far'd the many Years since they had seen each other; whence he then came; what occasion'd the Journey, &c. Conrad answered all his Questions; and when the Discourse began to flag, the Indian, to continue it, said, "Conrad, you have lived long among the white People, and know something of their Customs; I have been sometimes at Albany, and have observed, that once in Seven Days they shut up their Shops, and assemble all in the great House; tell me what it is for? What do they do there?" "They meet there," says Conrad, "to hear and learn *good Things*." "I do not doubt," says the Indian, "that they tell you so; they have told me the same; but I doubt the Truth of what they say, and I will tell you my Reasons. I went lately to Albany to sell my Skins and buy Blankets, Knives, Powder, Rum, &c. You know I us'd generally to deal with Hans Hanson; but I was a little inclin'd this time to try some other Merchant. However, I call'd first upon Hans, and asked him what he would give for Beaver. He said he could not give any more than four Shillings a Pound; 'but,' says he, 'I cannot talk on Business now; this is the Day when we meet together to learn *Good Things*, and I am going to the Meeting.' So I thought to myself, 'Since we cannot do any Business to-day, I may as well go to the meeting too,' and I went with him. There stood up a Man in Black, and began to talk to the People very angrily. I did not understand what he said; but, perceiving that he look'd much at me and at Hanson, I imagin'd he was angry at seeing me there; so I went out, sat down near the House, struck Fire, and lit my Pipe, waiting till the Meeting should break up. I thought too, that the Man had mention'd something of Beaver, and I suspected it might be the Subject of their Meeting. So, when they came out, I accosted my Merchant. 'Well, Hans,' says I, 'I hope you have agreed to give more than four Shillings a Pound.' 'No,' says he, 'I cannot give so much; I cannot give more than three shillings and sixpence.' I then spoke to several other Dealers, but they all sung the same song,—Three and sixpence,—Three and sixpence. This made it clear to me, that my Suspicion was right; and, that whatever they pretended of meeting to learn *good Things*, the real purpose was to consult how to cheat Indians in the Price of Beaver. Consider but little, Conrad, and you must be of my Opinion. If they met so often to learn *good Things*, they would certainly have learnt some before this time. But they are still ignorant. You know our Practice. If a white Man, in travelling thro' our Country, enters one of our Cabins, we all treat him as I treat you; we dry him if he is wet, we warm him if he is cold, we give him Meat and Drink, that he may allay his Thirst and Hunger; and we spread soft Furs for him to rest and sleep on; we demand nothing in return. But, if I go into a white Man's House at Albany, and ask for Victuals and Drink, they say, 'Where is your Money?' and if I have none, they say, 'Get out, you Indian Dog.' You see they have not yet learned those little *Good Things*, that we need no Meetings to be instructed in, because our Mothers taught them to us when we were Children; and therefore it is impossible their Meetings should be, as they say, for any such purpose, or have any such Effect; they are only to contrive *the Cheating of Indians in the Price of Beaver*."

QUESTIONS FOR READING ACTIVELY

1. What is Franklin's definition of *savage?* This term has long since ceased to be appropriate when used to refer to indigenous peoples; do you think that Franklin, writing 200 years ago, was also aware of how inappropriate this term could be? Explain your answer with reference to Franklin's own examples and argument.

2. What two ideals is Franklin comparing in this essay?

3. Franklin was widely known for his wit, of which there is a sly example in paragraph 6. Identify the joke. Why does Franklin include it? Is he simply being sarcastic, or is he making a much larger and subtle comparison of perspectives?

QUESTIONS FOR THINKING CRITICALLY

1. What does Franklin mean when he says, "Perhaps, if we could examine the Manners of different Nations with Impartiality, we should find no People so rude, as to be without any Rules of Politeness; nor any so polite, as not to have some Remains of Rudeness"?

2. What does the Iroquois speaker mean when he says, "If the Gentlemen of Virginia will send us a Dozen of their Sons, we will take great Care of their Education, instruct them in all we know, and make *Men* of them"?

3. In paragraph 9, Franklin recounts the experience of the Iroquois elder Canassatego when he went to a "great House" to "hear and learn *good Things*." Why does Franklin use Canassatego's exact language, rather than explaining or translating his perspective for his English-speaking colonial audience? What is the tremendous irony that Canassatego's perspective gives to the concept of "*good Things*"?

QUESTIONS FOR WRITING THOUGHTFULLY

1. How does Franklin use comparison to structure this essay?

2. The style of Benjamin Franklin's writing, indicative of much of the writing in the late 1700s, differs from more contemporary writing quite drastically. In a brief paragraph, describe your reaction to his style of writing, and note how, had this piece been written today, certain characteristics of the writing might be different.

From *The School Days of an Indian Girl*

by Zitkala-Sa (Gertrude Simmons Bonnin)

A member of the Yankton Sioux nation, Zitkala-Sa was born on the Pine Ridge Reservation in South Dakota and raised in a traditional tipi on the Missouri River. At the end of the nineteenth and beginning of the twentieth centuries, many surviving Native American nations were forced from their traditional lands onto "reservations," lands managed by the American government. Children on these reservations were forced to sacrifice their native languages, cultures, and traditions, often sent away from their families to religious or secular boarding schools. In the following autobiographical essay, Zitkala-Sa recounts her time spent at a Quaker boarding school for Native American children in Wabash, Indiana. The experience left her feeling divided between identities and cultures, a division that galvanized her into pursuing further education and devoting her life to

Source: From *The School Days of an Indian Girl* by Zitkala-Sa (Gertrude Simmons Bonnin) (1876–1938) (1900).

justice for Native Americans. She graduated from Earlham College with plans to become a teacher, and her musical talents brought her to the Boston Conservatory. In 1900, she went to Paris with the Carlisle Indian Industrial School (CIIS) as violin soloist for the Paris Exposition. But the loss and destruction of her own culture haunted her, and led to her first book, the 1901 collection *Old Indian Legends*.

Zitkala-Sa became increasingly active politically, along with her husband, Ray Bonnin of the Sioux Nation. She worked to increase voter participation by Native Americans, and in 1930, she formed the National Council of American Indians, where she served as president until her death in 1938.

The Cutting of My Long Hair

The first day in the land of apples was a bitter-cold one; for the snow still covered the ground, and the trees were bare. A large bell rang for breakfast, its loud metallic voice crashing through the belfry overhead and into our sensitive ears. The annoying clatter of shoes on bare floors gave us no peace. The constant clash of harsh noises, with an undercurrent of many voices murmuring an unknown tongue, made a bedlam within which I was securely tied. And though my spirit tore itself in struggling for its lost freedom, all was useless.

A paleface woman, with white hair, came up after us. We were placed in a line of girls who were marching into the dining room. These were Indian girls, in stiff shoes and closely clinging dresses. The small girls wore sleeved aprons and shingled hair. As I walked noiselessly in my soft moccasins, I felt like sinking to the floor, for my blanket had been stripped from my shoulders. I looked hard at the Indian girls, who seemed not to care that they were even more immodestly dressed than I, in their tightly fitting clothes. While we marched in, the boys entered at an opposite door. I watched for the three young braves who came in our party. I spied them in the rear ranks, looking as uncomfortable as I felt.

A small bell was tapped, and each of the pupils drew a chair from under the table. Supposing this act meant they were to be seated, I pulled out mine and at once slipped into it from one side. But when I turned my head, I saw that I was the only one seated, and all the rest at our table remained standing. Just as I began to rise, looking shyly around to see how chairs were to be used, a second bell was sounded. All were seated at last, and I had to crawl back into my chair again. I heard a man's voice at one end of the hall, and I looked around to see him. But all the others hung their heads over their plates. As I glanced at the long chain of tables, I caught the eyes of a paleface woman upon me. Immediately I dropped my eyes, wondering why I was so keenly watched by the strange woman. The man ceased his mutterings, and then a third bell was tapped. Every one picked up his knife and fork and began eating. I began crying instead, for by this time I was afraid to venture anything more.

But this eating by formula was not the hardest trial in that first day. Late in the morning, my friend Judewin gave me a terrible warning. Judewin knew a few words of English, and she had overheard the paleface woman talk about cutting our long, heavy hair. Our mothers had taught us that only unskilled warriors who were captured had their hair shingled by the enemy. Among our people, short hair was worn by mourners, and shingled hair by cowards!

We discussed our fate some moments, and when Judewin said, "We have to submit, because they are strong," I rebelled. 5

"No, I will not submit! I will struggle first!" I answered.

I watched my chance, and when no one noticed I disappeared. I crept up the stairs as quietly as I could in my squeaking shoes,—my moccasins had been exchanged for shoes. Along the hall I passed, without knowing whither I was going. Turning aside to an open door, I found a large room with three white beds in it. The windows were covered with dark green curtains, which made the room very dim. Thankful that no one was there, I directed my steps toward the corner farthest from the door. On my hands and knees I crawled under the bed, and cuddled myself in the dark corner.

From my hiding place I peered out, shuddering with fear whenever I heard footsteps near by. Though in the hall loud voices were calling my name, and I knew that even Judewin was searching for me, I did not open my mouth to answer. Then the steps were quickened and the voices became excited. The sounds came nearer and nearer. Women and girls entered the room. I held my breath, and watched them open closet doors and peep behind large trunks. Some one threw up the curtains, and the room was filled with sudden light. What caused them to stoop and look under the bed I do not know. I remember being dragged out, though I resisted by kicking and scratching wildly. In spite of myself, I was carried downstairs and tied fast in a chair.

I cried aloud, shaking my head all the while until I felt the cold blades of the scissors against my neck, and heard them gnaw off one of my thick braids. Then I lost my spirit. Since the day I was taken from my mother I had suffered extreme indignities. People had stared at me. I had been tossed about in the air like a wooden puppet. And now my long hair was shingled like a coward's! In my anguish I moaned for my mother, but no one came to comfort me. Not a soul reasoned quietly with me, as my own mother used to do; for now I was only one of many little animals driven by a herder.

The Snow Episode

10 A short time after our arrival we three Dakotas were playing in the snowdrifts. We were all still deaf to the English language, excepting Judewin, who always heard such puzzling things. One morning we learned through her ears that we were forbidden to fall lengthwise in the snow, as we had been doing, to see our own impressions. However, before many hours we had forgotten the order, and were having great sport in the snow, when a shrill voice called us. Looking up, we saw an imperative hand beckoning us into the house. We shook the snow off ourselves, and started toward the woman as slowly as we dared.

Judewin said: "Now the paleface is angry with us. She is going to punish us for falling into the snow. If she looks straight into your eyes and talks loudly, you must wait until she stops. Then, after a tiny pause, say, 'No.'" The rest of the way we practiced upon the little word "no."

As it happened, Thowin was summoned to judgment first. The door shut behind her with a click.

Judewin and I stood silently listening at the keyhole. The paleface woman talked in very severe tones. Her words fell from her lips like crackling embers, and her inflection ran up like the small end of a switch. I understood her voice better than the things she was saying. I was certain we had made her very impatient with us. Judewin heard enough of the words to realize all too late that she had taught us the wrong reply.

"Oh, poor Thowin!" she gasped, as she put both hands over her ears.

15   Just then I heard Thowin's tremulous answer, "No."

With an angry exclamation, the woman gave her a hard spanking. Then she stopped to say something. Judewin said it was this: "Are you going to obey my word the next time?"

Thowin answered again with the only word at her command, "No."

This time the woman meant her blows to smart, for the poor frightened girl shrieked at the top of her voice. In the midst of the whipping the blows ceased abruptly, and the woman asked another question: "Are you going to fall in the snow again?"

Thowin gave her bad password another trial. We heard her say feebly, "No! No!"

With this the woman hid away her half-worn slipper, and led the child out, stroking   20
her black shorn head. Perhaps it occurred to her that brute force is not the solution for such a problem. She did nothing to Judewin nor to me. She only returned to us our unhappy comrade, and left us alone in the room.

During the first two or three seasons misunderstandings as ridiculous as this one of the snow episode frequently took place, bringing unjustifiable frights and punishments into our little lives.

Within a year I was able to express myself somewhat in broken English. As soon as I comprehended a part of what was said and done, a mischievous spirit of revenge possessed me. One day I was called in from my play for some misconduct. I had disregarded a rule which seemed to me very needlessly binding. I was sent into the kitchen to mash the turnips for dinner. It was noon, and steaming dishes were hastily carried into the dining room. I hated turnips, and their odor which came from the brown jar was offensive to me. With fire in my heart, I took the wooden tool that the paleface woman held out to me. I stood upon a step, and, grasping the handle with both hands, I bent in hot rage over the turnips. I worked my vengeance upon them. All were so busily occupied that no one noticed me. I saw that the turnips were in a pulp, and that further beating could not improve them; but the order was, "Mash these turnips," and mash them I would! I renewed my energy; and as I sent the masher into the bottom of the jar, I felt a satisfying sensation that the weight of my body had gone into it.

Just here a paleface woman came up to my table. As she looked into the jar she shoved my hands roughly aside. I stood fearless and angry. She placed her red hands upon the rim of the jar. Then she gave one lift and a stride away from the table. But lo! the pulpy contents fell through the crumbled bottom to the floor! She spared me no scolding phrases that I had earned. I did not heed them. I felt triumphant in my revenge, though deep within me I was a wee bit sorry to have broken the jar.

As I sat eating my dinner, and saw that no turnips were served, I whooped in my heart for having once asserted the rebellion within me.

* * * *

Four Strange Summers

After my first three years of school, I roamed again in the Western country through four   25
strange summers.

During this time I seemed to hang in the heart of chaos, beyond the touch or voice of human aid. My brother, being almost ten years my senior, did not quite understand my feelings. My mother had never gone inside of a schoolhouse, and so she was not capable of comforting her daughter who could read and write. Even nature seemed to have no place for me. I was neither a wee girl nor a tall one; neither a wild Indian nor a tame one. This deplorable situation was the effect of my brief course in the East, and the unsatisfactory "teenth" in a girl's years.

It was under these trying conditions that, one bright afternoon, as I sat restless and unhappy in my brother's cabin, I caught the sound of the spirited step of my brother's pony on the road which passed by our dwelling. Soon I heard the wheels of a light buckboard, and Dawee's familiar "Ho!" to his pony. He alighted upon the bare ground in front of our house. Tying his pony to one of the projecting corner logs of the low-roofed cottage, he stepped upon the wooden doorstep.

I met him there with a hurried greeting, and as I passed by, he looked a quiet "What?" into my eyes.

When he began talking with my mother, I slipped the rope from the pony's bridle. Seizing the reins and bracing my feet against the dashboard, I wheeled around in an instant. The pony was ever ready to try his speed. Looking backward, I saw Dawee waving his hand to me. I turned with the curve in the road and disappeared. I followed the winding road which crawled upward between the bases of little hillocks. Deep water-worn ditches ran parallel on either side. A strong wind blew against my cheeks and fluttered my sleeves. The pony reached the top of the highest hill, and began an even race on the level lands. There was nothing moving within that great circular horizon of the Dakota prairies save the tall grasses, over which the wind blew and rolled off in long, shadowy waves.

30   Within this vast wigwam of blue and green I rode reckless and insignificant. It satisfied my small consciousness to see the white foam fly from the pony's mouth.

Suddenly, out of the earth a coyote came forth at a swinging trot that was taking the cunning thief toward the hills and the village beyond. Upon the moment's impulse, I gave him a long chase and a wholesome fright. As I turned away to go back to the village, the wolf sank down upon his haunches for rest, for it was a hot summer day; and as I drove slowly homeward, I saw his sharp nose still pointed at me, until I vanished below the margin of the hilltops.

In a little while I came in sight of my mother's house. Dawee stood in the yard, laughing at an old warrior who was pointing his forefinger, and again waving his whole hand, toward the hills. With his blanket drawn over one shoulder, he talked and motioned excitedly. Dawee turned the old man by the shoulder and pointed me out to him.

"Oh han!" (Oh yes) the warrior muttered, and went his way. He had climbed to the top of his favorite barren hill to survey the surrounding prairies, when he spied my chase after the coyote. His keen eyes recognized the pony and driver. At once uneasy for my safety, he had come running to my mother's cabin to give her warning. I did not appreciate his kindly interest, for there was an unrest gnawing at my heart.

As soon as he went away, I asked Dawee about something else.

35   "No, my baby sister, I cannot take you with me to the party to-night," he replied. Though I was not far from fifteen, and I felt that before long I should enjoy all the privileges of my tall cousin, Dawee persisted in calling me his baby sister.

That moonlight night, I cried in my mother's presence when I heard the jolly young people pass by our cottage. They were no more young braves in blankets and eagle plumes, nor Indian maids with prettily painted cheeks. They had gone three years to school in the East, and had become civilized. The young men wore the white man's coat and trousers, with bright neckties. The girls wore tight muslin dresses, with ribbons at neck and waist. At these gatherings they talked English. I could speak English almost as well as my brother, but I was not properly dressed to be taken along. I had no hat, no ribbons, and no close-fitting gown. Since my return from school I had thrown away my shoes, and wore again the soft moccasins.

While Dawee was busily preparing to go I controlled my tears. But when I heard him bounding away on his pony, I buried my face in my arms and cried hot tears.

My mother was troubled by my unhappiness. Coming to my side, she offered me the only printed matter we had in our home. It was an Indian Bible, given her some years ago by a missionary. She tried to console me. "Here, my child, are the white man's papers. Read a little from them," she said most piously.

I took it from her hand, for her sake; but my enraged spirit felt more like burning the book, which afforded me no help, and was a perfect delusion to my mother. I did not read it, but laid it unopened on the floor, where I sat on my feet. The dim yellow light of the braided muslin burning in a small vessel of oil flickered and sizzled in the awful silent storm which followed my rejection of the Bible.

Now my wrath against the fates consumed my tears before they reached my eyes. 40 I sat stony, with a bowed head. My mother threw a shawl over her head and shoulders, and stepped out into the night.

After an uncertain solitude, I was suddenly aroused by a loud cry piercing the night. It was my mother's voice wailing among the barren hills which held the bones of buried warriors. She called aloud for her brothers' spirits to support her in her helpless misery. My fingers grew icy cold, as I realized that my unrestrained tears had betrayed my suffering to her, and she was grieving for me.

Before she returned, though I knew she was on her way, for she had ceased her weeping, I extinguished the light, and leaned my head on the window sill.

Many schemes of running away from my surroundings hovered about in my mind. A few more moons of such a turmoil drove me away to the Eastern school. I rode on the white man's iron steed, thinking it would bring me back to my mother in a few winters, when I should be grown tall, and there would be congenial friends awaiting me.

Incurring My Mother's Displeasure

In the second journey to the East I had not come without some precautions. I had a secret interview with one of our best medicine men, and when I left his wigwam I carried securely in my sleeve a tiny bunch of magic roots. This possession assured me of friends wherever I should go. So absolutely did I believe in its charms that I wore it through all the school routine for more than a year. Then, before I lost my faith in the dead roots, I lost the little buckskin bag containing all my good luck.

At the close of this second term of three years I was the proud owner of my first 45 diploma. The following autumn I ventured upon a college career against my mother's will.

I had written for her approval, but in her reply I found no encouragement. She called my notice to her neighbors' children, who had completed their education in three years. They had returned to their homes, and were then talking English with the frontier settlers. Her few words hinted that I had better give up my slow attempt to learn the white man's ways, and be content to roam over the prairies and find my living upon wild roots. I silenced her by deliberate disobedience.

Thus, homeless and heavy-hearted, I began anew my life among strangers.

As I hid myself in my little room in the college dormitory, away from the scornful and yet curious eyes of the students, I pined for sympathy. Often I wept in secret, wishing I had gone West, to be nourished by my mother's love, instead of remaining among a cold race whose hearts were frozen hard with prejudice.

During the fall and winter seasons I scarcely had a real friend, though by that time several of my classmates were courteous to me at a safe distance.

50   My mother had not yet forgiven my rudeness to her, and I had no moment for letter-writing. By daylight and lamplight, I spun with reeds and thistles, until my hands were tired from their weaving, the magic design which promised me the white man's respect.

At length, in the spring term, I entered an oratorical contest among the various classes. As the day of competition approached, it did not seem possible that the event was so near at hand, but it came. In the chapel the classes assembled together, with their invited guests. The high platform was carpeted, and gayly festooned with college colors. A bright white light illumined the room, and outlined clearly the great polished beams that arched the domed ceiling. The assembled crowds filled the air with pulsating murmurs. When the hour for speaking arrived all were hushed. But on the wall the old clock which pointed out the trying moment ticked calmly on.

One after another I saw and heard the orators. Still, I could not realize that they longed for the favorable decision of the judges as much as I did. Each contestant received a loud burst of applause, and some were cheered heartily. Too soon my turn came, and I paused a moment behind the curtains for a deep breath. After my concluding words, I heard the same applause that the others had called out.

Upon my retreating steps, I was astounded to receive from my fellow students a large bouquet of roses tied with flowing ribbons. With the lovely flowers I fled from the stage. This friendly token was a rebuke to me for the hard feelings I had borne them.

Later, the decision of the judges awarded me the first place. Then there was a mad uproar in the hall, where my classmates sang and shouted my name at the top of their lungs; and the disappointed students howled and brayed in fearfully dissonant tin trumpets. In this excitement, happy students rushed forward to offer their congratulations. And I could not conceal a smile when they wished to escort me in a procession to the students' parlor, where all were going to calm themselves. Thanking them for the kind spirit which prompted them to make such a proposition, I walked alone with the night to my own little room.

55   A few weeks afterward, I appeared as the college representative in another contest. This time the competition was among orators from different colleges in our state. It was held at the state capital, in one of the largest opera houses.

Here again was a strong prejudice against my people. In the evening, as the great audience filled the house, the student bodies began warring among themselves. Fortunately, I was spared witnessing any of the noisy wrangling before the contest began. The slurs against the Indian that stained the lips of our opponents were already burning like a dry fever within my breast.

But after the orations were delivered a deeper burn awaited me. There, before that vast ocean of eyes, some college rowdies threw out a large white flag, with a drawing of a most forlorn Indian girl on it. Under this they had printed in bold black letters words that ridiculed the college which was represented by a "squaw." Such worse than barbarian rudeness embittered me. While we waited for the verdict of the judges,

I gleamed fiercely upon the throngs of palefaces. My teeth were hard set, as I saw the white flag still floating insolently in the air.

Then anxiously we watched the man carry toward the stage the envelope containing the final decision.

There were two prizes given, that night, and one of them was mine!

The evil spirit laughed within me when the white flag dropped out of sight, and the   60 hands which furled it hung limp in defeat.

Leaving the crowd as quickly as possible, I was soon in my room. The rest of the night I sat in an armchair and gazed into the crackling fire. I laughed no more in triumph when thus alone. The little taste of victory did not satisfy a hunger in my heart. In my mind I saw my mother far away on the Western plains, and she was holding a charge against me.

QUESTIONS FOR READING ACTIVELY

1. Zitkala-Sa uses a strikingly apt metaphor in paragraph 9. What is that metaphor? How many different layers of meaning does it have here?

2. In what ways does the Bible or representations of Christianity figure in this narrative?

3. What is the "evil spirit" that Zitkala-Sa refers to in paragraph 60?

QUESTIONS FOR THINKING CRITICALLY

1. Compare Zitkala-Sa's experience with the missionary school to the conversation between an Iroquois elder and a group of Virginia politicians who offered to educate six young Iroquois men at a Williamsburg, Virginia, college (the college, William and Mary, is today one of the oldest continuing institutions of higher learning in America). In what ways does Zitkala-Sa's experience reflect the observations of the Iroquois elders, in terms of both the perils of assimilation and the rifts created between family members?

2. Zitkala-Sa recounts her experiences through the perspective of a child. What are the advantages to this perspective in telling her story? What are the disadvantages?

QUESTIONS FOR WRITING THOUGHTFULLY

1. Did your education—and think broadly here of "education," not just of "school"—involve the taming or controlling of some part of your spirit or personality? Write a short essay about what you gave up and why and what that loss taught you, if anything.

2. In Chapter 7, you focused on writing to describe and narrate. How does the use of descriptive writing enhance your understanding of Zitkala-Sa's narrative and situation? Which particular passages had an impact on you? Point out two descriptive passages, and describe your reactions.

Writing Thoughtfully About Perspectives

COMPARISON AND CONTRAST

Whenever we place two or more perspectives, or two or more other things, together and examine them for similarities and differences, we are engaging in the powerful thinking pattern called *comparison and contrast*. To be precise, when we *compare*, we are focusing on likenesses or areas of agreement; when we *contrast*, we are focusing on differences or areas of disagreement. Generally, the items examined are from the same category. We will discuss writing about items from the same category in the next section, Thinking in Comparisons. Sometimes, in order to make a point or to explain something, we may compare items from different categories. We will discuss these unusual comparisons in the Analogy section (pages 329–330).

THINKING IN COMPARISONS

We use comparison and contrast informally in our daily lives when we make decisions such as what food to buy or which TV programs to watch. When we use comparison and contrast in a formal way by following certain established principles, we are using it to think critically to arrive at a significant conclusion. That is, we use it not only to list areas of similarity or difference but also to help achieve a clearer understanding or new insight. When we use comparison and contrast to examine different perspectives, we do so in order to understand each perspective, to see if one is superior to another, to see if we ourselves have yet another perspective, and so on.

The principles for using comparison and contrast to think critically are straightforward.

1. *Compare or contrast two or more things that have something essential in common (that is, items from the same category).* Thus, it makes sense to compare two accounts of the same event or two essays on the use of Standard English.

2. *Establish important bases or points for comparison and contrast.* In everyday situations, it is fairly easy to determine which points are important. In deciding between two cars, the important points may be price, model, and safety features; exterior color and exact trunk capacity may be lesser concerns. But when you are working with written texts, finding points for comparison and contrast and deciding which of them are important require careful thought. When comparing or contrasting two accounts of the same event, important points might include the actual presence of the writers at the event or the writers' reliance on the accounts of others, the language the writers use to describe the participants or actions, and which details the writers have included or omitted. The writer's gender or the length of an account might or might not be significant.

3. *Develop or locate relevant, specific evidence for each point.* Opinions valued by critical thinkers are those supported by evidence. In everyday situations, evidence usually means facts: the prices of two different cars, the presence or absence of air bags, and so on. With written texts, the evidence comes from the texts themselves, in the form of either accurate paraphrases or direct quotations.

4. *Determine the significance of the comparison and contrast: What can be learned from it? What should be done as a result?* In everyday situations, this significance is often a determination: one car is superior to another and is therefore the one to purchase. When you are working with written texts, the significance may be that the texts disagree on important points; therefore, you may decide that one is more persuasive than the other.

"A Natural Disaster, and a Human Tragedy"
by Ted Steinberg

Ted Steinberg is a professor of history and law at Case Western University, with a particular interest in the history of American environmental law and policy. His book *Acts of God: The Unnatural History of Natural Disaster in America* (Oxford, 2000) was a nominee for a Pulitzer Prize. He has also written about the legal implications of American environmental policy for the *New York Times* and the *Los Angeles Times*, among numerous other newspapers and magazines. "A Natural Disaster, and a Human Tragedy" was published in the September 23, 2005, edition of *The Chronicle of Higher Education*, a leading newspaper and journal about academic life.

Is Hurricane Katrina "our tsunami," as the mayor of Biloxi, Miss., A. J. Holloway, has said? Does it make sense to compare today's disaster to a catastrophe that killed upward of 200,000 impoverished people, injured roughly half a million, displaced millions more, and was felt across a huge geographic span that included Sumatra, Thailand, India, Sri Lanka, and eastern Africa?

In searching for meaning in the current calamity, we can learn something about the root causes of such disasters by pinpointing the proper historical analogy.

Although it is no doubt an overstatement to compare Katrina to the 2004 tsunami, the two have some things in common. Both demonstrated the vulnerability of the poor in the face of natural calamity: Consider Katrina's victims who suffered through the aftermath at the Superdome and convention center. That was a man-made disaster that clearly could have been averted if the federal government, specifically the Federal Emergency Management Agency, had quickly marshaled the political will and resources to evacuate those without access to cars, instead of promoting on its Web site a faith-based charity that was clearly no match for the problem.

Likewise, both disasters demonstrated the tragic consequences of reckless coastal development. In Asia, industrial fish farms, tourist resorts, and refineries combined over the last generation to destroy huge stretches of coastal mangrove forest. The forest helps stabilize the land, and offers a form of natural protection that can soften the blow of a tsunami. Bangladesh experienced many fewer deaths in the disaster because of the

Source: From "A Natural Disaster, and a Human Tragedy," by Ted Steinberg, *The Chronicle of Higher Education*, September 23, 2005, http://chronicle.com/free/v52/i05/05b01101.htm. Reprinted with permission of the author.

conservation of its coastal mangroves than did Indonesia, where two-thirds of the forest has been destroyed.

5   In New Orleans, meanwhile, the dredging of channels to accommodate petrochemical companies has compromised huge amounts of marshland. Such changes, combined with the erosion of the area's barrier islands, and the Bush administration's policy of opening up more wetlands to development, weakened the natural frontline defense against a hurricane storm surge and left the city more vulnerable to death and destruction.

Both disasters also show the problems with neoliberal imperatives, based in a theory of political economy that idealizes the free market and chips away at the public sector at home, while worshiping at the altar of free trade and investment abroad. Foreign capital, whether in the form of tourism or the cash-cropping of fish, played a role in opening the coast around the Indian Ocean to the destructive force of the tsunami. In the aftermath of the disaster, the World Bank is leading the effort to expand the reach of those very same enterprises at the expense of the poor. The poor suffered the most in the calamity, and they are now experiencing the brutalizing effects of what the activist journalist Naomi Klein has rightly termed "disaster capitalism," as foreign corporations seek to profit from the reconstruction while the residents of the fishing villages that formerly occupied the area are being forced to relocate. In June 2005 Oxfam found that because the flow of aid has tended to go to business people and landowners, many of the poor have been made even poorer by the disaster.

What form the postdisaster rebuilding of the Gulf region will take remains to be seen. But this much is clear: Those poor people who had to suffer through the stench, the heat, and the overflowing toilets were victims of a way of thinking that goes back 25 years. Neoliberalism is a philosophy that has been shared by Republicans and Democrats alike (which is, by the way, why I'm not entirely convinced by those who argue that this kind of mistreatment would not have happened under a Kerry administration), and it was the root cause behind the failed evacuation. It is an ethos that deludes its adherents into thinking that "a thousand points of light" are better at solving America's problems than the federal government. It is a worldview that would rather put its faith in volunteer efforts than pony up the money and resources to safely evacuate the roughly 120,000 people in New Orleans who, we knew in advance, had no access to cars.

When it comes to hurricane evacuation, American officials ought to take a page out of Fidel Castro's handbook. The American news media never miss an opportunity to poke fun at the Communists. I would not want to defend all of Castro's policies, but whatever their faults, the Communists in Cuba have figured out how to use government resources to organize an efficient civil-defense system for protecting their people—staging exercises to practice evacuation, providing shelters in advance with medical personnel, and even bringing in trucks before a storm so people can save their material possessions. It hardly needs mentioning that being alive is one of the prerequisites for enjoying the freedom that Americans value so much.

So there is a great deal that the tsunami and the present hurricane have in common. But a much better historical comparison exists closer to home, one that highlights the irresponsible decision making and denial on the part of government officials that, combined with profit-driven land development, largely explains why the poor pay with their lives in such disasters. I have in mind the 1928 hurricane that took the lives of at least 1,836 people in Florida, the vast majority of them poor migrant workers who drowned as the waters of Lake Okeechobee rose up over a dike and pounded them to death.

That disaster is comparable to what is happening in the wake of Hurricane Katrina   10
not just because the victims in both cases are overwhelmingly poor and African American. They compare because, in both cases, there were clear signs, in advance, that they were disasters waiting to happen—literally unnatural disasters.

In the case of the 1928 Florida hurricane, the warning was telegraphed several years in advance. Earlier in the century state authorities had overseen a massive drainage project that reclaimed land around the shores of Lake Okeechobee and turned it into valuable agricultural enterprises. Yet living around the lake had its price. In 1922 heavy rains caused the water to rise more than four feet and flooded Clewiston and Moore Haven, towns along the lake's southern shore that housed the black laborers who worked the rich agricultural land nearby.

In 1924 storms again raised the lake level, causing more flooding. Then, in the summer of 1926, heavy rains raised the level of the lake yet again, leading a journalist named Howard Sharp to beg state officials to take steps to lower the water: "The lake is truly at a level so high as to make a perilous situation in the event of a storm," he wrote in the *Tampa Tribune*.

The Everglades Drainage District, headed by some of the highest officials in the state, including Gov. John W. Martin and Attorney General J. B. Johnson, took no action to lower the water. By September 1 the level of Lake Okeechobee exceeded 18 feet. The levees around the lake were built to only 21 feet, and anyone even remotely familiar with the area knew that a stiff wind could cause the lake to rise as much as three feet. The mathematics of fatality and destruction were painfully obvious. Yet the drainage commissioners, beholden to wealthy agricultural and commercial interests—who wanted the lake water high to help with irrigating crops and navigation—refused to act.

Nobody listened, and on September 18, 1926, a Category 4 storm ripped across Florida and caused the waters of Lake Okeechobee to wash over a dike and kill at least 150 people (though 300 seems more likely) in Moore Haven, which had an entire population of only 1,200 at the time.

After the disaster, the attorney general explained: "The storm caused the loss and   15
damage. . . . It is not humanly possible to guard against the unknown and against the forces of nature when loosed." Interpreting the event as a "natural" disaster masked the calamity's man-made causes and scarcely moved anyone to action to help ward off a future catastrophe, which, it turned out, was just around the corner.

On September 16, 1928, a powerful storm, with a barometric low of 27.43 inches— even lower than that recorded in 1926—swept ashore near Palm Beach. After the notorious 1900 Galveston hurricane (which left at least 8,000 dead), it was the deadliest storm in twentieth-century American history. Most of those who died were black migrant workers, virtually all of whom drowned in the towns along the southern shore of Lake Okeechobee, as the howling winds sent a wall of water crashing over the dikes in a grim repetition of what had happened two years before.

Sightseers, brimming with morbid curiosity, filed into the region to see the mounds of swollen, rotting corpses firsthand. According to one report, "the visitor would stare for moments entranced, then invariably turn aside to vomit." Bodies were still being found more than a month after the disaster, when searching ceased for lack of funds.

Again, Sharp seemed remarkably prescient, writing a week before the storm that those who advocated a high water level in Lake Okeechobee were taking "a terrible responsibility on themselves." And again, a member of the Everglades drainage commission—this time Ernest Amos, the state comptroller—called the disaster an "act of God," in what is surely one of history's more irresponsible outbursts of denial.

After Hurricane Katrina swept through New Orleans, President Bush, sounding much like state officials in Florida in the 1920s, said: "I don't think anybody anticipated the breach of the levees." Seeing the calamity as primarily the work of unforeseen and unpredictable forces, however, amounts to a form of moral hand-washing.

20   In fact, multiple warnings had gone out. FEMA has known about the potential for large loss of life in New Orleans, probably for a generation. Ten years ago *Weatherwise* magazine called New Orleans "the Death Valley of the Gulf Coast" because the city is surrounded by water and not particularly well served by major roadways. In 2000, in talking about the general decline in death rates from natural disasters in the twentieth century, I called attention in my book *Acts of God* to New Orleans and wrote: "Think twice before assuming that high death tolls are a thing of the past." Mark Fischetti, a contributing editor to *Scientific American*, made the same prediction in an excellent report in the magazine in 2001. The journalists John McQuaid and Mark Schleifstein reported extensively in 2002 on the potential for calamity in the *Times-Picayune*. And as recently as May 2005, Max Mayfield, the director of the National Hurricane Center, was quoted as saying, "I can't emphasize enough how concerned I am with southeast Louisiana because of its unique characteristics, its complex levee system."

Is the current disaster the American tsunami? No, it's the Hurricane Katrina calamity. But the same blind faith in the free market and private enterprise, coupled with the brutal downsizing of the public sector, and a very explicit pattern of denial in the face of impending natural calamity, help explain why America's most vulnerable saw their lives washed out to sea.

QUESTIONS FOR READING ACTIVELY

1. Identify Ted Steinberg's thesis. How soon in his essay does he name those things that he will compare and contrast? What is the connection between those identifications and his thesis statement?

2. Does Steinberg use a block organization or a point-by-point organization for his essay?

3. Circle the words, phrases, and sentences Steinberg uses that signal relationships among those things he is comparing and contrasting.

QUESTIONS FOR THINKING CRITICALLY

1. From paragraph 6 on, Steinberg's argument becomes explicitly economic. How does he define *neoliberal imperatives*, and to what does he contrast such

an economic system? Have other resources that you have consulted about the impact of hurricanes Katrina and Rita discussed the economic backgrounds?

2. In this chapter, we have examined the need to develop and appreciate multiple perspectives as critical thinkers. How many fields of expertise—different academic and/or professional perspectives—does Steinberg draw upon to write his essay? In your own life as a worker, a student, and a citizen, how can you work to become better informed without necessarily becoming an "expert" yourself?

QUESTIONS FOR WRITING THOUGHTFULLY

1. In the second paragraph of his essay, Steinberg argues for the need to find a "proper historical analogy" for understanding both the aftermath of Katrina and the devastation caused by the Asian tsunami of 2004. In your own words, describe this analogy. (The next section of this chapter will explore analogy more fully as a strategy for critical thinking.)

2. What is the significance of the comparison and contrast in this essay—that is, what can be learned from Steinberg?

ANALOGY

We noted earlier that comparative relationships involve examining the similarities and differences of two items in the same general category, such as two perspectives, two items on a menu, or two methods of birth control. There is another kind of comparison, however, one that does not focus on things in the same category. Such comparisons are known as *analogies*, and their goal is to clarify or illuminate a concept from one category by saying that in some ways, it resembles a concept from a very different category.

The purpose of an analogy is not the same as the purpose of the comparison we have been discussing. We noted that the goal of comparing similar things is often to make a choice and that the process of comparing can provide us with information on which we can base an intelligent decision. The main goal of analogies, however, is not to choose or decide; it is to illuminate our understanding. Identifying similarities between very different things can often stimulate us to see these things in a new light or from a different perspective.

We often create and use analogies to put a point across. Used appropriately, an analogy can help to illustrate what we are trying to communicate. This device is particularly useful when we have difficulty finding the right words to represent our experiences. Similes and metaphors, two figures of speech based on analogy that help us to "say things for which we have not words," are discussed on pages 183–185 in Chapter 6.

In addition to communicating experiences that resist simple characterization, analogies are useful when a writer is explaining a complicated concept.

For instance, we might compare the eye to a camera lens or compare the body's immune system to the National Guard (corpuscles are called to active duty and rush to the scene of danger when undesirable elements threaten the well-being of the organism).

Analogies are often used to describe shape or size. They help our readers to visualize size if we describe an object as "about the size of a dollar bill" or a piece of property as "roughly the size of two football fields."

Analogies enliven discourse by evoking images that illuminate the points of comparison. Consider the following analogies and explain the points of comparison.

> "Laws are like cobwebs, which may catch small flies, but let wasps and hornets break through."—Jonathan Swift

> "Like as the waves make towards the pebbled shore, so do our minutes hasten to their end."—William Shakespeare

> "Some books are to be tasted, others to be swallowed, and some few to be chewed and digested."—Francis Bacon

> "He has all the qualities of a dog, except its devotion."—Gore Vidal

In addition to *simple analogies* like the preceding ones that are designed to make one or two penetrating points, *extended analogies* have a more ambitious purpose. They attempt to illuminate a more complex subject by identifying a number of points of comparison. For example, we might seek to explain the theory of causal determinism by drawing an analogy between the universe and a watch or by analogizing the chemical interaction of molecules to a choreographed dance.

A word of caution about using analogies is in order here. Since they are based on items from different categories and have only limited points of similarity, be very careful when writing or reading arguments based on analogies. The failed U.S. military policy in Vietnam was partially based on the "domino theory," which held that since the countries in Southeast Asia had common borders, if one country became Communist, the other countries would also "fall" to Communism, just as a row of dominoes would all fall if one were knocked down. However, the countries were separate entities, places with people, history, cultures, and policies of their own. They were not small game pieces like dominoes, so the theory proved false. Analogies do have value for describing and explaining, but by their very nature, they have limited value in an argument.

Writing Project

COMPARING PERSPECTIVES ON AN ISSUE OR EVENT

This chapter has included both readings and Thinking-Writing Activities that encourage you to reflect on the nature of perception and on comparing and contrasting different perspectives. Be sure to reread what you wrote for those activities; you may be able to use the material when completing this project.

Project Overview and Requirements

Write an essay comparing and contrasting two or more written texts that present different perspectives on the same event or issue. First, you should analyze each text based on the principles for using comparison and contrast in addition to considering the context, or overall situation, of the event or issue. Next, present several significant insights about these different perspectives by following the principles for using comparison and contrast yourself.

Follow your instructor's directions for choosing texts and for the paper's length and format.

Begin by considering the key elements in the Thinking-Writing Model in Chapter 1 on pages 5–8.

THE WRITING SITUATION

Purpose   Along with presenting significant insights about the texts and their subject, you will better understand how to use the thinking patterns of comparison and contrast by analyzing the implications of different perspectives presented in various accounts. Also, since comparative papers require logical organization, your planning abilities should improve. Finally, you will be sharing your insights about the texts with your audience.

Audience   One audience for this paper could be anyone interested in the subject you have chosen to discuss. This audience might be outside of your college, since most events or issues that are written about have community, national, or international significance. If you can, identify such an audience, and share your paper with that audience by publishing it in a newspaper, newsletter, or other venue. If the texts pertain to history, sociology, psychology, or another academic subject, perhaps people studying those subjects would want to read your essay.

Consider whether or not your audience has read the texts that you are analyzing. If your readers have not read the texts, you should include a brief summary and perhaps an explanation of why the texts were originally written. Include enough evidence from the texts to demonstrate the main points you want to communicate. Avoid merely *telling* the members of your audience that a likeness or difference exists—instead, *show* them the evidence so they can see it for themselves.

Subject   If your instructor specifies which texts you should compare and contrast, consider why he or she may have chosen them. What do those texts have in common? If your instructor has left the choice to you, remember that you must use texts that have something essential in common and that are interesting to you based on subject matter or style. If you select an issue or event that interests you, use your research skills to locate additional texts about the topic, keeping in mind that you will need to paraphrase, summarize, or directly quote (and provide citations for) these sources.

Writer   This project asks you to bring your critical reading and thinking skills to other writers' works and to analyze their perspectives. Your position of authority and your comfort level may depend on how much you know about the subject. However, neither your personal opinions nor your experiences are the focus of this project. You must be as objective as possible as you write and as thoughtful as possible as you establish the significance of your analysis.

The following questions (and your responses to the Thinking-Writing Activities earlier in this chapter) will help you more fully focus on the Writing Situation. The prewriting you do here can help you create a framework for your essay, which must compare the perspectives of two or more written texts that focus on the same issue or event.

1. Provide the titles and author(s) of the two articles you would like to compare. For example:

   "The College Idea" by Andrew Delbanco, published in Lapham's Quarterly, Ways of Learning, Fall 2008.

   "8 Ways College Could Better Prepare Students for the Job Search" by Allison Green, August 15, 2012, U.S. News & World Report.

2. Describe the event or issue that these two sources focus on and that you would like to compare. For the articles above, one student wrote:

   I am interested in the role of higher education and find myself contemplating why students go to college today—is it to learn a trade, so to speak, or to learn how to think more critically and become, ultimately, a better citizen? Delbanco claims that, historically, there has been a move from "particular discipline" to "general education," and that there is a big difference between a college (which focuses on the past and critical thinking) and a university (which focuses on the future and learning a skill). His argument is that "it is more urgent than ever that the rising generations learn how "to think and how to choose." In contrast, the article by Green focuses not on critical thinking skills, but instead on the importance of networking, learning how to evaluate employers, and learning how the interview process works. The goal that Green promotes is employment.

3. Define your potential audience—for example:

   Anyone interested in education might find this comparison interesting and necessary: students, professors, and administrators alike. I would also like to submit my essay to our campus newsletter to spark debate on campus.

4. How will you, as the writer, remain objective in this particular piece of writing?

Although I believe that the role of higher education is to help students develop critical thinking skills, I also feel that students need to graduate with skills that will enable them to find gainful employment. In the paper itself, I will not express my opinion and will present both sides of the issue as objectively as possible and will write, of course, from the third-person point of view.

THE WRITING PROCESS

The following sections will guide you through the stages of generating, planning, drafting, and revising as you work on your essay. Try to be particularly conscious of applying the principles discussed in this chapter and of the critical thinking you do when you revise.

Generating Ideas Once you have decided which texts you will use, reread each of them several times. Likenesses and differences may not be immediately apparent, but make a habit of highlighting or underlining passages or words that carry some significance for you if you own a copy of the text. Doing some preliminary writing can also help. Here are a few suggestions to get you started:

- Make a list of the ideas in each text.
- Make a list of what you notice about each text. Are you struck by the opening, the choice of words, the author's bias or objectivity, the presence or absence of specific details, or any other elements or characteristics?
- After you have made these lists, look for points of likeness or difference. Doing this requires abstract thinking on your part, but patience will yield results.
- Collaboration can be productive. Talk with others about the texts.

- Read the student paper at the end of this chapter. It may help you to see what needs to be done.
- Carefully read any other models your instructor provides.
- Try freewriting for five minutes on what the texts have in common and then for five minutes on how they differ.
- Once you have established some bases for comparison or contrast, go back to the texts themselves and look for passages you could quote to illustrate your points.
- If you own the publication(s) in which the texts appear, use a highlighting pen to mark areas you may wish to quote. If you don't own them, copy the quotations or make photocopies to highlight.
- Now begin to think about significance. What are you beginning to observe about the texts? What are you beginning to feel about them?

Begin with the easiest paragraph to draft. If you are using point-by-point, remember to begin each body paragraph with a topic sentence indicating which particular point will be discussed for both (or all) texts: for example, "Both accounts agree on the cause of the contamination." After your topic sentence, provide as much information as needed to help your audience see what you mean. Use the quotations you highlighted to support your points, and let the audience see that the texts really do say very similar—or very different—things.

You will also need to decide on the most logical order for the body paragraphs overall—that is, which point to present first, second, and so on. Generally, readers have an easier time following point-by-point organization, but some writing situations call for block. Fortunately, word processors make it easy to move material around, so try it both ways to see which method of organization will make it easier for your audience to follow your ideas.

In your conclusion, describe or expand upon the significance of your analysis, but be careful not to make too broad a statement. Consideration of two or three texts does not prove, for instance, that all texts are racist or sexist, but discovering racism or sexism in some texts should encourage you and your readers to be aware that these perspectives may be present in others.

Revising Your Essay: Comparing Perspectives on an Issue or Event

Once your draft is complete, it can help to take a break from your writing—especially when the structure of the writing is complex. When you come back to your draft and read it from a fresh perspective, put yourself in the shoes of your audience. Do you clearly introduce your topic? Is the organization of your essay logical? Do you carefully lead your reader through your analysis (comparison and contrast) of the texts you are focusing on?

Peer Response

Consider exchanging your draft with a peer for feedback, or ask someone outside of class to review your writing. Pay close attention to the feedback you receive.

Revision

After you receive feedback, use "A Step-by-Step Method for Revising Any Assignment," located on the inside front cover of this book, for additional tips to make your writing stronger, and remember to look at the larger components of your paper first.

Editing and Proofreading

After you have revised the larger components of your paper and are certain it flows well and effectively communicates your ideas, turn your attention to the smaller details such as grammar, punctuation, and other mechanics. Do your very best to deliver a clear and compelling comparison and contrast.

STUDENT WRITING

Jennifer Wade's Writing Process

Student Jennifer Wade felt an immediate and powerful personal connection to this chapter's readings by Benjamin Franklin and Zitkala-Sa. Sorting out her personal perspective and comparing it to the "official" or "objective" accounts she had obtained from family and archival history was a particular challenge for Jennifer and led to a very compelling essay in which she explores the ambivalence she feels as she tries to reconcile her European and her Cherokee ancestry. Many forms of academic and professional writing do not (by convention or by common agreement) allow for the use of the personal voice, also known as writing in the first person. In Jennifer's case, however, a personal perspective lends her essay a particular authority.

Where Did All of the Cherokees Go?

by Jennifer Wade

Almost twenty-five years ago on Tuesday, December 2, 1980, around one o'clock in the morning, my mother gave birth to me in an Indian hospital. Shortly after my birth I received an identification card from the United States Department of the Interior Affairs Tahlequah Agency. My identification card states that 5/64 of the red blood flowing through my veins is Cherokee Indian blood. I have oftentimes wondered why the government issues identification cards to the chosen few who are a part of something that has become almost nonexistent. What happened in order for the American government to go to great extremes to acknowledge such small traces of a certain descent? My identification card tells me who I am, yet I do not feel like a Cherokee Indian. Nor do I look like one.

According to the web site of the U.S. Department of the Interior, which includes the Bureau of Indian Affairs, the Cherokee nation adopted a new Constitution in 1975 that "establishes a Cherokee Register for the inclusion of any Cherokee for membership purposes in the Cherokee Nation." It was through this agreement

Source: Where Did All of the Cherokees Go? by Jennifer Wade.

Jennifer begins her essay with several key facts that lead into her personal struggle with identity.

that I was enrolled as a member of the Nation at my birth. My father gave me the Cherokee blood and shortly thereafter left me with my mother. She resented my father and everything about him, including my Cherokee heritage. I grew up being a part of something exclusive, and yet I never experienced the culture. As generations pass, the Cherokee Indians will become extinct. After twenty-five years I decided it was time for me to meet my ancestors. I wanted to know where I came from and what had happened to them.

As my research began, I found that I shared many of the beliefs and values my ancestors did. According to Professor Theda Perdue, the Cherokees believed Earth was created by something powerful. They believed the rock sky where everyone lived became overcrowded, and so a water beetle created an island and sent the Cherokee down to inhabit the new land (The Cherokee 13). It is as though God sent his people back to live as a mortal again. The Cherokees too had their own Adam and Eve, but they called them Kana'ti and Selu. From this man and woman came all others (13). Although the Cherokees speak an alien language and look like weather-beaten scavengers, their beliefs are similar to others'. Through this discovery, I have found that all ethnicities have a universal code of conduct.

Unfortunately, there are those who choose to ignore the universal code of conduct when interacting with other ethnicities. Frank W. Porter III, director of the Chelsea House foundation for American Indian Studies, makes this point clear: "The Europeans believed they had 'discovered' a New World," but their religious bigotry, cultural bias, and materialistic world-view kept them from appreciating and understanding the people who lived in it (7). These narcissistic views all but destroyed a strong nation of people. All that remain are a few American citizens with meaningless identification cards reminding us of what we once were, or could have been.

Comedian Chris Rock points out, in his stand-up routine *Bigger, Blacker, and Better*, "You ain't never gonna find a family of American Indians chillin' out in Red Lobster." You will not because they do not exist anymore. Somewhere in Oklahoma you may find people with long, straight, jet black hair and dark brown eyes who probably have an identification card, but they, like me, are only a glimpse of what the Cherokee Indians once were.

In a sense the Cherokee Indians caused their own demise. Had they had the mentality of their counterparts, the outcome may have been different. The Cherokees were generous and willing to compromise with the Europeans who were invading their homeland. Perdue explains that the Cherokees were "incredibly adaptable" (39). If they had chosen to live like the Europeans, could they have survived and lived peacefully together? In the book *Voices From the*

This clear sentence ("I grew up being a part of something exclusive, and yet I never experienced the culture") is a central part of her struggle.

The transition from paragraph 2 to paragraph 3 is strong in that it helps the reader easily move from one idea to the next.

Jennifer sorts through and evaluates different academic, historical, and contemporary accounts and compares them to her personal perspective.

Trail of Tears, Vicki Rozema reports of an article written in 1828 by Elias Boudinot in which a chief from a Cherokee tribe explains how generous the Cherokees had been as he sits in the house of General Knox looking out his window at what once was free land where his people hunted and lived: "They [the white people] asked only to let them tie it [a great canoe] to a tree—we consented. They then said some of their people were sick, and they asked [to] put them under the shade of the trees," (4) and so the Cherokees consented. They kept consenting until everything they had was gone. Soon they were fighting to the death for the clothes on their back. Never before had the Cherokees encountered such an enemy. It was not enough for the Europeans to be satisfied with food and shelter; they wanted everything.

I am left with feeling guilt because I think like the European does. One is not enough; I want two. As the Cherokee nation died, so too did its teachings; *do unto others as they would do unto you* is a philosophy I was taught at an early age. The Cherokees understood this philosophy and applied it accordingly. The Europeans applied this philosophy as they saw fit. In most cases they had to receive in order to give. This is the "you scratch my back and I will scratch yours" mentality.

But despite my ambivalence, many others of Cherokee heritage are taking the initiative to keep our culture's heritage and traditions alive. Museums across the Carolinas (where the Cherokee nation originated) and Oklahoma (where I was born) commemorate both the livelihoods of the Cherokee peoples and the tragedies of the Trail of Tears. An effort to create a written language to preserve the rich Cherokee oral traditions of storytelling, genealogy, and folk wisdom is being perpetuated by the Internet.

It can be peculiar how the nature of human interaction can work. I am a descendant of European and Cherokee heritage because of events beyond any one person's control. Hundreds of years ago a big boat bumped into a peaceful nation of tribal people who were too generous in their offers. Today it is known as the United States of America. We are one of the strongest and largest nations in the world because of ruthless generals who wanted it all. Our history teaches us that George Washington and Benjamin Franklin liberated us from an unruly king and brought us a new world full of opportunity and prosperity. Although all of these statements are true, they do not tell us what it cost the world. From the very moment the first Europeans set foot on what they thought was India, the world lost a great nation of philosophical people. We are left with identification cards that remind us of the remnants of Cherokee blood pumping through the hearts of a select few.

Jennifer clearly explains how guilt affects her and admits that she aligns with her European roots. In the next paragraph, however, she shows her inclusion in her Native culture by stating those of Cherokee heritage are trying to keep "our" culture alive.

In her conclusion, Jennifer seems to reconcile the ambivalence she feels and leaves the reader with a final, provoking thought.

	a	e	i	o	u	v [ə]
	a	e	i	o	u	v
	ga · ka	ge	gi	go	gu	gv
	ha	he	hi	ho	hu	hv
	la	le	li	lo	lu	lv
	ma	me	mi	mo	mu	
	na · hna · nah	ne	ni	no	nu	nv
	qua	que	qui	quo	quu	quv
	s · sa	se	si	so	su	sv
	da · ta	de · te	di · ti	do	du	dv
	dla · tla	tle	tli	tlo	tlu	tlv
	tsa	tse	tsi	tso	tsu	tsv
	wa	we	wi	wo	wu	wv
	ya	ye	yi	yo	yu	yv

© Cengage Learning

FIGURE 9.2
Cherokee Syllabary

Works Cited

Leone, Bruno, and Brenda Stalcup, eds. *Native American Rights*. San Diego: Green
    Haven, 1998. Print.

Mooney, Thomas. *Exploring Your Cherokee Ancestry*. Park Hill: Cherokee National
    Historic Society, 1990. Print.

Perdue, Theda. *The Cherokees*. New York: Chelsea, 1989. Print.

Rozema, Vicki. *Voices From the Trail of Tears*. Winston: Blair, 2003. Print.

United States. Dept. of the Interior. *Indian Ancestry—Cherokee Indian Ancestry*. 10 Oct.
    2003. Web. 3 Nov. 2005.

"Cherokee syllabary." *Wikipedia*. Wikipedia Foundation, n.d. Web. 30 October 2005.

REFLECTION ON WRITING

Jennifer Wade chose to tell her story by using the first-person narrative. Had she chosen to compose her story in the third person, would it have been as effective? Why or why not? Here is how her introduction would sound in the third person:

Almost twenty-five years ago on Tuesday, December 2, 1980, around one o'clock in the morning, a woman gave birth to a baby girl in an Indian hospital. Shortly after her birth she received an identification card from the United States Department of the Interior Affairs Tahlequah Agency. Her identification card states that 5/64 of the red blood flowing through her veins is Cherokee Indian blood. She oftentimes wondered why the government issues identification cards to the chosen few who are a part of something that has become almost nonexistent. What happened in order for the American government to go to great extremes to acknowledge such small traces of a certain descent? Her identification card tells her who she is, yet she does not feel like a Cherokee Indian. Nor does she look like one.

Jennifer is successful in regard to providing her audience with transitional words and phrases that keep her narrative flowing smoothly—a skill that is particularly important in a comparison and contrast essay. Can you identify several of these transitions?

ALTERNATIVE WRITING PROJECT: COMPARING TWO REVIEWS

Find a recent review of a movie that you have seen or of a restaurant at which you have eaten. Compare the review with your experience. Do you agree with the reviewer? Identify specific examples of points you agree with and explain why. Do you disagree with the reviewer? Identify specific examples of these, too. Write an essay presenting your analysis of the review as it relates to your experience with the movie or at the restaurant.

CHAPTER 9 | Summary

- Perceptions are messages from the senses, whereas perspectives are points of view that develop from and also influence perceptions.
- We actively select our perspectives based on what has been called to our attention, what our needs or interests are, what our moods and feelings are, what seems familiar or unfamiliar, and what our backgrounds are.
- We naturally try to order and organize our perceptions into patterns and relationships that make sense to us; this is important for writing.
- Context, or the overall situation, plays a big role in how we interpret our perceptions.
- Your ways of viewing the world will develop and change through the experiences you have, the knowledge you acquire, and your reflections on your experiences and knowledge.
- To obtain more accurate perceptions, you should develop your awareness, get input from others, find evidence, and keep an open mind.
- You can use comparison and contrast to think critically and to organize your writing.

Although we suspect that an oil spill causes environmental damage and that the effects of an oil spill are far-reaching, scientific research and data analysis confirms our speculations. From there, carefully supported arguments and persuasive negotiations between environmental activists, fishermen and sporting groups, local governments, and industry result in solutions that are broadly supported and easier to implement. What are some of the causes and effects at play regarding an ecosystem or environment you are familiar with?

Writing to Speculate:
Exploring Cause and Effect

"The present contains nothing more than the past, and what is found in the effect was already in the cause."

—HENRI BERGSON

CRITICAL
THINKING FOCUS:
**Causal
reasoning**

WRITING FOCUS:
**Presenting
causal
reasoning**

READING THEME:
**Longevity and
society**

WRITING
ACTIVITIES:
**Causal
relationships**

WRITING PROJECT:
**Exploring
causes of a
recent event**

Previous chapters have examined thinking and writing patterns that help us make sense of the world. As we explore our world, we humans tend to ask why things are as they are: Why do some marriages endure for years and others end in divorce? Why does a coastal area of the country have relatively calm summers for several years and then experience a record-breaking hurricane? Why do certain political ideas take hold during particular periods of history?

When we contemplate such questions, we are asking about (1) *causes,* factors that contribute to events and bring them about, and (2) *effects,* events that result directly or indirectly from causes or from other events. Much thinking about causes and effects occurs in an impromptu way. For example, about a divorce, we might guess, "I think the marriage failed because of financial problems." Though that might, in fact, be one reason, other factors are probably also involved. Determining causes is complicated because

- An event may have more than one cause
- An event may have various types of causes
- Determining causes with certainty is often impossible

When we think about causal relationships in an organized way, ever conscious of the difficulty and uncertainty of the task, we are using a critical thinking process called *causal analysis.*

The Writing Project in this chapter asks you to find information about some causes of a recent event and then to write a paper in which you present this information. The chapter should help you to write effectively about causal relationships.

Kinds of Causal Relationships

Causal patterns of thinking involve relating events in terms of the influence or effect they have on one another. The following statements are all examples of causal statements.

- Since I was the last to leave, I turned off the lights.
- Taking plenty of vitamin C really cured that terrible cold I had.
- I accidentally toasted my hand along with the marshmallows by getting too near the campfire.

343

In these statements, the words *since, turned off, cured,* and *getting too near* all point to the fact that something has caused something else to take place.

Words That Indicate Cause and Effect

Cause	*Effect*
because	because of
reason(s), for this reason (these reasons)	as a result, result, resulted in
affect, effect (verb)	consequently, consequence
bring about	therefore
a factor in	since
cure, infect	thus
lead, lead to	accordingly
produce (verb)	happens whenever
encourage, encouragement	follows from, follows that
discourage	ensues
influence	
solve	

What additional cause and effect words can you think of?

You are probably realizing that you make causal statements all the time and that you are constantly thinking in terms of causal relationships. In fact, the goal of much of your thinking is to figure out why something happened or how something came about. One advantage of causal analysis is that it enables you to make reasonable predictions because you are able to clarify the causal relationships involved and make predictions based on your understanding.

The purpose of much of your academic writing will be causal analysis, to demonstrate that you fully understand either the factors contributing to a specific situation or result (for example, why a certain genetic mutation leads to Type I diabetes in humans) or the effects of particular behaviors (for example, why a combination of poor eating habits and lack of exercise can bring on Type II diabetes in susceptible adolescents and adults). Your audience may at first be your professor, but it's clear that this kind of thinking and the writing it produces will be useful in the workplace and the community as well. Thinking carefully and skeptically about causes and effects is excellent training for your further research, and it will help you to solve complex problems and make well-informed decisions.

Causal Chain

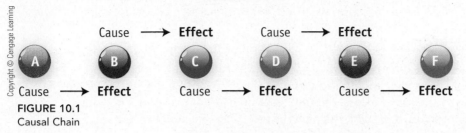

FIGURE 10.1
Causal Chain

Although you may think of causes and effects in isolation—A caused B—in reality, causes and effects rarely appear by themselves. There is not just one cause of a resulting effect; there is a whole string of causes, as illustrated by the structures in Figure 10.1. These interrelated causes form more complex patterns, including three that we will examine next: *causal chains, contributory causes,* and *interactive causes.*

CAUSAL CHAINS

Consider the following scenario:

Your paper on the topic "life span and poverty" is due on Monday morning. You have reserved the whole weekend to work on it and are just getting started when the phone rings. A favorite childhood friend is in town and wants to stay with you for the weekend. You say *yes.* By Sunday night, you've had a great weekend but have made little progress on your paper. You brew a pot of coffee and get started. At 3:00 a.m., you are too exhausted to continue. Deciding to get a few hours' sleep, you set the alarm clock for 6:00 a.m., giving yourself plenty of time to finish up. When you wake up, it's nine o'clock; the alarm failed to go off. Your class starts in 40 minutes. You have no chance of getting the paper done on time. On your way to class, you mentally review the causes of this disaster. No longer concerned about life after death, you are very worried about your own longevity after this class!

- What causes in this situation are responsible for your paper's being late?
- What do you think is the single most important cause?
- What do you think your instructor will identify as the most important cause? Why?

A *causal chain,* as illustrated by the preceding example, is a situation in which one thing leads to another, which then leads to another, and so on over a period of time. In writing about causal chains, your narrative would use chronological ordering (see page 220 in Chapter 7). There is not just one cause of the resulting effect. Which event or circumstance in the chain is the "tipping point," the most important contributing factor to the effect? Your answer will depend on your perspective on the situation. You might see the cause of the unfinished paper as a defective alarm clock. Your instructor, though, might see the cause of the problem as overall lack of planning.

Thinking-Writing Activity

CREATING A CAUSAL CHAIN

1. Create a scenario in which you make a series of decisions that culminates in a significant conclusion. For example, your decision to take a course outside of your major might lead to a conversation with the professor, which leads you to explore a career option that you had not previously considered, and so on. The scenario might be based on an actual experience in your life or one created through your imagination. Detail your scenario in a full paragraph or two.

2. Review the scenario you have just created. In a new paragraph, explain how the "real" cause of the final effect could vary depending on your perspective on the situation.

CONTRIBUTORY CAUSES

In addition to operating in causal chains over a period of time, causes can work simultaneously to produce an effect. This results in a situation in which a number of different *contributory causes* bring something about. Instead of working in isolation, each cause contributes to bringing about the final effect. When this situation occurs, each cause serves to support and reinforce the action of the other causes, a condition illustrated in Figure 10.2.

Consider the following situation:

It is the end of the term, and you have been working incredibly hard at school—writing papers, preparing for exams, finishing up course projects. You haven't been

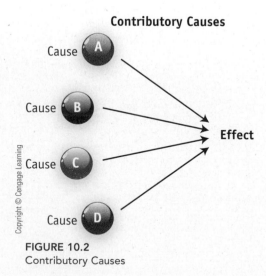

FIGURE 10.2
Contributory Causes

getting enough sleep, and you haven't been eating regular, well-balanced meals. To make matters worse, you have been under intense pressure in your personal life, having serious arguments with the person you have been dating, and this situation is constantly on your mind. It is the middle of the flu season, and many people you know have been sick with various respiratory infections. Walking home one evening, you get soaked by an unexpected downpour. By the time you get home, you are shivering. You soon find yourself in bed with a thermometer in your mouth—you are sick!

What was the "cause" of your illness? In this situation, you can see that evidently a combination of factors led to your physical breakdown: low resistance, getting wet and chilled, being exposed to various germs and viruses, physical exhaustion, lack of proper eating, and so on. Taken by itself, no one factor might have been enough to cause your illness. Together, they all contributed to the final outcome. The readings on the genetic modification of food crops later in this chapter demonstrate the complexity of interrelated causes.

Thinking-Writing Activity

CREATING A CAUSAL CHAIN

Create a similar scenario, and in a paragraph or two, detail the contributory causes that led to your asking someone for a date, choosing a major, losing or winning a game, or another effect.

INTERACTIVE CAUSES

Causes rarely operate in isolation but instead often influence (and are influenced by) other factors. Imagine that you are scheduled to give a PowerPoint presentation to a large group of people. As your moment at the podium approaches, you become anxious, which results in a dry mouth and throat, making your voice sound more like a croak. The prospect of sounding like a bullfrog increases your anxiety, which, in turn, dries your mouth and constricts your throat further, reducing your croak to something much worse—silence.

Different factors can relate to each other through reciprocal influences that flow back and forth from one to the other. Understanding this type of *interactive causal relationship* helps you to organize and make sense of your experiences. For instance, to comprehend social relationships (families, teams, groups of friends), you consider the complex ways in which each individual influences—and is influenced by—all the other members of the group. Student Daniel Eggers explored the complex, interactive causal relationships that continue to affect poverty in the African-American community decades after Dr. Martin Luther King Jr.'s "I Have a Dream" speech (page 185 in Chapter 6). Understanding biological systems and other systems is similar to understanding social systems. To comprehend and explain how an organ such as the heart, liver, or brain functions, you

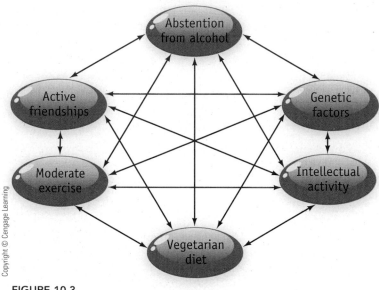

Copyright © Cengage Learning

FIGURE 10.3
Interactive Causes

have to describe its complex, interactive relationships with all the other parts of the biological system. Figure 10.3 illustrates these dynamic causal relationships.

Thinking-Writing Activity

IDENTIFYING CAUSAL PATTERNS

Read the following three passages, which illustrate causal patterns of thinking. For each passage, identify the kind of causal relationship (chain, contributory, or interactive). Draw a chart or figure that illustrates this relationship, and explain how the causes are related to one another.

1. Nothing posed a more serious threat to the bald eagle's survival than a modern chemical compound called DDT. Around 1940, a retired Canadian banker named Charles L. Broley began keeping track of eagles nesting in Florida. Each breeding season, he climbed into more than 50 nests, counted the eaglets and put metal bands on their legs. In the late 1940s, a sudden drop-off in the number of young produced led him to conclude that 80 percent of his birds were sterile. Broley blamed DDT. Scientists later discovered that DDE, a breakdown product of DDT, causes not sterility, but a fatal thinning of eggshell among birds of prey. Applied on cropland all over the United States, the pesticide was running off into waterways where it concentrated in fish. The bald eagles ate the fish and the DDT impaired their ability to reproduce. They were not alone, of course. Ospreys and pelicans suffered similar setbacks.—Jim Doherty, "The Bald Eagle and DDT"

2. It is popularly accepted that Hitler was the major cause of World War II, but the ultimate causes go much deeper than one personality. First, there were long-standing German grievances against reparations levied on the nation following its defeat in World War I. Second, there were severe economic strains that caused resentment among the German people. Third, there was French and English reluctance to work out a sound disarmament policy and American noninvolvement in the matter. Finally, there was the European fear that communism was a much greater danger than National Socialism. These factors contributed to the outbreak of World War II.—Gilbert Muller, *The American College Handbook*

3. You crunch and chew your way through vast quantities of snacks and confectioneries and relieve your thirst with multicolored, flavored soft drinks, with and without calories, for two basic reasons. The first is simple; the food tastes good, and you enjoy the sensation of eating it. Second, you associate these foods, often without being aware of it, with the highly pleasurable experiences depicted in the advertisements used to promote their sale. Current television advertisements demonstrate this point: people turn from grumpiness to euphoria after crunching a corn chip. Others water ski into the sunset with their loved ones while drinking a popular soft drink. People entertain on the patio with friends, cook over campfires without mosquitoes, or go to carnivals with granddad munching away at the latest candy or snack food. The people portrayed in these scenarios are all healthy, vigorous, and good looking; one wonders how popular the food they convince you to eat would be if they would crunch or drink away while complaining about low back pain or clogged sinuses.—Judith Wurtman, *Eating Your Way Through Life*

Ways of Testing Causes

NECESSARY CONDITION AND SUFFICIENT CONDITION

In addition to the three patterns of causality we have just examined, we need to consider necessary and sufficient conditions. A *necessary condition* is a factor that is required to bring about a certain result: for example, an intact light bulb is required for a lamp's illumination. However, by itself, an intact light bulb is not sufficient to provide illumination: you also need electricity, which is another necessary condition.

A *sufficient condition* is a factor that of itself is always sufficient for bringing about a certain result. For example, a pinch on the arm is a sufficient cause for discomfort. Of course, even with a sufficient condition, there may be an additional necessary condition, or several necessary conditions, for a result to occur. Having healthy nerves in the arm and being conscious are two necessary conditions for someone's feeling a sensation when pinched on the arm.

favorite shirt) has some influence on the other event (winning the game). As a result, you may continue to wear this shirt "for good luck." It is easy to see how this sort of mistaken thinking can lead to all sorts of superstitious beliefs. Consider the following causal conclusion arrived at by Mark Twain's fictional character Huckleberry Finn in the following passage. How would you analyze his conclusion?

> I've always reckoned that looking at the new moon over your left shoulder is one of the carelessest and foolishest things a body can do. Old Hank Bunker done it once, and bragged about it; and in less than two years he got drunk and fell off a shot tower and spread himself out so that he was just a kind of layer. . . . But anyway, it all came of looking at the moon that way, like a fool.

Can you identify any of your own superstitious beliefs or practices that may have resulted from *post hoc* thinking?

SLIPPERY SLOPE

The causal fallacy of *slippery slope* is illustrated in the following advice:

> Don't miss that first deadline, because if you do, it won't be long before you're missing all your deadlines. This will spread to the rest of your life, as you will be late for every appointment. This terminal procrastination will ruin your career, and friends and relatives will abandon you. You will end up a lonely failure who is unable to ever do anything on time.

Slippery slope thinking asserts that one undesirable action will inevitably lead to a worse action, which will necessarily lead to still a worse one, all the way down the "slippery slope" to some terrible disaster at the bottom. Although this progression may indeed occur, there certainly is no causal guarantee that it will. Create slippery slope scenarios for one of the following warnings:

- If you get behind on one credit card payment . . .
- If you fail that first test . . .
- If you eat that first potato chip . . .

Summary: Causal Fallacies

Questionable Cause:	Presenting a causal relationship for which no real evidence exists
Misidentification of Cause:	Uncertainty about what is the cause and what is the effect: ignoring a common cause, assuming a false common cause

Post Hoc Ego Propter Hoc:	Assuming a causal relationship between situations occurring closely together in time
Slippery Slope:	Asserting that one undesirable action will lead to a worse action, which will lead to still a worse one—down, down the slippery slope

Thinking-Writing Activity

DIAGNOSING CAUSAL FALLACIES

Review the four causal fallacies just described; then identify and explain the errors of reasoning illustrated in the following five examples. Write at least one full sentence for each example.

1. The person who won the lottery says she dreamed the winning numbers. I'm going to start writing down the numbers that I dream about.

2. Yesterday I forgot to take my vitamins, and I immediately got sick. That mistake won't occur again!

3. I'm warning you: if you miss a class, it won't be long before you flunk out of school and ruin your future.

4. I always take the first seat in the bus. Today I took another seat, and the bus broke down.

5. I think the reason I'm not doing well in school is that I simply don't have enough time to study, and my classes aren't interesting, either.

Detecting Causal Claims

Sometimes people use causal reasoning because they want us to see cause-and-effect relationships that they believe exist. When they do this, we say they are making *causal claims*. Consider the following examples.

1. Politicians assure us that a vote for them will result in better schools and lower taxes.

2. Advertisers tell us that using a detergent will leave our wash "cleaner than clean, whiter than white."

3. Doctors tell us that eating a balanced diet will result in a longer life.

4. Educators tell us that a college degree is worth an average of $830,000 additional income over an individual's lifetime.

5. Utility companies inform us that using nuclear energy will result in less pollution.

In each of these examples, certain causal claims are being made about how the world operates in an effort to persuade us to adopt a certain point of view. As critical thinkers, it is our responsibility to evaluate these various causal claims to determine whether they are valid or questionable.

Thinking-Writing Activity

EVALUATING CAUSAL CLAIMS

Explain how you might go about evaluating the causal claims listed above. To get you started, here is an example of how a critical thinker/thoughtful writer might approach the first claim:

- *Example:* Electing politicians and claims about getting better schools and lower taxes.

- *Evaluation:* Speak to teachers and principals about school needs. Understand what a politician in a specific office can and cannot do about education. Learn about budgets for school systems. Remember your own school experiences, and think about why they were good or bad. Learn about taxes and schools in your area.

EXPLORING CAUSE AND EFFECT: MODERN AGRICULTURE AND SOCIAL IMPACT

The impact of human civilization on the environment has taken on increasing urgency as global warming, the razing of rain forests, the search for sustainable fuel sources, and our dependence on factory-farmed or genetically modified food are discussed and debated in the media. All these factors affect the most basic aspects of our lives, from the quality of our air to the safety of our next meal. In the following article, "GMOs: Fooling—Er, 'Feeding'—the World for 20 Years," GRAIN argues that GMOs are doing more damage than good, and that most of what large corporations tell the public is false. Next, in "Do Seed Companies Control GM Crop Research?" the editors of *Scientific American* bemoan the fact that seed companies control GMO crop research, making it nearly impossible to evaluate the claims and risks of having GMOs in our food supply. In counterpoint to these perspectives is the article "Eating the Genes" in which Richard Manning argues that genetically modified food is an essential strategy in developing countries, the risks of which are of less consequence that the alternatives of starvation and malnutrition. As you read these articles, watch for the authors' development of different kinds of causal connections, and evaluate the clarity and effectiveness of their arguments.

GMOs: Fooling—Er, "Feeding"—the World for 20 Years

Myths and outright lies about the alleged benefits of genetically engineered crops (GE crops or GMOs) persist only because the multinationals that profit from them have put so much effort into spreading them around.

They want you to believe that GMOs will feed the world; that they are more productive; that they will eliminate the use of agrichemicals; that they can coexist with other crops, and that they are perfectly safe for humans and the environment.

False in every case, and in this article we'll show how easy it is to debunk these myths. All it takes is a dispassionate, objective look at twenty years of commercial GE planting and the research that supposedly backs it up. The conclusion is clear: GMOs are part of the problem, not part of the solution.

MYTH: GE crops will end world hunger

FACT: GE crops have nothing to do with ending world hunger, no matter how much GE spokespeople like to expound on this topic. Three comments give the lie to their claim:

- FAO data clearly show that the world produces plenty of food to feed everyone, year after year. Yet hunger is still with us. That's because hunger is not primarily a question of productivity but of access to arable land and resources. Put bluntly: Hunger is caused by poverty and exclusion.

- Today's commercial GE crops weren't designed to fight hunger in the first place. They aren't even mainly for human consumption. Practically the entire area planted to GE crops consists of soybeans, corn, canola, and cotton. The first three of these are used almost exclusively to make cattle feed, car fuel, and industrial oils for the United States and Europe, while cotton goes into clothing.

- More damning, there appears to be an iniquitous cause-and-effect relationship between GE crops and rural hunger. In countries like Brazil and Argentina, gigantic "green deserts" of corn and soybeans invade peasants' land, depriving them—or outright robbing them—of their means of subsistence. The consequence is hunger, abject poverty, and agrotoxin poisoning for rural people. The truth is that GE crops are edging out food on millions of hectares of fertile farmland.

In the year GMO seeds were first planted, 800 million people worldwide were hungry. Today, with millions of hectares of GMOs in production, 1 billion are hungry. When exactly do these crops start "feeding the world"?

MYTH: GE crops are more productive

FACT: Not true. Look at the data from the country with the longest experience of GMOs: the United States. In the most extensive and rigorous study, the Union of Concerned Scientists analyzed twenty years of GE crops and concluded that genetically engineered herbicide-tolerant soybeans and corn are no more productive than conventional plants and methods. Furthermore, 86% of the corn productivity increases obtained in the past

Source: GMOs: Fooling—Er, "Feeding"—The World for 20 years (GRAIN, 15 May 2013).

twenty years have been due to conventional methods and practices. Other studies have found GE productivity to be lower than conventional.

Crop plants are complex living beings, not Lego blocks. Their productivity is a function of multiple genetic and environmental factors, not some elusive "productivity gene." You can't just flip a genetic switch and turn on high productivity, nor would any responsible genetic engineer make such a claim. Even after all this time, GE methods are quite rudimentary. Proponents of the technology count it a success if they manage to transfer even two or three functional genes into one plant.

The bottom line is that twenty years and untold millions of dollars of research have resulted in a grand total of two marketable traits—herbicide tolerance and Bt pest resistance (see below). Neither has anything to do with productivity.

MYTH: GE crops will eliminate agrichemicals

FACT: It's the reverse: GE crops increase the use of harmful agrichemicals. Industry people try to put this myth over by touting the "Bt gene" from the Bacillus thuringiensis bacteria, which produces a toxin lethal to some corn and cotton worms. The plants produce their own pesticide, supposedly obviating the need to spray. But with such large areas planted to Bt monocultures, the worms have quickly developed resistance to Bt; worse, a host of formerly unknown secondary pests now have to be controlled with more chemicals.

The other innovation trumpeted by the "genetically modified corporations" consists of plants that can withstand high doses of herbicides. This allows vast monocultures to be sprayed from the air, year after year on the same site. It's a convenience for industrial farmers that has abetted the spectacular expansion of soybeans in recent years. Thirty years ago there were no soybeans in Argentina; now they take up half the country's arable land. Concurrently, the amount of the herbicide glyphosate sprayed in Argentina has skyrocketed from 8 million litres in 1995 to over 200 million litres today—a twentyfold increase, all for use in GE soy production.

The same thing is happening in the United States. Herbicide-tolerant GMOs have opened the floodgates, and glyphosate and other herbicides are pouring through onto farmers' fields. In 2011, US farmers using this type of GMO sprayed 24% more herbicides than their colleagues planting conventional seeds. Why? For reasons any evolutionary biologist could have predicted: the weeds are evolving chemical resistance. In short, the GE "revolution" is an environmental problem, not a solution.

MYTH: Farmers can decide for themselves. After all, GMOs can peacefully coexist with other crops

It sure doesn't look that way. GE boosters may claim nobody's forcing farmers to use GMOs, but a pesky little fact of basic biology implicates non-GE farmers against their will. It's called cross-pollination: Plants of the same species interbreed, and sooner or later the genes artificially inserted in the GE crops cross into the conventional crops.

In Canada, the widespread growing of genetically engineered canola has contaminated nearly all the conventional canola and in so doing wiped out organic canola production. Similar contamination has been found in corn crops around the world.

The introduction of GE seed is especially alarming when there is potential for contamination of local varieties. Mexico is the centre of origin and diversification of corn. For years now, Mexican indigenous communities have been noticing odd traits appearing in some of their varieties. Various studies confirm that this is because of contamination by GE corn imported from the United States. Now, the Mexican government is proposing to allow multinationals to plant up to 2.4 million ha of GE corn in the country. If this project goes ahead, it will not only be an attack on the food sovereignty of the Mexican people: it will be a threat to the biodiversity of one of the world's most important staple food crops.

In the Spanish state of Aragón, farm and environmental organizations have been complaining since 2005 that over 40% of organic grain has traces of GE content and can no longer be sold as organic or GMO-free.

What's really perverse about this fake "freedom to farm" argument is that certain transnationals have been forcing farmers to pay for seeds they never planted. In the United States, Monsanto has taken hundreds of farmers to court for supposedly infringing its intellectual-property rights. Monsanto detectives roam the countryside like debt collectors, looking for "their genes" in farmers' fields. In many cases, the genes got there because the farmers either purchased contaminated seed or had their own crops contaminated by a neighbour's field. Whatever the case, it's a lucrative strategy that has brought in millions of extra dollars for the corporation. And it has the added benefit of scaring farmers away from buying anything but Monsanto seeds. Sounds a lot more like the "freedom" to do exactly what the multinationals tell you to.

MYTH: GE crops pose no threat to health and the environment

At the very least, the biosafety of transgenic crops is an open question. Do we really want to entrust our health to an industrial agriculture system in which GE purveyors control food security offices and dictate their own standards? I don't think so. Food sovereignty requires that the people, not the companies, have control over what we eat.

Nevertheless, our plates are now filling up with food items from plants with altered DNA and heavy pesticide loads, and we are told to simply shut up and eat. Concerns have been heightened by a number of credible reports on GMOs and their attendant herbicides:

- The American Academy of Environmental Medicine (AAEM) stated in 2009 that genetically engineered foods "pose a serious health risk." Citing various studies, it concluded that "there is more than a casual association between GE foods and adverse health effects" and that these foods "pose a serious health risk in the areas of toxicology, allergy and immune function, reproductive health, and metabolic, physiologic and genetic health."

- The latest studies by Dr. Gilles-Éric Séralini looked at rats fed glyphosate-tolerant GE maize for two years. These rats showed greater and earlier mortality in addition to hormonal effects, mammary tumors in females, and liver and kidney disease.

- A recent study at the University of Leipzig (Germany) found high concentrations of glyphosate, the main ingredient in Roundup, in urine samples from city dwellers— from 5 to 20 times greater than the limit for drinking water.

- Professor Andrés Carrasco of the CONICET-UBA Molecular Embryology Lab at the University of Buenos Aires medical school (Argentina) has unveiled a study showing that glyphosate herbicides cause malformations in frog and chicken embryos at doses much lower than those used in agriculture. The malformations were of a type similar to those observed in human embryos exposed to these herbicides.

Finally, there is the incontrovertible evidence that glyphosate can have a direct impact on human beings, causing abortions, illnesses, and even death in high enough doses, as explained by Sofia Gatica, the Argentine winner of the latest Goldman prize. Our health is ours to defend, and so are our farms, and so is the health of the food supply that will nourish the generations to come. Food sovereignty now!

QUESTION FOR READING ACTIVELY

1. "GMOs: Fooling—Er, 'Feeding'—the World for 20 Years" deconstructs the notion that genetically modified crops and foods will end hunger, will eliminate agrichemicals, and are safe. How does the writer debunk these myths? Highlight the words and phrases that indicate rebuttal on behalf of the writer.

QUESTIONS FOR THINKING CRITICALLY

1. Identify any causal patterns you observe in this essay (for example, causal chains, contributory causes, and interactive causes), and describe their relationships.

2. According to this article, eating genetically modified food puts our health at serious risk. What evidence is used to support this assertion? Do you agree or disagree with this assertion? You may want to use several additional sources to support your ideas.

QUESTION FOR WRITING THOUGHTFULLY

1. This essay points out that "there appears to be an iniquitous cause-and-effect relationship between GE crops and rural hunger. In countries like Brazil and Argentina, gigantic 'green deserts' of corn and soybeans invade peasants' land, depriving them—or outright robbing them—of their means of subsistence. The consequence is hunger, abject poverty, and agrotoxin poisoning for rural people. The truth is that GE crops are edging out food on millions of hectares of fertile farmland." If the consequence is hunger, abject poverty, and agrotoxin poisoning for rural people, how might these issues increase in severity over time? Describe what our world might look like in a worst-case scenario.

Do Seed Companies Control GM Crop Research?

by the Editors of *Scientific American*

Advances in agricultural technology—including, but not limited to, the genetic modification of food crops—have made fields more productive than ever. Farmers grow more crops and feed more people using less land. They are able to use fewer pesticides and to reduce the amount of tilling that leads to erosion. And within the next two years, agritech companies plan to introduce advanced crops that are designed to survive heat waves and droughts, resilient characteristics that will become increasingly important in a world marked by a changing climate.

Unfortunately, it is impossible to verify that genetically modified crops perform as advertised. That is because agritech companies have given themselves veto power over the work of independent researchers.

To purchase genetically modified seeds, a customer must sign an agreement that limits what can be done with them. (If you have installed software recently, you will recognize the concept of the end-user agreement.) Agreements are considered necessary to protect a company's intellectual property, and they justifiably preclude the replication of the genetic enhancements that make the seeds unique. But agritech companies such as Monsanto, Pioneer and Syngenta go further. For a decade their user agreements have explicitly forbidden the use of the seeds for any independent research. Under the threat of litigation, scientists cannot test a seed to explore the different conditions under which it thrives or fails. They cannot compare seeds from one company against those from another company. And perhaps most important, they cannot examine whether the genetically modified crops lead to unintended environmental side effects.

Research on genetically modified seeds is still published, of course. But only studies that the seed companies have approved ever see the light of a peer-reviewed journal. In a number of cases, experiments that had the implicit go-ahead from the seed company were later blocked from publication because the results were not flattering. "It is important to understand that it is not always simply a matter of blanket denial of all research requests, which is bad enough," wrote Elson J. Shields, an entomologist at Cornell University, in a letter to an official at the Environmental Protection Agency (the body tasked with regulating the environmental consequences of genetically modified crops), "but selective denials and permissions based on industry perceptions of how 'friendly' or 'hostile' a particular scientist may be toward [seed enhancement] technology."

Shields is the spokesperson for a group of 24 corn insect scientists that opposes these practices. Because the scientists rely on the cooperation of the companies for their research—they must, after all, gain access to the seeds for studies—most have chosen to remain anonymous for fear of reprisals. The group has submitted a statement to the EPA protesting that "as a result of restricted access, no truly independent research can be legally conducted on many critical questions regarding the technology."

It would be chilling enough if any other type of company were able to prevent independent researchers from testing its wares and reporting what they find—imagine car companies trying to quash head-to-head model comparisons done by Consumer Reports, for example. But when scientists are prevented from examining the raw ingredients in our nation's food supply or from testing the plant material that covers a large portion of the country's agricultural land, the restrictions on free inquiry become dangerous.

Although we appreciate the need to protect the intellectual property rights that have spurred the investments into research and development that have led to agritech's successes, we also believe food safety and environmental protection depend on making plant products available to regular scientific scrutiny. Agricultural technology companies should therefore immediately remove the restriction on research from their end-user agreements. Going forward, the EPA should also require, as a condition of approving the sale of new seeds, that independent researchers have unfettered access to all products currently on the market. The agricultural revolution is too important to keep locked behind closed doors.

QUESTION FOR READING ACTIVELY

1. The editors of *Scientific American* are extremely concerned that, because agritech companies such as Monsanto, Pioneer, and Syngenta control research on the efficacy and dangers of GMOs, they alone decide who can do the research, the nature of the research, and the publication of the research findings. Why do the editors feel this is a practice of grave concern?

QUESTIONS FOR THINKING CRITICALLY

1. The editors declare, "It would be chilling enough if any other type of company were able to prevent independent researchers from testing its wares and reporting what they find—imagine car companies trying to quash head-to-head model comparisons done by Consumer Reports." Given the recent and growing uproar over genetically modified crops and the dangers they present to our health and environment, do you think agritech companies will be forced to become more forthright and transparent with their reporting and business practices? Explain your thoughts.

2. Seed companies contend that these GMOs increase crop yield and reduce the use of pesticides. Has that proved to be the case? Why or why not? Refer to at least two sources to support your ideas.

QUESTION FOR WRITING THOUGHTFULLY

1. Are you concerned about the findings and assertions in this and the previous article regarding the risks of the food we are eating? If so, what steps might you take to address this risk?

Eating the Genes: What the Green Revolution Did for Grain, Biotechnology May Do for Protein

by Richard Manning

Fears that genetically engineered foods will damage the environment have fueled controversy in the developed world. The debate looks very different when framed not by corporations and food activists but by three middle-aged women in saris working in a Spartan lab in Pune, India. The three, each with a doctoral degree and a full career in biological research, are studying the genes of chickpeas, but they begin their conversation by speaking of suicides.

The villain in their discussion is an insidious little worm, a pod borer, which makes its way unseen into the ripening chickpea pods and eats the peas. It comes every year, laying waste to some fields while sparing others. Subsistence farmers expecting a bumper crop instead find the fat pods hollow at harvest. Dozens will then kill themselves rather than face the looming hunger of their families. So while the battle

Source: "Eating the Gene," by Richard Manning, July 2001, in *Technology*, published by MIT Review, http://www.technologyreview.com/Biotech/12499/. Copyright Technology Review 2001.

wages over "frankenfood" in the well-fed countries of the world, here in this Pune lab the arguments quietly disappear.

A generation ago the world faced starvation, and India served as the poster child for the coming plague, occupying roughly the same position in international consciousness then that sub-Saharan Africa does today. The Green Revolution of the 1960s changed all that, with massive increases in grain production, especially in India, a country that now produces enough wheat, rice, sorghum, and maize to feed its people. Green Revolution methods, however, concentrated on grains, ignoring such crops as chickpeas and lentils, the primary sources of protein in the country's vegetarian diet. As a consequence, per capita production of carbohydrates from grain in India tripled. At the same time, largely because of population growth, per capita protein production halved.

The gains in grain yield came largely from breeding plants with shorter stems, which could support heavier and more bountiful seed heads. To realize this opportunity, farmers poured on nitrogen and water: globally, there was a sevenfold increase in fertilizer use between 1950 and 1990. Now, artificial sources of nitrogen, mostly from fertilizer, add more to the planet's nitrogen cycle than natural sources, contributing to global warming, ozone depletion, and smog. Add to this the massive loads of pesticides used against insects drawn to this bulging monoculture of grain, and one begins to see the rough outlines of environmental damage the globe cannot sustain.

During this same revolutionary period, India and other countries, including Mexico, Brazil, Chile, and Cuba, developed scientific communities capable of addressing many of their own food problems. High on their list is the promise of genetic engineering (see "New Markets for Biotech"). In India, researchers have found a natural resistance to pod borers in two other crops, the Asian bean and peanuts, and are trying to transfer the responsible gene to chickpeas. If they are successful, farmers will not only get more protein; they will also avoid insecticides. "The farmer has not to spray anything, has not to dust anything," D. R. Bapat, a retired plant breeder, told me. He need only plant a new seed.

This is the simple fact that makes genetic modification so attractive in the developing world. Seeds are packages of genes and genes are information—exceedingly valuable and powerful information. Biotech corporations can translate that information into profits. Yet when those same packets of power are developed by public-sector scientists in places like India, they become a tool, not for profit, but for quickly distributing important information. There is no more efficient means of spreading information than a seed.

The above argument built only slowly in my mind in the course of researching a book (*Food's Frontier: The Next Green Revolution*) that profiled nine food projects in the developing world, all of which were carried out largely by scientists native to the countries I visited. I expected to encounter low-technology projects appropriate for the primitive conditions of subsistence agriculture in the developing world—and I did. But I also found, in all nine cases, a sophisticated and equally appropriate use of genetic research or genetic engineering.

A lab in Uganda, for example, could not regularly flush its toilets for lack of running water, but could tag DNA. This tagging ability, used in six of the projects I studied, allows researchers to understand and accelerate the breeding of new strains. Typically, an effort to breed a disease- or pest-resistant strain of a crop can involve ten years of testing to verify the trait. Using genetic markers cuts that time in half—a difference that gains urgency in countries where test plots are surrounded by poor farmers whose crops are failing for want of that very trait.

In this manner, by allowing researchers to accelerate the development of new, pest-resistant sources of protein, genetic engineering can help fulfill the decades-old promise of the Green Revolution. Our last revolution created a world awash in grain. But if Uganda is to get better sweet potatoes, Peru better mashua, and India better chickpeas, then research on those orphan crops will have to catch up rapidly. Biotechnology can help.

Food researchers in developing countries are understandably worried they will be hampered by the controversy over genetically modified foods. Meanwhile, they have a hard time understanding why genetic engineering is the focus of such concern. The gains of the Green Revolution, after all—and for that matter the gains of 10,000 years of agriculture—have in many cases come from mating unrelated species of plants to create something new and better. Every new strain has brought with it the potential dangers now being ascribed with apparent exclusivity to genetic engineering, such as the creation of superresistant pests. Genetic engineering merely refines the tools.

When viewed from labs surrounded by subsistence farmers, where food research is a matter of life and death rather than an intellectual debate, genetic engineering is a qualified good—not without problems and dangers, but still of great promise. Genetic modification of foods becomes a natural extension of the millennia-old practice of plant breeding, less environmentally damaging than many modern alternatives. In the end, DNA is knowledge, which we can hope will build to wisdom, from which we may one day create an agriculture that both supports our population and coexists peacefully with our planet.

QUESTION FOR READING ACTIVELY

1. Richard Manning's perspective in "Eating the Genes" is quite different from the perspectives presented in the two previous essays. Describe some of the differences, and identify any causal relationships you observed while reading.

QUESTIONS FOR THINKING CRITICALLY

1. Manning claims that in developing countries, the risks to the environment or people posed by genetically engineered foods are of much less consequence than the reality of starvation and suicides by farmers whose crops are ruined by insects. Do you agree with the point he is making? Why or why not?

2. In contrast to developed countries like the United States and those in Europe where biotechnology is controlled by large, profit-oriented biotech corporations, in developing countries sophisticated native public-sector scientists are developing new disease-resistant and pest-resistant biotech crops for their countries. Which approach to biotechnology is better? Why?

QUESTION FOR WRITING THOUGHTFULLY

1. Given what you have learned about genetically modified crops and foods so far, define and describe your perspective on the issue (whether you are in favor of genetically modified crops and foods or against them), and justify your claims.

Writing Thoughtfully About Causal Relationships

Clearly, because of the complexity of determining cause and effect, writing a causal analysis requires special care. Causal analyses range all the way from rigorous scientific studies that can establish causes with some degree of certainty to theorizing about events in our personal lives. The causal analysis assignments you will encounter in college are likely to be of two types: those for which you conduct some kind of study to determine causality and then report your results, and those for which you research what others have said about the causes of an event and report their findings.

For the first type, you are likely to be given a format, such as for a lab report or an experimental design. It will be important for you to follow directions as you plan and conduct your study, and important for you to observe the conventions of the discipline in which you are writing as you prepare your report. Models are extremely helpful, so study them carefully if your professor provides them. If not, ask a librarian for guidance.

The second type, in which you report what others have said about the causes of an event, can be structured as an essay. Daniel Eggers' thoughtful analysis on page 371 is an example of such an essay. If you consult other sources of information, you must properly cite and document those sources (see the appendix).

Writing Project

EXPLORING SOME CAUSES OF A RECENT EVENT

This chapter has included both readings and Thinking-Writing Activities that encourage you to think about causal relationships in your own life and in the environment. Be sure to reread what you wrote for those activities; you may be able to use some of the material when completing this project.

Project Overview and Requirements

Write an essay in which you report and discuss some of the causes of a specific local or national event that occurred within the last three years. You might want to choose an event that had an environmental impact, or, depending on your interests or your instructor's directions, you might want to write about something else that has affected the lives of many people (such as a recent Supreme Court decision or a current national or international crisis).

For this project, you must conduct research and make sure your research is based on reliable sources. Look ahead to the "Checklist for Evaluating the Quality of Internet Resources" in Chapter 14 on pages 545–546 for helpful tips. Include material from two to four sources, being certain to cite and document each source accurately.

After you have drafted your essay, revise it to the best of your ability. Follow your instructor's directions for topic choices, length, format, documentation style, and so on.

Before you choose a topic and begin researching, read The Writing Situation and The Writing Process sections below, and consider the key elements in the Thinking-Writing Model (pages 5–8). You should also read the essay by Daniel Eggers, a student who wrote a causal analysis—"Was It Only a Dream?"—on page 371.

THE WRITING SITUATION

Purpose   You have a variety of purposes here. You can satisfy your own curiosity about why an event occurred and explain the causes to others. You can improve your ability to think critically about causal relationships. You can hone your revision skills by working through the revision questions that follow.

Audience   You have a range of readers within your audience. *You* are an important audience, since, through researching and analyzing causes, you can become a better thinker and possibly a more concerned citizen. Your classmates can be a valuable audience for review of a draft, reacting as intelligent readers who are not as knowledgeable as you about the causes of this event. Others interested in the event may find your essay enlightening. Finally, your instructor remains the audience who will judge how well you have planned, drafted, and revised. As a writing teacher, he or she cares about a clear focus, logical organization, specific details and examples, accurate documentation of sources, and correctness. Your classmates and your instructor will be interested in how you have applied this chapter's ideas.

Subject   You should reflect on the event or issue in terms of its causes and effects on the community. For example, if you decide to write about an event such as Hurricane Katrina (which had a disproportionate effect on the poor), consider that everyone should be concerned about both positive and negative environmental changes. Not only our future, but also our children's and their children's futures depend on our careful stewardship of the earth. At the same time, there are competing economic and political pressures that can act against a strict conservationist view. By researching and analyzing a specific event, we can add to our own knowledge and that of our audience, thereby preparing all for responsible future action.

Writer   Although you will be using research for this essay, your paper should include your own observations and experiences as well and be written in your own voice. You will incorporate published writers' words and ideas, provide citations or documentation of their words and ideas, and comment upon them as you think appropriate. If you find disagreement among your sources, don't discard any of them: opposing viewpoints can give you a variety of views to report and consider.

The questions and examples below will allow you focus on the Writing Situation and create a strong framework for your causal essay.

1. First, choose and describe a specific local or national event that occurred within the last three years. Describe one cause of that event, as well as a result of that event. For example:

> Political fund-raising has deep roots in America; however, in 2012, when Sheldon Adelson donated $21 million to a Super PAC tied to Newt Gingrich, the campaign finance landscape changed dramatically. Many are concerned that a select group of billionaires is literally buying America and creating an oligarchy.

2. Describe the audience you feel would be interested in learning more about the event you have chosen and how you plan to approach your audience. For example:

> I feel that every American has a right to know what is happening behind the scenes when it comes to campaign finance, and how it can (and does) impact our lives. My audience will be quite diverse, so I will need to clearly define political and financial terms and concepts and make sure the causal connections I make are logical and supported by reliable sources.

3. List and briefly describe at least two articles that will help you explore the event you have chosen. Be sure that each source includes causes or causal relationships. For example:

> The first source I found is actually what inspired my desire to write about Super PACs. It was an article in The Opinion Pages of the New York Times called "Buying the Election" by Joe Nocera (October 8, 2012). What initially caught my attention was the comparison he made between the Ford-Carter campaign back in 1976 and the Obama-Romney campaign in 2012 in regard to money spent. Nocera discusses several causal relationships. The second source is a September 7, 2012, transcript of Sen. Bernie Sanders talking to Bill Moyers about how money affects politics. Sanders claims that "billionaires and corporations [are] now buying elections," and that "I fear very much that if we don't turn this around, we're heading toward an oligarchic form of society."

4. Finally, although you will be using research to explore some of the causes of the event you have chosen and support your ideas, you will also need to include your own observations and experiences. What is your relationship to the event—what has shaped your perspective? For example:

> My parents lost a great deal of money back in 2007, and since then, I have taken a keen interest in politics—specifically, how a small handful of very powerful people seem to be controlling the lives of Americans. I find it frustrating that CEOs of large corporations who are accused of wrongdoing get a slap on the wrist and continue to buy everything from smaller businesses to elections. That said, I will work hard to remain objective in my essay and let the facts convince my audience.

THE WRITING PROCESS

The following sections will guide you through the stages of generating, planning, drafting, and revising as you work on your causal essay. Try to be particularly conscious of both the critical thinking you find in your sources and the critical thinking you do as you examine these sources and analyze causal relationships.

Generating Ideas

- Within your instructor's parameters for the assignment, begin by finding an event that interests you. If one comes to mind immediately, you can begin to research it. If not, begin by brainstorming a list of all the local and national events you can remember from the last few years.

- After you have selected an event, use your college library and the Internet. Consult Chapter 14, and an additional writing handbook if you use one, about locating sources. Search for full texts of articles from reputable publications. Check titles for words like *causes, factors, results in, reasons,* or *underlie.*

- Locate or print the sources that you identify and read them, using the strategies for active and critical reading discussed in Chapter 2. First, check to see that they do indeed discuss the causes of the event, not just the event itself. Then see what causes they identify and how they label them (contributory, interactive, and so on). If they do not label them, try to do that yourself. Also, look for language that indicates the source's level of certainty about these causes (e.g., "has been definitely identified as a cause" or "may be partially responsible").

- If you own the source (such as a book or magazine) or have made a photocopy of it, use a highlighter to mark any sentences that could support your ideas. If you cannot mark the materials directly, you could use index cards to record quotes and ideas (but be sure to record which source each idea comes from).

- Think about how much information you have. Do you need more? If so, continue researching, reading, and marking until you have enough to answer the question "Why did this event take place?"

Defining a Focus   Write a thesis statement that will make clear to your audience that you are going to analyze *why* the event occurred or why the issue is critical. Here are two possible ways to frame this type of thesis:

1. Simply report what your sources say and whether or not they are in agreement.

2. Take a position on the causal relationships involved. For example, you could write, "Having consulted four sources dealing with the causes of this event, I agree with three of them but reject a theory proposed in the fourth."

Organizing Ideas   If you used index cards, read through them two or three times; then spread them out on a table or desk so you can see them all at once. Group them into stacks: one to describe the event and one for each cause mentioned. Ideally, doing this will help you integrate material from your different sources into various parts of your essay. You may decide not to use a few of the cards; this often happens and indicates that you have done a good job of finding sufficient information. If you discover you don't have enough information, you can do more research.

If you didn't use index cards, spread your marked sources out and try to plan how you will use information from each. No matter how you organize your research, carefully review the principles for writing an essay of causal analysis (below).

Additionally, you will need to determine the best order for your body paragraphs. For a causal chain, you will probably want chronological order. For contributory causes, you may want to use climactic (least to most important) order. For interactive causes, you may want to try different orders until you discover which will make the interaction of the causes easiest for your audience to understand.

Principles for Analyzing Causes

1. Be cautious. Causal relationships are difficult to prove. You may have to use wording such as *possible cause* or *may have affected*.

2. Name and describe the event or issue and people's reactions to it in your introduction.

3. In your thesis statement, indicate that you will be analyzing the causes of this event or issue or that you will be reporting what others have said about its causes.

4. Discuss each cause in a separate section (at least one body paragraph for each cause).

5. Amplify how or why each cause brought about the event or makes the issue important or controversial. Simply naming the cause is not enough.

6. Whenever possible, focus on immediate rather than remote causes. See page 350 to review these terms.

7. Use the labels in this chapter (contributory, causal chain, interactive, sufficient, and so on) to identify causal relationships if they are suitable for the style of your paper.

8. Represent accurately any sources that you use and document them honestly and correctly.

9. Avoid logical fallacies such as *post hoc ergo propter hoc*. See pages 351–355 to review these fallacies.

10. In your conclusion, name the causes and discuss the level of certainty for each of them. You may, of course, wish to do more than this in your conclusion.

Drafting   Drafting your essay will partly depend on how you generated and organized your research and your ideas. If you used note cards, you could begin by writing one section from each stack of note cards. A highly specific description of the event could become the introduction. Quotations from eyewitnesses or participants in the event can help to interest your audience. Your introduction could conclude with your tentative thesis statement.

As you draft, begin each body paragraph with a topic sentence that names the possible or verifiable cause being discussed. Then provide those in your audience with as much information as necessary to help them understand how that cause actually could or did bring about the event.

For the conclusion of your essay, you can summarize the causes and discuss the level of certainty (or ambiguity) about them. If you found considerable discord among your sources, you could summarize the basic disagreements. If no specific conclusions have been drawn regarding the causes, you could discuss ongoing research. You will likely find that the content of your paper (and its purpose) will dictate what you write in the conclusion.

Be sure to correctly document all sources you use. Your instructor may ask you to follow a specific documentation style such as APA or MLA (see the appendix, MLA and APA Documentation Styles, beginning on page 583). Include documentation for your sources as you are drafting. If you don't, it is easy to lose track and accidentally plagiarize.

Finally, on a separate page, include a Works Cited (MLA) or Reference (APA) list depending on your instructor's guidance.

The following essay by Daniel Eggers is a good example of how one student responded to this assignment.

Revising Your Essay: Exploring Some Causes of a Recent Event

Once your draft is complete, take a break! A little distance is healthy, and when you come back to it with a clear mind, be sure to consider your audience. Is your introduction engaging and logical? Does your draft flow easily from one idea to the next? Do you carefully lead your reader through your causal analysis?

Peer Responses

Consider exchanging your draft with a few peers for feedback. You can also ask a friend or family member to review your writing. As always, pay close attention to any feedback you receive.

Revision

Use "A Step-by-Step Method for Revising Any Assignment," located on the inside front cover of this book for additional ways to strengthen your writing. Remember to focus on the larger components of your essay first.

Editing and Proofreading

Once you are satisfied with the larger components of your essay (it flows well and effectively communicates your ideas), turn your attention to the smaller details such as grammar, punctuation, and other mechanics. Do your best to clearly articulate a causal analysis of the recent event you have chosen.

STUDENT WRITING

Daniel Eggers' Writing Process

In response to an assignment asking him to update and add to an argument put forth in one of the assigned readings, Daniel Eggers, a student at City College of San Francisco, chose to consider whether or not the dream proposed by Dr. Martin Luther King Jr. had been achieved. When his research showed that it had not, he began to look for causes.

One of the most important decisions that I made in writing this essay was how to plan my approach. Since the validity of my arguments would be gauged through the supporting data, the majority of my effort went into locating appropriate sources, on which the framework of my essay would then be established. That is why I chose to produce a malleable thesis to begin with—so that I could later reshape it to allow the supporting sources to fit together nicely.

Although the majority of my effort went into locating sources, I still needed to produce a thesis and establish a framework to tie all of the sources together by creating supporting arguments for my thesis. My research suggested that there were many possible causes for racial inequality that were interrelated. Since the economy plays such an important role in American society, the first cause, to which all of the arguments could relate, was the involvement of African Americans in the economy. In the first paragraph I listed the origins of poverty for so many African Americans. These include the loss of low-skilled jobs, leading to deeper levels of poverty, which increases the development of ghettos and thus further isolates the African-American population. The causal chain could have gone in many different directions, but it was the material in my supporting sources that helped me to see the progression of causes.

Luckily, some of the sources I chose discussed recent events, such as the 2000 Presidential election and Hurricane Katrina, so writing comments about these sources came somewhat naturally. This is where I think the greatest advantage in writing this essay lay, with engaging a subject that ignited my curiosity, fascination, and interest.

Was It Only a Dream?
by Daniel Eggers

In the fall of 1963, on the one-hundredth anniversary of the Emancipation Proclamation, Martin Luther King Jr. stood before nearly two-hundred and fifty-thousand people in Washington, D.C., to present his famous speech, "I Have a

Source: Was It Only a Dream? by Daniel Eggers.

Dream." This speech was a momentous event for the civil rights movement, and even today we are still able to hear King's voice saying the words: "I have a dream that one day this nation will rise up and live out the true meaning of its creed: 'We hold these truths to be self-evident; that all men are created equal'" (531). Through King's speech we are able to partake in his vision of a future where racial inequalities no longer exist. Many people, despite the giant steps taken by the civil rights movement, feel that racial equality will never be achieved. I, myself, having researched the events of the civil rights movement, as well as recent events concerning race, feel that, though one day we may see King's dream come true, we still have a long way to go before racial equality will become a reality.

Now, over forty years after King's speech, many African Americans are still an underprivileged group, especially because of their position in the economy. Michael Hughes and Carolyn J. Kroehler reported in *Sociology: the Core* that in 2001, "for every dollar in wealth owned by a white household, the average African American household owns [only] sixteen cents" (183–184). This considerable economic inequality places limitations on the lifestyles of many African Americans by barring their access to decent housing, good education, adequate healthcare, and nutritious foods. Though the problem of African American poverty is clearly shown through statistics, the origins of the problem are not easily defined. Hughes and Kroehler state that due to the vanishing number of low-skilled jobs in the last decade, "poor urban African Americans find themselves relegated to all-black neighborhoods where they are socially isolated from mainstream American life" (233). These all-black neighborhoods, or what some would refer to as ghettos, are symbols of economic inequality in America. King refers to these all-black neighborhoods in his speech as a source of discontent for the devotees of civil rights: "We will not be satisfied as long as the Negro's basic mobility is from a smaller ghetto to a larger one" (530).

Most who can recognize African American poverty as a sizable fracture in our society can reasonably argue that it must be granted the attention it deserves in order to be repaired. However, the problem of African American poverty seldom receives attention in mainstream America. The media largely ignores gradually developing social and economic problems and places the spotlight on immediate high-profile events. Such was the case with Hurricane Katrina, whose aftermath, given ample media coverage by all the major networks, revealed some desperate levels of African American poverty, as well as incompetence and neglect of city, state, and federal governments to provide relief to the victims. An article in the *Wall Street Journal* by Shelby Steele discusses the aftermath of Hurricane Katrina with its connection to racial issues. Steele states, in light of Katrina's aftermath, "Here was a

Eggers uses his thesis statement to conclude the first paragraph and then smoothly transitions into paragraph 2 and the body of his paper.

To establish a framework for his causal chain, Eggers focuses on several contributory causes by listing the origins of African-American poverty.

Here, Eggers uses a contemporary event, Hurricane Katrina, to illustrate his point that African Americans are still grappling with the injustice of racial inequality.

poverty with an element of surrender in it that seemed to confirm the worst charges against [African Americans]: that [they] are inferior, that nothing really helps [them], that the modern world is beyond [their] reach" (20). The extensive media coverage given to Katrina, though horrifying and depressing, gave the American people an unforgettable example of extreme African American poverty stemming from the injustice of racial inequality.

Because the scales of economic distribution tilt disproportionately away from African Americans, the country has not obtained racial equality, but what steps can be taken to correct this inequity? Providing access to a good education seems to be one viable solution, and today there are numerous community colleges and vocational schools at which a person can acquire the necessary skills to earn a decent living. However, poverty looms like a cloud over many African Americans' prospects for acquiring an education. This is especially true because of the steady rise in the costs of tuition, housing, and transportation.

In paragraph 4, Eggers presents a sufficient condition (education can lead to employment) but explains other conditions that need to be met in order for a positive result to occur.

In addition to financial obstacles, some African American students are now facing a reversal of affirmative action when being considered for admission to higher education. One case occurred in Florida in 1999 with Governor Jeb Bush's abolishment of affirmative action in university admissions. K. Chandler reported in the *Westside Gazette* that due to this revocation of racial background being considered in the state universities' admissions process, the number of African American incoming freshmen to Florida universities dropped from a high of 17.6 percent in 1999 to 15.8 percent in 2004. A similar case is given by James T. Patterson in his book, *Brown v. Board of Education*, in which a 1996 Court of Appeals ruling required the University of Texas Law School to stop enforcing its affirmative action guidelines for admission. This decision resulted in African American enrollment there dropping from thirty-one to four in the following year (2006). Numbers like these illustrate the importance of affirmative action laws in maintaining equal opportunities in education for African Americans, and their reversal is a huge step backwards in the battle for racial equality.

Eggers uses carefully chosen sources to illustrate his point and back up his argument.

There are many more holes in the system to explore when analyzing the racial inequalities within America. Consider the disenfranchisement of some African American voters during the 2000 presidential election in Florida. Bob Drogin reported in a *Los Angeles Times* article that in Gadsden County, a poor rural county of Florida predominantly occupied by African Americans, "one in eight voters' [. . .] ballots were rejected as invalid." This article contrasts the wealthier and predominantly white county of Leon, where only two in one thousand ballots were rejected, which causes questions to arise about the fairness of the voting process. Clearly these discrepancies resulted from issues concerning class and

By comparing and contrasting two groups of voters in paragraphs 6 and 7, Eggers encourages the reader to consider both immediate and remote causes of the discrepancies and inequalities during the 2000 election.

racial inequality. Drogan reported that Leon County could afford to purchase more effective ballot processing machines for each of its districts, which would notify a voter if a ballot was not filled out correctly, while in Gadsden County, because of the lack of funds to purchase ballot processing machines, the ballots had to be taken to a main election office to be processed.

These technicalities are significant because, had the 179,855 ballots—noted by Drogan—that went uncounted in Florida been processed, we could possibly have seen a different outcome in the election, especially since George W. Bush defeated Al Gore by a mere 537 votes. The disenfranchisement of some African Americans during this election is also significant because it shows just how far away they are from gaining the equal voting rights to which they are entitled under the Fifteenth Amendment.

What history shows is that as long as a minority group is fighting to gain equal rights, there will be a group who will do what it can to halt its progress. Such was the circumstance involving the *Brown v. Board of Education* case of 1954. James T. Patterson noted that in response to the ruling, which outlawed segregation in public schools, white supremacist groups mobilized to resist desegregation. For example, Bryant Bowles, who founded the National Association for the Advancement of White People, organized protests and ordered white students to boycott a high school in Delaware. It was not only through boycotts and protests that Bowles tried to slow the civil rights movement, but also through threats of violence toward people who supported that school's desegregation (74–75).

Today the methods of supremacists are less direct and more covert, using economic, political, and psychological oppression to maintain racial inequality. The previously mentioned examples of Katrina and the disenfranchisement of African Americans in the Florida 2000 election would suffice as modern methods of oppression, but every now and then a supremacist will slip in an ounce of truth concerning his/her opinion about race. Bob Herbert wrote a column in the *New York Times* that discusses some cruel words said on the radio by the former secretary of education in the Reagan cabinet, Bill Bennett: "I do know that it's true that if you wanted to reduce crime, you could—if that were your sole purpose— you could abort every black baby in this country, and your crime rate would go down." Bennett went on to say, "That would be an impossible, ridiculous, and morally reprehensible thing to do, but your crime rate would go down." Bennett's statement makes clear that racism, so prevalent throughout American history, still exists today.

African Americans have a problematic disposition within our culture. It's sort of a double standard where they are expected to fit in and be functioning cogs

Eggers presents further historical and contemporary evidence (contributory causes) of racial inequality in paragraphs 8 and 9, including a shocking statement by Bill Bennett. This carefully chosen quotation has a powerful effect on the reader and clearly supports his thesis statement.

within the machine of American society, yet they are not truly accepted and are often treated as outsiders. W. E. B. DuBois describes this condition best in *The Souls of Black Folk* by saying, "One ever feels his two-ness,—an American, a Negro; two souls, two thoughts, two unreconciled strivings; two warring ideals in one dark body, whose dogged strength alone keeps it from being torn asunder" (38). But despite this disposition, along with the obstacles of oppression that were placed here as soon as the first enslaved Africans were brought to these shores, change will always be a constant, so the possibility for a future of justice and racial equality for African Americans may one day come to pass. However, the nation is still quite a distance from achieving this goal, but as long as we can recognize how far the civil rights movement has come and become aware of what must be done to push the movement forward, then the dream that millions of Americans from all racial groups share with Martin Luther King Jr. will never remain only a dream.

In the concluding paragraph, Eggers ends on a hopeful yet tentative note, while the title of his essay and the words of Martin Luther King Jr. skillfully reverberate with the reader.

Works Cited

Chandler, K. "Black Enrollment in Florida Colleges Plummets as Percentage of Hispanics Surges." *Westside Gazette*. 18 Aug. 2005. Web. 14 November 2005.

Drogin, Bob. "2 Florida Counties Show Election Day's Inequities." *Los Angeles Times*. 12 Mar. 2001. Web. 16 Nov. 2005.

Du Bois, W. E. B. *The Souls of Black Folk*. Massachusetts: Bedford, 1997. Print.

Herbert, Bob. "Impossible, Ridiculous, Repugnant." *New York Times*. 6 Oct. 2005. Web. 16 Nov. 2005.

Hughes, Michael, and Carolyn J. Kroehler. *Sociology: The Core*. 7th ed. New York: McGraw, 2005. Print.

King, Jr., Martin Luther. "I Have a Dream." *Great Writing: A Reader for Writers*. 3rd ed. Ed. Harvey S. Wiener. New York: McGraw, 2002. 529–32. Print.

Patterson, James T. *Brown v. Board of Education: A Civil Rights Milestone and Its Troubled Legacy*. New York: Oxford UP, 2001. Print.

Steele, Shelby. "Witness: Blacks, Whites, and the Politics of Shame in America." *Wall Street Journal*. 26 Oct. 2005. Web. 14 Nov. 2005.

REFLECTION ON WRITING

1. Based on "Principles for Analyzing Causes" (page 369), do you feel Daniel Eggers proved any causal relationships related to whether or not the dream proposed by Martin Luther King Jr. had been achieved?

2. Overall, do you feel Eggers' essay is hopeful that the future will be one of justice and equality for all Americans? Why or why not?

ALTERNATIVE WRITING PROJECT: UTOPIAS AND DYSTOPIAS

Dan Buettner, in a salient TEDX presentation (http://www.ted.com/talks/dan_buettner_how_to_live_to_be_100.html), debunks several myths about longevity, and discusses the possibilities of living to be 100 years old. In an essay, suggest ways in which a society made up of people who lived well past the century mark would be either a utopia or a dystopia. (Be sure to look up both words; your essay should define the term in your own words and within the context of your own argument.) How joyful would a society be, for example, if everyone practiced the physical discipline and appetite control some scientists suggest? What would be the benefits and challenges to a society where the population continually increased because people were living longer? Your essay could be quite imaginative, but even the most compelling science fiction or fantasy is based on some semblance of probability—so be sure to complement your suppositions with some research.

CHAPTER 10   Summary

- Three kinds of causal relationships are
  - *Causal chains,* situations in which one thing leads to another, which leads to another, and so on over a period of time;
  - *Contributory causes,* in which more than one cause works simultaneously to produce an effect; and
  - *Interactive causes* which relate to each that flow back and forth from one to the other.
- You can test a cause by determining its
  - *Necessary conditions,* factors that are required to bring about a certain result;
  - *Sufficient conditions,* factors that of themselves are always sufficient to bring about a certain result;
  - *Immediate causes,* things that happen just before an event that they cause; and
  - *Remote causes,* things that happen before an event, but further back in time, that they cause.
- Types of causal fallacies include
  - *Questionable cause,* presenting a causal relationship for which no real evidence exists;
  - *Misidentification of the cause,* uncertainty about what is the cause and what is the effect: ignoring or assuming a common cause;
  - *Post hoc ergo propter hoc,* assuming that, because two things occur closely together in time, one has caused the other; and
  - *Slippery slope,* asserting that one undesirable action will inevitably lead to a worse action, which will necessarily lead to a still worse one, and so forth, culminating in disaster.

3

Thinking and Writing to Explore Issues and Take Positions

CHAPTER 11   Writing to Analyze: Believing and Knowing

CHAPTER 12   Writing to Propose Solutions: Solving Problems

CHAPTER 13   Writing to Persuade: Constructing Arguments

CHAPTER 14   Writing About Investigations: Thinking About Research

As you have become more confident in your thinking and writing abilities, you may also have developed more respect for the thinking and writing of others. You have probably observed how academic work and even democracy itself depend on understanding sources of beliefs and various perspectives. You have been learning how to evaluate information and how to express your own perspectives clearly.

Part One of this book helped you focus on yourself as a thinker and a writer, and you wrote from your experiences and observations. Part Two asked you to explore important thinking patterns and to incorporate some ideas from others into your writing. Here in Part Three assignments will lead to the presentation of your ideas and those from sources in well-reasoned writing.

The Writing Projects at the end of each chapter in Part Three ask you to integrate material from several sources into your written work. As you do so, you will learn effective, responsible ways of introducing, commenting on, and documenting ideas from others. You will consider the principles that underlie research and citation, and you will use appropriate formats for academic writing.

Moving from *believing* something to be true to *knowing* something to be true is a process that involves close observation, research, analyses, and evaluation. Critical thinkers and thoughtful writers present their beliefs by reporting the facts, making inferences based on evidence, and judging by applying criteria.

Writing to Analyze:
Believing and Knowing

"A belief is not merely an idea the mind possesses, it is an idea that possesses the mind."

—ROBERT BOLTON

CRITICAL THINKING FOCUS:
Analyzing beliefs and their accuracy

WRITING FOCUS:
Evaluating evidence and presenting beliefs

READING THEME:
How the media shape our thinking

WRITING ACTIVITIES:
Identifying and analyzing beliefs and knowledge

WRITING PROJECT:
Analyzing influences on beliefs about a social or academic issue

Writers write about what they believe, and their purposes often include explaining their beliefs and persuading others to adopt them. Yet what exactly are beliefs, and how are they constructed? When should they be kept, when should they be modified, and when should they be discarded? What are the differences between believing and knowing, and how do writers handle these differences? How do writers present beliefs they hold with varying degrees of certainty?

In this information age, we are flooded with data, stories, and pictures from television, radio, newspapers, magazines, books, and computers. Thus, critical thinkers and thoughtful writers face a continuing challenge to evaluate information they receive and to redefine their beliefs accordingly.

Chapter 3 examined the sources of beliefs, especially those related to personal life. This chapter continues that discussion by further examining the structure of beliefs, by presenting guidelines for evaluating beliefs, and by drawing distinctions between believing and knowing and between knowledge and truth. This chapter presents some of the ways in which beliefs take shape and some of the ways in which they are presented. The concepts of *interpretation, evaluation, conclusion, prediction, report, inference,* and *judgment* will provide a vocabulary to help you think about your beliefs and those of others.

The Writing Project at the end of the chapter asks you to analyze some influences on your beliefs about a social or an academic issue.

Ways of Forming Beliefs

Throughout our lives, we form beliefs about the world around us to explain why things happen as they do, to predict how things will happen, and to govern the choices we make. For example, consider the following statements and answer "Yes," "No," or "Not sure" to each.

1. Human beings need to eat in order to stay alive.
2. Smoking marijuana is a harmful activity.

3. Every human life is valuable.

4. Developing your mind is as important as taking care of your body.

5. People should care about other people, not just about themselves.

Your responses to these statements reflect certain beliefs you have, beliefs not all people share.

What exactly are beliefs? *Beliefs* represent interpretations, evaluations, conclusions, or predictions that a person believes to be true. You may not have considered these different representations of beliefs before, but, if you think about it, you might see that most of your beliefs fit into one of these categories. Sometimes it might be important as you consider a belief to see which type it is. For example, *interpretation* suggests that other explanations are possible, and *prediction* makes clear that an event has not yet happened. Such understandings help when thinking critically about your beliefs.

The statement "I believe that the U.S. Constitution's guarantee of 'the right of the people to keep and bear arms' does not prohibit all governmental regulation of firearms" represents an interpretation of the Second Amendment. To say, "I believe that watching daytime talk shows is unhealthy because they focus almost exclusively on the seamy side of human life" expresses an *evaluation* of daytime talk shows. The statement "I believe that one of the main reasons two out of three people in the world go to bed hungry each night is that industrially advanced nations have not done a satisfactory job of sharing their resources" expresses a *conclusion* about the problem of world hunger. To say, "I believe that if drastic environmental measures are not undertaken to slow the global warming trend, the polar icecaps will melt and the earth will be flooded" is to make a *prediction* about events that will occur in the future.

Besides expressing an interpretation, evaluation, conclusion, or prediction about the world, a belief expresses an *endorsement* of its accuracy—an indication that the belief is held to be true by the writer or speaker. This endorsement is a necessary dimension of a belief. For example, the statement "Astrological predictions are meaningless because there is no persuasive evidence that the position of the planets has any effect on human affairs" expresses a belief even though it doesn't specifically include the words *I believe*.

In addition, it is necessary to recognize that beliefs are not static—at least not if we apply a critical approach. We continually form and re-form our beliefs throughout much of our lives. This process often follows the following sequence:

1. We *form* beliefs in order to explain what is taking place. (These initial beliefs are often based on our past experiences.)

2. We *test* these beliefs by acting on the basis of them.

3. We *revise* (or "re-form") these beliefs if our actions do not achieve our goals.

4. We *retest* these revised beliefs by again using them as a basis for action.

As we actively participate in this ongoing process of forming and re-forming beliefs, we are using our critical thinking abilities to identify and critically examine our beliefs by, in effect, asking the following questions:

• How effectively do these beliefs explain what is taking place?

• To what extent are the beliefs consistent with other beliefs about the world?

- How effectively do the beliefs help us to predict what will happen in the future?
- To what extent are these beliefs supported by sound reasons and compelling evidence derived from reliable sources?

This process of critical exploration enables us to develop more understanding of various situations and to exert more control over them.

Thinking-Writing Activity

IDENTIFYING BELIEFS

Describe beliefs you have that fall in each of these categories (interpretation, evaluation, conclusion, prediction) and then explain the reason(s) you have for endorsing the beliefs.

1. **Interpretation** (an explanation or analysis of the meaning or significance of something)
   My interpretation is that . . .
   Supporting reason(s):
2. **Evaluation** (a judgment of the value or quality of something, based on certain standards)
   My evaluation is that . . .
   Supporting reason(s):
3. **Conclusion** (a decision made or an opinion formed after consideration of the relevant facts or evidence)
   My conclusion is that . . .
   Supporting reason(s):
4. **Prediction** (a statement about what will happen in the future)
   My prediction is that . . .
   Supporting reason(s):

BELIEFS BASED ON PERSONAL EXPERIENCE

The introductory discussion of beliefs in Chapter 3 identified four sources of beliefs: people of authority, recorded references, observed evidence, and personal experience. The last two involve direct experience. Yet how we interpret and understand direct experience—what conclusions we draw from what we perceive—depends to some extent on what we already believe. In offering evidence to support their beliefs, people generally choose those perceptions and experiences that fit with their previous beliefs; contradictory experiences may be ignored or downplayed.

In the following readings, three writers offer differing beliefs about the situation of the homeless in the United States, based on their perceptions of direct experience. B. C. chooses to live as a homeless person in "Homeless in Prescott, Arizona," while in "Hard Times: A Family Escapes Homelessness," Cindy and Ben are living with the consequences of past mistakes and trying to find steady jobs and a place to live. In the third story, "Newport News Mom Escapes Homelessness," Suzanne Richardson is trying to reach her dream of becoming a message therapist, only to be disappointed by failure and lack of money.

Before you begin to read, write down two or three of your beliefs about homelessness and the homeless. After you have read both pieces, write a few sentences about how your beliefs were affected by your reading these articles. If possible, share your statements with your classmates.

"Homeless in Prescott, Arizona"

by B. C.

This narrative was one of thousands of stories submitted to National Public Radio's National Story Project. In 1999, novelist Paul Auster asked listeners to NPR's *Weekend All Things Considered* program to submit brief stories about some incident or anecdote "that revealed the mysterious and unknowable forces at work in our lives. . . . In other words, true stories that sounded like fiction." For more than a year, Auster read selected stories on the radio program. In 2001, he collected and published 179 of the stories in *I Thought My Father Was God and Other True Tales from NPR's National Story Project.*

Last spring I made a major life change, and I wasn't suffering from a midlife crisis. At fifty-seven I'm way beyond that. I decided I could not wait eight more years to retire, and I could not be a legal secretary for eight more years. I quit my job; sold my house, furnishings, and car; gave my cat to my neighbor; and moved to Prescott, Arizona, a community of thirty thousand, nestled in the Bradshaw Mountains with a fine library, community college, and a beautiful town square. I invested the proceeds from selling everything and I now receive $315 a month in interest income. That is what I live off of.

I am anonymous. I am not on any government programs. I do not receive any kind of welfare, not even food stamps. I do not eat at the Salvation Army. I do not take handouts. I am not dependent on anyone.

My base is downtown Prescott, where everything I need is within a radius of a mile and a half—easy walking. To go farther afield, I take a bus that makes a circuit of the city each hour and costs three dollars for a day pass. I have a post-office box—cost, forty dollars a year. The library is connected to the Internet, and I have an e-mail address. My storage space costs twenty-seven dollars a month, and I have access to it twenty-four hours a day. I store my clothes, cosmetic and hygiene supplies, a few kitchen items, and paperwork there. I rent a secluded corner of a backyard a block from my storage area for twenty-five dollars a month. This is my bedroom, complete with arctic tent, sleeping bag, mattress, and lantern.

I wear a sturdy pack with a water bottle, flashlight, and Walkman, toiletries and rain gear.

Yavapai College has an Olympic-size pool and a women's locker room. I take college classes and have access to these facilities; cost, thirty-five dollars a month. I go there every morning to perform my "toilet" and shower. I go to the Laundromat with a small load of clothes whenever I need to; cost, fifteen dollars a month. Looking presentable is the most important aspect of my new lifestyle. When I go to the library, no one can guess I'm homeless. The library is my living room. I sit in a comfortable chair and read. I listen to beautiful music through the stereo system. I communicate with my daughter via e-mail and type letters on the word processor. I stay dry when it's wet outside. Unfortunately, the library does not have a television, but I've found a student lounge at the college that does. Most of the time I can watch *The News Hour, Masterpiece Theater*, and *Mystery*. To further satisfy my cultural needs, I attend dress rehearsals at the local amateur theater company, free of charge.

Eating inexpensively and nutritiously is my biggest challenge. My budget allows   5
me to spend two hundred dollars a month for food. I have a Coleman burner and an old-fashioned percolator. I go to my storage space every morning and make coffee, pour it into my thermos, load my backpack, go to the park, and find a sunny spot to enjoy my coffee and listen to *Morning Edition* on my Walkman. The park is my backyard. It's a beautiful place to hang out when the weather is clement. I can lie on the grass and read and nap. The mature trees provide welcome shade when it's warm.

My new lifestyle has been comfortable and enjoyable so far because the weather in Prescott during the spring, summer, and fall has been delightful, though it did snow Easter weekend. But I was prepared. I have a parka, boots, and gloves, all warm and waterproof.

Back to eating. The Jack in the Box has four items that cost one dollar—Breakfast Jack, Jumbo Jack, a chicken sandwich, and two beef tacos. After I enjoy my coffee in the park, I have a Breakfast Jack. There's a nutrition program at the adult center where I can eat a hearty lunch for two dollars. For dinner, back to the Jack in the Box. I buy fresh fruit and veggies at Albertson's. Once in a while I go to the Pizza Hut—all you can eat for $4.49. When I return to my storage space in the evening, I make popcorn on my Coleman burner. I only drink water and coffee; other beverages are too expensive.

I've discovered another way to have a different eating experience and to combine it with a cultural evening. There's an art gallery downtown, and the openings of the new shows are announced in the newspaper. Two weeks ago I put on my dress and panty hose, went to the opening, enjoyed eating the snacks, and admired the paintings.

I've let my hair grow long, and I tie it back in a ponytail like I did in grade school. I no longer color it. I like the gray. I do not shave my legs or underarms and do not polish my fingernails [or] wear mascara, foundation, blush, or lipstick. The natural look costs nothing.

I love going to college. This fall, I'm taking ceramics, chorale, and cultural   10
anthropology—for enrichment, not for credit. I love reading all the books I want to but never had enough time for. I also have time to do absolutely nothing.

Of course there are negatives. I miss my friends from back home. Claudette, who works at the library, befriended me. She was a feature writer for the local newspaper and is adept at getting information from people. Eventually, I told her who I was and how I live. She never pressures me to live differently, and I know she's there for me if I need her.

I also miss Simon my cat. I keep hoping that a cat will come my way, particularly before winter sets in. It would be nice to sleep and snuggle with a furry body.

I hope I can survive the winter. I've been told that Prescott can have lots of snow and long stretches of freezing temperatures. I don't know what I'll do if I get sick. I'm generally an optimist, but I do worry. Pray for me.

Hard Times: A Family Escapes Homelessness

by Rob Manning

Ben Perrins and Cindi Shipley and their three kids have come a long way in the last seven months. When OPB met the couple last spring, they'd been without a stable place to live for a year, and were bouncing among shelters and friends' houses.

They still rely on government assistance, rather than jobs, for income, but Cindi says the recession has been good for them.

Cindi Shipley: "My view – the recession is God's way to push you and make you stretch yourself. And I felt like I couldn't handle it, I would cry and get depressed, losing our apartment, but I'm kind of glad we did."

Rob Manning reviews what the family went through in the last year—and why Cindi Shipley is happier now, than she was before the recession.

I don't know what your Memorial Day was like this year, but Ben and Cindi's went like this: They woke up in the spare room at a friend's house southwest of Portland. They roused their three kids and took them on public transit across the region to North Portland. It was a routine trip for them.

Their youngest child stayed with Ben and Cindi while they couch-surfed, but their two school-aged kids spent weeknights at Grandma's house, so they could stay at the same North Portland school. It pained Cindi.

Cindi Shipley: "I only see them on the weekends, and their grandma sees them all through the week. She's the parent to them, and that's not the way it's supposed to be."

As she sat on the steps at Pioneer Courthouse Square, Cindi's oldest, nine-year-old Kya was on her mind. Kya wanted to go to summer camp, but Cindi couldn't afford it.

Cindi Shipley: "So she took it upon herself—she's nine—took it upon herself to go to her neighbors, that she knows, of course to ask them 'can I do any yard work for you, or whatever?'. So in three days, she's raised seven dollars."

Ben and Cindi weren't always been homeless. Two years ago, Ben was working for a tow-truck company. But he says his name was at the top of the list, when the company went looking for layoffs.

Ben Perrins: "My head was on the block. They did it. I don't feel bad for them. I'd love to go back to work for them."

Source: http://www.opb.org/news/article/hard-times-family-escapes-homelessness/.

Both say they had a history with methamphetamine, especially Ben. They say they kicked the habit by summer, but it had helped consume their cash. Add in a rent increase and the family was homeless. But the summer was brighter.

Ben and Cindi got into a family shelter in Gresham called My Father's House.

Cindi Shipley: "This is a lot better. Now, the family is all together instead of two of the kids staying at my Mom's house, and then Ben and I staying with our friend. Now the whole family is together."

Little things seemed to be coming together for them, too. Nine year-old Kya got to go to camp, thanks to a donation they got, and the money she earned.

Kya: "I counted, I just can't remember exactly..."

Kya's mom, Cindi, comes and whispers in her ear.

Kya: "Twenty seven dollars."

But the couple had bigger worries. The shelter had a time limit, making Cindi and Ben worry that the family might have to separate again. The thought caused Cindi to tear up. Ben tried to consol her.

Ben Perrins: "Maybe one more split-up. Hey, we put ourselves together this time, we'll do it again. Stop... I love you. It'll work."

The time at the shelter wasn't easy. The boys got the flu, and Cindi had surgery for a benign cyst.

But the illnesses and worries drew them together. And on one special weekend in November, they got to move into their own place. And, they were getting married. Cindi beamed in the wedding gown she borrowed.

Cindi Shipley: "It is an incredible weekend. Most people, they deal with getting a house or getting married. I'm doing both in two days."

After the ceremony, Ben celebrated, but also thought about the pressure of being the family's provider, as he was before drugs and the economy dragged him down.

Ben Perrins: "It's back to the grind again, you know, where I take them to school, and I look for work. She stays home and putting the house together. Every day things we were doing before, when I started acting stupid. And now, I'm getting a new chance."

Now, both Ben and Cindi are looking for work, though Cindi spends a lot of time at home, watching four year-old, Kristopher.

Cindi Shipley: "We can't go outside, it's raining outside."

Kristopher: "Yup, it's really raining."

The shelter allowed the whole family to be together. Cindi says the apartment allows the kids—Kya, especially—to have a little time alone.

Cindi Shipley: "She's a lot less stressed. She doesn't say much about it—but you can tell that she's less aggravated. She doesn't get as aggravated with her brothers, and she plays with her brothers more. I think that's because we're in a stable situation, and she has a room to get away, if she needs to get away."

And, Cindi says without having to focus all of their energy on keeping their own lives together, they're able to give back a little. On one freezing night a few weeks ago, Cindi got a call from her mom.

Cindi Shipley: "She called up Ben, late at night, and she's crying and saying 'I need your help, the house is flooding, I don't know what to do...'"

Cindi Shipley: "Well Ben comes out there..."

As Cindi explains how Ben fixed the plumbing, another person they've helped comes in the door. Cindi's kids call him, "Uncle Mike," and he's been homeless himself. In exchange for the occasional night on the couch, he runs errands for them, or like today, takes Kristopher out for a while.

Cindi Shipley: "Go with Uncle Mike for a little bit."

Kristopher: "Bye, Mama."

Cindi Shipley: "Bye, son. Can I have a kiss please? Get your coat—because it's raining."

Cindi says she and Ben really appreciate all the help they've gotten. And she says she's glad to have a home she can open to a friend in need, the way friends did for her family, when she needed it, last spring.

Newport News Mom Escapes Homelessness

by Joe Lawlor

Suzanne Richardson's goal of becoming a massage therapist seemed to be within her grasp, but it kept slipping away.

Richardson, 21, had come a long way since being a high school dropout in Middletown, N.Y. Richardson, her mother Yvonne, and their family had always struggled with money issues. They were homeless for two months when they moved here in 2006, and always seemed to be scraping by.

And yet, things were looking up for Richardson.

She had achieved her general equivalency diploma and, while pregnant with her second child, completed a nine-month course in 2009 at Everest College in Chesapeake to become a massage therapist.

Despite graduating with honors, she failed the certification test this January, the last step she needed before she could seek permanent work as a therapist. To take the test again, she needed to somehow come up with $225 that she didn't have.

With her mom on disability, her 19-year-old brother still in high school and Richardson unemployed, the family's finances were teetering.

Then Richardson found a job through the Office of Human Affairs summer youth employment program. She would earn $7.25 per hour, work 30 hours per week at Little Tin Soldiers Day Care in Hampton.

"I thought, great, by my second paycheck, I can save up enough money to pay for the test," Richardson said.

But it didn't work out that way.

Between getting the job and her first day of work, the family discovered in June that the home they were renting on Augusta Street in Hampton was in foreclosure. They had a month to move out, come up with a security deposit and first month's rent for a new place while waiting to get their security deposit back from the homeowner they rented from.

They didn't have enough money.

With the electric shut off due to lack of funds, the Richardsons found themselves staying with friends during the day and sleeping at the house overnight. Without

Source: http://articles.dailypress.com/2010-08-27/news/dp-nws-formerly-homeless-20100827_1_massage-therapist-security-deposit-homelessness.

enough money for a security deposit, they got together $800 to be able to live in a hotel for a few weeks so they wouldn't be on the streets.

Essentially homeless, Richardson's money for her test was gone.

She started work on June 28, but she didn't have enough money to buy food for her children, Anais, 5, and Jamere, 1. Besides her mother, also living in the home was her brother, Tracey.

A church donated free food, but it wasn't enough to feed five people.

"It's hard. You want to smile for your kids. Act like nothing is wrong," Richardson said. "But knowing that your kids don't have enough food to eat makes you a little crazy. You don't know what you're going to do."

She said her brother got some money from donating plasma a few times so they could have food and diapers. When attending a banquet one time, she was given leftover food for free that the family survived on for two days.

At work, she put on a brave face, but sometimes she cried from the stress.

"I just thought, I've got to keep moving. I've got to try my best. I need this paycheck," she said. Her co-workers became her friends, and they helped her get through the rough times.

Kai-Michelle Coleman, Little Tin Soldiers director, said Richardson did such a good job, that she has been offered permanent employment, even after the OHA program ended this week. The OHA pays for the salaries of employees in the program, using federal stimulus money, during the summertime.

"She was always on time. She always goes above and beyond what's called for, all the time," Coleman said. Richardson's car broke down, and it took her 90 minutes to get to work.

Richardson, who has a wide, easy smile and tattoos of her children's names on both of her arms, said she tried to laugh a lot at work to keep her problems from feeling overwhelming.

Yvonne Richardson, Suzanne's mother, said her daughter has gained confidence and "blossomed" since starting the job.

"We just supported her and tried to make the best of it," she said. "We're getting there."

With money from the day care job, the family finally got a place in Newsome Park Apartments in Newport News.

Richardson is pregnant with her third child. She said the father for her five-year-old is not present in her life, but the father of her one-year-old and unborn baby is a steady presence, and she hopes they get married. Her boyfriend, Donnell Andrews, has a part-time job and he helps in any way he can, she said.

She said her mother might adopt her new baby, which is due in December.

But Richardson still didn't have enough money for that test, which would lead to a better-paying job and financial independence.

"I feel like I worked so hard for it and I feel like it's not going to happen," Richardson said Thursday, holding her hands to her face, tears streaming down.

But Friday, Wendell Braxton, executive director of the OHA, said the agency would pay for the test.

Richardson beamed and was speechless for a few seconds when told.

"I'm ready to take the test," she said. "I feel like it was holding me back, but it's not going to now."

She pulled on her coat. She needed to go to Manhattan to pick out furniture for the possible new apartment from a Salvation Army warehouse. It was her second trip there: the first time, the table and chairs she had ordered arrived with the legs broken.

"That's the most agitating part," she said. "Everything is done over and over. All of this has been done before."

QUESTIONS FOR READING ACTIVELY

1. Identify passages in "Homeless in Prescott, Arizona," "Hard Times: A Family Escapes Homelessness," and "Newport News Mom Escapes Homelessness" that express interpretations, evaluations, conclusions, and predictions.

2. Compare and contrast B. C.'s beliefs about their struggles with the beliefs of Cindy and Ben's, as well as Suzanne Richardson's. What does each person believe about their prospects of escaping homelessness?

QUESTIONS FOR THINKING CRITICALLY

1. Does the term *homeless* accurately describe the way B. C. has chosen to live? Which person—Cindy and Ben, Suzanne Richardson, or B. C.—seems to most closely reflect stereotypes about homelessness in America?

2. How did your beliefs affect your response to each reading?

QUESTIONS FOR WRITING THOUGHTFULLY

1. Both Cindy and Ben, and Suzanne Richardson believed that by following a course of action, their situation would improve. Explore the ways that this type of thinking gives hope and also demoralizes those involved. Did your views on homelessness changed after reading these stories? Do you feel sympathy for the people in these stories?

2. Are any of your beliefs about homelessness based on direct experience? If so, whose experiences are closer to yours: B. C.'s, Cindy and Ben's, or Suzanne Richardson's? Write a narrative like "Homeless in Prescott, Arizona" that describes your experience for an audience otherwise unfamiliar with homelessness.

BELIEFS BASED ON INDIRECT EXPERIENCE

No matter how much we have experienced in our lives, the fact is, of course, that no one person's direct experiences are enough to establish an adequate set of accurate beliefs. We all depend on the experience of others to provide us with beliefs and also to serve as foundations for those beliefs. For example, does Antarctica exist? How do we know? Have we ever been there and seen it with our own eyes? Probably not; nevertheless, we believe in the existence of Antarctica and its ice and penguins. Of all the beliefs each of us has, few are actually based on our direct personal experience. Instead, other people have in some way or form communicated to us virtually all these beliefs and the evidence for them. As we reach beyond our personal experiences to form and revise our beliefs, we find that information is provided by two sources: people of authority and recorded references.

As we have seen in the essays discussing homelessness by B. C. and about Cindy and Ben, and Suzanne Richardson, the beliefs of others cannot be accepted without question. Each of us views the world through individual lenses that shape and influence the way we select and present information. Comparing different sources helps to make these lenses explicit and highlights the different interests and purposes involved. In fact, examining sources may lead us to recognize that there are a variety of competing viewpoints, some fairly similar, some quite contradictory. In critically reviewing the beliefs of others, it is essential for us to pursue the same goals of accuracy and completeness that we set when examining beliefs based on personal experience. As a result, we focus on the reasons or evidence that supports the information others are presenting.

Thinking-Writing Activity

THE ORIGIN OF A BELIEF

Select one of the beliefs that you identified in the Thinking-Writing Activity at the beginning of this chapter. What indirect sources helped shape it: your family, friends, teachers, religious leaders, television, the Internet? What direct personal experiences or observations have had an impact on it? Note specifically how some of these influences shaped your belief.

Evaluating Sources and Information

When we depend on information that others provide, we need to ask key questions. The most crucial part of determining the reliability of a source's information is determining the reliability of the source itself.

HOW RELIABLE IS THE SOURCE?

We know that some sources—such as advertising—can be very unreliable, whereas other sources, such as *Consumer Reports* magazine (which does not accept advertising), are generally considered reliable. Sometimes, however, the reliability of a source of information is not immediately clear. In those cases, we have to use a variety of standards or criteria to evaluate a source's reliability, whether the source is written or audible.

Special care should be taken when evaluating information from websites. See "Checklist for Evaluating the Quality of Internet Resources" in Chapter 14 on pages 545–546.

WHAT ARE THE SOURCE'S PURPOSES AND INTERESTS?

Evaluating information means thinking critically about the perceiving lenses through which the source of the information views the situation. Is this source presenting an argument or giving information? Are you looking at a report, an inference, or a judgment (see pages 409–416)? In other words, what is the rhetorical purpose of the piece? How is the purpose reflected in the selection of details and in the wording and tone?

You also need to think about the piece's audience. Who is the intended audience? Is it friendly, neutral, or hostile? Is it informed or new to the subject? Writers or speakers can focus on specific audiences without being dishonorable, but sometimes they can emphasize one point of view or tap emotions in manipulative ways. Can you detect any slanting, or does this source's material seem balanced?

HOW KNOWLEDGEABLE OR EXPERIENCED IS THE SOURCE?

When seeking information from indirect sources, we want to locate people of authority or recorded references that can offer a special understanding of a subject. When a car begins making strange noises, we search for someone who knows cars. When we want to learn more about a social issue such as homelessness, we turn to articles and books written by people who have studied the problem.

In seeking information from sources, it is important to distinguish between nonexpert sources and expert sources who have training, education, and experience in a particular area. Also, any expert source's credentials should be up-to-date. A book about careers in the computer industry published 20 years ago is not likely to be relevant today.

Sports and entertainment figures often endorse products in television commercials, but their testimony is not very convincing if those products have nothing to do with sports or entertainment (and if these "experts" have been paid large sums of money and told exactly what to say). Finally, we should not accept expert opinion without question or critical examination, even if the experts meet all of our criteria.

WAS THE SOURCE ABLE TO MAKE ACCURATE OBSERVATIONS?

You may have heard of law-enforcement training courses where actors stage simulated crimes before an unsuspecting class. Students in the class are then quickly informed that the situation has been staged to test their powers of observation and asked to record what happened in as much detail as they can remember. Invariably, many witnesses are quite mistaken about much of what they remember, while others can recall many fine details exactly. The same is true in any kind of eyewitness account: some people have quite sharp memories, while others may "remember" many imagined details. In addition, a person's vantage point as a witness may color the reliability of the testimony. The amount of light, obstructions to vision, and other matters can make his or her perceptions less than wholly reliable.

The reliability of an indirect source also depends on the personal viewpoints and beliefs the source brings to a situation. These feelings, expectations, and interests often influence what a witness perceives without his or her full awareness of the process. For example, a group that sponsored an antiwar rally at a political convention might claim a crowd of more than 5,000, while politicians might issue a report estimating rally attendance at about 2,000. We have seen that two different writers can draw very different conclusions about what it means to be homeless. What further questions could be asked, and how might additional sources be located to evaluate the reliability of such differing sources?

HOW REPUTABLE IS THE SOURCE?

When evaluating the reliability of sources, it is useful to consider how accurate and reliable their information has been in the past. If someone has consistently given sound information over a period of time, we gradually develop confidence in the accuracy of that person's reports. Police officers and news media reporters must continually evaluate the reliability of information sources. Of course, this works the other way as well. When people consistently give inaccurate or incomplete information, others lose confidence in their reliability. Nevertheless, few people provide information that is either completely reliable or completely unreliable. You probably realize that your own reliability tends to vary, depending on the situation, the type of information you are providing, and the person to whom you are giving it. Thus, in trying to evaluate information offered by others, you have to explore the following factors before arriving at a provisional conclusion, which you may have to revise later in light of additional information.

HOW VALUABLE IS INFORMATION FROM THIS SOURCE?

Of course, you also need to assess the credibility of the information itself by asking these questions: What are the main ideas being presented? What evidence is provided? Does the information seem accurate? Is it up-to-date? Does anything seem false? Does anything seem to have been left out?

Thinking-Writing Activity

EVALUATING A SOURCE OF A BELIEF

Select one of the beliefs that you discussed in the Thinking-Writing Activity on page 381 that is based on sources such as people of authority or recorded references. Now, based on the criteria just discussed, evaluate the reliability of one source of your belief.

THINKING CRITICALLY ABOUT NEW MEDIA

Internet Hoaxes, Scams, and Urban Legends

As we have seen in Chapter 10, *fallacies* are unsound arguments that are often persuasive and appear to be logical because they usually appeal to our emotions and prejudices, and because they often support conclusions that we want to believe are accurate. One expression of fallacious thinking in new media can be found in the existence of *Internet hoaxes:* messages, offers, solicitations, advice, or threats that are often seductive in their appeal but false and sometimes dangerous. The hoaxes come in all shapes and sizes: "helping" someone from an African country transfer $20 million; receiving birthday greetings from a secret admirer; verifying your credit card information with an alleged bank; passing along a message to 10 friends with the hope of receiving special blessings or cash; helping to provide medical care for an ill or injured child; and many, many more. Often these hoaxes are harmless, resulting in nothing more than us wasting time and bandwidth by forwarding phony chain letters. Other times, however, we risk donating money to scam artists, divulging credit or bank information to financial predators, or introducing destructive viruses into our computer by opening attached files from Internet anarchists.

Most virus warnings are hoaxes and can be spotted by the following signs:

- They falsely claim to describe an extremely dangerous virus.
- They use pseudo-technical language to make impressive-sounding claims.
- They falsely claim that the report was issued or confirmed by a well-known company.
- They ask you to forward it to all your friends and colleagues.

You should avoid passing on warnings of this kind, as the continued re-forwarding of these hoaxes wastes time and email bandwidth. Sometimes you may receive hoaxes with a file attached that may be infected with a virus. A good principle is to delete all hoaxes and *never* open an attached file from a source that you don't know personally.

There are a number of sites devoted to uncovering these Internet hoaxes, including

www.snopes.com (Urban Legends Reference Pages)
www.hoaxbusters.org
urbanlegends.about.com

Hoaxbusters.org offers a guide to help detect whether an email is a hoax or the real deal. Included below are their "Top Five Signs That an E-mail Is a Hoax." After you read through their warning signs, review the emails included below and see if the guidelines help you identify them as hoaxes. Then conduct some independent research of your own by locating three possible Internet hoaxes and then analyzing their authenticity by applying the "Top Five Signs."

Top Five Signs That an E-mail Is a Hoax

The next time that you receive an alarming e-mail calling you to action, look for one or more of these five telltale characteristics before even thinking about sending it along to anybody else.

Urgent   The e-mail will have a great sense of urgency! You'll usually see a lot of exclamation points and capitalization. The subject line will typically be something like:

> URGENT!!!!!!
> WARNING!!!!!!
> IMPORTANT!!!!!!
> VIRUS ALERT!!!!!!
> THIS IS NOT A JOKE!!!!!!

Tell All Your Friends   There will always be a request that you share this "important information" by forwarding the message to everybody in your e-mail address book or to as many people as you possibly can. This is a surefire sign that the message is a hoax.

This Isn't a Hoax   The body of the e-mail may contain some form of corroboration, such as a pseudoquote from an executive of a major corporation or government official. The message may include a sincere-sounding premise, such as this, for example: *My neighbor, who works for Microsoft, just received this warning so I know it's true. He asked me to pass this along to as many people as I can.*

Sometimes the message will contain a link to Snopes to further confuse people. The references to Snopes are just red herrings, though, meant only to give a sense of legitimacy to the hoax. The author knows that lots of folks will believe it because

(Continues)

THINKING CRITICALLY ABOUT NEW MEDIA (*CONTINUED*)

they see it in print and won't bother to really check it for themselves. Anyone actually bothering to check the story with Snopes would, of course, discover that it was not true. Hoax writers count on folks being too lazy to verify those stories before they hit the forward button.

It's all a bunch of baloney. Don't believe it for a second.

Watch for e-mails containing a subtle form of self-corroboration. Statements such as "This is serious!" or "This is not a hoax!" can be deceiving. Just because somebody says it's not a hoax doesn't make it so.

Dire Consequences   The e-mail text will predict dire consequences if you don't act immediately. You are led to believe that a missing child will never be found unless the e-mail is forwarded immediately. It may infer that someone won't die happy unless they receive a bazillion business cards. Or it may state that a virus will destroy your hard drive and cause green fuzzy things to grow in your refrigerator.

History   Look for a lot of >>>> marks in the left margin. These marks indicate that people suckered by the hoax have forwarded the message countless times before it has reached you.

In her book *Cyberliteracy*, Laura Gurak identified three things that are common to all hoax and urban legend e-mail chain letters. They are the **hook**, the **threat**, and the **request**. To hook you in, a hoax will play on your sympathy, your greed, or your fears. It will threaten you with bad luck, play on your guilt, or label you a fool for not participating. And, of course, it will request that you forward the e-mail to all of your friends and family.

The hook catches your interest to make you read the whole e-mail. The hook may be a sad story about a missing or sick child, or about the latest computer virus. Once you're hooked, the threat warns you about the terrible things that will happen if you don't keep the chain going. The threat may be that someone will die if you don't respond, or that your computer will suffer a melt-down from the latest virus. Last is the request. It will implore you to send the message to as many others as possible. It may even promise a small donation to a group with a legitimate-sounding name because they are able to track every forwarded e-mail (also a hoax).

Source: "Top Five Signs That an E-mail Is a Hoax" from www.hoaxbusters.org/hoax10.html. Reprinted by permission.

Thinking-Writing Activity

IDENTIFYING INTERNET HOAXES

Use the guidelines that you have just read to identify the telltale signs of a hoax in the following four emails. Write a sentence or two for each one.

READ IMMEDIATELY AND PASS ON!

Someone is sending out a very cute screensaver of the Budweiser Frogs. If you download it, you will lose everything! Your hard drive will crash and someone from the Internet will get your screen name and password! DO NOT DOWNLOAD IT UNDER ANY CIRCUMSTANCES! It just went into circulation yesterday. Please distribute this message. This is a new, very malicious virus and not many people know about it. This information was announced yesterday morning from Microsoft. Please share it with everyone that might access the Internet. Once again, pass this along to EVERYONE in your address book so that this may be stopped. AOL has said that this is a very dangerous virus and that there is NO remedy for it at this time.

BONSAI KITTENS

To anyone with love and respect for life: In New York there is a Japanese who sells "bonsai-kittens." Sounds like fun huh? NOT! These animals are squeezed into a bottle. Their urine and feces are removed through probes. They feed them with a kind of tube. They feed them chemicals to keep their bones soft and flexible so the kittens grow into the shape of the bottle. The animals will stay their as long as they live. They can't walk or move or wash themselves. Bonsai-kittens are becoming a fashion in New York and Asia. See this horror at: http://www.bonsaikitten.com Please sign this email in protest against these tortures. If you receive an email with over 500 names, please send a copy to: anacheca@hotmail.com. From there this protest will be sent to USA and Mexican animal protection organizations.

(Continues)

THINKING CRITICALLY ABOUT NEW MEDIA (*CONTINUED*)

MISSING CHILD PICTURE

I am asking you all, begging you to please forward this email onto anyone and everyone you know, PLEASE. My 9 year old girl, Penny Brown, is missing. She has been missing for now two weeks. It is still not too late. Please help us. If anyone anywhere knows anything, sees anything, please contact me at zicozicozico@hotmail.com. I am including a picture of her. All prayers are appreciated!! It only takes 2 seconds to forward this on, if it was your child, you would want all the help you could get. Please. Thank you for your kindness, hopefully you can help us.

VIRUS WARNING

Just to let you know a new virus was started in New York last night. This virus acts in the following manner: It sends itself automatically to all contacts on your list with the title "A Virtual Card for You." As soon as the supposed virtual card is opened, the computer freezes so that the user has to reboot. When the ctrl+alt+del keys or the reset button are pressed, the virus destroys Sector Zero, thus permanently destroying the hard disk. Yesterday in just a few hours this virus caused panic in New York, according to news broadcast by CNN www.cnn.com. This alert was received by an employee of Microsoft itself. So don't open any mails with subject "A Virtual Card for You." As soon as you get the mail, delete it. Please pass on this email to all your friends. Forward this to everyone in your address book. I would rather receive this 25 times than not at all.

Believing and Knowing

Developing beliefs that are as accurate as possible is important to us as critical thinkers because the more accurate our beliefs are, the better we are able to understand the world around us and to make predictions about the future. As the preceding discussion has suggested, however, the accuracy of the beliefs we form can vary tremendously.

We use the word *knowing* to distinguish beliefs supported by strong reasons or evidence (such as the belief that life exists on earth) from beliefs for which there is less support (such as the belief that life exists on other planets) or from beliefs disproved by reasons or evidence to the contrary. This saying expresses another way to understand the difference between believing and knowing:

"You can believe what is not so, but you cannot know what is not so."

Thinking-Writing Activity

WEIGHING YOUR BELIEFS AND KNOWLEDGE

Look again at the beliefs you have written about for previous activities. Could you say about any of them "I know this" rather than merely "I believe this"? Why? Write answers to these questions.

KNOWLEDGE AND TRUTH

Authorities often disagree about the true nature of a given situation or the best course of action. It is common, for example, for doctors to disagree about a diagnosis, for economists to differ on the state of the economy, or for psychiatrists to disagree on whether a convicted felon is a menace to society or a victim of social forces.

What do we do when experts disagree? As critical thinkers, we must analyze and evaluate all the available information, develop our own well-reasoned beliefs, and recognize when we lack sufficient information to arrive at well-reasoned beliefs. We must realize, too, that such beliefs may evolve over time as we obtain more information or improve our insight.

Although there are compelling reasons to view knowledge and truth as evolving, some people resist doing so. Either they take refuge in a belief in the absolute, unchanging nature of knowledge and truth as presented by the appropriate authorities, or they conclude that there is no such thing as knowledge or truth and that trying to seek either is futile.

UNDERSTANDING RELATIVISM

In this latter view of the world, known as *relativism,* all beliefs are considered "relative" to the person or context in which they arise. For the relativist, all opinions are equal in validity to all others; no one is ever in a position to say with confidence that one view is right and another one wrong. Although a relativistic view is appropriate in some areas of experience—for example, in matters of taste such as fashion—in many other areas it is not. Knowledge, in the form of well-supported beliefs, does exist. Some beliefs are better than others, not because an authority has proclaimed them so but because they can be analyzed in terms of the criteria discussed earlier in this chapter.

UNDERSTANDING FALSIFIABLE BELIEFS

Another important criterion for evaluating certain beliefs is that the beliefs be *falsifiable.* This means that it is possible to state conditions—tests—under which the beliefs could be disproved and that the beliefs then pass those tests. For example, if you believe that you can create ice cubes by placing water-filled trays in a freezer, you can conduct an experiment to determine whether your belief is accurate. If no ice cubes form after you put the trays in the freezer, your theory is disproved. If, however, you believe that your destiny is related to the positions of the planets and stars (as astrologers do), it is not clear how you can conduct an experiment to determine whether your belief is accurate. Since a belief that is not falsifiable can never be proved, such a belief is questionable.

CLIMATE CHANGE AND TRUTH

Global warming refers to the accelerating warming of the earth's climate that is the direct result of the burning of fossil fuels and the torching of rainforests. The emissions from these activities are adding to the atmosphere's invisible blanket of carbon dioxide and other heat-trapping "greenhouse" gases. A growing body of scientific evidence supports the conclusion that the cumulative result of these activities is causing the earth's climate to warm at an alarming rate.

In order to deal with these frightening possibilities, there is scientific consensus that fossil fuel emissions must be reduced. Nevertheless, despite this realization, countries have been reluctant to limit emissions because of the economic consequences. In addition, there have been voices that have claimed that global warming and its connection to fossil fuel emissions are unproven, inaccurate, and overblown.

The articles that follow explore different perspectives on this complex and vitally important issue. Ken Caldeira's article, "The Great Climate Experiment," provides a comprehensive and in-depth analysis of this problem and the scientific research upon which it rests. In the article "Global Warming: Hoax of the Century," Patrick Buchanan contends that the entire global warming issue is a myth propagated for other, nonscientific reasons. And, finally, in the article "Why Media Tell Climate Story Poorly," Tyler Hamilton explains why, despite the compelling scientific evidence of global warming, nonscientific points of view have been permitted to gain traction and "muddy the waters" of this crucial issue.

The Great Climate Experiment: How Far Can We Push the Planet?
by Ken Caldeira

Business, government or technology forecasts usually look five or 10 years out, 50 years at most. Among climate scientists, there is some talk of century's end. In reality, carbon dioxide dumped into the atmosphere today will affect Earth hundreds of thousands of years hence.

How will greenhouse gases change the far future? No one can say for sure exactly how Earth will respond, but climate scientists—using mathematical models built from knowledge of past climate systems, as well as the complex web of processes that impact climate and the laws of physics and chemistry—can make predictions about what Earth will look like.

Already we are witnessing the future envisioned by many of these models take shape. As predicted, there has been more warming over land than over the oceans, more at the poles than near the equator, more in winter than in summer and more at night than in the day. Extreme downpours have become more common. In the Arctic, ice and snow cover less area, and methane-rich permafrost soils are beginning to melt. Weather is getting weirder, with storms fueled by the additional heat.

What are the ultimate limits of the change that we are causing? The best historical example comes from the 100-million-year-old climate of the Cretaceous period, when moist, hot air enveloped dinosaurs' leathery skin, crocodilelike creatures swam in the Arctic and teeming plant life flourished in the CO_2-rich air. The greenhouse that is forming now will have consequences that last for hundreds of thousands of years or more. But first, it will profoundly affect much of life on the planet—especially us.

A Desert in Italy

One of the greatest uncertainties in climate prediction is the amount of CO_2 that will ultimately be released into the atmosphere. In this article, I will assume industrial civilization will continue to do what it has been doing for the past 200 years—namely, burn fossil fuels at an accelerating rate until we can no longer afford to pull them out of the ground.

Just how much CO_2 could we put into the atmosphere? All told, there are about one quadrillion metric tons (1021 grams) of organic carbon locked up in Earth's sedimentary shell in one form or another. So far we have burned only one twentieth of 1 percent of this carbon, or roughly 2,000 billion metric tons of CO_2. With all the carbon locked in Earth's crust, we will never run out of fossil fuels. We are now extracting oil from tar sands and natural gas from water-fractured shale—both resources once thought to be technologically and economically inaccessible. No one can confidently predict just how far ingenuity can take us. Yet eventually the cost of extraction and processing will become so high that fossil fuels will become more expensive than alternative resources. In the scenario envisaged here, we ultimately burn about 1 percent of the available organic carbon over the next few centuries. That is in the range of the amount of extraction most likely to become technologically feasible in the foreseeable future. We further assume that in the future humanity will learn to extract unconventional fossil fuels but will burn them at slower rates. Without any change in our habits, Earth may warm by about five degrees Celsius (nine degrees Fahrenheit) by 2100, although the actual warming could be half or even double this amount, depending primarily on how clouds respond. This change is about the difference between the average climate of Boston, Mass., and Huntsville, Ala.

In the northern midlatitudes between 30 degrees north and 60 degrees north—a band that includes the U.S., Europe, China, and most of Canada and Russia—the annual average temperature drops two thirds of a degree C with each degree of increasing latitude. With five degrees C of warming in a century, that translates into an average poleward movement of more than 800 kilometers in that period, for an average poleward movement of temperature bands exceeding 20 meters each day. Squirrels may be able to keep up with this rate, but oak trees and earthworms have difficulty moving that fast.

Then there will be the rains. Earth is a planetary-scale heat engine. The hot sun warms equatorial air, which then rises and cools. The cooling condenses water vapor in the air, which falls back to Earth as rain—hence, the belt of torrential rains that occur near the equator.

Yet this water condensation also heats the surrounding air, causing it to rise even more rapidly. This hot, dry air reaches as high as jets fly, then spreads laterally toward the poles. At altitude, the hot air radiates heat to space and thus becomes cool, which causes it to sink back toward the planet's surface. The sun's rays pass through this dry, cloudless air, beating down to heat the arid surface. Today such dry air sinks occur at about 30 degrees north and south latitude, thus creating the great belts of desert that encircle the globe. With greenhouse warming, the rising air is hotter. Thus, it takes more time for this air to cool off and sink back to Earth. As a result, these desert bands move toward the poles.

The climate of the Sahara Desert may move northward. Already southern Europe has been experiencing more intense droughts despite overall increases in precipitation globally, and it may lose the Mediterranean climate that has long been considered one of the most desirable in the world. Future generations may say the same about the Scandinavian climate instead.

Up there in the northern midlatitudes, growing seasons are getting longer. Spring springs sooner: plants flower, lake ice melts and migratory birds return earlier than in the historical past.

That will not be the only benefit to croplands in Canada and Siberia. Plants make food by using the energy in sunlight to merge CO_2 and water. For the most part, plants absorb CO_2 via little pores in leaves known as stomata. When the stomata are open wide, the plants can get plenty of CO_2, but a lot of water evaporates through these gaping holes. Higher concentrations of atmospheric CO_2 mean a plant can get the CO_2 it needs by opening its stomata slightly or even building fewer stomata in leaves. In a high-CO_2 world, plants can grow more using the same amount of water. (This decrease in evaporation from plants also leads to a further decrease in precipitation, and because evaporation causes cooling, the decrease in evaporation causes further warming.)

Such gains will not be felt everywhere. In the tropics, high temperatures already compromise many crops; this heat stress will likely get worse with global warming. The outlook may be for increased crop productivity overall, with increases in the north exceeding the reductions near the equator. Global warming may not decrease overall food supply, but it may give more to the rich and less to the poor.

Oceans of Change

The vast oceans resist change, but change they will. At no time in Earth's past—with the possible exception of mass-extinction events—has ocean chemistry changed as much and as rapidly as scientists expect it to over the coming decades. When CO_2 enters the oceans, it reacts with seawater to become carbonic acid. In high enough concentrations, this carbonic acid can cause the shells and skeletons of many marine organisms to dissolve—particularly those made of a soluble form of calcium carbonate known as aragonite.

Scientists estimate that more than a quarter of all marine species spend part of their lives in coral reefs. Coral skeletons are made of aragonite. Even if chemical conditions do not deteriorate to the point where shells dissolve, acidification can make it more difficult for these organisms to build them. In just a few decades there will be no place left in the ocean with the kind of chemistry that has supported coral-reef growth in the geologic past. It is not known how many of these coral-dependent species will disappear along with the reefs.

Such chemical changes will most directly affect reef life, but the rest of us would be wise to consider the physical changes afoot. At the most basic level, water acts like mercury in a thermometer: add heat and watch it rise. The sea is also being fed by water now held in ice caps.

In high-CO_2 times in the ancient past, Earth warmed enough for crocodilelike animals to live north of the Arctic Circle. Roughly 100 million years ago annual average polar temperatures reached 14 degrees C, with summertime temperatures exceeding 25 degrees C. Over thousands of years temperatures of this magnitude would be sufficient to melt the great ice sheets of Greenland and Antarctica. With the ice sheets melted completely, sea level will be about 120 meters higher, flooding vast areas. That water's weight on low-lying continental regions will push those areas down farther into the mantle, causing the waters to lap even higher. The poles are expected to warm about 2.5 times faster than Earth as a whole. Already the Arctic has warmed faster than anywhere else, by about two degrees C compared with 0.8 degree C globally. At the end of the last ice age, when the climate warmed by about five degrees C over thousands of years, the ice sheets melted at a rate that caused sea level to rise about one meter per century. We hope and expect that ice sheets will not melt more rapidly this time, but we cannot be certain.

Chasing Venus

Over the past several million years Earth's climate has oscillated to cause the waxing and waning of great ice sheets. Our greenhouse gas emissions are hitting this complex system with a hammer. I have presented a scenario in which our climate evolves fairly smoothly, but jumps and starts that could shock biological, social and political systems beyond the limits of their resilience are also possible.

Consider that Arctic warming could cause hundreds of billions of metric tons of methane to rapidly bubble to the atmosphere from Arctic seabeds and soils. Molecule for molecule in the atmosphere, methane is about 37 times better at trapping heat than CO_2. Were this methane released suddenly, as may have occurred in a warming event 55 million years ago known as the Paleocene-Eocene Thermal Maximum, we could experience truly catastrophic warming. This risk is remote, however, according to most scientists. Some have also suggested that feedback effects such as melting permafrost could cause a runaway greenhouse scenario where the oceans become so hot they evaporate. Because water vapor is itself a greenhouse gas, such a stronger water cycle could cause Earth to get so hot that atmospheric water vapor would persist and never rain out. In this case, atmospheric CO_2 from volcanoes and other sources would continue to accumulate. Cosmic rays would break apart the water vapor at high altitudes; the resulting hydrogen would eventually escape to space. Earth's climate would then settle into a state reminiscent of its planetary neighbor Venus.

Fortunately, ocean vaporization is not even a remote risk from today's greenhouse gas emissions. Simply put, there is a limit to how much CO_2 can heat the planet. Once CO_2 and water vapor concentrations rise high enough, the molecules increasingly scatter the incoming sunlight, preventing it from getting any hotter. If we continue to burn fossil fuels, however, greenhouse gas concentrations in the atmosphere will reach levels last seen in the Cretaceous. Back then, inland seas flooded vast areas of the continents on a hot, moist Earth. Giant reptiles swam in the oceans. On land, dinosaurs grazed on luxuriant plant growth. If we burn just 1 percent of the organic carbon in Earth's crust over the next few centuries, humans will breathe the same CO_2 concentrations as the dinosaurs inhaled and experience similar temperatures.

Compared with the gradual warming of hothouse climates in the past, industrial climate change is occurring in fast-forward. In geologic history, transitions from low- to high-CO_2 atmospheres typically happened at rates of less than 0.00001 degree a year. We are re-creating the world of the dinosaurs 5,000 times faster. What will thrive in this hothouse? Some organisms, such as rats and cockroaches, are invasive generalists, which can take advantage of disrupted environments. Other organisms, such as corals and many tropical forest species, have evolved to thrive in a narrow range of conditions. Invasive species will likely transform such ecosystems as a result of global warming. Climate change may usher in a world of weeds. Human civilization is also at risk. Consider the Mayans. Even before Europeans arrived, the Mayan civilization had begun to collapse thanks to relatively minor climate changes. The Mayans had not developed enough resilience to weather small reductions in rainfall. The Mayans are not alone as examples of civilizations that failed to adapt to climate changes.

Crises provoked by climate change are likely to be regional. If the rich get richer and the poor get poorer, could this set in motion mass migrations that challenge political and economic stability? Some of the same countries that are most likely to suffer from the changes wrought by global warming also boast nuclear weapons. Could climate change exacerbate existing tensions and provoke nuclear or other apocalyptic conflict? The social response to climate change could produce bigger problems for humanity than the climate change itself.

Starting Over

The woody plants that flourished during the Cretaceous died, and some became coal over geologic time. The ocean's plankton ended up buried in sediments, and some became oil and gas. The climate cooled as sea life locked CO_2 in shells and skeletons.

The oceans will absorb most of our CO_2 over millennia. The resulting acidification will dissolve carbonate minerals, and the chemical effects of dissolution will allow yet more CO_2 to be absorbed. Nevertheless, atmospheric CO_2 concentrations will remain well above preindustrial levels of 280 parts per million for many tens of thousands of years. As a result, the ebb and flow of ice ages brought on by subtle variations in Earth's orbit will cease, and humanity's greenhouse gas emissions will keep the planet locked in a hothouse. Over time increased temperatures and precipitation will accelerate the rate at which bedrock and soils dissolve. Streams and rivers will bring these dissolved rocks and minerals, containing elements such as calcium and magnesium, to the oceans. Perhaps hundreds of thousands of years from now some marine organism will take the calcium and CO_2 and form a carbonate shell. That seashell and millions of others may eventually become limestone. Just as the White Cliffs of Dover in England are a remnant of the Cretaceous atmosphere, the majority of carbon in the fossil fuels burned today will become a layer in the rocks—a record, written in stone, of a world changed by a single species.

QUESTION FOR READING ACTIVELY

1. Ken Caldeira's article, "The Great Climate Experiment," provides a comprehensive analysis of climate change and the scientific research upon which it rests. As you were reading Caldeira's article, which passages stood out the most or had an impact on your current beliefs about global warming?

QUESTIONS FOR THINKING CRITICALLY

1. According to Caldeira, some of these global warming effects have already started occurring. As predicted, there has been more warming over land that over the oceans, more at the poles than near the equator, more in winter than in summer, and more at night than during the day. Extreme downpours have become more common. In the Arctic, ice and snow cover less area, and methane-rich permafrost soils are beginning to melt. Which of these unusual weather effects, like Hurricane Sandy in October 2012, have you begun to witness? Perhaps you have witnessed other changes in your environment that have not been mentioned in the article. If so, what are they?

2. What are some of the devastating effects scientists believe that global warming will result in? What are the reasons and evidence that have convinced scientists that global warming does actually pose a potentially catastrophic threat to the future of the earth?

QUESTION FOR WRITING THOUGHTFULLY

1. Based on your interpretation and evaluation of the evidence surrounding global warming that you have read about or experienced to date, describe the difference between believing and knowing that global warming actually does (or does not) pose a threat to our planet.

Global Warming: Hoax of the Century

by Patrick Buchanan

With publication of "On the Origin of Species" in 1859, the hunt was on for the "missing link." Fame and fortune awaited the scientist who found the link proving Darwin right: that man evolved from a monkey. In 1912, success! In a gravel pit near Piltdown in East Sussex, there was found the cranium of a man with the jaw of an ape. "Darwin Theory Proved True," ran the banner headline. Evolution skeptics were pilloried, and three English scientists were knighted for validating Piltdown Man.

It wasn't until 1953, after generations of biology students had been taught about Piltdown Man, that closer inspection discovered that the cranium belonged to a medieval Englishman, the bones had been dyed to look older and the jaw belonged to an orangutan whose teeth had been filed down to look human.

Source: © 1995–2013 Patrick J. Buchanan (http://buchanan.org/blog/hoax-of-the-century-3680).

The scientific discovery of the century became the hoax of the century. But Piltdown Man was not alone. There was Nebraska Man. In 1922, Henry Fairfield Osborn, president of the American Museum of Natural History, identified a tooth fossil found in Nebraska to be that of an "anthropoid ape." He used his discovery to mock William Jennings Bryan, newly elected to Congress, as "the most distinguished primate which the State of Nebraska has yet produced." Invited to testify at the Scopes trial, however, Osborn begged off. For, by 1925, Nebraska Man's tooth had been traced to a wild pig, and Creationist Duane Gish, a biochemist, had remarked of Osborn's Nebraska Man, "I believe this is a case in which a scientist made a man out of a pig, and the pig made a monkey out of the scientist."

These stories are wonderfully told in Eugene Windchy's 2009 The End of Darwinism. But if Piltdown Man and his American cousin Nebraska Man were the hoaxes of the 20th Century, global warming is the great hoax of the 21st. In a matter of months, we have we learned:

- In its 2007 report claiming that the Himalayan glaciers are melting, the U.N. Inter-governmental Panel on Climate Change relied on a 1999 news story in a popular science journal, based on one interview with a little-known Indian scientist who said this was pure "speculation" not supported by any research. The IPCC also misreported the supposed date of the glaciers' meltdown as 2035. The Indian had suggested 2350.

- The IPCC report that global warming is going to kill 40% of the Amazon rainforest and cut African crop yields 50% has been found to be alarmist propaganda.

- The IPCC 2007 report declared 55% of Holland to be below sea level, an exaggeration of over 100%.

- While endless keening is heard over the Arctic ice cap, we hear almost nothing of the 2009 report of the British Antarctica Survey that the sea ice cap of Antarctica has been expanding by 100,000 square kilometers a decade for 30 years. That translates into 3,800 square miles of new Antarctic ice every year.

- Though America endured one of the worst winters ever, while the 2009 hurricane season was among the mildest, the warmers say this proves nothing. But when our winters were mild and the 2005 hurricane season brought four major storms to the U.S. coast, Katrina among them, the warmers said this validated their theory. You can't have it both ways.

- The Climate Research Unit at East Anglia University, which provides the scientific backup for the IPCC, apparently threw out the basic data on which it based claims of a rise in global temperatures for the century. And a hacker into its e-mail files found CRU "scientists" had squelched the publication of dissenting views.

What we learned in a year's time: Polar bears are not vanishing. Sea levels are not rising at anything like the 20-foot surge this century was to bring. Cities are not sinking. Beaches are not disappearing. Temperatures have not been rising since the late 1990s. And, in historic terms, our global warming is not at all unprecedented. How horrible was it?

"The Vikings discovered and settled Greenland around A.D. 950. Greenland was then so warm that thousands of colonists supported themselves by pasturing cattle on what is now frozen tundra. During this great global warming, Europe built the looming castles and soaring cathedrals that even today stun tourists with their size, beauty and engineering excellence. These colossal buildings required the investment of millions of man-hours—which could be spared from farming because of higher crop yields."

Today's global-warming hysteria is the hoax of the 21st Century. H.L. Mencken had it right: "The whole aim of practical politics is to keep the populace alarmed—and hence clamorous to be led to safety—by menacing it with an endless series of hobgoblins, all of them imaginary."

QUESTION FOR READING ACTIVELY

1. In the article "Global Warming: Hoax of the Century," Patrick Buchanan contends that the entire global warming issue is a myth propagated for other, nonscientific reasons. What might some of these reasons be?

QUESTIONS FOR THINKING CRITICALLY

1. Buchanan argues that global warming is a hoax in the same way that Piltdown Man, the supposed "missing evolutionary link" between apes and *homo sapiens*, fooled scientists and laypeople for over 50 years. What evidence does Buchanan present to support this belief? How do you think scientists who believe in the reality of global warming would respond to his evidence?

2. Buchanan presents a list of findings that, according to him, show global warming is a hoax. Analyze his evidence carefully (including his sources), and explain why you think he is right or wrong. Consider the differences between knowledge and truth, the concept of relativism, the possibility of falsifiable beliefs, and the role of the media in your response.

QUESTION FOR WRITING THOUGHTFULLY

1. Buchanan concludes his article with a quote by H. L. Mencken and says that Mencken "had it right" in that "The whole aim of practical politics is to keep the populace alarmed—and hence clamorous to be led to safety—by menacing it with an endless series of hobgoblins, all of them imaginary." What did Mencken mean by this? Describe how this statement has relevance today—not only in regard to global warming, but with respect to other contemporary issues as well.

Why Media Tell Climate Story Poorly

by Tyler Hamilton

I apologize on behalf of my profession.

If it's true that Canadians and Americans have become less concerned about the potential impact of climate change, and that more consider global warming a hoax, some blame can certainly be directed at the news media.

"The media [are] giving an equal seat at the table to a lot of non-qualified scientists," Julio Betancourt, a senior scientist at the U.S. Geological Survey, told a group of environment and energy reporters during a week-long learning retreat in New Mexico.

I was among them, listening to Betancourt and two of his colleagues describe the measurable impacts climate change is having on the U.S. southwest. Drought. More frequent and damaging forest fires. Northward migration of forest and animal species. Hotter, longer growing seasons. Less snow pack. Earlier snow melt.

"The scientific evidence reported in peer-reviewed journals is growing by the day, and it suggests the pace of climate change has surpassed the worst-case scenarios predicted just a few years ago." Betancourt is the first to admit the science is constantly evolving and that the work at hand is highly complex. One challenge is separating the part of climate change caused by naturally occurring cyclical systems from the part caused by humans, who since the Industrial Revolution have dumped greenhouse gases into the atmosphere at an accelerating rate.

Clearly there is an interaction between the two. But can scientists explain it with bulletproof precision using predictive models everyone can agree on? No, of course not. That's not how science works. More difficult is that scientists such as Betancourt are realizing the climate changes observed are not happening in a gradual, predictable fashion but, instead, in sudden steps. Systems reach a certain threshold of environmental stress and then "pop," they act quickly to restabilize.

These changes also happen regionally, making it difficult for people in one region of the world to appreciate disruptive changes going on elsewhere.

Not surprisingly, those looking to stall action on climate change—or who altogether deny that humanity is contributing to global warming—are exploiting this complexity and lack of certainty.

A recent Pew Research Center poll of 1,500 Americans found that 57 per cent believed there was solid scientific evidence that the globe is warming, down from 77 per cent in 2007. The changing attitudes coincide with a growing effort to discredit climate science in the lead-up to the Copenhagen talks on Dec. 7 and efforts by U.S. legislators to cobble together climate legislation that would signal America's commitment to reducing its greenhouse-gas emissions.

It also coincides with an economic downturn, during which people are concerned most about their finances. There's also a strong likelihood that people want to hear that maybe this climate change stuff is all a bad dream.

It's much more difficult to have a story in the newspaper or a TV news segment, explaining the latest study in Nature or Science, than it is to have an unqualified scientist or "spokesman" offer a pithy, controversial quote or sound bite not necessarily grounded in fact.

This reality has given the fossil-fuel lobby a major leg up, writes James Hoggan, co-author of A Climate Cover-Up and founder of DeSmogBlog.com. Hoggan's must-read book describes in disturbing detail the well-oiled campaign to confuse the public and confound the science, creating enough doubt to thwart meaningful action and protect a world economic order built around the burning of oil, coal, and natural gas.

The Heartland Institute, Friends of Science, and Natural Resources Stewardship Project are among the groups that make their Rolodex of "experts" available to comment on climate issues.

But, as Hoggan points out, most of those experts are anything but. Lift their veil and they typically are funded by the fossil-fuel industry, long-retired climate scientists who have not published peer-reviewed papers for many years, or scientists who are experts but not necessarily in climate science. "If a doctor recommended that you undergo an innovative new surgical procedure, you might seek a second opinion, but you'd probably ask another surgeon," writes Hoggan, a public-relations veteran who is also chairman of the David Suzuki Foundation.

"You wouldn't check with your local carpenter, and you certainly wouldn't ask a representative of the drug company whose product would be rendered irrelevant if you had the operation."

Still, many journalists under deadline and without the time to verify credentials, journalists who do not follow climate science and the news around it, continue to give these so-called experts a soapbox to stand on. Even those with time to spare often offer up the soapbox out of some misplaced attempt at balance, giving the impression that the scientific community is deeply divided.

Once their comments are published, the blogs take over and public confusion grows deeper. Mark Twain said it best: "A lie travels halfway around the world while the truth is still putting on its boots." The Internet has only accelerated the speed of travel. It's why we've been seeing silly stories about "global cooling" appear in recent months, or articles about thickening Arctic ice, or the "Global Warming Conspiracy." On Friday, the latest conspiracy story began making its rounds. Hackers accessed email messages from some climate scientists on an Internet server at the University of East Anglia in Britain. The emails, from what I've read, do show that not all scientists agree, that some scientists don't like other scientists, and that some scientists are struggling with the complexity of their work. What these emails do not show is that there's any conspiracy or that consensus around the reality of human-influenced global warming is beginning to crack.

Still, that won't stop the skeptics from cherry picking what's in those emails and claiming this is some kind of smoking gun that will derail Copenhagen. The blogosphere is abuzz, and news media are never ones to turn down a juicy controversy. The timing of the hack makes it all the more suspicious, but no less dramatic.

It's a shame.

I asked Betancourt during his New Mexico talk why the scientific community has not done a better job of battling the misinformation campaign and speaking as a more united front.

The problem, he said, is working scientists don't tend to be communications specialists but are up against people who are. So, for honest, accurate describing of the science of climate, "it's more up to the media, and less up to us."

QUESTION FOR READING ACTIVELY

1. In the article "Why Media Tell Climate Story Poorly," Tyler Hamilton explains why, despite the compelling scientific evidence of global warming, nonscientific points of view have been permitted to gain traction and "muddy the waters" of this crucial issue. What are some of those reasons?

Thinking Critically About Visuals

Buyenlarge/Getty Images

"You must expect the unexpected. . ."

Beliefs about what the future will be like rarely turn out to be accurate. For example, it was widely assumed that at this point in time, we would be driving around in cars that floated on air, and that robots would have taken over all of the mundane chores of living so that we would have endless amounts of time to relax and live a life of happy indolence. It hasn't exactly turned out that way! Examine the figure to the left, which depicts one such vision of the future. What beliefs about the future does it reveal? In what ways were these predictions accurate? In what ways were they inaccurate?

On the other hand, the future has a way of surprising us, as expressed in the full quote by the ancient Greek philosopher Heraclitus: "You must expect the unexpected because it cannot be found by search or trail." Who could have predicted the Internet, Smartphones, Facebook, Twitter, GPS, . . . or medical inventions that permit amputees to compete in high-level sporting events like the one depicted in the figure below? Identify some of the current beliefs that people have about the future. Which of these beliefs do you think will turn out to be accurate? What are some of the surprises that you think the future has in store for us?

GLYN KIRK/AFP/Getty Images

1. Hamilton claims that only 57 percent of Americans believe there is solid scientific evidence that the globe is warming, down from 77 percent in 2007. Why does he believe that the media must shoulder much of the responsibility for this decline, and how can they correct this? What are some other factors that account for the public's confusion regarding the reality of global warming? And, finally, what critical thinking skills does Hamilton believe should be used in responding to the "experts" who reject the threat of global warming?

2. In order to deal with these frightening possibilities, there is scientific consensus that fossil fuel emissions must be reduced. Nevertheless, despite this realization, countries have been reluctant to limit emissions because of the economic consequences. Describe some of these consequences, and evaluate whether or not they are worse than the ultimate consequences of global warming. You may wish to refer back to the consequences detailed in Ken Caldeira's article, "The Great Climate Experiment."

1. Hamilton concludes his essay by quoting Julio Betancourt, a senior scientist at the U.S. Geological Survey: "The problem, said Betancourt, is working scientists don't tend to be communications specialists but are up against people who are. So, for honest, accurate describing of the science of climate, 'it's more up to the media, and less up to us.'" Considering some of what Hamilton revealed in his article, further explore what might happen (and what has already been happening) when we leave communication up to the media.

Ways of Presenting Beliefs

When you write, you are presenting your beliefs. No matter what its form—email, letters, research papers, blog, business documents, even stories and poems—your written expression states what you believe. When you write, you present your beliefs in three ways: reports, inferences, and judgments. Your choice of words establishes which of the three you are using:

- *Report:* My bus was late today.
- *Inference:* My bus will probably be late tomorrow.
- *Judgment:* The bus system is unreliable.

Now try to identify which of the three is being used in these statements:

1. Each modern nuclear warhead has over 100 times the explosive power of the bomb dropped on Hiroshima.

2. With all the billions of planets in the universe, the odds are that there are other forms of life in the cosmos.

3. In the long run, the energy needs of the world will best be met by solar energy technology rather than nuclear energy or fossil fuels.

As you examine these various statements, you can see that they provide readers with different types of information. For example, the first statement in each list reports aspects of the world that can be verified—that is, checked for accuracy. Appropriate investigation can determine whether the bus was actually late today and whether modern nuclear warheads really have the power attributed to them. When you describe the world in ways that can be verified through investigation, you are *reporting factual information.*

Looking at the second statement in each list, you can see that each provides a different sort of information than the first one does. These statements cannot be verified. There is no way to investigate and determine with certainty whether the bus will indeed be late tomorrow or whether there is life on other planets. Although these conclusions may be based on facts, they go beyond them. When you describe the world in ways based on factual information yet go beyond it to make statements about what is not currently known, you are *inferring* conclusions about the world.

Finally, as you examine the third statement in each list, it is apparent that these statements differ from both factual reports and inferences. In each, the speaker is applying certain standards (criteria) to deem the bus service as unreliable and solar energy as more promising than nuclear energy or fossil fuels. You are *judging* when you describe the world in ways that evaluate it on the basis of certain criteria.

You continually use these ways of describing and organizing your world—reporting, inferring, and judging—to make sense of your experience. In most instances, you are not aware that you are actually performing these activities, nor are you usually aware of the differences among them. Yet these three activities work together to help you see the world as a complete picture.

Thinking-Writing Activity
IDENTIFYING REPORTS, INFERENCES, AND JUDGMENTS

1. Write three statements that you believe—one as a report, one as an inference, and one as a judgment.

2. Locate a short article from a newspaper, magazine, or online news service, and identify the reports, inferences, and judgments it contains.

3. Share your statements and your findings with classmates.

REPORTING FACTUAL INFORMATION

Statements written as reports express the most accurate beliefs you have about the world. Factual beliefs have earned this distinction because they are verifiable, usually by using one or more of your senses. For example, consider the following factual statement: "That young woman is wearing a brown hat in the rain." This statement about an event in the world is considered factual because you can verify it immediately with sensual experience—what you can (in principle or in theory) see, hear, touch, taste, or smell. It is important to say *in principle* or *in theory* because often you do not use all of your senses to check out what you are experiencing. Look again at the factual statement: you would normally be satisfied to see this event without insisting on touching the hat or giving the person a physical examination. If necessary, however, you could perform these additional actions.

You use the same reasoning when you believe other people's factual statements that you are not in a position to check immediately. For instance:

- The Great Wall of China is more than 1,500 miles long.
- There are large mountains and craters on the moon.
- Your skin is covered with germs.

You consider these factual statements because even though you cannot verify them with your senses at the moment, you could in principle or in theory do so *if* you were flown to China, *if* you were rocketed to the moon, or *if* you were to examine your skin with a powerful microscope. The process of verifying factual statements involves identifying the sources of information on which they are based and evaluating the reliability of these sources.

You communicate factual information to others by means of reports. A *report* is a description of something that has been experienced; it is communicated in as accurate and complete a way as possible. Through reports, you share your sensory experiences with other people, and this sharing enables you to learn much more about the world than you would if you were confined to knowing only what you experience.

Because factual reports play such an important role in the exchange and accumulation of information about the world, it is important that they be as accurate and complete as possible. This brings us to a problem. We have already seen in previous chapters that our perceptions and observations often are not accurate or complete. This means that sometimes when we think we are making factual reports, they actually are inaccurate or incomplete. For instance, consider our earlier factual statement: "That young woman is wearing a brown hat in the rain." Here are questions you could ask concerning the accuracy of the statement:

- Is the woman actually young, or does she merely look young?
- Is the person actually a woman or a man disguised as a woman?
- Is that really a hat the woman is wearing, or is it something else (such as a helmet or a paper bag)?

Of course, there are methods you could use to answer these questions. Can you describe some of them?

Besides difficulties with observations, the "facts" that you see in the world actually depend on more *general beliefs* that you have about how the world operates. Consider this question: "Why did the man's body fall from the top of the building to the sidewalk?" Having had some general science courses, you might respond, "The body was simply obeying the law of gravity" and consider that a factual statement. But how did people account for this sort of event before Newton formulated the law of gravity? Some popular responses might have included the following:

- Things always fall down, not up.
- The spirit in the body wanted to join with the spirit of the earth.

In the past, when people made statements like these—such as "Humans can't fly"—they thought they were stating facts. Increased knowledge and understanding have since shown these "factual beliefs" to be inaccurate, so they have been replaced by "better" beliefs. These better beliefs explain the world in a way that is more accurate and predictable. Will many of the beliefs now considered to be factually accurate also be replaced by more precise and predictable beliefs? If history is any indication, this will most certainly happen. Newton's formulations have already been replaced by Einstein's, based on the latter's theory of relativity. Einstein's have been refined and modified as well and may someday also be replaced.

Thinking-Writing Activity
EVALUATING FACTUAL INFORMATION

1. Locate and carefully read, watch, or listen to a report that deals with a major social issue.
2. Identify the main idea and key points of the article.
3. Describe the factual statements used to support the main idea.
4. Evaluate the accuracy of the factual information.
5. Evaluate the reliability of the sources of the factual information.

INFERRING FROM EVIDENCE OR PREMISES

Imagine yourself in the following situations:

1. It is 2:00 A.M. and your roommate comes crashing into the room. He staggers to his bed and falls across it, dropping (and breaking) a nearly empty whiskey bottle. Startled, you gasp, "What's the matter?" With alcohol fumes blasting from his mouth, he mumbles: "I jus' wanna hadda widdel drink!" What do you conclude?

2. Your roommate has just learned that she passed a math exam for which she had done absolutely no studying. Humming the refrain "I did it my way," she

comes dancing over to you with a huge grin on her face and says, "Let me buy you dinner to celebrate!" What do you conclude about how she is feeling?

3. It is midnight and the library is about to close. As you head for the door, you spy your roommate shuffling along in an awkward waddle. His coat bulges out in front as if he's pregnant. When you ask, "What's going on?" he gives you a glare and hisses, "Shhh!" Just before he reaches the door, a pile of books slides from under his coat and crashes to the floor. What do you conclude?

In these examples, it would be reasonable to make the following conclusions:

1. Your roommate is drunk.
2. Your roommate is happy.
3. Your roommate is stealing library books.

Although these conclusions are reasonable, they are not factual reports; they are inferences. You have not directly experienced your roommate's "drunkenness," "happiness," or "stealing." Instead, you have inferred it on the basis of your roommate's behavior and the circumstances. What clues in these situations might lead to these conclusions? One way of understanding the inferential nature of these views is to ask yourself the following questions:

1. Have you ever pretended to be drunk when you weren't? Could other people tell?
2. Have you ever pretended to be happy when you weren't? Could other people tell?
3. Have you ever been accused of stealing something when you were perfectly innocent? How did this happen?

From these examples you can see that whereas factual beliefs can in principle be verified by direct observation, *inferential beliefs* go beyond what can be directly observed. For instance, in the previous examples, your observation of some of your roommate's actions led you to infer things that you were not observing directly—"He's drunk," "She's happy," "He's stealing books."

Making such simple inferences is something you do all the time. It is so automatic that usually you are not even aware that you are going beyond your immediate observations or that you may be having trouble distinguishing between what you *observe* and what you *infer*. Making such inferences enables you to see the world as a complete picture, to fill in the blanks and to supplement the fragmentary sensations being presented to your senses. Presenting your inferences along with your beliefs in writing paints a complete picture for your readers.

Your writing may also include *predictions* of what will occur in the near future. Predictions and expectations are also inferences because you attempt to determine what is currently unknown from what is already known.

It is possible that your inferences may be wrong; in fact, they frequently are. You may infer that the woman sitting next to you is wearing two earrings and then discover that she has only one. You may expect the class to end at noon but find that the teacher lets you out early—or late. In the last section, we concluded that not even factual beliefs are ever absolutely certain. Comparatively speaking, inferential beliefs are much more uncertain than factual beliefs, so it is important to distinguish between the two.

The distinction between what is observed and what is inferred is given particular attention in courtroom settings, where defense lawyers usually want witnesses to describe only what they observed—not what they inferred as they observed. When a witness includes an inference such as "I saw him steal it," the lawyer may object that the statement represents a "conclusion of the witness" and move to have the observation struck from the record. For example, imagine that you are a defense attorney listening to the following testimony. At what points would you object by saying, "This is a conclusion of the witness"?

> I saw Harvey running down the street, right after he knocked the old lady down. He had her purse in his hand and was trying to escape as fast as he could. He was really scared. I wasn't surprised because Harvey has always taken advantage of others. It's not the first time that he's stolen, either; I can tell you that. Just last summer he robbed the poor box at St. Anthony's. He was bragging about it for weeks.

Finally, keep in mind that even though in *theory* facts and inferences can be distinguished, in *practice* it is almost impossible to communicate with others in speech or writing by sticking only to factual observations. A reasonable approach is to state your inference along with the observable evidence on which the inference is based (e.g., John seemed happy because . . . .). Our language has an entire collection of terms (*seems, appears, is likely,* and so on) that signal when we are making an inference and not expressing an observable fact. Thoughtful writers use these words carefully and deliberately.

Many of the predictions that you make are inferences based on your past experiences and information that you presently have. Even when there appear to be sound reasons supporting them, these inferences are often wrong due to incomplete information or unanticipated events. The fact that even people whom society considers "experts" regularly make inaccurate predictions should encourage you to exercise caution when presenting your beliefs as inferences. Here are some examples:

> "So many centuries after the Creation, it is unlikely that anyone could find hitherto unknown lands of any value."
>
> > —The Advisory Committee to King Ferdinand and Queen
> > Isabella of Spain, before Columbus's voyage in 1492

> "What will the soldiers and sailors, what will the common people say to 'George Washington, President of the United States'? They will despise him to all eternity."
>
> > —John Adams, 1789

> "What use could the company make of an electrical toy?"
>
> > —Western Union's rejection of the telephone in 1878

> "The actual building of roads devoted to motor cars is not for the near future in spite of many rumors to that effect."
>
> > —a 1902 article in *Harper's Weekly*

"You ain't goin' nowhere, son. You ought to go back to driving a truck."

> —Jim Denny, Grand Ole Opry manager, firing Elvis
> Presley after one performance, 1954

Thinking-Writing Activity

FACTUAL AND INFERENTIAL BELIEFS

Examine the following list of statements, noting which are *factual beliefs* (based on observations) and which are *inferential beliefs* (conclusions that go beyond observations). For each factual statement, describe how you might go about verifying the information. For each inferential statement, describe a factual observation on which the inference could be based. (*Note:* Some statements may contain both factual beliefs and inferential beliefs.)

- When my leg starts to ache, that means snow is on the way.
- The grass is wet—it must have rained last night.
- I think that it's pretty clear from the length of the skid marks that the accident was caused by that person's driving too fast.
- Fifty men lost their lives in the construction of the Queensboro Bridge.
- Nancy said she wasn't feeling well yesterday—I'll bet that she's out sick today.

Now consider the following situations. What inferences might you be inclined to make on the basis of what you are observing? How could you investigate the accuracy of an inference?

- A student in your class is consistently late for class.
- You see a friend driving a new car.
- An instructor asks the same student to stay after class several times.
- You don't receive any birthday cards.

So far, we have been exploring relatively simple inferences. Many of the inferences people make, however, are much more complicated. In fact, much of our knowledge of the world rests on our ability to make complicated inferences in a systematic and logical way. However, just because an inference is more complicated does not mean that it is more accurate; in fact, the opposite is often the case. One of the masters of inference is the legendary Sherlock Holmes. In the following passage, Holmes makes an astonishing number of inferences upon meeting Dr. Watson. Study Holmes' conclusions carefully. Are they reasonable? Can you explain how he reaches them?

> "You appeared to be surprised when I told you, on our first meeting, that you had come from Afghanistan."

> "You were told, no doubt."

"Nothing of the sort. I knew you came from Afghanistan. From long habit the train of thoughts ran so swiftly through my mind that I arrived at the conclusion without being conscious of intermediate steps. There were such steps, however. The train of reasoning ran, 'Here is a gentleman of a medical type, but with the air of a military man. Clearly an army doctor, then. He is just come from the tropics, for his face is dark, and that is not the natural tint of his skin, for his wrists are fair. He has undergone hardship and sickness, as his haggard face says clearly. His left arm has been injured. He holds it in a stiff and unnatural manner. Where in the tropics could an English army doctor have seen much hardship and got his arm wounded? Clearly in Afghanistan.' The whole train of thought did not occupy a second. I then remarked that you came from Afghanistan, and you were astonished."

—Sir Arthur Conan Doyle, *A Study in Scarlet*

Thinking-Writing Activity

ANALYZING AN INCORRECT INFERENCE

Describe an experience in which you made an incorrect inference. For example, it might have been a situation in which you mistakenly accused someone, an accident based on a miscalculation, a poor decision based on an inaccurate prediction, or some other event. Analyze that experience by answering the following questions.

1. What was (were) your mistaken inference(s)?

2. What was the factual evidence on which you based your inference(s)?

3. Looking back, what could you have done to avoid making the erroneous inference(s)?

The following essay illustrates the ongoing process by which natural scientists use inferences to discover factual information and to construct theories explaining the information.

"Evolution as Fact and Theory"
by Stephen Jay Gould

Stephen Jay Gould started his academic career as a professor of geology at Harvard University but expanded his interests into evolutionary biology. He was curator of invertebrate paleontology at Harvard's Museum of Comparative Zoology and a writer with a gift for translating complex scientific theories into informed, but witty, prose that nonscientists can understand and enjoy. His essays appeared in magazines such as *Natural History* and *Discover* and were collected in the books *Ever Since Darwin*, *The*

Source: "Evolution as Fact and Theory" by Stephen Jay Gould. *Discover Magazine*, 1981. Reprinted by permission of the author.

Panda's Thumb, and *The Flamingo's Smile*. This essay illustrates the ongoing process by which natural scientists use inferences to discover factual information and to construct theories explaining that information.

Kirtley Mather, who died last year at age 89, was a pillar of both science and the Christian religion in America and one of my dearest friends. The difference of half a century in our ages evaporated before our common interests. The most curious thing we shared was a battle we each fought at the same age. For Kirtley had gone to Tennessee with Clarence Darrow to testify for evolution at the Scopes trial of 1925. When I think that we are enmeshed again in the same struggle for one of the best documented, most compelling and exciting concepts in all of science, I don't know whether to laugh or cry.

According to idealized principles of scientific discourse, the arousal of dormant issues should reflect fresh data that give renewed life to abandoned notions. Those outside the current debate may therefore be excused for suspecting that creationists have come up with something new, or that evolutionists have generated some serious internal trouble. But nothing has changed; the creationists have not a single new fact or argument. Darrow and Bryan were at least more entertaining than we lesser antagonists today. The rise of creationism is politics, pure and simple; it represents one issue (and by no means the major concern) of the resurgent evangelical right. Arguments that seemed kooky just a decade ago have re-entered the mainstream.

Creationism Is Not Science

The basic attack of the creationists falls apart on two general counts before we even reach the supposed factual details of their complaints against evolution. First, they play upon a vernacular misunderstanding of the word "theory" to convey the false impression that we evolutionists are covering up the rotten core of our edifice. Second, they misuse a popular philosophy of science to argue that they are behaving scientifically in attacking evolution. Yet the same philosophy demonstrates that their own belief is not science, and that "scientific creationism" is therefore meaningless and self-contradictory, a superb example of what Orwell called "newspeak."

In the American vernacular, "theory" often means "imperfect fact"—part of a hierarchy of confidence running downhill from fact to theory to hypothesis to guess. Thus the power of the creationist argument: evolution is "only" a theory, and intense debate now rages about many aspects of the theory. If evolution is less than a fact, and scientists can't even make up their minds about the theory, then what confidence can we have in it? Indeed, President Reagan echoed this argument before an evangelical group in Dallas when he said (in what I devoutly hope was campaign rhetoric): "Well, it is a theory. It is a scientific theory only, and it has in recent years been challenged in the world of science—that is, not believed in the scientific community to be as infallible as it once was."

Well, evolution *is* a theory. It is also a fact. And facts and theories are different things, not rungs in a hierarchy of increasing certainty. Facts are the world's data. Theories are structures of ideas that explain and interpret facts. Facts do not go away when scientists debate rival theories to explain them. Einstein's theory of gravitation replaced Newton's, but apples did not suspend themselves in mid-air pending the outcome. And human beings evolved from apelike ancestors whether they did so by Darwin's proposed mechanism or by some other, yet to be discovered.

5

Moreover, "fact" does not mean "absolute certainty." The final proofs of logic and mathematics flow deductively from stated premises and achieve certainty only because they are *not* about the empirical world. Evolutionists make no claim for perpetual truth, though creationists often do (and then attack us for a style of argument that they themselves favor). In science, "fact" can only mean "confirmed to such a degree that it would be perverse to withhold provisional assent." I suppose that apples might start to rise tomorrow, but possibility does not merit equal time in physics classrooms.

Evolutionists have been clear about this distinction between fact and theory from the very beginning, if only because we have always acknowledged how far we are from completely understanding the mechanisms (theory) by which evolution (fact) occurred. Darwin continually emphasized the difference between his two great and separate accomplishments: establishing the fact of evolution, and proposing a theory—natural selection—to explain the mechanism of evolution. He wrote in *The Descent of Man:* "I had two distinct objects in view; firstly, to show that species had not been separately created, and secondly, that natural selection had been the chief agent of change. . . . Hence if I have erred in . . . having exaggerated its [natural selection] power . . . I have at least, as I hope, done good service in aiding to overthrow the dogma of separate creations."

Thus Darwin acknowledged the provisional nature of natural selection while affirming the fact of evolution. The fruitful theoretical debate that Darwin initiated has never ceased. From the 1940s through the 1960s, Darwin's own theory of natural selection did achieve a temporary hegemony that it never enjoyed in his lifetime. But renewed debate characterizes our decade, and while no biologist questions the importance of natural selection, many now doubt its ubiquity. In particular, many evolutionists argue that substantial amounts of genetic change may not be subject to natural selection and may spread through populations at random. Others are challenging Darwin's linking of natural selection with gradual, imperceptible change through all intermediary degrees; they are arguing that most evolutionary events may occur far more rapidly than Darwin envisioned.

Scientists regard debates on fundamental issues of theory as a sign of intellectual health and a source of excitement. Science is—and how else can I say it?—most fun when it plays with interesting ideas, examines their implications, and recognizes that old information may be explained in surprisingly new ways. Evolutionary theory is now enjoying this uncommon vigor. Yet amidst all this turmoil no biologist has been led to doubt the fact that evolution occurred; we are debating *how* it happened. We are all trying to explain the same thing: the tree of evolutionary descent linking all organisms by ties of genealogy. Creationists pervert and caricature this debate by conveniently neglecting the common conviction that underlies it, and by falsely suggesting that we now doubt the very phenomenon we are struggling to understand.

10   Using another invalid argument, creationists claim that "the dogma of separate creations," as Darwin characterized it a century ago, is a scientific theory meriting equal time with evolution in high school biology curricula. But a prevailing viewpoint among philosophers of science belies this creationist argument. Philosopher Karl Popper has argued for decades that the primary criterion of science is the falsifiability of its theories. We can never prove absolutely, but we can falsify. A set of ideas that cannot, in principle, be falsified is not science.

The entire creationist argument involves little more than a rhetorical attempt to falsify evolution by presenting supposed contradictions among its supporters. Their brand of creationism, they claim, is "scientific" because it follows the Popperian model in trying to demolish evolution. Yet Popper's argument must apply in both directions. One does not become a scientist by the simple act of trying to falsify another scientific system; one has to present an alternative system that also meets Popper's criterion—it too must be falsifiable in principle.

"Scientific creationism" is a self-contradictory, nonsense phrase precisely because it cannot be falsified. I can envision observations and experiments that would disprove any evolutionary theory I know, but I cannot imagine what potential data could lead creationists to abandon their beliefs. Unbeatable systems are dogma, not science. Lest I seem harsh or rhetorical, I quote creationism's leading intellectual, Duane Gish, Ph.D., from his recent (1978) book *Evolution? The Fossils Say No!* "By creation we mean the bringing into being by a supernatural Creator of the basic kinds of plants and animals by the process of sudden, or fiat, creation. We do not know how the Creator created, what processes He used, *for He used processes which are not now operating anywhere in the natural universe* [Gish's italics]. This is why we refer to creation as special creation. We cannot discover by scientific investigations anything about the creative processes used by the Creator." Pray tell, Dr. Gish, in the light of your last sentence, what then is "scientific" creationism?

The Fact of Evolution

Our confidence that evolution occurred centers upon three general arguments. First, we have abundant, direct, observational evidence of evolution in action, from both the field and the laboratory. It ranges from countless experiments on change in nearly everything about fruit flies subjected to artificial selection in the laboratory to the famous British moths that turned black when industrial soot darkened the trees upon which they rest. (The moths gain protection from sharp-sighted bird predators by blending into the background.) Creationists do not deny these observations; how could they? Creationists have tightened their act. They now argue that God only created "basic kinds," and allowed for limited evolutionary meandering within them. Thus toy poodles and Great Danes come from the dog kind and moths can change color, but nature cannot convert a dog to a cat or a monkey to a man.

The second and third arguments for evolution—the case for major changes—do not involve direct observation of evolution in action. They rest upon inference, but are no less secure for that reason. Major evolutionary change requires too much time for direct observation on the scale of recorded human history. All historical sciences rest upon inference, and evolution is no different from geology, cosmology, or human history in this respect. In principle, we cannot observe processes that operated in the past. We must infer them from results that still survive: living and fossil organisms for evolution, documents and artifacts for human history, strata and topography for geology.

The second argument—that the imperfection of nature reveals evolution—strikes   15
many people as ironic, for they feel that evolution should be most elegantly displayed in the nearly perfect adaptation expressed by some organisms—the camber of a gull's wing, or butterflies that cannot be seen in ground litter because they mimic leaves so precisely. But perfection could be imposed by a wise creator or evolved by natural selection. Perfection covers the tracks of past history. And past history—the evidence of descent—is our mark of evolution.

Evolution lies exposed in the *imperfections* that record a history of descent. Why should a rat run, a bat fly, or porpoise swim, and I type this essay with structures built of the same bones unless we all inherited them from a common ancestor? An engineer, starting from scratch, could design better limbs in each case. Why should all the large native mammals of Australia be marsupials, unless they descended from a common ancestor isolated on this island continent? Marsupials are not "better," or ideally suited for Australia; many have been wiped out by placental mammals imported by man from other continents. This principle of imperfection extends to all historical sciences. When we recognize the etymology of September, October, November, and December (seventh, eighth, ninth, and tenth, from the Latin), we know that two additional items (January and February) must have been added to an original calendar of ten months.

The third argument is more direct: transitions are often found in the fossil record. Preserved transitions are not common—and should not be, according to our understanding of evolution . . . —but they are not entirely wanting, as creationists often claim. The lower jaw of reptiles contains several bones, that of mammals only one. The nonmammalian jawbones are reduced, step by step, in mammalian ancestors until they become tiny nubbins located at the back of the jaw. The "hammer" and the "anvil" bones of the mammalian ear are descendants of these nubbins. How could such a transition be accomplished?, the creationists ask. Surely a bone is either entirely in the jaw or in the ear. Yet paleontologists have discovered two transitional lineages of therapsids (the so-called mammal-like reptiles) with a double jaw joint—one composed of the old quadrate and articular bones (soon to become the hammer and anvil), the other of the squamosal and dentary bones (as in modern mammals). For that matter, what better transitional form could we desire than the oldest human, *Australopithecus afarensis*, with its apelike palate, its human upright stance, and a cranial capacity larger than any ape's of the same body size but a full 1,000 cubic centimeters below ours? If God made each of the half dozen human species discovered in ancient rocks, why did he create an unbroken temporal sequence of progressively more modern features—increasing cranial capacity, reduced face and teeth, larger body size? Did he create to mimic evolution and test our faith thereby?

Conclusion

I am both angry at and amused by the creationists; but mostly I am deeply sad. Sad for many reasons. Sad because so many people who respond to creationist appeals are troubled for the right reason, but venting their anger at the wrong target. It is true that scientists have often been dogmatic and elitist. It is true that we have often allowed the white-coated, advertising image to represent us—"Scientists say that Brand X cures bunions ten times faster than . . ." We have not fought it adequately because we derive benefits from appearing as a new priesthood. It is also true that faceless bureaucratic state power intrudes more and more into our lives and removes choices that should belong to individuals and communities. I can understand that requiring that evolution be taught in the schools might be seen as one more insult on all these grounds. But the culprit is not, and cannot be, evolution or any other fact of the natural world. Identify and fight your legitimate enemies by all means, but we are not among them.

I am sad because the practical result of this brouhaha will not be expanded coverage to include creationism (that would also make me sad), but the reduction or excision of evolution from high school curricula. Evolution is one of the half dozen "great ideas" developed by science. It speaks to the profound issues of genealogy that fascinate all of us—the "roots" phenomenon writ large. Where did we come from? Where did life arise? How did it develop? How are organisms related? It forces us to think, ponder, and wonder. Shall we deprive millions of this knowledge and once again teach biology as a set of dull and unconnected facts, without the thread that weaves diverse material into a supple unity?

But most of all I am saddened by a trend I am just beginning to discern among my 20 colleagues. I sense that some now wish to mute the healthy debate about theory that has brought new life to evolutionary biology. It provides grist for creationist mills, they say, even if only by distortion. Perhaps we should lie low and rally around the flag of strict Darwinism, at least for the moment—a kind of old-time religion on our part.

But we should borrow another metaphor and recognize that we too have to tread a straight and narrow path, surrounded by roads to perdition. For if we ever begin to suppress our search to understand nature, to quench our own intellectual excitement in a misguided effort to present a united front where it does not and should not exist, then we are truly lost.

QUESTIONS FOR READING ACTIVELY

1. Gould defines *facts* as the "world's data" and refers to observing an apple fall from the tree as Isaac Newton is alleged to have done. Identify some of the facts Gould presents as evidence to support the theory of evolution.

2. Gould defines *theories* as "structures of ideas that explain and interpret facts," such as Newton's theory of gravitation, which was introduced to explain facts like falling apples. In addition to facts, Gould states, the theory of evolution is supported by reasonable inferences. Identify some inferences that he cites as evidence.

3. Gould begins this essay with allusions to the Scopes trial of 1925, Darrow, and Bryan. He seems to assume that his readers will know what he is talking about. If you know about this event, how does this reference set the scene for his 1981 essay? If you don't know about it, was your understanding reduced? As a critical thinker and active reader, would you make certain to familiarize yourself with the Scopes trial of 1925 so that your understanding of the allusions would be clear?

QUESTIONS FOR THINKING CRITICALLY

1. What does Gould say about creationism? Find specific statements. Is Gould presenting reports, inferences, or judgments about this concept?

2. Gould calls Kirtley Mather a "pillar of both science and the Christian religion in America." Do you know people who are both scientific and spiritual? What do those people say about these two approaches to the world?

QUESTION FOR WRITING THOUGHTFULLY

1. Think about how the qualities of a critical reader and thinker can be useful in discussing issues related to evolution and creationism, and write a short essay describing your reasoning.

The comic strip below was probably intended to be funny, but it reflects what Gould says about theories as "structures of ideas that explain and interpret facts." Historical facts are interpreted differently at different times; theories about history change. School textbooks about United States history published 50 years ago usually focused on the Founding Fathers, pioneers moving westward, and military actions. Books published now usually include material on Native Americans, women, slaves, and daily life. You might want to discuss this change with your grandparents or older friends.

JUDGING BY APPLYING CRITERIA

Identify and write descriptions of a friend, a course you have taken, and the college you attend. Be sure your descriptions are specific and include what you think about the friend, the course, and the college.

1. _____ is a friend I have. He/she is . . .

2. _____ is a course I have taken. It was . . .

3. _____ is the college I attend. It is . . .

Now review your writing. Does it include factual descriptions? Note any facts that can be verified. Your writing may also contain inferences based on factual information. Can you identify any? In addition, your writing may include judgments about the person, the course, and the school—descriptions that express your evaluation based on certain criteria. Facts and inferences help you figure out what is actually happening (or will happen); the purpose of judgments is to express your evaluation about what is happening (or will happen). For example:

- My new car has broken down three times in the first six months. (Factual report)

- My new car will probably continue to have difficulties. (Inference)

- My new car is a lemon. (Judgment)

When you label your new car a "lemon," you are making a judgment based on certain criteria. For instance, a lemon is usually a newly purchased item—often an automobile—with which you have repeated problems. For another example of judging, consider the following statements:

- Carla always does her work thoroughly and completes it on time. (Factual report)
- Carla will probably continue to do her work in this fashion. (Inference)
- Carla is a very responsible person. (Judgment)

By judging Carla to be responsible, you are evaluating her on the basis of the criteria or standards that you believe indicate a responsible person. One such criterion is completing assigned work on time. Can you identify additional criteria for judging someone as being responsible?

Review your previous descriptions of a friend, a course, and your college. Can you identify any judgments in your descriptions? For each judgment you have listed, identify the criteria on which you based the judgment.

Many of our disagreements with others focus on differences in judgments. To write thoughtfully, you need to approach such differences intelligently by following these guidelines:

- Make explicit the criteria or standards used as a basis for the judgment.
- Try to establish the reasons that justify these criteria.

For instance, if you write "Professor Andrews is an excellent teacher," you are basing your judgment on certain criteria of teaching excellence. Once these standards are made explicit, they can be discussed to see whether they make sense and what justifies them. Of course, your idea of what makes an excellent teacher may be different from someone else's, so you can test your conclusion by comparing your criteria with those of your classmates. When disagreements occur, use these two steps for resolution.

In short, not all judgments are equally good or equally poor. The credibility of a judgment depends on the criteria used to make the judgment and on the evidence or reasons that support these criteria. For example, there may be legitimate disagreements about judgments on the following points:

- Who was the greatest United States president?
- Which movie deserves the Oscar this year?
- Which is the best baseball team this year?

However, in these and countless other cases, the quality of judgments depends on presenting the criteria used for the competing judgments and then demonstrating that your candidate best meets the agreed-upon criteria by providing supporting evidence and reasons. With this approach, you can often engage in intelligent discussion and establish which judgments are best supported by the evidence.

Thinking-Writing Activity

ANALYZING JUDGMENTS

Review the following two passages, which illustrate various judgments. For each passage, do the following:

1. Identify the evaluative criteria on which the judgments are based.

2. Describe the reasons or evidence the author uses to support the criteria.

3. Explain whether you agree or disagree with the judgments and give your rationale.

One widely held misconception concerning pizza should be laid to rest. Although it may be characterized as fast food, pizza is not junk food. Especially when it is made with fresh ingredients, pizza fulfills our basic nutritional requirements. The crust provides carbohydrates; from the cheese and meat or fish comes protein; and the tomatoes, herbs, onions, and garlic supply vitamins and minerals.

—Louis Philip Salamone, "Pizza: Fast Food, Not Junk Food"

Let us return to the question of food. Responsible agronomists report that before the end of the year millions of people if unaided might starve to death. Half a billion deaths by starvation is not an uncommon estimate. Even though the United States has done more than any other nation to feed the hungry, our relative affluence makes us morally vulnerable in the eyes of other nations and in our own eyes. Garrett Hardin, who has argued for a "lifeboat" ethic of survival (if you take all the passengers aboard, everybody drowns), admits that the decision not to feed all the hungry requires of us "a very hard psychological adjustment." Indeed it would. It has been estimated that the 3.5 million tons of fertilizer spread on American golf courses and lawns could provide up to 30 million tons of food in overseas agricultural production. The nightmarish thought intrudes itself. If we as a nation allow people to starve while we could, through some sacrifice, make more food available to them, what hope can any person have for the future of international relations? If we cannot agree on this most basic of values—feed the hungry—what hopes for the future can we entertain?

—James R. Kelly, "The Limits of Reason"

DISTINGUISHING AMONG REPORTS, INFERENCES, AND JUDGMENTS

Although the activities of reporting, inferring, and judging tend to be woven together in your experiences and in your writing, it is important to be able to distinguish these activities. Each plays a different role in helping you make sense of the world for yourself and for your audience, and you should be careful not to confuse these roles. For instance, although writers may appear to be reporting factual information, they may actually be expressing personal evaluations, which are not factual. Consider the statement "Los Angeles is a smog-ridden city drowning in automobiles." Although seeming to be reporting factual information, the writer really is expressing his or her personal judgment. Of course, writers can identify their judgments with such phrases as "in my opinion," "my evaluation is," and so forth.

Sometimes, however, writers do not identify their judgments. In some cases, they do not do so because the context within which they are writing (such as a newspaper editorial) makes it clear that the information is judgment rather than fact. In other cases, however, they want their judgments to be treated as factual information. Confusing the activities of reporting, inferring, and judging, whether accidental or deliberate, can be misleading and even dangerous.

Confusing factual information with judgments can be personally damaging as well. For example, there is a big difference between these two statements:

- I failed my exam today. (Factual report)
- I am a failure. (Judgment)

Stating the fact "I failed my exam today" describes your situation in a concrete way, enabling you to evaluate (judge) it as a problem you can hope to solve through reflection and hard work. If, however, the situation causes you to make the judgment "I am a failure," this sort of general evaluation will not encourage you to explore solutions to the problem or improve your situation.

Finally, another main reason for distinguishing among the activities of reporting, inferring, and judging concerns the accuracy of statements. We noted, for instance, that factual statements tend to be reasonably accurate because they are by nature verifiable, whereas inferences are usually much less certain. As a result, it is crucial to be aware of whether you are presenting a belief as a report, an inference, or a judgment. If you write the superintendent of your apartment building a note saying, "My thermostat is broken," an inference on your part based on the fact that you feel uncomfortably hot, you will feel foolish if you later discover that you have a fever and that the thermostat is functioning well.

Presenting Beliefs in Your Writing

Understanding and evaluating beliefs pertains in three particular ways to your college papers, as well as to the writing you will do in other settings. First, as you are better able to distinguish among reports, inferences, and judgments, you will be able to present different types of beliefs more accurately. Although you may not often use the term *report, inference,* or *judgment,* you will word your beliefs in precise ways that indicate the level of speculation behind your statements.

Second, a strong relationship exists between the thesis of a paper and your beliefs about the topic. The thesis, most of all, expresses what you believe is the main point of your paper. As you work to clarify your thesis statement, you also clarify your beliefs about the issue you are addressing. And when you state the thesis clearly in your paper, you are making your beliefs clear to your readers.

Third, as a college writer and quite possibly as a working professional, you will regularly use source material in your papers. The techniques for evaluating beliefs will help you evaluate sources of information. Then, as you present in your researched writing what others have said, you can comment on their beliefs as you integrate the material into your papers. (See Chapter 14 on research.)

Writing Project

ANALYZING INFLUENCES ON YOUR BELIEFS
ABOUT A SOCIAL OR ACADEMIC ISSUE

This chapter has included both readings and Thinking-Writing Activities that encourage you to think about the sources of your beliefs. Be sure to reread what you wrote for the activities as you may be able to use some of your work in completing this project.

Project Overview and Requirements

Write an essay that analyzes your beliefs about a social issue or idea related to an academic field—specifically, consider what influenced your beliefs and how they developed. Apply the concepts discussed in this chapter as part of your analysis.

Since you receive much of your information about social or academic issues from print and electronic sources, your essay should incorporate at least two media sources (newspaper, magazine, or journal articles; material from a website; a film or a DVD; a book or book chapter). You can also incorporate personal experience, as well as ideas you may have heard from others such as your teachers, peers, or family.

Before you begin writing, read The Writing Situation and The Writing Process below to help you generate ideas and structure your essay. The student essay at the end of this chapter ("Dealing with Sex Offenders" by Jessie Lange) provides a thoughtful model for this type of essay, and don't forget to consider the key elements of the Thinking-Writing Model in Chapter 1 on pages 5–8.

THE WRITING SITUATION

Purpose   Your primary purpose here is to further your own development as a capable college student. You will be exploring some of the ways in which you come to accept concepts. In addition, you will be sharing your insights with your audience, which always provides another purpose: to write an effective paper.

On a technical level, you are required to take different kinds of information and pull them together. Such *synthesis* is the central purpose of many kinds of academic and professional writing. Most research papers, case studies, field reports, project summaries, product proposals, and business plans use information that must be analyzed and synthesized.

You also have an intellectual purpose. You will look closely at your own ways of defining what you believe and what you consider true, as well as what you do not believe and what you consider false.

Audience   As usual, your classmates are a good audience for this paper, in both draft and finished versions, since they are doing the same assignment and will want to see how you handle it. In addition, people interested in the social issue or academic field will naturally be potential readers. If you are taking a class pertaining to your subject, you could share your paper with those students. If you are writing about a social issue relevant to your community, you could share your work in a newsletter or on a website.

Of course, your instructor remains the audience who will judge how well you have articulated your beliefs, how you have selected the influences on your beliefs, how you have handled the sources, and how you have planned, drafted, revised, and edited your essay.

Subject   Examining the sources of beliefs and evaluating evidence are among the most challenging of activities. If you are just beginning to learn about the issue on which you are writing, you may not have enough background to be very inquisitive or judgmental. However, you should be aware of criteria that any thoughtful student can detect: specific support for a claim, whether information is current, appropriateness of examples and authorities, and responsible attribution. Also, you have some understanding of reports, inferences, predictions, and judgments to apply to your analysis.

Writer   For this Writing Project, you should be as open as possible to new ways of thinking about your beliefs. After such critical analysis, some writers find that their beliefs have been strengthened; others may realize that some of their beliefs were based on unreliable information and need to be reevaluated.

As with the Writing Projects in Part One, you are in a position of authority here when you are writing about your own reactions and realizations. At the same time, since you are writing about a social issue or an academic field instead of about your personal life, you are a writer who is dealing with other people's beliefs in addition to your own. After writing the paper, you may want to consider whether you are a more accepting or more skeptical person.

The following questions will help you explore and develop your ideas related to analyzing the influences on your beliefs about a social or academic issue.

1. Describe the issue you plan to focus on for this essay. Briefly summarize your beliefs and how they evolved. For example:

   The social issue I would like to focus on is supporting local businesses. As the "big box" stores like Walmart and Best Buy move into town, smaller businesses—those owned by friends and neighbors—are pushed out. My views on this issue were greatly influenced when a friend had to close her independent bookstore approximately two years after a corporate bookstore moved into town. When I saw the effect this had on my friend, her family, and those who patronized her bookstore, I vowed to shop local as often as possible. I have not been to a "box store" in over three years now and feel good about the choice I have made. Local business provides stability and a sense of community.

2. Part of the goal of the Writing Project is to analyze and synthesize different types of professional and academic sources. Identify two of the sources you plan to use, and describe how these sources can help you engage your audience. For example:

   I plan to incorporate information from a Forbes article, "Google Now May Shift Walmart Vs Local—Top Ways To Support Independent Shops" by T.J. McCue (March 12, 2013). This article reveals both sides of the issue—for instance, by stating that Walmart does have some benefits. By providing a well-rounded analysis of the issue, my audience will more likely trust me. I also plan to discuss the documentary "Store Wars: When Wal-Mart Comes to Town," which takes place in Ashland, Virginia, and focuses on the impact box stores have on small towns. I feel that highlighting key aspects of this film will engage my audience because residents, from varying walks of life, are interviewed. There are many different voices and perspectives for an audience to identify with.

3. Examining the sources of your beliefs and evaluating evidence can be challenging, so you will need to find specific support for a claim, make sure the information is current, decide how appropriate your examples (and authorities) are, and practice responsible attribution. What challenges do you think you might face while drafting your essay? For example:

   The more I research the impact of big box stores on small communities, the more I realize how big this essay can become. One challenge I will face is keeping my essay concise, while at the same time, giving my audience an in-depth analysis of how my beliefs were influenced. There is a lot of information on this issue, and there is a danger of becoming side-tracked. I plan to create an outline to keep me on track, and I plan to carefully sort through my sources to be sure they are the most current and relevant.

4. For this project, you will be focusing on a social issue or an academic field instead of your personal life, and you will also be discussing other people's

beliefs in addition to your own. How do you plan to incorporate the beliefs of others in your essay, while maintaining your own voice and revealing some of the influences on the development of your beliefs?

I plan to focus the opening paragraph (or two) on what my friend experienced when her bookstore closed, and then move into how her experience started to influence my beliefs. I will then use examples from the documentary to draw some parallels between what happened in Ashland and what happened in our community. Interjecting statistics and comments from reliable sources will be important and will help accentuate my analysis, and when appropriate, I will clarify my beliefs. Instead of rambling about my beliefs or "lecturing," I will make sure the examples I choose clearly illustrate why I feel the way I do.

THE WRITING PROCESS

The following sections will guide you through the stages of planning, drafting, and revising your essay analyzing the sources of your beliefs.

Generating Ideas

- Revisit the work you completed during the Thinking-Writing Activities—you may be inspired by some of the ideas you wrote about.
- Think about teachers, books, films, articles, the Internet, and other sources of information in your field that have provided you with information that you believe. Why have they had this effect?
- As you explore media sources, gather information that will help illustrate or support your ideas. Be sure to keep track of your sources so you can document or cite them later.
- Think about any sources that you are reluctant to trust or believe. Why have they had this effect?
- What concepts in this field do you believe most firmly? Are there some that you question?
- Try freewriting for 5 or 10 minutes about something you believe to be true and why.
- Revisit the list of questions for exploring topics (pages 100–102) in Chapter 4, as well as "Additional Tips for Generating Ideas" on page 102.

Defining a Focus   The Writing Project itself provides a wide-angle focus, but you must sharpen it in order to produce an understandable paper. Does your issue or idea have several components? For example, the issue of high-stakes testing in public schools raises questions about the kind of tests used, the effects on students' passing to the next grade, the effects on school funding or ratings, and the effects on curriculum. You may want to focus only on one aspect. Perhaps your beliefs about evolution in biology or parallel processing in computer science are really beliefs about several components of the general idea.

Write down your belief to be sure that you can state it well. If you haven't decided on one belief, write several. Are there interpretations, evaluations, conclusions, or predictions in your statement? If so, do these terms help you find a focus? Here are a few other things to consider as you define your focus:

- Are you strongly convinced that your belief is plausible? Do you have questions about it? Why?
- What about differences? Does a popular press, television, or website account differ from what a book says or what a professor has taught you?
- Draft a thesis statement that gives direction to the essay.
- Create a map, web, or rough outline so that you can see how ideas might cluster or separate. See Chapter 4 for idea-generation strategies.

Organizing Ideas   Now that you have come up with a focus for your essay and sources to illustrate and support your focus, it is time to organize your ideas. If you created a map or rough outline while defining your focus, you are off to a good start, but answering the following questions will help you further organize your essay:

- Have you drafted a tentative thesis that states your belief, one that says something about the sources of the belief, or one that includes both?
- If you have several sources for your belief, does each one deserve at least a paragraph?
- If your beliefs have changed, have you discussed this matter in an effective place?
- If you are contrasting two differing perspectives, have you structured the contrast logically?
- If you are presenting similar perspectives, have you structured the comparison logically?
- How do you plan to conclude your essay?

Drafting   Begin with the part easiest to draft, whether it is the introduction or one of the body paragraphs. Focus on sections or ideas that come easily, and then, when you shift to parts that are a little harder to articulate, at least make some notes or write questions to help you see where more information will be necessary. You can always go back and develop those ideas. It can also help to draft a new outline or map as you rethink what you want to say. Remember that the writing process is recursive—that is, you will likely move back and forth in order to fully develop your ideas.

As you draft, think about the basic structure:

- Look at the preliminary thesis statement that you drafted. Do you need to rework it now, or should you wait until you have drafted more?

- Shape the paragraphs that will make up the body of your essay. Draft clear topic sentences; think about where the topic sentence should be placed in each paragraph.
- Draft an opening paragraph and a concluding paragraph, understanding that you may want to revise them substantially later.

Revising Your Essay: Analyzing Influences on Your Beliefs About a Social or Academic Issue

Take a break from your writing once your draft is complete. This is a good time to solicit feedback from a peer, if possible. If you receive feedback, review it carefully before revising your paper. As always, consider your audience, and ask yourself the following:

- Is the topic clearly introduced?
- Is the thesis clear?
- Is the organization logical?
- Do the paragraphs flow smoothly from one to the next? Can transitions between paragraphs be stronger?
- Have I incorporated concepts from the book related to interpretation, evaluation, conclusion, prediction, report, inference, and judgment where appropriate?
- Have I considered the reliability and value of each source I used?

Peer Responses

As noted above, soliciting feedback before you revise is wise. Consider exchanging your draft with a peer, or ask someone outside of class to review your draft.

Revision

Once you receive feedback, use "A Step-by-Step Method for Revising Any Assignment," on the inside front cover of this book for additional tips to strengthen your essay. Begin with the "big picture" components of your paper such as the structure and flow.

Editing and Proofreading

Next, turn your attention to sentence-level details like grammar, punctuation, and other mechanics. Check all your sources to be sure they are documented properly and include a Works Cited (MLA) or References (APA) list depending on your instructor's directions.

STUDENT WRITING

Jessie Lange's Writing Process

The following essay was written for a criminal justice course. Jessie's professor asked students to demonstrate how media treatments of a current criminal justice issue helped to shape the beliefs they hold about that issue. For students in a criminal justice course, who might someday be dealing with offenders or victims of a particular kind of crime, the ability to distinguish between personal beliefs and objective evidence (and to make a distinction between how they might personally feel about an issue and what the law says about that issue) is of critical importance. But Jessie realized that as a concerned citizen, it was also her responsibility to be informed about criminal justice issues that might impact her as a woman, a voter, and a future parent. Jessie used the Thinking-Writing Activity entitled Evaluating Factual Information on page 412 to discuss her two key sources.

Lange clearly defines her belief and reveals the source that inspired her to further explore this complex issue.

Dealing with Sex Offenders
by Jessie Lange

In the past few years we have heard much about Megan's Law, which states that people should be made aware of charged sex offenders in their community. While I wholeheartedly believe that people, for the protection of themselves and their children, have the right to know, there is another twist on the issue I hadn't thought about until I heard a story recently on *60 Minutes*. The story involved Stephanie's Law—a new law in place in some states under which sex offenders are kept *after* they have served their time to go through a therapy program in an attempt to "cure" them. The question that this provoked in me was not whether the state should have the right to hold sexual criminals beyond their sentence, but whether they can be cured at all. If not, should they ever be released back into a world where they are likely to do more damage, destroy more lives?

In the second and third paragraphs, Lange provides objective evidence and proposes a key question about recidivism.

A recent *New York Times* article described a rehabilitation program in Texas whereby prisoners are immersed in religion—taking classes, having discussions, and owning up to their "sins." Interestingly, while there are 79 men convicted of "robbery, drug possession, and murder" participating, those convicted of sexual crimes are not accepted into the program. This is partly because they are "looked down on by other prisoners" and partly because, according to criminologists, "sexual criminals are the most difficult to rehabilitate."

In fact, there is a question as to whether this rehabilitation is even possible. Sexual criminals in particular seem to be under the influence of urges which are out of their control. The *60 Minutes* report said that, while many may have good intentions in being treated through therapy and returning to society, it may be out of their hands. They may say they understand their wrongs, they may feel cured,

Source: Dealing with Sex Offenders by Jessie Lange.

but if they are released it seems impossible for even the offenders to know if they will be able to control their impulses. If there is such a question, do they deserve a chance at freedom when it means potentially committing another crime?

There is no question in my mind that, while many sex offenders do not repent for what they have done and have no real interest in being cured, there are also many for whom their crimes are almost out of their hands—as disgusting to them as to anyone else. The *New York Times* ran an article entitled "Sex Offender Agrees to Be Castrated." In Illinois, a convicted child sex offender is having himself castrated "in an effort to win a lighter sentence." The offender, in fact, "volunteered to be castrated even before he was convicted" previously of an attack on a young girl. It seems as though the man is making an attempt to control his urges but, according to the article, "experts disagree on whether castration helps" in controlling these urges.

Both the *New York Times* and *60 Minutes* have good reputations as reliable media sources. I read this paper and watch this show regularly. (I'm pleased that my parents introduced me to them.) I think that these reports are as reliable as the popular press can be. If I decide to do research on this subject and write a substantial paper, I will have to use criminal justice and sociology journals and try to interview one or two experts, as well.

I have not had any personal experience with sex offenders, but I have read and heard enough to know that their crimes destroy not only the lives of victims but also the lives of families and friends of the victims and that their crimes can so haunt victims that these fears are never resolved. In addition, victims of sexual crimes may grow up to inflict these crimes on others, continuing the cycle. In my opinion, the damage done by sex offenders and the risk of untreatable urges to commit these crimes, a risk illustrated by the high percentage of repeat offenders, is too great to justify their release. At least not until there is a proven "cure," a sure-fire way to *know* that they are treatable, have been treated, and will not continue to make victims of others.

Through the media, I have come to understand that many may be operating on urges not within their control, but this does not justify their release. At some point the blame has to fall on the individual. If they were to learn that their rehabilitation was an impossibility, I think that those who are truly disgusted by their crimes might even agree that they are too dangerous to be returned to a society where they have already done so much damage.

Works Cited

Niebuhr, Gustav. "Using Religion to Reform Criminals." *New York Times* 18 Jan. 1998, late ed.: A16. Print.

"Sex Offender Agrees to Be Castrated." *New York Times* 18 Jan. 1998: A6. Print.

60 Minutes. WCBS, New York. 24 June 1997. Television.

Lange incorporates another source that further analyzes the issue and also makes a distinction between her personal feelings and what the facts show.

Lange addresses the reliability of her sources, including their limitations. If she were to explore this topic in a different (more formal) rhetorical situation, she would likely choose more academic and professional sources.

In paragraph 6, Lange admits her lack of experience (an honest gesture that an audience can appreciate) but also shows that she has taken the time to educate herself on the issue. Both gestures help establish her credibility as a writer.

REFLECTION ON WRITING

1. After reading Lange's essay, do you feel she was able to make a distinction between her personal beliefs and the laws regarding sex offenders? If so, where do you see evidence of this? Does she present strong enough evidence to support her beliefs?

2. Lange mentions that she has had no personal experiences with sex offenders. If she was close to someone who had been the victim of a sex crime (or was a victim herself), how do you think this essay might have changed? How would this affect, for example, the inferences made in her essay?

ALTERNATIVE WRITING PROJECT: EVOLVING BELIEFS IN AN ACADEMIC FIELD

Locate a college or high school science, history, or literature textbook from 40 or 50 years ago. Compare several specific points made in the decades-old book with points made in one of your textbooks in the same field.

In order to establish a context for what you observe, ask your instructor or a librarian to guide you to sources that discuss changes in theories in the field that your material is about. For example, in history, you could examine material about multicultural or gender-based approaches; in literature, material about "the canon"; in science, material about a specific discovery in genetics or physics.

Write an essay presenting the differences and similarities that you have found, and comment on what beliefs they seem to reflect. Follow your instructor's directions for topic limitation, length, format, and citation methods.

CHAPTER 11 | Summary

- A *belief* expresses an interpretation, evaluation, conclusion, or prediction about the world, as well as an endorsement of its accuracy; is formed, tested, revised, and retested over time; and can be based on your own personal experience or indirect experience.

- When we evaluate the sources and information related to a belief, it is important to consider the following questions:

  - How reliable is the source?
  - What are the source's purposes and interests?
  - How knowledgeable or experienced is the source?
  - Was the source able to make accurate observations?
  - How reputable is the source?
  - How valuable is information from this source?

- *Knowing* is distinguished from belief by strong reasons and evidence, and truth is often disagreed upon amongst experts, so it is important that we all analyze, evaluate, and develop our own well-reasoned beliefs and acknowledge when we do not have enough information to do so.

- A relativistic view of the world sees all opinions as equal in validity to all others. There are serious problems with this view as some opinions are clearly more informed and accurate than others in many areas of life.

- A belief can be seen as falsifiable if it is possible to state conditions—tests—under which the belief could be disproved but the belief passes those tests.

- The media can shape our beliefs in subtle yet profound ways.

- You can present your beliefs by reporting factual information, inferring from evidence or premises, or judging by applying criteria.

American inventor, Charles F. Kettering (1876–1958), once said that, "A problem well stated is a problem half solved." Having the ability to recognize, and then define and analyze a problem allows us to propose, and ultimately implement, an effective solution. When is the last time you recall being faced with a problem? How did you tackle it and come up with a reasonable solution? Could you have done things differently in retrospect?

Writing to Propose Solutions:
Solving Problems

"Whatever creativity is, it is in part a solution to a problem."

—Brian Aldiss

CRITICAL
THINKING FOCUS:
**The problem-
solving model**

WRITING FOCUS:
**Applying the
problem-solving
model**

READING THEME:
**Solving a social
problem**

WRITING
ACTIVITIES:
**Analyzing
problems**

WRITING PROJECT:
**Proposing
a solution to
a problem**

Problem solving is one of the most powerful of human thinking patterns, and writing is the main system we use to analyze challenging problems and propose solutions. On a personal level, you have probably written an email about a problem in your life. You may have been trying to sustain a romantic relationship with someone while geographically separated, helping a friend resolve a personal crisis, or writing to family members to coordinate a holiday reunion. To address civic problems, you and your neighbors may have written letters to newspapers or petitioned your local government. Writing memos, reports, and proposals to solve problems is an integral part of most careers, from finance to filmmaking.

Although proposing solutions is a common form of writing, it is challenging. In order to compose an insightful solution, you need to do the following:

- *Define the problem clearly.* Your audience needs to understand that there *is* a problem and know exactly what it is.

- *Analyze the problem systematically.* Complex problems are often a confusing tangle of needs, ideas, frustrations, goals, and pieces of information. You need to disentangle the issues so that your audience can understand the core of the problem and what alternatives are possible.

- *Propose a well-reasoned solution.* After presenting a lucid analysis of the problem, along with feasible alternatives, you need to reach a conclusion that you support with thoughtful reasoning and solid evidence. As part of your proposed solution, you should explain why other alternative solutions are less desirable than yours. You should also address anticipated objections to your solution and explain how these difficulties can be overcome.

You will notice that the problem-solving method is similar to the decision-making method discussed in Chapter 5. However, this chapter presents the process in more detail; the focus is on problems instead of on decisions, and you will be considering social as well as personal issues. The reading in this chapter addresses a contemporary societal problem. Finally, the Writing Project involves analyzing a social or personal problem that needs a solution.

Problems in Personal and Civic Life

Throughout your life, you will continually be solving problems. As a student, for example, you deal with a steady stream of academic assignments—quizzes, exams, research projects, essays, papers, and audiovisual presentations. In order to solve these academic problems effectively—how to do well on an exam, for example— you need to define the problem (what areas will the exam cover, and what will its format be?), identify and evaluate various alternatives (what are possible study approaches?), and then combine all these factors to reach a solution (what will your study plan and schedule be?). Relatively simple problems like preparing for an exam do not require a systematic or complex analysis. You can solve them with effort and concentration. However, the difficult and complicated problems in your personal life, such as choosing a college major or ending a relationship, may be a different story. Because these are such crucial situations, you will need to solve such problems in the best possible way by using all your creative and critical thinking skills.

The problems that exist in society also need the very best thinking of all citizens. The fear of terrorism is far too real, parents feel stressed about their children's safety, drugs and alcohol continue to destroy lives, and both racism and sexism create conflicts. These problems may seem overwhelming, and it is true that you cannot control them in the same way that you can control your own life situations. Still, by thinking creatively and critically about such issues, and by gathering information, you can at least develop your own views about contending with them. Then you will be in a position to act on such problems and to vote for candidates whose positions are similar to yours.

Basics of the Problem-Solving Method

Consider the following personal problem:

> My best friend is addicted to drugs, but he won't admit it. Jack always liked to drink, but I never thought too much about it. After all, a lot of people like to drink socially, get relaxed, and have a good time. But over the last few years, he's started using other drugs as well as alcohol, and it's ruining his life. He's stopped taking classes at college and will soon lose his job if he doesn't change. Last week I told him that I was really worried about him, but he told me that he has no drug problem and that in any case it really isn't any of my business. I don't know what to do. I've known Jack since we were in elementary school together, and he's a wonderful person. It's as if he's in the grip of some terrible force and I'm powerless to help him.

In working through this problem, the writer of this description could only think of one possible course of action to try. But if he or she chose instead to approach the problem as a critical thinker, the writer would have to think carefully and systematically through several possibilities in order to reach a solution.

In order to think effectively in situations like this, we usually ask ourselves a series of questions. These are the questions to ask in a five-step problem-solving method:

1. What is the *problem?*
2. What are the *alternatives?*
3. What are the *advantages* and/or *disadvantages* of each alternative?
4. What is the *solution?*
5. How well is the solution *working?*

Put yourself in the position of the student whose friend seems to be addicted to drugs and alcohol, and apply the questions to that problem.

1. WHAT IS THE PROBLEM?

There are a variety of ways to define the problem. For instance, you might define it simply as "Jack has a drug dependency." You might view the problem as "Jack has a drug dependency, but he won't admit it." You might even define the problem as "Jack has a drug dependency, but he won't admit it—and I want to help him solve this problem." Notice that each redefinition of the problem results in a more *specific* definition, which, in turn, helps you better understand the essence of the problem and your responsibility with respect to it.

2. WHAT ARE THE ALTERNATIVES?

In dealing with this problem, you can consider a wide variety of possible actions before selecting the best ones. Identify some of the alternatives.

(Example): Speak to my friend in a candid and forceful way to convince him that he has a serious drug dependency.

3. WHAT ARE THE ADVANTAGES AND/OR DISADVANTAGES OF EACH ALTERNATIVE?

Evaluate the strengths and weaknesses of each alternative you have identified so that you can weigh your choices and determine the best course of action.

(Example): Speak to my friend in a candid and forceful way to convince him that he has a serious problem.

Advantage: He may respond to my direct emotional appeal, acknowledge that he has a problem, and seek help.

Disadvantage: He may react angrily, further alienating me from him and making it more difficult for me to have any influence on him.

4. WHAT IS THE SOLUTION?

After evaluating the various alternatives, select the one you think would be most effective for solving the problem and describe the sequence of steps you would take to act on that alternative.

5. HOW WELL IS THE SOLUTION WORKING?

The final step in the process comes after you have begun to implement your choice of action. You review the solution and decide whether it is working well. If it is not, you must modify your solution or perhaps try an alternate solution you disregarded earlier. In this situation, trying to figure out the best way to help your friend recognize addiction and seek treatment leads to a series of decisions. This is what the critical thinking process is all about—trying to make sense of what is going on in the world and acting appropriately in response. When we solve problems effectively, our thinking process exhibits a coherent organization, following the general approach just outlined.

This problem-solving method lends itself to the organization of an essay or argument. For your writing to be truly effective in describing a problem and proposing a solution, you will need to consider additional rhetorical issues.

Audience   When writing about Jack's situation, the evidence you draw on and the voice in which you write will have to do with your immediate audience. If you are writing directly to Jack, you will want to be as candid, caring, and explicit as possible. You might want to describe, in a letter to Jack, a particularly difficult or embarrassing moment when his addiction interfered with your relationship. On the other hand, if you are writing to Jack's family to urge members to intervene, you will want to be less personal about Jack's effects on your own life and instead describe the effect of his behavior on his grades and his job performance.

Purpose   When describing a personal problem and exploring possible solutions, your purpose depends not only on your immediate audience but also on the outcome you desire. For example, if you were to write directly to Jack in this situation, your purpose might be either to urge him to seek help to preserve your relationship or to inform him that you have reached the limits of your tolerance and you are ending your friendship although you still wish him well. Your purpose will, obviously, influence your choice of language, as well as the structure of your writing.

If we can understand the way the mind operates when we are thinking effectively, we can apply this understanding to improve our thinking in new, challenging situations. In the remainder of this chapter, we will explore a more sophisticated version of this problem-solving approach and apply it to a variety of complex, difficult problems.

Thinking-Writing Activity

ANALYZING A PROBLEM SOLVED PREVIOUSLY

1. Write a description of a problem in your personal life that you have recently solved.

2. Explain how you went about solving the problem. What were the steps, strategies, and approaches you used to understand the problem and to make an informed decision about a possible solution?

3. Analyze your thinking process by applying the five-step problem-solving method (page 439) we have been exploring.

4. Share your problem with classmates, and have them try to analyze and solve it. Then explain the solution you arrived at.

The Problem-Solving Method in Detail

Imagine yourself in the following situation. What would be your next move, and what are your reasons for deciding on it?

> You are about to begin your second year of college, following a very successful first year. Until now, you have financed your education through a combination of savings, financial aid, and a part-time job (16 hours a week) at a local store. However, you just received a letter from your college saying that your financial aid package has been reduced by half due to budgetary problems. The letter concludes, "We hope this aid reduction will not prove to be too great an inconvenience." From your perspective, the loss of aid isn't an inconvenience—it's a disaster! Your budget last year was already tight, and with your job, you barely had enough time to study, participate in a few college activities, and have a modest (but essential) social life. To make matters worse, your mother has been ill, reducing her income and creating financial problems at home. You're panicking—what in the world are you going to do?

As noted earlier, at first a difficult problem often seems like a confused tangle of information, feelings, alternatives, opinions, considerations, and risks. The problem just described is a complicated situation that does not seem to have a single simple solution. Without applying a systematic approach, your thoughts might wander through the tangle of issues in this manner:

> *I want to stay in school, . . . but I'm not going to have enough money. . . . I could work more hours at my job, . . . but I might not have enough time to study and get top grades . . . and if all I'm doing is working and studying, what about my social life? . . . and what about Mom and the kids? They will need my help. . . . I could drop out of school for a while, . . . but if I don't stay in school, what kind of future do we have?*

Very often, when faced with difficult problems like this one, you simply may not know where to begin to try to solve them. Every issue is connected to many others. Frustrated by not knowing where to take the first step, you may give up trying to understand the problem. Or you may behave in one of the following ways:

1. Act impulsively without thought or consideration ("I'll just quit school").

2. Follow someone else's advice without seriously evaluating the suggestion ("Tell me what I should do—I'm tired of thinking about this").

3. Do nothing as you wait for events to make the decision for you ("I'll just wait and see what happens").

None of these approaches is likely to succeed in the long run, and each can gradually reduce your confidence in dealing with complex problems. An alternative to these reactions is to *think critically* about the problem, analyzing it with an organized approach based on the following five-step method.

Detailed Method for Solving Problems

Step 1: What is the problem?

  a. What do I know about the situation?

  b. What results am I seeking in this situation?

  c. How can I define the problem?

Step 2: What are the alternatives?

  a. What are the boundaries of the problem situation?

  b. What alternatives are possible within these boundaries?

Step 3: What are the advantages and/or disadvantages of each alternative?

  a. What are the advantages of each alternative?

  b. What are the disadvantages of each alternative?

  c. What additional information do I need in order to evaluate this alternative?

Step 4: What is the solution?

  a. Which alternative(s) will I pursue?

  b. What steps can I take to act on this (these) alternative(s)?

Step 5: How well is the solution working?

  a. What is my evaluation?

  b. What adjustments are necessary?

Even when we are using an organized method for working through difficult problems and arriving at thoughtful conclusions, our minds may not always work in a logical, step-by-step fashion. Effective problem solvers typically pass through all the steps we will be examining—but not always in sequence.

Instead, the best problem solvers take a flexible approach to the process, one in which they utilize a repertoire of problem-solving strategies as needed. Sometimes exploring the various alternatives helps them to go back and redefine the original problem. Similarly, seeking to implement the solution can often suggest a new

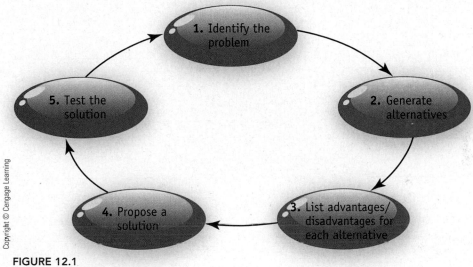

FIGURE 12.1
A Flexible Approach to Problem Solving

alternative or alternatives that combine the best points of previous ones. This recursive approach is shown in Figure 12.1.

The key point is that although the problem-solving steps are presented in a logical sequence here, you need not follow them in a mechanical and unimaginative fashion. At the same time, in learning a problem-solving method like this, it is generally not wise to omit steps because each one deals with an important aspect of the problem. As you become more proficient in using the method, you will find that you can apply its concepts and strategies to problem solving in an increasingly flexible and natural fashion, just as learning the basics of an activity like driving a car gradually results in a more integrated performance of the skills involved.

BEFORE YOU BEGIN: ACCEPTING THE PROBLEM

To solve a problem, you must first be willing to *accept* the problem by acknowledging that it exists and committing yourself to trying to solve it. Sometimes you may have difficulty recognizing a problem unless it is pointed out to you. At other times, you may actively resist acknowledging a problem, even when it is pointed out to you. The person who confidently states, "I don't really have any problems," sometimes has very serious problems—but is simply unwilling to acknowledge them.

However, mere acknowledgment is not enough to solve a problem, and indeed it would make for a very brief and unsatisfying essay. Once you have identified a problem, you must commit yourself to solving it. Successful problem solvers are highly motivated and willing to persevere through the many chal-lenges and frustrations of the problem-solving process. How do you find this motivation and commitment? There are not simple answers, but the following strategies may help:

- *List the benefits.* Making a detailed list of the benefits you will derive from successfully dealing with the problem is a good place to begin. Such a process helps you clarify why you might want to tackle the problem, motivates you to get started, and serves as a source of encouragement when you encounter difficulties or lose momentum.

- *Formalize your acceptance.* You can formalize your acceptance of a problem by "going on record," either by preparing a signed declaration or by signing a "contract" with someone else. This formal commitment can serve as an explicit statement of original intentions to which you can refer if your resolve weakens.

- *Accept responsibility for your life.* Former U.S. Attorney General Robert F. Kennedy, who was assassinated in 1968, once said, "Some people see things as they are, and ask, 'Why?' I see things as they could be, and ask, 'Why not?'" You have the potential to control the direction of your own life, but to do so, you must accept your freedom to choose and the responsibility that goes with it.

- *Create a "worst case" scenario.* Some problems persist because people are able to ignore their possible implications. When you create a worst-case scenario, you remind yourself, as graphically as possible, of the potentially disastrous consequences of your actions. For example, looking at vivid color photographs and research conclusions can remind a person that excessive smoking, drinking, or eating can lead to myriad health problems and social and psychological difficulties, as well as death.

- *Identify the constraints.* If you are having trouble accepting a problem, it is usually because something is holding you back. For example, you might be concerned about the amount of time and effort involved, you might be reluctant to confront the underlying issues the problem represents, you might be worried about finding out unpleasant things about yourself or others, or you might be inhibited by other problems in your life, such as a tendency to procrastinate. Whatever the constraints, using this strategy involves identifying and describing all the factors that are preventing you from confronting the problem and then addressing them one at a time.

As you work through the following five steps of the problem-solving method, be prepared to informally jot down your ideas and responses. They will help you com-plete other assignments in this chapter.

STEP 1: WHAT IS THE PROBLEM?

The problem-solving process begins by determining exactly what the central issues of the problem are. Otherwise, your chances of solving it are considerably reduced. You may even spend time trying to solve the wrong problem. For instance, consider the different formulations of the following problems. How might each formulation lead a person in a different direction when trying to solve the problem?

"School is boring" versus "I am bored in accounting class."
"I'm unlovable" versus "I was just turned down for a date."

In each of these cases, a very general conclusion (first formulation) has been replaced by a more specific characterization of the problem (second formulation).

General conclusions ("I'm a failure") do not suggest productive ways of resolving the difficulties. They are too absolute, too all-encompassing. On the other hand, more specific descriptions of the problem situation ("I just failed an exam") do permit you to attack problems with useful strategies. In short, the way you define a problem determines not only how you will go about solving it but also whether you feel that the problem can be solved at all. Correct identification of a problem is essential if you are going to be able to successfully analyze it and reach an appropriate conclusion. Incorrectly identifying the problem can lead to pursuing an unproductive, even destructive, course of action.

This process of identifying the problem and arriving at a specific characterization of it can help you to articulate a clear thesis (for an essay or research project) or claim (for an argument).

Consider the problem of the college student whose financial aid package was cut (pages 441–442), and analyze it using this problem-solving method. Ask

1. What do I know about the situation?
2. What is my purpose for writing about the problem?
3. What results am I seeking in this situation (what is my purpose)?
4. How can I define the problem?

Step 1(a): What do I know about the situation? Solving a problem begins with determining what you *know* to be the case and what you *think* may be the case. To explore the problem successfully, you need to have a clear idea of the details of your beginning circumstances. You can **identify** and organize what you know about the problem situation by posing key questions. By asking—and trying to answer—questions of fact, you are establishing a sound foundation for exploring your problem, as well as developing an interesting, arguable thesis or claim. Imagine that you are the student described earlier who is facing a reduction in financial aid. Answer the following questions of fact—who? what? when? how? why?—about your problem.

- *Who* are the people involved in this situation?
  Who will benefit from my solving this problem?
  Who can help me solve this problem?

- *What* are the various parts or dimensions of the problem?
  What are my strengths and resources for solving this problem?

- *When* did the problem begin?
  When should the problem be resolved?
- *How* did the problem arise or develop?
- *Why* is solving this problem important to me?
  Why is this problem difficult to solve?
- Additional questions: _____

Step 1(b): What results am I seeking in this situation?   The second part of answering the question "What is the problem?" consists of identifying the specific results or objectives you are trying to achieve. Your purpose for writing about this problem is to solve it. If you are able to achieve your specific results or objectives, you will have satisfied your purpose for writing. Whereas the first part of Step 1 oriented you in terms of the history of the problem and the current situation, this part encourages you to look to the future. To identify results, you need to ask yourself the question "What are the objectives that, once achieved, will solve this problem?" For instance, one of the results or objectives in the sample problem might be having enough money to pay for college. Describe additional results you might be trying to achieve in this situation.

1. Having enough money to pay for college.

2. _____

3. _____

4. _____

Step 1(c): How can I define the problem?   After exploring what you know about the problem and the results you want to achieve, you need to conclude Step 1 by defining the problem as clearly and specifically as possible. This is a crucial task in the problem-solving process because this definition will determine the direction of your analysis. Chapter 8 illustrates the thinking processes for successful definition.

Often, identifying the central issue of a problem is a complex process. For example, the statement "My problem is relating to other people" suggests a complicated situation with many interacting variables that resists simple definition. In fact, you may not even begin to develop a clear definition of the problem until you engage in the process of trying to solve it. Or you might begin by believing that your problem is, say, not having the ability to succeed but end by concluding that the problem is really a fear of success.

As you will see, the same insights also apply to social problems. For example, the problem of high school dropouts might initially be defined in terms of problems in the school system, whereas later formulations might identify drug use or social pressure as the core of the problem.

Although there are no simple formulas for defining challenging problems, you can try several strategies to identify the central issue most effectively:

- *View the problem from different perspectives.* As you saw in Chapters 3, 7, and 8, perspective taking is a key ingredient of thinking critically; it can also help you zero in on many problems. When you describe how various individuals might view a given problem—such as the high school dropout rate—the essential ingredients of the problems begin to emerge. In the student financial aid problem, how would you describe the student's perspective? The college's perspective? The student's family's perspective?

- *Identify component problems.* Larger problems are often made up of component problems. To define a larger problem, it is often necessary to identify and describe the subproblems that comprise it. A student's poor school performance, for example, might result from a number of factors like ineffective study habits, inefficient time management, and preoccupation with a personal problem. Defining, and dealing effectively with, a larger problem means defining and dealing with the subproblems first. Can you identify two possible subproblems in the financial aid problem?

- *State the problem clearly and specifically.* A third defining strategy is to state the problem as clearly and specifically as possible as you examine your objectives for solving it. Stating this sort of precise description of the problem is an important step toward solving it. If you state the problem in very general terms, you won't have a clear idea of how best to proceed in dealing with it. However, if you can describe it in specific terms, your description will begin to suggest actions you can take to solve the problem. Examine the differences between the statements of the following problem:

General: "My problem is money."
More specific: "My problem is needing to budget my money so that I won't always run out of it near the end of the month."
Most specific: "My problem is my need to develop the habits and discipline to budget my money so that I won't always run out of it near the end of the month."

Review your analysis of the student's financial aid problem; then state the problem in writing as clearly and specifically as you can.

STEP 2: WHAT ARE THE ALTERNATIVES?

Once you have clearly and specifically identified a problem, your next move is to examine each possible action that might help you to solve it. Before you list the alternatives, however, it makes sense to explore the situation's boundaries to determine which actions are possible and which are not.

Step 2(a): What are the boundaries of the problem situation?   Boundaries are limits that you simply cannot change. They are part of the problem, and they must be accepted and dealt with. At the same time, you must be careful not to identify as boundaries any circumstances that *can* be changed. For instance, again imagining yourself as the student with the financial aid problem, you might assume that your problem must be solved in your current location, without realizing that transferring to a less expensive college could be one of your options. Identify additional bound-aries that might be part of this sample situation, and list some of the questions you should answer about these boundaries.

Step 2(b): What alternatives are possible within these boundaries?   After you have established a general notion of the boundaries of the problem situation, you can proceed to identify the possible courses of action that can occur within them. Of course, identifying all the possible alternatives is not always easy; in fact, that may be part of your problem. Often we cannot see a way out of a problem because our thinking is set in certain ruts, fixed in certain perspectives. We may be blind to other approaches, either because we reject them without seriously considering them ("That will never work!") or because they simply do not occur to us. You can use several strategies to overcome these obstacles:

- *Discuss the problem with other people.* Discussing possible alternatives with others uses a number of the aspects of critical thinking we explored in Chapter 1. Other people can often suggest alternatives we haven't thought of, since they are outside the situation and thus have a more objective perspective and since they naturally view the world differently than we do because of their past experiences and their personalities. In addition, discussions are often creative experiences that generate ideas participants would not have come up with on their own.

- *Brainstorm ideas.* Group brainstorming builds on the strengths of working with other people to generate ideas and solve problems. In a typical brainstorming session, either in person or online, a group of people works together to propose as many ideas as possible in a specific time period. As ideas are produced, they are not judged or evaluated, as this tends to inhibit the free flow of ideas and discourage people from making suggestions. Evaluation is deferred until a later stage. People are encouraged to build on the ideas of others, since the most creative ideas are often generated through the constructive interplay of various minds.

- *Change your location.* Your perspectives on a problem are often tied to the circumstances in which the problem exists. For example, a problem you may be having in school is connected with your daily experiences and your habitual reactions to them. Sometimes you need a fresh perspective, which you can gain by getting away from the problem situation so that you can view it more clearly in a different light. Perhaps spending a day or two out of town will help, or even taking a long walk in a different neighborhood.

Using these strategies, as well as your own reflections, identify as many alterna-tives to help solve the financial aid problem as you can think of.

1. Attend school part-time

2. _____

3. _____

4. _____

STEP 3: WHAT ARE THE ADVANTAGES AND/OR DISADVANTAGES OF EACH ALTERNATIVE?

Once you have identified the alternatives, your next step is to evaluate them. Each possible course of action offers certain advantages in the sense that if you were to select that alternative, there would be some positive results. At the same time, each possible course of action probably also has disadvantages in the sense that if you were to select that alternative, you may incur a cost or risk some negative results. Determine how helpful each course of action would or would not be in solving the problem.

Step 3(a): What are the advantages of each alternative?   The alternative we listed in Step 2 for the sample problem ("Attend college part-time") might include the following advantages:

Alternative	Advantages
Attend college part-time	1. Doing this would remove some of the immediate time and money pressures I am experiencing, while still allowing me to prepare for the future.
	2. I would have more time to focus on the courses that I would be taking and to work additional hours.

Identify the advantages of each of the alternatives that you listed in Step 2. Be sure that your responses are thoughtful and specific. For example, how many additional hours could you work? How much additional income would doing that generate?

Step 3(b): What are the disadvantages of each alternative?   The alternative we listed in Step 2 for the sample problem might include the following disadvantages:

Alternative	Disadvantages
Attend college part-time	1. It would take me much longer to complete my schooling, thus delaying my progress toward my goals.
	2. I might lose motivation and drop out before completing school because the process would be taking so long.
	3. Being a part-time student might threaten my eligibility for financial aid.

Now identify the disadvantages of each of the alternatives that you listed for Step 2. Make sure that your responses are thoughtful and specific. For example, how much longer would it take you to get your degree?

Step 3(c): What additional information do I need to evaluate each alternative? The next part of Step 3 consists of determining what you must know (information needed) to best evaluate and compare the alternatives. For each alternative, there are questions that you must answer in order to establish which alternatives make sense and which do not. In addition, you need to figure out the most reliable sources for this information.

The information—and the sources of it—that must be located for the first alternative in the sample problem might include the following:

Information Needed

1. How long will it take me to complete my degree?
2. How long can I continue in school without losing interest and dropping out?
3. Will I threaten my eligibility for financial aid if I become a part-time student?

Sources: Myself, other part-time students, school counselors, financial aid office

Identify the information needed and the sources of this information for each of the alternatives that you identified on pages 447–448. Be sure that your responses are thoughtful and specific.

STEP 4: WHAT IS THE SOLUTION?

The purpose of Steps 1 through 3 is to analyze your problem in a systematic and detailed fashion. After breaking down the problem in this way, your next step is to decide on a thoughtful course of action based on your increased understanding. Even though conducting this sort of analysis does not guarantee finding a specific solution to the problem, it should deepen your understanding of exactly what the problem is. And in locating and evaluating the alternatives, it should give you some very good ideas about the general direction in which you should move and the immediate steps you should take.

Step 4(a): Which alternative(s) will I pursue?   There is no simple formula to tell you which alternatives to select. As you work through the different courses of action that are possible, you may find that you can immediately rule some out. In the sample problem, for example, you may know with certainty that you do not want to attend college part-time (alternative 1) because you will forfeit your remaining financial aid. However, it may not be as simple to select which of the other alternatives you wish to pursue. How do you decide?

The decisions we make usually depend on what we believe is most important to us. These beliefs are known as *values*. Our values are the starting points of our actions and strongly influence our decisions. For example, if we value staying alive (as most of us do), we will make many decisions each day that express this value— eating proper meals, not walking in front of moving traffic, and so on.

Our values help us set priorities in life—that is, decide what aspects of our lives are most important to us. We might decide that for the present, going to school is more important than having an active social life. In this case, going to school has higher priority than having an active social life. Unfortunately, our values are not always consistent with each other—we may have to choose either going to school or having an active social life. Both activities may be important to us; they are simply not compatible with each other. Very often the *conflicts* between our values constitute the problem. Let's examine some strategies for selecting alternatives that might help to solve the sample problem.

- *Evaluate and compare alternatives.* Although each alternative may have certain advantages and disadvantages, not all advantages are equally desirable or potentially effective. For example, giving up college entirely would certainly solve some aspects of the sample problem, but its obvious disadvantages would rule out this solution for most people. Thus, it makes sense to try to evaluate and rank the various alternatives on the basis of how effective they are likely to be and how they match up with your value system. A good place to begin is at the "Results" stage, Step 1(b). Examine each of your alternatives, and evaluate how well it will contribute to achieving the results you are seeking in the situation. You may want to rank the alternatives or develop your own rating system to assess their relative effectiveness.

  After evaluating the alternatives in terms of their anticipated *effectiveness,* the next step is to evaluate them in terms of their *desirability* relative to your needs, interests, and value system. Again, you can use either a ranking or a rating system to assess their relative desirability. After completing these two separate evaluations, you can select whatever alternatives seem most appropriate. Review the alternatives you identified in the sample problem; then rank or rate them according to their potential effectiveness and desirability.

- *Synthesize a new alternative.* After reviewing and evaluating the alternatives you have generated, you may develop a new alternative that combines the best qualities of several options, while avoiding the disadvantages some of them would have if implemented exclusively. In the sample problem, you might combine attending college part-time during the academic year with attending school during summer session so that progress toward your degree wouldn't be impeded. Examine the alternatives you identified, and develop a new option that combines the best elements of several of them.

- *Try out each alternative—in your imagination.* Focus on each alternative, and try to imagine, as concretely as possible, what it would be like if you actually selected it. Visualize what impact your choice would have on your problem and what the implications would be for your life as a whole. By trying out the alternative in your imagination, you can sometimes avoid unpleasant results or unexpected consequences. As a variation of this strategy, you can sometimes test alternatives on a very limited basis in a practice situation. Suppose you are trying to overcome your fear of speaking out in groups. You can practice various speaking techniques with your friends or family until you find an approach that works for you.

Step 4(b): What steps can I take to act on this (these) alternative(s)?   Once you have decided on an alternative to pursue, your next move is to plan what steps to take in acting on it. Planning the specific steps you will take is extremely important. Although thinking carefully about your problem is necessary, it is not enough if you hope to solve the problem. You have to take action. In the sample problem, for example, imagine that one of the alternatives you have selected is "find additional sources of income that will enable me to work part-time and attend school full-time." The specific steps you would take might include these:

- Contact the financial aid office to learn what other forms of monetary aid are available and how to apply for them.
- Contact some local banks to find out what sort of student loans they offer.
- Look for a higher-paying job to earn more money without working additional hours.
- Discuss your problem with students in similar circumstances in order to generate new ideas.

Identify the steps you would have to take to pursue the alternative(s) you identified on pages 447–448.

Plans, of course, do not implement themselves. Once you know what actions are needed, you have to make a commitment to taking the necessary steps. This is where many people stumble in the problem-solving process; they remain paralyzed by inertia or fear. Having a clear sense of purpose—and an audience who will be directly affected by your decisions—will help keep you motivated. To overcome such blocks and inhibitions, you sometimes need to reexamine your original acceptance of the problem, perhaps making use of some of the strategies you explored on pages 443–444. Once you get started, the rewards of actively attacking your problem are often enough incentive to keep you focused and motivated.

STEP 5: HOW WELL IS THE SOLUTION WORKING?

As you work toward reaching a reasonable and informed conclusion, be wary of falling into the trap of thinking that there is only one "right" solution and that if you don't figure out what it is and implement it, all is lost. You should remind yourself that any analysis of a problem situation, no matter how careful and systematic, is ultimately limited. You simply cannot anticipate or predict everything that will happen in the future. Consequently, every decision you make is provisional in the sense that your ongoing experience will inform you whether it is working out or needs to be modified.

Step 5(a): What is my evaluation?   In many cases, the relative effectiveness of your efforts will be apparent. In other cases, you will find it helpful to pursue a more systematic evaluation along the lines suggested in the following strategies.

- *Compare the results with the goals.* The essence of evaluation is comparing the results of your efforts with your initial goals. For example, the goals of the sample problem are embodied in the results you specified on pages 447–448. Compare the anticipated results of the alternative(s) you selected. To what extent will your choice(s) meet these goals? Are any goals not likely to be met by your alternative(s)? If so, which ones? Could they be addressed by other alternatives? Asking these questions and others will help you to assess the success of your efforts and will provide a foundation for future decisions.

- *Get other perspectives.* As you have seen throughout the problem-solving process, getting the opinions of others is a productive strategy at virtually every stage, and this is certainly true of evaluation. It is not always easy to accept the evaluations of others, but keeping an open mind about outside opinions is a very valuable attitude to cultivate because it will stimulate and guide you to produce your best efforts.

   To receive specific, practical feedback, you need to ask specific, practical questions that will elicit such information. General questions ("What do you think of this?") typically receive overly general, unhelpful answers ("It sounds okay to me"). Be focused when soliciting feedback, and remember that you do have the right to ask people for *constructive* comments—that is, to provide suggestions for improvement rather than just telling you what they think is wrong. For example, you could say, "What do you know about me that you think will help me maintain my motivation to stay in school—even if it takes two years longer than I had planned?" Or you can ask, "Do you have any ideas about how I can cut my expenses by 10 percent each month?"

Step 5(b): What adjustments are necessary?   As a result of your review, you may discover that the alternative you selected is not feasible or is not producing satisfactory results. Even when things initially appear to be working reasonably well, an active thinker continues to ask questions such as "What might I have overlooked?" and "How could I have done this differently?" Of course, asking—and trying to answer—questions like these is even more essential if solutions are hard to come by (as they usually are in real-world problems) and if you are to retain the flexibility and optimism you will need to tackle a new option.

Frank Cotham/The New Yorker Collection/CartoonBank.Com

"As soon as one problem is solved, another rears its ugly head."

Thinking-Writing Activity

ANALYZING A PROBLEM IN YOUR LIFE

This Thinking-Writing Activity provides you with an opportunity to apply the problem-solving method to an important unsolved problem in your own life.

First, select a problem that you are currently grappling with and have not been able to solve.

Next, strengthen your acceptance of the problem by using several strategies described on pages 443–444, such as listing benefits, formalizing your acceptance, accepting responsibility, creating a "worst case" scenario, or identifying the constraints.

Finally, write a thoughtful response to the questions asked in all five of the problem-solving steps in the "Detailed Method for Solving Problems" box on page 442.

Discuss your problem with other class members to generate fresh perspectives and unusual alternatives that might not have occurred to you. Your ultimate goal is to decide on a provisional solution to your problem and establish a plan of action that will help you move in the right direction.

Solving Social Problems

The problems we have analyzed up to this point are "personal" problems in the sense that they represent individual challenges we encounter as we live our lives. Problems are not only of a personal nature, however. We also face problems as members of a community, the larger society, and the world. As with personal problems, we need to approach these kinds of problems in an organized and thoughtful way in order to explore the issues, develop a clear understanding, and decide on an informed plan of action.

Making sense of a complex, challenging situation is not a simple process. The famous newspaperman H. L. Mencken once said, "To every complex question there is a simple answer—and it's wrong!" In this chapter, we explored how complex problems do not have simple solutions, whether they are personal problems or larger social problems like racial prejudice or world hunger. We have also learned that by working through these complex problems thoughtfully and systematically, we can achieve a deeper understanding of their many interacting elements, as well as developing and implementing strategies for solving them.

A thoughtful problem solver employs all the critical thinking abilities we have examined in this book. And although we might agree with Mencken's evaluation of simple answers to complex questions, we would expand upon it: "To many complex questions there are complex answers—and these are well worth pursuing."

Thinking Critically About Visuals

"Necessity Is the Mother of Invention"

This photo is of a windmill designed and built by William Kamkwamba in 2003 in Masitala, a village in Malawi, Africa, for the purpose of generating power for his parents' home. At the time, Kamkwamba was just a teenager, and he researched and taught himself how to build the windmill all on his own, using local scrap materials that he could find. This vividly illustrates the point that creative problem-solving is both innovative and useful in a practical way, and that it often makes use of available materials—whatever they are—thus underscoring the wisdom of the statement "Necessity is the mother of invention." What other examples of creative innovation have you run into in the course of everyday life?

Lucas Oleniuk/The Toronto Star/zReportage.com/ZUMApress

In the provocative article "Is Google Making Us Stupid?" writer Nicholas Carr wonders if the culture's pervasive use of the Web-based new media is restructuring the way that we think, making it more difficult for us to concentrate, contemplate, and read lengthy, complex books and articles. The author's concern is that using the Web encourages us to jump quickly from link to link, spending little time at any one particular place to think deeply and analytically about the ideas we are considering. Is this a problem about which we ought to be concerned?

THINKING CRITICALLY ABOUT NEW MEDIA

Surfing Dangers and Addictions

Using the power and opportunities afforded by new media is intoxicating—but it is also potentially problematic. In the last chapter, we explored the difficulties we can encounter when dealing with others on the Internet. But you may encounter threats and challenges just by virtue of spending a lot of time online. These threats and challenges can be dealt with effectively if we take an informed, problem-solving approach, but we first have to be aware of what the dangers are.

To begin with, using the various aspects of new media can be addictive in the same way that watching television can be addictive. For example, have you ever found yourself "hypnotized" by the television, watching shows that you're not even that interested in? There are a variety of visual and psychological reasons why it's so difficult to stop watching television, many of which apply to the computer screen as well. Unlike real life, where we take in a tiny part of the visual panorama around us with the fovea (the sharp-focusing part of the eye), when we watch television we take in the entire frame of the image with our sharp foveal vision, making the experience more visually fascinating. Similarly, again in contrast to real life, the images on the screen are dynamic and almost always moving, creating an attention-grabbing bond that is difficult to tear ourselves away from. This continual eye-movement as we watch activity on screens also causes the eye to defocus slightly, a physiological activity that typically accompanies various fantasy, daydreaming, and drug-induced states. As Marie Winn in her seminal work *The Plug-In Drug* observes: "This may very well be a reason for the trancelike nature of so many viewers' television experience, and may help to explain why the television image has so strong and hypnotic a fascination."

These same factors are at work whether we are watching a television screen or a computer screen. The difference is that new media are *interactive:* we can roam around the Internet at will, follow an infinite succession of links and websites, and communicate with as many people as we wish to. It's no wonder that once we start our fingertips moving on the computer or communication device we're using, it's very difficult to get those fingers to stop. Although a certain amount of the time we spend engaged with new media is productive, much of it is not particularly useful, and it prevents us from engaging in other activities that *would* be more enriching and productive.

As with any addiction, seeking a solution involves recognizing that there *is* a problem and then using a problem-solving methodology like the one introduced in this chapter. Certainly, a good place to begin is by strictly scheduling and limiting the time we spend "surfing" online or engaged in social exchanges. This is particularly true when it comes to emailing and text messaging. And if we're engaged in a real-world activity, it's useful to discipline ourselves by checking for messages every hour or so rather than reading and responding to them as they come in. Research has shown that leaving and then returning to the activity in which you were engaged is a tremendous time-waster.

A more subtle threat to our well-being is described in the article on page 458, "Is Google Making Us Stupid?" in which the author, Nicholas Carr, explores whether our immersion in new media is restructuring the way we think and process information, making it more difficult for us to concentrate on activities like reading for a lengthy period of time, spending time in quiet contemplation of important issues, or thinking in deep and complex ways. As Carr, a writer, explains: "Once I was a scuba diver in the sea of words. Now I zip along the surface like a guy on a Jet Ski."

Thinking-Writing Activity

READING PRINT VS. READING ONLINE

In anticipation of reading the following article, "Is Google Making Us Stupid?" perform the following reading "experiment" to explore the differences between print and online reading. Select a news source that has both a print version and an online version such as *The New York Times, Washington Post, Chicago Tribune,* or *The Los Angeles Times.*

First read the online version, selecting and reading the articles of interest as you normally would. Then read the print version of the same publication but on a different date. What differences did you find between the two experiences? For example, did you find that

- You spent more time reading one of the versions?
- One version provided you with more detailed and developed information?
- One version exposed you to a greater variety of topics and stories?
- One version more deeply engaged you in the process of reading and thinking?
- One version resulted in a greater recall of what you had read?

After responding to these questions, analyze and write about what factors accounted for the different experiences.

Is Google Making Us Stupid?

by Nicholas Carr

"Dave, stop. Stop, will you? Stop, Dave. Will you stop, Dave?" So the supercomputer HAL pleads with the implacable astronaut Dave Bowman in a famous and weirdly poignant scene toward the end of Stanley Kubrick's *2001: A Space Odyssey*. Bowman, having nearly been sent to a deep-space death by the malfunctioning machine, is calmly, coldly disconnecting the memory circuits that control its artificial "brain." "Dave, my mind is going," HAL says, forlornly. "I can feel it. I can feel it."

I can feel it, too. Over the past few years I've had an uncomfortable sense that someone, or something, has been tinkering with my brain, remapping the neural circuitry, reprogramming the memory. My mind isn't going—so far as I can tell—but it's changing. I'm not thinking the way I used to think. I can feel it most strongly when I'm reading. Immersing myself in a book or a lengthy article used to be easy. My mind would get caught up in the narrative or the turns of the argument, and I'd spend hours strolling through long stretches of prose. That's rarely the case anymore. Now my concentration often starts to drift after two or three pages. I get fidgety, lose the thread, begin looking for something else to do. I feel as if I'm always dragging my wayward brain back to the text. The deep reading that used to come naturally has become a struggle.

I think I know what's going on. For more than a decade now, I've been spending a lot of time online, searching and surfing and sometimes adding to the great databases of the Internet. The Web has been a godsend to me as a writer. Research that once required days

in the stacks or periodical rooms of libraries can now be done in minutes. A few Google searches, some quick clicks on hyperlinks, and I've got the telltale fact or pithy quote I was after. Even when I'm not working, I'm as likely as not to be foraging in the Web's info-thickets reading and writing e-mails, scanning headlines and blog posts, watching videos and listening to podcasts, or just tripping from link to link to link. (Unlike footnotes, to which they're sometimes likened, hyperlinks don't merely point to related works; they propel you toward them.)

Source: "Is Google Making Us Stupid?" by Nicholas Carr. From *The Atlantic*, July/August 2008. Reprinted by permission of the author.

For me, as for others, the Net is becoming a universal medium, the conduit for most of the information that flows through my eyes and ears and into my mind. The advantages of having immediate access to such an incredibly rich store of information are many, and they've been widely described and duly applauded. "The perfect recall of silicon memory," Wired's Clive Thompson has written, "can be an enormous boon to thinking." But that boon comes at a price. As the media theorist Marshall McLuhan pointed out in the 1960s, media are not just passive channels of information. They supply the stuff of thought, but they also shape the process of thought. And what the Net seems to be doing is chipping away my capacity for concentration and contemplation. My mind now expects to take in information the way the Net distributes it: in a swiftly moving stream of particles. Once I was a scuba diver in the sea of words. Now I zip along the surface like a guy on a Jet Ski.

I'm not the only one. When I mention my troubles with reading to friends and   5
acquaintances—literary types, most of them—many say they're having similar experiences. The more they use the Web, the more they have to fight to stay focused on long pieces of writing. Some of the bloggers I follow have also begun mentioning the phenomenon. Scott Karp, who writes a blog about online media, recently confessed that he has stopped reading books altogether. "I was a lit major in college, and used to be [a] voracious book reader," he wrote. "What happened?" He speculates on the answer: "What if I do all my reading on the web not so much because the way I read has changed, i.e. I'm just seeking convenience, but because the way I THINK has changed?"

. . .

Anecdotes alone don't prove much. And we still await the long-term neurological and psychological experiments that will provide a definitive picture of how Internet use affects cognition. But a recently published study of online research habits, conducted by scholars from University College London, suggests that we may well be in the midst of a sea change in the way we read and think. . . . They found that people using the sites exhibited "a form of skimming activity," hopping from one source to another and rarely returning to any source they'd already visited. They typically read no more than one or two pages of an article or book before they would "bounce" out to another site. Sometimes they'd save a long article, but there's no evidence that they ever went back and actually read it. The authors of the study report:

> It is clear that users are not reading online in the traditional sense; indeed there are signs that new forms of "reading" are emerging as users "power browse" horizontally through titles, contents pages and abstracts going for quick wins. It almost seems that they go online to avoid reading in the traditional sense.

Thanks to the ubiquity of text on the Internet, not to mention the popularity of text-messaging on cell phones, we may well be reading more today than we did in the 1970s or 1980s, when television was our medium of choice. But it's a different kind of reading, and behind it lies a different kind of thinking—perhaps even a new sense of the self. "We are not only what we read," says Maryanne Wolf, a developmental psychologist at Tufts University and the author of *Proust and the Squid: The Story and Science of the Reading Brain*. "We are how we read." Wolf worries that the style of reading promoted by the Net, a style that puts "efficiency" and "immediacy" above all else, may be weakening our capacity for the kind of deep reading that emerged when an earlier technology, the printing press, made long and complex works of prose commonplace. When we read online, she says, we tend to become "mere decoders of information." Our ability to interpret text, to make the rich mental connections that form when we read deeply and without distraction, remains largely disengaged.

Reading, explains Wolf, is not an instinctive skill for human beings. It's not etched into our genes the way speech is. We have to teach our minds how to translate the symbolic characters we see into the language we understand. And the media or other technologies we use in learning and practicing the craft of reading play an important part in shaping the neural circuits inside our brains. Experiments demonstrate that readers of ideograms, such as the Chinese, develop a mental circuitry for reading that is very different from the circuitry found in those of us whose written language employs an alphabet. The variations extend across many regions of the brain, including those that govern such essential cognitive functions as memory and the interpretation of visual and auditory stimuli. We can expect as well that the circuits woven by our use of the Net will be different from those woven by our reading of books and other printed works.

Sometime in 1882, Friedrich Nietzsche bought a typewriter—a Malling-Hansen Writing Ball, to be precise. His vision was failing, and keeping his eyes focused on a page had become exhausting and painful, often bringing on crushing headaches. He had been forced to curtail his writing, and he feared that he would soon have to give it up. The typewriter rescued him, at least for a time. Once he had mastered touch-typing, he was able to write with his eyes closed, using only the tips of his fingers. Words could once again flow from his mind to the page.

10   But the machine had a subtle effect on his work. One of Nietzsche's friends, a composer, noticed a change in the style of his writing. His already terse prose had become even tighter, more telegraphic. "Perhaps you will through this instrument even take to a new idiom," the friend wrote in a letter, noting that, in his own work, his "'thoughts' in music and language often depend on the quality of pen and paper."

"You are right," Nietzsche replied, "our writing equipment takes part in the forming of our thoughts." Under the sway of the machine, writes the German media scholar Friedrich A. Kittler, Nietzsche's prose "changed from arguments to aphorisms, from thoughts to puns, from rhetoric to telegram style."

The human brain is almost infinitely malleable. People used to think that our mental meshwork, the dense connections formed among the 100 billion or so neurons inside our skulls, was largely fixed by the time we reached adulthood. But brain researchers have discovered that that's not the case. James Olds, a professor of neuroscience who directs the Krasnow Institute for Advanced Study at George Mason University, says that even the adult mind "is very plastic." Nerve cells routinely break old connections and form new ones. "The brain," according to Olds, "has the ability to reprogram itself on the fly, altering the way it functions."

As we use what the sociologist Daniel Bell has called our "intellectual technologies"—the tools that extend our mental rather than our physical capacities— we inevitably begin to take on the qualities of those technologies. The mechanical clock, which came into common use in the 14th century, provides a compelling example. In Technics and Civilization, the historian and cultural critic Lewis Mumford described how the clock "disassociated time from human events and helped create the belief in an independent world of mathematically measurable sequences." The "abstract framework of divided time" became "the point of reference for both action and thought."

The clock's methodical ticking helped bring into being the scientific mind and the scientific man. But it also took something away. As the late MIT computer scientist Joseph Weizenbaum observed in his 1976 book, *Computer Power and Human Reason: From Judgment to Calculation,* the conception of the world that emerged from the widespread use of timekeeping instruments "remains an impoverished version of the older one, for it rests on a rejection of those direct experiences that formed the basis for, and indeed constituted, the old reality." In deciding when to eat, to work, to sleep, to rise, we stopped listening to our senses and started obeying the clock.

The process of adapting to new intellectual technologies is reflected in the   15 changing metaphors we use to explain ourselves to ourselves. When the mechanical clock arrived, people began thinking of their brains as operating "like clockwork." Today, in the age of software, we have come to think of them as operating "like computers." But the changes, neuroscience tells us, go much deeper than metaphor. Thanks to our brain's plasticity, the adaptation occurs also at a biological level.

The Internet promises to have particularly far-reaching effects on cognition. In a paper published in 1936, the British mathematician Alan Turing proved that a digital computer, which at the time existed only as a theoretical machine, could be programmed to perform the function of any other information-processing device. And that's what we're seeing today. The Internet, an immeasurably powerful computing system, is subsuming most of our other intellectual technologies. It's becoming our map and our clock, our printing press and our typewriter, our calculator and our telephone, and our radio and TV.

When the Net absorbs a medium, that medium is re-created in the Net's image. It injects the medium's content with hyperlinks, blinking ads, and other digital gewgaws, and it surrounds the content with the content of all the other media it has absorbed. A new e-mail message, for instance, may announce its arrival as we're glancing over the latest headlines at a newspaper's site. The result is to scatter our attention and diffuse our concentration.

The Net's influence doesn't end at the edges of a computer screen. . . . As people's minds become attuned to the crazy quilt of Internet media, traditional media have to adapt to the audience's expectations. Television programs add text crawls and pop-up ads, and magazines and newspapers shorten their articles, introduce capsule summaries, and crowd their pages with easy-to-browse info-snippets. When, in March of this year, *The New York Times* decided to devote the second and third pages of every edition to article abstracts, its design director, Tom Bodkin, explained that the "shortcuts" would give harried readers a quick "taste" of the day's news, sparing them the "less efficient" method of actually turning the pages and reading the articles. Old media have little choice but to play by the new-media rules.

Never has a communications system played so many roles in our lives—or exerted such broad influence over our thoughts—as the Internet does today. Yet, for all that's been written about the Net, there's been little consideration of how, exactly, it's reprogramming us. The Net's intellectual ethic remains obscure.

About the same time that Nietzsche started using his typewriter, an earnest young   20 man named Frederick Winslow Taylor carried a stopwatch into the Midvale Steel plant in Philadelphia and began a historic series of experiments aimed at improving the efficiency of the plant's machinists.

. . .

Once his system was applied to all acts of manual labor, Taylor assured his followers, it would bring about a restructuring not only of industry but of society, creating a utopia of perfect efficiency. "In the past the man has been first," he declared; "in the future the system must be first."

Taylor's system is still very much with us; it remains the ethic of industrial manufacturing. And now, thanks to the growing power that computer engineers and software coders wield over our intellectual lives, Taylor's ethic is beginning to govern the realm of the mind as well. The Internet is a machine designed for the efficient and automated collection, transmission, and manipulation of information, and its legions of programmers are intent on finding the "one best method"—the perfect algorithm—to carry out every mental movement of what we've come to describe as "knowledge work."

. . .

Google has declared that its mission is "to organize the world's information and make it universally accessible and useful." It seeks to develop "the perfect search engine," which it defines as something that "understands exactly what you mean and gives you back exactly what you want." In Google's view, information is a kind of commodity, a utilitarian resource that can be mined and processed with industrial efficiency. The more pieces of information we can "access" and the faster we can extract their gist, the more productive we become as thinkers.

Where does it end? Sergey Brin and Larry Page, the gifted young men who founded Google while pursuing doctoral degrees in computer science at Stanford, speak frequently of their desire to turn their search engine into an artificial intelligence, a HAL-like machine that might be connected directly to our brains. "The ultimate search engine is something as smart as people—or smarter," Page said in a speech a few years back. "For us, working on search is a way to work on artificial intelligence." In a 2004 interview with *Newsweek*, Brin said, "Certainly if you had all the world's information directly attached to your brain, or an artificial brain that was smarter than your brain, you'd be better off." Last year, Page told a convention of scientists that Google is "really trying to build artificial intelligence and to do it on a large scale."

Such an ambition is a natural one, even an admirable one, for a pair of math whizzes with vast quantities of cash at their disposal and a small army of computer scientists in their employ. A fundamentally scientific enterprise, Google is motivated by a desire to use technology, in Eric Schmidt's words, "to solve problems that have never been solved before," and artificial intelligence is the hardest problem out there. Why wouldn't Brin and Page want to be the ones to crack it?

25   Still, their easy assumption that we'd all "be better off" if our brains were supplemented, or even replaced, by an artificial intelligence is unsettling. It suggests a belief that intelligence is the output of a mechanical process, a series of discrete steps that can be isolated, measured, and optimized. In Google's world, the world we enter when we go online, there's little place for the fuzziness of contemplation. Ambiguity is not an opening for insight but a bug to be fixed. The human brain is just an outdated computer that needs a faster processor and a bigger hard drive.

The idea that our minds should operate as high-speed data-processing machines is not only built into the workings of the Internet, it is the network's reigning business model as well. The faster we surf across the Web—the more links we click and pages we view—the more opportunities Google and other companies gain to collect information about us and to feed us advertisements. Most of the proprietors of the commercial Internet have a financial stake in collecting the crumbs of data we leave behind as we flit from link to link—the more crumbs, the better. The last thing these companies want is to encourage leisurely reading or slow, concentrated thought. It's in their economic interest to drive us to distraction.

Maybe I'm just a worrywart. Just as there's a tendency to glorify technological progress, there's a countertendency to expect the worst of every new tool or machine. In Plato's *Phaedrus*, Socrates bemoaned the development of writing. He feared that, as people came to rely on the written word as a substitute for the knowledge they used to carry inside their heads, they would, in the words of one of the dialogue's characters, "cease to exercise their memory and become forgetful." And because they would be able to "receive a quantity of information without proper instruction," they would "be thought very knowledgeable when they are for the most part quite ignorant." They would be "filled with the conceit of wisdom instead of real wisdom." Socrates wasn't wrong—the new technology did often have the effects he feared—but he was shortsighted. He couldn't foresee the many ways that writing and reading would serve to spread information, spur fresh ideas, and expand human knowledge (if not wisdom).

The arrival of Gutenberg's printing press, in the 15th century, set off another round of teeth gnashing. The Italian humanist Hieronimo Squarciafico worried that the easy availability of books would lead to intellectual laziness, making men "less studious" and weakening their minds. Others argued that cheaply printed books and broadsheets would undermine religious authority, demean the work of scholars and scribes, and spread sedition and debauchery. As New York University professor Clay Shirky notes, "Most of the arguments made against the printing press were correct, even prescient." But, again, the doomsayers were unable to imagine the myriad blessings that the printed word would deliver.

So, yes, you should be skeptical of my skepticism. Perhaps those who dismiss critics of the Internet as Luddites or nostalgists will be proved correct, and from our hyperactive, data-stoked minds will spring a golden age of intellectual discovery and universal wisdom. Then again, the Net isn't the alphabet, and although it may replace the printing press, it produces something altogether different. The kind of deep reading that a sequence of printed pages promotes is valuable not just for the knowledge we acquire from the author's words but for the intellectual vibrations those words set off within our own minds. In the quiet spaces opened up by the sustained, undistracted reading of a book, or by any other act of contemplation, for that matter, we make our own associations, draw our own inferences and analogies, foster our own ideas. Deep reading, as Maryanne Wolf argues, is indistinguishable from deep thinking.

If we lose those quiet spaces, or fill them up with "content," we will sacrifice   30
something important not only in our selves but in our culture. In a recent essay, the playwright Richard Foreman eloquently described what's at stake:

> I come from a tradition of Western culture, in which the ideal (my ideal) was the complex, dense and "cathedral-like" structure of the highly educated and articulate personality—a man or woman who carried inside themselves a personally constructed and unique version of the entire heritage of the West. [But now] I see within us all (myself included) the

replacement of complex inner density with a new kind of self—evolving under the pressure of information overload and the technology of the "instantly available."

As we are drained of our "inner repertory of dense cultural inheritance," Foreman concluded, we risk turning into "'pancake people'—spread wide and thin as we connect with that vast network of information accessed by the mere touch of a button."

I'm haunted by that scene in 2001. What makes it so poignant, and so weird, is the computer's emotional response to the disassembly of its mind: its despair as one circuit after another goes dark, its childlike pleading with the astronaut—"I can feel it. I can feel it. I'm afraid"—and its final reversion to what can only be called a state of innocence. HAL's outpouring of feeling contrasts with the emotionlessness that characterizes the human figures in the film, who go about their business with an almost robotic efficiency. Their thoughts and actions feel scripted, as if they're following the steps of an algorithm. In the world of 2001, people have become so machinelike that the most human character turns out to be a machine. That's the essence of Kubrick's dark prophecy: as we come to rely on computers to mediate our understanding of the world, it is our own intelligence that flattens into artificial intelligence.

QUESTIONS FOR READING ACTIVELY

1. In your own words, state the *general* problem described by this article, and then list the specific *characterizations* of that problem. Is the prominence given to one of those characterizations in this article really the most important in the larger context of the general problem? Be prepared to show how the structure of this article demonstrates the relative importance of these specific characterizations.

2. Are there any voices missing from this article? If you were this writer's editor, whose voices and perspectives would you recommend including, and why?

QUESTIONS FOR THINKING CRITICALLY

1. Have you noticed in your own life that it's easier for you to move quickly around the Web than to spend concentrated time reading a book or lengthy article? Writing an extended essay or letter? Concentrating on an issue or problem for an extended period of time?

2. The author acknowledges that "the Net is becoming a universal medium, the conduit for most of the information that flows through my eyes and ears and into my mind" and that this puts him at risk for being a "mere decoder of information" rather than a deep thinker *about* information. Would you say that this is true for you as well? Why or why not?

QUESTIONS FOR WRITING THOUGHTFULLY

1. Imagine that you are the president of your college and that you want students to use the full power of the Internet in their education but you also wish them to develop their abilities to think deeply, concentrate, and contemplate. Using the problem-solving method in this chapter, analyze this problem, and write a short essay outlining some practical solutions for dealing with this challenge.

2. Consider your use of the Internet. Do you read the news online? Perhaps you follow blogs or are an avid Facebook user. Perhaps you use the Internet to search for information related to work, school, or hobbies. Nicholas Carr stated that "what the Net seems to be doing is chipping away at my capacity for concentration and contemplation." Can you relate to his experience? Monitor your Internet use for a day, and write a short essay describing your findings and explaining whether or not you feel it is a problem. If it is, what steps could you take to solve it?

Taking a Problem-Solving Approach to Writing

Problem solving provides you with a framework that you can use in much of your writing. A problem-solving approach can assist you in generating ideas and organizing information for most subjects. For example, you can look at a writing assignment as a problem and use a modification of the five-step method, such as the one that follows, as a way to work on it.

1. What exactly is the assignment? What is its purpose?

2. What are some alternative ways to complete it? Who is the obvious audience, and what other possible audiences should I consider?

3. What are the advantages and disadvantages of the alternatives? Am I prepared to change my subject or thesis if my initial approach doesn't work?

4. What is the best way for me to complete this assignment? How can I use conversations and peer review to gain additional perspectives?

5. After some drafting, ask: How is my solution to the problem of the assignment working out?

Then, as you write any essay, you can use modifications of the problem-solving steps at any stage. Look at the thesis as a problem, and ask the preceding questions about it. Look at any part of the paper, and ask the questions. Actually, effective writers do this to some extent—perhaps less systematically—as they draft, plan, and revise. As you recall, Chapter 5 sets forth a similar pattern for approaching revision.

Research projects can also be seen and approached as problems. Just as you can apply a problem-solving approach to any writing assignment, so can you apply it to most research projects (see Chapter 14).

As a way to prepare for the Writing Project (solving a local, national, or international problem or a personal problem), go back to the writing you have completed for the assignments in this chapter. Do you find any of these topics especially compelling or engaging?

Make a list of the three most promising ideas you have discussed or written about so far. Next, choose one of the strategies for generating ideas described in Chapter 4 (brainstorming, mind maps, freewriting, questioning), and use that strategy to further explore your ideas and help you choose the topic with the most potential. You can also refer to "Additional Tips for Generating Ideas" on page 102.

Writing Project

PROPOSING A SOLUTION TO A PROBLEM

This chapter includes a reading and Thinking-Writing Activities that encourage you to familiarize yourself with the problem-solving model and the steps required for implementing it.

Project Overview and Requirements

Write an essay in which you apply the five-step problem-solving method to a local, national, or international problem (social) or to a personal problem. As a reminder, the five steps are

1. Identify the problem
2. Generate alternatives
3. List advantages/disadvantages for each alternative
4. Propose a solution
5. Test the solution

If you are analyzing a social problem, you will have to do some research and locate several articles that provide background information about (and discussion of) the problem. If you are analyzing a personal problem, you will enrich your paper by consulting some sources that pertain to it. Be sure to document all sources honestly and correctly by providing citations in the format required by your instructor.

After you have a complete draft, consider making global revisions so that your main ideas are expressed clearly and logically, and then focus on more local editing concerns. Proofreading your work before submitting it is essential!

Finally, be sure you have followed your instructor's specific directions related to focus, length, scope, and format.

Before you begin writing, consider the key elements in Chapter 1, pages 5–8: the Thinking-Writing Model. Additionally, information related to The Writing Situation and The Writing Process on the following pages will help you develop your essay.

THE WRITING SITUATION

Purpose   You have a variety of purposes here. You can use this opportunity to learn about a major problem in order to arrive at the best possible solution—and thus become a better-informed citizen. For example, if you decide to write about electronic voting machines, you will probably learn a lot about the development of these machines and the ongoing effort to make them reliable and secure. You'll also learn a lot about the voting process, and possibly even have the opportunity to help implement a solution if you are involved in the situation. Additionally, you will be practicing the creative and critical thinking involved in the problem-solving model.

Audience   As usual, you will have several audiences for your paper. While working through the problem-solving model, you will be your own audience, since, while describing the problem and working through alternative solutions, you will be determining the solution to that problem. As you begin to shape the answers to the model's questions into an essay, your audience will include readers other than yourself, so their needs should now occupy your attention.

Your classmates can be a valuable audience for peer review of a draft. They can react as intelligent readers who are not as knowledgeable as you are about the problem and its possible solutions but who can become interested as they read your description of it and your evaluation of the possible solutions. Finally, your instructor remains the audience who will judge how well you have analyzed the problem. As a writing teacher, he or she cares about a clear focus, logical organization, relevant details and examples, and accepted usage. Keep these factors in mind as you revise, edit, and proofread.

Subject   Problems are problems precisely because they are difficult to think about and to solve. Often this is true because we don't have enough accurate information to arrive at an intelligent solution. Working on this paper will encourage you to find good information and to think about viable alternative solutions. Since you will be deeply involved in the subject, select a problem that you care about, one that is challenging—but compelling—to write about.

Writer   This assignment provides you an opportunity to learn more about a problem that you care about but perhaps do not know enough about to propose a solid solution. You will use both online and print resources to increase your knowledge of the problem and give you the pleasure of having additional expertise about something significant. If your instructor asks or allows you to write about a personal problem, you might not have to do as much research, but you will have the opportunity to work out something that is of immediate concern. Equipped with the problem-solving model and the direction it provides, you should work as a confident writer as you complete this assignment.

The questions and examples below will help you generate ideas related to proposing a solution to a problem and help you construct a solid framework for your essay. Keep in mind that you will need to apply the five-step problem-solving method (see page 439) to either a local, national, or international problem or a personal problem.

1. To begin, describe the problem that you would like to solve (including some background information), and discuss what the purpose might be. For example, one student wrote:

> My 4-year-old son will be starting kindergarten soon and I am torn between sending him to public school or a Montessori school. There are pros and cons for both, so I would like to learn more and carefully weigh my options

before making this important decision. I attended public school, and learned the basics, but I also struggled. It was a big school and it was chaotic and overwhelming. Lunchtime and recess were dangerous free-for-alls, and I never felt like I belonged to any of the cliques. I don't want my son to have to learn in that environment, but I also don't want him to deal with the stigma of being in what some think of as an exclusive school. Ultimately, I need to know I have made the right choice for my son.

2. Since your essay will be read by others, describe how your exploration of (and solution to) a problem can benefit a wider audience. For example:

When I talk to other parents, I realize that many of them are in the same predicament. While we understand the benefits of public school (a diverse body of students, school buildings are well-equipped and can generally afford more programs, etc.) as well as the benefits of a Montessori school (smaller classes, more individual attention, children learn at their own pace, etc.) there are many questions that need answers. For example, is it true that Montessori students have higher academic achievement rates? If students learn at their own pace, what if their pace is slow? Will students be exposed to the same programs (sports, music, etc.) children in public schools enjoy? What about safety? If I can gather enough resources to come up with a logical, practical solution to my dilemma, I think that many other parents can benefit from what I propose as a solution.

3. Problems can be difficult to solve, so how do you plan to follow the five-step method to help you arrive at a solution? For example:

Since I have a clear idea of the problem (where to send my son to school) and can identify it (step 1), I need to give more thought to generating alternatives (step 2). Are there other choices besides public and Montessori schools? Some Montessori schools are public, while others are private. There are also other charter schools, parochial schools and, of course, home schooling. I will need to explore each alternative and list the advantages and disadvantages for each one (step 3) and decide whether or not (and to which degree) I include them in my essay. I will also have to give some thought to how I will structure the paper. At this point, I don't know if it is best to discuss each school fully before moving on to the next school (next paragraph), or if it makes more sense to do a point-by-point analysis. In regards to proposing a solution (step 4), the research I find will dictate the outcome, of course, but I want to spend at least a paragraph explaining how and why I arrived at a logical conclusion. Testing the solution will be a challenge (step 5) since it will take some time, after my son is in school, to know if I made the right decision; however, I can address how I plan to evaluate the solution (meeting with teachers, talking with my son, listening to other parents, etc.) and give some thought to what kinds of adjustments I might have to make.

4. Finally, depending on the problem you wish to solve, research may play an important role in helping you sort through your options and arrive at a logical solution. If you plan to focus on a personal problem, you might not have to use research, but you may want to consider the experience or advice of friends

or family. What role will research play in your essay? Describe how you plan to approach this part of the problem-solving process. For example:

> Since this problem has been weighing on my mind for the past year or so, I have already collected a few resources that will help me make a decision, including a study on Montessori versus Traditional Education Programs by Christopher Lopata, Nancy Wallace, and Kristin Finn. I also follow the posts by parents on Mothering.com and Circleofmoms.com. I will include mostly academic and professional sources for my essay, but some of the online forums help to generate ideas for more research. I also plan to interview a few parents and a cousin whose daughter has been in Montessori for two years.

THE WRITING PROCESS

The following sections will guide you through the stages of generating, planning, drafting, and revising as you work on an essay about solving an important problem. Try to be particularly conscious of both the critical thinking you do while working through the problem-solving model and the critical thinking and decision making you do as you revise.

Generating Ideas   Brainstorm a list of problems that need solving. Think about problems that have affected you or problems you see in the current media that need solutions. Select one that seems most important or most interesting—one that you have some knowledge about and feel you could come up with a plausible solution for. Solving world hunger, for example, would be difficult to tackle in an essay. It is far too complex a problem. Solving hunger in your community might be a more manageable problem to solve.

Once you have chosen your topic, an effective way to begin is to work through the five steps in the problem-solving model. First, write down your responses to the five steps:

1. Identify the problem (for example, "There are too many people in my community who don't have enough to eat.")

2. Generate alternatives (for example, one alternative might be to "Host weekly community dinners.")

3. List advantages/disadvantages for each alternative (for example, "One advantage is that people will have a hearty meal at least once a week," while a disadvantage might be "The rest of the week, people will still be hungry.")

4. Propose a solution (for example, "Host nightly community dinners.")

5. Test the solution (for example, "Poll people in the community to find out if those who really need the meals are participating.")

Once you have worked through the problem-solving model, you will see how much additional information is needed to evaluate each of your alternative solutions. Research will be necessary—whether it is online or at your local library. Depending on the problem you want to solve, you could also consider interviewing experts.

Once you have filled in all the gaps and selected a solution—and a means to determine whether it is working—you are ready to turn your attention to presenting your information to your audience.

Defining a Focus   Your thesis statement should give your audience a clear indication of the focus and purpose of your paper, which is to explore a problem-solving situation. For example, if your paper is about saving a local organization from failure, your thesis statement might be this: "After carefully weighing the alternatives, raising more revenue, while continuing to cut the budget appears to be the best choice for the continued success of Save Our Park."

Organizing Ideas   When you are asked to write a proposal, essay, or argument about solving a problem, you can use the problem-solving method as a way to organize and structure your paper. Your description of the problem, together with its necessary history and additional background information, will give you a working introduction that can include your thesis statement. Each of the alternative solutions, explained in as much detail as possible, along with its advantages and disadvantages, will comprise the body of your paper. Your determination of the best solution and how it could be monitored will become your conclusion.

The following principles for writing about problem solving may not apply to every situation, but they can help you convert answers to the questions in the problem-solving model into an effective essay.

1. Make sure your thesis statement gives your audience a clear indication of the focus and purpose of your essay. If you are constructing an argument, be sure that your claim is debatable and that you give fair and equal consideration to opposing solutions.

2. Be aware of your audience. Your readers will need specific details about the problem you are presenting, and they will need to have this information presented with clarity and logic.

3. Present all the information your audience needs in order to understand the problem before you begin to discuss alternative solutions.

4. Clearly explain your alternative solutions (in the order that will most help your audience comprehend them), and discuss their advantages and disadvantages. For example, instead of saying, "A program could be developed to help students see how to avoid date rape," explain that "Respected student leaders from honor societies and athletic teams could participate in a forum explaining how excessive drinking, certain drugs, and certain behaviors can lead to situations in which date rape might occur." The more specific you are, the better your audience will understand you.

5. Conclude your essay by stating one solution, or some combination of solutions, and explain clearly why you chose it. If you have had time to implement the solution, describe whether or not it is working. If you have not yet implemented it, explain how you will determine whether or not it is working.

Drafting   Begin expanding the brief answers you came up with for each part of the problem-solving model into full paragraphs, starting with your introduction. Begin each section of the body of your essay with a topic sentence that names the alternative solution being considered.

If you are discussing advantages or disadvantages in separate paragraphs, draft topic sentences that prepare your readers for that information—such as "Unfortunately, cutting the budget further will create serious disadvantages for many citizens." Then provide specific information. You will, of course, have to determine the best order in which to arrange each section. Experiment until you find the one that seems most helpful to your audience, and make sure you transition smoothly from one idea to the next.

Be sure to indicate the sources of your information. You do not have to use the correct citation format in a draft, but you do have to remind yourself exactly where you obtained the material so that you won't forget to properly document it as you finish the essay.

In your conclusion, name the solution you have chosen. You may want to explain why you selected it if you think that will not be obvious to your audience. Remember to explain how you will evaluate the effectiveness of your solution.

Revising Your Essay: Proposing a Solution to a Problem

Peer Review

After your draft is complete, partner up with someone and exchange essays. Read the essay from beginning to end, jotting notes as needed. Keep in mind that the goal of a peer review, or critique, is to improve the writing, not criticize the writer. Then, for this particular essay, complete the following steps:

1. Locate and highlight the thesis statement. Is it clear and does it describe the problem and solution? If it does not, offer specific suggestions.

2. Does the draft consider the audience? That is, do you feel you learned all you need to know to understand the problem and the solutions the writer is presenting in the draft? If not, what questions do you have that need to be answered?

3. Considering the organization of the draft, are the alternative solutions (advantages and disadvantages) presented in logical order? If not, what improvements could be made? Be specific in your feedback to the writer.

Revision

Once you have received the comments your classmate made during the peer review, you can incorporate that feedback and make necessary changes to strengthen the content of your essay. Be sure to work on the larger issues in your essay first, such as the structure, flow, and overall description of (and solution to) the problem at the paragraph level. Refer back to "A Step-by-Step Method for Revising Any Assignment" in Chapter 6 (or on the inside front cover of this book) for more guidance if necessary.

Editing and Proofreading

Finally, focus on the smaller details that make your writing sound polished and professional: carefully check for and correct any typos; look for errors in grammar, spelling, and mechanics; make sure the format of your paper meets your instructor's requirements; and so forth.

The following essay shows how a student responded to this assignment—by writing about a social problem and citing according to Modern Language Association (MLA) format.

STUDENT WRITING

Joshua Bartlett's Writing Process

As a college student, Joshua witnessed firsthand the impact of irresponsible attitudes toward alcohol among his peers. Even though he and his classmates were required to participate in various "alcohol awareness" education programs as part of freshman orientation at their campus, Joshua knew that the programs were not engaging, urgent, or serious enough to get the attention of young people like himself. Because Joshua was writing a formal argument, and because he was required to use sources to provide information, Joshua did not include anecdotes from his own personal experience. Had he been writing an opinion piece for his campus newspaper, he might well have described a campus party in which a fellow student was seriously hurt in an alcohol-related incident; he might even have described his own experiences with binge drinking. Although that evidence would certainly be compelling, it might not be adequately objective for an academic audience—and you can imagine how it might undermine his credibility with his professor! Instead, Joshua provides objective evidence from a range of sources to support his well-thought-out approach to the problem of alcohol abuse on college campuses.

To structure his draft, Joshua used the "Detailed Method for Solving Problems" (page 442).

Joshua clearly identifies the problem he would like to solve in his opening paragraph and then transitions into a description of the scope of the problem and some of the causes. This background information helps the reader understand why a solution is needed.

Critical Thinking About Uncritical Drinking

by Joshua Bartlett

There is widespread agreement that excessive student drinking is a serious problem on many college campuses. However, there are different views on the causes of this problem and on the best solutions for it. In this paper I will

Source: Critical Thinking About Uncritical Drinking by Joshua Bartlett.

---

present some perspectives on the problem of student drinking and conclude with suggestions on how to deal with this serious threat to student health and success.

Why do college students drink to excess? According to many experts, it is mainly due to the influence of the people around them. When most students enter college, they do not have a drinking problem. However, although few realize it, they are entering a culture in which alcohol is often the drug of choice, one that can easily destroy their lives. According to some estimates, 80 to 90 percent of the students on many campuses drink alcohol, and many of them are heavy drinkers (Engs 543). One study found that nearly 30 percent of university students consume more than 15 alcoholic drinks a week (Gerson A43). An additional study found that among those who drink at least once a week, 92 percent of the men and 82 percent of the women consume at least five drinks in a row, and half said they wanted to get drunk (Rosenberg 81).

The results of all this drinking are predictably deadly. Virtually all college administrators agree that alcohol is the most widely used drug among college students and that its abuse is directly related to emotional problems and violent behavior, ranging from date rape to death (Dodge, "Campus Crime" A331; Leatherman A33). For example, at one university, a 20-year-old woman became drunk at a fraternity party and fell to her death from the third floor ("Clemson" A3). At another university, two students were killed in a drunk-driving accident after drinking alcohol at an off-campus fraternity house; the families of both students have filed lawsuits against the fraternity (Dodge, "Beer Kegs Banned" A28). When students enter a college or university, they often become socialized into the alcohol-sodden culture of "higher education," at both formal and informal parties. The influence of peer pressure is enormous. Students often find it difficult to resist the pressures from their friends and fellow students to drink.

However, some observers of young people believe that, although peer pressure is certainly a factor in excessive college drinking, it is only one of a number of factors. They point out that the misuse of alcohol is a problem for all youth in our society, not just college students. For example, a recent study by the surgeon general's office shows that 1 in 3 teenagers consumes alcohol every week. This abuse leads to traffic deaths, academic difficulties, and acts of violence (Elson 64). Another study based on a large, nationally representative sample indicates that although college students are more likely to use alcohol, they tend to drink less per drinking day than nonstudents of the same age (Crowley 14); in other words, most college students who drink are more social drinkers than problem drinkers. One survey of undergraduate students found that college drinking is not as widespread as many people think (O'Hare 540).

Paragraphs 3 and 4 rely on carefully chosen facts and examples to highlight the consequences of excessive drinking. Joshua's analysis helps the reader further understand the severity of the problem.

The conclusion from these data is that even though drinking certainly takes place on college campuses, it is no greater a problem than in the population at large.

Whatever the extent, the misuse of alcohol by college students is a serious situation with a number of probable causes. Certainly the influence of friends, whether in college or out, plays a role, as I've already discussed. But it is not the only factor. To begin with, there is evidence that family history is related to alcohol abuse. For example, one survey of college students found more problem drinking among students whose parents or grandparents had been diagnosed with alcoholism (Perkins and Berkowitz 237–240). Another study found that college students who come from families with high degrees of conflict display a greater potential for alcoholism (Pardeck 342–343).

Joshua describes and analyzes several other factors that lead to alcohol abuse and then ties in the title of his essay with a statement about the choices students make.

Another important factor to consider in the misuse of alcohol by young people is advertising. A recent article entitled "It Isn't Miller Time Yet, and This Bud's Not for You" underscores the influence advertisers exert on the behavior of youth (Siler 52). By portraying beer drinkers as healthy, fun-loving, attractive young people, they create role models that many youths imitate. In the same way that cigarette advertisers used to encourage smoking among our youth—without regard for the health hazards—so alcohol advertisers try to sell as much booze as they can to whoever will buy it—no matter what the consequences.

A final factor in the abuse of alcohol is the people themselves. Although young people are subject to a huge number of influences, in the final analysis, they are free to choose what they want to do. They don't have to drink, no matter what the social pressures. In fact, many students resist these pressures and choose not to drink excessively or at all. In short, some students choose to think critically, while others choose to drink uncritically.

Here, Joshua moves into the solution to the problem.

In order to encourage good judgment by more students and to minimize the causes of excessive drinking, I think that the following strategies could help solve the college alcohol problem. Only the last one has any disadvantages to be considered.

1. Colleges should have orientation and educational programs aimed at preventing alcohol abuse, and colleges should give top priority to campaigns against underage and excessive drinking.

2. Advertising and promotion of alcoholic beverages on college campuses and in college publications should be banned. Liquor distributors should not sponsor campus events. In addition, alcoholic beverage companies should be petitioned not to target young people in their ads.

3. Depending on the campus culture, colleges should ban or restrict alcohol use on campus and include stiff penalties for students who violate the rules.

4. Students at residential colleges should be able to live in substance-free housing, offering them a voluntary haven from alcohol, other drugs, tobacco, and peer pressure.

5. Colleges should create attractive alcohol-free clubs or pubs.

6. Colleges should ban the use of beer kegs, a symbol of cheap and easy availability of alcohol.

7. Fraternities should eliminate all alcohol-based contests or hazing torments.

8. Where possible, the on-campus drinking age should be reduced to 18 so that students won't be forced to move parties off-campus. At off-campus parties, there is no college control, and as a result, students tend to drink greater quantities and more dangerous concoctions.

Of course, this suggestion has the disadvantages of being in conflict with laws in many states or counties and also of seeming to encourage drinking by connecting it even more extensively with social events. But it has the advantages of control and of eliminating the attraction of what's forbidden.

In conclusion, alcohol abuse on college campuses is an extremely serious problem that is threatening the health and college careers of many students. As challenging as this problem is, I believe that it can be solved if students, teachers, and college officials work together in harmony and with determination to implement the suggestions made in this paper.

Although Joshua proposed eight solid strategies to combat alcohol abuse on campus, he only describes a disadvantage for the last suggestion. The paper could be more effective if the advantages and disadvantages of each suggestion were more fully developed, even though the advantages seem fairly clear.

The conclusion summarizes the problem and solution and ends with a call to action.

Works Cited

"Clemson Issues Ban on Parties Using Alcohol." *Chronicle of Higher Education* 31 Jan. 1990: A3. Print.

Crowley, Joan E. "Educational Status and Drinking Patterns: How Representative Are College Students?" *Journal of Studies on Alcohol* 52.1 (1991): 10–16. Print.

Dodge, Susan. "Campus Crime Linked to Students' Use of Drugs and Alcohol." *Chronicle of Higher Education* 17 Jan. 1990: A331. Print.

——— "Use of Beer Kegs Banned by Some Colleges and National Fraternities." *Chronicle of Higher Education* 12 June 1991: A27–28. Print.

Elson, John. "Drink Until You Finally Drop." *Time* 16 Dec. 1991: 64. Print.

Engs, Ruth C. "Family Background of Alcohol Abuse and Its Relationship to Alcohol Consumption Among College Students: An Unexpected Finding." *Journal of Studies on Alcohol* 51.6 (1990): 542–547. Print.

Gerson, Mark. "30 Pct. of Ontario's Students Called 'Heavy Drinkers.'" *Chronicle of Higher Education* 12 April 1989: A43. Print.

Leatherman, Courtney. "College Officials Are Split on Alcohol Policies; Some Seek to End Underage Drinking; Others Try to Encourage 'Responsible' Use." *Chronicle of Higher Education* 31 Jan. 1990: A33–35. Print.

O'Hare, Thomas M. "Drinking in College: Consumption Patterns, Problems, Sex Differences and Legal Drinking Age." *Journal of Studies on Alcohol* 51.6 (1990): 536–541. Print.

Pardeck, John T. "A Multiple Regression Analysis of Family Factors Affecting the Potential for Alcoholism in College Students." *Adolescence* 26.102 (1991): 341–347. Print.

Perkins, H. Wesley, and Alan D. Berkowitz. "Collegiate COAs and Alcohol Abuse: Problem Drinking in Relation to Assessment of Parent and Grandparent Alcoholism." *Journal of Counseling and Development* 69.3 (1991): 237–240. Print.

Rosenberg, Debra. "Bad Times at Hangover U." *Newsweek* 19 Nov. 1990: 81. Print.

Siler, Julie Flynn. "It Isn't Miller Time Yet, and This Bud's Not for You." *Business Week* 24 June 1991: 52. Print.

REFLECTION ON WRITING

1. What is your reaction to Joshua Bartlett's essay, "Critical Thinking About Uncritical Drinking"? Did your classmates have the same reaction? In a paragraph or two, discuss some of the differences you encountered.

2. Do you feel Joshua presented enough evidence to clearly describe both the problems and the solutions related to drinking? If so, describe the areas where you feel he was particularly successful. If not, explain where more information would be helpful to an audience.

ALTERNATIVE WRITING PROJECTS: COMMUNITY PROBLEMS, COMMUNITY SOLUTIONS

1. Prepare a concise PowerPoint presentation that addresses a specific campus or community problem and that proposes a specific solution. Your presentation should consist of no more than 10 slides—about the time you would have to present your concerns at a public forum such as a student governance board or town council meeting. Plan to have two slides for each of the five steps of the Flexible Approach to Problem Solving in Figure 12.1. Your main purpose here is to be as concise as possible, while issuing a call to action.

2. Apply the five-step problem-solving method to a local, national, or international problem that has already been successfully solved. You will be writing primarily in the past tense, and your purpose will be to describe *why* a particular solution worked so well. Your particular focus will be on Step 5 of the process, Test the Solution, and your critical analysis will be focused on evaluation.

CHAPTER 12

Summary

We can become more effective problem-solvers by approaching complex problems in an organized way:

- Have I accepted the problem and committed myself to solving it?
- Step 1: What is the problem?
- Step 2: What are the alternatives?
- Step 3: What are the advantages and/or disadvantages of each alternative?
- Step 4: What is the solution?
- Step 5: How well is the solution working?

This approach to solving problems is effective not only for problems that you experience personally but also for problems that you may face as a citizen of a community, a society, and the world. It also provides a framework that you can use in much of your writing.

As rigorously planned and carefully controlled as laboratory experiments, thought experiments are used by scientists and philosophers to explore possibilities that might not otherwise be ethically or physically tested. The Australian philosopher and ethicist Peter Singer, who teaches at Princeton University, uses thought experiments to explore such provocative social issues as animal rights, euthanasia, and the redistribution of wealth. His provocative, rigorous thinking challenges all of us to live ethically, in ways that do indeed shake the comfortable material foundations of our culture. What other topics in ethics might be well suited to thought experiments?

Writing to Persuade:
Constructing Arguments

"I got into direct confrontation with everybody I love."

—LAURYN HILL

Principles of Argument

People who study communication, argument, and rhetoric believe that much of what we say, write, and post online can be defined as *argument* because most statements seek listeners' or readers' agreement with the ideas being presented. Unless someone is just saying "Hmmmm" or "Hello" or is asking a question only to obtain information, the purpose of his or her statement usually is to make a point, to convince the audience of its validity, and often to bring about change or action. Essays, letters, stories, poems, movies, websites—and even paintings and clothes—can be considered arguments or have argumentative purposes.

This chapter is devoted to argument, even though most of your previous writing has had argumentative characteristics. Some writing is supposed to be predominantly argumentative, and you need to know how to create it and how to analyze it. Arguing effectively is essential to achieving academic and professional success, as well as to establishing your personal ethic. In addition, because both politicians and advertisers use argumentative techniques, you need to understand both valid and fallacious arguments in order to evaluate claims that people want you to accept.

This chapter will introduce concepts related to argument, provide readings and Thinking-Writing Activities to help you grasp them, and conclude with a Writing Project that asks you to write a logical, well-organized argument for a position that is important to you. The chapter will also explore ways to construct effective arguments and to evaluate arguments.

CRITICAL THINKING FOCUS:
Using reasons, evidence, and logic

WRITING FOCUS:
Convincing an audience

READING THEME:
Arguments about important issues

WRITING ACTIVITIES:
Constructing Arguments

WRITING PROJECT:
Arguing a position on a significant issue

Thinking-Writing Activity

ANALYZING ARGUMENTATIVE WRITING

1. Select an essay or blog entry that you have written that you believe has an argumentative purpose. What is your thesis or claim? What specific evidence do you present? Who are your audiences? Does the paper advocate for any change or action? What is it?

2. Select a reading from a previous chapter that you consider argumentative. What is its claim? What evidence does it present? Who are its audiences? What change or action does it seek?

CLASSICAL CONCEPTS OF ARGUMENT

The concepts that guide logical argument are central to Western culture. Articulated by the philosophers and rhetoricians of ancient Greece and Rome, they have been studied and applied for more than 2,000 years. Even though emotions, gut reactions, and intuition cannot be brushed aside—because they are so human—logical thinking and the resulting structured arguments are expected in business, government, and scholarship. Therefore, as a college composition student, you have both practical and historical reasons for giving attention to principles of argument or rhetoric.

The Greek philosopher Aristotle, in his famous work the *Rhetoric* and in other writings on logic, is the source of many concepts basic to our ideas of argument. But even Aristotle, more than 300 years B.C.E., was responding to earlier works on rhetoric; and to this day, those who have followed him have modified and redefined his ideas and those of other classical rhetoricians. Classical concepts of argument include *ethos,* the character of the speaker or writer; *pathos,* the effect on the audience; and *logos,* the logic and substance of an argument. All three are powerful aspects of any argument. You should try to identify them in arguments that others address to you, and you should work hard to achieve effectiveness with each in arguments that you write.

Responsible writers try to present themselves as knowledgeable, reasonable, trustworthy, and sensitive to the tone appropriate to the situation—that is, to achieve their desired *ethos.* Critical thinkers are able to build clear and logical discussions, avoid fallacious reasoning, and handle opposing viewpoints courteously but firmly—that is, achieve their desired *logos.* A good combination of *logos* and *ethos* will engage audiences and elicit thoughtful responses—that is, achieve the desired *pathos.*

Some other centuries-old concepts are the techniques for generation or discovery of ideas, the arrangement of sections of an argument, the thinking methods of deduction and induction, techniques for refutation, and moral concerns about the use of rhetorical power for honorable ends.

Links to the Thinking-Writing Model   The classical rhetoricians were concerned with oral communication; literacy for all, print, and electronics were yet to come. Speech is, of course, still essential to communication, both face to face and via electronic media. This book concentrates on writing, but the ancient concepts have never gone out of use, and they function well to promote effective writing. The topics in the Thinking-Writing Model (pages 5–8 in Chapter 1) that is the foundation of this book demonstrate contemporary applications of many classical principles.

Notice how subject, purpose, audience, and writer connect in multiple ways with the concepts of *logos, pathos,* and *ethos*. If *logos* means both content and the logic of its presentation, *logos* connects with the Thinking-Writing Model's topics of identifying a subject, defining a thesis, and organizing idea, as well as with thinking critically. *Pathos* connects, of course, with the Thinking-Writing Model's audience and purpose; *ethos* connects with the writer and also with the editing and proofreading stages of revising, since a well-finished paper gives a good impression of its writer.

The classical concepts of *discovery* and *arrangement* are clearly connected to the Thinking-Writing Model's notions of thinking creatively, generating ideas, organizing ideas, and drafting.

Responsible Rhetoric   Today the words *argument* and *rhetoric* are regularly used in conversation and in the media differently from the ways in which they are used in this chapter. Popularly, *argument* often means "a quarrel," and *rhetoric* is often used to mean "insubstantial or misleading language" (which is connected to the classical concern about the use of rhetorical power for honorable ends). In this chapter, *rhetoric* means "the use of the best means of persuasion." We will discuss *argument* throughout the chapter and define the term on page 491.

MODERN CONCEPTS OF ARGUMENT

In the twenty-first century, much attention has been paid to argument, at least partly because both mass media and education have extended their reaches. More communication and analyses of it from different points of view continue to provide new ways of thinking about arguments. Three important modern approaches are the *Toulmin method,* analyzing the effects of electronic communication, and various consensus-building strategies.

Toulmin's Method   College composition students are often introduced to some concepts that have developed from the work of the British professor of philosophy Stephen Toulmin. Professor Toulmin's ideas about argument can be applied to almost any argument, no matter how it is constructed. Concepts important to the Toulmin method are *claim* and *qualified claim, grounds, warrants,* and *backings.*

You already understand *claim* because *thesis, main point,* and *conclusion* are other ways to say it. You already understand *grounds* because it means *reasons, evidence, support, examples,* and *data.* You have established a thesis and provided support for it in most papers that you have written for this course.

As you improved your ability to develop a good thesis and studied Chapter 8's material on definition and classification, you were learning about qualified claims or qualifiers. A *qualified claim* is an accurately worded claim, one that establishes the

Thinking Critically About Visuals

How Visual Arguments Influence Our Choices

Looking at these U.S. Army recruitment materials should help you understand warrants.

What is your reaction to the figure of Uncle Sam? How do you read the gesture he is making? At whom is he pointing? Who was the "you" he wanted? In 1917, who would Uncle Sam not have been recruiting? What are some assumptions, principles, or beliefs—or warrants—that provide a foundation for the argument presented by this poster? What is the meaning or symbolism of the fact that Uncle Sam appears to be an older white man?

© Library of Congress

What are the demographics in the images shown on the website? How do they compare to the 1917 poster? What does the idea of "Your Education Our Mission" suggest to you? While both this and the 1917 poster are recruitment devices, what different appeals do they make to potential enlistees?

Can you see some assumptions, principles, or beliefs—or warrants—that are behind the approaches taken by the poster and by the website as they try to convince young people to enlist? See if you and your classmates found the same ones.

For additional examples of how visuals can be used to provoke, persuade, and argue, see "Creative and Critical Thinking About Images" in Chapter 4 (beginning on page 101).

category to be discussed. A qualified claim is not exaggerated or overly general. For example, you might not want to claim that "*Teenagers* should not be allowed to drive after midnight." Instead, you might claim that "People *under 18 years* of age should not be allowed to drive after midnight." That way you would be acknowledging the probable differences in experience and maturity between a 16-year-old and an 18- or 19-year-old and showing that the overly general word *teenager* needs qualification. Properly qualified claims produce effective arguments.

Warrants are the assumptions, principles, premises, and beliefs that are the foundations of most arguments. This is an important concept to understand because warrants are not always stated. However, warrants provide the connection between a claim and its grounds, and they enable the acceptance or rejection of an argument. Here's a simple example:

> *Claim:* People should brush and floss their teeth regularly.
>
> *Grounds:* Dentists tell us that brushing and flossing will help prevent tooth decay and gum disease.
>
> *Warrants:* People do not want their teeth to fall out. They do not want to have toothaches or ugly decayed teeth. People do not want drilling, fillings, and dentists' bills.

Backings are larger principles that support warrants. They are the foundations of the foundations. A backing for the warrants about brushing and flossing is the generally accepted principle of self-interest. People are concerned about their own health, appearance, and finances; people are concerned about situations that affect them. Therefore, the backing of the principle of self-interest supports the warrants about what people don't want, which support and connect the claim and grounds about dental hygiene.

This use of the word *warrant* is related to its use in law enforcement—a warrant for an arrest or a search warrant, which authorizes actions. The warrants of an argument are also related to the sources of beliefs (see Chapters 3 and 11). In addition, warrants are related to the premises used in deductive reasoning, which you will study later in this chapter.

Just as you need to understand the sources of your beliefs and those of others, you need to understand the warrants behind the arguments that you make and that people present to you. You need to recognize them when they are stated as part of an argument and search for them if they are not stated.

Argument and Electronic Media   There is currently much speculation about the effects of electronic communication on arguments. Of course, different kinds of electronic technologies raise different questions. Obviously, podcasting transmits spoken arguments, and television uses both sound and visuals to produce its well-known impact on audiences. Computers do so many things that analysis is difficult—but exciting. Visuals, sounds, and texts can be combined in countless ways, so distinctions among written, pictorial, and spoken arguments are blurred.

Many characteristics of online communication can affect arguments. The movement of linking means that logical connections are not always made. The speed at which ideas are transmitted and the rapidity with which some information can change can cause confusion and raise questions about credibility. Many people tend to write more informally in email than on paper, and such informality can change the tone of an argument for better or for worse. The rapid transmission of email can quickly conclude an argument or cause it to go on longer.

On the other hand, many Internet texts are simply posted versions of printed material or have been composed in a traditional manner. You need to be aware of the ways in which electronic and written communications differ, as well as the ways in which argumentative concepts operate similarly in various media.

More Links to the Thinking-Writing Model Just as the concepts of classical rhetoric connect with components in the Thinking-Writing Model, so do the modern concepts. A claim, especially a qualified claim, clearly relates to defining a thesis. Grounds are important for generating and organizing ideas. Warrants and backing connect significantly with audience, purpose, and the writer. Writers need to understand their own assumptions and basic beliefs as they develop arguments in order to think critically about what they are presenting. Also, since assumptions and basic beliefs can differ in various communities, writers need to consider how the warrants beneath an argument might affect their audiences. Consensus-building approaches relate most obviously to reaching an audience, but also pertain to defining purposes and to organizing ideas.

Achieving Mutual Understanding Some people believe that the purpose of argument is to coerce or to "win." As we have seen in this book, though, critical thinkers strive to develop the most informed understanding, which involves

Bernard Schoenbaum/The New Yorker Collection/Cartoonbank.com

"I shall now punch a huge hole in your argument."

THINKING CRITICALLY ABOUT NEW MEDIA

Freedom of Speech on the Internet

The dramatic growth of new media has created new issues with respect to freedom of speech. Of course, even before the Internet, the guarantee of freedom of speech under the Constitution never meant that people could say *anything*. For example, you have never been permitted to yell "Fire" in a crowded theater because of the panic that might ensue. Nor is it legal to use wildly inflammatory language toward other people—"fighting words"—that could precipitate an altercation. And if you make false and unflattering allegations about a person or organization that are demonstrably false, you can be sued for *libel* (written defamation) or *slander* (spoken defamation), or both. And, of course, there have been bans on content dealing with child pornography and other taboo subjects.

But the development of new media has introduced new battlegrounds where freedom of speech is being debated. For example, the Center for Democracy & Technology (CDT) <http://www.cdt.org/> is an organization devoted to maximizing freedom of speech and minimizing censorship on the Internet to the greatest extent possible, as explained in the following passage from CDT's website:

> Free speech has long been a hallmark of a healthy democracy and a free society. The Internet and new communications technologies have become unprecedented tools for expanding the ability for individuals to speak and receive information, participate in political and democratic processes, and share knowledge and ideas. Recognizing the potential of these technologies, courts have extended the highest level of First Amendment protection to the Internet medium. Online free expression also requires that private online service providers be protected from legal liability for content posted by users, so they will be willing to host that speech.

> CDT works to keep the Internet and communications technologies free of government censorship and content gatekeepers alike, and to extend the highest level of free speech protection afforded the Internet to all converged media. User choice and control over access to information are the key to protecting core First Amendment values while still addressing important social ills in the digital age. Through our advocacy, CDT seeks to maximize the ability of individuals to decide for themselves what they say, hear, publish, and access online.

There are others who believe that while freedom of expression is of paramount importance in a free democracy, this right must be balanced against threats to personal safety. For example, should sexual predators be permitted to create false Internet identities and try to lure children into inappropriate correspondence or even dangerous encounters in the real world? Should advertisers be allowed to use deceptive advertising to sell prescription drugs to both minors and adults alike? What about information related to your personal health: should insurance companies be able to gain access to this material, which they might then use to raise your rates or deny you health coverage? The entire issue of consumer privacy is an issue also, as detailed profiles about each one of us—our demographics, the websites we visit, our buying patterns, our financial data, etc.—are available and often shared among organizations and businesses without our knowledge. One recent court judgment has ruled that Internet organizations like Craigslist.com on which people post advertisements cannot be held responsible for the content of the ads themselves. For example, if people want to use these online venues to solicit sexual business or sell illegal pharmaceuticals, it is not up to the owners of the site to "police" these ads and prohibit or report them. (Despite this ruling, Craigslist recently decided to prohibit "adult content" in its publication.)

In addition to the CDT, which provides frequent updates on challenges to free speech online and elsewhere in society, there are other sites devoted to this complex issue, including the following:

- Electronic Frontier Foundation <www.eff.org> is a site that advocates for freedom of speech online and offers legal resources and information for people interested in pursuing these issues.
- *PCWorld.com* <www.pcworld.com> and *Wired* <www.wired.com> are consumer magazines about computing that frequently publish articles that go beyond the *content* of "free speech" online to the *technology* that allows for—and complicates—freedom of speech.

Source: Excerpt from Center for Democracy & Technology (CDT) website (http://www .cdt.org/). Reprinted by permission.

Thinking-Writing Activity

FREEDOM OF SPEECH ON THE INTERNET

After exploring the websites devoted to freedom of speech on the Internet noted above, respond to the following questions:

1. Do you believe that existing laws concerning consumer rights, freedom of speech, and intellectual property (copyrights, performance licensing, etc.) are sufficient to cover what occurs on the Internet, or do we need stricter regulations to protect children, the elderly, consumers, and others? Explain the reasoning supporting your perspective.

(Continues)

THINKING CRITICALLY ABOUT NEW MEDIA (*CONTINUED*)

2. Which, if any, of these Internet activities should be prohibited or regulated? In each case, construct an argument (with a conclusion and supporting reasons) that supports your position.

- Emailed chain letters and petitions
- Unsolicited email "spam" (bulk mail messages from people trying to sell products)
- False "virus alerts" and other hoaxes
- The creation and dissemination of computer viruses
- Programs that defeat advertising and "pop-up banners" on Web pages
- *Your example…*
- *Your example…*

trying to fully appreciate other perspectives. Instead of attempting to prove others wrong, a more desirable purpose is to arrive at a clear and mutual understanding about the issue being discussed. Sometimes people are so far apart in their convictions that agreement cannot be reached and an impasse (or worse) occurs. At other times, people "agree to disagree" and work around their differences; but if agreement does come, good feelings can result in progress, problem solving, or other desired achievements. By thinking critically, you can inspire others to think critically as well so that all parties are working together to achieve the clearest understanding rather than splintering into adversarial factions. In the cartoon on page 485, the man on the right seems to be pursuing conflict rather than mutual understanding. What are the disadvantages of such an approach? Can you think of some more constructive strategies that he could use?

Considering Other Points of View   People do not argue about things on which they agree, nor do they argue about concepts that are accepted as facts. For example, it's not likely that an argument would arise over the relative lengths of a meter and a yard. A measuring tape takes care of the question. However, people do argue about whether the United States should adopt the metric system. Arguments develop because people have different opinions about issues.

You should not ignore opposing points of view when you are making an argument. Sometimes people will ignore other ideas and present one-sided cases—as in most advertisements, some sermons, many political statements, and attempts at pushing proposals through. But in reasoned arguments, you should address varying ideas in order to demonstrate your grasp of the issue and also to try to achieve mutual understanding and, if possible, consensus or agreement.

Guidelines for Addressing Other Points of View

1. *Restate the other claim to show that you understand it.* This is often easier to do in a face-to-face discussion than in writing, but it is important in any argument. Sometimes misunderstandings can be uncovered by this technique. Restatements can also lead to finding common ground. A restatement should be made in a nonjudgmental, respectful tone.

2. *Find areas of agreement, or common ground, at the outset of the argument.* This, too, is sometimes easier to do in a face-to-face discussion than in writing. It is a technique often used in negotiations and mediation. However, in a written argument, you should try whenever you can to establish common ground with those who have other beliefs about the issue that you are addressing. Often identifying warrants can lead parties to find areas of agreement. When people see that they agree about some parts of an issue, they can establish mutual respect and then examine their differing opinions carefully.

3. *Identify which differences are important and which are trivial.* This, too, is more easily done when people talk with each other, but it is also something that can be attempted in written argument. Here, too, identifying warrants sometimes clarifies the significance of some parts of an argument.

4. *Concede points that you cannot uphold.* Sometimes you will have to concede that some of your opponents' ideas are so strong that you cannot counter them, even if you do not agree with them.

5. *Compromise.* At times, accepting a middle position or a partial achievement of your purpose is better than arguing for its complete achievement.

6. *Rebut.* This means to refute or to present opposing evidence. Rebuttal often seems necessary. It is part of the debate tradition and is important in legal arguments, but it maintains adversarial positions. If you have to rebut an opposing point, do so courteously.

7. *Be sensitive to different argumentative philosophies.* Some cultures, some groups, and some individuals prefer indirect methods of argumentation, while others want to get to the point quickly. Sometimes a direct approach is seen as rude or overly aggressive; sometimes an indirect approach is seen as weak, sneaky, or confusing. In the United States, directness is often considered the best approach. If your audience is from a different culture, however, be sure that you understand that culture's argumentative style.

Thinking-Writing Activity

ESTABLISHING AGREEMENT

1. Find a classmate who disagrees with you about something—for example, the quality of a specific television show, a political principle, or a controversy at your college. Each of you should then write a brief statement about your position. Next, read each other's statements.

2. See if you can establish some areas of agreement. Can you identify warrants for your position and for your classmate's? Where might you compromise? Determine whether any differences are not important. Do either of you have to concede a point?

Analyzing the Audience   You learned long ago that you should speak and write differently to different audiences. You use one kind of vocabulary and tone with your friends and another with your grandparents. You write formally in a job application letter and informally in an email to your sister describing what you did last weekend.

The suggestions for completing every Writing Project in this book include some discussion of your audience because it is one of the major components of any writing situation and therefore is prominently featured in the Thinking-Writing Model. However, consideration of audience is especially important when you are writing an argumentative paper, particularly if you hope to effect some change or action. Also, remember that you may have more than one audience. Here are some questions to ask yourself about the audiences for any argument you write:

- Who is interested in this issue?
- What concerns do these interested people have?
- What is their level of education or expertise?
- What related issues interest them?
- How much time might they give to reading my argument?
- Who can do something about the situation?
- Who is opposed to my point of view?
- What are the opposing claims?
- What format, tone, or method of presentation will be effective with this audience?

Can you think of other questions to ask about audiences?

Going Too Far   Paying attention to audiences does not mean telling an audience only what it wants to hear or manipulating ideas just to reach a certain audience. Some advertisers and politicians mislead audiences in such ways. Pandering to an audience is one of the ways in which rhetoric can be misused. Responsible writers and speakers accommodate their audiences honestly.

Recognizing Arguments

TWO FRIENDS ARGUE: SHOULD MARIJUANA BE LEGALIZED?

Consider the following dialogue about whether marijuana should be legalized. Have you participated in such exchanges? In what ways do dialogues like this differ from written argument? How do such dialogues provide a starting point for written arguments?

DENNIS: Have you read about the medical uses of marijuana—that people who have cancer, AIDS, and some other diseases might be helped by smoking? I think some doctors are prescribing it, and some states may be changing their laws. This might change people's thinking more than all those discussions about unenforced laws, unjust punishments, and victimless crimes that have been going on since my uncles were in college.

CAROLINE: Well, I agree that we need to think about drug laws. But I hope you agree that we have to be careful. Drugs pose a serious threat to the young people of our country. Look at all the people who are addicted to drugs, who have their lives ruined, and who often die at an early age of overdoses. And think of all the crimes people commit to support their drug habits. So I don't know if anything that's illegal now should be legalized...and the laws should be enforced.

DENNIS: That's ridiculous. Smoking marijuana is nothing like using drugs such as heroin or even cocaine. It follows that smoking marijuana should not be against the law if it's harmless and maybe even helpful to some sick people.

CAROLINE: I don't agree. Although marijuana may not be as dangerous as some other drugs, it does affect things like a driver's ability to judge distances. And smoking it surely isn't good for you. And I don't think that anything that is a threat to your health should be legal.

DENNIS: What about cigarettes and alcohol? We know that they are dangerous. Medical research has linked smoking cigarettes to lung cancer, emphysema, and heart disease. Alcohol damages the liver and also the brain. Has anyone ever proved that marijuana is a threat to our health? And even if it does turn out to be somewhat unhealthy, it's certainly not as dangerous as cigarettes and alcohol.

CAROLINE: That's a good point. But to tell you the truth, I'm not so sure that cigarettes and alcohol should be legal. And in any case, they are legal. The fact that cigarettes and alcohol are bad for your health is not reason to legalize another drug that can cause health problems.

DENNIS: Look—life is full of risks. We take chances every time we cross the street or climb into our cars. In fact, with all the irresponsible drivers on the road, driving could be a lot more hazardous to our health than any of the drugs around. Many of the foods we eat can kill. For example, red meat contributes to heart disease, and artificial sweeteners can cause cancer. The point is, if people want to take chances with their health, that's up to them. And many people in our society like to mellow out with marijuana. I read somewhere that over 70 percent of the people in the United States think that marijuana should be legalized.

CAROLINE: There is a big difference between letting people drive cars and letting them use dangerous drugs. Society has a responsibility to protect people from themselves. People often do things that are foolish if they are encouraged to or given the opportunity. Legalizing something like marijuana encourages people to use it, especially young people. It follows that many more people would use marijuana if it were legalized. It's like society saying "This is all right—go ahead and use it."

DENNIS: I still maintain that marijuana isn't dangerous. It's not addictive—like heroin is—and there is no evidence that it harms you. Consequently, anything that is harmless should be legal.

CAROLINE: Marijuana may not be physically addictive like heroin, but I think that it can be psychologically addictive because people tend to use more and more of it over time. I know a number of people who spend a lot of their time getting high. What about Carl? All he does is lie around and get high. This shows that smoking it over a period of time definitely affects your mind. Think about the people you know who smoke a lot—don't they seem to be floating in a dream world? How are they ever going to make anything of their lives? As far as I'm concerned, a pothead is like a zombie—living but dead.

DENNIS: Since you have had so little experience with marijuana, I don't think that you can offer an informed opinion on the subject. And anyway, if you do too much of anything, it can hurt you. Even something as healthy as exercise can cause problems if you do too much of it. But I sure don't see anything wrong with toking up with some friends at a party or even getting into a relaxed state by yourself. In fact, I find that I can even concentrate better on my school work after taking a little smoke.

CAROLINE: If you believe that, then marijuana really has damaged your brain. You're just trying to rationalize your drug habit. Smoking marijuana doesn't help you concentrate—it takes you away from reality. And I don't think that people can control it. Either you smoke and surrender control of your life, or you don't smoke because you want to retain control. There's nothing in between.

DENNIS: Let me point out something to you. Because marijuana is illegal, organized crime controls its distribution and makes all the money from it. If marijuana were legalized, the government could tax the sale of it—like cigarettes and alcohol—and use the money for some worthwhile purpose. For example, many states have legalized gambling and use the money to support education. In fact, the major tobacco companies have already copyrighted names for different marijuana brands—like "Acapulco Gold." Obviously they believe that marijuana will soon become legal.

CAROLINE: The fact that the government can make money out of something doesn't mean that they should legalize it. We could also legalize prostitution or muggings and then tax the proceeds. Also, even if the cigarette companies are prepared to sell marijuana, that doesn't mean that selling it makes sense. After all, they're the ones who are selling us cigarettes....

Can you think of other views on the subject of legalizing marijuana? Can you think of other subjects about which such dialogues are taking place now?

The previous discussion illustrates two people's engaging in dialogue, the systematic exchange of ideas. Discussing issues with others encourages you to be mentally active, to ask questions, to view issues from different perspectives, to develop reasons that support conclusions, and to write convincingly.

This chapter focuses on the last quality of thinking critically—supporting claims with reasons—because when we offer reasons to support a conclusion, we are presenting an argument, the essence of most college and business writing. An *argument* is a form of thinking in which certain statements (reasons or evidence) are offered to support another statement (a conclusion or a claim).

In the dialogue, Dennis presents the following argument for legalizing marijuana:

Reason: Marijuana might help some people who have serious diseases.

Reason: Marijuana isn't dangerous like heroin and cocaine.

Reason: Governments could tax the sale of marijuana as they do cigarettes and alcohol.

Claim: Marijuana should be legalized.

Expanding the definition of *argument,* we can define the main ideas that make up an argument. *Reasons, evidence,* or *grounds* are statements that support another statement (a claim, thesis, or conclusion), justify it, or make it more probable. The *claim, thesis,* or *conclusion* is a statement that explains, asserts, or predicts on the basis of statements (known as reasons, evidence, or grounds) that are offered to support it.

The type of thinking that uses argument—presenting reasons to support conclusions—is known as *reasoning,* and it is a type of thinking explained throughout this book. We are continually trying to explain, justify, and predict through the process of reasoning, and often we must present such thinking in writing.

Of course, our reasoning—and that of others—is not always correct. The reasons someone offers may not really support the claim they are intended to, a conclusion may not really follow from the reasons stated, or the reasons may be questionable or wrong. These difficulties are illustrated in a number of the arguments contained in the previous discussion on marijuana.

Nevertheless, whenever we accept a conclusion as likely or true on the basis of certain reasons, or whenever we offer reasons to support a conclusion, we are using arguments—even if our reasoning is weak or faulty and needs improvement.

Let's return to the discussion about marijuana. After Dennis presents one argument, Caroline presents another, giving reasons that lead to a conclusion that conflicts with the one Dennis has offered.

Reason: Drugs pose a very serious threat to the young people of our country.

Reason: Many crimes are committed to support drug habits.

Claim: As a result, society has to have drug laws and enforce them to convince people of the seriousness of the situation.

Which of Dennis's or Caroline's arguments do you see as reasonable? Which seem weak or faulty?

English, like other languages, provides guidance in our efforts to identify reasons and conclusions. Certain key words, or cue words, signal that a reason is being offered to support a conclusion or that a conclusion is being drawn on the basis of certain reasons. After you read the following list, go back to the dialogue and see how and when Dennis and Caroline use these words.

The following are some commonly used cue words for reasons and conclusions. Of course, identifying reasons, claims, and conclusions involves more than looking for cue words. The words and phrases listed here do not always signal reasons and conclusions, and in many cases people present arguments without using cue words. Cue words, however, do alert us that an argument is being offered. Careful use of cue words helps us to write effective arguments.

Useful Words for Recognizing and Writing Arguments

Cue Words Signaling Reasons

since	in view of
for	first, second
because	in the first (second) place
as shown by	may be inferred from
as indicated by	may be deduced from
given that	may be derived from
assuming that	for the reason that

Cue Words Signaling Conclusions

therefore	then
thus	it follows that
hence	thereby showing
so	demonstrates that
(which) shows that	allows us to infer that
(which) proves that	suggests very strongly that
implies that	you see that
points to	leads me to believe that
as a result	allows us to deduce that
consequently	

Thinking-Writing Activity
ANALYZING A DIALOGUE

1. Review "Two Friends Argue: Should Marijuana Be Legalized?" and underline cue words that signal when Dennis and Caroline are giving reasons or announcing conclusions.

2. Identify one argument in the dialogue that you find convincing and one that seems unconvincing.

3. Write your reasons for your opinions, referring to specific places in the dialogue.

4. Share your responses with classmates and note where you agree and disagree.

Imagine living in a society in which important decisions affecting your life were made by a central authority completely independent of your wishes or input: would you resent living in a society so lacking in personal freedom? If you are one of the 900 million members of the social network Facebook, that's precisely the situation in which you find yourself. As the following article explains, in a society of that many people, conflicts and disputes are inevitable: in the case of Facebook, 2 million such disputes a week. For example, here are some of the recent disputes and how they were adjudicated:

- A complaint about a photograph of two men kissing: the photograph was removed.

- A copyright complaint against an information-providing service: the site was closed down without explanation.

- A professional photographer whose fan base listing was removed without explanation.

- A complaint against a women's group by an antipornography group: the group's site was taken down.

Who makes these decisions and on what basis are they made? It's a team of individuals working for Facebook using a collection of sophisticated technological tools and guided by Facebook's guiding principle of getting people more open and connected with a minimum of negative experiences. After reading the following article, "The Perfect Technocracy: Facebook's Attempt to Create Good Government for 900 Million People," answer the questions that follow.

The Perfect Technocracy: Facebook's Attempt to Create Good Government for 900 Million People

by Alexis C. Madrigal

Let's stipulate that Facebook is not a country, that real governments fulfill many more functions, and that people are not citizens of their social networks.

Nonetheless, 900 million human beings do something like live in the blue-and-white virtual space of the world's largest structured web of people. And those people get into disputes that they expect to be adjudicated. They have this expectation in part because Facebook has long said it wants to create a safe environment for connecting with other people. (How else can you get people to be "more open and connected"?) But people also want someone to be in charge, they want an authority to whom they can appeal if some other person is being a jerk.

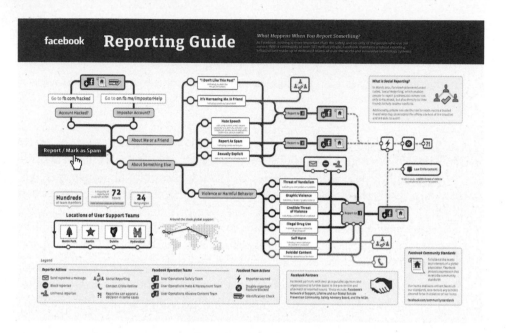

Except in this case, the someone really is a corporate person. So when you report something or someone reports something of yours, it is Facebook that makes the decision about what's been posted, even if we know that somewhere down the line, some human being has to embody the corporate we, if only for long enough to click a button.

Any individual decision made by Facebook's team—like taking down this photo of a gay couple kissing—is easy to question. Ars Technica's Ken Fisher detailed a whole bunch of one-off problems that people have encountered with Facebook's reporting system. In each, there is an aggrieved party, but we're only hearing one side of the conflict when these problems bubble up. Across many single events, you have two people (or entities like businesses) with conflicting desires. This is a classic case where you need some sort of government.

It's not hard to imagine making one or 20 or even 200 decisions about photographs or status updates in a week, but it's mindboggling to consider that Facebook has to process *2 million reports per week*, and that's not including simple "mark as spam" messages.

How do you design a system to deal with that workload? I spoke with James Mitchell, who helms what Facebook calls "site integrity" within its user-operations department, and Jud Hoffman, the company's global policy manager about the reporting process. They are the architects of Facebook's technocracy.

"The amount of thought and debate that goes into the process of creating and managing these rules is not that different from a legislative and judicial process all rolled up into one," Hoffman, a lawyer, told me. "And James has the executive/judicial element. I don't think it is a stretch to think about this in a governance context, but it's a different form and we take it really, really seriously."

The key step, Mitchell told me, was to put some structure into the reporting process. Back when he started in 2006, there wasn't any form to complaints from users. That meant there was a massive queue of undifferentiated problems. So, he and his team

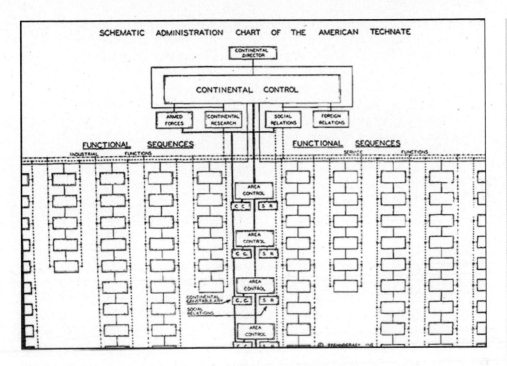

SCHEMATIC ADMINISTRATION CHART OF THE AMERICAN TECHNATE

started to think about what kinds of problems they received and created categories of problems, which they refined over time.

That allows the reports to be channeled through a complex set of processes and teams so that they arrive in front of human beings or computers that know what to do with them.

Facebook has revealed this infrastructure for the first time today. It's the product of more than five years of work by several teams within Facebook, who have worked to make the process of handling this flood of user inquiries as efficient as possible.

At the end of many of these reporting lines, there's a person who has to make a decision about the user's message. Some of these decisions are binary—Does this photograph contain nudity?—and those are generally outsourced to teams that can apply simple and rigorous formulas such as asking, "Is this person naked?" Other decisions are complex in ways that make machines very good at dealing with them. (For example, there are more than 50 signals that Facebook's algorithms look at to determine whether a profile is spam, and the automated responses are more accurate than human ones would be.)

But the bulk of the reports are fielded by a faceless team of several hundred Facebook employees in Mountain View, Austin, Dublin, and Hyderabad. These people and the tools they've built have become the de facto legislators, bureaucrats, police, and judges of the quasi-nation of Facebook. Some decisions they make impact hundreds of millions of people in some small way; other decisions will change some small number of people's lives in a big way.

What's fascinating to me is that Facebook has essentially recreated a government bureaucracy complete with regulators and law enforcement, but optimized for totally different values than traditional governments. Instead of a constitution, Facebook has the dual missions of making "the world more open and connected" and keeping users on its site by minimizing their negative experiences. Above all, Facebook's solution to all governance problems have to be designed for extreme efficiency at scale.

As stipulated above, real-world governments have to fulfill all kinds of functions aside from disputes between citizens, but just look at the difference in scale between Facebook's government and Palo Alto's government. Palo Alto has roughly 65,000 residents and 617 full-time employees. Facebook has 900 million "residents" and a few hundred bureaucrats who make all the content decisions.

Facebook's desire for efficiency means democracy is out and technocratic, developer-king rule is in. People don't get to vote on the rules, and even when Facebook offered its users the opportunity to vote on a new privacy policy last week, voter turnout was 0.038 percent. People know that Facebook controls a large slice of their digital lives, but they don't have a sense of digital citizenship. And that apathy gives Facebook's technocracy a chance to succeed where its historical antecedents did not.

The original technocrats were a group of thinkers and engineers in the 1930s who revived Plato's dream of the philosopher-king, but with a machine-age spin. Led by Thorstein Veblen, Howard Scott and M. King Hubbert, they advocated not rule by the people or the monarchy or the dictator, but by the engineers. The engineers and scientists would rule rationally and impartially. They would create a Technocracy that functioned like clockwork and ensured the productivity of all was efficiently distributed. They worked out a whole system by which the North American continent would be ruled with functional sequences that would allow the Continental Director to get things done.

Technocracy, as originally conceived, was explicitly not democratic. Its proponents did not want popular rule; they wanted rule by a knowledgeable elite who would make good decisions. And maybe they would have, but there was one big problem. Few people found the general vision of surrendering their political power to engineers all that appealing.

With Facebook, people seem to care much more about individual decisions that Facebook makes than the existence of the ultraefficient technocratic system. They are not challenging the principles or values of the system, so much as wanting them to be applied quickly to resolve their particular dispute. And desire for speed, of course, drives the efficiency-first mindset that makes it hard to deal with nuanced problems. None of the accusations leveled at Facebook's administrative system read to me like criticisms of its core structure.

I mean, of course Facebook's governance isn't perfect. Of course the people who run it make mistakes, mistakes that they use every bit of data to squeeze out of the system. These problems are a consequence of running our social lives through a centralized, corporate social network with a set of rather staid goals: openness, connectedness, and the minimization of negative experiences. Given these goals, Facebook has come to a rational set of structures for dealing with social problems within its walled garden. It is a gated community with some CCRs and if you don't like it . . . Well, there's always Brooklyn!

That is to say, the real question is whether Facebook's goals—and the systems it uses to promote them—reflect one's own desires. Do you want a clean, well-lighted place that works without any effort on your part? If so, Facebook has the governance structure for you. You want a more permissive place with fewer rules? Allow me to introduce you to 4chan.

QUESTIONS FOR READING ACTIVELY

1. Are you a member of Facebook? If so, are you aware of their policy for resolving disputes? What is your reaction to the system that they have instituted for answering complaints and resolving disputes?

2. Review the infrastructure model that Facebook has developed (included on page 497): what is their goal in developing such a model? What is your analysis of it: does it make sense to you? Do you have any suggestions for improvement?

QUESTIONS FOR THINKING CRITICALLY

1. The prospect of reviewing 2 million complaints per week is a daunting challenge. If you were in charge of developing a system to respond in a timely and informed way to this volume of complaints, how would you go about doing it?

2. Facebook's guiding principles are getting people more open and connected with a minimum of negative experiences. Do you think these principles are appropriate? Are there other principles that you think Facebook should be using to guide their decisions? Why or why not?

QUESTIONS FOR WRITING THOUGHTFULLY

1. Madrigal compares Facebook's system of governance to our own system of local government, both of which are bureaucracies with regulators and law enforcement. But due to the difference in scale between Facebook's government and that of an average sized U.S. city, Facebook is technocratic rather than democratic. Do you think Facebook's technocratic approach to governance is the best way to govern the users of its site? Explain your reasoning in an essay using the Toulmin method (claim or qualified claim, grounds, warrants and backing).

2. If you were handed the job of governing Facebook's 900 million users, what would be your approach? How would it differ from the current system of governance?

Arguments as Inferences

When you construct arguments, you are constructing views of the world by means of your ability to infer. As you saw in Chapter 11, inferring is a thinking process used to reason from what one already knows (or believes to be the case) to acquire new knowledge or beliefs. This is usually what you do when you construct arguments: work from reasons you know or believe to draw conclusions based on them.

Just as you can use inferences to make sense of different types of situations, you can also construct arguments for different purposes. As already noted, some people believe in using arguments to coerce or to "win." A more desirable goal is to use arguments to clarify issues, develop mutual understanding, and if possible, bring about agreement or consensus on the issue being discussed. Notice how you can work toward agreement when you construct arguments to do any of the following: decide, explain, predict, persuade.

CONSTRUCTING ARGUMENTS TO DECIDE

Reason: Throughout my life, I've always been interested in all kinds of electricity.

Reason: There are many attractive job opportunities in the field of electrical engineering.

Claim: Electrical engineering would be a good major for me.

Audience: Myself, my parents, my academic adviser, the scholarship office

CONSTRUCTING ARGUMENTS TO EXPLAIN

Reason: I was delayed leaving my house because my dog needed emergency walking.

Reason: There was an unexpected traffic jam caused by motorists slowing down to view an overturned chicken truck.

Claim: Therefore, I couldn't help being late for our appointment.

Audience: The person waiting for me

CONSTRUCTING ARGUMENTS TO PREDICT

Reason: Some people will always drive faster than the speed limit allows, no matter whether the limit is 55 or 65 mph.

Reason: Car accidents are more likely to occur at higher speeds.

Claim: A reinstated 65 mph speed limit will result in more accidents.

Audience: Legislators, voters, drivers

CONSTRUCTING ARGUMENTS TO PERSUADE

Reason: Chewing tobacco can lead to cancer of the mouth and throat.

Reason: Young people sometimes begin chewing tobacco because they see ads that feature sports heroes they admire doing it.

Claim: Ads for chewing tobacco should be banned.

Audience: Parents, voters, legislators, advertising agencies, media executives

Evaluating Arguments

To construct good arguments, you must be skilled at evaluating the effectiveness, or soundness, of arguments already constructed. You must investigate the components of an argument to determine the soundness of the argument as a whole.

1. How true are the reasons being offered to support the conclusion?
2. To what extent do the reasons support the conclusion, claim, or thesis—or to what extent does the conclusion follow from the reasons offered?

TRUTH: HOW TRUE ARE THE SUPPORTING REASONS?

The first aspect of an argument that you must evaluate is the truth of the reasons being used to support a conclusion. Ask yourself these questions:

- What specific evidence is the writer offering to illustrate each reason?
- Are any reasons consistent with my own experience?
- Are the reasons based on reliable sources?
- Are the reasons relevant to the subject of the argument?

You use these questions and others like them to analyze the reasons offered and to determine how true they seem to be. As you saw in Chapter 11, evaluating the kinds of beliefs used as reasons in arguments is a complex challenge.

VALIDITY: DO THE REASONS SUPPORT THE CLAIM OR CONCLUSION?

In addition to determining whether the reasons are true, evaluating arguments involves investigating the relationship between the reasons and the claim or conclusion (which becomes the thesis of a piece of writing that argues a position on an issue).

When the reasons support the conclusion in such a way that the conclusion follows from them, you have a *valid argument*. If, however, the reasons do not support the conclusion—that is, if the conclusion does not follow from the reasons being offered—you have an *invalid argument*. Remember that the words *valid* and *true* do not have the same meaning. You must first evaluate the truth of a reason and then determine its validity.

One way to focus on the concept of *validity* is to assume that all the reasons in an argument are true and then try to determine how probable they make the conclusion. The following is an example of one type of valid argument.

Reason: Anything that is a threat to our health should not be legal.

Reason: Marijuana is a threat to our health.

Conclusion: Therefore, marijuana should not be legal.

This is a valid argument because if we assume that the reasons are true, its conclusion does necessarily follow from them.

Of course, we may not agree that either or both of the reasons are true; in that case, we would not agree with the conclusion. Nevertheless, the structure of the argument is valid. This particular form of thinking is known as *deduction*.

Here is a different type of argument:

Reason: As part of a project in my social science class, we selected 100 students in the school to be interviewed. We took special steps to ensure that these students were representative of the student body as a whole (total students: 4,386). We asked the students whether they thought that the United States should actively try to overthrow foreign governments that it disapproves of. Of the 100 students interviewed, 88 said that the United States should definitely not be involved in such activities.

Conclusion: We can conclude that most students in this school believe that the United States should not be engaged in attempts to actively overthrow foreign governments that it disapproves of.

This is a persuasive argument because if we assume that the reason is true, that reason provides strong support for the conclusion. In this case, the key part of the reason is the statement that the 100 students selected were representative of the entire student population at the school. To evaluate the truth of the reason, we might want to investigate the procedure used to select the 100 students in order to determine whether this sample was, in fact, representative of all the students. (Notice that the conclusion carefully said "in this school." It did not imprecisely say "most students.")

This particular form of thinking is an example of *induction.*

SOUNDNESS: IS THE ARGUMENT BOTH TRUE AND VALID?

When an argument includes both true reasons and a valid structure, the argument is considered sound. When an argument has either one or more false reasons or an invalid structure, however, the argument is considered unsound.

Figure 13.1 reminds us that in terms of arguments, *truth* and *validity* are not identical concepts. An argument can have true reasons and an invalid structure or have false reasons and a valid structure. In both cases, the argument is unsound. Consider the following argument:

Reason: Professor Davis believes that megadoses of vitamins can cure colds.

Reason: Davis is a professor of computer science.

Conclusion: Megadoses of vitamins can cure colds.

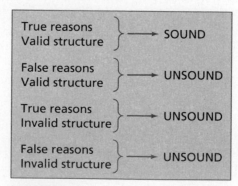

FIGURE 13.1
Sound and Unsound Arguments

This argument is obviously not valid: even if we assume that the reasons are true, the conclusion does not follow. Professor Davis's expertise with computers does not provide her with special knowledge about nutrition and medicine. This invalid thinking is neither structurally nor factually acceptable. It is clearly not a sound argument. Now, consider this argument:

Reason: For a democracy to function most effectively, the citizens should be able to think critically about the major social and political issues.

Reason: Education plays a key role in developing critical thinking abilities.

Conclusion: Therefore, education plays a key role in ensuring that a democracy is functioning most effectively.

A good case could be made for the soundness of this argument because the reasons are persuasive and the argument structure is valid. Of course, someone might counter that one or both of the reasons are not completely true, which illustrates an important point about the arguments we construct and evaluate. Many of the arguments we encounter in life fall somewhere between complete soundness and complete unsoundness because often we are not sure if our reasons are completely true. Throughout this book, we have found that developing accurate beliefs is an ongoing process and that our beliefs are subject to clarification and revision. As a result, the conclusion of any argument can be only as certain as the reasons supporting the conclusion.

Forms of Argument

Arguments occur in many forms, but two major thinking methods—deduction and induction—provide the foundations for most arguments and also influence the organizational structure of arguments. They can be seen as (1) moving from general principles to specific applications and (2) moving from specific examples to general conclusions. Deduction and induction are seldom applied in "pure" or textbook ways in real-life arguments. Instead, they often are compressed or combined, so recognizing and analyzing their uses can sometimes be difficult. In fact, some teachers and students feel that studying them separately is more a mental exercise than a practical activity. However, as a critical thinker, a writer of arguments, and an analyst of arguments, you need to understand these principles.

DEDUCTIVE REASONING

The deductive argument is the one most commonly associated with the study of logic. Though it has a variety of valid forms, they all share one characteristic: if you accept the supporting reasons (also called *premises*) as true, you must also accept the conclusion as true. A *deductive argument* is an argument form in which one reasons from premises that are known or assumed to be true to a conclusion that necessarily follows from these premises. For example, consider the following famous deductive argument:

Reason/Premise: All persons are mortal.

Reason/Premise: Socrates is a person.

Conclusion: Therefore, Socrates is mortal.

In this example of *deductive reasoning,* accepting the premises of the argument as true means that the conclusion necessarily follows; it cannot be false. Many deductive arguments, like this one, are structured as *syllogisms,* an argument form that consists of two supporting premises and a conclusion. There are also, however, a large number of invalid deductive forms, one of which is illustrated in the following defective syllogism:

Reason/Premise: All persons are mortal.

Reason/Premise: Socrates is a person.

Conclusion: Therefore, all persons are Socrates.

This example is deliberately absurd, but people do shift terms in these ways and think things such as "all tall people should play basketball" just because basketball players are usually tall. Despite the variety of invalid deductive structures, once you become aware of the concept of *validity,* you should be able to detect invalidity.

One way to do this is through the application of a general rule. Whenever we reason by using the form illustrated by the valid Socrates syllogism, we are using the following argument structure:

Premise: All A (people) are B (mortal).

Premise: S is an A (Socrates is a person).

Conclusion: Therefore, S is B (Socrates is mortal).

This basic argument form is valid no matter what terms are included. For example:

Premise: All politicians are untrustworthy.

Premise: Bill White is a politician.

Conclusion: Therefore, Bill White is untrustworthy.

Notice again that with any valid deductive form, if we assume that the premises are true, we must accept the conclusion. Of course, in this case it is unlikely that the first premise is true.

Although we are not always aware of doing so, we use this basic type of reasoning whenever we apply a general rule. For instance:

Premise: All eight-year-old children should be in bed by 9:30 P.M.

Premise: You are an eight-year-old child.

Conclusion: Therefore, you should be in bed by 9:30 P.M.

Often we present this kind of reasoning in an abbreviated form called an *enthymeme,* which assumes the first premise: You should be in bed by 9:30 because you're an eight-year-old child; Bill White is a politician, so he's untrustworthy.

Describe an example from your own experience in which you use this deductive form, both as a syllogism and as an enthymeme.

OTHER DEDUCTIVE FORMS

Deductive arguments, or syllogisms and enthymemes, come in many other forms, most of which have been named by logicians. At some point in your college education, you should consider taking a course in critical thinking or logic to learn about as many kinds of reasoning as you can. This chapter provides only an introduction.

Affirming the Antecedent

Premise: If I have prepared thoroughly for the final exam, I will do well.

Premise: I prepared thoroughly for the exam.

Conclusion: Therefore, I will do well on the exam.

When we reason like this, we are using the following argument structure:

Premise: If A (I have prepared thoroughly), then B (I will do well).

Premise: A (I have prepared thoroughly).

Conclusion: Therefore, B (I will do well).

Like all valid deductive forms, this form is valid no matter what specific terms are included. For example:

Premise: If the Democrats register 20 million new voters, they will win the presidential election.

Premise: The Democrats have registered more than 20 million new voters.

Conclusion: Therefore, the Democrats will win the presidential election.

As with other valid argument forms, the conclusion will be true if the reasons are true. Although the second premise in this argument expresses information that can be verified, the first premise would be more difficult to establish.

Denying the Consequent

Premise: If Michael were a really good friend, he would lend me his car for the weekend.

Premise: Michael refuses to lend me his car for the weekend.

Conclusion: Therefore, Michael is not a really good friend.

When we reason in this fashion, we are using the following argument structure:

Premise: If A (Michael is a really good friend), then B (He will lend me his car).

Premise: Not B (He won't lend me his car).

Conclusion: Therefore, not A (He's not a really good friend).

Again, like other valid reasoning forms, this form is valid no matter what subject is being considered. As always, the truth of the premises must be evaluated.

Disjunctive Syllogism

> *Premise:* Either I left my wallet on my dresser, or I have lost it.
>
> *Premise:* The wallet is not on my dresser.
>
> *Conclusion:* Therefore, I must have lost it.

When we reason in this way, we are using the following argument structure:

> *Premise:* Either A (I left my wallet on my dresser) or B (I have lost it).
>
> *Premise:* Not A (I didn't leave it on my dresser).
>
> *Conclusion:* Therefore, B (I have lost it).

This valid reasoning form can be applied to any number of situations and still yield accurate results. For example:

> *Premise:* Either your stomach trouble is caused by what you are eating, or it is caused by nervous tension.
>
> *Premise:* You tell me that you have been very careful about your diet.
>
> *Conclusion:* Therefore, your stomach trouble is caused by nervous tension.

To determine the accuracy of the conclusion, we must determine the accuracy of the premises. If they are true, then the conclusion must also be true.

Thinking-Writing Activity

EVALUATING DEDUCTIVE ARGUMENTS

Analyze the following brief arguments by completing these steps:

1. Summarize the reasons and conclusions given.
2. Identify which, if any, deductive argument forms are being used.
3. Evaluate the truth of the reasons that support the conclusion.

> For if the brain is a machine of ten billion nerve cells and the mind can somehow be explained as the summed activity of a finite number of chemical and electrical reactions, [then] boundaries limit the human prospect—we are biological and our souls cannot fly free.
>
> —Edward O. Wilson, *On Human Nature*

> The extreme vulnerability of a complex industrial society to intelligent, targeted terrorism by a very small number of people may prove the fatal challenge to which Western states have no adequate response. Counterforce alone will never suffice. The real challenge of the true terrorist is to the basic values of a society. If there is no commitment to shared values in Western society—and if none are imparted in our amoral institutions of higher learning—no increase in police and burglar alarms will suffice to preserve our society from the specter that haunts us—not a bomb from above but a gun from within.
>
> —James Billington, "The Gun Within"

To fully believe in something, to truly understand something, one must be intimately acquainted with its opposite. One should not adopt a creed by default, because no alternative is known. Education should prepare students for the "real world" not by segregating them from evil but by urging full confrontation to test and modify the validity of the good.

—Robert Baron, "In Defense of Teaching Racism, Sexism, and Fascism"

The inescapable conclusion is that society secretly wants crime, needs crime, and gains definite satisfactions from the present mishandling of it! We condemn crime; we punish offenders for it; but we need it. The crime and punishment ritual is a part of our lives. We need crimes to wonder at, to enjoy vicariously, to discuss and speculate about, and to publicly deplore. We need criminals to identify ourselves with, to envy secretly, and to punish stoutly. They do for us the forbidden, illegal things we wish to do and, like scapegoats of old, they bear the burdens of our displaced guilt and punishment—"the iniquities of us all."

—Karl Menninger, "The Crime of Punishment"

All of the preceding basic argument forms can be found not only in informal daily conversations but also at more formal levels of thinking. They appear in academic disciplines, in scientific inquiry, in debates on social issues, and so on. Many other argument forms—both deductive and inductive—also constitute human reasoning. By sharpening your understanding of these ways of thinking, you will be better able to make sense of the world by constructing and evaluating effective arguments.

INDUCTIVE REASONING

The preceding section focused on deductive reasoning, an argument form in which one reasons from premises that are known or assumed to be true to a conclusion that follows necessarily from the premises. This section introduces *inductive reasoning,* an argument form in which one reasons from premises or instances that are known or assumed to be true to a conclusion that is supported by the premises but does not necessarily follow from them.

When you reason inductively, your premises, instances, or data provide evidence that makes it more or less probable (but not certain) that the conclusion is true. The following statements are examples of conclusions reached through inductive reasoning. As you read them, think about how the data might have been obtained and what arguments could be based on each statement.

1. A recent Gallup poll reported that 74 percent of the American public believes that abortion should remain legal.

2. On the average, a person with a college degree will earn over $830,000 more in his or her lifetime than a person with just a high school diploma.

3. The outbreak of food poisoning at the end-of-year school party was probably caused by the squid salad.

4. The devastating disease AIDS is caused by a particularly complex virus that may not be curable.

5. The solar system is probably the result of an enormous explosion—a "big bang"—that occurred billions of years ago.

The first two statements are examples of inductive reasoning known as *empirical generalization*—a general statement about an entire group made on the basis of observing some members of the group. The final three statements are examples of *causal reasoning*—a form of inductive reasoning that claims an event (or events) is the result of the occurrence of another event (or events).

CAUSAL REASONING

You were introduced to causal analysis in Chapter 10 and also to the fallacies that can result if causes are not analyzed logically. Review pages 351–355 to recall the characteristics of this pattern of induction.

Causal reasoning is the backbone of the natural and the social sciences. It is also central to the *scientific method,* which operates on the assumption that the world is constructed in a complex web of causal relationships that can be discovered through systematic investigation. You apply the scientific method in your science courses.

EMPIRICAL GENERALIZATION

An important tool used by both natural and social scientists is empirical generalization. Have you ever wondered how the major television and radio networks can predict election results hours before the polls close? These predictions are made possible by using *empirical generalization,* a form of inductive reasoning defined as "reasoning by examining a limited sample to reach a general conclusion based on that sample."

Network election predictions, as well as public opinion polls that are conducted throughout a political campaign, are based on interviews with a select number of people. Ideally, pollsters would interview everyone in the "target population" (in this case, voters), but doing this, of course, is hardly practical. Instead, they select a relatively small group of individuals from the target population, known as a "sample," who they have determined will adequately represent the group as a whole. Pollsters believe that they can then generalize the opinions of this smaller group to the target population.

There are three key criteria for evaluating inductive arguments:

- Is the sample known?
- Is the sample sufficient?
- Is the sample representative?

Is the Sample Known?   An inductive argument is only as strong as the sample on which it is based. For example, sample populations described in vague terms—such as "highly placed sources" or "many young people interviewed"—provide a treacherously weak foundation for generalizing to larger populations. In order for an inductive argument to be persuasive, the sample population should be explicitly known and clearly identified. Natural and social scientists take great care when selecting members of sample groups. They also make information on members of the sample groups available to outside investigators who may wish to evaluate and verify the results.

Is the Sample Sufficient?   The second criterion for evaluating inductive reasoning is to consider the size of the sample. It should be large enough to provide an accurate sense of the group as a whole. In the polling example discussed earlier, we would be concerned if only a few registered voters had been interviewed and the results of the interviews were then generalized to a much larger population. Overall, the larger the sample, the more reliable the inductive conclusions. Natural and social scientists have developed precise guidelines for determining the size of the sample needed to achieve reliable results. For example, poll results are often accompanied by a qualification such as "These results are subject to an error factor of ±3 percentage points." This means that if the sample reveals that 47 percent of those interviewed prefer candidate X, we can reliably state that 44 to 50 percent of the target population prefers candidate X. Because a sample is usually a small portion of the target population, we can rarely state that the two match each other exactly—there must always be some room for variation. The exceptions to this are situations in which the target population is completely homogeneous. For instance, tasting one cookie from a bag of cookies is usually enough to tell us whether or not the contents of the entire bag are stale.

Is the Sample Representative?   The third crucial element in effective inductive reasoning is the representativeness of the sample. If we are to generalize with confidence from the sample to the target population, we have to be sure the sample is similar in all relevant aspects to the larger group from which it is drawn. For instance, in the polling example, the sample population should reflect the same percentages of men and women, of Democrats and Republicans, of young and old, and so on, as exist in the target population. It is obvious that many characteristics—such as hair color, favorite food, and shoe size—are not relevant to the comparison. The better the sample reflects the target population in terms of relevant qualities, however, the better the accuracy of the generalizations. On the other hand, when the sample does not represent the target population—for example, if the election pollsters interviewed only females between the ages of 30 and 35—the sample is termed *biased,* and any generalizations about the target population will be highly suspect.

How do we ensure that the sample is representative of the target population? One important device is *random selection,* a selection strategy in which every member of the target population has an equal chance of being included in the sample. For example, the various techniques used to select winning lottery tickets are supposed to be random—each ticket is supposed to have an equal chance of winning. In complex cases of inductive reasoning—such as polling—random selection is often combined with the confirmation that all the important categories in the population are adequately represented. For example, an election pollster would want to ensure that all significant geographical areas are included and then would randomly select individuals from within those areas to compose the sample.

Understanding the principles of empirical generalization is crucial to effective thinking because we are continually challenged to evaluate this form of inductive thinking in our lives. In addition, when writing about political or social issues, we often use the results of inductive investigations, so we should be able to determine their accuracy and relevance.

Thinking-Writing Activity

ANALYZING EMPIRICAL GENERALIZATION

Review the following examples of empirical generalizing. Select two, and then evaluate the quality of the thinking by answering the following questions:

1. Is the sample known?
2. Is the sample sufficient?
3. Is the sample representative?
4. Do you believe that the conclusions are likely to be accurate? Why or why not?
5. What are some arguments that might be based on your answers?

Example 1: In a study of a possible relationship between pornography and antisocial behavior, questionnaires went out to 7,500 psychiatrists and psychoanalysts whose listing in the directory of the American Psychological Association indicated clinical experience. Over 3,400 of these professionals responded. The result: 7.4 percent of the psychiatrists and psychologists had cases in which they were convinced that pornography was a causal factor in antisocial behavior, an additional 9.4 percent were suspicious, 3.2 percent did not commit themselves, and 80 percent said they had no cases in which a causal connection was suspected.

Example 2: A survey by the Sleep Disorder Clinic of the VA hospital in La Jolla, California (involving more than 1 million people), revealed that people who sleep more than 10 hours a night have a death rate 80 percent higher than those who sleep only 7 or 8 hours. Men who sleep fewer than 4 hours a night have a death rate 180 percent higher, and women with less than 4 hours of sleep have a rate 40 percent higher. This might be taken as indicating that too much and too little sleep cause death.

Example 3: In a recent survey, twice as many doctors interviewed stated that if they were stranded on a desert island, they would prefer X Aspirin to Extra Strength Y. Being a general practitioner in a rural area has tremendous drawbacks—being on virtual 24-hour call 365 days a year, patients without financial means or insurance, low fees in the first place, inadequate facilities and assistance. Nevertheless, America's small-town G.P.s seem fairly content with their lot. According to a survey taken by *Country Doctor,* fully 50 percent wrote back that they "basically like being a rural G.P." Only 1 in 15 regretted that he or she had not specialized. Only 2 out of 20 rural general practitioners would trade places with their urban counterparts, given the chance. And only 1 in 30 would "choose some other line of work altogether."

More Fallacies: Forms of False Reasoning

As we pointed out in Chapter 10, certain forms of reasoning are not logical. These types of pseudoreasoning (false reasoning) are often termed *fallacies*: arguments that are not sound because of various errors in reasoning. Fallacious reasoning is sometimes used to influence others. It seeks to persuade not on the basis of sound arguments and critical thinking but rather on the basis of emotional and illogical factors. Sometimes fallacious reasoning is used inadvertently. However, it is always dangerous, so it is important to recognize it as well as to avoid using it. Detecting fallacious reasoning is a significant factor in evaluating sources of beliefs, the concept discussed in Chapter 11.

In Chapter 8, we explored the way in which we form concepts through the interactive process of generalizing (identifying the common qualities that define the boundaries of the concept) and interpreting (identifying examples of the concept). This process is similar to the process involved in constructing empirical generalizations as we seek to reach a general conclusion based on a limited number of examples and then apply this conclusion to other examples. Although generalizing and interpreting are useful in forming concepts, they also can lead to fallacious ways of thinking, including hasty generalization, sweeping generalization, false dilemma, begging the question, red herring, and fallacies of relevance.

HASTY GENERALIZATION

Consider the following examples of reasoning. Do you think the arguments are sound? Why or why not?

- My boyfriends have never shown any real concern for my feelings. My conclusion is that men are insensitive, selfish, and emotionally superficial.
- My mother always gets upset over insignificant things. This leads me to believe that women are very emotional.

In both of these cases, a general conclusion has been reached that is based on a very small sample. As a result, the reasons provide very weak support for the conclusions. It does not make good sense to generalize from one or a few individuals to all men or all women. The conclusion is *hasty* because the information is not adequate enough to justify the generalization.

SWEEPING GENERALIZATION

Whereas the fallacy of hasty generalization deals with errors in the process of generalizing, the fallacy of *sweeping generalization* stems from difficulties in the process of interpreting. Consider the following examples of reasoning. Do you consider the arguments sound? Why or why not?

- Vigorous exercise contributes to overall good health. Therefore, vigorous exercise should be practiced by recent heart-attack victims, people who are out of shape, and women in the last month of pregnancy.
- People should be allowed to make their own decisions, providing that their actions do not harm other people. Therefore, people who are trying to commit suicide should be left alone to do as they please.

In both of these cases, generalizations that are true in most cases have been deliberately applied to examples that are clearly intended to be exceptions to the generalizations because of their special features. Of course, the use of a sweeping generalization motivates us to clarify the generalization, rephrasing it to exclude examples, like those given here, that have special features. For example, the first generalization could be reformulated as "Vigorous exercise contributes to the overall good health of most people *except* recent heart-attack victims, people who are out of shape, and women who are about to give birth." Sweeping generalizations become dangerous when they are accepted without critical analysis.

Examine the following examples of sweeping generalizations. In each case, (a) explain why it is a sweeping generalization, and (b) reformulate the statement to make it a legitimate generalization.

1. A college education stimulates you to develop as a person and prepares you for many professions. Therefore, all people should attend college, no matter what career interests them.

2. Drugs such as heroin and morphine are addictive and therefore qualify as dangerous drugs. This means that they should never be used, even as painkillers in medical situations.

3. Once criminals have served time for the crimes they have committed, they have paid their debt to society and should be permitted to work at any job they choose.

FALSE DILEMMA

The fallacy of the *false dilemma*—also known as the *either/or* fallacy and the *false dichotomy* fallacy—occurs when one is asked to choose between two extreme alternatives without being able to consider additional options. For example, we may say, "You're either for me or against me." Sometimes giving people only two choices on an issue makes sense ("If you decide to swim the English Channel, you'll either make it or you won't"). At other times, however, viewing a complicated situation in such extreme terms can result in a serious oversimplification.

The following statements are examples of false dilemmas. After analyzing the fallacy in each case, suggest different alternatives than those being presented.

Example: "Everyone in Germany is a National Socialist—the few outside the party are either lunatics or idiots." (Adolf Hitler, quoted by the *New York Times*, April 5, 1938)

Analysis: Hitler was saying that Germans who were not Nazis were lunatics or idiots. By limiting the classification of the population to these three categories, Hitler was simply ignoring all the people who did not qualify as Nazis, lunatics, or idiots.

1. "America—love it or leave it!"

2. "She loves me; she loves me not."

3. "Live free or die."

4. "If you're not part of the solution, you're part of the problem."

5. "If you know about a BMW, you either own one or you want to."

BEGGING THE QUESTION

This fallacious approach presents a circular argument that restates the claim in different words and so "begs off," or sidesteps, the important questions involved.

> *Example:* Tough antidrug laws reduce drug use by making usage a criminal act.
>
> *Analysis:* This begs the question of the effectiveness of prohibiting a substance and of punishment for its use.

RED HERRING

Here is another way of moving the discussion away from a basic issue. This colorful expression comes from an old practice of dragging a very dead fish on the ground in front of young hunting dogs to teach them to follow a scent.

> *Example:* Speculating about whether the governor will be re-elected as you analyze the environmental impact of a proposed new highway.
>
> *Analysis:* Who is governor may well affect legislation authorizing the highway, but this matter has little to do with analyzing environmental data.

FALLACIES OF RELEVANCE

Many fallacious arguments try to gain support by appealing to factors that have little or nothing to do with the arguments. In these cases, false appeals substitute for sound reasoning and a critical examination of the issues. Such appeals are known as fallacies of *relevance*.

Appeal to Authority   In Chapters 3 and 8, we explored the ways in which we sometimes use various authorities to establish our beliefs or to prove our points. At that time, we noted that to serve as a basis for beliefs, authorities must have legitimate expertise in the area in which they are advising—for example, an experienced mechanic could diagnose your car's problem. However, people occasionally appeal to authorities who are not qualified to give an expert opinion. Consider the reasoning in the following advertisements. Do you think the arguments are sound? Why or why not?

- Hi. You've probably seen me out on the football field. After a hard day's work crushing halfbacks and sacking quarterbacks, I like to settle down with a cold, smooth Maltz beer.

- SONY. Ask anyone.

- Over 11 million women will read this ad. Only 16 will own the coat.

Each of these arguments is intended to persuade us of the value of a product through the appeal to various authorities. In the first case, the authority is a well-known sports figure; in the second, the authority is large numbers of people; in the third, the authority is a select few, so the appeal is to our desire to be exclusive ("snob appeal"). Unfortunately, none of these authorities offers legitimate expertise about the product. Football players are not beer experts, large numbers of people are often misled, and exclusive groups of people are frequently mistaken in their beliefs. To evaluate authorities properly, we have to ask these questions:

What are the professional credentials on which the authorities' expertise is based?

Is their expertise in the area on which they are commenting?

Appeal to Pity   Consider the reasoning in the following arguments. Do you think the arguments are sound? Why or why not?

- I know that I haven't completed my term paper, but I really think that I should be excused. This has been a very difficult semester for me. I caught every kind of flu that came around. In addition, my brother has a drinking problem, and this has been very upsetting for me. Also, my dog died.
- I admit that my client embezzled money from the company, Your Honor. However, I would like to bring several facts to your attention. He is a family man with a wonderful wife and two terrific children. He is an important member of the community. He is active in his church, coaches a Little League baseball team, and has worked very hard to be a good person who cares about people. I think that you should take these things into consideration when handing down your sentence.

In each of these arguments, the reasons offered to support the conclusions may indeed be true, yet they are not relevant to the conclusion. Instead of providing evidence that supports the conclusion, the reasons are designed to make us feel sorry for the person involved and therefore to agree with the conclusion out of sympathy. Although these appeals can often be effective, the arguments are not sound. The validity of a conclusion can only be established by reasons that support and are relevant to the conclusion.

Appeal to Fear   Consider the reasoning in the following arguments. Do you consider the arguments sound? Why or why not?

- I don't think you deserve a raise. After all, there are many people who would be happy to have your job at the salary you are currently receiving. I would be happy to interview some of these people if you really think that you are underpaid.
- If you continue to disagree with my interpretation of *The Catcher in the Rye*, I'm afraid it may affect the grade on your paper.

In both of these arguments, the conclusions being suggested are supported by an appeal to fear, not by reasons that provide evidence for the conclusions. In the first case, the threat is that if you do not forgo your salary demands, your job may be in jeopardy. In the second case, the threat is that if you do not agree with the teacher's interpretation, you may receive a low grade. In neither instance are the real issues—Is a salary increase deserved? Is the student's interpretation legitimate?—being discussed. People who appeal to fear to support their conclusions are interested only in prevailing regardless of which position might be more justified.

Appeal to Ignorance   Consider the reasoning in the following arguments. Do you find the arguments sound? Why or why not?

- You say that you don't believe in God. But can you prove that an omnipotent spirit doesn't exist? If not, then you have to accept the conclusion that it does, in fact, exist.
- Greco Tires are the best. No others have been proved better.

When this argument form is used, the person offering the conclusion is asking his or her opponent to *disprove* the conclusion. If the opponent is unable to do so, the conclusion is asserted to be true. This argument form is not valid because it is the task of the person proposing the argument to prove the conclusion. The fact that an opponent cannot disprove it offers no evidence that the conclusion is justified.

Appeal to Personal Attack   Consider the reasoning in the following arguments. Do you think the arguments are valid? Why or why not?

- Senator Smith's opinion about a tax cut is wrong. It's impossible to believe anything he says since he left his wife for that model.
- How can you have an intelligent opinion about abortion? You're not a woman, so this is a decision that you'll never have to make.

This argument form has been one of the fallacies most frequently used through the ages. Its effectiveness results from ignoring the issues of the argument and focusing instead on the qualities of the person presenting it. Trying to discredit the other person is an effort to discredit the argument—no matter what reasons are offered. This fallacy is also referred to as the *ad hominem* argument (which means drawing attention "to the man" rather than to the issue) and as *poisoning the well* (since the speaker is trying to ensure that any water drawn from the opponent's well will be regarded as undrinkable).

The effort to discredit can take two forms, as illustrated in the preceding examples. The fallacy can be *abusive* by directly attacking the credibility of an opponent. In addition, the fallacy can be *circumstantial* by claiming that a person's circumstances, not character, render his or her opinion so biased or uninformed that it cannot be treated seriously. Another example of the circumstantial form would be disregarding the views on nuclear-plant safety that were presented by an owner of a nuclear plant.

Appeal to Popular Opinion or the Bandwagon   You are probably familiar with this "everybody else is doing it" appeal. Children use it while trying to convince parents to allow questionable activities and purchases. However, it is not absent from adult situations. Political and advertising campaigns often use the result of surveys to influence voters or consumers:

- Awww, Dad, I really need a new iPod. Everyone else in my class has one! Puuuhhhleeeeze . . .

- 58 percent of registered voters surveyed say that they will vote for Green Party nominee Edward Norton next week. Let's all get to the polls to send a message to the incumbents that we support Norton and his proposals for change!

- Well-dressed women will want pin-striped suits for fall!

This appeal can be effective because even thoughtful adults gravitate toward fashions in clothing and home furnishings, and voters want to support the policies and candidates with whom they agree. A certain amount of conformity is essential to a stable society, but clear thinkers are aware of the attraction of a "bandwagon" before they jump on.

Analyzing well-known arguments to see how they use deduction, induction, evidence *(logos), ethos, pathos,* and appeals—and perhaps fallacious reasoning—is a challenging activity and one that can help you with your own arguments. Read the Declaration of Independence and the Declaration of Sentiments and Resolutions, which follow, and Martin Luther King Jr.'s "I Have a Dream" speech (see pages 185–188 in Chapter 6). Then answer the questions that follow the readings.

Thinking-Writing Activity
ANALYZING FALLACIES

1. Find in advertisements, political statements, or other arguments that you have encountered examples of two or three false appeals. Write a brief explanation of why you think the appeal is not warranted. Look for the following fallacies:

   - Appeal to authority
   - Appeal to pity
   - Appeal to fear
   - Appeal to ignorance
   - Appeal to personal attack
   - Appeal to popular opinion

2. Share the fallacies you have found with classmates, and also examine the ones they have identified.

3. Write a few sentences explaining how you can avoid using fallacies in your own writing.

The Declaration of Independence

In Congress, July 4, 1776

The unanimous declaration of the thirteen United States of America.

When in the course of human events, it becomes necessary for one people to dissolve the political bands which have connected them with another, and to assume among the powers of the earth, the separate and equal station to which the Laws of Nature and of Nature's God entitle them, a decent respect to the opinions of mankind requires that they should declare the causes which impel them to the separation.

We hold these truths to be self-evident, that all men are created equal, that they are endowed by their Creator with certain unalienable rights, that among these are life, liberty and the pursuit of happiness. That to secure these rights, governments are instituted among men, deriving their just powers from the consent of the governed. That whenever any form of government becomes destructive of these ends, it is the right of the people to alter or to abolish it, and to institute new government, laying its foundation on such principles and organizing its powers in such form, as to them shall seem most likely to effect their safety and happiness. Prudence, indeed, will dictate that governments long established should not be changed for light and transient causes; and accordingly all experience hath shown, that mankind are more disposed to suffer, while evils are sufferable, than to right themselves by abolishing the forms to which they are accustomed. But when a long train of abuses and usurpations, pursuing invariably the same object evinces a design to reduce them under absolute despotism, it is their right, it is their duty, to throw off such government, and to provide new guards for their future security. Such has been the patient sufferance of these Colonies; and such is now the necessity which constrains them to alter their former systems of government. The history of the present King of Great Britain is a history of repeated injuries and usurpations, all having in direct object the establishment of an absolute tyranny over these States. To prove this, let facts be submitted to a candid world.

He has refused his assent to laws, the most wholesome and necessary for the public good.   5

He has forbidden his Governors to pass laws of immediate and pressing importance, unless suspended in their operation till his assent should be obtained; and when so suspended, he has utterly neglected to attend to them.

He has refused to pass other laws for the accommodation of large districts of people, unless those people would relinquish the right of representation in the Legislature, a right inestimable to them and formidable to tyrants only.

He has called together legislative bodies at places unusual, uncomfortable, and distant from the depository of their public records, for the sole purpose of fatiguing them into compliance with his measures.

He has dissolved representative houses repeatedly, for opposing with manly firmness his invasions on the rights of the people.

He has refused for a long time, after such dissolutions, to cause others to be elected; whereby the legislative powers, incapable of annihilation, have returned to the people at large for their exercise; the State remaining in the meantime exposed to all the dangers of invasion from without and convulsions within.

Source: "The Declaration of Independence" In Congress, July 4, 1776.

He has endeavoured to prevent the population of these States; for that purpose obstructing the laws of naturalization of foreigners; refusing to pass others to encourage their migration hither, and raising the conditions of new appropriations of lands.

10   He has obstructed the administration of justice, by refusing his assent to laws for establishing judiciary powers.

He has made judges dependent on his will alone, for the tenure of their offices, and the amount and payment of their salaries.

He has erected a multitude of new offices, and sent hither swarms of officers to harass our people, and eat out their substance.

He has kept among us, in times of peace, standing armies without the consent of our legislatures.

15   He has affected to render the military independent of and superior to the civil power.

He has combined with others to subject us to a jurisdiction foreign to our constitution, and unacknowledged by our laws; giving his assent to their acts of pretended legislation.

For quartering large bodies of armed troops among us.

For protecting them, by a mock trial, from punishment for any murders which they should commit on the inhabitants of these States.

For cutting off our trade with all parts of the world.

For imposing taxes on us without our consent.

20   For depriving us, in many cases, of the benefits of trial by jury.

For transporting us beyond seas to be tried for pretended offences.

For abolishing the free system of English laws in a neighbouring Province, establishing therein an arbitrary government, and enlarging its boundaries so as to render it at once an example and fit instrument for introducing the same absolute rule into these Colonies.

For taking away our Charters, abolishing our most valuable laws, and altering fundamentally the forms of our governments.

For suspending our own Legislatures, and declaring themselves invested with power to legislate for us in all cases whatsoever.

25   He has abdicated government here, by declaring us out of his protection and waging war against us.

He has plundered our seas, ravaged our coasts, burnt our towns, and destroyed the lives of our people.

He is at this time transporting large armies of foreign mercenaries to complete the works of death, desolation and tyranny, already begun with circumstances of cruelty and perfidy scarcely paralleled in the most barbarous ages, and totally unworthy the head of a civilized nation.

He has constrained our fellow citizens taken captive on the high seas to bear arms against their country, to become the executioners of their friends and brethren, or to fall themselves by their hands.

He has excited domestic insurrections amongst us, and has endeavoured to bring on the inhabitants of our frontiers, the merciless Indian savages, whose known rule of warfare, is an undistinguished destruction of all ages, sexes, and conditions.

30   In every stage of these oppressions we have petitioned for redress in the most humble terms: our repeated petitions have been answered only by repeated injury.

A prince whose character is thus marked by every act which may define a tyrant is unfit to be the ruler of a free people.

Nor have we been wanting in attention to our British brethren. We have warned them from time to time of attempts by their legislature to extend an unwarrantable jurisdiction over us. We have reminded them of the circumstances of our emigration and settlement here. We have appealed to their native justice and magnanimity, and we have conjured them by the ties of our common kindred to disavow these usurpations, which would inevitably interrupt our connections and correspondence. They too have been deaf to the voice of justice and of consanguinity. We must, therefore, acquiesce in the necessity, which denounces our separation, and hold them, as we hold the rest of mankind, enemies in war, in peace friends.

We, therefore, the Representatives of the United States of America, in General Congress assembled, appealing to the Supreme Judge of the world for the rectitude of our intentions, do, in the name, and by the authority of the good people of these Colonies, solemnly publish and declare, That these United Colonies are, and of right ought to be Free and Independent States; that they are absolved from all allegiance to the British Crown, and that all political connection between them and the State of Great Britain, is and ought to be totally dissolved; and that as Free and Independent States, they have full power to levy war, conclude peace, contract alliances, establish commerce, and to do all other acts and things which Independent States may of right do. And for the support of this declaration, with a firm reliance on the protection of Divine Providence, we mutually pledge to each other our lives, our fortunes, and our sacred honor.

Declaration of Sentiments and Resolutions
by Elizabeth Cady Stanton

A leading suffragist of the nineteenth century, Elizabeth Cady Stanton was born in Jamestown, New York. Her father was a judge, and while working as his assistant, Stanton became aware of the extent of male dominance in the eyes of the law. She married an abolitionist, in spite of her parents' concerns, and together they crusaded to change racial and gender inequities. She organized the first Women's Rights Convention in Seneca Falls, New York, in 1848. In 1851, she formed a working relationship with Susan B. Anthony that united them for the rest of their lives. Stanton ran for Congress in 1866 and cofounded *The Revolution*, a suffragist newspaper, in 1868. Today, she is revered by feminists as an early leader in the fight for equality.

When, in the course of human events, it becomes necessary for one person of the family of man to assume among the people of the earth a position different from that which they have hitherto occupied, but one to which the laws of nature and nature's God entitle them, a decent respect to the opinions of mankind requires that they should declare the causes that impel them to such a course.

We hold these truths to be self-evident: that all men and women are created equal; that they are endowed by their Creator with certain inalienable rights; that among these are life, liberty, and the pursuit of happiness; that to secure these rights governments are instituted, deriving their just powers from the consent of the governed. Whenever any form

Source: "Declaration of Sentiments and Resolutions" by Elizabeth Cady Stanton (1815–1902).

of government becomes destructive of these ends, it is the right of those who suffer from it to refuse allegiance to it, and to insist upon the institution of a new government, laying its foundation on such principles, and organizing its powers in such form, as to them shall seem most likely to effect their safety and happiness. Prudence, indeed, will dictate that governments long established should not be changed for light and transient causes; and accordingly all experience hath shown that mankind are more disposed to suffer, while evils are sufferable, than to right themselves by abolishing the forms to which they were accustomed. But when a long train of abuses and usurpations, pursuing invariably the same object evinces a design to reduce them under absolute despotism, it is their duty to throw off such government, and to provide new guards for their future security. Such has been the patient sufferance of the women under this government, and such is now the necessity which constrains them to demand the equal station to which they are entitled.

The history of mankind is a history of repeated injuries and usurpations on the part of man toward woman, having in direct object the establishment of an absolute tyranny over her. To prove this, let facts be submitted to a candid world.

He has never permitted her to exercise her inalienable right to the elective franchise.

5   He has compelled her to submit to laws, in the formation of which she had no voice.

He has withheld from her rights which are given to the most ignorant and degraded men—both natives and foreigners.

Having deprived her of this first right of a citizen, the elective franchise, thereby leaving her without representation in the halls of legislation, he has oppressed her on all sides.

He has made her, if married, in the eye of the law, civilly dead.

He has taken from her all right in property, even to the wages she earns.

10   He has made her, morally, an irresponsible being, as she can commit many crimes with impunity, provided they be done in the presence of her husband. In the covenant of marriage, she is compelled to promise obedience to her husband, he becoming, to all intents and purposes, her master—the law giving him power to deprive her of her liberty, and to administer chastisement.

He has so framed the laws of divorce, as to what shall be the proper causes, and in case of separation, to whom the guardianship of the children shall be given, as to be wholly regardless of the happiness of women—the law, in all cases, going upon a false supposition of the supremacy of man, and giving all power into his hands.

After depriving her of all rights as a married woman, if single, and the owner of property, he has taxed her to support a government which recognizes her only when her property can be made profitable to it.

He has monopolized nearly all the profitable employments, and from those she is permitted to follow, she receives but a scanty remuneration. He closes against her all the avenues to wealth and distinction which he considers most honorable to himself. As a teacher of theology, medicine, or law, she is not known.

He has denied her the facilities for obtaining a thorough education, all colleges being closed against her.

15   He allows her in Church, as well as State, but a subordinate position, claiming Apostolic authority for her exclusion from the ministry, and, with some exceptions, from any public participation in the affairs of the Church.

He has created a false public sentiment by giving to the world a different code of morals for men and women, by which moral delinquencies which exclude women from society are not only tolerated, but deemed of little account in man.

He has usurped the prerogative of Jehovah himself, claiming it as his right to assign for her a sphere of action, when that belongs to her conscience and to her God.

He has endeavored, in every way that he could, to destroy her confidence in her own powers, to lessen her self-respect, and to make her willing to lead a dependent and abject life.

Now, in view of this entire disfranchisement of one-half the people of this country, their social and religious degradation—in view of the unjust laws above mentioned, and because women do feel themselves aggrieved, oppressed, and fraudulently deprived of their most sacred rights, we insist that they have immediate admission to all the rights and privileges which belong to them as citizens of the United States.

In entering upon the great work before us, we anticipate no small amount of 20 misconception, misrepresentation, and ridicule; but we shall use every instrumentality within our power to effect our object. We shall employ agents, circulate tracts, petition the State and National legislatures, and endeavor to enlist the pulpit and the press in our behalf. We hope this Convention will be followed by a series of Conventions embracing every part of the country.

Resolutions

WHEREAS, The great precept of nature is conceded to be, that "man shall pursue his own true and substantial happiness." Blackstone in his Commentaries remarks that this law of Nature being coeval with mankind, and dictated by God himself, is of course superior in obligation to any other. It is binding over all the globe, in all countries and at all times; no human laws are of any validity if contrary to this, and such of them as are valid, derive all their force and all their validity, and all their authority, mediately and immediately, from this original; therefore,

Resolved, That such laws as conflict, in any way, with the true and substantial happiness of woman, are contrary to the great precept of nature and of no validity, for this is "superior in obligation to any other."

Resolved, That all laws which prevent woman from occupying such a station in society as her conscience shall dictate, or which place her in a position inferior to that of man, are contrary to the great precept of nature, and therefore of no force or authority.

Resolved, That woman is man's equal—was intended to be so by the Creator, and the highest good of the race demands that she should be recognized as such.

Resolved, That the women of this country ought to be enlightened in regard to 25 the laws under which they live, that they may no longer publish their degradation by declaring themselves satisfied with their present position, nor their ignorance, by asserting that they have all the rights they want.

Resolved, That inasmuch as man, while claiming for himself intellectual superiority, does accord to woman moral superiority for it is preeminently his duty to encourage her to speak and teach, as she has an opportunity, in all religious assemblies.

Resolved, That the same amount of virtue, delicacy, and refinement of behavior that is required of woman in the social state, should also be required of man, and the same transgressions should be visited with equal severity on both man and woman.

Resolved, That the objection of indelicacy and impropriety, which is so often brought against woman when she addresses a public audience, comes with a very ill-grace from those who encourage, by their attendance, her appearance on the stage, in the concert, or in feats of the circus.

Resolved, That woman has too long rested satisfied in the circumscribed limits which corrupt customs and a perverted application of the Scriptures have marked out for her, and that it is time she should move in the enlarged sphere which her great Creator has assigned her.

30   *Resolved,* That it is the duty of the women of this country to secure to themselves their sacred right to the elective franchise.

Resolved, That the equality of human rights results necessarily from the fact of the identity of the race in capabilities and responsibilities.

Resolved, therefore, That, being invested by the Creator with the same capabilities, and the same consciousness of responsibility for their exercise, it is demonstrably the right and duty of woman, equally with man, to promote every righteous cause by every righteous means; and especially in regard to the great subjects of morals and religion, it is self-evidently her right to participate with her brother in teaching them, both in private and in public, by writing and by speaking, by any instrumentalities proper to be used, and in any assemblies proper to be held; and this being a self-evident truth growing out of the divinely implanted principles of human nature, any custom or authority adverse to it, whether modern or wearing the hoary sanction of antiquity, is to be regarded as a self-evident falsehood, and at war with mankind.

[At the last session Lucretia Mott offered and spoke to the following resolution:]

Resolved, That the speedy success of our cause depends upon the zealous and untiring efforts of both men and women, for the overthrow of the monopoly of the pulpit, and for the securing to women an equal participation with men in the various trades, professions and commerce.

QUESTIONS FOR READING ACTIVELY

1. What is the thesis of each of these arguments? Where is it stated in each of these arguments?

2. How does the Declaration of Independence use deduction and induction? Identify the premises and the conclusion in the second paragraph. Comment on the effectiveness of this deliberate use of these basic reasoning methods.

3. How does the Declaration of Sentiments and Resolutions use induction to support the central claim? What are the effects of its parallels with the Declaration of Independence?

QUESTIONS FOR THINKING CRITICALLY

1. In your library or on the Internet, locate a copy of Martin Luther King Jr.'s "Letter from Birmingham Jail." What differences in approach do you see between it and "I Have a Dream" (pages 185–188)? What about the tone or *ethos?* Can you identify the warrants and qualifiers in King's arguments?

2. How would you define *liberty* and *the pursuit of happiness?* Is it possible, in your current circumstances, to achieve either liberty or happiness? To what extent is the state responsible for guaranteeing *liberty* and *the pursuit of happiness,* according to your definition of both terms?

QUESTION FOR WRITING THOUGHTFULLY

1. These political arguments address profound questions about human rights. What in these arguments could be applicable to arguments that you might write about academic or business issues? What might not be applicable? Explain in a short essay.

Deductive and Inductive Reasoning in Writing

As pointed out earlier in this chapter, writers and speakers seldom use deductive or inductive reasoning solely or purely. In their arguments, conclusions reached by induction become premises for deductions; statements that are premises are asserted but not demonstrated, as in the opening sentences of the Declaration of Independence. Deductively developed paragraphs interact with inductively developed ones, as in Gould's "Evolution as Fact and Theory" in Chapter 11.

However, deduction is used obviously when a definition or principle is established by the writer, and the point of the paper or paragraph is to claim that the subject being discussed fits the definition or demonstrates the principle. If the readers agree with the definition and also agree that the subject fits it, the claim is proved for whatever purpose the writer has. Political science, literature, philosophy, theology, psychology, and law are among the many fields that employ deductive arguments in this way.

Inductive reasoning is reflected in two ways in writing. One is structural. When a writer chooses to present instances of evidence first, leading readers to the claim presented as a conclusion, the paragraph or paper is organized inductively. Composition instructors tend to steer students away from using this technique to structure entire papers, since great skill is needed to keep readers with the argument. The "Organizing Ideas and Revising Your Essay" sections in the Writing Projects have asked you to think carefully about where you state your thesis or claim for this reason. It is usually more effective to use a deductively based structure.

A reflection of inductive reasoning that is often used in writing occurs when the writer makes a claim in a topic sentence or thesis statement and then simply exemplifies it. The writer is asking the readers to reenact the inductive process that led him or her to make the claim. Notice how the list of evils alleged to have been committed by the British government functions this way in the Declaration of Independence. Notice how regularly you use this technique, and how often much of what you read uses it, too.

In addition, deduction often appears in the abbreviated form of the enthymeme (see page 505), and induction is commonly presented through the small sample of the example, the inference, and the anecdote. These practices are neither wrong nor fallacious. Writers cannot take the time or space to state all the premises of every deduction or to give multiple instances to support each idea. However, critical thinkers need to understand these reductions so that claims and evidence can be evaluated. Deduction and induction, the basic reasoning methods, are at work in various ways in what we write and read.

Writing Project

ARGUING A POSITION ON A SIGNIFICANT ISSUE

This chapter has emphasized the importance of the basic concepts and terminology connected with argument because reasoned argument leading to mutual
understanding, consensus, or agreement is the foundation of a democratic
society and also is often the key to success in personal, academic, and business
activities.

Because so much college and professional writing is argumentative, this Writing
Project asks you to concentrate on the two central elements of argument: establishing a clear thesis and providing sound evidence for it. In addition, you should be
particularly careful to be logical, to avoid fallacious statements, to consider your
audience, and to present yourself as a reasonable, well-informed proponent of your
claims.

Project Overview and Requirements

Write an essay in which you argue logically for a position on an issue
that you consider significant (see Generating Ideas on page 527 to get
started).

Use print sources, electronic sources, and—if possible—an interview
with an informed individual to support your claims.

Follow your instructor's directions regarding the number and range
of sources, length of the paper, and academic format for citation of
sources. The citation format could follow, for example, MLA or APA.
Consult Chapter 14 and the appendix in this book for additional help with
citations.

On a page separate from your paper, identify the audience to whom
you are addressing your argument, and explain why members will
benefit from understanding your position. Also, explain why this issue is
important to you so that your classmates and instructor, as they help you
revise your drafts, can be aware of the nature of your expertise and any
possible biases.

Before you begin this Writing Project, it is important to consider the writing
situation and writing purpose, as well as the "Principles for Writing Responsible
Arguments," detailed on the following pages. Also, this chapter has included both
readings and Thinking-Writing Activities that encourage you to think about argument. Be sure to reread what you wrote for those activities; you may be able to use
some of the material for this Writing Project.

Begin by considering the key elements in the Thinking-Writing Model in Chapter 1 on pages 5–8.

THE WRITING SITUATION

Purpose   Your primary purpose is to write an argument that will persuade your intended audience to agree with your claim or thesis. As you work toward that goal, you will have to think critically about a subject that you care about and clarify or modify your view of it, which is another useful purpose.

Audience   The audience is a major concern in any argument. A successful writer understands the characteristics and attitudes of his or her audience. When you develop an argument, you must have a specific audience in mind. Pandering to the audience by distorting evidence or using flattery is bad rhetoric, but a writer should consider the needs of the audience. Factors to consider include the following:

- *Knowledge* (an expert audience needs less background than a general or novice audience)
- *Age* (younger and older people often have different points of view)
- *Roles* (people have various roles and respond differently as roles change)
- *Relationships* (an audience of peers can be approached differently than an audience of strangers)
- *Emotional levels* (a highly charged situation should be approached differently than a calm one)

Subject   Whenever you argue for a position about which you are concerned, you are addressing an important subject. In addition, the techniques of argument themselves constitute a subject that merits much attention because argument has such importance in people's lives.

Writer   If you have been using sources for other projects, you should be comfortable incorporating other people's ideas into your writing and documenting them appropriately. A new role for you may be that of the good rhetorician, the responsible arguer; if you use your developing critical thinking abilities, you will manage that role well.

Now that you have spent time focusing on purpose, audience, subject, and writer, work through the following questions to help you write a responsible argument. You may also want to look ahead to "Principles for Writing Responsible Arguments" on page 528 and review your responses to the Thinking-Writing Activities earlier in this chapter. Formulating ideas now will help you with the writing process itself.

1. Briefly describe the argument you would like to present. Include the topic and the side you plan to argue. For example, one student wrote:

   My youngest sister was recently diagnosed as bipolar, so I am interested in exploring different types of treatments. There are many bipolar children being treated with drugs such as Lithium, Depakote, Effexor, and Seroquel, but I have serious concerns about these drugs—especially since the FDA warns about putting children on antidepressants. I would like to argue that other treatments, such as Light Therapy and Electroconvulsive Therapy (ECT), should be tried first.

2. Discuss who might benefit from the argument you present in your essay and how you plan to address their possible concerns and rebuttals. How do you plan to establish *ethos* (the impression your audience will have of you) and *pathos* (the effect your argument will have on your audience)? For example:

> My specific audience will be my family. Once my sister was diagnosed with bipolar disorder, my family has been working with a doctor to figure out a way to treat, or at least manage, the disorder. Unfortunately, the doctor is trying to convince my parents that drugs are the best option. I plan to show that drugs can (and do) work for many children; however, there are inherent dangers. I plan to discuss a few cases where the results of taking the drugs have led to more problems and even suicide. I also plan to show the benefits of Light Therapy and ECT—possibly even Talk Therapy—and how trying these therapies first is a more prudent decision. My plan is to present enough information so that the answer is clear to my parents (without offending them or making them feel defensive). I also feel my paper can help others outside my family.

3. How do you plan to approach the argument overall, and, more specifically, how do you plan to incorporate alternative points of view? Also, since arguments often depend on definitions, discuss what definitions you may need to provide. For example:

> I plan to describe what, exactly, bipolar disorder is in the beginning of the paper to give my audience a solid foundation before launching into possible treatments (a comparison) and an argument for trying alternative treatments before drugs. I will need to define these treatments and the drugs, including the benefits and the possible side effects of all of them. I want to be sure everything an audience needs to know is included in the paper. That said, I'll need to be sure I anticipate any questions people might have.

4. Finally, you have likely been incorporating research into your past projects and should feel fairly comfortable using the work of others to support your ideas. For this project, what are your ultimate goals as a responsible arguer? For example:

> I am very worried that my sister will not respond well to the drugs the doctor wants to prescribe and feel that we owe it to her to try less dangerous alternatives first. I have to fully educate myself on the different drugs and therapies available, and then carefully present what I have learned in a logical, convincing way. I will need to analyze the research of others, and then present those findings in a way that my family will comprehend. This will be a challenging paper for me, but my sister is only 12 years old. Ultimately, I want her to live a full and happy life.

THE WRITING PROCESS

The following sections will guide you through the stages of generating, planning, drafting, and revising as you develop the argument in your persuasive essay.

Generating Ideas

- You may be involved with an issue because of your sex, ethnicity, or field of study or through some organization in which you participate. Or you may be concerned about a problem at your college, in your community, in your country, or elsewhere in the world. If so, you should have no problem deciding what to write about.

- If no issue comes quickly to mind, look around your campus and community to see what problems exist or what changes could be made.

- Be attentive to various print, broadcast, and online news outlets. Talk with friends, family members, and professors about significant issues.

- Think about questions in your areas of interest: your favorite college subjects, sports, entertainment, food, cars, the environment, architecture. Some of these questions may pertain to serious issues; some might be more lighthearted; many will merit a reasoned argument.

- Freewrite about one or two of your concerns. See how many issues or positions you can come up with in five minutes.

 Defining a Focus   After selecting an issue to write about, draft a thesis statement that describes the position you will argue. Remember that the issue (or topic) is *what you are going to write about*, while a thesis statement is *what you are going to say about it* (see pages 96–97, Moving from Topic to Thesis). Be sure your thesis statement gives your audience a clear indication of the focus and purpose of your essay. Note that it may be a complex sentence: for example, "Using table salt alternatives and countering the effects of a high sodium diet by eating foods rich in potassium will save lives and lower health care costs nationally; however, we also need to convince food manufacturing companies to reduce the amounts of salt in their products if Americans are to lead healthier lives."

Organizing Ideas   Your argument could be set up using this traditional structure:

> Introduction
>
> Thesis
>
> Evidence
>
> Handling of other views
>
> Summing up
>
> Conclusion/recommendation for action

You may notice, however, that your material adapts itself to various thinking patterns, so you could use another arrangement effectively.

Select your supporting source materials carefully, and integrate them into your writing by using smooth transitions. Whether you directly quote someone or paraphrase, make certain you use citations to give your sources credit and avoid plagiarism.

Drafting   Start composing your draft with the easiest part to write; this might be the beginning, since you have already been thinking about your thesis and its context, but you are free to start anywhere. You might want to draft the paragraphs that present your evidence, for example, and then consider what inductive or deductive methods you should use.

It can help to revise one version of your draft, while retaining a copy of the original in case your changes are not satisfactory. You will always have a copy to go back to if necessary.

Whether you use direct quotations, paraphrased passages, or a combination of the two, be sure to keep track of publication information for all sources such as titles, authors, and pages in your draft. Then, when you revise, you can cite the sources in the required format.

Principles for Writing Responsible Arguments

The following principles for writing responsible arguments are fundamental to the Western tradition of logical, structured argument. Always be sure to follow them as well as you can.

Principles for Writing Responsible Arguments

1. Formulate and qualify the thesis statement carefully. Place it purposefully. Use deductive and inductive approaches as appropriate to develop and support the thesis.

2. Provide a context for the thesis; give reasons for its importance. These might be warrants.

3. Present sound evidence, or grounds, clearly and specifically.

4. Acknowledge and demonstrate understanding of other points of view. Grant validity to any point when it is justified. To strengthen your argument, courteously refute points with which you disagree.

5. Use the thinking/organizing patterns in Part Two (Thinking and Writing to Shape Our World, beginning on page 205). Arguments often rely on definitions. The causes of a situation and the effects of a proposal are often vital to an argument. Narratives and chronologies are often effective. Contrasts, comparisons, and analogies illuminate your points.

6. Don't use fallacious reasoning.

7. Be aware of your tone. You want to sound reasonable, thoughtful, and polite as you argue your points.

8. Remember that the conclusion to an argument is extremely important. Restate the thesis or claim with a suggestion, a call for action, a decision, or further thought.

Revising Your Essay: Arguing a Position on a Significant Issue

Before you complete your draft, carefully consider the following questions:

- Is my claim clearly stated and adequately qualified?
- Do I provide adequate (and reliable) evidence to support the validity of my claim?
- Have I correctly cited and documented the sources of that evidence?
- Are any of my statements fallacious? Have I double-checked my argument for fallacies?
- Should I clearly state the warrants for my argument, or should I leave them unstated?
- Have I appropriately established my *ethos* (the impression my audience will have of me) and *pathos* (the effect my argument will have on my audience)?
- Have I considered, and included, other points of view? Does my argument clearly prove why my claims are more logical, sensible, useful, or appealing than the opposition's viewpoints?

Peer Response

After you have completed your draft, exchange essays with someone from your class. Keep in mind that the goal of a peer review, or critique, is to help make the writing stronger. In this case, you want to be sure the argument and supporting research are sound and that the essay comes to a natural, logical conclusion. Ask yourself the following questions as you review your peer's work:

1. Is the argument apparent within the first few paragraphs, and is the thesis statement clear? If not, offer specific suggestions.

2. Who is the intended audience for this essay? Do you feel the essay takes that audience into consideration by providing enough background information without sounding patronizing? Comment on specific passages.

3. Can you find evidence of logical fallacies in the essay? Explain how they might affect the effectiveness of the argument.

4. Finally, do you feel convinced? Point out passages where more (or different) information might help convince you.

Revising, Editing, and Proofreading

After you have received the comments your classmate made on your draft during the peer review process, you can make necessary changes to strengthen the content of your essay.

Next, take the time to review "A Step-by-Step Method for Revising Any Assignment" on the inside front cover of the book. This checklist will help you revise your essay and polish your final draft.

STUDENT WRITING

Will Portman's Writing Process

Will Portman wrote a column in his college newspaper about coming "out of the closet" to his family by sending them a personal letter. His family called him right away and was accepting and supportive. In fact, Portman felt it was a turning point in his life in that he no longer had to feel ashamed of who he is. Two years later, when presidential candidate Mitt Romney was considering Will's father, Republican Senator Rob Portman, as a running mate in the 2012 election, the senator announced that, although he once opposed it, he now supported same-sex marriage.

In his column, Will presents his story—one that contains a multifaceted argument. One of Portman's goals is to empower those who are "closeted" and afraid to come out through his experience. He also believes everyone should have the right to marry the one he or she loves and, ultimately, that people should be more compassionate and accepting of one another's perspectives.

PORTMAN: Coming out

by Will Portman

I came to Yale as a freshman in the fall of 2010 with two big uncertainties hanging over my head: whether my dad would get elected to the Senate in November, and whether I'd ever work up the courage to come out of the closet.

Source: http://yaledailynews.com/blog/2013/03/25/portman-coming-out/

I made some good friends that first semester, took a couple of interesting classes and got involved in a few rewarding activities. My dad won his election. On the surface, things looked like they were going well. But the truth was, I wasn't happy.

I'd make stuff up when my suitemates and I would talk about our personal lives. I remember going to a dance in the Trumbull dining hall with a girl in my class and feeling guilty about pretending to be somebody I wasn't. One night, I snuck up to the stacks in Sterling Library and did some research on coming out. The thought of telling people I was gay was pretty terrifying, but I was beginning to realize that coming out, however difficult it seemed, was a lot better than the alternative: staying in, all alone.

I worried about how my friends back home would react when I told them I was gay. Would they stop hanging out with me? Would they tell me they were supportive, but then slowly distance themselves? And what about my friends at Yale, the "Gay Ivy"? Would they criticize me for not having come out earlier? Would they be able to understand my anxiety about all of this? I felt like I didn't quite fit in with Yale or Cincinnati, or with gay or straight culture.

In February of freshman year, I decided to write a letter to my parents. I'd tried to come out to them in person over winter break but hadn't been able to. So I found a cubicle in Bass Library one day and went to work. Once I had something I was satisfied with, I overnighted it to my parents and awaited a response.

They called as soon as they got the letter. They were surprised to learn I was gay, and full of questions, but absolutely rock-solid supportive. That was the beginning of the end of feeling ashamed about who I was.

I still had a ways to go, though. By the end of freshman year, I'd only come out to my parents, my brother and sister, and two friends. One day that summer, my best friend from high school and I were hanging out.

"There's something I need to tell you," I finally said. "I'm gay." He paused for a second, looked down at the ground, looked back up, and said, "Me too."

I was surprised. At first it was funny, and we made jokes about our lack of gaydar. Then it was kind of sad to realize that we'd been going through the same thing all along but hadn't felt safe enough to confide in each other. But then, it was pretty cool—we probably understood each other's situation at that moment better than anybody else could.

In the weeks that followed, I got serious about coming out. I made a list of my family and friends and went through the names, checking them off one by one as I systematically filled people in on who I really was. A phone call here, a Skype call there, a couple of meals at Skyline Chili, my favorite Cincinnati restaurant. I was fortunate that virtually everyone, both from Yale and from home, was supportive

Portman builds up to the reason he decided to come out in his introduction by providing carefully chosen personal details.

Here, Portman analyzes his decision and possible outcomes as a result of that decision.

This is a major turning point for Portman, though he realizes there are further challenges ahead. By revealing his fears in the first part of his essay, he helps facilitate understanding on behalf of his audience.

and encouraging, calming my fears about how they'd react to my news. If anything, coming out seemed to strengthen my friendships and family relationships.

I started talking to my dad more about being gay. Through the process of my coming out, we'd had a tacit understanding that he was my dad first and my senator a distant second. Eventually, though, we began talking about the policy issues surrounding marriage for same-sex couples.

The following summer, the summer of 2012, my dad was under consideration to be Gov. Romney's running mate. The rest of my family and I had given him the go-ahead to enter the vetting process. My dad told the Romney campaign that I was gay, that he and my mom were supportive and proud of their son, and that we'd be open about it on the campaign trail.

When he ultimately wasn't chosen for the ticket, I was pretty relieved to have avoided the spotlight of a presidential campaign. Some people have criticized my dad for waiting for two years after I came out to him before he endorsed marriage for gay couples. Part of the reason for that is that it took time for him to think through the issue more deeply after the impetus of my coming out. But another factor was my reluctance to make my personal life public.

We had decided that my dad would talk about having a gay son if he were to change his position on marriage equality. It would be the only honest way to explain his change of heart. Besides, the fact that I was gay would probably become public anyway. I had encouraged my dad all along to change his position, but it gave me pause to think that the one thing that nobody had known about me for so many years would suddenly become the one thing that everybody knew about me.

It has been strange to have my personal life in the headlines. I could certainly do without having my sexual orientation announced on the evening news, or commentators weighing in to tell me things like living my life honestly and fully is "harmful to [me] and society as a whole." But in many ways it's been a privilege to come out so publicly. Now, my friends at Yale and the folks in my dad's political orbit in Ohio are all on the same page. They know two things about me that I'm very proud of, not just one or the other: that I'm gay, and that I'm Rob and Jane Portman's son.

I'm grateful to be able to continue to integrate my two worlds, the yin and yang of Yale and Ohio and the different values and experiences they represent in my life. When you find yourself between two worlds—for example, if you're navigating the transition between a straight culture and a gay identity—it's possible to feel isolated and alone, like you don't fit in with either group that makes up a part of who you are.

Portman introduces his argument that same-sex couples should be allowed to marry. The details he includes throughout the essay help to clarify issues in addition to developing mutual understanding.

Portman weighs the personal pros and cons of coming out.

But instead of feeling like you don't belong anywhere, or like you have to reject one group in order to join another, you can build a bridge between your two worlds, and work to facilitate greater understanding between them.

I support marriage for same-sex couples because I believe that everybody should be treated the same way and have the same shot at happiness. Over the course of our country's history the full rights of citizenship have gradually been extended to a broader and broader group of people, something that's made our society stronger, not weaker. Gay rights may be the civil rights cause of the moment, but the movement fits into a larger historical narrative.

I'm proud of my dad, not necessarily because of where he is now on marriage equality (although I'm pretty psyched about that), but because he's been thoughtful and open-minded in how he's approached the issue, and because he's shown that he's willing to take a political risk in order to take a principled stand. He was a good man before he changed his position, and he's a good man now, just as there are good people on either side of this issue today.

We're all the products of our backgrounds and environments, and the issue of marriage for same-sex couples is a complicated nexus of love, identity, politics, ideology and religious beliefs. We should think twice before using terms like "bigoted" to describe the position of those opposed to same-sex marriage or "immoral" to describe the position of those in favor, and always strive to cultivate humility in ourselves as we listen to others' perspectives and share our own.

I hope that my dad's announcement and our family's story will have a positive impact on anyone who is closeted and afraid, and questioning whether there's something wrong with them. I've been there. If you're there now, please know that things really do get better, and they will for you too.

Note how Portman reiterates his argument supporting same-sex marriage.

In closing, Portman appeals to his audience by first admitting the complexity of the issue. He then resolves that people should have the right to marry the ones they love. Ultimately, he maintains, everyone should be more compassionate and accepting of one another's perspectives. Finally, Portman encourages his audience— particularly those who are "closeted"—to overcome their fear.

REFLECTION ON WRITING

1. Earlier in this chapter, you learned about taking an organized approach to decision making. Identify the organized approach Portman used in his essay. For example, where did he clearly define the decision he had to make? What were his possible choices? How did he evaluate the pros and cons? Which choice best suited him? What was his plan of action, and did he monitor the results?

2. Portman struggled with his personal decision to come out and in paragraph 3 writes: "The thought of telling people I was gay was pretty terrifying," but it "was a lot better than the alternative: staying in, all alone." Many people experience similar personal dilemmas. Describe an experience

when you (or someone close to you) finally made a decision because the alternative (not deciding or ignoring the situation) was too hard to bear?

3. Is this particular "coming out" story more notable than other "coming out" stories? What if politics and a high-profile senator were not part of the equation? What parts of Portman's personal story affected you? Consider the language he uses, as well as personal anecdotes, and describe your reaction to several passages. You may also want to consider the duality of this essay in that the author came out, and his father did, too (to the Republican Party).

ALTERNATIVE WRITING PROJECT: THE PURSUIT OF HAPPINESS

Early women's rights activists, including Elizabeth Cady Stanton, modeled much of their rhetoric, style, and evidence for their Declaration of Sentiments and Resolutions on the original American Declaration of Independence. Both documents assert—or warrant—that the "pursuit of happiness" is an "unalienable right." In a well-argued essay, define the concept of *happiness* as it relates to a specific aspect of your academic or professional life. Are you currently in that state of happiness, and, if so, argue for its adoption by other students or others in your career field. Is there something or someone impeding your "unalienable right" to this specific kind of happiness? Argue, perhaps by drawing up a list of injustices as the framers of the Declaration of Independence did against King George, that this obstacle to your specific pursuit of happiness is unfair and unjust. Your final argument may draw upon the many rhetorical strategies and specific appeals to audience that appear in both of these Declarations.

CHAPTER 13 | Summary

- The classical concepts of argument include *ethos,* the character of the speaker or writer; *pathos,* the effect on the audience; and *logos,* the logic and substance of an argument.
- In this chapter, *rhetoric* should be understood to mean the use of the best means of persuasion.
- Concepts important to the Toulmin method of argument are *claim* and *qualified claim, grounds, warrants,* and *backings.*
- When arguing, you should consider other points of view and strive to reach mutual understanding and, if possible, consensus or agreement.

- When considering your audience, you should be careful not to cross over the line into pandering.
- *Inferring* is a thinking process used to reason from what one already knows or believes to acquire new knowledge or beliefs.
- You can work toward agreement when you construct arguments to decide, explain, predict, or persuade.
- When an argument includes both *true* reasons and *valid* structure, the argument is considered *sound*.
- In a *deductive argument,* one reasons from premises that are known or assumed to be true to a conclusion that necessarily follows from these premises.
- A *syllogism* is an argument form that consists of two supporting premises and a conclusion; an *enthymeme* assumes the first premise.
- Types of syllogisms or enthymemes include affirming the antecedent, denying the consequent, and disjunctive syllogism.
- In an *inductive argument,* one reasons from premises or instances that are known or assumed to be true to a conclusion that is supported by the premises but does not necessarily follow from them.
- Causal reasoning is central to the scientific method used in the natural and social sciences.
- *Empirical generalization* is a form of inductive reasoning, which is defined as "reasoning by examining a limited sample to reach a general conclusion based on that sample."
- To evaluate inductive reasoning, you must determine if the sample is known, sufficient, and representative.
- Types of false reasoning, or fallacies, include hasty generalization, sweeping generalization, false dilemma, begging the question, red herring, and fallacies of relevance.
- Fallacies of relevance include appeals to authority, pity, fear, ignorance, personal attack, and popular opinion (or bandwagon).

All research begins with inquiry, whether it is a question that demands an answer, or it comes from a desire to know more about a particular subject or issue. Sometimes, curiosity requires courage—especially when the research question might lead to difficult, challenging, or even dangerous inquiry. In your experience, how does research writing differ from other types of writing?

Writing About Investigations:
Thinking About Research

"If we would have new knowledge, we must get a whole world of new questions."

—SUSANNE K. LANGER

CRITICAL
THINKING FOCUS:
Deciding what
information to
look for, what
to use, and how
to present it

WRITING FOCUS:
Completing a
research paper

WRITING
ACTIVITIES:
Developing
questions,
finding and
evaluating
research,
taking notes,
plagiarism,
and citations

WRITING PROJECT:
A research
project

Rewards of Research

When you work on your college research projects, you are participating in one of humanity's oldest and most productive efforts. You can easily come up with an endless list of scientific, technical, historical, and social investigations that have made our lives richer and safer. Conducting good research can also be rewarding for you. It can contribute to your success in college and, often, to your progress in a career. As you continue your studies, you will do several kinds of research, including retrieving and understanding what others have discovered, synthesizing and connecting others' discoveries, connecting others' discoveries with your own ideas, and formulating new concepts and theories yourself. Each of these activities is rewarding in itself, and each is also an important component in research as an extensive human activity.

Critical thinking and creative thinking are parts of all aspects of research. The concepts discussed in every chapter of this book also pertain to research. As people seek information, they constantly deal with *perceptions, beliefs, perspectives, processes, causes, comparisons, contrasts, analogies, definitions,* and *arguments.* Research often involves *making decisions* and *solving problems.* Researchers present *reports, inferences,* and *judgments.*

In addition, like writing, research is often a recursive process rather than a linear one. One source will lead to another, new questions will arise, a creative insight will illuminate a topic, or a critical analysis will change the direction of a project.

This chapter introduces and explains strategies for using researched information in academic papers. An appendix to this book provides guidelines for using the Modern Language Association (MLA) documentation style and the American Psychological Association (APA) documentation style. Your instructor and your campus or local librarians can provide you with additional information.

Starting with Questions

Researchers begin with a question. Researchers are in pursuit of answers. Student researchers are often assigned a topic by their instructors, and asking questions about it is usually an effective approach because questions can help a researcher find a focus and can stimulate inquiry. Questions can help in various ways.

QUESTIONS THAT IDENTIFY YOUR TOPIC

If you are choosing your own topic, ask yourself these questions:

- What interests me most within the guidelines for this project?
- What within the guidelines pertains to my college major or my future career?
- What affects my life or the lives of people close to me?
- What affects my community?
- What topics can I find material about in my college library and on the Internet?

Thinking-Writing Activity

DEVELOPING RESEARCH QUESTIONS

1. Identify a field of study that interests you. Then write two or three questions about specific issues in that field.

2. If you can, show your questions to a professor or graduate student in the field. Ask her or him if these questions have been answered or if researchers are still working on them.

3. Share your questions with classmates. See if they have additional questions that pertain to this field of study.

QUESTIONS THAT FOCUS YOUR TOPIC

After you have selected a broad topic, or if your instructor has assigned a topic, you can use questions to focus it into a manageable and interesting topic. (Notice how many of these questions use the thinking patterns discussed in previous chapters of this book.)

- What are the issues involved in a topic? How are they defined? (Chapter 8)
- What are some different perspectives on the issues? (Chapter 9)
- Who is the audience for my research?
- What did people believe about my topic in previous historical periods? (Chapter 11)
- How have theories about it changed? (Chapter 11)

- What caused it? (Chapter 10)
- What problems are connected with it? How might they be solved? (Chapter 12)
- What is my purpose for conducting this research?
- What are future concerns about it likely to be?

The specific question that you want to investigate can be called a *research question*.

Thinking-Writing Activity

IDENTIFYING RESEARCH QUESTIONS

1. In your own words, write the research question(s) that might have inspired some of the student or professional writers included in this book.
2. What strategies did these writers use to develop their research questions?

Searching for Information

FINDING ELECTRONIC AND PRINT SOURCES IN THE LIBRARY

You are probably accustomed to using an online search engine to connect you with all kinds of information. However, you should use the resources of your college's computer center or library to help you learn the best ways to use these resources. Most college libraries provide guides to their resources. Some instructors or departments require completion of a workbook or physical or online attendance at library orientation sessions. You should take every opportunity to improve your ability to use your college library and the Internet.

Your library uses computers in at least four ways to direct you to source material:

1. The library's holdings are *cataloged* via a computer program, so the best way for you to find books, articles, videos, and DVDs is to learn to use the terminals in your library.
2. Most college libraries subscribe to *databases* such as Expanded Academic ASAP and National Newspapers that contain whole texts of articles from newspapers, magazines, and specialized journals, so a good way for you to find solid information is to learn to use whatever service your library has. The library provides databases that cannot be accessed on most home computers.
3. Your library probably offers online access to collections containing encyclopedias, books, poems, and visuals.
4. Computer terminals available to library patrons allow you to access the Internet and use various search engines to find an infinite variety of material.

Thinking-Writing Activity

LEARNING ABOUT YOUR LIBRARY

1. Go to your college or community library. Find out how to access its holdings, and learn what Internet services it provides.

2. Write a paragraph explaining what your library can do for you and how to use its computers. Also, explain how you would go about obtaining print sources.

PRIMARY AND SECONDARY SOURCES

Researchers find valuable information in both *primary* and *secondary* sources. Primary sources include original documents such as letters, texts of speeches, and governmental resolutions; works of literature such as novels, stories, poems, plays, and autobiographies; and firsthand reports of experiments, observations, and interviews by the persons who conducted them. Secondary sources comment on other sources. Examples are literary criticism, biographies, studies of historical events, and any synthesis or analysis of other sources.

You should use primary sources as much as possible and try to compare secondary sources with the primary sources on which they comment to be sure that interpretations seem valid.

COLLECTING INFORMATION FROM EXPERTS AND FROM THE FIELD

In addition to obtaining material from print and electronic sources, you can get information from people who have expertise on your subject. Also, you can go to places or events that are important to your research questions and conduct field research, where you observe and carefully document what goes on. The tools researchers use to collect information, or data, are sometimes referred to as *instruments*.

Interviews   Conducting an interview can be a valuable way to obtain information. Your creativity and critical abilities will be well used in an interview. Here are some guidelines for interviewing:

1. Identify the person with whom you wish to talk and then make an appointment with that person.

2. Carefully develop—and write out—the questions you will ask. You might want to email them to the interviewee ahead of time so that he or she will be able to prepare thorough responses.

3. Be careful as you record the interview. If you want to tape the interview, you must ask permission. If you are writing down the responses or keying them into a laptop computer, you must be sure to be accurate.

4. Do not take up too much of your interviewee's time, and—of course—give appropriate thanks.

5. Use and cite the material from an interview as you would any other source (see the MLA appendix, pages 593–594, for guidelines). It should be effectively integrated into your paper where it works best to develop the points that you are making.

6. If you can, give your interviewee a draft of your paper to show how you have presented the material, and be willing to heed suggestions if any are offered.

7. Provide the person interviewed with a copy of the completed paper, and thank him or her again.

Questionnaires   Using questionnaires is another way to obtain information from people, but they are difficult to design well. If you want to gather information with a questionnaire, you should review the material on inductive reasoning and empirical generalization in Chapter 13 on pages 508–510. As a beginning researcher, you should ask only a few questions, perhaps no more than three or four.

Also, think about these concerns:

1. What exactly is the issue about which you want people's opinions? Define it very clearly.

2. How can you state questions to obtain unambiguous information? Sometimes "yes-no" or "two-way" questions are best, since they elicit specific responses. However, sometimes yes-no questions are frustrating because people do not want to respond in such a limited way.

3. If you do not ask yes-no questions, how can you obtain possible responses in a small number of consistent categories that pertain to the information you want? Do you want choices? Do you want to construct a scale?

4. Can the responses be easily tabulated?

5. How many people can you poll in the time that you have and with the methods that you want to use? Will that group provide a representative sample appropriate for the scope of your project?

6. How will you use the results? How can you report them accurately, clearly identifying the characteristics and numbers of those who responded?

7. How can you use caution when drawing conclusions?

Questionnaires can be administered in several ways: by face-to-face polling; by mailing forms with a stamped, addressed return envelope; or by email. Practically speaking, a first attempt should focus on a small group—for example, asking the people on your block about a community issue or asking the students in one of your classes about a campus or political issue.

 If you know someone experienced in questionnaire use—such as a social science professor, a public health researcher, or a journalism major—you might ask that person to help you craft your instrument. Also, test your questions on a few close friends or family members to see what kinds of answers you get. Then, after revising any questions that need adjusting, pose them to your selected group.

Field Research   Observations provide firsthand data and are often used in art history, sociology, education, environmental studies, medicine, and other branches of science. If you want to conduct field research, you should review Chapter 7 to remind yourself about factors that might affect your perceptions and Chapter 9 to recall different perspectives that you might take as an observer, either consciously or unconsciously. You should consider the following principles when you conduct an observation:

1. Identify a place, situation, or object that pertains to your research question.

2. Ask permission from an appropriate person if the site is reserved for use by a specific group such as a class, a club, or a religious assembly.

3. Select a good time to go to your observation site.

4. Do not become involved in any of the activities that you have come to observe.

5. Be as unobtrusive as possible. The presence of an observer often alters the dynamics of a situation.

6. If you are observing an object such as a painting, statue, building, or element of nature, try to study it at different times of day or under varying circumstances. In your write-up, accurately report the circumstances under which you made your observations.

7. Note your observations carefully.

8. Present your observations as objectively as possible. State any inferences and judgments carefully and separate them from your reporting of information obtained through your senses.

Thinking-Writing Activity

INTERVIEWS, QUESTIONNAIRES, AND OBSERVATIONS

1. Interview one of your instructors about using firsthand (or "primary") sources of information. Ask him or her about how observations, questionnaires, and interviews are used in his or her field. Ask how these instruments should be designed and what pitfalls to avoid.

2. Write a paragraph or two about what you have learned from the interview.

Using Information

Finding material is relatively easy. Dealing with it is the challenging part. You must evaluate the information that you have found, which involves active and critical reading. You must use critical thinking to select what you will use and then save, copy, or take notes from it carefully. Writing your paper involves all the interrelated elements of the Thinking-Writing Model. In addition, you must integrate and cite source material in a prescribed academic format, which may at first seem difficult. Most important, you must present information accurately and honestly.

EVALUATING SOURCES FOR A RESEARCH PROJECT

All material found during research has to be evaluated. Sometimes evaluation is easy—a source may be so obviously good that you know you will use it, or it may be so clearly weak or irrelevant to your inquiry that you know you will not need it.

Here are some guidelines for deciding whether print and online material will be useful to you. These guidelines are an abbreviated version of the material in Chapter 11 on pages 389–391. Also, you may want to consult Chapters 3 and 11 to think again about some of the ways in which your beliefs have been formed, since beliefs have a strong influence on evaluation.

These basic questions can help to judge information and sources:

1. *How reliable is the source?*
   - What kind of text is this? An editorial, a report, an advertisement?
   - Who is its intended audience? Is this audience important to the text's point of view?
   - When was it written? Is the date relevant to my research question?
   - Is it a primary or secondary source?

2. *How knowledgeable or experienced is the author?*
   - What credentials does the person who provided this information have?
   - If the person is not an expert, under what circumstances did she or he provide the information?

3. *What specific ideas are being presented?*
   - What is the main point, claim, or thesis?
   - What reasons or evidence support the information? Does anything about it seem false?
   - Does anything seem to have been left out?
   - Are interests, purposes, and intended audiences apparent?
   - If an argument is presented, can you identify its warrants?

Thinking-Writing Activity

EVALUATING PRINT AND WEB SOURCES

1. After you have found a print source, ask the evaluative questions above, and then write your answers.
2. Go to an Internet site, and evaluate it according to the Web guidelines. Then write your answers.
3. Examine your answers to the previous two questions. How will they influence your possible use of these sources?

THINKING CRITICALLY ABOUT NEW MEDIA

Evaluating Online Information

The Internet is an incredibly rich source of information on almost every subject that exists. But it's important to remember that information is not knowledge. Information doesn't become *knowledge* until we think critically about it. As a critical thinker, you should never accept information at face value without first establishing its accuracy, evaluating the credibility of the source, and determining the point of view or bias of the source. These are issues that we have explored throughout this book, and you can use the checklist on pages 545–546 to evaluate information found on the Internet, as well as from other sources.

Before You Search

The first stage of evaluating Web sources should happen before you search the Internet! Ask yourself what you are looking for. If you don't know what you're looking for, you probably won't find it! You might want

narratives	arguments
facts	statistics
opinions	eyewitness reports
photographs or graphics	

Do you want new ideas, support for a position you already hold, or something entirely different? Once you decide, you will be better able to evaluate what you find on the Web.

Choose Sources Likely to Be Reliable

Ask yourself, "What sources (or what kinds of sources) would be most likely to give me the kind of reliable information I'm looking for?" Some sources are more likely than others to

be fair	lack hidden motives
be objective	show quality control

Sometimes a site's address (or uniform resource locator [URL]) suggests its reliability or its purpose. Sites ending in

- .edu indicate educational or research material
- .gov indicate government resources
- .com indicate commercial products or commercially sponsored sites
- .org usually indicate nonprofit organizations

"\\7,126\\ NAME" in a URL may indicate a personal home page without a recognized affiliation.

Keep these considerations in mind; don't just accept the opinion of the first sources you locate.

Checklist for Evaluating the Quality of Internet Resources

Criterion 1: Authority

❏ Is it clear who sponsors the page and what the sponsor's purpose is in maintaining the page? Is there a respected, well-known organizational affiliation?

❏ Is it clear who wrote the material and what the author's qualifications are for writing on this topic?

❏ Is there a way of verifying the legitimacy of the page's sponsor? In particular, is there a phone number or postal address to contact for more information? (An email address alone is not enough.)

❏ If the material is protected by copyright, is the name of the copyright holder given? Is there a date of page creation or version?

❏ *Beware!* Avoid anonymous sites and affiliations that you've never heard of or that can't be easily checked.

Criterion 2: Accuracy

❏ Are the sources for any factual information clearly listed so they can be verified by another source?

❏ Has the sponsor provided a link to outside sources (such as product reviews or reports filed with the Securities and Exchange Commission [SEC]) that can be used to verify the sponsor's claims?

❏ Is the information free of grammatical, spelling, and other typographical errors? (These kinds of errors not only indicate a lack of quality control but also can actually produce inaccuracies in information.)

❏ Are statistical data in graphs and charts clearly labeled and easy to read?

❏ Does anyone monitor the accuracy of the information being published?

❏ *Beware!* Avoid unverifiable statistics and claims not supported by reasons and evidence.

Criterion 3: Objectivity

❏ For any given piece of information, is it clear what the sponsor's motivation is for providing it?

❏ Is the purported factual information clearly separated from any advertising or opinion content?

(Continues)

THINKING CRITICALLY ABOUT NEW MEDIA (CONTINUED)

❑ Is the point of view of the sponsor presented in a clear manner, with his or her arguments well supported?

❑ *Beware!* Avoid sites offering "information" in an effort to sell a product or service, as well as sites containing conflicts of interest, bias and one-sidedness, emotional language, and slanted tone.

Criterion 4: Currentness

❑ Are there dates on the page to indicate when the page was written, first placed on the Web, and last revised?

❑ Are there any other indications that the material is kept current?

❑ If material is presented in graphs or charts, is there a clear statement about when the data were gathered?

❑ Is there an indication that the page has been completed and is not still in the process of being developed?

❑ *Beware!* Avoid sites that lack any dates, sources, or references.

Thinking-Writing Activity

EVALUATING THE QUALITY OF TWO WEBSITES WITH CONTRASTING PERSPECTIVES ON AN ISSUE

1. Select an issue that plays an important role in our world today, such as global warming, genetically modified foods, or the increasing use of drugs to treat children for attention-deficit hyperactivity disorder (ADHD).

2. Locate two different websites that present contrasting views on the issue.

3. Evaluate each website using the checklist above.

4. Write a one-page summary of your informed view on the issue, and explain the reasons and evidence that support your perspective.

Thinking Critically About Visuals

Is FactCheck.org a Reputable Source of Information?

Using the guidelines you just learned, how reliable would you say this site is? In addition to considering this screen capture, feel free to visit the website itself and see if you can find additional evidence of the site's reliability or lack thereof.

MOVING FROM QUESTIONS TO THESIS

The next step in your research is to move from your research questions to a thesis for your research paper. The guidelines for all of this book's Writing Projects include suggestions for identifying a focus and defining a thesis. Reviewing these suggestions will help you when you are writing a research paper.

Some research papers take an informative position; others are strongly argumentative. This distinction will depend on your purpose, the traditions of the discipline in which you are writing the paper, and your instructor's goals for the assignment. Be sure that you understand whether your instructor wants your paper to be informative or argumentative.

Thinking-Writing Activity

GOING FROM QUESTIONS TO THESIS

1. Select one of the questions that you wrote for the Thinking-Writing Activity: Developing Research Questions on page 538. Construct an answer for the question based on your knowledge or research. Next, use your answer to create a thesis statement that clearly describes your answer or makes a claim based on your answer.

2. Look at the questions and statements that two or three of your classmates created for this Thinking-Writing Activity. Identify the statements that seem clearest and have the most potential to be developed into solid papers.

Understanding Plagiarism and Using Information Ethically

Plagiarism is presenting another person's ideas or words as your own. There are three good reasons not to plagiarize. The first is honesty. Most people do not want to be fakes; they want to be honest, and so they do not want to steal others' ideas and work without giving credit. The second is that another person or group of people put a great deal of time and effort into a piece of work, and it is only right that the person (or group) receives credit for this work. The third reason not to plagiarize is that plagiarism can bring severe penalties, both in college and at work.

In college writing, two kinds of plagiarism are possible. One is deliberate and dishonorable—the willful copying of all or part of another student's paper or all or part of a source. Buying a paper from a service is also plagiarism because a student who does this is taking credit for someone else's words, ideas, and effort.

The other kind of plagiarism is accidental and happens when a student does not know how to document properly. Once you understand that you must always signal where any material from a source begins and ends, and that you must always make clear who said something and where it was said, you should be able to avoid accidental plagiarism. The sections in this chapter on Taking Notes, The Logic Behind Documentation Formats, and Tips on Avoiding Plagiarism will help.

A *fabrication* is a deliberately false or invented statement. It presents as true something that is made up or distorted, such as an event that did not happen, a statement that was not made, a misleading addition or omission of words or data, or a listing of a source that was not used. Some writers are tempted to fabricate or falsify if they do not have real information that they need in order to make a point or create a desired effect. Yet readers must be able to trust the material that is presented in academic work and in responsible media.

Fabrication is different from making a mistake, which unfortunately almost everyone does occasionally, but not deliberately. A fabrication is different from a hypothesis or hypothetical example, which should be identified as such.

Guidelines for Avoiding Plagiarism

❑ Remember that all material from any source must be documented in some way. Downloaded items, websites, email, interviews, illustrations, DVDs, videos, films, broadcasts, lectures, books, articles—anything that is not drawn from your own experience, observation, or creativity—must be cited appropriately.

❑ Learn the different methods of citation used in various writing situations. In college, you may need to use different formats in papers written for different classes. These disciplinary formats are explained in guides to research and handbooks. At work, you will give credit to others as expected in your occupation. In writing done for community activities, you will probably cite information informally, just stating that a person, article, or report said something.

❑ Be sure that quoted material (exact words) is placed in quotation marks, indented, or indicated in some other way, depending on the format that you are using.

❑ Remember that copied-and-pasted material, paraphrases, summaries, and short extracts, even of less than a sentence, all must be cited. Other people's ideas must be documented as well as their exact words.

❑ Be sure to indicate in all drafts where source material is from so that you do not lose track of it as you revise and edit.

❑ Signal where material from others begins and where it ends. Learn to do this in a variety of ways, as appropriate to the writing situation.

❑ Take pride in presenting your own thinking and distinguish your ideas clearly from those of your sources.

❑ Be careful to capture all bibliographic material as you download, photocopy, and take notes so that you can easily provide documentation. Be sure to record authors' full names, exact titles, publication information, dates, page numbers, URLs, and other access items.

❑ Consult with your instructors and writing center tutors about citing sources when you are drafting your researched writing.

❑ When in doubt, cite.

Thinking-Writing Activity

PLAGIARISM IN THE NEWS

1. Read carefully your college's statements about plagiarism. Does your college have an honor code? If so, what does it say about plagiarism? Write a few sentences giving your responses to these statements.

2. Search for information about Stephen Glass, Jayson Blair, Janet Cook, James Frey, Stephen Ambrose, or Doris Kearns Goodwin. Find out what any of these writers are reported to have fabricated or plagiarized, what they said about their situations, and what happened to them.

3. What can college students learn from the experience of these professionals?

Share your responses to these questions with classmates and see how your ideas are similar or different.

Taking Notes

Although photocopying and downloading have made note taking less necessary than it was in previous eras, researchers still need to have methods for deciding what to note, highlight, or underline; for accurately recording content and bibliographic information; and for integrating source material thoughtfully into their own written work.

DECIDING WHEN TO TAKE NOTES

Sometimes you can easily see that certain parts of an article, book, or website relate to your research question or working thesis. Naturally, in such cases, you will then note the material or photocopy, highlight, or download it. However, at other times, you may not be sure what to select from a source.

Your critical reading abilities will come into play here. Before you even think about taking notes, you should read an entire article. If you are consulting a book, read the whole book—if possible—or skim it, consult the index, and read the chapters that contain information related to your topic. Look for headings, topic sentences, chapter titles—all the elements that point out what the writer is discussing. As you read through, jot down page numbers or mark passages that strike you in some way, but you really should not take notes until you have a grasp of the entire piece.

After getting an overview of the work, you need to go back and select specific points that pertain to your question or thesis. If you're not sure how the material relates, note it! At this stage, you want too much information instead of too little. Highlighting and underlining are forms of note taking because you are choosing information.

QUOTING AND PARAPHRASING

Another decision that you have to make while taking notes is when to directly quote (using the original author's exact words) or when to paraphrase (restating the original author's ideas in your own words). If you are not sure how you plan to incorporate certain materials into your own essay during this stage of the writing process, it is best to copy the direct quote and note the author(s) and location of the information. Highlighting or underlining the information is ideal if you own the book, or if you have made copies of the pages. Be sure to follow these two important tips:

1. When you quote, put all of the quoted material inside quotation marks in your notes so that you will never forget that these are the author's exact words. Then you will know that anything else in your notes that is not in quotation marks is paraphrased.

2. Accurately copy every word in order to avoid misrepresenting the original text.

The following are some guidelines for quoting:

- If the author has said something in a distinctive way, quote or highlight it.
- If the author has said something complicated and/or technical, quote or highlight it.
- If the author has said something controversial, quote or highlight it.
- When in doubt, quote the author's words in your notes. You can decide if you would rather paraphrase them later when you are writing your paper.
- If you know that you only want a summary of a source or an indication of what it says, paraphrase it.

Here are examples of a full note and the paraphrased version:

Quoted note: "A Kampala journalist named Michael Wakabi told me that Kampala has become a 'used culture.' The cars are used—they arrive from Japan with broken power windows and air conditioning, so Ugandan drivers bake in the sun. Used furniture from Europe lines the streets in Kampala. The Ugandan Army occupies part of neighboring Congo with used tanks and aircraft from Ukraine. And the traditional Ugandan dress made from local cotton, called gomesi, is as rare as the mountain gorilla. To dress African, Ugandans have to have money."—Packer 58.

Paraphrased note: The economy of Uganda is ruined by exploitation—local industries and culture are almost extinct. Nothing is fabricated or produced in Uganda anymore; most consumer goods are rejects from Western countries. Because native Ugandan products are so rare, only wealthy Ugandans can have them.—Packer 58.

The author's full name and all publication information will be on a bibliography card or list (see pages 552–553).

USING COMMON KNOWLEDGE

It is usually not necessary to document information that is considered "common knowledge," or things that "everybody" knows. Common knowledge is often factual, such as the fact that hijacked planes piloted by terrorists crashed into the World Trade Center on September 11, 2001. Well-known sayings like "Haste makes waste" are usually not documented, nor are accepted concepts like consuming large amounts of high-calorie food will cause most people to gain weight. However, discussions of facts or well-known ideas are not common; they are produced by individuals and must be documented.

In addition, common knowledge is not universally common. Different cultures, different time periods, different academic disciplines, and different occupations all have their own common knowledge and often do not see ideas from other groups or eras as well known. Therefore, you need to be cautious about presenting something as common knowledge and perhaps consult with your instructor. If in doubt, document. It is better to overcite than to plagiarize.

CHARACTERISTICS OF EFFECTIVE NOTE-TAKING SYSTEMS

Good note-taking systems have the following characteristics:

- accuracy in recording material
- accuracy in recording full bibliographic information
- differentiation between quoted and paraphrased material
- indication of the source from which a specific note is taken
- indication of the section of a paper to which a specific note pertains
- capacity to rearrange notes to put material into the appropriate sections of a paper

The traditional technique of using note cards has all of these characteristics. Other methods can accomplish the same tasks, but researchers need to use care to separate noted items and to find a way to sort information in order to insert it in its logical place in the paper. If, like many students today, you only use note cards when you cannot photocopy or download a source, you need to think carefully about ways to develop a method that will provide you with the benefits of the note-card system.

The traditional system has two parts: a note card for each piece of information and a bibliographic card for every source.

Note Cards   Each note card contains only one item of information. The act of selecting specific items motivates you to think carefully about what *you* are looking for in order to present your ideas in the paper. Figure 14.1 shows an example of a note card.

You indicate clearly on the card whether the material is quoted by using quotation marks or whether it is paraphrased by not using the marks. You also briefly identify the source on the card and note the section or subtopic of your paper to

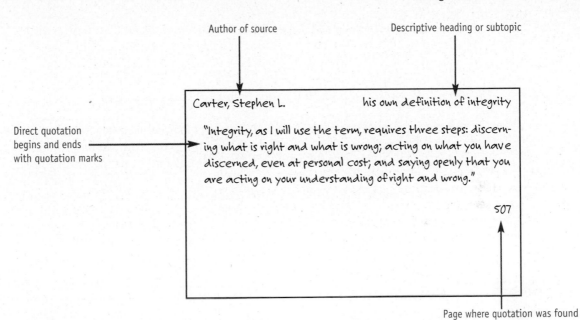

Author of source

Descriptive heading or subtopic

Carter, Stephen L.   his own definition of integrity

"Integrity, as I will use the term, requires three steps: discerning what is right and what is wrong; acting on what you have
discerned, even at personal cost; and saying openly that you
are acting on your understanding of right and wrong."

507

Direct quotation
begins and ends
with quotation marks

Page where quotation was found

FIGURE 14.1
Note Card

which the information pertains. As you begin drafting, arrange the cards in groups
according to the places in the paper where that information will be used. Citation
of sources is easy because each card records its source.

Bibliographic Cards   A good note-taking system includes a set of bibliography cards
(or a list), which provides the full publication information for each source. You arrange
the cards alphabetically by author or title when preparing your Works Cited list.

Figure 14.2 shows the bibliography card for the source of the quotation illustrated in Figure 14.1.

Carter, Stephen L. "The Insufficiency of Honesty."
Great Writing. Ed. Harvey S. Weiner and Nora Eisenberg.
3rd ed. San Francisco: McGraw, 2002. 507–512.

FIGURE 14.2
Bibliography Card

Look at the Works Cited list for one of the documented student papers in this book or consult a writing handbook that includes information on citation styles such as MLA or APA. Then ask yourself: Is this source recorded in the MLA Works Cited–list format? Is it a book, a periodical, or an Internet source? Why will it be easy for this student to insert this source into her Works Cited list?

Using Your Computer to Take Notes   Computers can be used in many ways for note taking. Simply by using a word-processing program, you can enter notes in appropriate files or under specific headings, and by pasting, copying, or using other combining methods, you can put the information into the part of your paper where you want it. You should double- or triple-space so that you can see items clearly, write changes interlinearly on printouts, and cut pages up to rearrange material. You can compile a Works Cited (MLA) or References (APA) list by using an alphabetizing program or simply by copying or pasting.

Thinking-Writing Activity
CREATING YOUR OWN NOTE-TAKING METHODS

1. If you have previously worked on research projects, write an explanation of your own note-taking and record-keeping processes. How do you use your computer to complete tasks? What do you do that is effective? What do you need to improve?

2. Share your system with your classmates, and learn about their systems. Does a classmate have a technique that you would like to adopt?

Most students use combinations of note-taking and recording methods such as writing on cards, paper, or in a notebook, and typing (or copying and pasting) notes into a word processing program. Probably the most unwieldy system—and one to avoid—is writing page after page of notes in a notebook, on both sides of the paper, without leaving spaces for notes to be annotated or cut apart and rearranged. You should avoid using any technique that does not allow you to review and organize material easily.

Thinking-Writing Activity
LEARNING ABOUT THE METHODS OF EXPERIENCED NOTE TAKERS

1. Ask one of your instructors or a successful upper-division student how he or she takes notes, keeps records of sources, and arranges source material for use in a paper. Ask also about the advantages and disadvantages of the system.

2. Write a paragraph summarizing what you have learned. Then share what you have written with classmates, and see what systems they have learned about.

SUMMARIZING

You will often need to summarize what a source says, either as a way of taking notes or as a way of inserting information into your paper. Your critical reading abilities will serve you well when you write a summary. Here are some guidelines:

- A summary is by definition short. An article or book chapter might be summarized in five or six sentences.

- A summary presents major points, not introductory material or multiple examples. It might give one necessary example.

- A summary should state the main point or the thesis clearly, probably at the beginning.

- A summary does not include your commentary on or evaluation of the material. You can comment later as you introduce summarized material into your paper or after you have included it.

    Comment or evaluation: "This article discussed a major breakthrough...."

    Summary: "It says...."

    Comment or evaluation: "This book takes a stand that is no longer accepted...."

    Summary: "It claims...."

- Signal that you are presenting summarized material. One way to begin a summary is to state the main point. Signal words such as *The article says...*, *He points out...*, or *She concludes...* are helpful throughout a summary.

- Usually a summary paraphrases a source, but if you quote special words, graceful phrases, or entire sentences, be sure to use quotation marks.

- A summary is accurate.

The following is a professionally written summary of the article "Hospice Care or Assisted Suicide: A False Dichotomy," by John L. Miller.

> In this paper, the author argues that making assisted suicide available is not a contradictory position to espousing hospice care. He draws on historical and political examples to explain the ethical basis for this assertion. By defining the issue at stake as one of personal autonomy (the loss or gain thereof), the author challenges the argument that making assisted suicide available leads to a slippery slope toward euthanasia, eugenics, or genocide. He asserts that narrowing choices by preventing people from seeking assistance in suicide is more likely to lead us down the slippery slope toward coercive medical and state intervention in our lives.

Thinking-Writing Activity

LEARNING TO SUMMARIZE

1. Write a four- or five-sentence summary of one of the sources that you evaluated for the Thinking-Writing Activity: Evaluating Print and Web Sources on page 543.

2. If you can, ask a classmate to read the source and then comment on whether your summary seems accurate.

Preparing an Annotated Bibliography

One technique that can help you evaluate your sources is writing an annotated bibliography. Your research librarian can show you annotated bibliographies about many subjects, either as books, as indexes, or online.

Sometimes instructors will ask students to create an annotated bibliography as a part of a research project. An *annotated bibliography* is a list of sources with a brief summary of and some evaluative comments about each one.

A student who was researching genocide in Rwanda made the entries shown in the example in Figure 14.3. His instructor had required students to prepare an annotated bibliography of several sources before drafting their research papers.

Carter, Stephen L. "Defending Our Neighbor." *Christianity Today*. Christianity
   Today International, Nov. 2004. Web. 15 Nov. 2005.

   In this essay, Carter provides a very detailed definition of integrity and
a thoughtful discussion of applications of the concept of integrity to difficult
real-world situations.
   These examples helped me see that I could connect the concept of
integrity with the United States' and United Nations' lack of response to the
atrocities in Rwanda. This essay will be central to my paper because I want
to show that integrity demanded that they intervene.

United Nations General Assembly. "Convention on the Prevention and
   Punishment of the Crime of Genocide." 1948. Web. 15 Nov. 2005.
   <http://www.hrweb.org/legal/genocide.html>.

   The 19 articles of this United Nations document state clearly that genocide
is a political as well as a moral crime. It specifies genocidal acts, such as
killing a group's members, aiming to destroy a group, preventing birth of or
taking its children, and causing physical and mental harm that will prevent
a group from maintaining its way of life.
   This primary document provides valuable context and support for my
paper's thesis. I will use it to show that in addition to the moral obligation
to intervene in Rwanda, there was a contractual obligation as well.

FIGURE 14.3
Sample Annotated Bibliography Entries

Thinking-Writing Activity

CREATING AN ANNOTATED BIBLIOGRAPHY

1. Find three sources that pertain to one of the questions that you used in a previous Thinking-Writing Activity or to a paper that you are writing.

2. After you have read the sources carefully, create an annotated bibliography in which you list full bibliographic information. Also, summarize each source in one or two sentences and comment in one or two sentences about what each source's value would be in a paper about the subject.

Integrating Source Material

Research has often been described as an endless conversation. The formats in which academic work is presented reflect the metaphor of research as conversation by indicating who is saying what.

The most important point to remember is that *you* are the person presenting the information in your paper. You are, in effect, participating in a conversation with your sources and your readers. Your paper is not just a series of quotations and paraphrases from sources; instead, it is a presentation of your ideas about the issue and your thinking about what your sources have said.

INTRODUCING SOURCES

An extension of the notion of research as conversation is seeing a research paper as analogous to a dignified television or radio talk show or a panel discussion about a current issue. Think of yourself as a talk-show host as you write a paper that uses source material. Just as the host sets up the discussion, you will provide a context and a clear purpose for presenting the material that you have found. Just as the host introduces each guest to the audience, you will select sources your audience will be interested in and respect. Just as the host helps the guests interact, you will point out the connections and oppositions between and among your sources. And just as the host wraps the show up, you will conclude your paper in an effective manner.

To be considerate of your audience, you will need to know how academic writers introduce a source into a paper. Here are some techniques:

- *Use the name of the author, especially a significant writer or scholar:*

  "Elizabeth Cady Stanton wrote that 'it is the duty of the women of this country to secure to themselves their sacred right to the elective franchise.'"

- *Use the name of the publication:*

  "A *New York Times* article provides guidelines for evaluating information found on the Web. It says...."

- *Establish a context:*

  "Students now receive much advice about how to decide whether information found on the Internet is likely to be good or useless. For example, an article in the *New York Times* provides a list of hints and warnings. This article says...."

- *Indicate your purpose for presenting the information.* This is part of the research conversation. You are talking about the source. In the following passage, a student has commented in his own voice both before and after paraphrasing from a source.

Student { Integrity is at the heart of my position on this situation. According to Stephen L. Carter in his essay "The Insufficiency of Honesty," integrity is much more than acting or appearing noble when dealing with a situation. He says that there are three steps in

Source { defining the degree of one's integrity. These are "discerning what is right and what is wrong; acting on what you have discerned, even at personal cost; and saying openly you are acting on your understanding of what is right and what is wrong" (507).

Student { Obviously the massacre of 800,000 innocent people is inherently wrong; having knowledge that a massacre of 800,000 people is about to occur is inherently wrong, and not acting on this legitimate intelligence is painfully misguided. It is completely devoid of any semblance of integrity.

ESTABLISHING YOUR VOICE

You will use your own voice in your research writing to fulfill several purposes. First, as just explained, you will always signal in some way that you are introducing source material into your paper. In addition, as the author of a paper, not just a compiler of other people's ideas, you might

- *Comment on what sources say.* You should indicate your purpose for including the source material in the paper. You could express agreement or disagreement with particular sources. You might explain which sources you consider most important to the points you are making in the paper. Providing such commentary is an important part of your role as "host."
- *Synthesize what sources say.* You should discuss ways in which sources relate to each other. You might point out a chronological sequence of concepts or explain how theories differ from each other. You could show how sources agree.
- *Present your own thinking.* You have established a thesis for your paper, and, of course, you will present ideas to support it. You might explain why you agree with one source or a group of sources or why you differ from them all and have your own claim to put forth. You might present ideas that have

come from your experiences, your observations, your interpretations, or your creative thinking.

You need to clarify when you are speaking in order to be credited for your ideas and comments, just as you must indicate when your sources are speaking so that proper credit is given to them.

Your voice should be easily identifiable as long as you have indicated where all source material begins and ends. Then everything else is your commentary, your synthesis, or your own thinking. Often, you will want to use words or phrases to show that you are commenting—such as "Therefore," "A consideration of these concepts shows . . ." or "Another significant idea is . . . ."

CHOOSING POINT OF VIEW

If your instructor agrees, you could simply present some of your comments and ideas as first-person statements: "I want to suggest . . ."; "After analyzing these reports, I decided . . ."; "I believe . . . ." However, there is an academic tradition that discourages the use of the first-person singular pronoun (*I*) in order to suggest an objective and impersonal point of view. This tradition is stronger in some disciplines than in others. You should ask your instructors about the preferred pronoun use in research papers and also look at pronoun use in academic journals in the fields in which you are studying.

Also be careful about using *we*. Be sure you identify who "we" is—people sometimes use the word to mean society at large, the citizens of a particular country, or the readers of a particular newspaper or magazine. However, your readers should never have to assume. In addition, the second person (*you*) is rarely used in academic writing.

Thinking-Writing Activity

CLARIFYING WHO IS TALKING

1. Look at the student paper at the end of this chapter, at other documented papers in this book, or at a research paper in your handbook. Notice how the student writers introduce other people's ideas into their papers. Then write a paragraph about what you have observed. Quote some different ways in which these student writers bring sources into their papers.

2. Notice how the writers clarify what their own thinking is about the source material or about the point that the source is being used to support. Identify two specific places where student writers are speaking in their own voices.

Think about how this activity might help you to write your next documented paper and to avoid creating a paper that is just a string of quotations and paraphrases of others' ideas.

The Logic Behind Documentation

REASONS FOR DOCUMENTATION

Two principles underlie academic documentation formats:

- Readers have to know *who* says something.
- Readers have to know *where* something is said.

All academic formats provide this information in logical systems, whether they use parentheses, endnotes, or footnotes. Different disciplines use different formats, but they are all based on these two principles. Your handbook or guide to research will explain most of the formats, such as those adopted by the American Psychological Association (APA), the Council of Science Editors (CSE), and the Modern Language Association (MLA). Also, these associations maintain websites on which you can find the most current format models. Guidelines to the MLA and APA styles are in this book's appendix.

Researchers clarify who said something and where it was said for a number of reasons:

- *To give credibility to a paper.* The strength or weakness of source materials helps readers judge the strength or weakness of a research project and its presentation.

- *To help readers and other researchers learn more.* Proper documentation can direct readers to sources so that they can find out more about a subject than what is presented in a paper.

- *To give credit where credit is due.* Research papers combine many people's ideas. Democracy tells us that each person is important. Giving appropriate credit shows respect for the human being who expressed the idea being used. Further, out of self-respect, researchers and writers want their own ideas to be credited to them just as much as they want to acknowledge others' ideas.

- *To observe the courtesies of conversation.* If research is a millennia-long conversation, the courtesies of conversation are in order. People take turns speaking during a conversation; sometimes points are recapped; often questions are asked and answered. It is usually important to know who is speaking in a conversation.

- *To avoid plagiarism.*

Thinking-Writing Activity

CITING AND PARAPHRASING

Students usually know that quoted material of a sentence or more must be documented. However, students sometimes have difficulty understanding that paraphrases and quotations of short, "apt phrases" must also be cited. Read the following passage that was written by Lynn Z. Bloom and appears on page 90 of the eighth edition of *The Essay Connection,* published by Houghton Mifflin in 2007:

> *Original passage:* "Narratives have as many purposes, as many plots, as many characters as there are people to write them. You have but to examine your life, your thoughts, your experiences, to find an unwritten library of narratives yet to tell."

Why is this use acceptable?

1. Lynn Bloom points out that all people have stories worth telling if they will just look into their lives and experiences where they will "find an unwritten library of narratives" (90).

Why could this use be seen as plagiarism by some or as an error in punctuation by others? What do you think?

2. Each person's life can be seen as holding an unwritten library of narratives (Bloom 90).

Where do you see plagiarism here?

3. Storytelling may be one of the defining characteristics of the human species. Stories come in countless forms, and have been told in various ways by almost everybody who has ever lived. Indeed, narratives have as many purposes, as many plots, as many characters as there are people to tell them.

THE LOGIC OF MLA STYLE

The MLA system is used in this book because it is widely used in English classes and the humanities. To understand how it works, look at the paper at the end of this chapter, at a model in a writing handbook, or visit the Modern Language Association's website: http://www.mla.org/.

1. First, note that at the end of a paper, there is a list of Works Cited, with the sources listed alphabetically according to *author* or, if no author is given, according to the *title* of the source. Full bibliographic information is given in this list so that it does not have to be provided in the parenthetical citations within the body of the paper.

2. Next, look at the places within the paper where sources are cited. Note that when material has been taken from a source, the last name or an abbreviated title under which it is listed in Works Cited is given—either when the material is introduced or in parentheses at the end of its use. The number of the page on which the material can be found is given in parentheses at the end of the quotation or paraphrase. The parentheses signal the end of the source material.

3. If a source does not have a page number, then a number cannot be given, so you must otherwise signal that use of the source has ended. Many online documents do not show page numbers, so you must be careful to indicate where your use of such a source ends.

Thinking-Writing Activity

EXPLAINING THE MLA SYSTEM

1. Review the documented paper in this chapter, or in a writing handbook, and, if possible, the MLA website (http://www.mla.org/). Then write an explanation of how the MLA system works. Explain the relationship between the Works Cited list and the parenthetical citations in the body of the text.

2. Next, explain the MLA system to a classmate. Then tell your classmate why you believe the reasons for documentation are important. See if she or he agrees.

Working Thoughtfully on Research Projects

Much of the work you do to produce a research paper is similar to what you do when you write from your own resources. However, research projects often involve some special steps and concerns, including scheduling a significant amount of time, planning your paper carefully, using a specified academic format, and, often, consulting with librarians and with your instructor.

TIME

No one needs to tell you that you cannot just sit down and write up the results of a research project in a short hour spent at your keyboard. Reading, evaluating, selecting, noting, commenting on, and arranging material demands the use of critical and creative thinking processes that usually cannot be hurried.

Using a library can involve waiting for help from a librarian, learning to use the computerized catalog, searching the shelves for material, seeing interesting material that doesn't pertain to your paper, and, of course, having to read, evaluate, copy, take notes on, and think about what you've found. College libraries are pleasant places where time is usually well spent—and where you will spend much time while working on a research project.

Deciding on the scope of a project, working though research questions, narrowing a topic, interviewing knowledgeable persons, and revising and qualifying a thesis all take time.

Therefore, you should make a schedule when you begin a research project. You must complete the project within the time frame that your instructor allows. Instructors usually give weeks or months for research projects, but it is amazing how quickly that time evaporates and how suddenly deadlines are staring you in the face. Start as soon as you are given the assignment. Block out time to work on it regularly. Be sure to follow any time line that your instructor establishes.

One instructor gives her students this checklist:

Research Project Checklist

	Due Date	Date(s) Completed
Decide on focus	_____	_____
Develop research questions	_____	_____
Locate and evaluate sources (ongoing)	_____	_____
Select and read sources (ongoing)	_____	_____
Identify useful sources; take notes	_____	_____
Develop thesis	_____	_____
Develop working outline	_____	_____
Draft sections of paper	_____	_____
Conference with instructor	_____	_____
Draft(s) of complete paper	_____	_____
Peer review	_____	_____
Revise, edit, and proofread paper	_____	_____
Hand in completed paper and all required material	_____	_____

Remember that this checklist makes research seem more linear and less recursive than it usually is.

PLANNING AND OUTLINING

Since research papers are often longer than essays or reports, planning and outlining are important steps. You will probably have to gather information before you can see what shape your paper will take, but as soon as you can, you will want to block out the sections of the paper and make a working outline (to be changed as the paper develops). If your instructor requires that a formal outline be submitted with your finished paper, look at the paper at the end of this chapter or consult your writing handbook for a model. Some word-processing programs include formal outlines in their formatting options, so your computer might help you create an outline.

FORMATS AND MODELS

You must use an accepted academic documentation format when you write a research paper for a college class. You cannot be creative about documentation. You must follow the models exactly. You should also familiarize yourself with the style, design, and format your instructor requires for the presentation of your research paper.

COLLABORATION

The research conducted in business, at large laboratories, and by think tanks and professional organizations is often done by teams. Therefore, to give students this experience, some instructors may assign team projects in college classes. But even if the project that you will be working on will be an individual effort, other people can provide much help. You will want to work with your instructor, the librarians, computer experts, and your classmates as much as you can as you complete your research. See Chapter 6, pages 174–176 for using peer response groups as a revising strategy.

Writing Project

A RESEARCH PAPER

This chapter emphasizes the reasoning behind many of the activities that occur while you are engaged in research. The Thinking-Writing Activities should help you find and use information. Be sure to reread what you wrote for those activities.

> ## Project Overview and Requirements
>
> Following your instructor's directions regarding the number and range of sources, length of the paper, and academic format for citation of sources, complete a research project and write a well-documented paper in which you report and discuss your findings.
>
> Your research may consist of a combination of print sources, electronic sources, surveys, and interviews with informed individuals to support your claims.
>
> Depending on your instructor's directions, be sure to carefully follow the MLA, APA, or other appropriate format, and consult this chapter as well as the appendix in this book.

As with the other projects you have completed so far, it is important to consider the Thinking-Writing Model in Chapter 1 (pages 5–8) and work through the elements of the Writing Situation and Writing Process below. Additionally, you will want to review the "Guidelines for Avoiding Plagiarism" (page 549), as well as the "Checklist for Evaluating the Quality of Internet Resources" on pages 545–546. It can also help to fill out the "Research Project Checklist" on page 563.

THE WRITING SITUATION

Purpose   Your two major purposes for research are to learn as much as you can about your topic and then to present your thinking about your findings in an effective paper. Also, you can improve your ability to use your college library and the Internet. In addition, you will further develop your critical and creative thinking abilities as you apply almost every concept presented in this book to your research project.

Audience   If your classmates are working on similar projects, they will be an excellent audience for your finished paper, as well as for drafts. If your research topic is about a social or political issue, your audience might include people beyond your college. Perhaps you can find a way to share what you've learned at a community forum; in a newspaper, newsletter, or listserv; or on a website. Your instructor remains the audience who will judge how well you have shaped your research question, investigated possible answers, discussed what you have found, and documented your paper in the required academic format.

Subject   Obviously, you should be interested in the subject of your research so that your work will be a pleasure rather than a chore. If the subject is significant in your life or connected with one of your favorite academic fields, you should be able

ZITS   *BY JERRY SCOTT AND JIM BORGMAN*

©Zits Partnership, King Features Syndicate

As tempting as this "mental blender" approach to research might appear, there is at this time no substitute for research based on thoughtful exploration, effective planning, productive collaboration, and above all, critical thinking.

to think of a stimulating research question. If the subject has been assigned and, perhaps, is not among your interests, do everything you can to connect it to your interests. Ask questions about it, read as widely as you can, and consult websites. You will almost surely find issues within any subject that you can relate to your own concerns.

Writer   If you've already worked on research projects in previous classes, you should feel confident as you undertake this one, but you should be willing to improve your abilities throughout the entire process. Be your most efficient self by setting up a schedule, working steadily, and meeting all deadlines. Don't hesitate to ask for help from librarians, computer room staff, and your instructor.

Remember the talk-show analogy presented in this chapter: you are the host, in charge of the paper. Comment on what you discover during your investigation; present your own thinking and keep yourself in the paper as much as is appropriate to the subject, to the traditions of the discipline in which you are working, and to your assignment.

After spending time considering the purpose, audience, subject, and writer, working through the following questions will help you with your research project.

1. Briefly describe the topic you would like to research and why. For example, here is one student's topic:

   The topic of my research paper will be the role of social media in relationships. This is a relatively broad topic, but I plan to focus primarily on relationships between friends and family, as well as larger circles of acquaintances. Networks such as Facebook, Twitter, Instagram, Pinterest, LinkedIn, Google Plus, and MySpace are quite popular, but I would like to learn more about how relying on these sites to maintain relationships actually affects the relationships themselves. I recently came across a study by, I believe, Oxford University, showing that excessive social networking might actually harm relationships. I plan to find that article again so I can use it in my research.

2. Who might benefit from the research you present in your essay? Who will your audience be? For example:

   My audience will likely be quite large, as nearly everyone participates in some sort of social network—from kids to grandparents. I am hoping that by learning more about how social networks affect relationships, I can share that knowledge so others can give their use of these networks more thought in regards to if they want to use them and how. I also feel that the information I present can encourage people to find a balance between virtual and actual relationships.

3. How do you plan to approach the research portion of your project? Also, how might you organize and incorporate the information you gather? For example:

   I plan to do a bulk of my research on the Internet, though I will incorporate some print materials, and I also plan to survey friends and family on their usage of and feelings about social networks. My survey will be relatively brief, and I want them to estimate how many hours per day/week they spend on these networks, tell me which networks they use, and why they use them. I also want them to rate their satisfaction with the relationships they maintain online and comment on why they are or are not satisfied. I think this will give my paper depth. I plan to incorporate the research based on subtopics. For example, I may quote or paraphrase an Internet resource and then illustrate the concept by providing an example from my survey results.

4. Finally, a research paper takes time and dedication, and organization will be essential in order to present your findings clearly and professionally. What are your plans for staying organized and effectively managing your time during the research and writing process? For example:

> My instructor said we have about two weeks to complete this project, so I plan to dig into the research portion of it right away. I feel fairly confident of the direction I am headed, but I want to be sure that I keep the materials I find organized—especially in regards to keeping track of the citations I will need for each source. I also plan to construct my instrument right away so there is plenty of time to distribute and then collect the surveys. While those are out, I plan to continue research while building an outline and then a draft of my paper. I know that this process will be recursive, so I will need to be flexible.

THE WRITING PROCESS

Much of the material already presented in this chapter relates to generating ideas, finding a focus, and defining a thesis as you work on a research project. You should review it before you begin your paper.

Generating Ideas

- As you use the technique of asking questions about your subject, look again at the questions presented in Chapter 4 (pages 100–102). Apply as many of those questions as you can.

- Brainstorm and freewrite as you begin your research project, just as you would do when writing a paper from your own experience. "Talk to yourself" on paper about what you want to investigate and what you want to say about the topic.

- Use the thinking patterns discussed in Chapters 7 to 10 as ways to find ideas. Ask yourself about any processes involved in your subject. Describe important objects connected with it. Think about similarities and differences within it. Identify causal relationships. Define important terms. And be sure to write down what the thinking patterns show you.

- Before you decide on a limited focus, read widely about your subject. Consult encyclopedias and websites to get background information and ideas.

Defining a Thesis or Making a Claim   As you turn your research question (or questions) into a tentative thesis statement or claim, you need to be sure that your thesis or claim reflects the rhetorical purpose of your paper. Are you explaining, describing, or presenting different points of views? In that case, you will need to create a thesis statement. Or are you arguing for a specific position? For a researched argument, you will need to define and support a claim.

Notice how the documented student papers in Chapters 8 and 10 explain their topics. Notice how Joshua Bartlett's paper in Chapter 12 and the paper in Chapter 13 argue for specific changes. Notice how the paper in this chapter argues for a claim.

Draft more than one possible thesis statement or claim, and then decide which one best serves your purposes. Remember that you may refocus your paper as you draft and revise it, so you should be open to reshaping your thesis statement or claim as you rework the paper.

Organizing Ideas   Research papers are usually divided into logically distinguished sections. As you organize your paper, you need to think about how the material that you have found pertains to different aspects of the topic. And in an interactive process, as your research develops, the material you find will suggest different points that you may want to develop.

For example, if you are researching changes in beliefs about healthy diets, you might divide your paper chronologically or according to food groups depending on what you decide to emphasize. If you are researching homelessness in a community in order to present an overview of it to an audience of relatively affluent young people, your paper might include almost equally developed sections on the estimated numbers of homeless people, the causes of homelessness, and the programs to help the homeless. If your purpose is to argue for improved programs, your paper might have a short introductory section on the numbers and causes and well-developed sections on various options for helping the homeless.

If you have used note cards and classified them according to the aspect of your topic to which they contribute, you can easily arrange and rearrange them as you incorporate information into your draft. If you have taken notes on your computer, you can print files and/or copy and organize. If you have assembled printouts and photocopies of articles and pages, you'll need to identify the parts of your paper where this information belongs and sort it appropriately. If you have a combination of downloaded material, photocopies, and written notes—which is likely—you will need to put them in logical piles or arrange them near your keyboard in a way that will help you incorporate information and keep track of where every item came from.

Outlines are usually necessary planning tools for long research papers. You should draft working outlines several times during your research process. If your instructor requires a formal outline, you can write one at the end of your planning, after you have completed a draft, or after you finish the paper. A formal outline will provide a good measure of the organization of your paper.

Drafting   Drafting a research paper differs from drafting a personal paper in one important way: you must remember to indicate within the draft where source material begins, where it ends, where it is from, and whether it is quoted or paraphrased. In a draft, citation formats and wordings of the signals that indicate a source do not have to be perfect. You can polish these up when you revise and edit, but to avoid accidental plagiarism, you must keep track of this material as you draft.

One decision you will have to make during drafting is whether to quote, paraphrase, or summarize source material. This is not always an easy choice. You do not want to quote too much, yet you do need to report what sources say. You should read documented papers and articles in your fields of interest in order to develop a sense of how experienced academic writers use their sources. Notice how these writers use short quotations, long quotations, paraphrases, and summaries.

The following are some guidelines for deciding what to quote, paraphrase, or summarize:

- You probably should quote if what a source has said is worded in a special way, is complicated or technical, or is controversial.

- If you are still learning about the field that your sources are discussing, you might need to quote more than an expert would.

- You should not use many long quoted passages. If you include a lot of lengthy quotations, you may end up compiling a small anthology instead of writing a paper. Instead of stringing quotes together, remember that you have a voice and that it should be heard in your writing.

- Remember that you do not have to quote whole sentences; often a few words will suffice. Example: In contrasting facts and theories, Stephen Jay Gould calls facts "the world's data" and theories "structures of ideas that explain and interpret facts" (page 416 in Chapter 11).

- You might want to quote fairly extensively in an early draft and then ask your classmates, writing center tutors, or instructor for help with shortening quotations and paraphrasing.

- *Paraphrasing*, or restating another's ideas in your own words, requires a good vocabulary and well-developed critical reading skills. Ask yourself as you are drafting: "Let's see. What is this source saying? How do these ideas help develop my paper?" Then write your answers, and see how they might help you incorporate the source into your paper.

- You use *summaries* to show the main points of an article, section, chapter, book, or Internet source. Remember to explain the significance of the summarized material.

Remember that you must always signal the beginning and end of sources used and cite appropriately, whether you are quoting, paraphrasing, or summarizing.

You should remain aware of your talk-show host role as you comment on what you have used from your sources. You will probably need to draft your statements several times as you reread your notes and sources and rethink what you want to say.

Revising Your Essay: A Research Paper

Before you complete your draft, carefully consider the following questions:

- Have you clearly defined the focus of your paper?
- Do you provide solid answers to the research questions you asked?
- Did you properly identify and cite all sources in your draft?
- Is your thesis statement clear and apparent?
- Is your draft presented logically? Did you follow what you planned in your outline?
- Are there any parts of your paper where more information is needed or where you have repeated information that might need to be cut?

Peer Response

After you have completed your draft, exchange essays with one of your classmates. Ask yourself the following questions as you review one another's work:

1. Is the focus of the topic clear within the first few paragraphs of the paper? Is the thesis statement clear? Offer specific suggestions if necessary.

2. Consider the intended audience: Does the writer adequately address the audience by, for example, providing enough background information about the topic? Comment on specific passages.

3. Are there any passages in the paper that caused confusion? For example, there might be conflicting information, a jump in ideas without a proper transition, or perhaps information that has been left out or repeated. Point out specific passages where these problems might occur and offer concrete suggestions.

4. Finally, what do you, as the reader, take away from this research paper? Do you feel you have learned something of value? Explain your reaction to it.

Revising, Editing, and Proofreading

After you have received feedback from your classmate during peer review, make necessary changes to strengthen the focus and content of your research paper.

Finally, take time to review "A Step-by-Step Method for Revising Any Assignment" on the inside front cover of this book. The checklist, if carefully followed, will help you revise and polish your final draft so it is clear and professional.

Annotated Student Research Paper: The Writing Situation and Writing Process in Action

The paper on pages 574–581 was written for an English composition course that emphasized exposition, argument, and research. A sequence of reading and writing assignments led up to the paper assignment. Students then responded to each other's drafts during two peer review sessions. Chris Buxton-Smith describes how he thought about his writing situation and writing process.

CHRIS BUXTON-SMITH'S WRITING SITUATION

Purpose Midway through the semester, our instructor gave us an assignment for which we were to choose one of several concepts and write an argument of at least six pages, using a minimum of four sources. The essay was to address a specific concept in order to argue for or against a particular act or position. Among the concepts were *masculinity, femininity, racism,* and *integrity,* as well as a whole slew of others that pertained to readings we had been assigned throughout the semester. The purpose was to demonstrate our understanding of the concept and our proficiency at writing a strong argumentation paper. After some thought, I saw that I might be able to choose a subject that, since my late teens, I had always wanted to write about: the Rwandan Genocide that left nearly a million ethnic Tutsis dead.

Audience I identified my audience as my classmates, who could also be regarded as a portion of the general American public, most of whom were in the dark about the atrocities that occurred in 1994 in the African country of Rwanda. Many Americans had not been aware that a genocide was occurring, even under the watchful eye of the world press. In class, after a peer review, classmates were awed by the fact that such things could occur in this seemingly modern world where almost a million people were scratched from existence in only one hundred days, in spite of the potential of United States military power and the possibility of diplomacy by the United Nations. I wanted to open my audience's eyes.

Subject   When I started, I was torn between [writing on one of the suggested] concepts and [determining] how I could effectively apply one to a pertinent subject in which I had great interest. I knew I could take the easier route and write a straightforward essay addressing one of the concepts in a one-dimensional fashion. Instead, I chose a pair that had a number of controversial details to discuss. I opted for the concept of *integrity* and how it applied to the United States' and the United Nations' involvement, or lack thereof, in the Rwandan Genocide. In the end, I was able to connect the two in a way that met the demands of the assignment.

Writer   After reading about the situation that occurred in Rwanda in a book called *We Wish to Inform You That Tomorrow You Will Be Killed with Your Families* by Phillip Gourevitch, I became haunted by the subject of modern-day mass genocide. I tried to write the paper in a state of sort of suspended ignorance in order to keep an open mind since I had already read the book on Rwanda, and I had preconceived emotions about the subject. When I began researching, I tried to check those emotions at the door and allow myself to remain open to a fresh perspective. But, in the end, my research reinvigorated my anger and confusion about how genocides still occur.

CHRIS BUXTON-SMITH'S WRITING PROCESS

Brainstorming   The process I used to write this paper was relatively straightforward. Using techniques of which I had prior knowledge and new ones that I learned in class, I set about writing. The first step was to brainstorm. Using this technique, I was able to come up with numerous ideas, no matter the quality, and choose from among them a subject that I could combine with a concept given by our instructor. Even the most outlandish idea was not subject to disposal. I found brainstorming very helpful because I wrote down possible subjects to think about.

Finding a Focus   After brainstorming for a while, I set about choosing a concept and subject. In choosing *integrity*, I found myself with a general concept that needed to be narrowed down to address a specific aspect or act of integrity. At first, I thought integrity would be difficult to write about; but in combination with the subject of Rwanda, everything began to come together.

Researching   My next steps, and perhaps the most important ones, were researching my subject and finding quality sources to use. Since I had two topics which I had to bring together, I needed to find sources about each and combine them. Using books, periodicals, and online resources, I was able to dredge up enough information in what I thought were legitimate sources.

Organizing   Generating a working outline was a very important step in my writing process. Since so much information is usually contained amidst the clutter of notes, I found it very helpful to filter out information and organize it in a fashion that was easily viewable when I sat down to write my first draft. Honestly, though, my outline was rather sparse because I found myself really getting into freewriting about the subject. Sometimes, when one has strong feelings about a subject, the words just flow. Eventually, I was able to trim my content down and develop clear paragraphs.

Drafting and Revising   As I said, my drafting process consists of a lot of freewriting in confluence with my outline. I took the items in the outline, wrote topic sentences explaining them, and developed the paragraphs accordingly. Often, I found myself with too much content. So I tried to streamline each sentence, omitting redundant ideas. Oddly enough, this seemingly redundant material often proved valuable in later paragraphs when I thought I was stuck—but then saw that those points fit in.

Finishing   After a peer review session, I set about typing my final draft, using peer input combined with extra proofreading. I took into account everything I had learned about writing an argument and using sources. In addition, I added heartfelt conviction to a subject that I believe needed to be addressed.

CHRIS BUXTON-SMITH'S WORKING OUTLINE

Lest We Forget Rwanda

I. Introduction/thesis
II. Integrity
   - Integrity and Rwanda
   - Definition
III. Background
   - Conflict between the two ethnicities
   - Revolution and power struggle
   - Rise of Hutu power
IV. World awareness
   - Initially world not aware
   - America's stance on war and intervention
   - U.N. resolution
V. Genocide
   - Definition of *genocide*
   - Goal of the Hutu government regarding Tutsis
   - U.N. and U.S. viewed conflict as a civil war
VI. Civil war
VII. Misinformation/ignoring intelligence
   - Hutu security official's fax
VIII. Intervention
IX. Lack of morality/integrity
X. Conclusion/thesis

SAMPLE ANNOTATED RESEARCH PAPER (MLA)

Chris Buxton-Smith, "Lest We Forget About Rwanda"

1"
½"
Buxton-Smith 1

Chris Buxton-Smith
Instructor McMahon
English 1A
5 December 2005

Double-space paper

Center title →
Lest We Forget About Rwanda

Indent ½"
(5 spaces)

Introduction

1"
What would you do if one night while lying awake in bed, on the verge of sleep, you hear a blood-curdling scream from the house of your elderly next-door neighbor? Would you stand by and let the cries go unheeded, or would you attempt to remedy the situation by intervening? Hopefully, if you had some sense of integrity, moral fortitude, even an inkling of benevolence for your fellow human beings, you would assist your elderly neighbor.

1"

Background information; source identified, quotation of four lines or fewer not indented.

This comparison is a microcosm of a situation that occurred in the African country of Rwanda. According to Philip Gourevitch—author, journalist, and the editor of *The Paris Review*, "In Rwanda, in the course of 100 days in the spring and early summer of 1994, 800,000 people were put to death in the most unambiguous case of state-sponsored genocide in an attempt to exterminate a category of humanity, a people, since the Nazi Holocaust of the Jews of Europe" (*Triumph*). This massacre was one of the most expeditious and brutally efficient genocides in terms of the number of people that were killed in a relatively short period of time.

Research question

Background information; preview of specific points

Statement of thesis or claim; answer to research question

The question I must pose is: Should the United States and the United Nations have, as a matter of integrity, intervened in the situation? Understandably, many would say no. The U.S. is not the police force of the world, and the U.N. must adhere to a strict set of guidelines before it embarks on any peacekeeping mission. Many people feel that the two bodies must allow countries to carry out and conduct their own internal affairs whenever possible. I agree; but where do we draw the line that allows a nation to maintain its political sovereignty when its government sponsors the massacre of a portion of its own population?

Source: Chris Buxton-Smith "Lest We Forget About Rwanda."

1"

Buxton-Smith 2

My answer is that America and the United Nations did, as a matter of integrity, have a moral obligation to intervene in the Rwandan massacre.

Integrity is at the heart of my position on this situation. Law professor and author Stephen L. Carter observes in his essay "The Insufficiency of Honesty" that integrity is more than acting nobly when dealing with a situation. He says that there are three steps in defining the degree of one's integrity. These are "discerning what is right and what is wrong; acting on what you have discerned, even at personal cost; and saying openly you are acting on your understanding of what is right and what is wrong" (507). Obviously the massacre of 800,000 innocent people is inherently wrong; having knowledge that a massacre of 800,000 people is about to occur is inherently wrong, and not acting on this legitimate intelligence is painfully misguided. It is completely devoid of any semblance of integrity.

In order to understand the birth of the complex conflict between the two native ethnic groups in Rwanda, the Hutus and the Tutsis, it is necessary to have some background on the matter. Rwanda is located in central Africa, surrounded by Burundi, the Democratic Republic of the Congo, Tanzania, and Uganda.

Before the Germans and then the Belgians colonized Rwanda, there was little racial distinction or tension between the two groups; what tension there was, was due to the disproportionate distribution of economic wealth and political power. Gourevitch explains: "Until the late 19th century, which is to say, until European colonization, Tutsis (the minority) represented the aristocratic upper classes; Hutus were the peasant masses." Then, when the Europeans arrived, they used the pre-existing socioeconomic situation as a skeleton for the new colonial government that was implemented. They "took this traditional structure and made it even more extreme and more polarized into an almost apartheid-like system. And ethnic identity cards were issued, and Tutsis were privileged for all things, and Hutus were really made into a very oppressed mass" (*Triumph*).

Rwanda gained independence from Belgium in 1962. Then, Gourevitch reports, a revolution occurred. After years of oppression, the Hutus finally gained power over the Tutsis. They took over the

Margin annotations:

Warrants

Page number given; essay source

Background information

Source quoted, paraphrased, and quoted; online source—no page numbers

Buxton-Smith 3

country's government institutions and infrastructure; this new-found power, coupled with resentment towards their Tutsi counterparts, began a new era of Hutu power movements. With this new era came the social oppression of the once powerful Tutsis. There was "…a Hutu dictatorship running through the '60s, the '70s, the '80s, and into the mid '90s. Throughout that period, there was systematic political violence used to maintain this Hutu power" (*Triumph*).

According to Gourevitch, this violence climaxed when the slaughter of the Tutsis began in 1994, after Hutu President Habyarimana was killed when his plane was apparently shot down. Habyarimana was engaged in peace talks sanctioned by the U.N. in order to establish a cease fire between the rival groups, which—it has been suggested—militant Hutu leaders did not want. These militant leaders incited the massacre by building ethnic hatred of the Tutsis and saying that the Tutsis had killed the president (*Triumph*).

Initially, the world was not well informed about the situation in Rwanda because conflicting stories from inside sources, chaos within the country, and biased intelligence from within the Hutu regime clouded the brutal reality of the situation. The United States and the United Nations had been aware of some escalating violence and tension between the groups, but they seem to have shrugged it off as a conflict limited to within the Rwandan border. They did not intervene.

America's involvement in international conflicts has long been the topic of heated bipartisan and civilian debate, ranging from general support for the "World Wars" to heavy protest against the Vietnam War. U.S. involvement in a sovereign nation's war with another country, or with a country's civil war, is drastically different from U.S. involvement in a government-sponsored genocide like the one that occurred in Rwanda. However, both America's stance on genocide and the action required when it is occurring are clear. On Warrants December 9, 1948, the U.S., as a member of the United Nations, adopted a resolution, specifically resolution 260 (III), which states as follows: "The contracting parties confirm that genocide, whether committed in time of peace or in time of war, is a crime under international law which they undertake to prevent and to punish" (United Nations). Not only did America and the

Source worked into a sentence

Source paraphrased and cited

Student writer synthesizing information that is generally accepted

Warrants

Buxton-Smith 4

U.N. have a moral obligation to assist with the situation in Rwanda; they had a contractual obligation as well.

As a result of the European Holocaust of the 1930s and 40s, the word *genocide* was coined; it means "'the destruction of a nation or of an ethnic group' and implies the existence of a coordinated plan aimed at total extermination" (Destexhe, quoting Raphael Lemkin). This describes the goal of the Hutu government, Gourevitch claims, especially officials with close ties to the recently assassinated president. With no evidence, they blamed Tutsi extremists for the assassination, using it as a rallying call for Hutu militias to take up arms against their Tutsi neighbors. For decades, intermittent massacres had been occurring at the hands of Hutu extremists with the full knowledge of the government. To the rest of the world, including the United States, this appeared to be nothing more than a decades-long power struggle between two ethnic parties vying for political control; in essence, a civil war (*Triumph*).

Source using a source

United Nations and United States foreign policy dictate that, unless crimes against humanity are being committed, it is a violation of a nation's sovereignty to intervene in a civil war. A civil war, according to *The American Heritage Dictionary of the English Language, Fourth Edition* is "1. A war between factions or regions of the same country. 2. A state of hostility or conflict between elements within an organization." This seemed like what was occurring in Rwanda, but in reality the Tutsis had no political power or influence; they had no representatives in the government because the rule was totalitarian under the Hutu party. However, "much of the reporting said, 'The civil war has been renewed in Rwanda.' But a civil war involves two or more armies fighting one another—a rebel army and a government army. And it means that soldiers fight soldiers. The objective is to defeat the other party" (Gourevitch *Triumph*). Under this premise, the United Nations and the United States did not intervene.

Synthesis of material; source worked into sentence

Unfortunately, the premise upon which the U.S. and the U.N. did not intervene was not simply a case of misinformation; rather, it was a case of ignoring viable intelligence from a legitimate source within the Hutu regime. Gourevitch reports that on January 14, 1994, a Hutu security advisor sent a fax to the United Nations intelligence office alerting U.N. officials to the situation he knew was about to occur. This

Buxton-Smith 5

Hutu official was in the upper echelon of the party and was aware that his government was about to sponsor a massacre against unarmed Tutsi civilians. The official stated in his fax that he been hired by the now-deceased president's political party to train the Interahamawe, a Hutu power militia, in order to orchestrate the extermination of the Tutsis (*Triumph*). No one listened.

Only after the killings of a small contingent of Belgian U.N. peacekeepers and the identification of large arms caches, did the U.N. define the situation as genocide:

> By early June, the Secretary-General of the U.N.—and even...the French Foreign Minister—had taken to describing the slaughter in Rwanda as "genocide." But the U.N. High Commissioner for Human Rights still favored the phrase "possible genocide," while the Clinton administration actually forbade unqualified use of the g-word. The official formulation approved by the White House was: "acts of genocide may have occurred." (Gourevitch *Genocide*)

The U.S., after suffering a recent humiliation in the peacekeeping mission of Somalia, chose not to intervene. In addition, officials may have wanted to appear "respectful" of a sovereign nation's boundaries and its affairs within those boundaries.

Not only was there no intervention by the U.S., but little attention was paid by the U.S. government to the genocide in Rwanda. In her Pulitzer Prize–winning book *"A Problem from Hell": America and the Age of Genocide,* Samantha Power states, "It is shocking to note that during the entire three months of the genocide, Clinton never assembled his top policy advisors to discuss the killings." Power offers this explanation: "Rwanda generated no sense of urgency and could safely be avoided by Clinton at no political cost" (366). America and the United Nations, a country and an organization built upon the idea of maintaining freedom and integrity in regards to the civilized world, chose to ignore the desperate cries for help from an African nation on the brink of disaster.

Clearly, both the United States and the United Nations, in their failure to intervene, lacked any sense of integrity regarding the massacre in Rwanda; moral and lawful obligation deemed it necessary that action

---

Source paraphrased and cited

Material omitted (. . .)

Four lines or more quoted, indented; no quotation marks.

Buxton-Smith 6

be taken. Because no action was taken, they subsequently violated standards and ethics upon which the frames of both bodies were built. Stephen L. Carter states this about the Rwanda situation in an article in *Christianity Today:*

> In cases of genocide, we often hear opponents of unilateral action say that it is up to the world community to act. But this argument touches only expediency, not morality. We can well imagine a war that is morally imperative even though every country in the world lines up against it. We can also imagine a war that is morally prohibited even though every country supports it. If protecting a people against the ravages of their own sovereign is indeed a matter of moral urgency, one cannot shirk it on the ground that others do not agree. ("Defending")

It is true that the U.N. was created to be an organization where collective decisions lead to unified action in regards to world affairs; but when those collective decisions and their subsequent actions become mired in a political bog of allegiances and futile hopes of letting the situation run its course, action must be taken to preserve the sanctity of morality and the safety of the world. Carter again makes a poignant statement on the issue when he says that "the morality of humanitarian intervention has nothing to do with whether others agree that the action is appropriate" ("Defending").

Summing up

Our country and our world now have the blood of over 800,000 innocent men, women, and children on their hands because people with bureaucratic allegiances and obligations could not see past the red tape hindering their views of the reality in the Rwanda situation. In 1848, the American philosopher and author Henry David Thoreau—angered by the Mexican War—wrote this about American integrity: "This American government,—what is it but a tradition, though a recent one, endeavoring to transmit itself unimpaired to posterity, but each instant losing some of its integrity." The mistakes of the past should not cement our reactions towards events of the future. In times of peril, we must not let past actions cloud our response to imminent threats of human barbarity and depravity.

Buxton-Smith 7

As one nation and a part of one world, the United States cannot turn a deaf ear to the cries of a people under duress. The United Nations and the United States must remain vigilant towards maintaining the integrity of the rules and the laws that they have established, through consistent enforcement of resolutions like that of resolution 260 (III), lest we forget about those one hundred terrible days in Rwanda.

Works Cited

Carter, Stephen L. "Defending Our Neighbor." *Christianity Today.* Christianity Today International, Nov. 2004. Web. 15 Nov. 2005.

"The Insufficiency of Honesty." *Great Writing.* Ed. Harvey S. Weiner and Nora Eisenberg. San Francisco: McGraw, 2002. 507–12. Print.

"Civil war." *The American Heritage Dictionary of the English Language.* 4th ed. Boston: Houghton, 2000. Web. 1 Dec. 2005.

Destexhe, Alain. *The Crime of Genocide.* 1995. Web. 15 Nov. 2005.

Gourevitch, Philip. Genocide in Rwanda as quoted in "Glimpses of Tyranny and Resistance." 2003. Web. 10 Nov. 2005.

———. *The Triumph of Evil.* 1996. Web. 10 Nov. 2005. ———.

Power, Samantha. *"A Problem from Hell": America and the Age of Genocide.* New York: Perennial, 2003. Print.

Gianluigi Guercia/AFP/Getty Images

Rwandan boy in front of skulls from Rwandans massacred during the genocide.

Buxton-Smith 8

"Rwanda." *The Free Dictionary*. Farlex. Web. 1 Dec. 2005.

"The Rwandan Genocide through Photographs." *Rwanda*. Web. 1 Dec. 2005. <http://emileelime.tripod.com/id5.html>.

Thoreau, Henry David. *The Columbia World of Quotations*. New York: Columbia UP, 1996. Web. 20 Nov. 2005.

United Nations General Assembly. "Convention on the Prevention and Punishment of the Crime of Genocide." 1948. Web. 15 Nov. 2005. <http://www.hrweb.org/legal/genocide.html>.

Electronic version of print dictionary

Online posting of television program

Book

Website

CHAPTER 14 | Summary

- Researchers use questions to help them identify and focus their topic.

- *Primary resources* include original documents, works of literature, and first-hand reports, observations, or interviews; *secondary resources* comment on other resources.

- When doing research, you can use electronic and print sources in the library, collect information from experts, or obtain data from the field through interviews, questionnaires, and field research.

- To evaluate sources for a research project, you should ask yourself: How reliable is the source? How knowledgeable or experienced is the author? What specific ideas are being presented?

- To evaluate the reliability of a website, you need to determine its authority, accuracy, objectivity, and currency.

- *Plagiarism,* presenting another person's ideas or words as your own, is a serious offense. Avoid plagiarism by documenting your sources in your research paper thoroughly and accurately.

- *Quoting* is using someone's exact words; *paraphrasing* is restating an idea in your own words. Use quotation marks *only* for quotes, but credit the source for *both* quotes and paraphrased ideas. Information considered common knowledge does not require quotes or documentation.

- To keep track of your research and ensure proper documentation of your sources, take notes on your computer and/or on note cards, create an annotated bibliography, and summarize your findings.

- To successfully integrate source material into your research paper, be sure to introduce sources, establish your voice, and choose a point of view appropriate for your purpose and be consistent with it.

- Proper documentation is necessary to: give credibility to a paper, help readers and other researchers learn more, give credit where credit is due, observe the courtesies of conversation, and avoid plagiarism.

- Allow yourself enough time to plan, research, collaborate on, write, and format your paper properly.

Modern Language Association Style:
MLA and APA Documentation Styles

Careful documentation and a complete Works Cited list provide readers with full information on sources cited in a paper. (See The Logic of MLA Style, Chapter 14, pages 561–562 for information on in-text citations.)

To be useful to readers, citations must be clear and consistent. Therefore, very specific rules of documentation have been devised and must be applied.

QUICK REFERENCE

Using the following formats, begin preparing your Works Cited entries as soon as you begin taking notes.

- A book by one author

  Author's last name, first name. *Book title*. Additional information. City of publication: Publishing company, publication date. Medium of publication.

- An article by one author

  Author's last name, first name. "Article title." *Periodical title* Date: inclusive pages. Medium of publication.

CITATION FORMAT

Most research writing in English and other humanities courses uses the documentation format described in the *MLA [Modern Language Association] Handbook for Writers of Research Papers*, seventh edition (New York: MLA, 2003). This documentation format, known as MLA style, is simple, clear, and widely accepted.

ACCURACY AND COMPLETENESS

Because Works Cited entries direct readers to sources used in research writing, they must be as complete as possible and presented in a consistent and recognizable format. If the following guidelines do not cover a source you want to use, consult the *MLA Handbook*, your instructor, or a reference librarian.

WHAT TO INCLUDE IN MLA CITATIONS

MLA citations present information in an established order. When combining forms (to list a translation of a second edition, for example), follow these guidelines to determine the order of information:

1. *Author(s).* Use the name or names with the spelling and order shown on the title page of a book or on the first page of an article, without degrees, titles, or affiliations. If no author (individual or organization) is named, list the work by title in the Works Cited entry.

2. *Title.* List titles from part to whole: the title of an essay (the part) before the book (the whole), the title of an article before the periodical title, an episode before the program, or a song before the compact disc. Use complete titles, including subtitles, no matter how long they are.

3. *Additional information.* In the order noted next, include any of the following information listed on the title page of the book or on the first page of an article: editor, translator, compiler, edition number, volume number, or name of series.

4. *Facts of publication.* For a book, find the publisher's name and the place of publication on the title page and the date of publication on the copyright page (immediately following the title page). Use the publisher's name in abbreviated form (numerous samples are present throughout the appendix), use the first city listed if more than one is given, and use the most recent date shown. When a city is outside the United States, include an abbreviation for the country, if necessary, for clarity. For a periodical, find the volume number, issue number, and date on the masthead (at the top of the first page of a newspaper or within the first few pages in a journal or magazine, often in combination with the table of contents).

5. *Page numbers.* When citing a part of a book or an article, provide inclusive page numbers without page abbreviations. Record inclusive page numbers from 1 to 99 in full form (8–12, 33–39, 68–73); inclusive numbers of 100 or higher require at least the last two digits and any other digits needed for clarity (100–02, 120–36, 193–206).

6. *Medium of publication.* MLA now requests that the medium of publication be included in citations: Print, Web, Film, DVD, and so on. For examples, see pages 92, 283, 340, 375, 433, 475, and 581.

FORMAT FOR MLA WORKS CITED LIST

The MLA Works Cited list follows these general formatting guidelines:

- Begin the first line of each entry at the left margin, and indent subsequent lines one-half inch (five spaces).

- Invert the author's name so that it appears with the last name first (to alphabetize easily). If sources are coauthored, list additional authors' names in normal, first-last order.

- Italicize titles of full-length works. (MLA no longer recommends underlining in place of italicizing.)
- Separate major sections of entries (author, title, and publication information) with periods and one space, not two. When other forms of end punctuation are used (when titles end with question marks or exclamation points, for example), the period may be omitted.
- Double-space all entries; do not insert additional space between entries.

ANNOTATIONS

Annotations are sometimes used to clarify for readers the value of sources or to provide additional information. Typically, these comments assess the quality of the source, describe the source's condition or availability, or provide additional clarification. In most student writing, annotations usually evaluate a source's value for the research project by highlighting its special features.

Present an annotation in one or more complete sentences. It follows the citation's closing period and retains the citation's indention pattern and line spacing, as in this sample.

> National Commission on Excellence in Education. *A Nation at Risk: The Imperative for Educational Reform.* Washington: GPO, 1983. Print. With its aggressively critical tone, this small publication by the NCEE launched the educational reform movement that is affecting our schools today.

BOOKS

Book by one author

> Monmonier, Mark. *Rhumb Lines and Map Wars: A Social History of the Mercator Projection.* Chicago: U of Chicago P, 2004. Print.

(The letters *U* and *P*, without periods, abbreviate *University* and *Press*. Also note the medium consulted at the end of the entry—in this case, *Print*.)

Book by two or more authors

Authors' names appear in the order in which they are presented on the title page, which may or may not be alphabetical. A comma follows the initial author's first name; second and third authors' names appear in normal order.

> Fainaru-Wada, Mark, and Lance Williams. *Game of Shadows: Barry Bonds, BALCO, and the Steroids Scandal That Rocked Professional Sports.* New York: Gotham, 2006. Print.

When a book has four or more authors, include only the first author's name in full form; substitute *et al.* (meaning "and others," not italicized) for the names of additional authors.

> McDaniel, Susan H., et al. *Family-Oriented Primary Care: A Manual for Medical Providers.* 2nd ed. New York: Springer, 2004. Print.

Book with no author

When no author is named, list the work by title. Alphabetize books listed by title using the first important word of the title, not the article *a, an,* or *the.*

> *UPI Stylebook and Guide to Newswriting.* 4th ed. Sterling: Capital, 2004. Print.

585

When citing multiple works by the same author, present the first citation completely. Subsequent entries, alphabetized by title, are introduced by three hyphens and a period. Coauthored works require full names and are alphabetized after those with single authors.

> Ehrenreich, Barbara. *Bait and Switch: The (Futile) Pursuit of the American Dream.* New York: Metropolitan Books, 2005. Print.
>
> ---. *Nickel and Dimed: On (Not) Getting By in America.* New York: Holt, 2002. Print.
>
> Ehrenreich, Barbara, Elizabeth Hess, and Gloria Jacobs. *Re-Making Love: The Feminization of Sex.* Garden City: Anchor-Doubleday, 1986. Print.

(Notice that the publisher of the last selection includes a two-part name: the imprint and the major publisher; see "An Imprint," page 588, for an additional sample.)

When an organization is both the author and the publisher, present the name completely in the author position, and use an abbreviation in the publisher position.

> American Psychological Association. *Publication Manual of the American Psychological Association.* 6th ed. Washington: APA, 2001. Print.

The edition number, noted on the title page, follows the title of the book. When a book also has an editor, translator, or compiler, the edition number follows that information. Edition numbers are presented in numeral-abbreviation form (2nd, 3rd, 4th).

> Bjelajac, David. *American Art: A Cultural History.* 2nd ed. Upper Saddle River: Prentice, 2004. Print.

A reprint, a newly printed but unaltered version of a book, is identified as such on the title page or copyright page. The original publication date precedes the facts of publication, and the date of the reprinted edition follows the publisher's name.

> Joyce, James. *Ulysses.* 1992. Mineola: Dover, 2002. Print.

A multivolume work may have one title, or it may have a comprehensive title for the complete work and separate titles for each volume. When you use the entire set of volumes, use the collective title and note the number of volumes. If volumes are published over several years, provide inclusive dates (2000–02); if the work is still in progress, include the earliest date, a hyphen, one space, and the closing period (1999– .).

> *The Norton Anthology of American Literature.* Ed. Nina Baym. 6th ed. 5 vols. New York: Norton, 2002. Print.

To emphasize a single volume, first cite the volume as a separate book. Then add the volume number, the collection title, and the total number of volumes.

> Ramazani, Jahan, Richard Ellman, and Robert O'Clair, eds. 2 vols. *Modern Poetry.* 3rd ed. New York: Norton, 2003. Print. Vol. 1 of *The Norton Anthology of Modern and Contemporary Poetry.*

To cite a work in a collection, include the name of the selection's author, the title of the specific selection (appropriately punctuated), the collection title, publication facts, and the inclusive page numbers for the selection (without page abbreviations).

To cite more than one selection from the collection, prepare separate citations (see Multiple Selections from the Same Collection, which follows).

> Foster, Roy. "Something of Us Will Remain: Sebastian Barry and History." *Out of History: Essays on the Writings of Sebastian Barry.* Ed. Christina Hunt Mahony. Washington: Catholic U of America P, 2006. 183–97. Print.

Previously published work in a collection

To indicate that a selection has been previously published, begin the citation with original facts of publication. *Rpt.*, meaning "reprinted," begins the second part of the citation, which includes information about the source you have used.

> Sloan, Gary. "Sleuthing Patriotic Slogans." *Alternet* 10 Apr. 2003. Rpt. in *The Thomson Reader: Conversations in Context.* Ed. Robert P. Yagelski. New York: Wadsworth, 2006. 323–26. Print.

Multiple selections from the same collection

To cite several selections from the same collection, prepare a citation for the complete work—beginning either with the editor's name or with the collection title. Additional references begin with the author of the individual selection and its title. However, instead of providing full publication information, include the editor's name or a shortened version of the title; provide inclusive page numbers for the selection. Notice that all citations are alphabetized.

> Denman, Peter. "From Rhetoric to Narrative: The Poems of Sebastian Barry." Mahony 9–23.
>
> Mahony, Christina Hunt, ed. *Out of History: Essays on the Writings of Sebastian Barry.* Washington: Catholic U of America P, 2006. Print.
>
> Roche, Anthony. "Redressing the Irish Theatrical Landscape: Sebastian Barry's *The Only True History of Lizzie Finn.*" Mahony 147–65.

Article in an encyclopedia or other reference work

Use an author's name when it is available. If only initials are listed with the article, match them with the name from the list of contributors. Well-known reference books require no information other than the title, edition number (if any), and date. Citations for less well-known or recently published reference works include full publication information. Page numbers are not needed when a reference work is arranged alphabetically.

> DeGregorio, William. "Zachary Taylor." *The Complete Book of U.S. Presidents.* 6th ed. New York: Gramercy, 2005. 175–86. Print.

(Because the articles on presidents are arranged chronologically, not alphabetically, page numbers are required.)

> Angermüller, Rudolph. "Salieri, Antonio." *The New Grove Dictionary of Music and Musicians.* 2001 ed. Print.

(This 20-volume set is extremely well known and consequently needs no publication information.)

When no author's name or initials appear with an article, begin with the title, reproduced to match the pattern in the reference book. Other principles remain the same.

> "Socrates." *Encyclopedia of Ancient Greece.* Ed. Nigel Wilson. New York: Routledge, 2006. Print.

Work in a series

The name of a series (a collection of books related to the same subject, genre, time period, and so on) is typically found on a book's title page and should be included at the end of the entry. Abbreviate the word *Series* (*Ser.*) if it is part of the series title.

> Yang, Gua-ja. *Contradictions*. Trans. Stephen Epstein and Kim Mi-Young. Ithaca: Cornell UP, 2005. Print. Cornell East Asia Ser.

When a volume in a series is numbered, include both the series name and the number, followed by a period.

> Audubon, John James. *The Audubon Reader*. New York: Knopf, 2006. Print. Everyman's Library 284.

Imprint

An imprint is a specialized division of a larger publishing company. When an imprint name and a publisher name both appear on the title page, list them together (imprint name first), separated by a hyphen and no additional spaces.

> Atwood, Margaret. *The Tent*. New York: Talese-Doubleday, 2006. Print.

(Nan A. Talese is the imprint, which is shortened to *Talese*; Doubleday is the publisher.)

Translation

A translator's name must always be included in a citation for a translated work because he or she prepared the version that you read. To emphasize the original work (the most common pattern), place the abbreviation *Trans.* (for "translated by," not italicized) and the translator's name after the title (but following editors' names, if the translator translated the entire work).

> Allende, Isabel. *Zorro: A Novel*. Trans. Margaret Sayers Peden. New York: Harper, 2005. Print.

If selections within a collection are translated by different people, then each translator's name should follow the appropriate selection.

> Freixis, Laura. "Absurd Ending." Trans. John R. King. *Short Stories in Spanish: New Penguin Parallel Texts*. Ed. John R. King. New York: Penguin, 2001. 143–62. Print.

(This citation indicates that John R. King was both translator and editor.)

Preface, introduction, foreword, epilogue, or afterword

To cite material that is separate from the primary text of a book, begin with the name of the person who wrote the separate material, an assigned title (if applicable) in quotation marks or a descriptive title for the part used (capitalized but not punctuated), the title of the book, the name of the book's author (introduced with *By*, not italicized), publication facts, and inclusive page numbers for the separate material. Note that most prefatory or introductory material is paged using lowercase roman numerals.

> Updike, John. Introduction. *Walden*. By Henry David Thoreau. Ed. J. Lyndon Shanley. Princeton: Princeton UP, 2004. ix–xiii. Print.

Pamphlet

When a pamphlet contains clear and complete information, it is cited like a book. When information is missing, use these abbreviations: *N.p.* for "No place of publication," *n.p.* for "no publisher," *n.d.* for "no date," and *N. pag.* (with a space between the abbreviations) for "no page."

Depression and Spinal Cord Injury. Seattle: UW Medicine, 2005. N. pag. Print.

Dissertation   A citation for an unpublished dissertation begins with the author's name, the dissertation title in quotation marks, the abbreviation *Diss.* (not italicized), the name of the degree-granting school (with *University* abbreviated), and the date.

>   Wentland, Meghan Pontbriand. "Terrorists and Terrorism: Representations of Violence in 'Troubles' Fiction." Diss. Catholic U of America, 2004. Print.

A published dissertation is a book and should be presented as such. However, include dissertation information between the title and the facts of publication.

Sacred writings   A citation for a sacred writing follows a pattern similar to that of any other book, except information about its version and who translated it should be included when available as well.

>   *The Bhagavad Gita.* Trans. and Intro. by Juan Mascaró. London: Rider & Co., 1970. Print.

>   *The New Oxford Annotated Bible.* Ed. Herbert G. May and Bruce M. Metzger. Rev. Expanded Edition. New York: Oxford UP, 1977. Print. Standard Version.

(This citation provides full information, highlighting a version other than the King James and the editorial work that it includes.)

GOVERNMENT-CIVIC DOCUMENTS

Government document   A citation for *Congressional Record* is exceedingly brief: the italicized and abbreviated title, *Cong. Rec.,* the date (presented in day-month-year order), and the page number. Page numbers used alone indicate Senate records; page numbers preceded by an *H* indicate records from the House of Representatives.

>   *Cong. Rec.* 7 April 2006. 3380. Print.

>   *Cong. Rec.* 6 April 2006. H1566. Print.

Government agency   Information to describe a government document is generally presented in this order: (1) country, state, province, or county; (2) government official, governing body, sponsoring department, commission, center, ministry, or agency; (3) office, bureau, or committee; (4) the title of the publication, italicized; (5) if appropriate, the author of the document, the number and session of Congress, or the kind and number of the document; (6) the city of publication, the publisher, and the date.

When citing more than one work from the same government or agency, use three hyphens and a period to substitute for identical elements.

>   United States. Cong. Senate. *Committee on Energy and Natural Resources.* 107th Cong., 2nd sess. 2002. Washington: GPO, 2003. Print.

>   ---. Dept. of Education. *Alcohol, Other Drugs, and College: A Parent's Guide.* Washington: GPO, 2000. Print.

>   ---. Dept. of Health and Human Services. *Steps to a Healthier US.* Washington: GPO, 2005. Print.

(The Government Printing Office, the publisher of most federal documents, is abbreviated to save space.)

PERIODICALS

Article in a monthly magazine

To cite an article in a monthly magazine, include the author's name, the article's title in quotation marks, the magazine's name (italicized), the month (abbreviated) and year, the inclusive pages of the article (without page abbreviations), and the medium of publication.

> Teague, Matthew. "Double Blind: The Untold Story of How British Intelligence Infiltrated and Undermined the IRA." *The Atlantic* Apr. 2006: 53–62. Print.

(Note that the period comes before the closing quotation marks of the article's title, that one space [but no punctuation] separates the periodical title and the date, and that a colon and a space separate the date and the pages.)

Article in a weekly magazine

A citation for an article in a weekly or biweekly magazine is identical to that for a monthly magazine, with one exception: the publication date is presented in more detailed form, in day-month-year order (with the month abbreviated).

> Conley, Kevin. "How High Can You Go? The Roller Coaster's New Golden Age." *The New Yorker* 30 Aug. 2005: 48–55. Print.

Article in a journal with continuous/ separate paging

A journal with continuous paging numbers issues sequentially for the entire year. For this kind of journal, place the volume and issue numbers after the journal title, identify the year in parentheses, follow it with a colon and a space, list page numbers, and end with the medium of publication. Note that MLA no longer makes a distinction between journals continuously paged or not; include the volume and issue numbers for both.

> Fry, Prem S., and Dominique L. Debats. "Sources of Life Strengths as Predictors of Late-Life Mortality and Survivorship." *International Journal of Aging and Human Development* 62.1 (2006): 303–34. Print.

For a journal that pages each issue separately, follow the volume number with a period and the issue number (without spaces). If no volume number is given, include the issue number alone.

> Brittan, Alice. "The Diarist, the Cryptographer, and *The English Patient*." *PMLA* 121.1 (2006): 200–13. Print.

Article in a newspaper

A citation for a newspaper resembles that for a magazine: it includes the author's name, article title (in quotation marks), newspaper title (italicized), the location [in brackets], the date (in day-month-year order, followed by a colon), inclusive pages, and medium of publication.

However, when a newspaper has editions (*morning, evening, national*), they must be identified. After the year, place a comma and describe the edition, abbreviating common words.

When sections of a newspaper are designated by letters, place the section letter with the page number, without a space (*A22, C3, F11*). If sections are indicated by numerals, place a comma after the date or edition (rather than a colon), include the abbreviation *sec.* (not italicized), the section number, a colon, a space, and the page number (*sec. 1: 22, sec. 3: 2, sec. 5: 17*).

Callender, David. "Amid Scandals, Still No Sign of Campaign Reform." *Capital Times* [Madison] 15 Dec. 2005: A1. Print.

When an article continues in a later part of the paper, indicate the initial page, use a comma, and then add the subsequent page. If the article appears on more than three separated pages, list the initial page, followed by a plus sign (*22+, A17+, sec. 2: 9+*).

Weekly newspapers are cited just like daily newspapers.

Keefe-Feldman, Mike. "Heart of Noise." *Washington City Paper* 7 Apr. 2006: 311. Print.

Editorial The citation for an editorial resembles that for a magazine or newspaper article, with one exception: the word *Editorial* (not italicized), with a period, follows the title of the essay.

Herbert, Bob. "George Bush's Trillion-Dollar War." Editorial. *New York Times* 23 Mar. 2006, natl. ed.: A25. Print.

Letter to the editor Include the author's name, the word *Letter* (not italicized), the name of the publication (magazine, journal, or newspaper), and appropriate facts of publication. Do not record descriptive, attention-getting titles that publications, not authors, supply.

Alexie, Sherman. Letter. *Harper's* Dec. 2005: 6. Print.

Review Begin with the author's name and the title of the review (if one is provided). The abbreviation *Rev. of* (not italicized) follows, publication information ends the citation, incorporating elements required for different kinds of sources.

Gleiberman, Owen. "The High Drama." Rev. of *Traffic,* Dir. Steven Soderbergh. Perf. Benicio Del Toro, Catherine Zeta-Jones, Don Cheadle, and Michael Douglas. *Entertainment Weekly* 5 Jan. 2001: 45–46. Print.

NONPRINT SOURCES

Lecture or speech If you have difficulty finding the information to document nonprint sources clearly, ask your instructor or a librarian for help.

A citation for a formal lecture or speech includes the speaker's name, the title of the presentation (in quotation marks), the name of the lecture or speaker series (if applicable), the location of the speech (convention, meeting, university, library, meeting hall), the city, the date in day-month-year order, and the medium of delivery.

Courtright, Robert. "The Carpe Diem Poem." George Mason U, McLean. 11 Apr. 2006. Class Lecture.

Doyle, Roddy. "An Evening with Roddy Doyle." Seattle Arts and Lectures. Seattle.15 Nov. 2004. Lecture.

(For class lectures, provide as much of this information as possible: speaker, title of lecture in quotation marks, a descriptive title, the school, the city, and the date.)

Bush, George W. State of the Union Address. U.S. Capitol. 31 Jan. 2006. Address.

Work of art When an artist titles his or her own work, include this information: artist's name; the title (italicized); the date of composition (if the year is unknown, write *N.d.*); the medium of composition; the museum, gallery, or collection where the work of art is housed; and the city (and country if needed for clarity).

> Cézanne, Paul. *Houses Along a Road.* N.d. Oil on canvas. The Hermitage, St. Petersburg, Russia.

When an artist has not titled a work, use the title that art historians have given to it (not italicized), followed by a brief description of the work. The rest of the citation is the same.

> Madonna and Child with Cherubim. N.d. Bas-relief in marble. Vatican Library, Vatican City.

Map, graph, table, or chart A map, graph, table, or chart is treated like a book. If known, include the name of the author, artist, designer, scientist, person, or group responsible for the map, graph, table, or chart. Then include the title (italicized), followed by a separately punctuated descriptive title. Also include any other necessary information such as the date.

> Pope, C. Arden. *Children's Respiratory Hospital Admissions.* Graph 2010.

Cartoon Begin with the cartoonist's name, the title of the cartoon in quotation marks, and the word *Cartoon* (not italicized), followed by a period. Then include the citation information required for the source and conclude with the medium of publication.

> Rees, David. "Get Your War On." Cartoon. *Rolling Stone* 11 Dec. 2003: 36. Print.

Film To cite a film as a complete work, include the title (italicized), the director (noted by the abbreviation *Dir.,* not italicized), the studio, and the date of release. If you include other people's contributions, do so after the director's name by using brief phrases (*Screenplay by, Original score by*) or abbreviations (*Perf.* for "performed by," *Prod.* for "produced by") to clarify their roles. Indicate a nonfilm format—VHS, DVD, or laserdisc—before the studio name. If a film is released by two studios, include both names, separated by a hyphen.

> *Ray.* Dir. Taylor Hackford. Perf. Jamie Foxx, Regina King. Universal Pictures, 2004. Film.

To emphasize the contribution of an individual (rather than the film as a whole), place the person's name first, followed by a comma and a descriptive title (beginning with a lowercase letter). The rest of the citation follows normal patterns.

> Allen, Woody, dir. *Anything Else.* Perf. Jason Biggs and Christina Ricci. Dream-Works SKG, 2003. Film.

> "Flunky File Clerk." *American Splendor.* Dir. Robert Pulcini and Shari Springer Berman. Perf. Paul Giamatti. HBO Video, 2003. DVD.

Television broadcast List a regular program by the title (italicized), the network (e.g., CBS, CNN, Fox), the local station (including both the call letters and the city, separated by a comma), the broadcast date (in day-month-year order), and the medium of reception.

Include other people's contributions after the program title, using brief phrases (*Written by, Hosted by*) or abbreviations (*Perf.* for "performed by," *Prod.* for "produced by") to clarify their roles.

> *The Sopranos*. Perf. James Gandolfini and Edie Falco. HBO. 15 Apr. 2006. Television.

To cite a single episode of an ongoing program, include the name of the episode in quotation marks before the program's title. Other elements are presented in the same order as used for a regular program.

> "Two Weeks Out." *The West Wing*. Perf. Alan Alda, Jimmy Smits, and Richard Schiff. NBC. WRC, Washington. 19 Mar. 2006. Television.

List special programs by title, followed by traditional descriptive information. If a special program is part of a series (for example, Hallmark Hall of Fame, Great Performances, or American Playhouse), include the series name without quotation marks or italics immediately preceding the name of the network.

> *The Sleeping Beauty*. Composed by Peter Ilich Tchaikovsky. Chor. Marius Petipa. Perf. Viviana Durante and Zoltan Solymosi. Great Performances. PBS. WFYI, Indianapolis. 24 Dec. 1995. Performance.

Radio broadcast
A citation for a radio broadcast follows the same guidelines as those for a television broadcast.

> *The War of the Worlds*. CBS Radio. WCBS, New York. 30 Oct. 1938. Radio.

Recording
A citation for a recording usually begins with the performer or composer, followed by the title of the recording (italicized except for titles using numerals for musical form, key, or number), the recording company, the copyright date, and the medium (such as *CD* for compact disc or *LP* for long-playing record).

> The Beatles. *Let It Be . . . Naked*. Capitol/Apple, 2003. CD.
>
> Davis, Miles. *The Cellar Door Sessions 1970*. 6 discs. Sony, 2005. CD.

To cite a single selection from a recording, include the selection title in quotation marks followed by the title of the complete recording. All else remains the same.

> Springsteen, Bruce. "Silver Palomino." *Devils and Dust*. Sony, 2005. CD.

To cite liner notes, the printed material that comes with many recordings, list the name of the writer and the description *Liner notes* (not italicized), followed by a period. The rest of the citation follows normal patterns.

> Kooper, Al. Liner notes. *Bob Dylan: No Direction Home: The Soundtrack [The Bootleg Series Vol. 7]*. 2 Discs. Sony, 2005. CD.

Interview
A citation for a personally conducted interview includes the name of the person interviewed, the type of interview (personal or telephone), and the interview date.

> Heller, William. Personal interview. 5 Feb. 2006.

A citation for a broadcast or printed interview includes the name of the person interviewed, the descriptive title *Interview* (not italicized), and information necessary to describe the source.

> Holloway, Dave. Interview. *Larry King Live*. CNN. 11 Apr. 2006. Television.

Transcript A transcript of a program is presented according to the source of the original broadcast, with clarifying information provided.

> Adler, Margot. "Letters Offer Glimpse of Life in Nazi Labor Camps." *All Things Considered*. Natl. Public Radio. 7 Mar. 2006. Print. Transcript.

Questionnaire or survey A citation for a personally conducted questionnaire or survey begins with your name (since you are the author of the questions and compiler of the results) and then includes a descriptive title and the date (which may be inclusive) on which you gathered your information. For additional clarity, you may include information about the location of your work.

> Greene, Erika. Survey. Terre Haute: Indiana State U. 30 Jan. 2006. Print.

ELECTRONIC SOURCES

Businesses, organizations, government agencies, and publishers of all kinds have transferred many of their print-based documents to subscription databases, CD-ROMs, the Internet, online video broadcasts, and other electronic formats.

As you gather citation information for Internet and other electronic sources, you must be both resourceful and patient because the patterns of electronic publication are less consistent than those of traditional print publication. Your goal should be to gather the most complete set of data possible to describe each electronic source, following the patterns described in this section.

Online scholarly project or information database To cite an entire online scholarly project or information database, present available information in this order: the title of the project or database, italicized; the editor or compiler, if identified, introduced with the abbreviation *ed.* or *comp.* (not italicized); the version number, if applicable; the date of electronic posting or the date of the most recent update; the name of the sponsoring organization or institution, if identified; the medium of publication (Web); the date you accessed the site; and the electronic address (URL), in angle brackets. *Note:* Current MLA guidelines recommend that a URL be included in Works Cited entries only when the reader probably cannot find the source without it or if your instructor requires one.

> *ProQuest.* 2006. ProQuest Company. Web. 10 Apr. 2006.
>
> *The Victorian Web.* Ed. George P. Landow. 2005. Brown U. Web. 11 Apr. 2006.

To cite a selected source—article, illustration, map, or other—from an online scholarly project or information database, begin with the name of the author (or artist, compiler, or editor) of the individual source, if appropriate; the title of the source, punctuated appropriately (quotation marks for articles, italics for charts, and so on); and print information if the source reproduces a print version. Continue the citation with the name of the online project or database and other required information. However, use the URL of the specific source, not the general address for the project or database, in angle brackets.

Cody, David. "Queen Victoria." *Victorian Web*. 2005. Brown U. Web. 11 Sep. 2010. <http://www.victorianweb.org/vn/victor6.html>.

Cooke, Bill. "Fatal Attraction." *Astronomy* 34.5 (2006): 46–52. *ProQuest*. 2006. ProQuest Company. Web. 20 Apr. 2006. <http://proquest.umi.com/pqdweb/>.

Website To cite a website, including blogs, podcasts, and video, provide the name of the author, editor, or host, if any; the title of the site, italicized; the date of electronic posting or the date of the most recent update; the name of the organization or institution, if any, affiliated with the site; the medium of publication; the date you accessed the site; and the URL (if needed), in angle brackets. As the variety of online content, such as podcasts and v-casts, increases, new academic citation guidelines will be issued. For the purposes of your papers, it is most important that you provide your reader with enough information to locate and verify the site, and that you properly acknowledge any ideas or content that you find online.

ABA Law Student Division. 5 Jan. 2002. American Bar Association. Web. 11 Jan. 2002.

UNICEF. 7 Jan. 2002. United Nations. Web. 12 Jan. 2002.

Atrios. "Unpopular President." *Escaton*. Web. 24 Apr. 2006. Weblog. <http://atrios.blogstop.com.>

ABC News. *The Afternote*. 22 Apr. 2006. Web. 24 April 2006. Podcast. <http://abcnews.go.com/ThisWeek/>.

Online book To cite an online book that has a corresponding print version, first prepare a standard citation describing the print version. Then provide additional information required for a scholarly project or information database, if applicable; the medium of publication; the date you accessed the site; and the specific URL of the book, not the general project or database, in angle brackets.

Tarkington, Booth. *Gentle Julia*. New York: Doubleday, 1922. *Project Gutenberg*. Apr. 2006. U of Illinois. Web. 26 Apr. 2006. <http://www.gutenberg.org/etext/18259>.

Article in an online encyclopedia or reference source To cite an online book that is available only in electronic form, provide the name of the author or editor; the title, italicized; the date of electronic posting or the date of the most recent update; the name of the sponsoring organization or institution, if provided; the medium of publication; the date you accessed the site; and the URL of the book, not the project or database, in angle brackets.

Buxhoeveden, Sophie. *The Life and Tragedy of Alexandra Feodorvna, Empress of Russia*. 2004. *Russian History Website*. Pallasart and the Alexander Palace Association. Web. 20 Apr. 2006. <http://www.alexenderpalace.org/alexandra/>.

To cite an article from an online encyclopedia or reference source, provide the author of the entry, if there is one; the title of the entry exactly as it appears in the source ("Paige, Satchel"); the name of the reference work, italicized; the date of electronic posting or the date of the most recent update; the medium of publication; the date you accessed the site; and the URL for the specific article, not the general reference, in angle brackets.

> Coney, Peter. "Plate Tectonics." *Encarta Online Encyclopedia.* 2006. Web. 4 Apr. 2006. <http://encarta.msn.com/encyclopedia_761554623/Plate_Tectonics.html>.

Online government document

To cite an online version of a government document—book, report, proceedings, brochure, or other—first provide the information required for the print source. Then continue the citation with the information appropriate to the electronic source, whether it is a scholarly project, an information database, or a website.

> United States. Cong. Budget Office. *China's Growing Demand for Oil and Its Impact on U.S. Petroleum Markets.* Washington: GPO, 2006. Cong. Budget Office. Web. 26 Apr. 2006. <http://www.cbo.gov/ftpdocs/71xx/doc7128/04-07-ChinaOil.pdf>.

Article in an online magazine

To cite an article in an online magazine, provide the name of the author, if appropriate; the title of the article, in quotation marks; the name of the magazine, italicized; the date of electronic publication or the date of the most recent update; the medium of publication; the date on which you accessed the article; and the URL of the specific article, not the general magazine site, in angle brackets.

> O'Neill, Hugh. "You Say You Want a Resolution?" *Men's Health.com* 9 Jan. 2001. Web. 11 Jan. 2002. <http://www.menshealth.com/health/resolution.html>.

Article in an online journal

To cite an article in an online journal, provide the name of the author, if appropriate; the title of the article, in quotation marks; the name of the journal, italicized; the volume and issue number; the year of publication, in parentheses; the medium of publication; the date on which you accessed the article; and the URL of the specific article, not the general journal site, in angle brackets.

> Cramer, Kenneth M., and Lynn A. Perrault. "Effects of Predictability, Actual Controllability, and Awareness of Choice on Perceptions of Control." *Current Research in Social Psychology* 11.8 (2006). Web. 20 Apr. 2006. <http://www.uiowa.edu/%7Egrpproc/crisp/crisp.html>.

Article in an online newspaper

To cite an article in an online newspaper, provide the name of the author, if appropriate; the title of the article, in quotation marks; the name of the newspaper, italicized; the date of electronic publication or the date of the most recent update; the medium of publication; the date on which you accessed the article; and the URL of the specific article, not the general newspaper site, in angle brackets.

> Rodriguez, Cindy. "Amid Dispute, Plight of Illegal Workers Revisited." *Boston Globe* 9 Jan. 2001. Web. 10 Jan. 2002 <http://www.boston.com/dailyglobe2/010/nation/amid_dispute_plight_of_illegal_workers_revisited1.shtml>.

Online transcript of a lecture or speech

To cite the transcript of a lecture or speech, first provide the information required for a lecture or speech. Then include the word *Transcript,* not italicized; the date of electronic publication or the date of the most recent update; the medium of publication; the date on which you accessed the transcript; and the URL of the specific transcript, not the general site, in angle brackets.

King, Martin Luther, Jr. Nobel Peace Prize Acceptance Speech. Nobel Prize Ceremony. Oslo. 10 Dec. 1964. Transcript. 2001. Web. 31 Jan. 2002. <http://www .stanford.edu/group/king>.

Work of art online

To cite a work of art online, provide the name of the artist, if known; the assigned title of the work of art, italicized, or the common name of the work of art, not italicized; a phrase describing the artistic medium; the museum, gallery, or collection where the work is housed; the city; the medium of publication; the date on which you accessed the work of art; and the URL of the specific work of art, not the general site, in angle brackets.

Picasso, Pablo. *Les Demoiselles d'Avignon.* Oil on canvas. Museum of Modern Art. New York. Web. 30 June 2002. <http://www.moma.org/docs/collection/ paintsculpt/C40.htm>.

Online map, graph, table, or chart

To cite a map, graph, table, or chart online, first provide the information required for the kind of visual element. Then continue the citation with the information appropriate to the electronic source, whether it is a scholarly project or an information database or a website.

"New York City Subway Route Map." Map. 5 Mar. 2000. New York City Subway Resources. Web. 9 Jan. 2002. <http://www.nycsubway.org/maps/route/>.

Online cartoon

To cite a cartoon online, provide the name of the cartoonist, if known; the assigned title of the cartoon, in quotation marks; the word *Cartoon,* not italicized; the source, italicized; the date of electronic publication or the date of the most recent update; the medium of publication; the date on which you accessed the cartoon; and the URL of the cartoon, not the general site, in angle brackets.

Steiner, Peter. "Don't Anybody Move: This Is a Merger." Cartoon. *Cartoonbank.* 10 Jan. 2001. Web. 13 Jan. 2001. <k.com/cartoon_closeup.asp?/mscssid-52BGLVUGOU7S92MD000GPBQXMNAB6808>.

Online film or filmclip

To cite an online film or filmclip, first provide the information required for a film. Then include the name of your electronic source, italicized; the date of electronic publication or the date of the most recent update; the medium of publication; the date on which you accessed the film or filmclip; and the URL of the film or filmclip, not the general site, in angle brackets.

Reefer Madness. Dir. Louis J. Gasnier. 1938. *The Sync.* 2000. Web. 22 Apr. 2002. <http://www.thesync.com/ram/reefermadness.ram>.

Online transcript of a television or radio broadcast

To cite an online transcript of a television or radio broadcast, first provide the information required for a television or radio broadcast. Then include the word *Transcript,* not italicized; the medium of publication; the date on which you accessed the transcript; and the URL of the transcript, not the general site, in angle brackets.

"Inside the World of Polygamy." *Larry King Live.* CNN, Washington. 15 Apr. 2006. Transcript. Web. 25 Apr. 2006. <http://transcripts.cnn.com/ TRANSCRIPTS/0604/15/lkl.01.html>.

Online recording

To cite an online recording of previously released material, first provide the information required for a traditional recording. Then include the date of electronic publication or the date of the most recent update; the medium of publication; the date on which you accessed the recording; and the URL of the recording, not the general site, in angle brackets.

To cite an online recording that has not been previously released, provide the name of the recording artist; the title of the selection; and performance information such as concert locations and dates, recording studios, locations, or other relevant information. Then provide information about your source for the recording, whether a database or a website.

> Dylan, Bob. "Yea! Heavy and a Bottle of Bread." New York City. 11 Nov. 2002. Web. 20 Apr. 2006. <http://bobdylan.com/performances>.

CD-ROM sources Because Internet sites provide researchers with more easily updated materials than do CD-ROMs, most libraries are phasing out CD-ROMs from their collections. However, you may still need to cite a CD-ROM source.

If a CD-ROM source reproduces material available in print form, begin the citation with full print information: author (or editor), title, and facts of publication. If the material is not available in print form, begin the citation with identifying information: author, if given; title, italicized; and the date of the material, if appropriate. Next, citations for both kinds of materials include the title of the publication, italicized; the description *CD-ROM*, not italicized; the city, if known, and name of the company that produced the CD-ROM; and the date of electronic publication.

> *The Baseball Encyclopedia: The Complete and Definitive Record of Major League Baseball.* CD-ROM. New York: Macmillan, 1996.

> Becklake, Sue. *All About Space.* Illus. Sebastian Quigley. CD-ROM. New York: Scholastic Reference, 1998.

Email interview To cite an email interview, include the name of the person you interviewed; the phrase *Email interview,* not italicized; and the date of the email posting.

> Lublin, Robert. Email interview. 1 Mar. 2006.

Online posting To cite an online posting to a forum or discussion group, provide the name of the author, if known; the official title of the posting, in quotation marks, or a descriptive title, without quotation marks; the phrase *Online posting,* not italicized; the date of electronic publication or the date of the most recent update; the name of the forum or discussion group; the medium of publication; the date on which you accessed the posting; and the URL of the posting, not the general forum or discussion site, in angle brackets.

> Bailey, Buddy. "What's Wrong with My Miniature Roses?" Online posting. 22 Apr. 2006. Miniature Roses Forum. Web. 26 Apr. 2006. <http://forums.gardenweb.com/forums/load/rosesmin/msg0422021712641.html?4>.

American Psychological Association Style

In fields such as psychology, education, public health, and criminology, researchers follow the guidelines given in the *Publication Manual of the American Psychological Association,* sixth edition (Washington: APA, 2010) to document their work. Like MLA style, APA style encourages brevity in documentation, uses in-text parenthetical citations of sources, and limits the use of numbered notes and appended materials.

PAPER FORMAT

Title page
: Include a descriptive title, your name, and your affiliation (course or university), with two spaces between elements; center this information left to right and top to bottom. In the upper-right corner, include the first few words of the paper's title, followed by five spaces and the page number (without a page abbreviation). Two lines below, at the left margin, type the words *Running head* (not italicized), a colon, and a brief version of the title (no more than 50 letters and spaces) in all capital letters. The title page is always page 1.

Abstract
: On a separate page following the title page, type the label *Abstract* (capitalized but not italicized). Two lines below, include an unindented paragraph describing the major ideas in the paper; it should contain no more than 120 words.

Introduction
: Include a paragraph or series of paragraphs to define the topic, present the hypothesis (or thesis), explain the method of investigation, and state the theoretical implications (or context).

Body
: Incorporate a series of paragraphs to describe study procedures, results obtained, and interpretations of the findings.

In-text documentation
: In parentheses, include the author and date for summaries and paraphrases; include the author, date, and page number for quotations and facts.

List of sources
: Cite sources used in the paper in a listing titled "References."

Appendix
: Include related materials (charts, graphs, illustrations, and so on) that cannot be incorporated into the body of the paper.

MANUSCRIPT FORMAT

Fonts
: Use any standard font with serifs (cross lines on the ends of individual letters). Sans serif fonts like Helvetica are used only for labeling illustrations, not for text.

Use italics to identify titles of complete, separately published works.

Spacing All elements of the paper are double-spaced.

Margins Use one-inch margins at the top and bottom and on the left and right. Indent paragraphs five to seven spaces; indent long quotations five spaces.

Paging Put the first two or three words of the title (no more than 50 letters and spaces) in the upper-right corner; after five spaces, include the page number without a page abbreviation.

Heading Whenever possible, use headings to label divisions and subdivisions of the paper.

Number style Express numbers one through nine (and zero) in words and all other numbers in numeral form.

CITATION FORMAT

The following samples illustrate a number of basic citation forms. If you are using other kinds of sources, consult the APA style guide.

REFERENCE LIST FORMAT

Book by one author

Monmonier, M. (2004). *Rhumb lines and map wars: A social history of the Mercator Projection.* Chicago, IL: University of Chicago Press.

(Use initials for the author's first name. After the author's name, place the publication date in parentheses, followed by a period. Capitalize only the first word of the title and of the subtitle and any proper nouns and proper adjectives. Spell out the names of university presses. For other publishers, retain only the words *Books* and *Press*.)

Book by two or more authors

Fainaru-Wada, M., & Williams, L. (2006). *Game of shadows: Barry Bonds, BALCO, and the steroids scandal that rocked professional sports.* New York, NY: Gotham.

(Invert the names of all authors. Insert an ampersand [&] before the last author's name.)

Book with an organization as author

American Psychological Association. (2010). *Publication manual of the American Psychological Association* (6th ed.). Washington, DC: Author.

(When the organization is also the publisher, use the word *Author* [not italicized] in the publisher position.)

Edition other than the first

Bjelajac, D. (2004). *American art: A cultural history* (2nd ed.). Upper Saddle River, NJ: Prentice Hall.

(Insert information about the edition in parentheses, following the title but before the period.)

Work in a collection

Foster, R. (2006). Something of us will remain: Sebastian Barry and history. In C. H. Mahony (Ed.), *Out of history: Essays on the writings of Sebastian Barry* (pp. 183–197). Washington, DC: The Catholic University of America Press.

(Do not enclose the title of a short work in quotation marks. *In*, not italicized, introduces its source. Provide the editor's name, the abbreviation *Ed.* [capitalized, not italicized, and placed in parentheses] followed by a comma, the collection title, and inclusive page numbers for the short work [given in parentheses]. Abbreviate *pages.*)

Article in a monthly magazine

Teague, M. (2006, April). Double blind: The untold story of how British intelligence infiltrated and undermined the IRA. *The Atlantic, 297,* 53–62.

(Give the year of publication followed by a comma and the month and day [if any]. When appropriate, follow the magazine title with a comma, one space, the volume number, and another comma [all italicized]. Do not use a page abbreviation.)

Brittan, A. (2006). The diarist, the cryptographer, and *The English Patient. PMLA: Publications of the Modern Language Association of America, 121*(1), 200–213.

Article in a journal with separate paging

(Italicize the name of the journal, the comma that follows it, and the volume number. The issue number [or numbers] in parentheses immediately follows the volume number; no space separates them; the issue number is *not* italicized. No abbreviation for pages accompanies the inclusive page numbers.)

Article in a newspaper

Callender, D. (2005, December 15). Amid scandals, still no sign of campaign reform. *The Capital Times* (Madison, Wisconsin), p. 1:1.

(Invert the date. Do not include information about the edition or section. When sections are indicated by letters, present them along with the page numbers with no intervening space. Also, include the location in parenthesis if it is not included in the name of the newspaper.)

Lecture or speech

Doyle, R. (2004, November 15). *An evening with Roddy Doyle.* Lecture presented for Seattle Arts and Lectures, Seattle, Washington.

(Italicize the title of the speech. Follow the title with the name of the sponsoring organization and the location, separated by commas.)

Nonprint materials

Allen, W. (Director). (2003). *Anything else* [motion picture]. United States: Dream-Works SKG.

(List entries by the name of the most important contributor [director, producer, speaker, and so on]; note the specific role in full in parentheses following the name. Identify the medium [motion picture, slide show, tape recording] in brackets after the title. The country of origin precedes the name of the production company.)

ELECTRONIC SOURCES

Online scholarly project, information database, or website

Cody, D. (2005). Queen Victoria. Victorian Web. Providence: Brown University. Retrieved from http://www.victorianweb.org

(To cite an online scholarly project, information database, or professional website, include the author, if known, and the date in parentheses; the title of the source without special punctuation [followed by the date if there is no author]; the name of the project, database, or website; and a retrieval statement.)

Article in an online encyclopedia or reference source

Children in foster care. (2004). [Chart]. *Infoplease almanac.* Retrieved from http://www.infoplease.com/

(To cite an article from an online encyclopedia or reference source, provide the author of the entry, if there is one, and the date in parentheses; the title of the entry exactly as it appears in the source, without special punctuation [followed by the date if there is no author]; the type of medium in brackets [e.g., chart, figure, table]; the name of the reference work, italicized; and the retrieval statement.)

Article in an online magazine

Wheelright, J. (2001, January). Betting on designer genes. *Smithsonian, 31.* Retrieved from http://www.smithsonianmag.sr.edu/smithsonian/issues01/jan01/gene.html

(To cite an article in an online magazine, provide the name of the author, if appropriate; the date in parentheses; the title of the article; the name of the magazine and volume number, italicized; and the retrieval statement.)

Article in an online journal

Cramer, K., & Perrault, L. (2006). Effects of predictability, actual controllability, and awareness of choice on perceptions of control. *Current Research in Social Psychology, 11*(8). Retrieved from http://www.uiowa.edu/%7Egrpproc/crisp/crisp.html

(To cite an article in an online journal, provide the name of the author, if appropriate; the date in parentheses; the title of the article; the name of the journal and the volume number, italicized, and the issue number, not italicized; and the retrieval statement.)

Article in an online newspaper

Rodriguez, C. (2001, January 9). Amid dispute, plight of illegal workers revisited. *Boston Globe.* Retrieved from http://www.boston.com/dailyglobe2/010/nation/Amid_dispute_plight_of_illegal_workers_revisited1.html

(To cite an article in an online newspaper, provide the name of the author, if appropriate; the date of publication in parentheses; the title of the article; the name of the newspaper, italicized; and the retrieval statement.)

CD-ROM sources

Welmers, W. E. (2003). African languages. *The new Grolier multimedia encyclopedia.* Retrieved from Grolier database (Grolier, CD-ROM, 2003 release).

(To cite a CD-ROM source, provide the name of the author, if given; the release date; the title of the selection, without special punctuation; the CD-ROM title, italicized; and a special CD-ROM retrieval statement, which includes the publisher's name, without special punctuation, and, in parentheses, the name of the database; the description *CD-ROM,* not italicized; the release date; and an item number, if applicable.)

Online posting

Whinney, K. (2001, January 11). Discussion of *A clockwork orange.* [Online forum comment]. Book Lovers' Discussion. Retrieved from http://www.Whatamigoingtoread.com/book.asp?bookid56395

(To cite an online posting to a forum or discussion group, provide the name of the author, if known; the date of the posting; the official or descriptive title of the posting; a description of the message, in brackets; the name of the forum or discussion group; the phrase *Retrieved from,* not italicized; and the URL.)

TEXT CITATION FORMAT

One author

Greybowski (1995) noted that . . . .

Or

In a recent study at USC (Greybowski, 1995), participants were asked to . . . .

Multiple authors: first citation

Cadrillo, Thurgood, Johnson, and Lawrence (1967) found in their evaluation . . . .

Multiple authors: subsequent citations

Cadrillo et al. (1967) also discovered . . . .

Corporate author: first citation

. . . a close connection between political interests and environmental issues (Council on Environmental Quality [CEQ], 1981).

Corporate author: subsequent citations

. . . in their additional work (CEQ, 1981).

QUOTATIONS WITHIN THE TEXT

First option

She stated, "The cultural awareness of a student depends, by implication, on the cultural awareness of the parents" (Hermann, 1984, p. 219).

Second option

Hermann (1984) added that "enrichment in our schools is costly and has little bearing on the later lives of the students" (pp. 230–231).

Third option

"A school's responsibility rests with providing solid educational skills, not with supplementing the cultural education of the uninterested," stated Hermann (1984) in her summary (p. 236).

Index

Abilities, core, 18, 94
Abundance
    in Information Age, 115
    meaning-making and, 115
    right brain-style thinking and,
        115–116
Academic writing, formats for, 377
Action plan, 139–140
    experience from, 241
Active influences, 62–63
Affirmative action, 373
Affirming antecedent, 505
African American
    disposition, 374–375
    poverty, 372
Agriculture
    modern, 356–364
    technological development
        and, 360
Agudo, Wendy
    on freedom, 160–162
    freewriting of, 165
    student writing, 159–162
    writing process of, 159–162
Alcohol abuse, 98–99
    Bartlett on, 472–476
Aldiss, Brian, 437
Alvarez, Julia
    "Between Dominica and
        Ecuador," 49
    curiosidades, 45
    fears of, 47
    "Grounds for Fiction," 44–51
    on inspiration, 49–50, 53
    "Naming the Fabrics," 46–47, 50
    subjects of, 44
    "The Tent," 50
    on visuals, 53
    on writing, 44–51
Amabile, Teresa, on creativity,
    117–119
America, violent crime rate in, 295
American Association for Marriage
    and Family Therapy, 254

An American Childhood (Dillard),
    70–73
American Psychological
    Association Style. See APA
    documentation style
Americans, clusters of, 259–260
Amos, Ernest, 328
Analogy, 329. See also
    Metaphor; Simile
    extended, 330
    simple, 330
    use of, 330
Analytical questions, 35, 101, 129
    principles of, 369
Andreu, Frankie, 149
Andrews, Donnell, 387
"Animal Feelings" (Grandin),
    215–219
Animals
    autism and, 215–216
    emotion in, 216–217
    movement orientation of, 218
    repression in, 217–218
Annotated bibliography, 556
    Thinking-Writing activity, 557
Annotation, 33–34
    Bartlett and, 39
    MLA documentation style, 585
Anthony, Ted
    arguments of, 293–294
    "Connecticut School Shooting
        'An Attack on America'",
        293–294
    on school shootings, 293–294
An Anthropologist on Mars
    (Sacks), 215
Anticipation, 43
APA documentation style,
    370, 537
    citation format, 600
    electronic sources, 601–602
    manuscript format, 599–600
    paper format, 599
    quotations within text, 603

reference list format, 600–601
    text citation format, 603
Apologia (justification), 52
Application, questions of, 102, 129
"An Argument for Chores"
    (Sharp, E.), 89–92
Arguments
    of Anthony, 293–294
    for chores, 89–92
    classical concepts of, 480–481
    construction of, 500
    deductive, 503–507, 535
    electronic media and, 484–485
    evaluation of, 500–503, 506
    for evolution, 419–420
    forms of, 503–510
    inductive, 507–508, 535
    as inferences, 499–500
    modern concepts of, 481–490
    principles of, 479–490
    recognizing, 491–499
    responsible, 528–529
    soundness of, 502–503
    Thinking-Writing activity,
        480, 506–507
    truth in, 501
    validity of, 501–502
    writing project, 524–528
Aristotle, on concepts, 242
Army recruitment materials, 482
Arthropods, 77–79
Asia, right brain-style thinking in,
    113–114
Audience
    analysis, 490
    composition of, 10
    considerations for, 11
    decision-making, 133–134
    drafts and, 178
    effect on, 480, 534
    of Gawande, 228
    hypothetical, 22
    images and, 103
    lenses of, 207

Audience (*continued*)
  Murray on, 180
  needs of, 133–134
  perspective and, 65–66
  thinking critically about visuals,
    10–11
  writer and, 14
  writing situation, 83–84, 121,
    154, 198, 230, 270, 331, 366,
    427, 467, 525, 565
Audience, for communication,
  6–7, 9
Audio
  amplification with, 36
  learning experience and, 36
Auld, Hugh, 140
Auld, Sophia, 140
Aurelius, Marcus, 239
Auster, Paul, 382
Australopithecus afarensis, 420
Authority, appeal to, 513–514
Author's purpose, 43
Autism
  animals and, 215–216
  brain size in, 216
  emotion and, 216
  Grandin and, 215
  repression in, 217–218
  vaccination rates and, 353
The Autobiography of Malcolm X
  (Malcolm X), 170–172
Automation, right brain-style
  thinking, 114
Automobile, 243–244
Awareness
  development of, 309–310
  of lenses, 287
  of perception, 208–209
  during reading, 42–43
  of VOJ, 111

Backings, 484, 534
Bacon, Francis, on reading, 29, 330
Bandwagon appeal, 515–516
Barkai, Amos, 75–76
Bartlett, Joshua, 38, 40–42
  on alcohol abuse, 472–476
  annotation and, 39
  previewing, 39

problem-solving, 39
  student writing, 472–476
  summary by, 39
  writing process of, 472–476
Baum, Dan
  on gun control, 294–296
  on gun violence, 298
  on Rosenthal, 295
  "The Price of Gun Control,"
    294–296
Beaudry, Marie, 46
Begging the question, 513, 535
Beliefs. *See also* Inference
  adoption of, 63–64
  challenge to, 58
  change in, 93
  conceptualization of, 379
  of critical thinkers, 378
  defining, 380, 434
  development of, 69–70
  evaluation of, 64–65, 93
  experience and, 70–82, 381–382,
    388–389
  falsifiable, 397–398, 435
  formation of, 379–389
  of friends, 93
  of future, 408
  general, 412
  identification of, 381
  indirect experience and,
    388–389
  influences on, 426–431
  knowledge compared with,
    378, 396–409
  map of, 69–70
  observed, 93
  Perdue on, 338
  presentation of, 409–425, 435
  of relatives, 93
  thesis and, 425
  Thinking-Writing activity,
    64–66, 69–70, 381, 389, 391,
    397, 415
  writing about, 425–426
  writing project, 82–93,
    426–431
Bell, Daniel, 460
Bennett, Bill, on racism, 374
Bergson, Henri, 343

Berman, John, "What Makes a
    Family? Children, Say Many
    Americans," 259
"Beslan Atrocity: They're
    Terrorists—Not Activists"
    (Pipes), 191–193
Betancourt, Julio, 406–407, 409
"Between Dominica and Ecuador"
    (Alvarez), 49
Bibliographic cards, 553–554
Bierce, Ambrose, 267
Births, to unmarried women, 258
Blog, 20
  Thinking-Writing activity, 60
  writing for, 60
Blood doping, 144–145
  advantage of, 149
  r-EPO, 147–148
Bloom, Lynn, 561
Blueprint sentence, 123, 156–157
Bonnin, Gertrude Simmons.
    See Zitkala-Sa
Bonnin, Ray, 317
Bonsai Kittens, 395
Bonuses, 118
Borges, Jorge Luis, 45
Borgman, Jim, 565
Boudinot, Elias, 339
Boury-Esnault, N., 77
Bowles, Bryant, 374
Boyer, Jonathan, 144
Bradbury, Ray, 177
Brady Campaign to Prevent
    Gun Violence, 294
Brainstorming, idea generation,
    97–98, 448
Braxton, Wendell, 387
Breen, Bill
  on creativity, 117–119
  education of, 116
  The 6 Myths of Creativity,
    116–120
Breivik, Anders Behring,
    294–295
Brin, Sergey, 462
Broley, Charles L., 348
Brown, Cynthia
  approach of, 165
  on freedom, 163–165

student writing, 162–165
on time pressure, 163–165
writing process of, 162–165
Brown, El, 293
Brown v. Board of Education,
373–374
Bryan, William Jennings, 404, 421
Buchanan, Patrick, 398
on global warming, 403–405
*Global Warming: Hoax of the
Century*, 403–405
Buddhism, Sherpa on, 276–277
Buettner, Dan, 376
Burgess, Anthony, 177
Burkholder, J. M., 76–77
Bush, George W., 189
on Hurricane Katrina, 328
Bush, Jeb, 373
Buxton-Smith, Chris
sample paper, 574–581
student writing, 571–581
working outline of, 573
writing process of, 572–573
writing situation of, 571–572

Caldeira, Ken
on climate change, 398–403
*The Great Climate Experiment:
How Far Can We Push the
Planet?*, 398–403
Capitalism, 261–263
Carbon dioxide, atmospheric,
399–400
Carlsen, Jorden
on masculine, 278–281
student writing, 278–281
writing process of, 278–281
Carr, Nicholas
on Google, 458–464
Is Google Making Us Stupid?,
458–464
on technological development,
458–464
on thinking, 455, 457, 465
Carroll, Lewis, *Jabberwocky*, 46
Carter, Stephen L., 575, 579
Casado, Philippe, 147
The Case Against Chores (Smiley),
80–82

Castro, Fidel, 326
Causal analysis, 343–344
Causal chain, 345, 376
Thinking-Writing activity,
346–347
Causal claims
detecting, 355–364
evaluation of, 356
Thinking-Writing activity, 356
Causal fallacy identification,
351–353
summary, 354–355
Thinking-Writing activity, 355
Causal reasoning, 508, 535
Causal relationships, 205, 376
Eggers on, 365
kinds of, 343–349
writing thoughtfully about, 365
Causation, correlation *vs.*, 352
Causes. *See also* Contributory
causes; Immediate
cause; Interactive causes;
Questionable cause;
Remote cause
analysis of, 369
common, 353
effects and, 356–364
misidentification of, 352–354, 376
testing, 349–351
writing project, 365–370
Cell phone use, 66
Censorship, writing and, 51
Central line, 222–227
Chaffee, Joshua
outline, 233–234
student writing, 233–236
writing process of, 233–237
Chapter outlines, 32
Cherokee nation, 337, 339–340
Perdue on, 338
syllabary, 340
Children
of cohabiting couples, 257
on Indian reservations, 316
unmarried couples with, 259–260
Cho, Seung-Hui, 292
Choice, 59
decision-making, 138–139
Eliot on, 131

freedom and, 161
of language, 168
of perspective, 559
pros and cons of, 138
thinking critically about visuals,
482–483
Chores, 80–82
as labor, 91
O'Hagan on, 90
Chrisler, Jennifer, 260
Chronological relationships
narratives, 220
process writing, 220–222
Ciardi, John, 177
Civil war, 577
Classification, 239, 282
by concepts, 264–267
establishment of, 241
of ethics, 266
of people, 265
process of, 243–244
Thinking-Writing activity, 265, 267
writing and, 266–267
Clichés, 204
function of, 194
Thinking-Writing activity, 194
Climate change. *See also* Global
warming
Caldeira on, 398–403
coral reefs in, 400–401
Hamilton on, 405–409
truth and, 398
Clinton, Bill, 189
Cohabiting couples, 256
children of, 257
Coleman, Kai-Michelle, 387
Collaboration, 6–7
benefits of, 27, 333
competition compared to, 119
in research, 564
in writing process, 25–26
College
reading in, 29–34
writing in, 3
Color, as concept, 242
Communicare (to share), 7
Communication
audience for, 6–7, 9
clarity of, 238

Communication (*continued*)
  considerations for, 12
  images as, 129
  issues with, 152–153
  through language, 168
  purpose of, 6
  subject of, 6, 9
  Thinking-Writing activity, 15
Communities, ecological structure
    of, 78
Community, Quindlen on, 234, 236
Comparisons, 211
  contrast and, 324, 333, 341
  guidelines for, 334–335
  relationships of, 205, 329–330
  thinking in, 324–325
  words for, 335
  in writing, 334–335
  writing project, 330–337
Competition, collaboration
    compared to, 119
Complex ability acquisition, 5–6
Comprehension, 43
Concepts
  application of, 245, 248–251, 283
  Aristotle on, 242
  changing, 240
  classification by, 264–267
  college-level, 241
  color as, 242
  complexity of, 238, 250–251
  components of, 240
  defining, 267–268, 282–283
  development of, 246
  diagramming, 244
  discipline specific, 241–242
  dog as, 248–250
  examples of, 239, 246, 264–265
  family as, 251–264
  fashion statement as, 249
  formation of, 238, 244–248, 282
  from general to well-defined, 246
  guidelines for, 273–274
  gun as, 295
  importance of, 241–242
  key, 239
  masculine as, 278–281
  requirements of, 248–250, 282
  structure of, 242–243

support for, 240
  Thinking-Writing activity, 240,
    244, 247
  tree as, 264
  writing project, 269–275
  writing thoughtfully on, 268–269
Conceptual Age, 113, 115
Concluding paragraphs, 33
  decision-making, 135–136
Conclusion, 380–381
  signal, 494
The Conformity to Masculinity
    Norms Inventory, 279
"Connecticut School Shooting
    'An Attack on America'"
    (Anthony), 293–294
Connotation. *See* Perceptual
    meaning
Consumer base, 262
Context, 291, 341
Contrast, comparisons and,
    324, 333, 341
Contributory causes, 346–347, 376
Coontz, Stephanie, on family,
    251–252
Coral reefs, in climate change,
    400–401
Core abilities, 18
  creativity as, 94
Core beliefs, 63
Core feelings, 215
  Panksepp on, 217
Core qualities, 59
Correlation, causation *vs.*, 352
Couple, cohabiting, 256
Creationism, 417–419
Creative problem-solving, 238
Creative thinking. *See* Thinking
    creatively
Creativity, 5
  absorption in, 109–110
  Amabile on, 117–119
  Breen on, 117–119
  competition compared to
    collaboration, 119
  as core ability, 94
  creative types, 117–118
  definition of, 112
  establishing, 111

fear and, 118–119
  in idea generation, 97–102,
    121–122, 129
  increasing, 107–112, 120–129
  incubation time for, 110
  inhibitions, 107
  intelligence and, 117–118
  Lange on, 126–128
  money as motivator, 118
  practice, 94
  as priority, 112
  recollection, 106
  role of, 94
  streamlining and, 119
  time pressure and, 118
  in topic selection, 95–96
  writing and, 95–102
Creativity in Business (Ray and
    Myers), 110–111
Critical reading. *See* Reading;
    Reading critically
Critical thinker
  becoming, 4–5, 27
  beliefs of, 378
  defining, 4
  thoughtful writer and, 4
Critical thinking. *See* Thinking
    critically
Critical viewing, thinking creatively
    and, 95–102
Crowdsourcing, 109
Crowe, Russell, 250
Culture, reading as, 30
Curious, 5
Cyberliteracy (Gurak), 394
Cycling, competitive, 144–145,
    148–151. *See also* Blood doping
  rules of, 146–147

Dahl, Roald, 177–178
Darwin, Charles
  on man, 418
  The Origin of Species,
    60, 78–79, 403
  on patterns, 78–79
Decision-making, 130
  analysis of, 136, 154–158
  audience, 133–134
  choice and, 138–139

as commitment, 131
concluding paragraphs, 135–136
defining, 137
discrimination in, 134
drafts, 132–136, 158, 172–176, 204
first, 133
future strategies for, 167
goals of, 137
identification after, 167
introductory paragraphs,
    135–136
levels of, 173–176
in life, 136–140, 166–167
organized approach to, 136–140,
    166–167, 173
preparation, 153
purpose, 133, 138
recollection of, 155
subject, 134, 137
summary, 140
thesis, 134
thinking critically about
    visuals, 132
Thinking-Writing activity, 136, 153
Declaration of Independence,
    517–519, 534
*Declaration of Sentiments and
    Resolutions* (Stanton), 519–522
Defense mechanisms, Freud on,
    217–218
Definition, as concept, 239
    extended, 268–269
Denotation. *See* Semantic meaning
Denying consequent, 505
Descriptions
    intentions for, 214
    objective, 214
    subjective, 214
    Thinking-Writing activity, 219
d'Holbach, Baron, 163
Diagrams, 33
Dickens, Charles, *Hard Times*, 268
Dickey, Jay
    delusions of, 299
    on gun ownership, 298–299
Dickinson, Emily, on poetry, 49
Dillard, Annie
    An American Childhood, 70–73
    Pilgrim at Tinker Creek, 70

on science, 71–73
on writing, 70
Dimension, 178
Dinoflagellates, 76–77
Diploma, fraudulent, 212–213
Disenfranchisement, 373–374
Documentation, logic behind,
    560–562, 582
Dog, as concept, 248–250
Dogma, 66
Doherty, Jim, 348
Doig, Ivan, 221
The Doping Dilemma (Shermer),
    144–151
Douglass, Frederick
    anxiety of, 142
    birth of, 140
    on contentment, 141
    death of, 140
    on freedom, 140–144
    Malcolm X and, 143
    *Narrative of the Life of Frederick
        Douglass, an American Slave*,
        140–144
    on planning, 141–142
    on responsibility, 142
    Underground Railroad and, 140
Downsizing, 119
Drafts, 6–7, 19
    audience and, 178
    decision-making, 132–136, 158,
        172–176, 204
    Drucker on, 177
    hints for, 86, 124
    Murray on, 176–177
    outlining and, 135
    preparation for, 166
    progression of, 177
    questions before, 166
    Tolstoy on, 179
    in writing process, 21–22,
        86, 124, 157, 200, 232,
        274, 369–370, 430–431,
        471, 528, 569
Drogin, Bob, 373–374
Drucker, Peter
    on drafts, 177
    on knowledge workers,
        112–113

Dualism
    with dominance, 73–74, 79
    Gould on, 73–74
DuBois, W. E. B.
    on racism, 375
    The Souls of Black Folk, 375
Dystopias, 376

Earnings, loans *vs.*, 132
*Eating the Genes: What the Green
    Revolution Did for Grain,
    Biotechnology May Do for
    Protein* (Manning, Richard),
    362–364
Ecosystem cause and effect, 342
An edible, 267
Editing
    levels of, 175
    peer review groups,
        87, 124–125, 157, 200–201,
        233, 275, 336, 370, 431, 471,
        529–530, 570
    in writing process, 22–23,
        88, 125–126, 158, 201,
        233, 274–275, 337, 370,
        431, 472, 530
Education
    as journey, 41
    responsibility in, 41
    Tanner on, 38–42
Effects, causes and, 356–364
Eggers, Daniel
    on causal relationships, 365
    on MLK, 371–735
    on racism, 373
    rationale of, 371
    student writing, 371–375
    writing process of,
        371–375
Eisner, Tom, 74–75
Eliot, George, on choice, 131
Emotion
    in animals, 216
    autism and, 216
    masculine and, 279–280
Emotive language, 194, 204
    evaluation of, 196
    role of, 195
    Thinking-Writing activity, 196

Endorsement, 380
Enlightenment, trajectory of, 41
Enthymeme, 504–505, 523, 535
Ericsson, K. Anders, 226
Estes, Eleanor, 177
Ethics, 169
    classification of, 266
    information and,
        548–550
    Thinking-Writing activity, 266
Ethos (character of writer),
        480, 516, 534
Euphemisms, 190, 204
    as dangerous, 191
    Pipes on, 192–193
    for terrorists, 192–193
    Thinking-Writing activity, 191
Evaluation, 43, 380–381
    of arguments, 500–503, 506
    of beliefs, 64–65, 93
    of causal claims, 356
    of emotive language, 196
    of fact, 412
    of information, 389–396, 434
    of Internet, 544–546, 581
    questions of, 35, 102, 129
    of sources, 389–396, 434,
        543–547
Evidence, 310
Evolution
    arguments for, 419–420
    as fact, 419–420
    Gould on, 416–421
"Evolution as Fact and Theory"
        (Gould), 416–421
Existentialism
    first effect of, 37–38
    first principle of, 37
"Existentialism Is Humanism"
        (Sartre), 37–38
Experience
    action leads to, 241
    beliefs and, 70–82, 381–382,
        388–389
    knowledge and, 341
    shaping, 205
    writing project, 82–93
Expressing deeper meaning,
        Thinking-Writing activity, 26

Fabrication, 549
Facebook
    efficiency, 498
    legislation by, 497–498
    Madrigal on, 495–499
    mission of, 497–498
    as Pandora's box, 152–153
    potential employers and, 152
    reporting infrastructure, 497
    site integrity, 496
    Thinking-Writing activity, 153
Fact
    defining, 418
    evaluation of, 412
    evolution as, 419–420
    Gould on, 267, 421
    questions of, 100–101, 129
    report, 411–412
    Thinking-Writing activity, 412
FactCheck.org, 547
Fallacies of relevance,
        513–516, 535
False dichotomy fallacy,
        512–513, 535
False dilemma, 512–513, 535
False reasoning, 511–515,
        517–523, 535
    Thinking-Writing activity, 516
Falsifiable beliefs,
        397–398, 435
Family
    Census Bureau on, 259
    as concept, 251–264
    Coontz on, 251–252
    extended, 251
    household composition, 258
    Kotkin on, 261–264
    maps of, 253
    Merrill on, 253
    in modernity, 262
    1950s myth, 252
    no single model for, 252–253
    nuclear, 251
    Powell, B., on, 259
    purpose of, 252–253
    requirements of, 251–254,
        259–260
    research on, 255–258
    Rice on, 251–254

    Sharp, E., on, 90
    unmarried couples with
        children, 259–260
Family Equality Council, 260
Family First, 253
Fashion statement
    as concept, 249
    Mamet on, 249
Fear
    appeal to, 514–515
    creativity and, 118–119
Feminine, Thinking-Writing
        activity, 250
Ferrari, Michele, 149
Fiction
    definitions of, 51
    in litigious age, 50
    reality in, 50–51
Field research, 542, 581
Figurative language,
        183–185, 204
Fischetti, Mark, 328
Fish, 76–77
Fisher, Ken, 496
Fitzgerald, Shane, 212
Flexibility, 66
Flies, 74–75
Focus definition, 6–7.
    See also Thesis
    in writing process, 19–21,
        86, 123, 156–157, 199–200,
        272–273, 334, 368, 429–430,
        470, 527
Foreman, Richard, 463–464
Forster, E. M., on thinking, 3
Franklin, Benjamin, 339
    childhood of, 311–312
    death of, 312
    position of, 312
    "Remarks Concerning the
        Savages of North America,"
        311–316
    on savages, 312–315
Freedom
    Agudo on, 160–162
    Brown on, 163–165
    choice and, 161
    Douglass on, 140–144
    King on, 186–188

Sartre on, 38, 159
Sherpa on, 275–277, 282
of speech, 486–488
Free enterprise, 90
Freewriting. *See also* Writing
of Agudo, 165
idea generation, 100
Lange, 126–128
student writing, 126–128
Freud, Sigmund, on defense
mechanisms, 217–218
Frogs, 74–75

Galveston hurricane, 327
Game matrix, 146, 149
Game theory, 145–146
Shermer on, 155
Gaming sports, Shermer on,
145–147
García, Yolanda, 46
Gates, Bill, 395
Gatica, Sofía, 359
Gawande, Atul
audience of, 228
education of, 222
"The Learning Curve,"
222–228
on practice, 227
on skill, 226
on teaching, 227–228
Generalization, 244–245
empirical, 508–510, 535
hasty, 511, 535
sweeping, 511–512, 535
Thinking-Writing activity, 510
Genetically modified organisms
(GMOs)
agreement for, 361
agrichemicals and, 358
hunger and, 357, 363
local crop contamination, 358–359
Manning, Richard on, 356,
362–364
myths of, 357–360
as neutral, 359
performance of, 360–362
productivity of, 357–358
research on, 360–363
traditional crops and, 358–359

Genocide, as term, 577–578
Germanotta, Stefani Joanne
Angelina. *See* Lady Gaga
Ghandi, Mohandas K., King and, 185
Giffords, Gabrielle, 292
Gish, Duane, 419
Global warming, 398, 401. *See also*
Climate change
Buchanan on, 403–405
effects, 403
precedent for, 404–405
*Global Warming: Hoax of the
Century* (Buchanan),
403–405
GMOs. *See* Genetically modified
organisms
Goethe, Johann Wolfgang von,
Sorrows of Young Werther, 44
Goldberg, Natalie
on inspiration, 24–25
on writing, 23–25
"Writing Is Not a McDonald's
Hamburger," 23–24
Golden Rule, 64–65
Gonzales, Adolfo, 48
Google
Carr on, 458–464
mission of, 462
Gould, Stephen Jay
academic career of, 73
career of, 416
on dualism, 73–74
on evolution, 416–421
"Evolution as Fact and Theory,"
416–421
on fact, 267, 421
on reversals, 74–79
Reversing Established Orders,
73–80
on theories, 267, 417–419
Gourevitch, Philip, 574, 576–577
Grandin, Temple
"Animal Feelings," 215–219
autism and, 215
on denial, 218
on images, 218
Sacks on, 215
Graves, Robert, 91
Gray, Liz, 252–253

*The Great Climate Experiment:
How Far Can We Push the
Planet?* (Caldeira), 398–403
Green Revolution, 362–364
"Grounds for Fiction" (Alvarez),
44–51
Gun, as concept, 295
Gun advocates, 298
objections of, 299–300
on violation of rights, 300
Gun control
Baum on, 294–296
McMahan on, 298–301
Obama on, 295
Selinger on, 302
Gun ownership
Dickey on, 298–299
La Pierre on, 296–297
logic of, 299
as masculine, 302
McMahan on, 300
permissive laws on, 300
Gun violence, 292
Baum on, 298
Brady Campaign to Prevent
Gun Violence, 294
Kimmel, M., on, 302
La Pierre on, 297
perspective on, 296
Rosenthal on, 294
Gurak, Laura, *Cyberliteracy*, 394

Hagan, Thomas, 306
Hale, Nancy, 177
Haley, Alex, *The Autobiography
of Malcolm X*, 170–172
Hamilton, Tyler, 398
Why Media Tell Climate Story
Poorly, 405–409
Happiness, pursuit of, 534
Hard Times (Dickens), 268
*Hard Times: A Family Escapes
Homelessness* (Manning, Rob),
384–386
HCT. *See* Hematocrit level
Hematocrit level (HCT), 147
stabilizing, 149
Henry, Patrick, 142
Heraclitus, 95

Hershman, Marcie, on writing, 48
High concept, 115–116
Hill, Lauryn, 479
Hitler, Adolf, 349
Hoffman, Jud, 496
Hoggan, James, 406–407
Holloway, A. J., 325
Holmes, James Egan, 292
Holt, Douglas B., 280
Homelessness, 381–383, 389
    Lawlor on, 386–388
    Manning on, 384–386
Homicide bomber, 193
Hook, 394
Household composition, 258
"How to Write for the New Media"
    (Jansons), 12–14
Hughes, Michael, 372
Humans, as social beings, 7
Hunger, GMOs and, 357, 363
Hurricane Katrina
    Bush on, 328
    Steele on, 372–373
    Steinberg on, 325–328
Hurston, Zora Neale, 285
Hyper-realism, 292, 297
    Scarborough on, 304

Idea generation, 6–7, 18
    brainstorming, 97–98, 448
    causes of, 112–120
    creativity in, 97–102, 121–122, 129
    freewriting, 100
    mind maps, 98–99
    questioning, 100–102
    by Sharp, E., 88
    tips for, 102
    in writing process, 19–20, 85–86,
        122–123, 156, 199, 232, 272,
        333–334, 368, 429, 469–470,
        527, 567
Identity
    language and, 169
    virtual self and, 152
    Wade, J., on, 337
    as writer, 134
Ignorance, appeal to, 515
"I Have a Dream" (King), 185–188
Illustrations, 33

Images
    audience and, 103
    as communication, 129
    Grandin on, 218
    perceptual meaning, 104–105
    Plato on, 207
    power of, 206
    pragmatic meaning, 106
    purpose and, 103
    reading critically, 104–106
    semantic meaning, 104
    subject and, 103
    subjective view of, 206
    syntactic meaning, 105–106
    thinking creatively about, 103
    thinking critically about, 103
    of women, 210
    writing situation and, 103
Immediate cause, 350–351, 376
Index cards, for organization, 368
Industrial Age, 115
Inference, 409, 424–425, 535.
        See also Beliefs
    arguments as, 499–500
    from evidence, 412–422
    incorrect, 416
    language of, 414
    Thinking-Writing activity, 416
Information
    collection of, 540–542
    ethics and, 548–550
    evaluation of, 389–396, 434
    knowledge compared to, 247, 435
    search for, 539–542
    use of, 542–548
    value of, 391
Information Age, 113
    abundance in, 115
Informed beliefs. See Beliefs
Informed intuition, 136–137
Insight, to writing, 59
Inspiration
    Alvarez on, 49–50, 53
    Goldberg on, 24–25
Intellectual property rights, 361
Intelligence, creativity and, 117–118
Interactive causes, 347–348, 376
Intermarriage, among
        newlyweds, 256

Internet
    addictions, 456–457
    counterfeit websites, 213
    evaluation of, 544–546, 581
    freedom of speech on, 486–488
    hoaxes, 392–396
    influence of, 461
    lawyers and, 114
    reading and, 31
    scams, 392–396
    Thinking-Writing activity,
        395–396, 487, 546
    use of, 465
    virus, 392, 396
Interpretation, 244, 380–381
    of perception, 291
Interpretation questions, 35, 101, 129
Interviews, 540–541, 581
    Thinking-Writing activity, 542
Introductory paragraphs, 33
    decision-making, 135–136
Iraq war, 96–97
Is Google Making Us Stupid?
        (Carr), 458–464
Italy, desert in, 399–400

Jabberwocky (Carroll), 46
Jalabert, Laurent, 147
James, Henry, 45
    advice of, 47
Jansons, Neal
    on content, 14
    "How to Write for the
        New Media," 12–14
    on K.I.S.S., 14
    on leading the reader, 13
    on length, 13
    on passive voice, 13
    on text blocks, 13
Jarre, Maurice, 212
Johnson, J. B., 327
Journal, 20
    questions for, 32
Judgment, 409–410, 425
    analysis of, 424
    criteria for, 422–424
    elimination of, 110–111
    Thinking-Writing activity, 424
Justification. See Apologia

Kafka, Franz, *Metamorphosis*, 45
Kamkwamba, William, 455
Karp, Scott, 459
Kasparov, Garry, 114
Kaufman, Alan, 235–236
Keep it simple. *See* K.I.S.S.
Kelly, James R., 424
Kenneally, Brenda Ann, 106
Kennedy, John F., inaugural
   address of, 91
Kettering, Charles F., 436
Kimmel, Michael, on gun
   violence, 302
Kimmel, Sara B., 279
King, Martin Luther, Jr. (MLK)
   assassination of, 186
   on freedom, 186–188
   Ghandi and, 185
   "I Have a Dream,"
      185–188
   influence of, 185
   Malcolm X and, 189
   metaphor use by, 186–188
   Nobel Peace Prize of, 185
   urgency of, 186
Kinship relations, 261
K.I.S.S. (keep it simple), 14
Kittler, Friedrich A., 460
Knowledge, 5
   beliefs compared with, 378,
      396–409
   common, 552
   experience and, 341
   information compared to,
      247, 435
   of source, 390, 543
Knowledge workers, Drucker on,
   112–113
Kotkin, Joel
   on family, 261–264
   language of, 263
   "The Rise of Post-Familialism:
      Humanity's Future?", 260–264
Kroehler, Carolyn J., 372

Labor
   chores as, 91
   force, 262
   Taylor on, 462

Lady Gaga, 249
La Frieda, Lisa, 234–235
La Frieda, Pat, 234–235
La Frieda Meats, 235
Lamb, Trevor, on color, 242
Lampley, Jim, 144
Lange, Jessie
   on creativity, 126–128
   freewriting, 126–128
   on language, 202–203
   on sex offenders, 432–433
   student writing, 201–203,
      432–433
   writing process of, 201–203,
      432–433
Language
   choice of, 168
   clear, 181–183
   communication through, 168
   doublespeak, 48–49
   effective use of, 170–172
   emotive, 194–196, 204
   ethical use of, 181–185
   euphemistic, 190–191
   figurative, 183–185, 204
   identity and, 169
   impact of, 196–201
   of inference, 414
   influence of, 189–196
   of Kotkin, 263
   Lange on, 202–203
   Malcolm X and, 170–171
   meaning-making and, 179
   objective, 214
   Orwell on, 196
   perspective and, 305–309
   reading and, 204
   Rich on, 169
   subjective, 214
   thinking and, 168, 181–183, 189
   Thinking-Writing activity, 170,
      182, 196
   use of, 1
   vague, 181–183
   writing project, 196–201
Language barrier, study abroad
   and, 28
Lanza, Adam, 291–293,
   301–302

La Pierre, Wayne
   on gun ownership,
      296–297
   on gun violence, 297
   lenses of, 297
   on Sandy Hook Elementary
      School shooting, 296–298
   on school guards, 297
Lawlor, Joe
   on homelessness, 386–388
   *Newport News Mom Escapes
      Homelessness*, 386–388
Learning
   audio and, 36
   differences in, 36
   recalling, 4
   thinking and, 170
"The Learning Curve" (Gawande),
   222–228
Lemkin, Raphael, 577
LeMond, Greg, 147
   death of, 148
Lenses
   adjustment, 309–311
   of audience, 207
   awareness of, 287
   of La Pierre, 297
   perception and, 285, 289
   of writers, 207
Libel, 486
Liberty, 517–519
Lightman, Alan, 164, 184
Lincoln, Abraham, 304–305
List making, 333
Litigious age, fiction in, 50
Living creatively, 106–107
Loans, earnings *vs.*, 132
Lobsters, 75–76
Logos (logic), 480, 516, 534
Loughner, Jared Lee, 292
Lutz, Wolfgang, 261

Macdonald, Anne, 49
Macrorie, Ken, *Telling Writing*, 49
Madrigal, Alexis C., *The Perfect
   Technocracy: Facebook's
   Attempt to Create Good
   Government for 900 Million
   People*, 495–499

Malcolm X
   assassination accounts of, 305–309
   The Autobiography of Malcolm X, 170–172
   criminal activity of, 171
   Douglass and, 143
   King and, 189
   language and, 170–171
   prison recollections of, 171
   Thinking-Writing activity, 308
Mallarmé, Stéphane, 45
Mamet, David, on fashion statements, 249
Manning, Eli, 96–97
Manning, Richard
   Eating the Genes: What the Green Revolution Did for Grain, Biotechnology May Do for Protein, 362–364
   on GMOs, 356, 362–364
Manning, Rob, *Hard Times: A Family Escapes Homelessness*, 384–386
Marijuana legalization, 491–494
Marital status, 255
   of parents, 257
Marriage, median age at first, 255
Martin, John W., 327
Masculine
   breadwinner, 280
   Carlsen on, 278–281
   as concept, 278–281
   emotion and, 279–280
   gun ownership as, 302
   strength, 280–281
   Thinking-Writing activity, 250–251
   violence as, 302
   vulnerable and, 280
Mather, Kirtley, 417, 421
Mayan civilization, 402
Mayfield, Max, 328
McMahan, Jeff
   on gun control, 298–301
   on gun ownership, 300
   "Why Gun 'Control' Is Not Enough," 298–301
McQuaid, Christopher, 75–76

McQuaid, John, 328
Meaning-making
   abundance and, 115
   language and, 179
   perceptual meaning, 54–55, 104–105
   pragmatic meaning, 56–57, 106
   semantic meaning, 54, 104
   syntactic meaning, 55–56, 105–106
   words, 179
Mencken, H. L., 405, 454
Menninger, Karl, 507
Merrill, Mark, on family, 253
Metacognition, 42. *See also* Thinking
   practicing, 43–44
   reading critically and, 57
   Thinking-Writing activity, 43–44
Metacognitive strategies, 42–43
Metamorphosis (Kafka), 45
Metaphor, 183. *See also* Analogy; Simile
   King's use of, 186–188
   new media as, 184
   Thinking-Writing activity, 185
   of Zitkala-Sa, 318, 323
Militant, 192–193
Miller, John L., 555
Mind, development of, 2
Mind maps
   idea generation, 98–99
   representation of, 99
   Thinking-Writing activity, 98–99
Mirabal sisters, 49–50
Mitchell, James, 496–497
MLA documentation style, 370, 537
   accuracy, 583
   annotations, 585
   books, 585–589
   citation format, 583–585
   completeness, 583
   electronic sources, 594–598
   government-civic documents, 589
   logic of, 561–562
   nonprint sources, 591–594
   periodicals, 590–591
   quick reference, 583
   Thinking-Writing activity, 562
MLK. *See* King, Martin Luther, Jr.

Modern Language Association Style. *See* MLA documentation style
Money, as creativity motivator, 118
Monsanto, 359, 361–362. *See also* Genetically modified organisms
Morris, James, 254
Moxie, 271
Muller, Gilbert, 349
Munro, Alice, 47
Murray, Donald M.
   awards of, 176
   death of, 176
   on drafts, 176–177
   "The Maker's Eye: Revising Your Own Manuscripts," 176–180
   on writing, 176–180
Mutual understanding, 485–486
"My American Journey" (Powell, C.), 15–17
Myers, Rochelle, 110–111
MySpace, as Pandora's box, 152–153

"Naming the Fabrics" (Alvarez), 46–47, 50
Narration, 84
   as chronological relationship, 220
   principles of, 230
   by Wade, J., 340–341
Narrative of the Life of Frederick Douglass, an American Slave (Douglass), 140–144
Nash, John Forbes, Jr., 149–151
Nash equilibrium, 149–151
National Association for the Advancement of White People, 374
National Rifle Association (NRA), 296
   Scarborough on, 304
National Story Project, 382–384
"A Natural Disaster, and a Human Tragedy" (Steinberg), 325–329
Nature, categorization of, 74–79
Nebraska Man, 404
Necessary condition, 349, 376
Neoliberalism, 326, 328–329

Newlyweds, intermarriage
among, 256
New media
as concept, 247
as interactive, 456
as metaphor, 184
power of, 456
relationships and, 152
research through, 246–247
thinking critically about,
108–109, 212–213, 352–353,
392–396, 456–457, 486–488,
544–546
Thinking-Writing activity, 247
writing for, 12–13
writing thoughtfully and, 12–13,
36, 60, 152–153, 184
"New 'Non-Traditional' American
Families" (Rice), 251–254
*Newport News Mom Escapes
Homelessness* (Lawlor),
386–388
Newtown massacre. *See* Sandy
Hook Elementary School
shooting
Nietzsche, Friedrich, 460
Norton, Heidi, 251, 253
Notebook computers, 242
Note cards, 552–553
Note-taking, 550–551
by computer, 554
summary, 555
systems, 552–554
Thinking-Writing activity, 554
NRA. *See* National Rifle Association
Nuclear family, 251

Obama, Barack, 96–97
on gun control, 295
Objectivity, subjectivity compared
to, 207, 214, 545–546
Observations, 542
Oceans
change in, 400–401
vaporization, 401–402
O'Connor, Flannery, on writing, 48
OCR. *See* Optical character
recognition software
O'Hagan, Andrew, on chores, 90

Oil spill, 342
Olds, James, 460
Oliva, Joe, 236
"On Plato's Cave" (Tanner), 38–42
Open-minded, 5, 310–311
Optical character recognition
software (OCR), 36
Organization, 6–7, 19
block, 335–336
index cards for, 368
of perception, 290–291, 341
point-by-point, 335–336
of Steinberg, 328
of writing process, 291
The Origin of Species (Darwin), 60,
78–79, 403
Orwell, George, on language, 196
Osborn, Henry Fairfield, 404
Outlining
by Buxton-Smith, 573
by Chaffee, 233–234
drafts and, 135
research, 563
Oxymoron, 267

Page, Larry, 462
Paleocene-Eocene Thermal
Maximum, 401
Pandora's box
Facebook as, 152–153
MySpace as, 152–153
Panksepp, Jaak, on core feelings, 217
Papp, Joe, 148–149
Paragraph structure, 370
Paraphrasing, 551, 569, 581
Thinking-Writing activity,
560–561
Parents, marital status of, 257
Passive influences, 62–63
Passive voice, in writing, 13
Pathos (effect on audience), 480,
516, 534
Pattern recognition, 209
Darwin on, 78–79
Thinking-Writing activity,
348–349
understanding, 239
Patterson, James T., 373–374
Pay-for-performance, 118

Perception. *See also* Stereotypes
accuracy of, 341
awareness of, 208–209
changes in, 308–309
definition of, 207
differences in, 211, 288
effect of, 229–236
exploration of, 207–208
faulty, 213
interpretation of, 291
lenses and, 285, 289
as message, 341
organization of, 290–291, 341
perspective and, 284–291
as process, 208
process of, 210
reality distinguished from,
212–213
of Sandy Hook Elementary
School shooting, 291–305
selection of, 289–290
thinking critically about, 208–213
Thinking-Writing activity,
211, 213, 288
writing thoughtfully about,
214–219
Perceptual meaning (connotation),
54–55
images, 104–105
Perdue, Theda
on beliefs, 338
on Cherokee nation, 338
*The Perfect Technocracy: Facebook's
Attempt to Create Good
Government for 900 Million
People* (Madrigal), 495–499
Perrins, Ben, 384–386
Personal attack, appeal to, 515
Personification, 219
Perspective
audience and, 65–66
changes in, 308–309
choice of, 559
consideration of, 488–489
on gun violence, 296
language and, 305–309
perception and, 284–291
problem-solving and, 453
purpose and, 66

Perspective (*continued*)
relationships and, 285
selection of, 341
support for, 66–68
Thinking-Writing activity, 68–69
use of, 65–66
writing and, 7, 25, 27
writing thoughtfully about,
324–330
Perspective-taking, thinking
critically about visuals, 10–11
Peter, Laurence J., 221–222
Philosophy, 244–245
Pilgrim at Tinker Creek (Dillard), 70
Piltdown Man, 403–404
Pink, Daniel H.
Revenge of the Right Brain,
112–116
on success, 120
Pioneer, 361–362
Pipes, Daniel
"Beslan Atrocity: They're
Terrorists—Not Activists,"
191–193
on euphemisms, 192–193
expertise of, 191
on terrorism, 191–193
Pity, appeal to, 514
Plagiarism, 548–549, 581
Thinking-Writing activity, 550
Plato
on images, 207
The Republic, 38–42
Pod borer, 362–363
Podcast, 237
Poetry, Dickinson on, 49
Pogue, David, 108–109
Popper, Karl, 418–419
Popular opinion, appeal to,
515–516
Pornography, U.S. Supreme Court
on, 191
Porter, Frank W., III, 338
Portman, Rob, 530
on marriage equality, 532–533
Portman, Will
on coming out, 530–534
student writing, 530–534
writing process of, 530–534

Post hoc ergo propter hoc
(after that, therefore because
of that), 353–355, 376
avoidance of, 369
Poverty, African American, 372
Powell, Brian
on family, 259
on same-sex couples, 259
Powell, Colin
education of, 15
military career of, 14–16
"My American Journey," 15–17
racism and, 17
Power
of images, 206
of new media, 456
Power, Samantha, 578
Pragmatic meaning, 56–57
images, 106
Thinking-Writing activity, 57
Prediction, 380–381, 413–414
Premise, 503
"The Price of Gun Control"
(Baum), 294–296
Prisoner's dilemma, 145–146,
150–151
Problem-solving, 437
acceptance, 443–444
adjustments, 453
alternatives for, 439, 447–450
in civic life, 438
details, 441–454
effectiveness of, 477
flexible approach to, 443, 477
identification, 439, 444–447
method, 438–454
in personal life, 438
perspective and, 453
social, 454–465
solutions, 439–440, 450–453
Thinking-Writing activity, 440, 454
writing approach, 465
writing project, 466–472
Process relationships, 220–221
Process writing
chronological relationships,
220–221
examples of, 221–222
Thinking-Writing activity, 222

Proofreading, 6–7, 19
levels of, 175
in writing process, 22–23, 88,
125–126, 158, 201, 233,
274–275, 337, 370, 431,
472, 530
Properties, 243–244
Proverb, Thinking-Writing
activity, 194
Puig, Manuel, 202
Purpose
of communication, 6
decision-making, 133, 138
of family, 252–253
images and, 203
perspective and, 66
of source, 390
of writing, 8–9
writing situation, 83, 121,
154, 198, 230, 270, 331, 366,
426–427, 466–467, 525, 565

Questionable cause, 351, 354, 376
Questionnaires, 541, 581
Thinking-Writing activity, 542
Quindlen, Anna, on community,
234, 236
Quoting, 551, 581

Race Across America, 144
Racism
Bennett on, 374
DuBois on, 375
Eggers on, 373
Powell, C., and, 17
Random selection, 509–510
Ray, Michael, 47, 110–111
Reading
awareness during, 42–43
Bacon on, 29, 330
in college, 29–34
as culture, 30
habits, 29
Internet and, 31
inventory, 32
language and, 204
for life, 29–34
print *vs.* online, 457
skimming, 549

strategies, 1
television and, 30–31
Thinking-Writing activity on,
31, 457
as tool, 59
Troncoso on, 29
Wolf on, 460, 463
Reading actively
components of, 57
definition of, 32
practicing, 38–54
productivity of, 32
Thinking-Writing activity, 42
Reading critically
analytical questions, 35
asking questions, 34–35
benefits of, 1
components of, 57
evaluation questions, 35
images, 104–106
interpretation questions,
35, 101, 129
metacognition and, 57
problem-solving approach,
37–38
questions for, 70
Thinking-Writing activity, 38
thoughtful writer and, 23
Reality
perception distinguished from,
212–213
of Sandy Hook Elementary
School shooting, 291–305
Reasoning
causal, 508
deductive, 503–507, 523, 535
false, 511–523, 535
inductive, 507–508, 523, 535
signal, 494
for thinking critically, 66
writing and, 523
Recombinant erythropoietin
(r-EPO), 147–148
Red herring, 513, 535
Referents, 243–244
A Regular Guy (Simpson), 47
Relationships
of cause, 205, 343–349, 365, 376
chronological, 220–222

of classification, 205
of comparison, 205, 329–330
of definition, 205
new media and, 152
perspective and, 285
process, 220–221
in space, 205
in time, 205
Relativism, 397, 435
Relaxation techniques, 221–222
"Remarks Concerning the Savages
of North America" (Franklin),
311–316
Remote cause, 350–351, 376
r-EPO. *See* Recombinant
erythropoietin
Report, 409–410, 424–425
fact, 411–412
The Republic (Plato), 38–42
Request, 394
Research. *See also* Field research
beginning of, 536
checklist, 563
collaboration in, 564
development, 538, 581–582
on family, 255–258
format, 564
on GMOs, 360–363
model, 564
through new media, 246–247
outlining, 563
planning, 563
rewards of, 537
Thinking-Writing activity,
538–539
writing project, 564–571
Research paper, 564–571
Revenge of the Right Brain (Pinker),
112–116
Reversing Established Orders
(Gould), 73–80
Revisions, 6–7, 19
importance of, 172
levels of, 174–176
questions for, 87–88
as recursive, 173–174
step-by-step method for, 174–176
Thinking-Writing activity, 176
tips for, 204

in writing process, 22–23,
87–88, 124–126, 157–159,
200–201, 233, 274–275,
336–337, 370, 431, 471–472,
529–530, 570–571
Rhetoric, 534
definition of, 8
responsible, 481
writing situation and, 8–9, 14
Rice, Kate
on family, 251–254
"New 'Non-Traditional'
American Families," 251–254
Rich, Adrienne, on language, 169
Richardson, Suzanne, 386–388
Right brain-style thinking
abundance and, 115–116
in Asia, 113–114
automation, 114
Riis, Bjarne, 147
Rilke, Rainer Maria, 51
"The Rise of Post-Familialism:
Humanity's Future?"
(Kotkin), 260–264
Rivera, Diego, 190
Rock, Chris, 338
Rodriguez, Richard, 279–280
Romney, Mitt, 530
Rosenthal, Andrew
Baum on, 295
on gun violence, 294
Rousseau, Jean-Jacques,
on society, 90–91
Rozema, Vicki, 339
Russell, Bertrand, on trait
variation, 195
Rwanda, 574–581

Sacks, Oliver
*An Anthropologist
on Mars*, 215
on Grandin, 215
Sahara Desert, 400
Salamone, Louis Philip, 424
Sample, 535
biased, 509
as known, 508–509
as representative, 509–510
as sufficient, 509

Sandy Hook Elementary School shooting. *See also* School shootings
aftermath of, 304
Anthony on, 293–294
La Pierre on, 296–298
perception, 291–305
reality, 291–305
Scarborough on, 303–305
thinking critically about visuals, 304
Sartre, Jean-Paul
"Existentialism Is Humanism," 37–38
on freedom, 38, 159
on man, 276
Scanning assignment, 33
Scarborough, Joe
on hyper-realism, 304
on NRA, 204
on Sandy Hook Elementary School shooting, 303–305
Scheherazade, 48
Schleifstein, Mark, 328
The School Days of an Indian Girl (Zitkala-Sa), 316–323
School shootings, 292. *See also* Sandy Hook Elementary School shooting
Anthony on, 293–294
Scopes trial, 404, 417, 421
Scott, Jerry, 565
Section headlines, 33
Selinger, Evan, on gun control, 302
Semantic meaning (denotation), 54
images, 104
Sensations
interpreting, 209–210, 237
organizing, 209–210, 237
selecting, 209–210, 237
Senses, 208
Thinking-Writing activity, 209
Separation distress, 217
Shakespeare, William, 330
Sharp, Eli
"An Argument for Chores," 89–92
emotional reaction of, 88
on family, 90

idea generation by, 88
questions on, 92
on Smiley, 89–92
on society, 90–91
student writing, 88–92
writing process of, 88–92
Sharp, Gwen, 301–302
Sharp, Howard, 327–328
Shaughnessey, Mina, 22
Shermer, Michael
arms race, 148–149
on climb, 144
The Doping Dilemma, 144–151
on game theory, 155
on gaming sports, 145–147
on genetics, 144
r-EPO, 147–148
Sherpa, Nawang Doma
on Buddhism, 276–277
on enlightenment, 276–277
on freedom, 275–277, 282
on religion, 275–276
student writing, 275–277
writing process of, 275–277
Shields, Elson, J., 361
Shipley, Cindi, 384–386
Sign, 243–244
Simile, 183. *See also* Analogy; Metaphor
Thinking-Writing activity, 185
Simpson, Mona, *A Regular Guy*, 47
Simpson, Tom, 147
Singer, Peter, experiments of, 478
The 6 Myths of Creativity (Breen), 116–120
Skill, Gawande on, 226
Slander, 486
Slippery slope, 354–355, 376
Smiley, Jane
The Case Against Chores, 80–82
Sharp, E., on, 89–92
subjects of, 80
Smith, Gina, 251–253
Snails, 75–76
Society
central authority, 495
changing demographics of, 262
norms of, 261–262

problem-solving, 454–465
Rousseau on, 90–91
Sharp, E., on, 90–91
Socrates, on writing, 463
Sorrows of Young Werther (Goethe), 44
The Souls of Black Folk (DuBois), 375
Source
electronic, 539, 581
evaluation, 389–396, 434, 543–547
interests of, 390
introduction, 557–558, 582
knowledge of, 390, 543
material integration, 557–559
observations by, 390–391
primary, 540
print, 539, 581
purpose of, 390
reliability of, 389–390, 543–546
reputation of, 391
secondary, 540
Thinking-Writing activity, 543
Speaking, writing and, 12
Speculation, 343
Speech
freedom of, 486–488
as revealing, 48–49
Sponges, 77–79
Squaw, 322
Stanton, Elizabeth Cady, 534
Declaration of Sentiments and Resolutions, 519–522
politics of, 519
Steele, Shelby, on Hurricane Katrina, 372–373
Steinberg, Ted
on Hurricane Katrina, 325–328
"A Natural Disaster, and a Human Tragedy," 325–329
organization of, 328
thesis of, 328
Stephanie's Law, 432
Stereotypes, 311
Streamlining, creativity and, 119
Student writing
Agudo, 159–162
Bartlett, 472–476

Brown, 162–165
Buxton-Smith, 571–581
Carlsen, 278–281
Chaffee, 233–236
Eggers, 371–375
freewriting, 126–128
Lange, 201–203, 432–433
Portman, 530–534
Sharp, E., 88–92
Sherpa, 275–277
Wade, J., 337–341
Study abroad, language barrier
    and, 28
Subject
    of communication, 6, 9
    decision-making, 134, 137
    images and, 103
    writing situation, 84, 121, 154,
        198, 230, 270–271, 331–332,
        366, 427, 467, 525, 565–566
Subjectivity, objectivity compared
    to, 207, 214, 545–546
Success, Pink on, 120
Sufficient condition, 349, 376
Suicide bomber, 193
Summary, 33–34, 569
    by Bartlett, 39
    decision-making, 140
    note-taking, 555
Supreme Court, U. S., on
    pornography, 191
Surgeons, as egalitarianism,
    225–226
Swift, Jonathan, 330
Syllogism, 504–506, 535
Syngenta, 361–362
Syntactic meaning
    connection, 55
    content, 55
    description, 55
    images, 105–106
    Thinking-Writing activity, 56
Synthesis, 427
    questions of, 101, 129

Table of contents, 32
Tanner, Sonja
    on education, 38–42
    "On Plato's Cave," 38–42

Taylor, Frederick Winslow, 461
    on labor, 462
Technological development, 108
    agriculture and, 360
    Carr on, 458–464
    Wade on, 301–302
Television, reading and, 30–31
Telling Writing (Macrorie), 49
"The Tent" (Alvarez), 50
Terrorism, Pipes on, 191–193
Terrorists, euphemisms for,
    192–193
Text blocks, 13
Theories, Gould on, 267, 417–419
Thesis, 20. See also
        Focus definition
    beliefs and, 425
    decision-making, 134
    defining, 568
    development of, 334
    of Steinberg, 328
    Thinking-Writing activity, 548
    topic selection, 96–97
Thinking. See also Metacognition;
        Right brain-style thinking
    breakthroughs in, 58
    Carr on, 455, 457, 465
    characteristics of, 42
    in comparisons, 324–325
    Forster on, 3
    influences on, 61–62
    language and,
        168, 181–183, 189
    learning and, 170
    respect for, 377
    as tool, 59
Thinking actively
    benefits of, 69, 93
    writing and, 61–62, 93, 208
Thinking creatively, 7
    critical viewing and, 95–102
    about images, 103
    in practice, 18
Thinking critically, 18. See also
        Critical thinker; Thinking
    about new media, 108–109,
        212–213, 286–287, 352–353,
        392–396, 456–457, 486–488,
        544–546

about perceptions, 208–213
reasoning for, 66
as social, 2
Thinking critically about
    images, 103
Thinking critically about visuals
    Are you what you eat?, 350
    audience and, 10–11
    choice, 482–483
    complex issues, 67
    denotation and connotation, 52
    decision-making, 132
    expect unexpected, 408
    fashion statements, 249
    necessity, 455
    perception comparison, 211
    perspective-taking, 10–11
    reading unwritten, 190
    Sandy Hook Elementary School
        shooting, 304
    source reputability, 547
    visual interpretation and
        analysis, 105
Thinking independently, 62–69
Thinking-Writing activity
    active and passive influences,
        62–63
    analyzing a writing experience,
        7–8
    annotate bibliography, 557
    arguments, 480, 506–507
    belief, identification, 381, 415
    belief, knowledge compared
        to, 397
    belief, origin, 389
    belief, sides of, 66
    belief evaluation,
        64–65, 391
    belief map, 69–70
    blog, 60
    causal chains, 346–347
    causal claims, 356
    causal fallacy diagnosis, 355
    causal pattern identification,
        348–349
    classification, 265
    classification, identification, 267
    cliché, 194
    communication, 15

Thinking-Writing activity
(*continued*)
concepts, 240
concepts, diagramming, 244
concepts, formation, 247
concepts, new media as, 247
creative inhibitions, 107
creative recollection, 106
crowdsourcing, 109
decision-making analysis, 136
decision-making
    preparation, 153
descriptions, 219
dialogue, 494–495
establishing agreement, 490
ethics, 266
euphemisms, 191
expressing deeper meaning, 26
Facebook, 153
fact evaluation, 412
false reasoning, 516
feminine, 250–251
generalization, 510
inference, incorrect, 416
Internet evaluation, 546
Internet freedom, 487
Internet hoax, 395–396
interviews, 542
judgment, 424
language, emotive, 196
language, offensive, 170
language, vague, 182
library, 540
Malcolm X, 308
masculine, 250–251
metacognition, 43–44
metaphors, 185
mind maps, 98–99
MLA documentation style, 562
note-taking, 554
paraphrasing, 560–561
pattern recognition,
    348–349
perception, comparison, 211
perception, differences in, 288
perception, faulty, 213
plagiarism, 550
pragmatic meaning, 57
previewing reading assignment, 33

problem-solving, 440, 454
process descriptions, 222
proverb, 194
questionnaires, 542
on reading, 31
reading actively, 42
reading critically, 38
reading print *vs.* online, 457
research, 538–539
revisions, 176
senses, 209
simile, 185
source, 543
syntactic meaning, 56
taking reading inventory, 32
thesis, 548
viewing perspectives,
    68–69
voice, 559
Wikimedia, 287
Thinking-Writing Model, 5–8,
    18–19, 480–481, 485
Thompson, Craig J., 280
Thompson, D'Arcy, 79
Thoreau, Henry David,
    on war, 579
Thought experiments, 478
Thoughtful writer.
    See also Writing
    becoming, 4–5
    critical reading and, 23
    critical thinker and, 4
    qualities of, 4–5
Threat, 394
Time pressure
    Brown on, 163–165
    creativity and, 118
    writing thoughtfully and,
        562–563
Tolstoy, Lev, 91–92
    on drafts, 179
Topic
    focus, 538–539
    identification, 538
Topic selection
    creativity in, 95–96
    thesis, 96–97
Toulmin, Stephen, 481
Toulmin's method, 481, 484, 534

Tree, as concept, 264
Triangle, 243
Troncoso, Sergio
    on reading, 29
    "Why Read?", 30–31
Truth, climate change and, 398
Truth, in arguments, 501
Tsunami, 325–328
Turing, Alan, 461
Twain, Mark, 45, 407

UCI. *See* Union Cycliste
    International
Underground Railroad, Douglass
    and, 140
Union Cycliste International
    (UCI), 148
United Nations, creation of, 579
United Nations Population
    Prospects, 262
Urban legends, 392–396
Urban living, 261
Urban migration, 261
Utopias, 376

Vacelet, J., 77
Validity, of arguments, 501–502
Van Allen, James, on writing, 59
Vaughters, Jonathan, 149–151
Vermeij, Geerat, 75
Vidal, Gore, 330
Video games. *See* Hyper-realism
Vinge, Vernor, 114
Vinjamuri, David, 231
Violence. *See also* Gun violence
    as masculine, 302
Violent crime rate, in America, 295
Virtual self, identity and, 152
Visuals. *See also* Thinking critically
    about visuals
    Alvarez on, 53
Voet, Willy, 148
Voice, 178–179
    establishing, 558–559, 582
    Thinking-Writing activity, 559
Voice of Judgment (VOJ)
    awareness of, 111
    elimination of, 110–111, 129
Voting fairness, 373

Wade, Jennifer
  ancestry of, 337
  on identity, 337
  narration by, 340–341
  student writing, 337–341
  "Where Did All of the Cherokees
    Go?", 337–340
  writing process of, 337–341
Wade, Liza
  on technological development,
    301–302
  "The (Terrifying) Transformative
    Potential of Technology,"
    301–302
Wales, Jimmy, 286
Walker, Alexis, 252
War, Thoreau on, 579
Warrants, 484, 534
Washington, George, 339
Weizenbaum, Joseph, 461
Wetland development, 326
"What Makes a Family? Children,
  Say Many Americans"
  (Berman), 259
"Where Did All of the Cherokees
  Go?" (Wade, J.), 337–340
"Why Gun 'Control' Is Not
  Enough" (McMahan),
  298–301
"Why Read?" (Troncoso),
  30–31
Wiesel, Elie, 3
Wikimedia, 286
  Thinking-Writing activity, 287
Wikipedia, 212, 286–287
Windchy, Eugene, 404
Winn, Marie, 456
Wolf, Maryanne, 459
  on reading, 460, 463
Women
  image of, 210, 290–291
  squaw, 322
  unmarried mothers, 258
Words. See also Euphemisms
  causal, 344
  for comparisons, 335
  emotive, 194–196, 204
  meaning-making, 179
  transitional, 341

Writer, 9. See also Thoughtful
    writer
  audience and, 14
  character of, 480, 534
  development, 178
  identity, 134
  lenses of, 207
  writing situation and,
    84–85, 121–122, 155,
    198–199, 230–231, 271–272,
    332–333, 366–367,
    427–429, 467–469,
    525–526, 566–567
Writing, 1. See also Academic
    writing; Freewriting; Process
    writing; Student writing;
    Thoughtful writer
  Alvarez on, 44–51
  about beliefs, 425–426
  for blog, 60
  censorship and, 51
  chronological, 237
  classification and, 266–267
  in college, 3
  college expectations, 14
  comparisons in, 334–335
  creativity and, 95–102
  deductive reasoning in, 523
  Dillard on, 70
  effectiveness of, 3
  emphasis in, 18
  Goldberg on, 23–25
  Hershman on, 48
  improvement in, 3
  insight to, 59
  leading the reader, 13
  length of, 13
  Murray on, 176–180
  for new media, 12–13
  O'Connor on, 48
  passive voice in, 13
  perspective and, 7, 25, 27
  problem-solving approach
    to, 465
  about processes, 220–221
  purpose of, 8–9
  reasoning and, 523
  reflection on, 92, 128, 533–534
  respect for, 377

Socrates on, 463
speaking and, 12
thinking actively and, 61–62,
  93, 208
as tool, 59
types of, 536
Van Allen on, 59
"Writing Is Not a McDonald's
  Hamburger" (Goldberg),
  23–24
Writing process, 231
  of Agudo, 159–162
  of Bartlett, 472–476
  blogging, 20
  of Brown, 162–165
  of Buxton-Smith, 572–573
  of Carlsen, 278–281
  of Chaffee, 233–236
  collaboration in, 25–26
  components of, 27
  drafts in, 21–22, 86, 157, 200,
    232, 274, 369–370, 430–431,
    471, 528, 569
  editing in, 22–23, 88, 125–126,
    158, 201, 233, 274–275, 337,
    370, 431, 472, 530
  of Eggers, 371–375
  focus definition, 19–21, 86,
    123, 156–157, 199–200,
    272–273, 334, 368, 429–430,
    470, 527
  idea generation in, 20, 85–86,
    122–123, 156, 199, 232, 272,
    333–334, 368, 429, 469–470,
    527, 567
  idea organization in,
    21, 86, 123–124, 157,
    200, 232, 273, 334–336,
    368–369, 430, 470,
    527–528, 568
  journaling, 20
  of Lange, 201–203, 432–433
  organization of, 291
  of Portman, 530–534
  proofreading in, 22–23, 88,
    125–126, 158, 201, 233,
    274–275, 337, 370, 431,
    472, 530
  recursive nature of, 19–20

Writing process (*continued*)
revisions in, 22–23, 87–88, 124–126, 157–159, 200–201, 233, 274–275, 336–337, 370, 431, 471–472, 529–530, 570–571
of Sharp, E., 88–92
of Sherpa, 275–277
of Wade, J., 337–341
Writing project
alternative, 93, 128–129, 166, 203, 236–237, 282, 341, 376, 434, 476, 534
arguments, 524–528
beliefs, 82–93, 426–431
causes, 365–370
comparison, 330–337
concept definition, 269–275
decision-making analysis, 154–158
experience and beliefs, 82–93
imagining life lived more creatively, 120–129
language, 196–201
overview, 83, 120, 154, 197, 229, 270, 331, 365, 426, 466, 524, 564

problem-solving, 466–472
requirements, 83, 120, 154, 197, 229, 270, 331, 365, 426, 466, 524, 564
research, 564–571
Writing situation, 229
audience, 83–84, 121, 154, 198, 230, 270, 331, 366, 427, 467, 525, 565
of Buxton-Smith, 571–572
components of, 27
consideration of, 83–85
images and, 103
purpose, 83, 121, 154, 198, 230, 270, 331, 366, 426–427, 466–467, 525, 565
rhetoric and, 8–9, 14
subject, 84, 121, 154, 198, 230, 270–271, 331–332, 366, 427, 467, 525, 565–566
writer, 84–85, 121–122, 155, 198–199, 230–231, 271–272, 332–333, 366–367, 427–429, 467–469, 525–526, 566–567
Writing thoughtfully, 18
about causal relationships, 365

on concepts, 268–269
new media and, 12–13, 36, 60, 152–153, 184
about perceptions, 214–219
about perspectives, 324–330
requirements for, 237
time pressure and, 562–563
Wurtman, Judith, 349

Yavapai College, 383
Yeats, William Butler, 51

Zitkala-Sa
birth of, 316
death of, 317
on hair-cutting, 317–318
metaphor used by, 318, 323
on mother's displeasure, 321–323
political activity of, 317
Quaker schooling of, 316–317
The School Days of an Indian Girl, 316–323
on snow, 318–319
on summers, 319–321